Here's what the critics Peter Rinearson's books on Microsoft Word:

"Peter Rinearson has written the best books on Microsoft Word."

Jim Seymour
PC Magazine

"Word owners should not be without Rinearson's book, even if they read no more than a tenth of it."

Erik Sandberg-Diment
The New York Times

"The thoroughness of Rinearson's book is awesome. If you're new to Word, the book will prove to be a long-term friend. And even if you're an experienced user, you will find something useful on nearly every page. WORD PROCESSING POWER WITH MICROSOFT WORD is the Word power user's book of choice—don't miss it."

John Dickinson
PC Magazine

"Almost every Word user from beginner to pro will find a treasure chest of information in this excellent, comprehensive book."

Clifton Karnes
Compute

"The definitive guide to Microsoft Word on the IBM PC. This comprehensive sourcebook can be read as a beginner's tutorial or employed nicely as an experienced user's reference. Experienced word processors new to Word will love it...beautifully produced."

Computer Book Review

"What sets the Rinearson book apart from most other works on Word—and computer books in general for that matter—is that it is not written for the computer user. It's for the person who happens to be using a computer to compose and edit words on a word processor. The distinction is important; it makes WORD PROCESSING POWER a much more entertaining and enlightening book."

Gordon McComb
New Accountant

"It's a winner....the book is a triumph of no-cute-stuff clarity, but Rinearson also throws in some unique conceptual approaches."

Lindsy Van Gelder
CompuServe

"WORD PROCESSING POWER by Peter Rinearson is one of the best guides to any program available."

Art Kleiner
San Francisco Bay Guardian

"The book is a 'must-read'....Rinearson's book includes tips that will give even the most experienced users a powerful head start when learning to use them....The tricks you learn are well worth the price of the book....It's a thorough, well-written beginner's guide to a writer's power tool. Don't use Word without it."

John Dickinson
PC Magazine

"A splendid book....If you use Word, you need this book. If you don't use Word, this book may persuade you to change."

Jim Seymour
Syndicated columnist

"The early chapters...almost supplant the manual."

Edward Mendelson
Yale Review

"A first-rate introduction to an innovative program."

William Fisher
Syracuse New Times

RUNNING
Microsoft® Word 5.5

RUNNING Microsoft® Word 5.5

Peter Rinearson

- **Complete Guide to Mastering Word's New Drop-Down Menus**
- **Example-Packed Introduction**
- **Handy Command Reference**
- **Expert Insights from the Author of *Word Processing Power with Microsoft Word***

The Authorized Edition

PUBLISHED BY
Microsoft Press
A Division of Microsoft Corporation
One Microsoft Way
Redmond, Washington 98052-6399

Copyright © 1991 by Peter Rinearson

All rights reserved. No part of the contents of this book may
be reproduced or transmitted in any form or by any means without
the written permission of the publisher.

Library of Congress Cataloging-in-Publication Data
Rinearson, Peter, 1954–
    Running word 5.5 / Peter Rinearson.
      p.   cm.
    Includes index.
    ISBN 1-55615-325-2
    1. Microsoft Word (Computer program)   2. Word processing.
I. Title.
Z52.5.M52R556   1991
652.5'.536--dc20   90-49855
                                                                        CIP

Printed and bound in the United States of America.

123456789 FGFG 32109

Distributed to the book trade in Canada by Macmillan of Canada, a division
of Canada Publishing Corporation.

Distributed to the book trade outside the United States and Canada by
Penguin Books Ltd.

Penguin Books Ltd., Harmondsworth, Middlesex, England
Penguin Books Australia Ltd., Ringwood, Victoria, Australia
Penguin Books N.Z. Ltd., 182–190 Wairau Road, Auckland 10, New Zealand

British Cataloging-in-Publication Data available.

The authors and publishers have made every effort to provide accurate, useful information. Please be aware that errors may exist, however, and that this book is offered without guarantees.

PostScript® is a registered trademark of Adobe Systems Incorporated. Aldus® and PageMaker® are registered trademarks of Aldus Corporation. MasterWord™ is a trademark of Alki Software Corporation. Paradox® is a registered trademark of Ansa Software, a Borland company. Apple® and Macintosh® are registered trademarks of Apple Computer, Incorporated. CHART-MASTER®, dBASE II®, dBASE III®, and dBASE IV® are registered trademarks of Ashton-Tate Corporation. AutoCAD® is a registered trademark of Autodesk, Incorporated. CompuServe® is a registered trademark of CompuServe, Incorporated. Epson® is a registered trademark of Epson America, Incorporated. Hercules® is a registered trademark of Hercules Computer Technology. Hewlett-Packard® and LaserJet® are registered trademarks of Hewlett-Packard Company. IBM® is a registered trademark of International Business Machines Corporation. ITC Avant Garde Gothic, ITC Century®, ITC Garamond®, ITC Souvenir®, ITC Zapf Chancery®, and ITC Zapf Dingbats® are registered trademarks of International Typeface Corporation. Park Avenue® is a registered trademark of Kingsley/ATF Type Corporation. Helvetica®, Palatino®, and Times® are registered trademarks of Linotype AG and its subsidiaries. 1-2-3® and Lotus® are registered trademarks of Lotus Development Corporation. Microsoft®, MS-DOS®, and Multiplan® are registered trademarks and Windows™ is a trademark of Microsoft Corporation. OS/2® is a registered trademark licensed to Microsoft Corporation. Graph-In-The-Box™ is a trademark of New England Software, Incorporated. Harvard® is a registered trademark of Software Publishing Corporation. Ventura Publisher® is a registered trademark of Ventura Software, Incorporated. Paintbrush® is a registered trademark of ZSoft Corporation.

Project Editors: Megan E. Sheppard and Ron Lamb
Technical Editor: Gerald Joyce
Acquisitions Editor: Marjorie Schlaikjer

To Jill

Contents

Acknowledgments   xi
Introduction   xiii

PART I   LEARNING

CHAPTER ONE:	Powers and Possibilities	3
CHAPTER TWO:	Concepts	19
CHAPTER THREE:	Getting Started: A Tutorial	33
CHAPTER FOUR:	The Screen: Menus and Documents	57
CHAPTER FIVE:	Using the Keyboard and Mouse	89
CHAPTER SIX:	Introducing Styles and Macros	103
CHAPTER SEVEN:	Introducing Graphics and Layout	131
CHAPTER EIGHT:	Keep in Mind	145

PART II   USING

CHAPTER NINE:	Introducing Commands	155
CHAPTER TEN:	File Commands	161
CHAPTER ELEVEN:	File Commands for Printing	193
CHAPTER TWELVE:	Edit Commands	207
CHAPTER THIRTEEN:	View Commands	229
CHAPTER FOURTEEN:	Insert Commands	245
CHAPTER FIFTEEN:	Format Commands	273
CHAPTER SIXTEEN:	Utilities Commands	319
CHAPTER SEVENTEEN:	Macro Commands	353
CHAPTER EIGHTEEN:	Window Commands	361
CHAPTER NINETEEN:	Help Commands	369

	PART III	MASTERING	
	CHAPTER TWENTY:	Speed	379
	CHAPTER TWENTY-ONE:	Navigation Aids	387
	CHAPTER TWENTY-TWO:	Glossaries	405
	CHAPTER TWENTY-THREE:	Macros	413
	CHAPTER TWENTY-FOUR:	Style Sheets	451
	CHAPTER TWENTY-FIVE:	Merge	465
	CHAPTER TWENTY-SIX:	Outlining	499
	CHAPTER TWENTY-SEVEN:	Indexes	523
	CHAPTER TWENTY-EIGHT:	Tables of Contents	537
	CHAPTER TWENTY-NINE:	Columns, Tables, and Forms	549
	CHAPTER THIRTY:	Graphics, Layout, and Positioning	583
	CHAPTER THIRTY-ONE:	Printing and Fonts	611
	PART IV	APPENDIXES	
	APPENDIX A:	Setting Up and Setting Options	627
	APPENDIX B:	Keyboard	641
	APPENDIX C:	Mouse	663
		Index	669

Acknowledgments

Many people at Microsoft provided me with insights into Word so that I could pass them along to you. The first came in 1983, when a friend at Microsoft, Jeff Raikes, introduced me to Word. Over the course of the three editions of an earlier book, *Word Processing Power with Microsoft Word*, I received generous help from people such as Richard Brodie, Greg Slyngstad, and Gerard Baz, all of whom played crucial roles in the creation and evolution of Word.

For this new book, a number of Microsoft people were generous to me. Among them were David Bangs, Melissa Birch, Duane Campbell, Ann Drews, Blas Garcia-Moros, Jodi Green, Greg Jones, Leslie Koch, Leo Nottenboom, Alex Price, Nina Roberts, Todd Roberts, Jeff Sanderson, Darrin Smith, Ruth Warren, and Bruce Williams.

At Microsoft Press, countless hours were poured into the book by people whose contributions were invisible to those not able to watch the process firsthand. Among those who contributed their time and effort were Judith Bloch, Jim Brown, Kim Eggleston, Peggy Herman, Ron Lamb, Carol Luke, Gerald Joyce, Debbie Kem, Deborah Long, Carolyn Magruder, Theresa Mannix, Cynthia Riskin, Megan Sheppard, Randy Thompson, Marjorie Schlaijker, Alice Copp Smith, and JoAnne Woodcock.

At Alki Software Corporation, where the companion software MasterWord was created, direct and indirect contributions to this book were made by Carolyn Pearson, Eric Berman, Dale Askew, and Lisa Askew.

Finally, my thanks to you, the users of Word. Over the years, your confidence in my books has made them best-sellers, and I appreciate your confidence very much.

Introduction

If you've used earlier editions of this book, titled *Word Processing Power with Microsoft Word*—watching them grow fatter as Word gained more features—you might be surprised at how slender this volume is. "Has the book lost something?" you might ask.

On the other hand, you might be struck by how thick this book is compared to some of the other titles on Word. "Is this book too advanced for me?" you might ask.

The answers to these questions are simple and encouraging and will help you use Word to best advantage.

Running Microsoft Word 5.5 is slimmer than before because Word is better than before. In fact, for many tasks and kinds of people, Word version 5.5 is arguably the best word processor ever created. Unlike previous versions, each of which has significant new capabilities, Word 5.5 has enhancements that are largely devoted to making the existing features easier to learn and use. The improved organization and intuitiveness of Word make using it more obvious and straightforward, with the result that this book is leaner without losing muscle.

For example, previous editions devoted three chapters to using multiple windows because the complexity of Word's Window commands obscured some of the benefits of using multiple windows. This edition has only one chapter on the topic because windows now are easier to use. Similarly, Word 5.0 offered three commands that let you transfer information from one file into another. Word 5.5 accomplishes the same ends with just one command. Word 5.5 has less to explain and less to learn—although if you're moving from an earlier version, you have a great deal to relearn.

Many books promise to make using computers simple, but often it's the books that end up being simple. For example, they will tell you that to print a document you simply use the Print command. But what if you have problems printing? Or you want to achieve a particular result with your printer and Word?

By analogy, how well can you find your way through a city with an oversimplified tourist map that shows only some of the important roads and few of the interesting side streets? This book contains tours and instructions but also teaches you to get from one place to another on your own—to really understand Word.

Like Word, the book offers a lot and lets you choose from it what you want:

- If you seek a straightforward book that covers Word's fundamentals, read only the chapters of Part I. Follow the hands-on tutorial in Chapter 3. Pay particular attention to Chapters 4 and 5. You can always look further into the book later, when you have a problem.

- If you want to make the transition from an earlier version of Word to version 5.5, four sections warrant special attention. Chapter 2 explains the nature of Word's cursor. Chapters 4 and 5 explore Word's new personality. Appendix B provides a comprehensive reference to accomplishing tasks with the keyboard. Appendix C translates the commands, terminology, and keystrokes of Word 5.0 into Word 5.5.
- If you want a reference to Word's commands, skim through Part I but concentrate on the chapters of Part II, which guide you through every command and answer many common questions.
- If you want to take full advantage of Word, delve into the chapters of Part III. These chapters aren't just for power users but for anyone who believes that a usable computer program is a combination of good design and abundant, clear information.

Running Microsoft Word 5.5 is a complete reference to Word for DOS, version 5.5. It is not meant as a guide to Word for Windows or Word for the Macintosh, nor does it dwell much on Word 5.0 except to help veteran users of Word adapt to this latest—and quite different—version. (If you intend to use Word 5.0, you need to obtain *Word Processing Power with Microsoft Word*. If you know an earlier version of Word, you'll find tips in this book that help you make the transition, and you'll frequently refer to Appendix C, which translates the commands, terminology, and keystrokes of the old Word into those of the new Word.)

The stages of learning Word 5.5 correspond roughly to the parts of this book—Learning, Using, and Mastering. Nothing is sacred about the book's organization, though. Skip around as you want.

As you become adept with Word you might find your productivity rising, your creative impulses freed, your printed work more attractive. Soon you won't think about Word much. You'll just use it.

Special Offer

MasterWord Offers Intelligent, Readable Help

If you like the approach and completeness of this book, you will find *MasterWord* invaluable. It is an eight-disk set of utilities, macros, and detailed help screens designed to make the use of Microsoft Word easier and more satisfying.

Created by Peter Rinearson and other Word experts, *MasterWord* contains:

- **Replacement Help Screens.** More than 2,500 help screens replace and greatly amplify the ones that come with Word 5.5. These screens of MasterWord Help cover each Word command, feature, dialog box, and message. There is special help for people who already know Word 5.0, WordPerfect, or WordStar. Also learn about DOS, printing, grammar, and other topics relevant to people who use Word.

- **ACT Buttons.** Find a description of what you want done, press its ACT button, and watch while MasterWord performs the task for you.

- **Macros.** More than 100 macros, each a new "command" or function. For example, one macro creates multicolumn tables, another prints addresses on envelopes, and another makes it easy to update a document's summary information.

- **Style Sheets.** A comprehensive set of 52 style sheets.

- **WordSet.** A control panel that gives you easy control of more than 100 aspects of Word, including screen colors.

- **MasterWord Calc.** A sophisticated calculator offers dozens of financial and math functions. Insert the results into a Word document.

- **MasterWord Seek.** Search your hard disk for files, by name or content. Browse through Word documents and other files.

- **Touch Me Not.** A password-protected screen saver.

- **Desktop Easy Reference.** Vital information about Word and MasterWord is presented in this unique 30-page guide. It lies flat or stands beside your keyboard, combining the best qualities of a keyboard template and a detailed reference card.

MasterWord works hand-in-hand with this book, providing the most valuable help available. Order *MasterWord* from Alki Software Corporation by calling 1-800-NOW-WORD or by using the postage-paid order card at the back of this book. The price is $99.95, which includes air shipping. Please indicate disk size.

Microsoft's foreign-language, medical, and legal spell-checking dictionaries are also available from Alki.

Alki Software Corporation, 219 First Ave. N., Suite 410, Seattle, WA 98109
Phone: 206-286-2600   Fax: 206-286-2785
Orders: 1-800-NOW-WORD (1-800-669-9673)

PART I
Learning

CHAPTER ONE

Powers and Possibilities

It is astounding how much personality can be packed into a little disk of plastic. At first, a computer is like a newborn child, full of undeveloped potential. But feed it a floppy disk—a seemingly nondescript bit of Mylar—and suddenly the computer grows up. It assumes a function. It becomes a tool, or a game, or even a companion. Its keyboard and screen take on distinctive features. If the software hidden on the disk is powerful and elegant, it transforms the computer utterly and gives a machine fashioned of switches and silicon a most pronounced and even pleasing personality.

Microsoft Word turns your computer into a dedicated, state-of-the-art word processor. Word is a powerful tool for writing, editing, and printing documents of all kinds—from memos to book manuscripts, from outlines to form letters, from screenplays to newsletters. It lets you work on several documents at once, and it takes much of the drudgery out of tasks such as footnoting, cross-referencing, indexing, and formatting. Because it checks spelling (and grammar) and can format and print documents following predetermined guidelines, Word handles troublesome details and frees you to concentrate on writing.

A MAGNIFICENT TYPEWRITER

Success comes at many levels with Word. At its simplest, you turn on Word, type for a while to create a file, and choose the File Print command to produce a paper copy. At this level, the way you use Word is obvious and there is little to learn. If what you want is a magnificent typewriter, an hour with this book is all you'll need.

Even if you're a beginner, at some point you're likely to want to venture at least a little further, to take Word to a more rewarding level. You'll want to store documents on disk, possibly revising them or changing their formats to suit special purposes.

You'll want Word to check your spelling or count the words in your document or show you what your page will look like *before* you print it. This is where the word processing powers of Word become important.

In time, you might decide to harness even more of Word's abundant potential. You might want to search through existing documents to create a list of those that contain particular phrases or write a cover letter and a report simultaneously or link the content of a document to information in another document or a spreadsheet. Perhaps you'll want to automate a common task so that with just a keystroke or two you can perform work that might otherwise take hours.

Word has many talents: footnoting, multiple-column layout, document annotation, the ability to insert and print spreadsheets and graphics, an aptitude for simple mathematics, and so on. You will use some of these features frequently, others intermittently, and some perhaps not at all. Word accommodates the needs and preferences of many kinds of people who perform many kinds of work.

WHY UPGRADE TO WORD 5.5?

Word 5.5 offers a wealth of capabilities but few that aren't in Word 5.0. If you're a happy user of version 5.0, you might ask: *"Why should I bother to upgrade?"*

You don't have to switch to version 5.5, but here are a few reasons you might choose to:

- Word 5.5 is more intuitive, which makes features both easier to learn and harder to forget. (For example: Command names are more descriptive; messages are more specific; commands and option names are "grayed" or "dimmed" when they are not available; and macros have been separated from other glossary entries, so they appear in their own list and have their own commands.) If versions 5.0 and 5.5 were houses, they would be of similar size and have the same number of rooms. But in 5.5 the floor plan would be more thoughtful, the rooms better organized, the light switches always at hand. The advantages? You get around quicker, tap potential more easily, and don't fumble in the dark for long.
- Version 5.5 has on-line help that is improved in three ways. First, help appears in a window that can remain on the screen while you work. Second, the help now includes hypertext links that let you jump freely from topic to topic. Third, version 5.5 offers roughly twice as much help information as version 5.0.

THE POSSIBILITIES

To succeed with any tool, it helps to understand what is possible. Through such an understanding, you can choose what to learn and what to ignore. You should know, for example, that Word can alphabetize lists. You don't have to learn the feature right away, and you might never need to use it, but unless you know that Word can alphabetize a long list in seconds, you might someday waste an hour doing it by hand.

This first chapter, then, is an account of what is possible with Microsoft Word 5.5. Remember, we're not interested quite yet in knowing how to do these things, only in knowing that they can be done and where you might look for more information. Because Word's features are for the most part reached through commands, the tasks are grouped under their command names. (The first word of each command tells you which menu holds that command.) And although these commands offer a wide array of powers, choosing any particular command requires only a few keystrokes or a click or two of a mouse button.

- Small enhancements have been incorporated into Word, including a word-counting feature and better support for many printers. Various invisible refinements, such as better management of memory, have been added too.
- Learning version 5.5 will prepare you for the future. Word 5.0 is based on an interface developed in 1982 and 1983. In contrast, Word 5.5 is based on Microsoft's vision of the future—a future in which most programs are used in fundamentally similar ways. This "drop-down menu interface" already is employed, with various adaptations, in Macintosh programs, Windows programs, and such other popular programs as Microsoft Works.
- Documents and style sheets for Word 5.5 are compatible with those of Word 5.0, making it easy to transfer work between the two programs. In an office setting, people can work together even though some of them continue to use Word 5.0. This compatibility also makes the transition from 5.0 to 5.5 easier.

If you don't know Word 5.0 already, there's little reason to learn it now. Jump right to Word 5.5 instead. If you do know version 5.0, what better time than the present to become comfortable with Word's new personality?

And to make the transition easier, this book has tips throughout for veteran Word users.

FILE COMMANDS

The File commands let you open and close documents and other files, find desired files on your disk, print a document or preview how it will look when printed, and either exit (quit) Word or run DOS commands without actually exiting Word. The File commands are discussed in detail in Chapters 10 and 11.

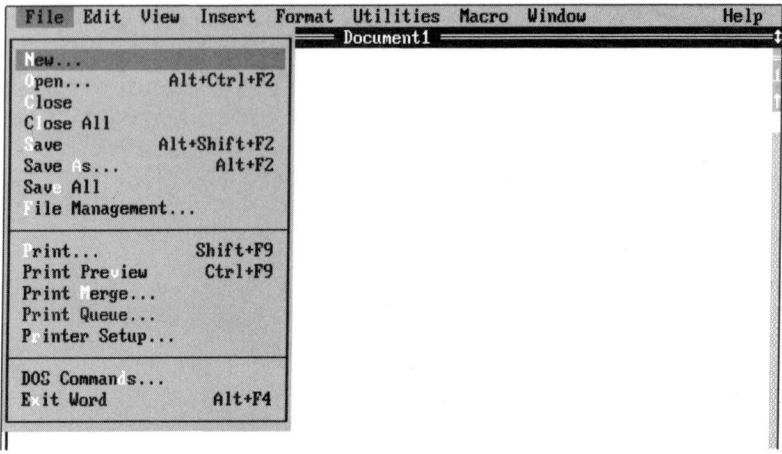

File New

Creates a new document or style sheet, opening a new window to accommodate it if the current window isn't empty. (A style sheet is a collection of formatting instructions that can be used to format one or more documents.)

File Open

Retrieves an existing document or style sheet and opens it for editing. Opens a new window, which overlaps the existing window.

File Close

Closes an existing window, including the document or style sheet it contains.

File Close All

Closes all windows and files, just as if you had exited Word and started again.

File Save

Saves the current document or style sheet, using its existing name.

File Save As

Saves the current document or style sheet after prompting you for a name.

File Save All

Saves all documents and other files on disk, protecting them against loss and at the same time freeing memory.

File File Management

Helps you find and load or print any document that meets criteria you specify. Word searches either document *summary sheets* (containing author's name, creation and last-saved dates, key words, and other relevant facts), the documents themselves, or both.

File Print

Prints the current document, or a desired portion of the document. Can also be used to print a style sheet or the current glossary. (The glossary is a collection of text entries and macros that you can modify and use as you desire.)

File Print Preview

Displays on the screen, exactly as they will print, the pages of a document (including their headlines, headers and footers, multiple-column layouts, graphics, and boxed paragraphs). Such immediate feedback allows you to fix problems or fine-tune a layout before you print it.

File Print Merge

Lets you print form letters and other documents that merge data with boilerplate text.

File Print Queue

Lets you control printing when one or more documents are queued to print. With the queue feature, you can work on a document even while Word is sending information to your printer.

File Printer Setup

Gives you a chance to give Word information about your printer and how it is hooked to your computer and lets you offer Word any special instructions you might have regarding printing. Used most often to switch between two printers.

File DOS Commands

Lets you run a DOS command—or if memory permits, another program—without actually exiting Word. If you are running Word under OS/2 instead of DOS, this command will appear as *OS/2 Commands* rather than as *DOS Commands*.

File Exit Word

Quits Word after alerting you of any unsaved documents or files.

EDIT COMMANDS

Edit commands let you delete or move text, insert boilerplate text from a special storage area called the glossary, reverse (undo) the effect of the most recent editing action, or search some or all of a document for either specified text or specified formatting. Edit commands are discussed in detail in Chapter 12.

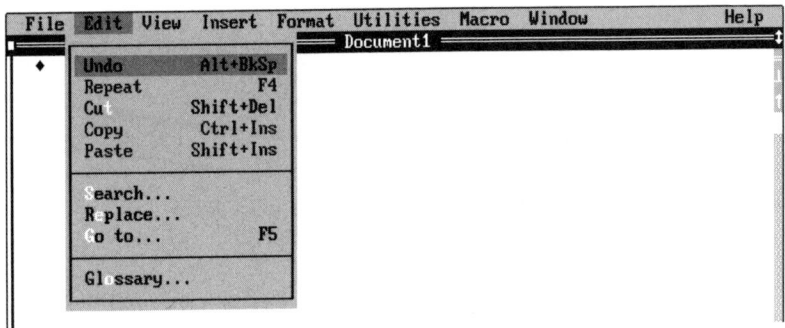

Edit Undo
Reverses the effect of a deletion or of virtually any other editing action.

Edit Repeat
Repeats the most recent editing or formatting action.

Edit Cut
Deletes highlighted text and places it in a special storage area called the *scrap*. The scrap is represented at the bottom of the screen by two braces { }. Text stored in the scrap can later be pasted into the same or a different document.

Edit Copy
Copies highlighted text and places it in the scrap. Unlike the Edit Cut command, which deletes the highlighted text from the document, the Edit Copy command leaves the original text unchanged but places a copy in the scrap.

Edit Paste
Inserts text from the scrap into your document, at the location of the cursor.

Edit Search
Searches for instances of either specific text or specific formatting.

Edit Replace
Searches for instances of either specific text or specific formatting and replaces them with other text or formatting.

Edit Go To
Lets you jump immediately to a specific page, electronic bookmark, footnote, or annotation.

Edit Glossary
Permits you to store, in a special memory, text you might want to reuse. You give a name to each item saved so that it can be retrieved. Each item saved in this way is a glossary entry; you can also save the collection of entries in the current glossary on disk, thereby creating a glossary file that you can load at a later date.

VIEW COMMANDS

View commands control whether certain kinds of elements appear on the screen. View commands are discussed in detail in Chapter 13.

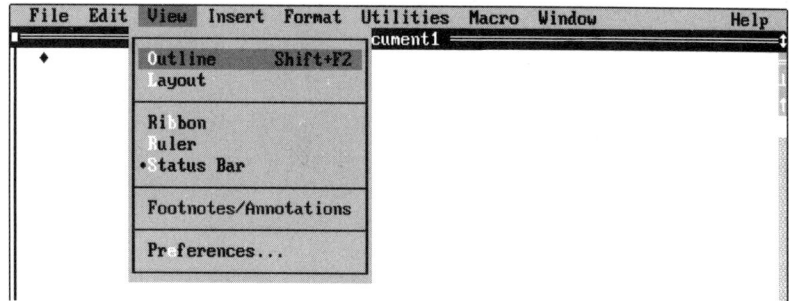

View Outline

Lets you look at and rearrange a document in an abbreviated, outline form. You can suppress the display of subordinate headings and text passages, permitting you to focus on—and rapidly reshape—the structure of what you are writing.

View Layout

Lets you view and edit your document in a special mode in which columns, graphics, and other elements appear in approximately the relationship they will have when printed. Although the File Print Preview command provides a truer approximation of the printed version, the View Layout command is a useful and accurate guide—and unlike the File Print Preview command, the View Layout command lets you edit your document while viewing it.

View Ribbon

Turns on or off the *ribbon,* a horizontal bar that appears directly below the menu bar. The ribbon shows, and lets you change, the style (if any) that governs the current paragraph, as well as the font, size, and certain other characteristics of any highlighted text or the text you are typing.

View Ruler

Turns on or off a ruler at the top of a window. The ruler shows the indentations and tab stops of the highlighted paragraph.

View Status Bar

Turns on or off the *status bar,* which spans the bottom of the screen and provides such information as the name of the current document and the page and column number of the cursor.

View Footnotes/Annotations

Opens or closes a special portion of a window dedicated to showing the text of footnotes and annotations. This *pane* uses some of the bottom portion of the document window.

View Preferences

Permits you to make a variety of choices about what is displayed on your screen, such as whether paragraph marks appear and what colors are used. Also, depending on your equipment, you might be able to choose how many lines of text your screen displays and whether Word runs in a graphics or a text mode.

INSERT COMMANDS

Insert commands let you insert into a document such elements as footnotes, page numbers, pictures, or an index. Insert commands are discussed in detail in Chapter 14.

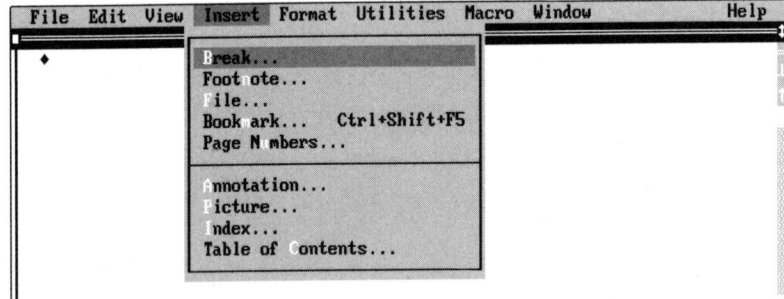

Insert Break

Inserts a special character into your document, indicating to Word that a new page, section, or column is to begin. Although Word will create new pages or columns without your inserting breaks, the Insert Break command gives you greater control over their locations.

Insert Footnote

Lets you insert a footnote reference mark into your document and then type the text of the corresponding footnote. Word will number footnotes if you want; if you move text that contains numbered footnote reference marks, Word will the renumber the reference marks accordingly.

Insert File

Inserts some or all of another document or spreadsheet into your current document.

Insert Bookmark

Lets you place an electronic "bookmark" in your text. (To return to the bookmark instantly, you use the Edit Go To command.)

Insert Page Numbers

Places a page number, at a position you specify, on each page or section of a document. Various numbering schemes, including roman numerals, are allowed.

Insert Annotation

Inserts an annotation in your document. An annotation is a special type of footnote, provided so that one or more people can make comments about elements in a document. Unlike a conventional footnote, which generally uses a number as its reference mark, an annotation can use initials or even a full name as a reference mark, thereby identifying the source of each comment. Furthermore, the Insert Annotation command can insert the date and time the comment was made.

Insert Picture

Inserts a graphics image into a document. The images can come from many sources, including leading software programs and scanners. In addition, computer screen images can be captured with Capture, a program that comes with Word, and imported into a document with this command.

Insert Index

Creates an index for your document and inserts it into the document. Coding must be placed in your document before this command can be used successfully.

Insert Table of Contents

Creates a table of contents for your document and inserts it into the document. The table of contents can be limited to headings from the document, or it can include other text that you specify in advance.

FORMAT COMMANDS

Word has many types of built-in formatting: double-spaced paragraphs, centered paragraphs, italic, bold, or underlined characters, and so on. So that you can refine or expand on these formatting opportunities, Word offers Format commands. Each command controls some aspect of a document's appearance.

The Format commands accept precise instructions about spacing and measurements, although they don't *require* precision. When you're creating something with exacting requirements, you can specify a margin or other measurement in inches, in pica-size or elite-size characters, in centimeters, or even in typographical points. For truly demanding circumstances, such as typesetting, Word is accurate to almost a thousandth of an inch (actually, to a "twip"—$\frac{1}{1440}$ of an inch).

Format commands are discussed in detail in Chapter 15.

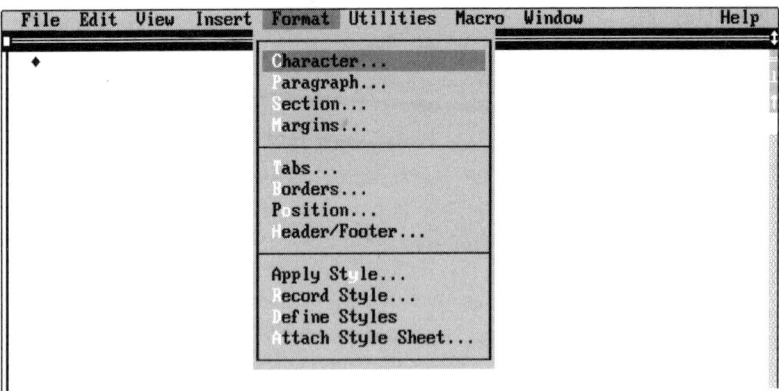

Format Character

Controls the appearance of printed characters, including their font, their size, and any of their other attributes (for example, whether they are italic, bold, or underlined).

Format Paragraph

Controls how the lines of a paragraph are laid out on the page. Indentations, centering, and line spacing are among the paragraph characteristics controlled by the Format Paragraph command.

Format Section

Offers you broad control over page appearance (presence or absence of line numbers, location of footnotes, and so on). You can have one, two, three, or even more columns on a page, and you can change the number of columns in the middle of the page.

Format Margins

Controls page margins; lets you print odd-numbered pages with a wide left margin and even-numbered pages with a wide right margin, providing a gutter that facilitates binding.

Format Tabs

Places tab stops in or removes them from a paragraph or paragraphs.

Format Borders

Boxes individual paragraphs, or places lines on one or more sides of a paragraph. Also lets you shade a paragraph, with shading available in those colors allowed by your printer (generally gray of various intensities).

Format Position

Enables you to specify an exact location for printed text or graphics. If you wish, other text can "flow" around elements that have been fixed to a specific position with this command.

Format Header/Footer

Lets you turn a paragraph into a *header* or *footer*—special text that prints at either the top or bottom of a series of pages. Page numbers, dates, and document titles are examples of text often included in headers and footers, which were called running heads in earlier versions of Word.

Format Apply Style

Lets you format a document rapidly and accurately by highlighting text and choosing an appropriate Format Apply Style command.

You can use ready-made styles or create them yourself as you go along. All styles needed for a particular document or class of documents are stored in a special file called a *style sheet*. To format a document with the assistance of an existing style sheet, you attach the style sheet to the document and then apply individual styles to the text as needed.

Format Record Style

Lets you record (as a *style*) an often-used type of formatting—such as a centered heading with bold characters—so that you can easily use it at a later time.

Format Define Styles

Opens a window that describes each style in the current style sheet. After this window is displayed, you can modify styles and their formatting.

Format Attach Style Sheet

Lets you specify which style sheet should be used to format the active document. See the preceding description of the Format Apply Styles command.

UTILITIES COMMANDS

Utilities commands give you access to a miscellaneous collection of features, including spell checking, alphabetizing, arithmetic calculations, word counting, and repagination. Utilities commands are discussed in detail in Chapter 16.

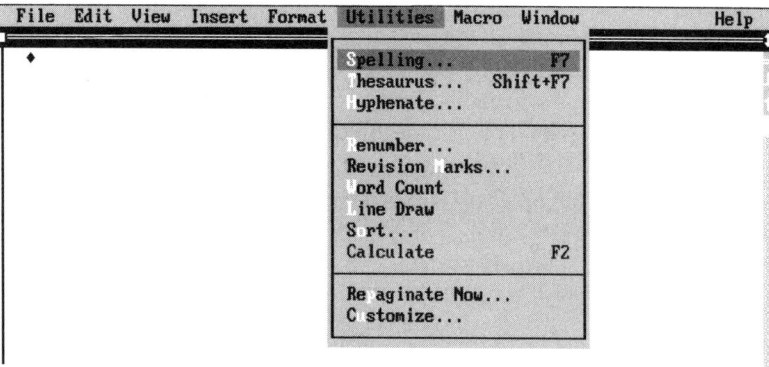

Utilities Spelling

Checks the spelling of your entire document (unless words are highlighted, in which case it checks only those words). When the spell checker doesn't recognize a word, it can propose a similar substitute from the word list or lists it consults.

Utilities Thesaurus

Offers a list of synonyms for a highlighted word and makes a substitution if you want.

Utilities Hyphenate

Hyphenates a multisyllabic word that would otherwise print at the beginning of a line. Once the word is hyphenated, the first part moves to the previous line, allowing more text to be squeezed onto a line. Word's hyphenation is of particular value when your text is *justified* (formatted to create straight left and right margins).

Utilities Renumber

Numbers or renumbers paragraphs or removes the numbering from the beginning of paragraphs.

Utilities Revision Marks

Lets you see all changes made in the most recent version of a document, by specially marking insertions and deletions and, optionally, drawing vertical bars in the margin wherever a change has been made.

Utilities Word Count

Counts the words in a document.

Utilities Line Draw

Lets you draw lines within a document.

Utilities Sort

Alphabetizes or places numbered paragraphs in numeric order.

Utilities Calculate

Performs simple arithmetic: addition, subtraction, multiplication, division, and the calculation of percentages.

Utilities Repaginate Now

Indicates where pages will break the next time the document is printed, and lets you confirm or adjust the breaks. Word keeps pagination up to date if you want, through a feature called *background pagination*. However, in certain situations you might want to turn background pagination off—in which case you use the Utilities Repaginate Now command to calculate page breaks.

Utilities Customize

Lets you control or influence the way Word operates and displays information. Through this command, for instance, background pagination is turned on or off, and the identity of the spelling dictionary is established.

MACRO COMMANDS

Macro commands let you record a series of keystrokes for later use or customize Word with special features that suit your particular needs. Macro commands are discussed in detail in Chapters 16, 17, and 23.

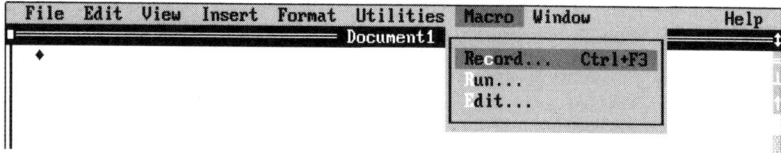

Macro Record

Lets you record a series of keystrokes as a *macro* with a name and a code that you can use to run the keystrokes later at extremely high speed.

Macro Run

Runs an existing macro so that you can accomplish a frequently performed task at high speed.

Macro Edit

Lets you edit an existing macro. Among the things you can do is add programming that lets the macro perform "intelligent" tasks—such as typing certain text in one situation but different text in another.

WINDOW COMMANDS

Window commands let you open, close, and move windows so that you can work on more than one document at a time or on more than one part of a document at a time. These windows, which are a feature of Microsoft Word, should not be confused with the product Microsoft Windows, which is a graphical extension to the MS-DOS operating system. Window commands are discussed in detail in Chapter 18.

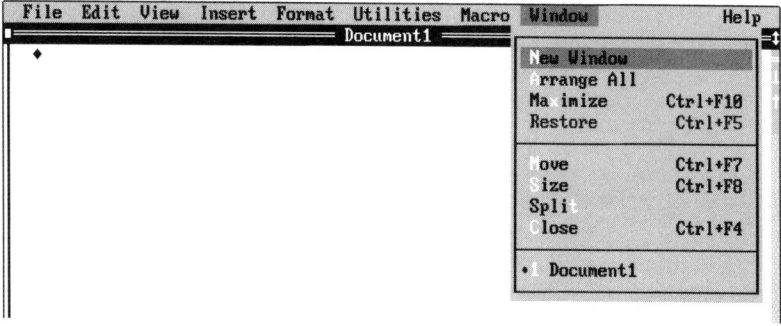

Window New Window

Opens a new window, which contains a copy of the current document. The new window overlaps any existing windows. To open a window that contains a different document, use the File Open command instead. To open a new window that doesn't contain a document, use the File New command.

Multiple windows are particularly useful when you are referring to more than one part of a long document, checking facts in a related document, moving text between documents or working on a document that contains many sections.

Window Arrange All

Arranges all windows so that none overlap each other; instead, they use relatively small regions of the screen. You can think of the window arrangement created by this command as a set of tiles, each butting against others but not overlapping them.

Window Maximize

Increases the size of the active window so that it takes up all of the document portion of the screen.

Window Restore

Reverses the effect of the Window Maximize command, causing a window that has been maximized to assume its former, smaller dimensions.

Window Move

Moves the active window on the screen. You can move most of a window completely off the screen, provided that its upper-left corner remains visible.

Window Size

Changes the size of the active window.

Window Split

Splits a window into two horizontal panes that can show independent views of the same document.

Window Close

Closes a window, removing it from the screen.

Window **Document names**

Lets you activate a window.

HELP COMMANDS

Help commands give you immediate on-screen assistance with various aspects of Word. Help screens are linked, allowing you to move among related topics with little difficulty. Help commands are discussed in detail in Chapter 19.

CHAPTER ONE: Powers and Possibilities 17

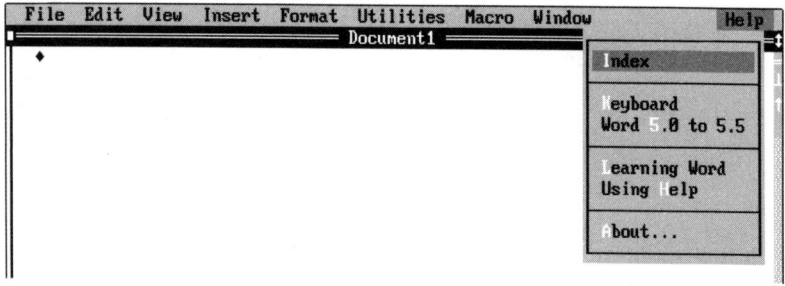

Help Index

Lists available kinds of online help. Keep choosing from the more specific sublists that appear; eventually, and with some luck, you get to a help screen that has the information you desire.

Help Keyboard

Describes the purposes and uses of keys and key combinations on the keyboard.

Help Word 5.0 to 5.5

Provides assistance with Word 5.5 for people who already know how to use version 5.0. Also helpful to people who know version 4.0.

Help Learning Word

Lets you run the interactive tutorial that comes with Word, without quitting Word.

Help Using Help

Provides brief instructions on use of the Help instructions.

Help About

Shows the version of Microsoft Word you are using, as well as the serial number of the specific copy you are using and the name of the person or organization to whom the copy is licensed by Microsoft. (When you install Word on your computer system before using it for the first time, it asks you to type your name; this is the name that appears when the Help About command is used.)

Obviously, Microsoft Word has many powers. So do you. Combine them to any extent you choose. As your experience grows, so will the pleasure of using Word. Keep in mind that you don't need to know every facet of Word to use it, any more than you have to master the piano before you find pleasure in sitting down to play. The important thing is to begin.

BEGIN AT THE BEGINNING

People tend to learn software in one of two ways. Some want to see the big picture before they begin; others want to jump in and start *doing* something. Although most chapters in this book will suit both kinds of learners, Chapters 2 and 3 have a special focus.

- Chapter 2 is designed to please the "big picture" people, who want to understand the nature of Word before they tackle the specifics. It presents 11 general concepts that will help you make better sense—and better use—of Microsoft Word.
- Chapter 3 is designed for people who want to jump right in and use Microsoft Word. It is a tutorial that helps you create, print, and save a document, as well as learn several of Word's basic operations.

Because it offers a foundation that will help you perform such vital tasks as *selecting* text and *formatting*, Chapter 2 is a must for all Word users. (You might prefer to read it quickly the first time and come back to it when you know Word a little better or if some aspect of Word puzzles you.) Work through Chapter 3 if you're new to Word, or if you're a fan of tutorials. If you're eager to become productive, Chapter 3 is a good place to begin.

CHAPTER TWO

Concepts

When you approach Word 5.5 from a broad perspective, the following 11 concepts are among those most critical to developing an understanding of Word's capabilities: They are the foundation for much of the information you'll learn throughout this book.

CONCEPT 1: SIX STEPS

When you create a document with Word, you work through six steps:

1. You *enter* the contents of a document on the screen by typing new text, loading previously typed text from disk, or both. You can even incorporate in your Word document spreadsheets or graphics images from other programs.
2. You *revise* the document, changing words and spellings or adding, subtracting, and moving passages.
3. You *format* the document, dictating its overall appearance—from individual characters to entire pages. You can also preview on the screen how the document will look when printed. You can then make changes as desired and preview the pages again.
4. You order Word to *print* one or more copies of part or all of the document. You can even merge information from a data document into a main Word document, creating a form letter or a series of other personalized documents.
5. You *save* the document on disk for reference or for later additional text entry, revision, formatting, and printing.
6. You *close* the window containing the document, or you quit Word.

Although these steps reflect a simplified Word model, you might sometimes follow this model exactly. For example, you might type (enter) a letter in a spurt of creativity and then revise its contents, format it to look like a letter instead of only lines of type, print it, store it on disk for reference, and close the file. Such an orderly process, however, is rare. You'll more likely mix up the steps at least a bit, possibly deciding some of the formatting in advance or revising as you write.

CONCEPT 2: SELECT-DO

Your instructions to Word are based on the concept of Select-Do. First you tell Word *where* within a document you want to do something, such as enter, revise, format, or in some cases, even print or store text. This is the Select part. Then you tell Word what *action* you want to take, such as deleting text or formatting it. This is the Do part.

Whereas many word processors require that you use different commands to delete a character, word, line, or block of text, Word simply says "Tell me where and how much, and then tell me what to do."

In general, the mouse lends itself to performing the Select part of Select-Do efficiently. You can select many parts of a document far more quickly with the mouse than with the keyboard. But an experienced user will find that executing many of the commands tends to be faster with the keyboard.

CONCEPT 3: A MULTIPURPOSE CURSOR

Most computer programs display a cursor—a small underline, vertical line, or rectangle of light that shows where you are on the screen. As you type, the cursor moves along, leaving a trail of characters behind it. You can also move the cursor without leaving a trail of characters, much as you can lift a pen from paper and place it elsewhere without leaving a trail of ink. Most often, you move the cursor by using the four direction (arrow) keys.

In Word 5.5, the cursor is a blinking underline that appears immediately to the right of the location at which anything you type will appear on screen. (The cursor is sometimes called the *insertion point*.)

The cursor serves a second purpose: It lets you highlight multiple characters, a word, a phrase, a line, a sentence, a paragraph, and so on. In fact, you can extend the cursor to highlight any number of characters, including every word, space, and punctuation mark in a document. Any text that is highlighted in this way is called a *selection*—the first element in the Select-Do process. (See Concept 2.)

Knowing how to take advantage of this multipurpose cursor is crucial to your success with Word 5.5.

Inserting Text with the Cursor

Other word processors, such as Microsoft Word for Windows and Microsoft Word for the Macintosh, have an insertion-point cursor, displayed as a vertical line between two characters on the screen. When you type a character into a document in one of these programs, it is inserted between the two letters—at the insertion point.

Word 5.5, like any character-based (non-graphical) application, is unable to display a vertical line between two characters. So Word 5.5 does the next-best thing: It places a blinking cursor under the character to the immediate right of the actual insertion point. You can think of the insertion point as being at the left end of the blinking underline.

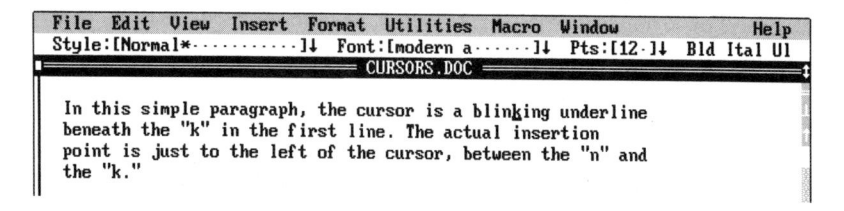

```
 File  Edit  View  Insert  Format  Utilities  Macro  Window              Help
 Style:[Normal*··········]↓  Font:[modern a······]↓  Pts:[12·]↓  Bld Ital Ul
════════════════════════════ CURSORS.DOC ══════════════════════════════════
  In this simple paragraph, the cursor is a blinking underline
  beneath the "k" in the first line. The actual insertion
  point is just to the left of the cursor, between the "n" and
  the "k."
```

Whenever the blinking cursor is visible, any character-formatting instructions you give Word are applied to the cursor rather than to existing text. (Character formatting is formatting that affects the font, size, boldfacing, underlining, or other characteristics of text.) Although the cursor itself does not reflect its character-formatting features, any new text you type is formatted in the style you specified.

For instance, if you want to insert the word *small* in bold characters before the word *blinking* in the preceding example, you start by moving the cursor to the first letter of the word *blinking*.

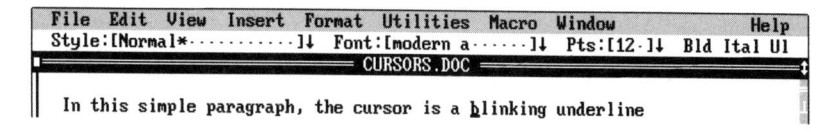

```
 File  Edit  View  Insert  Format  Utilities  Macro  Window              Help
 Style:[Normal*··········]↓  Font:[modern a······]↓  Pts:[12·]↓  Bld Ital Ul
════════════════════════════ CURSORS.DOC ══════════════════════════════════
  In this simple paragraph, the cursor is a blinking underline
```

Then turn on bold character formatting. (One method is to hold down the Ctrl key and press the B key.) This causes the cursor to be formatted as bold but doesn't directly affect the formatting of any existing text.

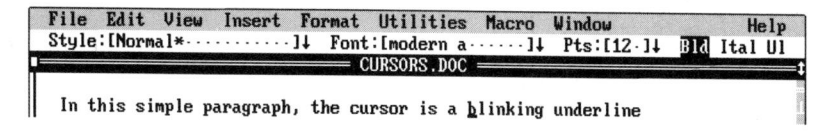

```
 File  Edit  View  Insert  Format  Utilities  Macro  Window              Help
 Style:[Normal*··········]↓  Font:[modern a······]↓  Pts:[12·]↓  Bld Ital Ul
════════════════════════════ CURSORS.DOC ══════════════════════════════════
  In this simple paragraph, the cursor is a blinking underline
```

Now type the word *small*, which will appear in your text in bold characters because the cursor is bold. The other text moves aside to allow the new text to be typed into place, with this result:

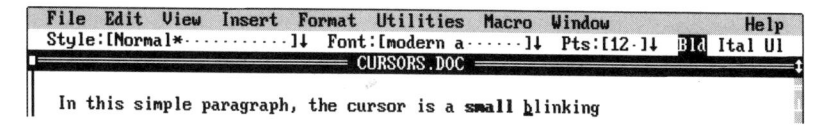

```
 File  Edit  View  Insert  Format  Utilities  Macro  Window              Help
 Style:[Normal*··········]↓  Font:[modern a······]↓  Pts:[12·]↓  Bld Ital Ul
════════════════════════════ CURSORS.DOC ══════════════════════════════════
  In this simple paragraph, the cursor is a small blinking
```

The cursor retains its bold formatting until you remove the formatting or move the cursor to a different location. (For information on moving the cursor, see Concept 5, later in the chapter.)

We've seen that the insertion-point cursor lets you pinpoint a single location in a document—the location where the next thing you type will appear. This location is smaller than a single character: It is like a slit in the fabric of your document, into which text can be inserted. We've also seen that by formatting the cursor before typing new text, you can dictate the character formatting of the new text.

But what if you want to change existing text in some way? How do you indicate a word that you want to delete or a sentence that you want to underline?

Selecting Text with the Cursor

To designate already-defined text for some subsequent action, you select it by extending the cursor. Selected text is highlighted, and for this reason the selection often is called the *highlight*—a selected sentence is the same as a highlighted sentence. After text is selected, you can delete it, format it, copy it to a special holding area called the *scrap*, define it as a Word *bookmark*, or even print it.

Chapter 5 explores several ways to select text with the keyboard and mouse, and Appendix B includes a list of keyboard methods. For now, we'll confine ourselves to two of these keyboard methods, one using the Shift key and the other using the F8 function key.

Selecting single characters

To select a single character of text, you hold down the Shift key and press either the Right or the Left direction key. If you press the Right direction key, the character to the right of the insertion point (the character above the blinking cursor) is highlighted. If you press the Left direction key, the character to the left of the insertion point (the character immediately before the blinking cursor) is highlighted. To select additional characters in either direction, continue holding down the Shift key while pressing either the Right or the Left direction key.

Extending the selection

To select text by units larger than characters, first press the extend-selection key, which in Word 5.5 is F8. (In previous versions of Word it was the F6 key.) After you have pressed F8, the letters *EX* appear on the second-to-last line of the screen, a line called the *status bar*. Figure 2-1 shows the full screen as it appears as soon as you press the F8 key the *first* time.

After you have pressed the F8 key the first time, direction keys and other keys that normally move the cursor extend the selection. For instance, if you press the Left direction key, the highlight is extended to the left. If you press the Esc key, Extend Selection mode turns off.

By pressing the F8 key more than once, you extend the selection by convenient amounts—a word, a sentence, a paragraph, or the whole document. If you select too much with this method, hold down the Shift key and press F8 to deselect.

CHAPTER TWO: Concepts

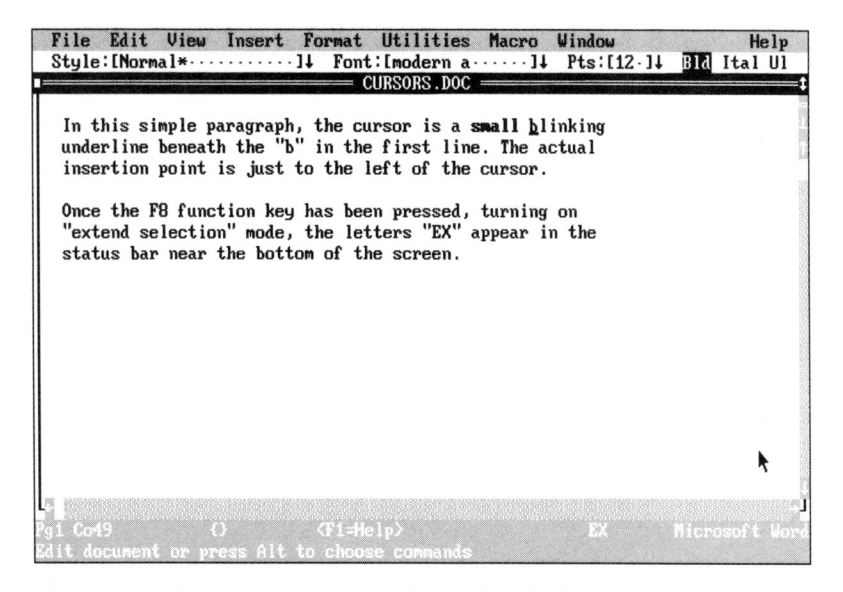

Figure 2-1. As soon as you press the F8 key the first time, the letters EX appear near the bottom of the screen (in the status bar). Pressing F8 additional times extends the selection.

The first time you press F8, Extend Selection mode turns on. The second time you press F8, the highlight extends a full word.

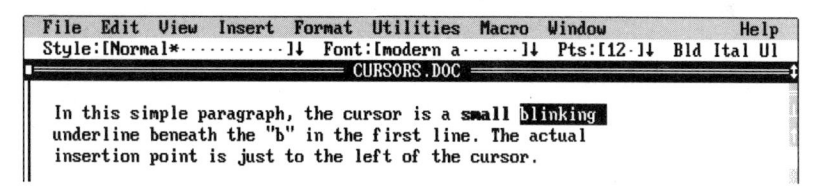

Word is clever. In the preceding example, the program has included the space following the word *blinking* as part of the selection. If you delete the selection, Word will delete the space along with the word. That's what you want because the space isn't needed in the sentence if the word has been removed. But if instead of deleting the selection, you format it—underline it, say—Word won't underline the space. Word knows you probably don't want to underline the space after a single underlined word.

If you press F8 a third time, the sentence containing the word is selected.

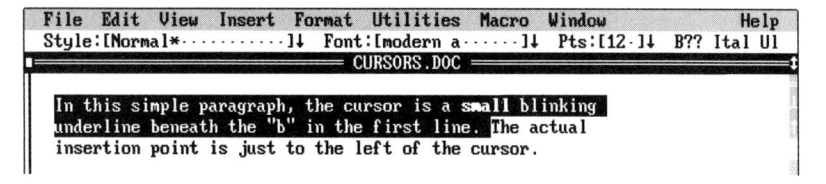

Notice in this example that the boldfaced word *small* still shows as bold even though the sentence containing it is highlighted.

If you press F8 yet another time, the entire paragraph is selected.

```
 File   Edit   View   Insert   Format   Utilities   Macro   Window              Help
 Style:[Normal*··········]↧  Font:[modern a······]↧  Pts:[12·]↧  B?? Ital Ul
═══════════════════════════════ CURSORS.DOC ═══════════════════════════════
In this simple paragraph, the cursor is a small blinking
underline beneath the "b" in the first line. The actual
insertion point is just to the left of the cursor.
```

If you were to press F8 a final time, the entire document would be selected. Two general rules govern use of the cursor:

♦ Whenever text is selected and you type a character or insert text into a document, the selection vanishes and the text is inserted at what was the beginning of the selection.

♦ You needn't select all of something when the action you want to take can be applied only to the whole. For example, you needn't select all of a paragraph to exercise the command that formats paragraphs: You can simply select a single character in it or position the insertion-point cursor inside it. By the same token, you needn't select a whole document to print it or to save it on disk; just be sure that if documents are in more than one window, the insertion point or selection is in the window of the document you want to print or save.

CONCEPT 4: SPACES AS CHARACTERS

There is a crucial difference between the absence of characters and the existence of characters that create blank spaces. Cryptographers know that the letter *e* is the most common letter in the English language. When you write something of any length, chances are it will contain more *e*'s than any other letter. But when you write on a computer, the most common character is the space. There's one between almost every pair of words.

Sometimes people don't understand why the cursor won't move to certain blank parts of the screen. This situation is most apparent when you first start Word and the document window on the screen is almost empty. At this time, the cursor is in the screen's upper left corner, at a small diamond (called the *end mark*) that marks the end of the document (which in this case happens to be the beginning of the document too). If you have a mouse, the mouse pointer might be on the screen somewhere, but all in all, the screen gives you a blank stare. And Word won't let you use the direction keys to move the selection because only characters can be selected and there aren't any on the screen yet.

Now imagine that you press the Spacebar 50 times, moving the selection (and the end mark with it) across the top row of the screen. The top row doesn't look too different now, nor does it look different from the blank lines below it. In reality, however, the top row is much different: It is filled with the 50 spaces you created with the Spacebar. To Word and your computer, these spaces are characters as much as *a*, *b*, and *c* and *1*, *2*, and *3* are characters; they simply print, both on screen and on paper, as spaces instead of as letters or numbers.

The Tab key is another key that creates a spacing character rather than a printing character. The tab character appears as a bar of light when it is selected because it is generally wider than a single character.

You can see on screen the difference between spacing characters and the absence of characters. Spacing characters appear on the screen if you use the View Preferences command to turn the Spaces check box on. Spaces made with the Spacebar show up as tiny dots, much smaller than periods.

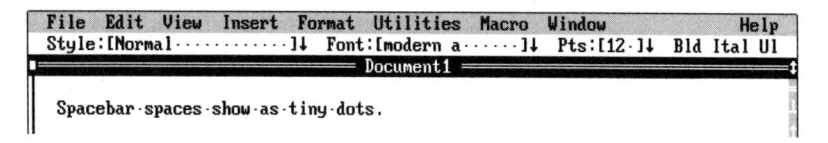

```
 File  Edit  View  Insert  Format  Utilities  Macro  Window              Help
 Style:[Normal············]↕  Font:[modern a······]↕  Pts:[12·]↕  Bld Ital Ul
════════════════════════════════ Document1 ═══════════════════════════════
 Spacebar·spaces·show·as·tiny·dots.
```

These dots also appear between words inside the scrap brackets at the bottom left of the screen, regardless of how the Options command is set.

CONCEPT 5: MOVING VERSUS CHANGING

There is a difference between simply moving your selection around in a document and actually changing the document.

Some beginners mistakenly try to use the Spacebar to move the cursor/selection/highlight across a line of text. It's an easy mistake to make. But while the computer's Spacebar moves the cursor to the right, it also adds spacing characters to the document as it goes. (If you've turned on Overtype mode by pressing the Ins key, the Spacebar overtypes existing characters instead of pushing them to the right.)

To move the selection without changing the document, much as you would scan a printed line without changing it, use either the mouse or the direction keys. To scroll through a long document, much as you'd page through a report or a book, use the PgUp or the PgDn key. These actions don't change the document's contents or format, so they aren't editing acts.

Most writing and editing involves both moving and changing: You move the cursor up a line to correct a misspelling, move it down a paragraph or two to refine an idea, and so on.

CONCEPT 6: CONTENT VERSUS FORMAT

Editing falls into two broad categories: establishing or changing *content* and establishing or changing *format*.

You control content by entering and revising text, including spacing characters. Content changes alter the substance but not the appearance of the document. Typing characters and deleting and inserting passages are examples of working with content.

Format, on the other hand, has nothing to do with substance and everything to do with appearance. Underlining characters, justifying or centering paragraphs, and setting page margins are examples of formatting.

One of Word's strengths lies in the way it can divorce content from format. You can change the content of a document without affecting its format, or the format without fiddling with content.

CONCEPT 7: THREE TYPES OF FORMATTING

Although the family of Format commands has many members, Word breaks formatting into three broad categories:

- Section formatting controls the overall appearance of pages, and it is applicable to a whole document or a major section of a document. You use the Format Section and Format Margins commands to specify characteristics such as page length and width, location of page numbers, and the dimensions of margins.
- Paragraph formatting controls how lines of text are laid out, and it applies to one or more whole paragraphs at a time. You can set paragraph indentation, centering, justification, and line spacing with the Format Paragraph command, or you can choose from among built-in paragraph formats that offer you popular choices at the touch of two keys.
- Character formatting controls the appearance of your text characters. A particular format can apply to as little as a single character or to as much as a whole document. The Format Character command applies such features as underlines, italics, and different fonts and type sizes to the characters you have selected. As an alternative to the command, built-in character formats offer you popular choices at the touch of two keys. (For example, holding down the Ctrl key and pressing the U key will underline the selected text.)

TIP FOR WORD VETERANS

- Section formatting was called Division formatting in all previous versions of Word for DOS.
- In previous versions of Word, you used built-in formats by holding down the Alt key and pressing a letter (such as U for underline). Beginning with Word 5.5, you use the Ctrl key rather than the Alt key for this purpose. For instance, Ctrl-U underlines.

CONCEPT 8: FORMAT AT ANY TIME

You can make formatting decisions before, during, or after typing a document:

- ♦ You can make formatting decisions in advance by creating or choosing a Word style sheet. As you type, you need only tell Word which styles (formatting rules) you want to use for various parts of the document.
- ♦ You can format while you create a document. If you specify a format as you type, it won't change: Letter after letter and page after page will have the same format until you specify otherwise.
- ♦ To format a document after writing and revising it, use the Select-Do model: First select the text to be formatted, and then apply the formatting with the Format commands or the built-in formats.

CONCEPT 9: FORMATTING CHEMICALS

You've already seen that Word divorces formatting from content. The benefit is efficiency and flexibility in formatting what you write. The disadvantage, for people who already know other word processors, is that Word's approach is not what they expect. To understand how Word applies formatting to content, think of a format as a chemical you spread on selected parts of your document.

Many word processors supply you with what amounts to a cup of pens. You use one pen to write normal characters, another to write italics, and so on. Formatting is a property of the pen that's in use. To change the appearance of what you write, you pick up a different pen. In a sense, Word lets you work this way if you want to: You can format the insertion-point cursor, as described in Concept 3, and then type text that is already formatted.

But to broaden your skills in formatting, think of the task in a different way.

In Word, imagine that you use a single pen for everything you write. The pen creates only content. To give the document the appearance you want, you use a "formatting chemical." One chemical underlines, another italicizes, another changes the size of type, and so forth. You can use several at the same time to combine formats for just the look you want. Your chemicals can be dabbed on a single character, or brushed over a passage or even a whole document. The underlying content never changes, but different formatting can utterly change the look of the document.

The key to skillful formatting is spreading the chemicals in such a way that they touch only the characters and paragraphs you want to format. If you've already finished writing and revising, you simply select the text and apply the chemical with a Format command, a built-in format, or a style from a style sheet.

To format while you write, you can apply formatting to the cursor in advance, or you can format a spot in your text and begin writing from that point. When you select a spot and format it, imagine you are dabbing the spot with a formatting chemical. As you type subsequent text, it gets smeared with the formatting chemical; any text you type will be formatted that way as long as you don't move the cursor away from the area treated with the chemical.

To achieve multiple formats within a single document, treat different passages with different formatting chemicals. Any writing you do in an area treated with a particular chemical will be given the same format.

Sounds easy, and it is, after you get the hang of it. But newcomers sometimes run into difficulties when they have treated different parts of a Word document with unlike formats. They become puzzled when they move the cursor away from the text that is formatted in the way they want. It seems to them that the formatting is changing of its own volition. If you fall into this situation on your road to mastering Word, remember that formatting exists only where it's been placed, either because you put it there or because it was "carried" there when you typed. These pointers may help too:

- Unless the cursor has been formatted, as described in Concept 3, all new text initially assumes the "look" of the position at which it is typed.
- If you use the mouse or the direction keys to move around in a document, you might accidentally move away from the formatting you want. Return to an area that has the formatting, and resume your work there if you can, or apply the desired formatting to your new location.
- Every character in a document is formatted in one way or another. If you don't give a character a specific font and size, Word gives it the "normal" (or "standard") format. The "normal" font is governed by your printer unless you are using a style sheet, in which case it is governed by the character-formatting portion of the Normal paragraph style. (More on this in Chapters 6 and 24.)

CONCEPT 10: DIRECT VERSUS INDIRECT

At times, Word is rather indirect. Instead of linking your actions directly to the effects they are intended to achieve, Word sometimes routes you through an intermediate step, in which your instructions or desires are translated. This approach provides numerous benefits, and it isn't troublesome because it's mostly invisible.

You can use Word productively for years and never know what's going on behind the scenes. But sometimes, when you want to take full advantage of the program or if you want to understand how the pieces of Word fit together, it helps to have at least a general understanding of what some Microsoft techies call *indirection*.

They may call it that, but I think of it as the "Blue Plate Special" approach. You know the scene: a short-order restaurant with a long counter and stools, a few tables, some scruffy linoleum. And on the wall is a sign proclaiming the Blue Plate Special. Meat loaf, with mashed potatoes and overcooked green beans, perhaps. The special changes daily, or maybe it doesn't. Regardless, regulars know they can order a whole meal just by calling out "Blue Plate Special."

This is an indirect, but efficient, way to give an order. Rather than directly specifying what you want—"meat loaf, with mashed potatoes and green beans"—you point to or call out the special. Whatever happens to be written on the sign becomes your order. In a sense, the sign translates your brief order into something specific and detailed that the kitchen can work on. And there can be more than one special, giving patrons a variety of easy choices. When a busload of people arrives all at one time, matters are sped up considerably if the server can simply jot down the name (or number) of a special for each patron.

Now let's step out of the diner and back to your computer.

Word is justly renowned for its ability to format the appearance of documents quickly and attractively. Most beginners with Word use *direct formatting,* in which they modify the text of their document the way they want it. Direct formatting creates a firm link between text and its format. But much of Word's effectiveness stems from its ability to format in an indirect way, using a style sheet.

When you use a style sheet, you store sets of specific, detailed formatting instructions as individual *styles.* Then you apply these styles to your document. Rather than saying "I want this line to be centered, uppercase, and boldface, with two blank lines before it and one blank line after it," you say "I want this line to be a *Heading 1* style." To turn a line into a heading, you simply hold down the Shift and Ctrl keys simultaneously and type a one-letter or two-letter code that tells Word you want to use the Heading 1 style. Word then interprets what you want and applies the combination of formats associated with the Heading 1 style. It's like ordering the Blue Plate Special instead of detailing all the particulars of what you want. This formatting is called *indirect* because the specific formatting instructions aren't applied to your document (even though it seems as if they are). The formatting really is stored in a style in the style sheet, and Word consults the style to know how to print what you have written.

Obviously, indirect formatting can be fast because you can specify so many details with one command. It also lends consistency to a document because all headings, for example, will be formatted identically (provided you use the same style for each of them). But there are less-obvious advantages to the indirect approach too. For example, if you have a long document with many headings and you want to add an underline to each of them, you can simply add the underline once (to the formatting of the Heading 1 style), and Word will instantly underline all of the headings formatted with this style. In a sense, it is like making a change to the Blue Plate Special sign instead of going around changing all the menus in the diner.

Another example of Word's indirect nature involves printers and typefaces. Word always wants to know what printer you are using, and it adjusts its list of available typefaces (called *fonts*) accordingly. Consequently, when you are choosing a typeface

---

TIP FOR WORD VETERANS

In earlier versions of Word, the quickest way to format text by using a style was to hold down the Alt key and type the style's one-character or two-character *key code.*

To use such a key code in Word 5.5, you hold down the Ctrl key and type Y followed by the code. Or you hold down Shift and Ctrl simultaneously and type the code.

for a document, the list of alternatives includes only those that your particular printer uses. Word gets the information it needs about the printer from the installed *printer file*, also called a *PRD file*.

But what if you format a document using one printer and later want to print it using a different printer that has different fonts? This is where Word's indirect approach is useful. When you format with a font such as Courier, the document itself seems to be directly formatted in Courier type. This is not the case. In reality, the document is formatted with one of 64 generic fonts—fonts that have names such as roman a or modern a or modern b. When you tell Word to format in Courier, it checks the printer file to see which generic font corresponds to Courier on your particular printer. It formats the document using the generic name rather than the specific name Courier. When you ask Word to show you the name of a font or when it comes time to print the document, Word knows only the generic font name. So it must translate again. It consults the printer file to see which actual font to use. If Courier on your printer is assigned to the generic font name *modern a*, Word consults the printer file when you print to translate this generic name back into Courier. If you switch printers (and hence printer files), Courier might no longer be available. But the new printer might well have a different font assigned to the generic name *modern a*, and so your document is printed to the best capabilities of the new printer. It's all indirect, but effective.

CONCEPT 11: WINDOWS VERSUS DOCUMENTS

This is intended especially for users of earlier versions of Word who are moving to Word 5.5.

In the past, Word has treated a window and a document as distinct entities. For example, you could open a window that did not contain a document, or you could clear a document from a window, leaving it empty. You could even replace the contents of a window by loading a different document from disk.

In contrast, Word 5.5 eliminates the distinction between a document and the window that displays it. In Word 5.5, a window and its document are inseparable: You cannot clear the document from the window or load a different document into the window. If one document is displayed and you load another document from disk, the newcomer appears in its own window on top of the first document. To display only one of these documents, you must close the window containing the first document and then open the other document. In other words, although Word 5.0 lets you use the Transfer Load command to replace one document with another, Word 5.5 requires that you use the File Close command to close the first document (and its window) before you use the File Open command to bring the new document to the screen (again, in its own window).

> NOTE: *You can load the same document into more than one window so that you can look at more than one part of it simultaneously. A document can be displayed in up to nine windows at once, but a given window can display only one document.*

Although this notion of a document and its window as a single entity might seem odd to veterans of Microsoft Word for DOS, the concept is familiar to users of Microsoft Word for the Macintosh and Microsoft Word for Windows: These other two programs have always treated documents and the windows that contain them as virtually one and the same.

CHAPTER THREE

Getting Started: A Tutorial

Starting Word is easy: Simply type *word* at the DOS prompt, and press Enter. Or, if you're using Microsoft Windows, double-click on the Word icon.

Once you've started the program, Word can be as simple to use as a typewriter and much more forgiving:

- Just type.
- If you make a mistake, press the Backspace key to erase it, and then type the correction.
- When you're done, print the result by holding down the Shift key and pressing the F9 key and then pressing the Enter key.
- If you want to save your work on disk, hold down the Alt and Shift keys simultaneously and press the F2 key. Type a name for the document if Word asks for one, and press Enter.

Quitting Word is easy too. Hold down the Alt key and press the F4 key. Word will exit to DOS or Windows. That's it.

Of course, by learning only a little more of Word than the bare essentials you can do a lot more than simply type and print documents. In this chapter you'll learn to use easy formatting that is built into Word to write, print, and save a good-looking document in a few minutes. Along the way you'll practice such tasks as selecting and deleting text.

NOTE: *This chapter is intended primarily for newcomers to Word. If you are an intermediate or advanced user and already have experience with version 5.5, you might want to skim the chapter for tips and skip the hands-on practice session.*

BUILT-IN SPEED FORMATS

Word's built-in formats, called *speed formats*, make creating attractive documents easy. By holding down the Ctrl key and pressing one other key, you can specify a wide variety of looks for what you write or edit. You can even combine speed formats for additional variety. In later chapters you'll learn other ways to format documents. But for the exercises in this chapter, let's rely on predefined speed formats because they're relatively flexible and quite simple to use. For many purposes, speed formats are all you need.

Recall from Chapter 2 the three main types of formatting: section, paragraph, and character. Word has built-in speed formats for each.

> **TIP**
>
> If you have macros installed in Word that have codes beginning with Ctrl, you might find it necessary to first press Ctrl+A to use speed-formatting keys. For example, if a macro is installed that has a code beginning with the letter C, you won't be able to press Ctrl+C to use the speed-formatting key for centering. Instead, you must press Ctrl+AC for centering.

The Built-In Section Format

Section formatting controls the layout of pages in a major section of a document. (A document's index might be a separate section with its own page layout, for example.) You can think of section formatting as "page formatting." You can also think of it as "document formatting" because many people rarely, if ever, break documents into more than one section.

Word has only one built-in section format. Because it is in effect unless you change it, you don't need to do anything to use it; Word will follow the guidelines of the built-in section format.

> **TIP FOR WORD VETERANS**
>
> The Ctrl key, not the Alt key, is used to signal to Word that you are using a speed-formatting key. Prior to Word 5.5, the Alt key was used almost exclusively for formatting, including speed formatting. But in version 5.5, the Alt key has been given over to choosing commands, and formatting tasks have been reassigned to the Ctrl key.

In the version of Word sold in the United States, the built-in section format has the following characteristics:

- Page length is 11 inches; page width is 8.5 inches.
- Automatic page numbering is turned off.
- If you turn on automatic page numbering, page numbers print 0.5 inch from the top of the page and 7.25 inches from the left edge of the page.
- Top and bottom page margins are each 1 inch.
- Left and right page margins are each 1.25 inches, providing you with a 6-inch–wide writing space.

NOTE: *If you prefer that Word use a different page format as its default, you have two choices. You can define a Normal Section style in a NORMAL style sheet, as described in Chapters 6 and 24. Or you can give Word new measurements for the default page size and margins of the built-in section format. This technique is covered in the Format Margins discussion in Chapter 15. This chapter assumes that default section formatting is* not *changed.*

Built-In Paragraph Formats

Paragraph formatting dictates how lines are laid out on the page. It is called paragraph formatting because it is imposed on a whole paragraph at a time. Unless you tell it otherwise or use a style sheet, Word gives every paragraph a "normal" paragraph format. This built-in format has the following characteristics:

- Text is aligned evenly (justified) on the left side. The right side of the paragraph is uneven (not justified).
- Text is not indented on the right or the left side. In other words, text extends all the way to the page margins. (This is not to say the text extends to the edge of the page. The page margins are governed by section formatting.)
- The first line of the paragraph has no indentation.
- Lines are single-spaced, six to the vertical inch.
- No extra space appears above or below the paragraph.
- Tab stops are preset evenly across the lines of the paragraph. The default spacing is every 0.5 inch, but you can change this distance with the Utilities Customize command.

TIP FOR WORD VETERANS

In version 5.5, you no longer can use the speed-formatting key F to indent the first line of a paragraph. (The F key is used as a speed-formatting key that lets you use the ribbon to indicate a font.)

Word offers 11 other built-in paragraph formats that alter the "normal" paragraph format. Each of these formats has its own speed-formatting key. A twelfth speed-formatting key, Ctrl+X, undoes all paragraph formatting and returns the selected paragraph or paragraphs to the "normal," built-in format. This lets you undo the cumulative effects of several speed-formatting keys.

Two additional speed-formatting keys, Ctrl+S and Ctrl+Y, permit you to format text easily using *styles*, which are combinations of formatting stored in a file called a *style sheet*. You'll be introduced to these methods in Chapters 4, 5, and 6.

The table in Figure 3-1 and the examples in Figure 3-2 show the built-in paragraph formats and their key combinations. Any paragraph or paragraphs that contain the cursor or are selected when you use a paragraph key code will be formatted according to the corresponding built-in format.

To obtain this paragraph formatting (appearance):	Press:
Normal paragraph (undoes formats)	Ctrl+X
Centered	Ctrl+C
Justified (right and left edges even)	Ctrl+J
Flush left (only left edge even)	Ctrl+L
Increase left indent one tab stop (nest)	Ctrl+N
Decrease left indent one tab stop (unnest)	Ctrl+M
Open spacing (blank line before paragraph)	Ctrl+O
For quotations, indent 0.5" from left and right	Ctrl+Q
Flush right (only right edge even)	Ctrl+R
Hanging indent (all but first line indented)	Ctrl+T
Single-spaced lines	Ctrl+1
Double-spaced lines	Ctrl+2

Figure 3-1. Built-in paragraph formats and speed-formatting keys.

```
Ctrl+X: This paragraph is in the "normal" built-in paragraph
format used by Word. Note that it is flush left, meaning
that only the left edges of the lines are even.

Ctrl+C: Now the paragraph is shown in the centered built-in
   format. Center the lines in a paragraph by selecting any
   character or characters in it and hold down the Ctrl key
             while pressing the letter C.

Ctrl+J: Now the paragraph has been justified. Each line
except the last is the same length. Extra spaces are placed
in the middle of the lines to make both ends line up.
```

Figure 3-2. Examples of built-in paragraph formats.

(continued)

Figure 3-2. continued

Ctrl+L: This paragraph shows the flush left style. It looks identical to the "normal" built-in paragraph format, but differs because it can be added on top of other paragraph formats, while the "normal" format replaces all other built-in paragraph formats.

> Ctrl+N: The combination Ctrl+N "nests" a paragraph one tab stop. That means its left indent increases one tab stop, relative to the way it was formatted before the built-in format was applied.

> Ctrl+N, Ctrl+J: This paragraph has both nesting and justification. To do this, apply one built-in format, and then the other.

Ctrl+M: The combination Ctrl+M is the opposite of Ctrl+N. Holding down the Stroll key and pressing the letter M reduces nesting by one tab stop, relative to the way the paragraph was before, or to the paragraph preceding it.

>> Ctrl+N, Ctrl+N: You can nest a paragraph two full tab stops by using the combination Ctrl+N twice. Each use causes a one-tab indentation for the whole paragraph — and all that follow it.

Ctrl+O: All of these paragraphs have open spacing — meaning there is a blank space before them. To achieve this, you use the built-in paragraph format Ctrl+O.

> Ctrl+Q: This format is handy for block quotations. It indents both the left and right paragraph indents by one tab stop. If you use it successively, the indents will get larger and larger.

Ctrl+R: This format is of less use than most. It lines up the right side of lines, and leaves the paragraph "ragged left." It is called the flush right built-in format.

Ctrl+T: This format simulates some fancy work with tabs. It is called a "hanging indent," because its first line has an outdent of one tab stop. Each time you press the Ctrl+T combination, the outdent increases one tab stop.

Ctrl+1: This paragraph shows the single-space style. It looks identical to the "normal" built-in paragraph format, but differs because it can be added on top of other paragraph formats, while the "normal" format replaces all other built-in paragraph formats.

Ctrl+2: Paragraphs can be double-spaced by using the built-

in format that has the key combination Ctrl+2. Select any

spot in the paragraph — or select many paragraphs — and

hold down the Ctrl key at the same time you press the 2 key.

Built-In Character Formats

Character formatting dictates how specific characters in your text appear when printed. Underlining and boldfacing are examples. If your computer equipment can display it and you are using a graphics mode, rudimentary character formatting is shown on the screen. However, Word displays all characters in the same font and size, regardless of how they will print.

Because character formatting affects individual characters, you must select all the characters first before formatting them. (Text selection was introduced in Concept 3 of Chapter 2.)

Eight speed-formatting keys let you apply built-in character formats singly or in combinations.

Two additional key combinations remove rather than add formats. One is Ctrl+Spacebar, and the other is Ctrl+Z. To contrast the effects of these key combinations, imagine that you have highlighted a sentence that is formatted with the Times Roman font, in the 10-point size, with both underlining and boldface.

- Pressing Ctrl+Spacebar removes all special character formatting from the selected characters, returning the characters to whatever your printer considers "normal." If your printer considers 12-point Courier to be "normal," the selected characters would become 12-point Courier and would not be underlined or boldfaced.
- Pressing Ctrl+Z removes all special character formatting except font and font size. The selected characters in our example would remain 10-point Times Roman but would no longer be underlined or boldfaced.

The built-in character formats are shown in the table in Figure 3-3 and the examples in Figure 3-4.

To obtain this character formatting (appearance):	Press:
Normal (undoes formats)	Ctrl+Spacebar
Normal (undoes all but font and size)	Ctrl+Z
Bold	Ctrl+B
Italic	Ctrl+I
Underline	Ctrl+U
Double underline	Ctrl+D
Small caps	Ctrl+K
Superscript	Ctrl+plus
Subscript	Ctrl+equal sign
Hidden	Ctrl+H

Figure 3-3. Built-in character formats and key codes.

CHAPTER THREE: Getting Started

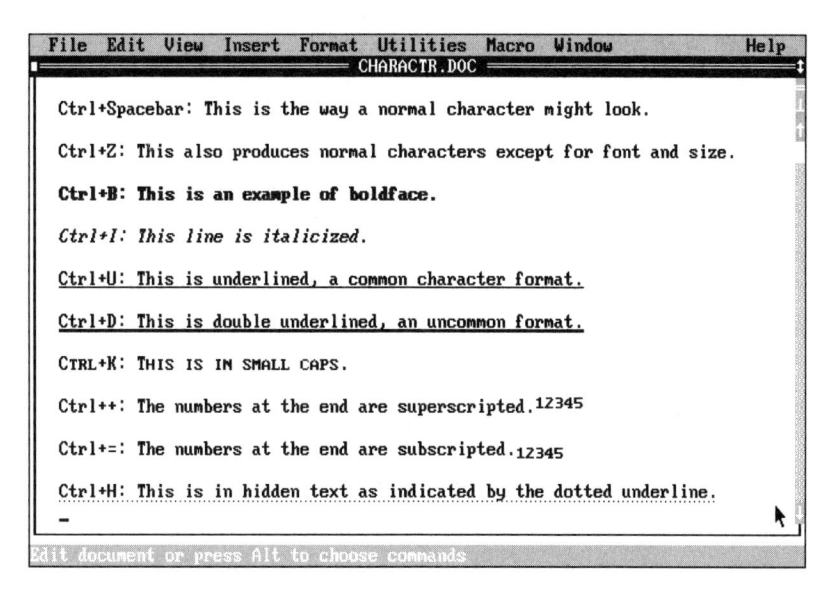

```
 File  Edit  View  Insert  Format  Utilities  Macro  Window              Help
                            CHARACTR.DOC
 Ctrl+Spacebar: This is the way a normal character might look.

 Ctrl+Z: This also produces normal characters except for font and size.

 Ctrl+B: This is an example of boldface.

 Ctrl+I: This line is italicized.

 Ctrl+U: This is underlined, a common character format.

 Ctrl+D: This is double underlined, an uncommon format.

 CTRL+K: THIS IS IN SMALL CAPS.

 Ctrl++: The numbers at the end are superscripted.12345

 Ctrl+=: The numbers at the end are subscripted.12345

 Ctrl+H: This is in hidden text as indicated by the dotted underline.

 Edit document or press Alt to choose commands
```

Figure 3-4. Examples of built-in character formats. (Characters formatted as "hidden" normally don't appear on the screen. When they do, they have a dotted or solid underline, or they appear in a different color.)

You can combine speed character formats with each other and also with speed paragraph formats. Like the paragraph formats, the speed character formats "toggle"—that is, if you press a speed-formatting key a second time, the format is turned off.

THE TUTORIAL

This tutorial teaches you how to take advantage of Word's built-in formats so that you can easily give a polished appearance to your documents. You'll write a short, informal memo, revise and format it, and then print and store it. The steps are fully explained, but if you want to experience uninterrupted activity with Word, go through the hands-on practice without stopping to absorb the discussion, and then return to read it carefully while the exercise is still fresh in your mind.

If Word is not already on your screen, type *word* and press Enter. The only character in Word's text area should be the diamond-shaped endmark.

Now let's use Word to create and print this memo:

```
                              Memo


         TO:  Horatio Toad, supervisor

         FR:  Ima Killjoy

         RE:  European Travel



              I've returned from a hectic trip to Europe, one I
         didn't request, you'll remember.  It was your idea to send me
         abroad on a scouting trip.  And it was on short notice.

              The streets were crowded.  There wasn't a shower in my
         room.  The sleeping car on the train to Amsterdam was a
         furnace.  It rained half the time.  I felt intimidated
         occasionally.

              So I have just one question, boss:  How soon may I go
         back?  I loved it!
```

To ensure that we're starting from the same place, tap the Esc key once or twice to be sure the cursor is in the text window.

BUT FIRST...

Before working with the program for the first time, you must either set up Word using the installation program called SETUP or be sure someone else has done it already. The setup procedure tailors Word to the characteristics of your video monitor and printer and prepares certain files that are otherwise unusable.

Appendix A explains the use of the SETUP program, discusses the role of the MasterWord WORDSET program, and explains how you can use Word itself to adjust options that you would otherwise control with SETUP or WORDSET. The appendix also explains the various ways to start Word, such as typing *word/l* to start Word and load the last document on which you worked.

CHAPTER THREE: Getting Started

Getting Ready

As a prelude to the tutorial, we will verify two of Word's settings to be sure that what you see on your screen matches the images that accompany the instructions here.

NOTE: *For simplicity, only keyboard methods are offered for these initial* Getting Ready *steps. Even if you have a mouse, please use the keyboard for just the first minute or so, while we get your copy of Word set up. Then you can use mouse methods for the many operations in the rest of the chapter.*

Step 1. With Word running, press the Alt key and then press the letter V. This displays the commands on Word's View menu.

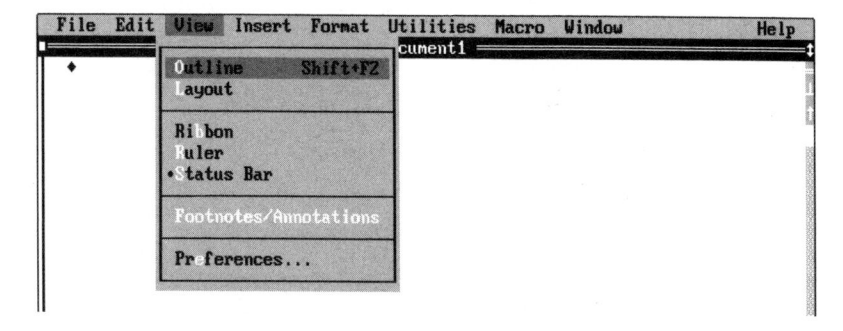

Step 2. Check to see if there is a dot before the word *Ribbon* in the View menu. In the sample screen illustration, there is no dot before *Ribbon* but there is a dot before *Status Bar*. A dot indicates that the named option is turned on. Our objective is to be sure the ribbon is on.

Step 3. If there *is* a dot before the word *Ribbon*, the ribbon is already on. In this case, press the Esc key to cancel the menu. On the other hand, if there is *no* dot before the word *Ribbon*, press the Down direction key until the word *Ribbon* is highlighted, and then press Enter to turn the ribbon on.

The ribbon offers information about the formatting of your document and gives you easy ways to change the formatting. After the ribbon is displayed, the top of the screen will look something like this:

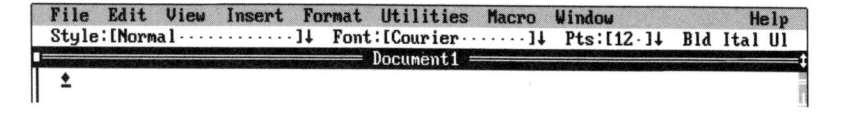

Step 4. Choose the View menu again by pressing Alt and then V. Then press the Down direction key six times to highlight the Preferences command.

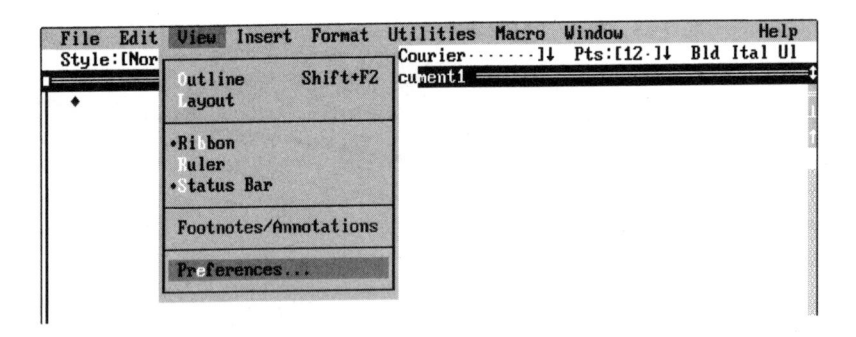

```
File  Edit  View  Insert  Format  Utilities  Macro  Window            Help
Style:[Nor                          Courier·······]↓ Pts:[12·]↓ Bld Ital Ul
            Outline     Shift+F2 cument1
            Layout

            •Ribbon
             Ruler
            •Status Bar

            Footnotes/Annotations

            Preferences...
```

Note that the word *Preferences* has three dots after it. This indicates that if you press Enter to choose the command you'll be shown a *dialog box* filled with various choices that pertain to the command. Any command name that ends in an ellipsis (...) leads to a dialog box.

Step 5. With the word *Preferences* highlighted on the View menu, press the Enter key to move to the View Preferences dialog box. This is what it looks like:

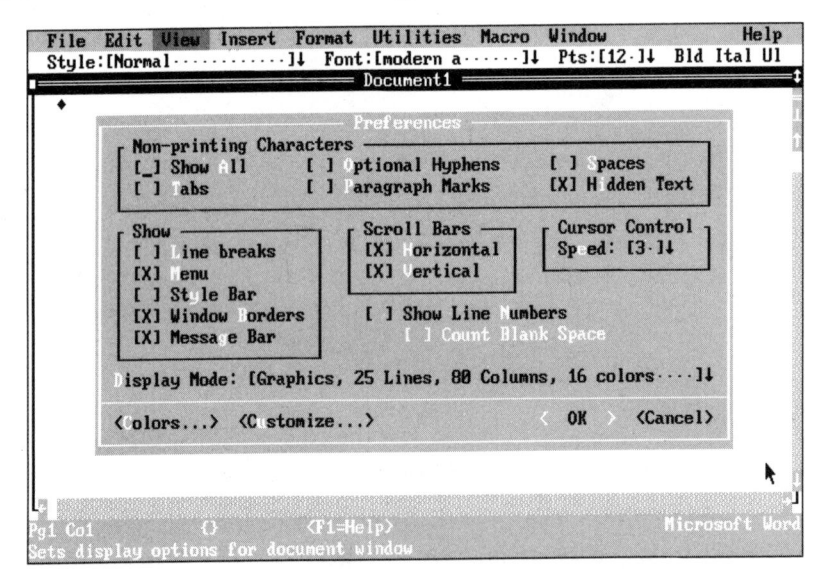

```
File  Edit  View  Insert  Format  Utilities  Macro  Window            Help
Style:[Normal············]↓ Font:[modern a······]↓ Pts:[12·]↓ Bld Ital Ul
                          ══ Document1 ══
   ┌──────────────── Preferences ────────────────┐
   │ ┌─ Non-printing Characters ─────────────────┐│
   │ │ [_] Show All       [ ] Optional Hyphens   [ ] Spaces       ││
   │ │ [ ] Tabs           [ ] Paragraph Marks    [X] Hidden Text  ││
   │ └───────────────────────────────────────────┘│
   │ ┌─ Show ──────────┐ ┌─ Scroll Bars ─┐ ┌─ Cursor Control ─┐│
   │ │ [ ] Line breaks │ │ [X] Horizontal│ │ Speed: [3·]↓    ││
   │ │ [X] Menu        │ │ [X] Vertical  │ └─────────────────┘│
   │ │ [ ] Style Bar   │ │                                    │
   │ │ [X] Window Borders│ [ ] Show Line Numbers              │
   │ │ [X] Message Bar │    [ ] Count Blank Space             │
   │ └─────────────────┘                                      │
   │ Display Mode: [Graphics, 25 Lines, 80 Columns, 16 colors····]↓│
   │                                                          │
   │ <Colors...> <Customize...>        < OK >   <Cancel>      │
   └──────────────────────────────────────────────────────────┘
Pg1 Co1         {}         <F1=Help>              Microsoft Word
Sets display options for document window
```

The dialog box lets you express preferences about a number of aspects of Word's personality. The topmost collection of choices appears under the heading *Non-printing Characters*. Each choice is controlled by a separate *check box*. In the sample illustration, the Paragraph Marks check box is not checked but the Hidden Text check box is checked.

Step 6. Press the Tab key three times to move to the choice labeled *Paragraph Marks*. If there is an X in this check box, paragraph marks will be displayed on the screen. In this case, press the Esc key to cancel the Preferences command. On the other hand, if there is not an X in this check box, press the Spacebar once to cause paragraph marks to display as symbols on the screen. Then press Enter to carry out the command.

This completes our check on how Word is set up. Many other choices can be made about the way Word looks and functions. See Appendix A for an overview.

Look Before You Type

Now we can begin to work with Word.

Step 1. Look at the format of the memo on page 40. Observe that all paragraphs have a blank line above them (open paragraph spacing). You want the document you are about to type to have the same format.

Step 2. Observe on your screen that the blinking cursor is under a diamond-shaped mark. This is called the *endmark*. It signifies the end of a file. When a file is new and empty, as is the one on your screen, the diamond is at both the beginning and the end of the file, because the file's beginning and its end are synonymous. Most of the time you want to keep away from the endmark or at least ignore it.

Step 3. With the cursor at the beginning of the document (and coincidentally on the endmark), hold down the Ctrl key and press O (the letter O, not a zero) to apply the built-in speed format for open paragraph spacing.

Whether you typed Ctrl+AO or just Ctrl+O, Word responds by

- Formatting the first paragraph of the document to have a blank line before it. On the screen, you see the cursor move down a line, reflecting this "open" formatting.
- Displaying a paragraph mark (¶).
- Pushing the endmark down a line below the cursor. It does this because the paragraph mark itself cannot be formatted.

This is what you should see at the top of your screen after you have used the Ctrl+O speed-formatting key to create open paragraph formatting:

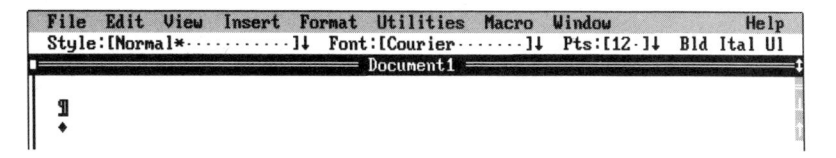

```
File  Edit  View  Insert  Format  Utilities  Macro  Window              Help
Style:[Normal*··········]↓  Font:[Courier·······]↓  Pts:[12·]↓  Bld Ital Ul
═══════════════════════════ Document1 ═══════════════════════════

      ¶
      ♦
```

Entering Text

You're ready to begin entering text.

Step 1. Type the word *Memo*, and press the Enter key to signify that you've reached the end of the paragraph. In this case, the paragraph is only a single line—indeed, a single word. The word is not centered, boldfaced, or underlined, although it will be before you're through. You'll come back later to format it.

Step 2. To create extra blank space in your document, press the Enter key again, thereby creating another paragraph. Notice that the cursor moves down two more lines and now is under the mark of the third paragraph. All of these paragraphs are formatted identically because they all were created from the paragraph you previously formatted to have open line spacing.

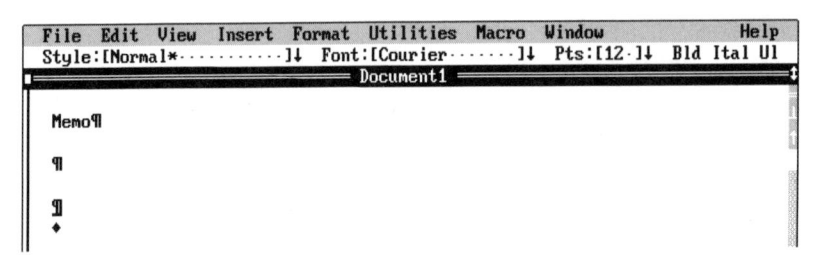

```
  File  Edit  View  Insert  Format  Utilities  Macro  Window           Help
  Style:[Normal*···········]↓  Font:[Courier········]↓ Pts:[12·]↓ Bld Ital Ul
═══════════════════════════════ Document1 ═══════════════════════════════
  Memo¶

  ¶

  ¶
  ◆
```

NOTE: *If you were now to press the Up direction key once, the cursor would move back up to the preceding paragraph. Anything you subsequently wrote in either paragraph would be formatted with open spacing. However, if you were to press the Down direction key once instead, the selection would move to the endmark, and anything you typed would assume the look of a "normal" paragraph: no open spacing. If you didn't understand what had happened, you might think that Word had somehow lost your formatting instructions. On the contrary, the formatting would still be there, but you'd have to move your cursor back up to a formatted paragraph in order to use it.*

Step 3. Type the next line:

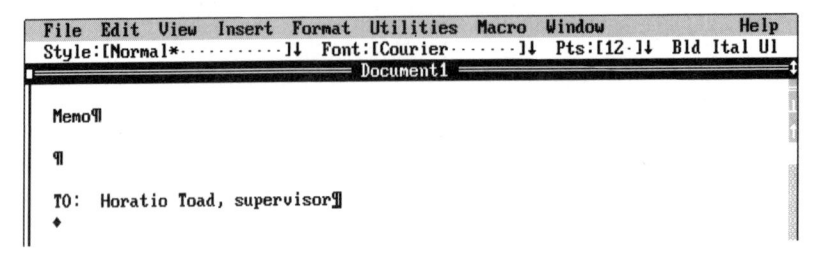

```
  File  Edit  View  Insert  Format  Utilities  Macro  Window           Help
  Style:[Normal*···········]↓  Font:[Courier········]↓ Pts:[12·]↓ Bld Ital Ul
═══════════════════════════════ Document1 ═══════════════════════════════
  Memo¶

  ¶

  TO:   Horatio Toad, supervisor¶
  ◆
```

CHAPTER THREE: Getting Started   45

To type the example exactly, follow *TO:* by pressing the Tab key to enter a tab character into the document. If you make a typing error, use the Backspace key to back up and erase it, and then retype it.

Step 4. Press the Enter key at the end of the line to end the paragraph and create a new one.

Step 5. Type the next two lines, pressing the Enter key at the end of each:

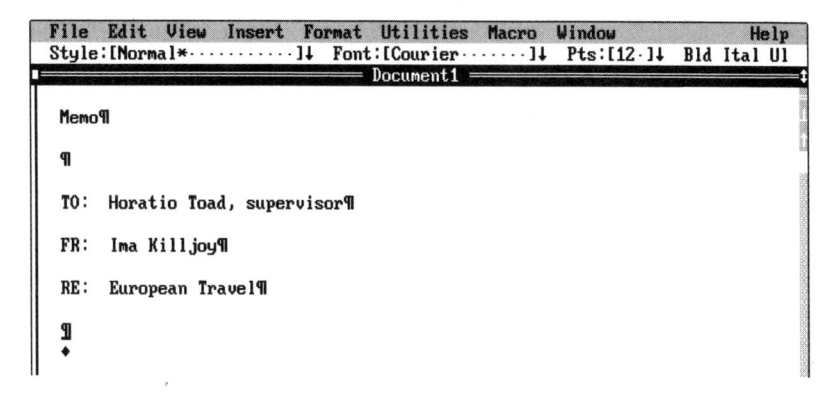

```
File  Edit  View  Insert  Format  Utilities  Macro  Window           Help
Style:[Normal*··········]↓  Font:[Courier·······]↓  Pts:[12·]↓ Bld Ital Ul
======================== Document1 ========================

Memo¶

¶

TO:    Horatio Toad, supervisor¶

FR:    Ima Killjoy¶

RE:    European Travel¶

¶
♦
```

Step 6. To create an extra blank line before beginning the body of the memo, press the Enter key one extra time.

Step 7. Type the first paragraph of the memo, as shown here:

```
I've returned from a hectic trip to Europe, a trip I didn't
request, you'll remember. It was your idea to send me abroad
on a scouting trip. And it was on short notice.¶
```

Do not press the Enter key at the end of each line. Word moves to the next line for you. Do press the Enter key once when you are at the end of the paragraph.

Step 8. Type the next paragraph. Remember to press the Enter key only at the end of the paragraph. Notice that when you reach the last line of the screen, Word scrolls one line up so that you continue to add text at the bottom of the document window.

When you're done, your screen should look something like this:

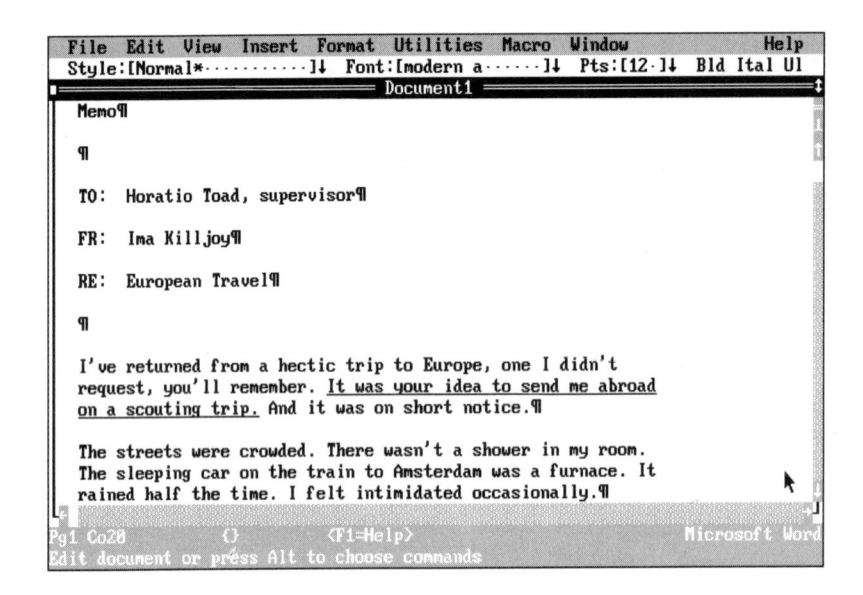

```
File   Edit   View   Insert   Format   Utilities   Macro   Window              Help
Style:[Normal*············]↓  Font:[modern a······]↓  Pts:[12·]↓  Bld Ital Ul
═══════════════════════════════ Document1 ═══════════════════════════════
Memo¶

¶

TO:   Horatio Toad, supervisor¶

FR:   Ima Killjoy¶

RE:   European Travel¶

¶

I've returned from a hectic trip to Europe, one I didn't
request, you'll remember. It was your idea to send me abroad
on a scouting trip. And it was on short notice.¶

The streets were crowded. There wasn't a shower in my room.
The sleeping car on the train to Amsterdam was a furnace. It
rained half the time. I felt intimidated occasionally.¶

Pg1 Co28         {}         <F1=Help>                    Microsoft Word
Edit document or press Alt to choose commands
```

Revising Content

Before you finish typing the memo, let's go back and practice revising the content of what you've already typed. Let's decide that the word *trip* is overused in the first paragraph. We'll eliminate the second instance of the word.

Step 1. Move the cursor to the word *a*, as shown here.

```
I've returned from a hectic trip to Europe, a trip I didn't
request, you'll remember. It was your idea to send me abroad
on a scouting trip. And it was on short notice.¶
```

You can move the cursor either with the direction keys or by rolling the mouse until the mouse pointer is on *a* and then clicking the left mouse button.

Step 2. Select (highlight) the text *a trip* (including the space after the *p* in *trip*).

Extending the selection

There are several ways to extend the selection to encompass all of *a trip*, including the following:

- Hold down the Shift key, and press the Right direction key repeatedly. As long as you continue to hold down the Shift key, direction keys extend the selection rather than move the cursor.
- Press the F8 key once to turn on Extend Selection mode, press the Right direction key repeatedly, and then press the Esc key to turn off Extend Selection mode.

CHAPTER THREE: Getting Started   47

- Press F8 once to extend the selection; then hold down the Ctrl key, and press the Right direction key twice. Each time you press Ctrl+Right, the highlight is extended to encompass another word.
- Point at the letter *a* with the mouse, hold down the Right direction key to select a word at a time, and move the mouse to the right so that the highlight is extended to encompass all of *a trip*.

This is how your line will look when the cursor is expanded into a highlight that selects both words (and the space following the second word):

```
I've returned from a hectic trip to Europe, a trip I didn't
request, you'll remember. It was your idea to send me abroad
on a scouting trip. And it was on short notice.¶
```

Deleting the selected text

Step 3. Press the Del key once. The Del key deletes whatever is selected—in this case, the words *a trip*.

Alternatively, with the mouse you can delete the highlighted text by using the Edit Cut command: (1) Move the mouse pointer to the word *Edit* in the menu of command names at the top of the screen, and click the left mouse button; (2) point at the word *Cut* and click again.

Notice that the Edit Cut command deletes text to the *scrap*, a special temporary storage area represented in the status bar at the bottom of the screen by brackets: {}. In contrast, pressing the Del key kills selected text—deleting it completely rather than sending it to the scrap. (You need to hold down the Shift key and press the Del key if you want to send the text to the scrap.)

No matter how you delete the phrase *a trip*, the cursor remains in the place within the paragraph, but the remaining text re-forms to fill the space left by the words you deleted:

```
I've returned from a hectic trip to Europe, I didn't
request, you'll remember. It was your idea to send me abroad
on a scouting trip. And it was on short notice.¶
```

Undoing an editing act

Step 4. To experience a handy feature, hold down the Alt key and press the Backspace key. This is one way to trigger Word's Undo command, which reverses virtually any editing action. In this case, as soon as you release the Alt key the previously deleted text is restored and highlighted.

```
I've returned from a hectic trip to Europe, a trip I didn't
request, you'll remember. It was your idea to send me abroad
on a scouting trip. And it was on short notice.¶
```

Alternatively, with the mouse you can point at the word *Edit* in the menu at the top of the screen and click the left button, and then point at the word *Undo* and click again.

Although restoring deleted text may be the most common use of the Undo command, Undo also is valuable as a means of reversing the effects of such acts as formatting changes.

Step 5. Repeat Step 4 in order to "undo the undo." When you run the Undo command a second time, you reverse the effect of its previous use. In this case, pressing Alt+Backspace again causes the words *a trip* to once again vanish from your document.

You can execute the command repeatedly so that you can compare two versions of the same passage.

Typing the replacement text

Step 6. To complete the revision, type the word *one* and put a space after it with the Spacebar. The inserted text appears to the immediate left of the cursor.

```
I've returned from a hectic trip to Europe, one I didn't
request, you'll remember. It was your idea to send me abroad
on a scouting trip. And it was on short notice.¶
```

Revising the content of what you write is just that easy.

Moving text to a new location

Although we're not going to do it in this tutorial, you might want to know how easy it is to move text from one location to another. It's just a variation on, and an extension of, the steps you've just taken.

First you select the text to be moved, just as you selected the text *a trip*, then you delete it to the scrap, as discussed in Step 3 above.

Finally, you move the cursor to the location to which you want to move the text, and insert it from the scrap. You can insert text from the scrap by using the Edit Paste command (Alt+EP) or by pressing either the Ins key or Shift+Ins. (Just as the method of deleting to the scrap is to press either Del or Shift+Del, so the method of inserting from the scrap is to press either Ins or Shift+Ins. See Step 3 above, or for details see the Chapter 5 discussion "Emulating Word 5.0 Keys.")

Revising Formatting

Now that you have had a little experience revising the content of a document, let's turn to revising formatting. We'll employ some of the speed-formatting keys introduced at the beginning of the chapter, using them to apply built-in speed formats to text that we've already typed.

CHAPTER THREE: Getting Started

Step 1. Move the cursor down one line so that it is within the sentence that begins *It was your idea*. Do this by pressing the Down direction key or by positioning the mouse pointer within the sentence and clicking the left mouse button.

Step 2. Select (highlight) the entire sentence. You can do this in several ways:

- Press the F8 key once to turn on Extend Selection mode, again to select the word containing the cursor, and then again to select the entire sentence. If you press the F8 key one too many times, the entire paragraph will become highlighted; reverse this by holding down the Shift key and pressing the F8 key.
- Point with the mouse at any letter in the sentence, hold down the Ctrl key, and click the left mouse button.

This is how the sentence looks when selected:

> I've returned from a hectic trip to Europe, one I didn't request, you'll remember. **It was your idea to send me abroad on a scouting trip.** And it was on short notice.¶

Observe that the space following the end of the sentence is selected too. Word is smart about this. If you press the Del key at this point, all of the selected characters will vanish, preventing extra spaces from appearing in the middle of the paragraph. But if instead of deleting the sentence you tell Word to format it, only the actual characters and the spaces *between* those characters will be formatted. For example, if you tell Word to underline the sentence, the underlining won't extend to the beginning of the sentence that follows it.

Speaking of underlining the highlighted sentence, let's do it.

Step 3. Hold down the Ctrl key and press the letter U. (Recall from early in the chapter that U is the speed-formatting key for the built-in underlining format.)

Word responds by underlining the highlighted text and by emphasizing the letters *Ul* at the right end of the ribbon at the top of the screen. The *Ul* stands for *underlining* and is one way Word lets you know about the formatting of your document.

Step 4. To see the underlining more clearly, move elsewhere in the document by pressing a direction key or by clicking a mouse button when the mouse pointer is away from the selected sentence. This converts the selection back into a cursor and reveals the underlining. And because the cursor/selection is no longer on underlined text, the *Ul* is no longer emphasized.

> I've returned from a hectic trip to Europe, one I didn't request, you'll remember. It was your idea to send me abroad on a scouting trip. And it was on short notice.¶

NOTE: *In certain modes, Word indicates the presence of underlined text by showing it in yellow or another color or in bold, as in the preceding screen example, rather than by showing an actual underline. (If you are running Word in a text mode and are using a monochrome monitor rather than a color one, the* Ul *in the ribbon might be your only visual cue that the underlined text is underlined.)*

Now let's do a little paragraph formatting. Specifically, let's center the word *Memo* at the top of the page, using the speed-formatting key Ctrl+C.

Step 5. Hold down Ctrl and press the Home key to move the cursor to the first character of the document, the *M* of *Memo*.

Step 6. Hold down the Ctrl key and press the letter C. This applies the built-in speed format for centering paragraphs—and the word *Memo* moves to the center of its line.

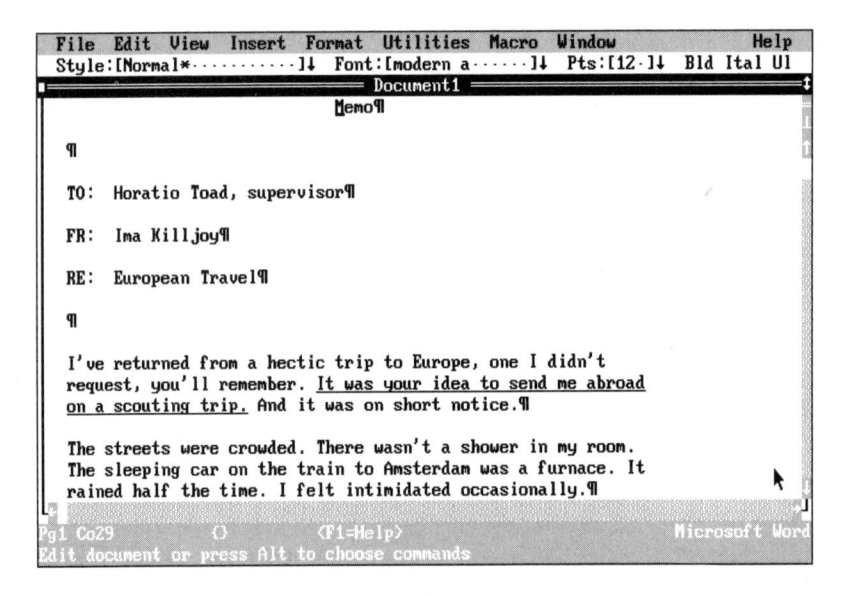

```
 File  Edit  View  Insert  Format  Utilities  Macro  Window           Help
 Style:[Normal*..........]↓ Font:[modern a.....]↓ Pts:[12 ]↓ Bld Ital Ul
═══════════════════════════ Document1 ═══════════════════════════
                              Memo¶

    ¶

    TO:  Horatio Toad, supervisor¶

    FR:  Ima Killjoy¶

    RE:  European Travel¶

    ¶
    I've returned from a hectic trip to Europe, one I didn't
    request, you'll remember. It was your idea to send me abroad
    on a scouting trip. And it was on short notice.¶

    The streets were crowded. There wasn't a shower in my room.
    The sleeping car on the train to Amsterdam was a furnace. It
    rained half the time. I felt intimidated occasionally.¶

 Pg1 Co29          {}         <F1=Help>                    Microsoft Word
 Edit document or press Alt to choose commands
```

Now we'll use character formatting on the word we just centered. First we'll boldface the characters with one built-in format; then we'll underline them with another.

Step 7. Select all characters in the word *Memo* by pressing F8 twice in a row or by clicking the right mouse button when the mouse pointer is on the word.

Step 8. Boldface the highlighted characters by holding down the Ctrl key and pressing B.

Step 9. Underline the same characters by holding down the Ctrl key and then pressing U.

This completes our formatting revisions to the existing text. But you still have one paragraph left to type before completing the memo.

CHAPTER THREE: Getting Started

Content and Formatting

For the final paragraph, you will create content and formatting at the same time by formatting the cursor before you type (as explained in Concept 3 of Chapter 2).

Step 1. Hold down the Ctrl key, and press the End key to move to the end of the document, which is the endmark.

You don't want to type text when your cursor is on the endmark, because it won't be formatted with the same open spacing that governs the rest of this document. So...

Step 2. Press the Left direction key, which will return you to the end of the previous line. This line ends a paragraph which is formatted appropriately.

Step 3. Press the Enter key to create a new paragraph. This paragraph will be formatted correctly because it was created from the previous paragraph.

Step 4. Type *So I have just one question, Boss:* and stop. Be sure to type a space after you type the colon.

Step 5. Now, to format the cursor so that it will underline the rest of the sentence as you type it, hold down the Ctrl key and press U.

Step 6. Type the rest of the sentence: *How soon may I go back?*

It is underlined as you type. (On some monitors you will see a different color or characters of a different intensity rather than underlining. But the printed version will have underlining.)

Step 7. At the end of the sentence, hold down the Ctrl key, and press the Spacebar. This speed-formatting key applies the built-in "normal" character format, thereby turning off the cursor's underlining.

Step 8. Type two spaces and then the last three words of the memo: *I loved it!* You're done.

Printing, Previewing, Saving, and Opening

You're done—that is, unless you want to print, preview, or save your document.

Printing a document

Printing what you've written is simple. Simply hold down the Shift key and press the F9 key. (Or you can choose the File Print command.) Word responds with this dialog box of choices:

```
         ┌──────────── Print ─────────────┐
         │ LaserJet Series II on COM1:        (HPLASER2.PRD) │
         │ Print: [Document·······]↓   ┌─ To ──────────────┐ │
         │ Copies: [1·············]    │ (•) Printer       │ │
         │ Paper Feed: [Continuous·]↓  │ ( ) File: [······]│ │
         │                             └───────────────────┘ │
         │ Page Range: [All········]↓  Pages: [············] │
         │ <Printer Setup...>  <Options...>    < OK >  <Cancel> │
         └───────────────────────────────────────────────────┘
```

Assuming that the printer listed at the top of the dialog box is correct and that Word has made no bad assumptions about what you want, press Enter to print the document.

Bad assumptions?

Word makes assumptions all the time. Almost every dialog box contains default settings, which you need to change only if Word has guessed wrong about your intentions. In the case of this sample dialog box, Word assumes you want to print on an HP LaserJet Series II printer that is connected to your printer's first parallel port (LPT1:) and that you want to print all of the current document (rather than just part of it, or rather than a style sheet or other file). You can correct Word's assumptions by altering any of these settings before pressing Enter to begin printing.

NOTE: *If your document fails to print, Word might not be set up properly. Refer to Appendix A, or see Chapters 11 and 31 for additional information on printing.*

Previewing before printing

Sometimes you might wonder exactly how a document will look after it is printed. You can satisfy this curiosity by printing the document, of course, but that takes paper and at least a little bit of time. (If your document contains graphics images, it might take quite a little time.)

But provided your computer is equipped with a graphics adapter (and almost all computers are these days), you can see an immediate, reduced-size, on-screen image of the printed page by simply holding down the Ctrl key and pressing the F9 key to use Word's Preview feature. Preview lets you view your document, one or two full pages at a time, as it will print. For example, this is what your memo might look like when previewed on a screen controlled by an adapter producing VGA (video graphics array) displays:

CHAPTER THREE: Getting Started   53

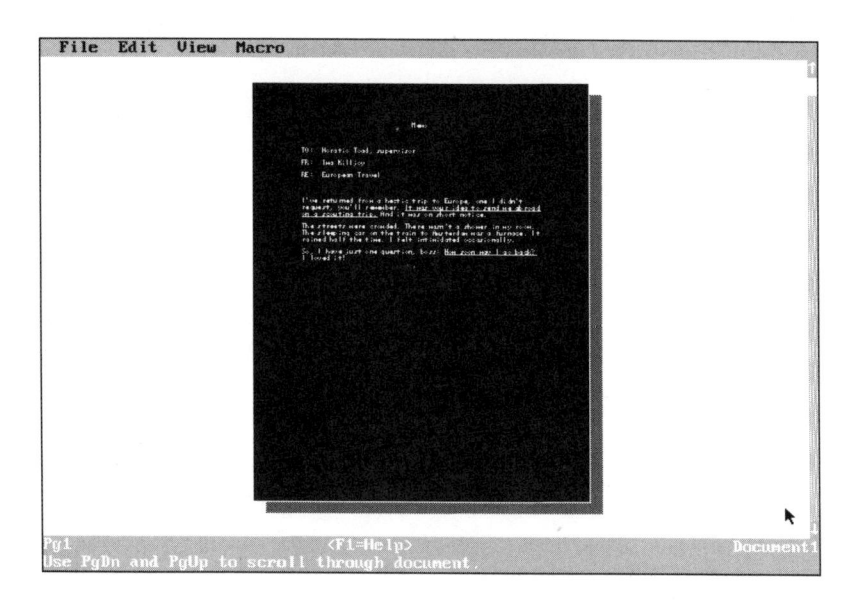

[screenshot of Word preview mode showing a document page with File/Edit/View/Macro menu, status line "Pg1 <F1=Help> Document1", and "Use PgDn and PgUp to scroll through document."]

The Preview feature is especially useful when you're creating tables or other fancy formatting that might require tweaking before it is just right. Rather than print the document numerous times as you adjust elements, preview it after each tentative change. Print it after you think you've got it right.

Saving on disk

To save a document on disk, use the File Save command. To do this, hold down the Alt and Shift keys and press F2, or simply hold down the Alt key and press FS (for File Save).

The first time you use the File Save command on a new document, Word presents you with the dialog box of the File Save As command. Word must have a name for a document before it can save it, and this dialog box allows you to supply a name. Type up to eight characters. (Word adds the *.DOC* extension to any name you type, unless you type a different extension, which is not recommended.)

For example, the Save As dialog box would look like this if you had typed the name *MEMO* but had not yet pressed the Enter key (or clicked the mouse on the OK button) to save the document:

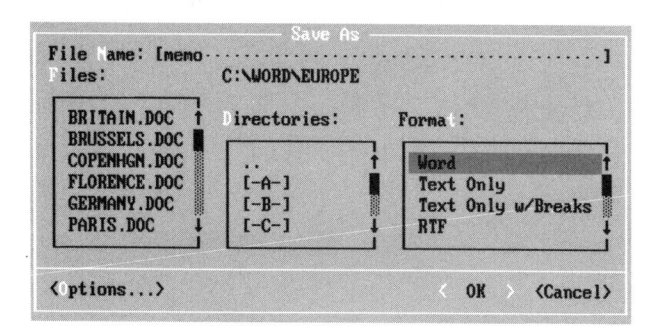

[screenshot of Save As dialog box: File Name: [memo], Files: C:\WORD\EUROPE, listing BRITAIN.DOC, BRUSSELS.DOC, COPENHGN.DOC, FLORENCE.DOC, GERMANY.DOC, PARIS.DOC; Directories: .., [-A-], [-B-], [-C-]; Format: Word, Text Only, Text Only w/Breaks, RTF; <Options...> <OK> <Cancel>]

In the example, the document has been created on the C drive in a directory called EUROPE. The directory already contains a number of files, the first few of which are listed in alphabetic order in the vertical box to the left.

After you press Enter (or choose the OK button from the dialog box), you might be presented with a second dialog box, labeled Summary. In this box you can type such optional information as a title and comments for your document.

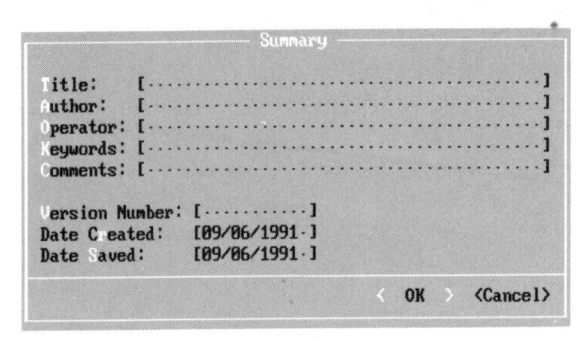

```
┌─────────────── Summary ───────────────┐
│ Title:     [·····························]│
│ Author:    [·····························]│
│ Operator:  [·····························]│
│ Keywords:  [·····························]│
│ Comments:  [·····························]│
│                                       │
│ Version Number: [··········]           │
│ Date Created:   [09/06/1991]           │
│ Date Saved:     [09/06/1991]           │
│                                       │
│                     < OK >  <Cancel>  │
└───────────────────────────────────────┘
```

It takes anywhere from a few seconds to a minute or more to fill in a summary sheet. If you don't want to bother, simply press Enter to finish saving your document. On the other hand, summary information can be valuable when you need a quick way to understand someone else's document or even when you're trying to find a particular document you wrote yourself. Word can search summary information on a whole collection of documents rapidly and compile a list of those that meet whatever criteria you specify. In any event, whether you fill in none, some, or all of the Summary dialog box, finish by pressing Enter.

NOTE: *After you've used the File Save command the first time, you will not be presented with the Save As or Summary dialog boxes again unless you request them. Instead, your document will be saved immediately whenever you press Alt+Shift+F2 or Alt+FS.*

To clear your work from the screen after saving it, use the Window Close command (press Alt followed by WC). If instead of clearing your work you want to put it aside temporarily while you work on something else, open a different document in a new window.

When you have two or more documents, you can switch between the windows by holding down the Ctrl key and pressing F6.

Opening a document

To open an existing document, use the File Open command (hold down Alt and Ctrl and press F2, or press Alt followed by FO). Type the name of the file you want to open. If you prefer to choose the name of the file to be opened from a list of existing files, press the Tab key once to move the cursor to the box containing document names, and

CHAPTER THREE: Getting Started

then use the direction keys (Down, Up, Right, and Left) to highlight the name of the desired document. After you have typed or selected the name of the desired file from the list, press Enter.

To open a new document so that you can start fresh with a blank document window, use the File New command (press Alt+FN). A dialog box asks whether you want to start a document or a style sheet; simply press Enter to start a new document.

Exiting Word

When you have finished using Word, hold down the Alt key and press the F4 key. Or use the File Exit Word command by pressing the Alt key and then pressing FX (for File eXit). If no new editing has occurred since you last saved the document, Word quits immediately. If your work has changed in the slightest since it was last saved, even if it's only been repaginated for printing, Word asks whether you want to save the edited version. You will see this message or a similar one:

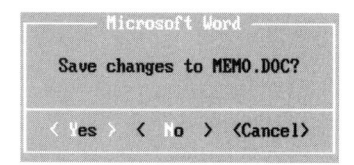

```
───── Microsoft Word ─────
Save changes to MEMO.DOC?

  < Yes >   < No >   <Cancel>
```

To save the latest version of the document under its existing name, press Y. To lose the editing changes made since you last stored the document on disk, press N. If you decide you're not ready to quit after all, press the Esc key.

CHAPTER FOUR

The Screen: Menus and Documents

Imagine that you are leaning over a desktop. You might see tools—a ruler, various pens, scissors, and a pot of paste—perhaps even a thesaurus, a dictionary, or an instruction book to one side. Handy reminders are posted in an eye-catching place. A top drawer holds paper clips and other useful aids. Nearby is a file drawer storing documents.

On top of the desk, dead center and commanding attention, is a document. Although you can see only one page of it, you could easily thumb through to other pages. Perhaps other documents rest under or to the side of the uppermost one.

Your Word screen is a tangible expression of this imaginary desktop. Its tools—such as a ruler and a menu of commands—let you do everything from changing the format of text to cutting and pasting passages in a new order to requesting synonyms or verifying spelling (potentially in any of several languages). A special help window offers instruction, and handy reminders appear across the bottom of the screen. Other tools are tucked out of sight, but not far away.

Commanding the center of the screen, displayed in a window, is a document. You can see at most a few paragraphs of it at one time, but you can easily scroll to any part of it. Perhaps additional documents lie beneath the uppermost window or in other windows to the sides.

Understanding the screen, with its menus and documents and other elements, is key to making the most of Word.

This chapter is divided into two sections. The first explores the regions at the top and bottom of the screen that display menus and other tools as well as information.

The second guides you through the central region of the screen, which is dedicated to displaying documents and other files. In fact, this chapter lays much of the groundwork for the concepts you'll learn in the rest of this book.

If you're reading this chapter for the first time, you might want to skim it for a sense of Word's personality. You can return later if you're puzzled by something you see on the screen or if you can't remember such things as the general procedures for using commands.

THE SCREEN AND ITS TOOLS

Figure 4-1 shows how a Word screen might look if a document called *Document1* were in the uppermost window (the "active" window).

By "uppermost," we mean the window that appears to be the closest to you, unobstructed by other documents or windows. We don't mean that the document is closest to the top of the two-dimensional screen, although in this case *Document1* happens to be that too. Implicit in the term is the idea that your screen represents a three-dimensional desktop, on which things can be piled in various orders.

At the right side of the screen, a portion of a help window peeks through from "underneath" the document window. Figure 4-2 shows how the same screen looks if the help window is made active.

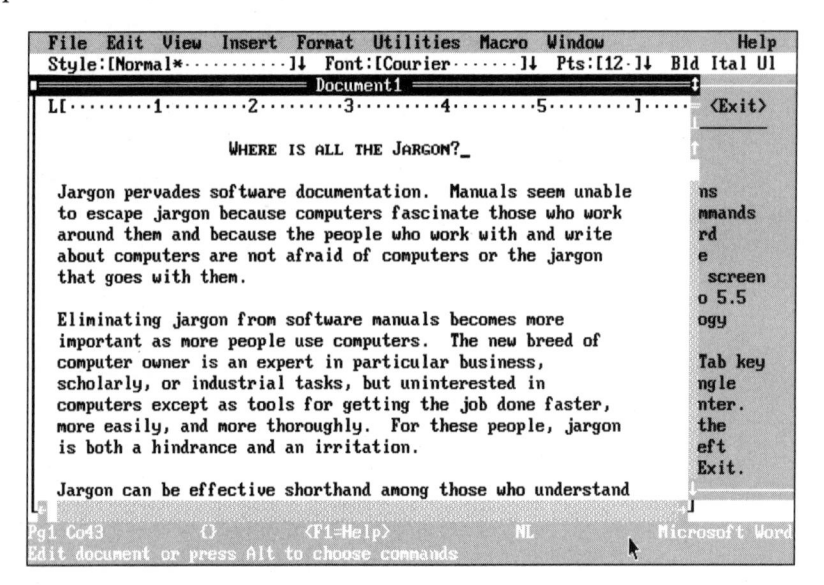

Figure 4-1. *Think of the Word screen as a desktop with a document and tools such as a ruler and a menu of commands. Partly concealed behind this document is a help window.*

CHAPTER FOUR: The Screen

In a sense, the tools from the desktop around the document window compete with the document and with each other for the scarce and valuable screen space. Word makes many elements available, and you control which of them to display. For example, turning off a screen element is akin to putting it in a desk drawer where it is out of sight but readily available.

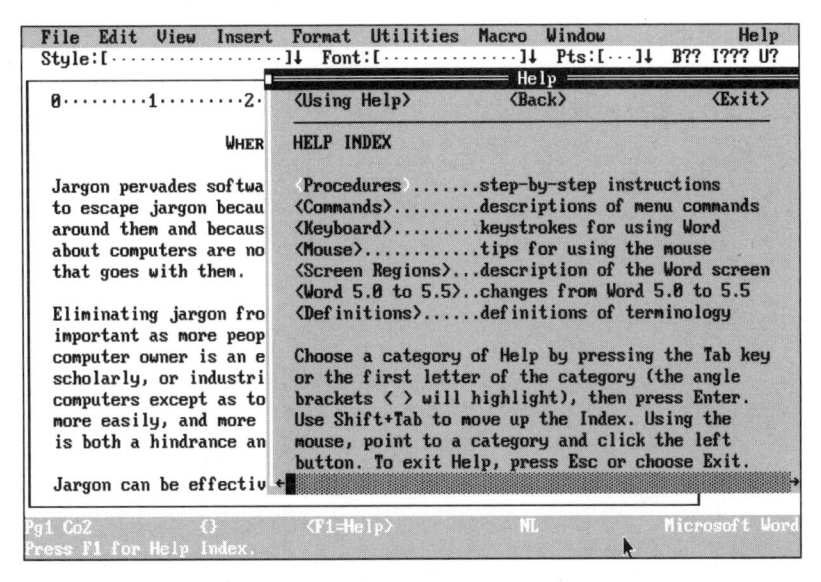

Figure 4-2. After you activate the help window, it seems to lie on top of the document. In this case, the help window is pushed partly off the screen, which makes it impossible to read, but you can move or resize it.

NOTE: *When you first work with Word 5.5, you might want to display most screen elements so that you get to know and take advantage of them. Later, as you learn which elements are most useful to you, you might want to turn others off. In fact, if you favor an uncluttered look, you can turn off virtually everything on the screen, leaving only a single document window without borders.*

With multiple document windows, you choose whether they overlap so that you can work with whichever is uppermost on the "pile," or whether the screen is divided into smaller window "tiles" that abut without overlapping. You can maximize any window so that it takes up all of the text area of the screen, covering any other windows. (Older versions of Word refer to this as "zooming" rather than as "maximizing.")

Let's examine the elements that surround a document window. With Figure 4-3 as our guide, we'll start at the top of the screen and work our way to the bottom, describing each element as we encounter it. Although the document area of Figure 4-3 contains a document that has no content yet, it is called *Document1* because that's the name Word assigns your first document that is not yet named.

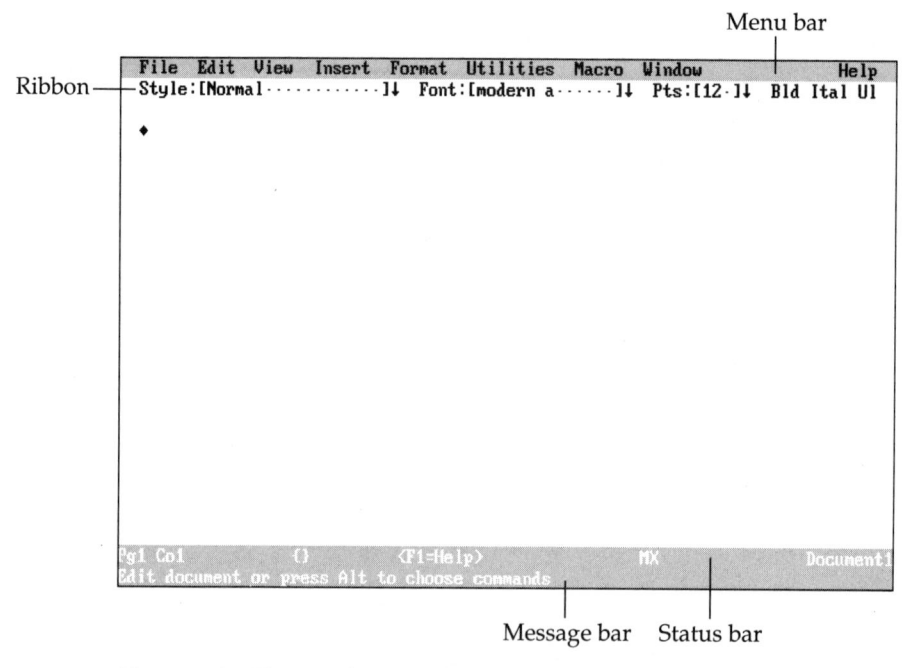

```
                                                    Menu bar
         File  Edit  View  Insert  Format  Utilities  Macro  Window        Help
Ribbon——Style:[Normal·········]↓  Font:[modern a······]↓  Pts:[12·]↓  Bld Ital Ul
         ♦




















        Pg1 Col      {}       <F1=Help>              MX              Document1
        Edit document or press Alt to choose commands
                                                |          |
                                           Message bar  Status bar
```

Figure 4-3. The Word screen, displaying a document that has no content. To achieve a screen this uncluttered, we've maximized the document window and turned off window borders and scroll bars. This chapter covers more about these kinds of choices later.

Menu Bar and Commands

The *menu bar* is the horizontal series of words that spans the very top of the screen, and it looks like this:

```
File  Edit  View  Insert  Format  Utilities  Macro  Window          Help
```

Each word in the menu bar, beginning with *File* and ending with *Help*, represents a family of commands. To activate the menu bar, either press the Alt key or click on the name of the desired command family with the mouse. Pressing the Alt key selects the first name in the menu bar (File):

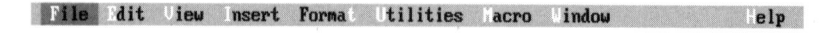

```
File  Edit  View  Insert  Format  Utilities  Macro  Window         Help
```

If you press Enter at this point, a list of all the File commands drops down from the menu bar. If instead you press the Right direction key, you select the next menu to the right—in this case, Edit.

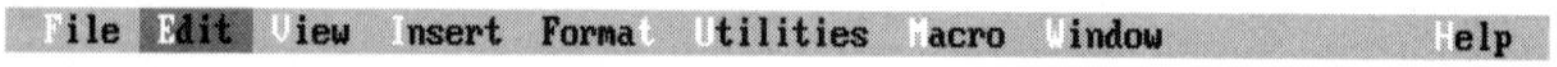

```
File  Edit  View  Insert  Format  Utilities  Macro  Window         Help
```

CHAPTER FOUR: The Screen   61

NOTE: *If you close all windows that contain documents or style sheets, the number of names in the menu bar is reduced to five: File, View, Utilities, Macro, and Help. This occurs because the other families of commands, such as Edit and Format, are relevant only when a document or style sheet is displayed.*

Drop-down menus

If you've ever used an Apple Macintosh, a Microsoft Windows program, or such other programs as Microsoft Works, you're already familiar with drop-down menus.

You can access Word's drop-down menus in several ways:

- Press Enter when the name *Edit* is highlighted, and the full list of Edit commands drops down onto your screen.
- Point at the name *Edit* with a mouse, and press the left mouse button. The Edit menu appears, almost as if it were dropping down from the menu bar (hence the term "drop-down menu").
- Press the Alt key to activate the menu bar, and then press the letter E, an *accelerator key*, or shortcut to drop down the menu. Figure 4-4 shows what the screen looks like with the Edit drop-down menu displayed.

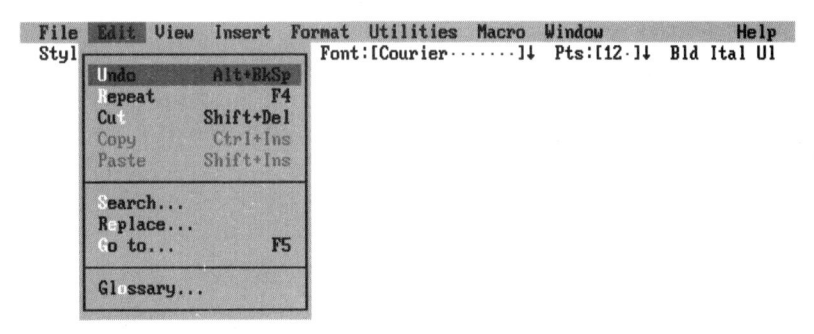

Figure 4-4. The Edit drop-down menu. Commands that are not available at the moment (Copy and Paste) are "grayed."

Accelerator keys

The accelerator keys are emphasized—displayed in bright white or a color such as red, or highlighted—when they are available. For example, when you press the Alt key to activate the menu bar, one letter is emphasized in each command: **F**ile **E**dit **V**iew **I**nsert Forma**t** **U**tilities **M**acro **W**indow **H**elp.

If you press an emphasized letter, Word takes you directly to its associated drop-down menu. To get to the File menu, you press Alt followed by F; to get to the Edit menu, you press Alt followed by E, and so forth. Except for Forma**t**, which uses *t* because *F* is used by File, the shortcut letter is the first letter of each menu name.

In the Edit drop-down menu, shown in Figure 4-4, the first command is Undo, which is highlighted. The highlight indicates that pressing Enter at this point will execute the Undo command.

The *U* of Undo is emphasized because it is the accelerator key for the command. If you press U when the Edit menu is displayed, the Undo command will execute. Similarly, R is the accelerator key for the Repeat command, which means the command will execute if the Edit menu is dropped down and you press R. Below the Repeat command on the Edit menu is the Cut command, which has the letter corresponding to its accelerator key (*t*) emphasized.

Command-key shortcuts

Accelerator keys are only the first of three keyboard shortcuts Word offers. The others are *command-key shortcuts* and *speed-formatting keys*.

- A command-key shortcut lets you carry out a command without accessing a menu. For example, to use the Undo command without first going to the Edit menu, hold down the Alt key and press the Backspace key. Not every command has a shortcut. Those that do list the shortcut next to the command name in the menu.
- The speed-formatting key, which was introduced in Chapter 3, is discussed again later in this chapter.

All three kinds of shortcut keys are reviewed in Chapter 5.

Grayed command names

Observe that the Edit menu's next two commands, Copy and Paste, appear lighter than the other commands. Commands that are grayed this way are not available at the moment; for one reason or another, you cannot choose them. For example, the Paste command is grayed now because nothing is available to paste into the blank document. However, as soon as text is cut or copied to the scrap storage area, the Paste command will become available and will cease being gray.

Commands that toggle

A few commands on the View menu toggle features on and off. In other words, if the feature was off before you used the command, choosing the command turns it on. And if it was on, choosing the command turns it off.

Such commands are displayed with dots to their immediate left when they are turned on. For example, the View menu here shows the Ribbon and Status Bar features turned on but Outline, Layout, and Ruler turned off.

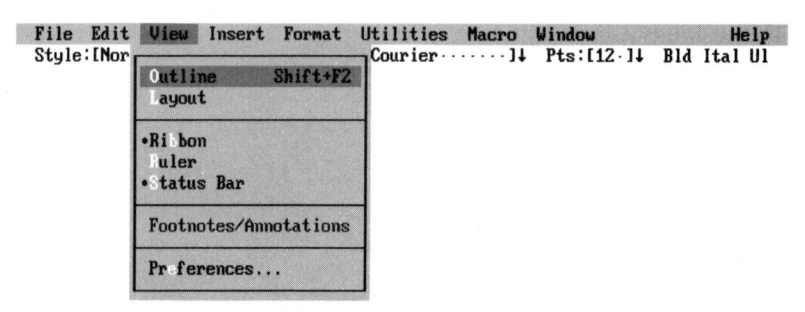

```
    File  Edit  View  Insert  Format  Utilities  Macro  Window              Help
    Style:[Nor                        Courier······]↓  Pts:[12·]↓  Bld Ital Ul
              Outline      Shift+F2
              Layout

             •Ribbon
              Ruler
             •Status Bar

              Footnotes/Annotations

              Preferences...
```

CHAPTER FOUR: The Screen

NOTE: *A dot also is used in the Window menu to indicate which document is active. The menu shows the names of the documents in all windows; the name of the document in the active window has a dot to its left.*

Dialog boxes

As can be seen in Figure 4-4, each of the last four choices in the drop-down Edit menu is followed by an ellipsis (three periods). An ellipsis indicates that choosing the command leads you to a collection of additional choices that let you refine how the command performs. These options appear in the center of the screen inside a bordered rectangle called a *dialog box*.

For example, if you choose the Search command from the Edit menu, Word displays the Search dialog box:

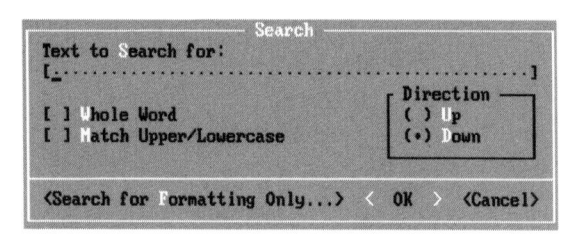

```
┌──────────────── Search ────────────────┐
│ Text to Search for:                    │
│ [.....................................]│
│                        ┌─ Direction ─┐ │
│ [ ] Whole Word         │ ( ) Up      │ │
│ [ ] Match Upper/Lowercase │ (•) Down │ │
│                        └─────────────┘ │
│ <Search for Formatting Only...>  < OK >  <Cancel> │
└────────────────────────────────────────┘
```

This particular dialog box contains an *entry field*, two *check-box fields*, and an *option-button field*, as well as three buttons.

Entry fields The first field, labeled *Text to Search for*, is an entry field. You enter text in it by typing. In this case, you type the word, words, or characters you want to locate in your document. For example, to find the next occurrence of the word *Europe*, you would type *Europe* and press the Tab key to move to the next field.

Entry fields in some dialog boxes offer drop-down lists of some or all of the possible entries for the field. These fields are marked with a down arrow. To see the drop-down list, you hold down the Alt key and press the Down direction key, or you click on the down arrow with the mouse. To move through the choices one at a time on such a list without dropping it down, repeatedly press the Down or the Up direction key.

Check-box fields The Search dialog box contains two check-box fields, labeled *Whole Word* and *Match Upper/Lowercase*. These represent independent options you can turn on or off. To mark a check box, you move to it and press the Spacebar. Word responds by marking it with an *X*:

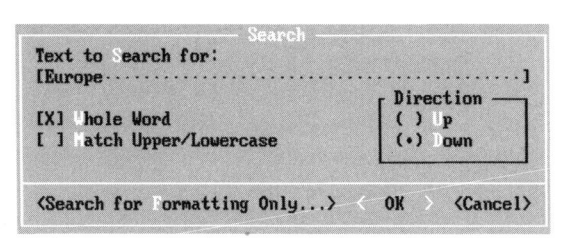

```
┌──────────────── Search ────────────────┐
│ Text to Search for:                    │
│ [Europe................................]│
│                        ┌─ Direction ─┐ │
│ [X] Whole Word         │ ( ) Up      │ │
│ [ ] Match Upper/Lowercase │ (•) Down │ │
│                        └─────────────┘ │
│ <Search for Formatting Only...>  < OK >  <Cancel> │
└────────────────────────────────────────┘
```

Check boxes have no relation to each other. You can mark any of them, none of them, or all of them.

Check boxes frequently have default settings: either on (with an X) or off (without an X). If the default is ambiguous, the check box will contain a hyphen rather than an X—for example, as with Format commands, in which a dialog box might attempt to reflect the formatting of selected text that is formatted partly one way and partly another way.

Check-box fields are represented on your screen with facing square brackets: [ ].

Option-button fields The Search dialog box contains one option-button field, labeled *Direction*. Option-button fields contain choices that are mutually exclusive: If you choose *Up*, you cannot choose *Down*, and vice versa.

When you move into an option-button field with the Tab key, you are taken to the current, or default, choice. You then can use the direction keys (Up or Down, Left or Right) to make a choice. If you move into an option-button field with the mouse or by pressing an accelerator key, you go directly to your choice.

Option-button fields are represented on your screen with a pair of facing parentheses: ( ). If a choice has been made in the field or if a default choice is available, it is marked with a dot between the parentheses.

Buttons The final line of any dialog box is set off by a horizontal line and contains an *OK* button, a *Cancel* button, and sometimes other buttons. You can identify a button because its text is enclosed within angle brackets, like this: *<Button text>*. Some buttons have accelerator keys; hold down the Alt key and press the emphasized letter to go directly to the button from anywhere in the dialog box.

The Search dialog box contains a button labeled *<Search for Formatting Only...>*. The dots indicate that choosing the button takes you directly to another dialog box, where you can make additional choices if you want.

The OK button is your way of signaling that the fields have been set as desired. Choosing it causes Word to execute the command.

If you decide not to use the command after all, press the Tab key until the brackets around the Cancel button are highlighted, like this:

```
─────────────────── Search ───────────────────
Text to Search for:
[Europe·······································]
                              ┌─ Direction ─┐
[X] Whole Word                │ ( ) Up      │
[ ] Match Upper/Lowercase     │ (•) Down    │
                              └─────────────┘

<Search for Formatting Only...>   < OK >   <Cancel>
```

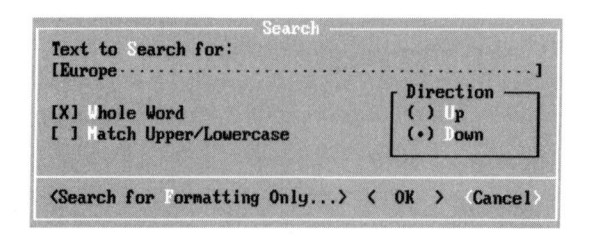

After the Cancel button is highlighted, press Enter. This cancels the command and lets you exit the dialog box. You can also press the Esc key to cancel the command.

Navigating within a dialog box There are two ways to move between the various fields and buttons in a dialog box:

- If you have a mouse, you can move directly to the field or button you want.
- To use a keyboard to move forward among the fields of a dialog box, press the Tab key. To move backward, press Shift+Tab.

NOTE: *In many dialog boxes you can use direction keys (Up, Down, Left, and Right) to move to a desired field or button, but a major drawback is that the Up and the Down direction keys change choices* within *certain entry fields—which means that as you try to navigate between fields you might unwittingly change settings. Hence, it is best to avoid using direction keys to move between fields or buttons.*

Speed-formatting keys

A *speed-formatting key* is a keyboard shortcut, a way to avoid using a menu and dialog box when you want to make certain common formatting choices. Instead of employing a menu or a command-key shortcut to navigate to the relevant field of a dialog box, you hold down the Ctrl key and press a letter or another character.

With few exceptions each speed-formatting key triggers one of Word's built-in speed formats (introduced in Chapter 3). For instance, the speed-formatting key for boldface is B. To turn on boldfacing, you hold down the Ctrl key and press B. (This is expressed in this book as Ctrl+B.) Using it eliminates the need to employ the Format Character command's dialog box, which you might otherwise use to turn boldfacing on or off.

NOTE: *If you are using macros or glossary entries that have codes beginning* Ctrl, *you might first have to press Ctrl+A in order to use a speed-formatting key. For instance, to apply boldfacing you would press Ctrl+AB instead of Ctrl+B. For details, see the discussion of the Ctrl key in the next chapter.*

At the beginning of Chapter 3, you were introduced to 27 speed-formatting keys, which employ most letters of the alphabet plus several symbols. They are summarized again in Chapter 5 and Appendix B. Most speed-formatting keys toggle a particular kind of formatting on and off, but three of them—Ctrl+F, Ctrl+P, and Ctrl+S—let you gain access to Word's ribbon so that you can make your formatting changes. And, as already noted, Ctrl+A is reserved as a prefix that lets you use a speed-formatting key even when it conflicts with a macro's control code, and Ctrl+Y lets you use any style from a style sheet.

The Ribbon

In a sense, the ribbon is akin to a special dialog box that is displayed while you are writing or editing. It contains fields—similar to those in a dialog box—that provide information and permit you to make formatting choices.

Only one ribbon exists, regardless of how many document windows are open. The ribbon reflects the formatting of any selected text in the active window, or the current format of the cursor. Accordingly, as you move around in your document or as you move from window to window, the information displayed in the ribbon might change.

When turned on, the ribbon appears at the top of the screen, below the menu bar. Typically, it looks like this:

```
Style:[Normal············]↕  Font:[modern a······]↕  Pts:[12·]↕  Bld Ital Ul
```

Character attributes (Bld Ital Ul)

At the far right of the ribbon are the letters *Bld Ital Ul*. Actually three separate abbreviations, these letters stand for "Bold Italic Underlined," and they will be emphasized if either the cursor or all of the selected text is formatted with one or more of these properties. The following sample ribbon indicates that italic text is in use:

```
Style:[Normal············]↕  Font:[modern a······]↕  Pts:[12·]↕  Bld [Ital] Ul
```

If text is selected and some of it is formatted one way and some of it another way, the ribbon will reflect this with question marks. For example, if only a portion of the selected text is bold, the letters *Bld* will be displayed as *B??*. Or, if all of the selected text is bold but only some of it is italic, the ribbon will display *Bld* in emphasized type and *I???* in non-emphasized type:

```
Style:[Normal············]↕  Font:[modern a······]↕  Pts:[12·]↕  [Bld] I??? Ul
```

Font and point size

Just as the ribbon reflects whether the cursor or selected characters are bold, italic, or underlined, it also shows you what typeface (*font*) and type size (measured in points) are in use.

Fonts and the printer file In the illustrations of the ribbon so far, you might have noticed that the font is shown as *modern a* and the font size as *12*. The name *modern a* is a generic name that, in this case, means "the normal font for the printer." The specific

---

TOGGLING THE RIBBON

When you first install Word, the ribbon is turned off. To turn it on (or to later turn it off—the procedure is the same), use one of two methods:

- Use the View Ribbon command (hold down the Alt key and press VB).
- Position the mouse cursor over the ⊥ symbol in the right border of the screen, and click the right mouse button.

Word remembers whether you want the ribbon on or off, even when you turn off your computer. (See Tip 9 in Chapter 8.)

CHAPTER FOUR: The Screen

font corresponding to *modern a* varies depending on the printer in use. After you install a printer file, *modern a* will change to reflect the default font for the printer—in this case, Courier:

```
Style:[Normal············]↓  Font:[Courier·······]↓  Pts:[12·]↓  Bld Ital Ul
```

If you don't want to use Courier, Word provides various means to switch to different fonts, provided your printer has them available. And one of the easiest ways to choose a new font is by using the ribbon.

The list box Look closely at the ribbon. You'll see three arrows pointing down. Each arrow indicates that the entry field to its left has an associated list box from which you can choose a finite group of options.

To activate the ribbon's entry field for fonts, use the speed-formatting key Ctrl+F (the F representing "Font"). The contents of the box (if any) will be highlighted, and the flashing cursor will move from the document to the box. This indicates that the entry field is active. Hold down the Alt key and press the Down direction key once to drop the Font entry field's list box onto the screen. If you have a mouse, an alternative method is available: Activate the entry field and simultaneously drop down its list box by pointing at the down arrow with the mouse and clicking the left mouse button.

When you drop down the Font field's list box, you'll see choices such as the following:

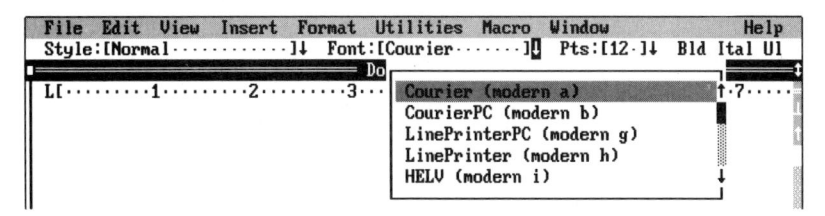

```
 File  Edit  View  Insert  Format  Utilities  Macro  Window              Help
 Style:[Normal············]↓  Font:[Courier·······]↓  Pts:[12·]↓  Bld Ital Ul
                            Do
 L[·········1·········2·········3··· Courier (modern a)          ↑·?····
                                     CourierPC (modern b)
                                     LinePrinterPC (modern g)
                                     LinePrinter (modern h)
                                     HELV (modern i)             ↓
```

Note that the default choice (Courier in this example) is highlighted in the list box and is followed on subsequent lines by alternatives. Each font name is listed with its generic name in parentheses. For example, Courier is listed as *Courier (modern a)*, and HELV is listed as *HELV (modern i)*.

TIP FOR WORD VETERANS

The printer file is called the "PRD file" or "printer-description file" in versions of Word prior to 5.5. Despite the name difference, the purposes of such files remain the same: to describe the printer's specific capabilities and to translate printing instructions from Word into a form that printer will comprehend. Printer files for Word 5.0 can be used with Word 5.5 but not vice versa.

- To change from one font to another, press the Down (or Up) direction key to highlight the font of your choice.

Press Enter to implement any change in the font and return to your document; press Esc to abandon any change and return to your document; or press Tab to move to the ribbon's Pts field. Or you can move to the Character dialog box, where you can refine your decisions regarding the font.

Character dialog box Recall that the Search dialog box is a collection of fields that govern the specifics of how Word executes the Edit Search command. Similarly, the Character dialog box contains fields that govern how Word executes the Format Character command. Normally, you reach the command by choosing Character from the menu bar's drop-down Format menu. But the speed-formatting key Ctrl+F gives you a shortcut.

Press Ctrl+F when the ribbon's Font list box is active (but the list box has not been dropped down), and the Character dialog box appears:

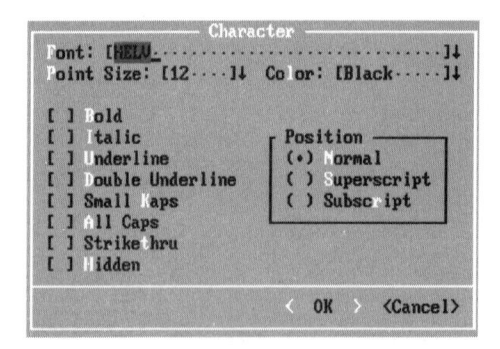

```
┌─────────────── Character ───────────────┐
│ Font: [HELV                           ]↓│
│ Point Size: [12   ]↓  Color: [Black  ]↓ │
│                                         │
│ [ ] Bold                                │
│ [ ] Italic          ┌─ Position ──────┐ │
│ [ ] Underline       │ (•) Normal      │ │
│ [ ] Double Underline│ ( ) Superscript │ │
│ [ ] Small Caps      │ ( ) Subscript   │ │
│ [ ] All Caps        └─────────────────┘ │
│ [ ] Strike Thru                         │
│ [ ] Hidden                              │
│                                         │
│                    <  OK  >   <Cancel>  │
└─────────────────────────────────────────┘
```

Like the Search dialog box, the Character dialog box contains entry fields (for font, size, and color), check boxes (for attributes such as bold, italic, or hidden text), and option buttons (to choose whether text will be normal, superscripted, or subscripted).

WHAT'S THE POINT?

If you're new to word processing, the term *point size* might not mean much to you yet. Chapter 31 includes samples of various fonts in several sizes, but for now simply remember that a typeface (font) is measured vertically in points, with 72 points equal to approximately 1 inch. A document that appears to have been created with a typewriter typically has 6 lines to the vertical inch, with the font 12 points tall. (An inch is 72 points; divide this by 6 lines and you get 12 points per line.) Fine print typically is 6 to 8 points tall, and newspapers typically print in 9-point, 10-point, or 11-point type. The font for the body of this book is 10-point Palatino.

CHAPTER FOUR: The Screen

One difference from the Search dialog box is that the entry fields of the Character dialog box all offer associated list boxes—if you press Alt+Down direction key or click with the mouse on the down arrow, a drop-down list of choices appears. In the case of the dialog box's Font field, the choices are identical to those already encountered in the ribbon's Font list box:

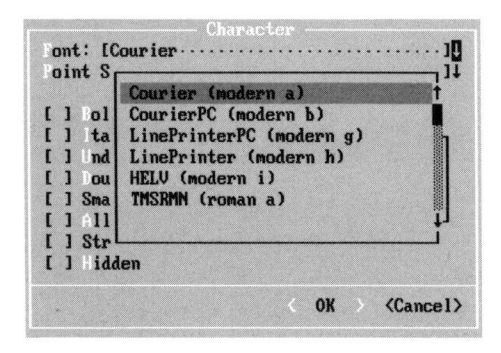

```
┌─────────────────────── Character ───────────────────────┐
│ Font: [Courier·······························]▐        │
│ Point S┌─────────────────────────────────┐ ]↓          │
│        │ Courier (modern a)              │↑            │
│ [ ] ol │ CourierPC (modern b)            │             │
│ [ ] ta │ LinePrinterPC (modern g)        │             │
│ [ ] nd │ LinePrinter (modern h)          │             │
│ [ ] ou │ HELV (modern i)                 │             │
│ [ ] Sma│ TMSRMN (roman a)                │             │
│ [ ] ll │                                 │↓            │
│ [ ] Str└─────────────────────────────────┘             │
│ [ ] idden                                              │
│                                                        │
│                       <  OK  >   <Cancel>              │
└────────────────────────────────────────────────────────┘
```

As previously observed, these font choices vary depending on which printer file is installed.

Point size To the right of the ribbon's Font entry field is the Pts entry field. If you haven't already made a choice of size with the Character dialog box, you choose a size for your font here—a decision influenced by the capabilities of your printer.

Word consults the currently installed printer file to learn which sizes are available for each font and, in turn, conveys this information to you on the ribbon.

To use the ribbon to choose a point size for a font, activate the Pts entry field by holding down the Ctrl key and pressing the P key. When the Pts entry field is active, hold down the Alt key and press the Down direction key to display a list of available font sizes. You can use the Up and the Down direction keys to choose a size.

If you're using a mouse, click the left button when the mouse is pointing at the list box's down arrow; the same choices appear.

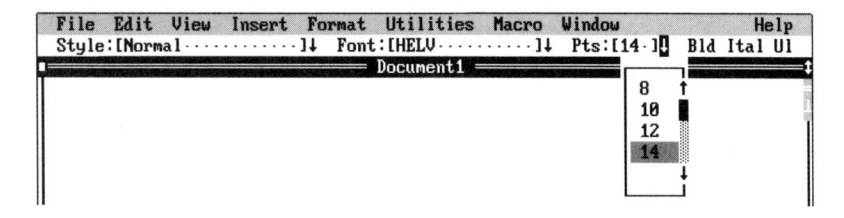

```
┌──────────────────────────────────────────────────────────┐
│ File  Edit  View  Insert  Format  Utilities  Macro  Window       Help │
│ Style:[Normal············]↓ Font:[HELV·········]↓ Pts:[14·]▐ Bld Ital Ul │
│═══════════════════════════ Document1 ═══════════════════│
│                                                  8   ↑  │
│                                                  10     │
│                                                  12     │
│                                                  14     │
│                                                      ↓  │
└──────────────────────────────────────────────────────────┘
```

To put your choice into effect, double-click on it with the mouse, or press the Enter key when it is highlighted.

As with the Fonts list box, you can shortcut directly to the Character dialog box from the Pts entry field: Simply press Ctrl+P when the Pts entry field is active. (This shortcut works only before the drop-down list is displayed.)

Style of the paragraph

At the left end of ribbon is the Style entry field. As its name implies, this shows you the style of the current paragraph. It lets you easily change the style, much in the way that the other entry fields in the ribbon let you change the font or point size of text.

"Fine and good," you say. "But what is a style?"

Styles A *style* is a collection of one or more formatting characteristics that is assigned a name and often given a one-character or two-character *key code*. After a style is created, it can be used and reused to format text almost effortlessly.

For example, when writing a letter, you might want a centered and underlined subject line near the top of the document, with a blank line before it. You could type the line and then manually center it and so forth, but why not instead use a style that does all the formatting at one time?

One way to create a style is to format a subject line the way you want it, applying whatever combination of formats you want, and then record the resulting amalgamation as a style. You'll learn about this technique, including how the ribbon can play a role, in Chapter 6.

A second way to create a style is to open a *style sheet*, which is a collection of styles stored together as a file, and define a new style with the formatting you want. You'll learn this technique in Chapter 24.

A third approach is not to create a style at all but to use an existing one from a style sheet that someone else has created. This approach is convenient if the style sheet is competently crafted from both technical and design standpoints. Such a style sheet will have one style for each element you might want in document—a style for normal paragraphs, a style for footnotes, styles for block quotations and tables, and so forth.

The next several paragraphs introduce the topic of style sheets. If you don't want to concern yourself with style sheets now, skip ahead to "The Status Bar."

A style sheet For purposes of introducing the Style list box in the ribbon, let's assume you are using an existing style from a style sheet. The style is for formatting subject lines and is from a style sheet in the product MasterWord. We'll assume you're working on a document to which the style sheet is attached (which means the style sheet is governing the document's overall appearance). Now let's choose a style for the line of text that contains the cursor.

To activate the Styles entry field, hold down Ctrl and press S. When the entry field is active, hold down the Alt key and press the Down direction key to drop down a list of choices such as this one:

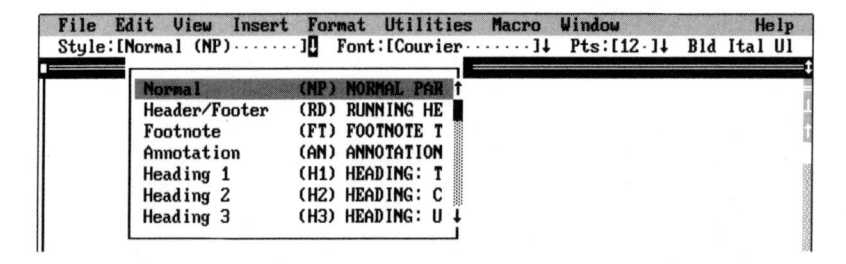

```
 File   Edit  View  Insert  Format  Utilities  Macro  Window            Help
 Style:[Normal (NP)······]▮  Font:[Courier······]↕  Pts:[12·]↕  Bld Ital Ul

                  ┌─────────────────────────────────┐
                  │ Normal          (NP) NORMAL PAR │↑
                  │ Header/Footer   (RD) RUNNING HE │
                  │ Footnote        (FT) FOOTNOTE T │
                  │ Annotation      (AN) ANNOTATION │
                  │ Heading 1       (H1) HEADING: T │
                  │ Heading 2       (H2) HEADING: C │
                  │ Heading 3       (H3) HEADING: U │↓
                  └─────────────────────────────────┘
```

Each of the list's seven lines displays the name of a style from the style sheet. Each line shows the style's I.D. (such as *Normal*), followed by its two-letter key code (such as *NP*) and the first few letters of a descriptive remark (such as *NORMAL PAR...* for "NORMAL PARAGRAPH").

Each style has a distinct purpose—the Normal style is used for standard body text in a document; the Header/Footer style is used for a header or footer (*running head*), which appears at the top (or bottom) of every page; the footnote style governs the font size and line layout of footnotes, and so forth.

To apply a style to whatever text is selected, you double-click on the style's name with the mouse, or you press the Down direction key until the style's name is highlighted. Then you press Enter.

Scrolling through styles The list box can display only seven styles at a time, but often, as in this case, more than seven styles are available. To see additional choices, you press the Down direction key until the names in the list box scroll upward; or you press the PgDn key to move to another seven names; or you use the mouse to operate the vertical *scroll bar*.

The vertical scroll bar is the shaded column at the right of the list box. At the bottom of the scroll bar is a down arrow, and at the top of the scroll bar is an up arrow. Scroll bars are used in many facets of Word, and you'll learn more about them in the discussion of the document window later in the chapter. For now, it is enough to know that you can scroll down through a list by clicking or holding down the left mouse button while pointing the mouse at the down arrow at the bottom of the scroll bar. Similarly, you scroll up by clicking on the up arrow.

As you move down through the styles in the list box, a highlight, called the *scroll box*, moves down the scroll bar to represent your progress. For example, if you are in the middle of the list of styles, the scroll box will be halfway down the vertical scroll bar, as it is here:

```
 File  Edit  View  Insert  Format  Utilities  Macro  Window           Help
 Style:[Paragraph 32 (SU) ·]   Font:[Courier······]  Pts:[12·]  Bld Ital Ul

           Paragraph 20     (BQ) BLOCK QUOT
           Paragraph 21     (CL) COMPLMNTRY
           Paragraph 22     (CO) COMPANY NA
           Paragraph 32     (SU) SUBJECT LI
           Paragraph 33     (O1) OUTLINE--F
           Paragraph 34     (O2) OUTLINE--S
           Paragraph 35     (O3) OUTLINE--T
```

Observe in this example that the style highlighted in the list box has as its I.D. *Paragraph 32*. Unlike the styles higher in the list box, the I.D. of this one doesn't suggest a particular purpose (such as *Normal* paragraphs or *Footnotes*). Rather, this style can be assigned to any kind of formatting purpose. Here it happens to be assigned the task of formatting subject lines in letters—a mission hinted at by the key code *SU* and the beginning of the remark *SUBJECT LI....*

To apply this style to text, you simply highlight the listing for the style and press Enter. Immediately, the selected text assumes the formatting stipulated by the style.

But what formatting is that?

Dialog box It's easy to look at a plain description of the formatting—merely press the speed-formatting key Ctrl+S when the Style entry field is active (but not after its drop-down list box is displayed). Word will take you to the Apply Style dialog box, as displayed in Figure 4-5.

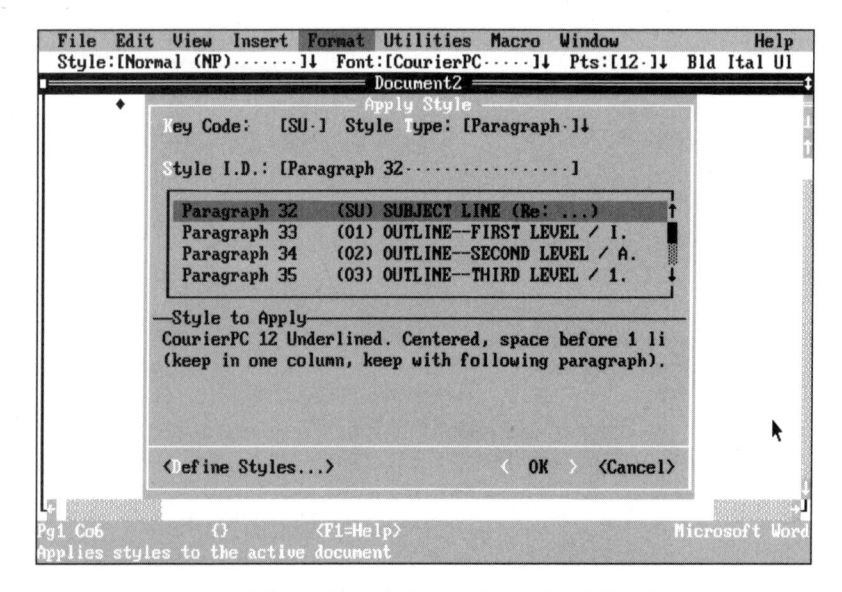

Figure 4-5. *The middle region of the Apply Style dialog box shows a list box containing styles from the style sheet, with one highlighted. Above the list are fields describing the name of the highlighted style, and below the list is a description of the style's formatting.*

At the top of the dialog box are three fields that describe aspects of the name of a style. In the middle of the dialog box is a list box containing a few styles from the style sheet. A scroll bar lets you see additional choices. One style's name is highlighted; this style is described elsewhere in the dialog box.

Below the list box is a plain description of the formatting associated with the highlighted style: *Courier 12 Underlined. Centered, space before 1 li (keep in one column, keep with following paragraph).* This is a somewhat terse way of saying that any paragraph formatted with this style will have the following characteristics:

- Text will be in the 12-point Courier font and underlined.
- Lines will be centered within the margins.
- A blank line will be inserted before the paragraph.

- Word will print all of the paragraph's lines on the same page or same column, never splitting it.
- Word will print the paragraph and at least the first two lines of the next paragraph on the same page (important for headings).

After you get used to formatting with styles, it is hard to go back to individually specifying each of the separate characteristics you want for a paragraph. But who says you have to go back? Now that the ribbon lets you apply styles from a handy list, styles are remarkably easy to keep track of and use.

The Status Bar

The status bar provides information about the status of Word and of your document. It stretches across the bottom of the screen, usually on the second-to-last line, although it can be turned off completely, or it can appear at the very bottom of the screen if the *message bar* is turned off.

The status bar typically looks like this:

`Pg1 Co32            {}         <F1=Help>           CL              Microsoft Word`

Or it might look like this:

`P3 S2 L17 C54       {My...eas} <F1=Help>SAVE       EX              Microsoft Word`

From left to right, here are the elements you might encounter in the status bar:

Pg 1 Co32 (or) ***P3 S2 L17 C54*** Word shows the number of the current page of your document (such as *Pg 1*) and the column number that contains your cursor (such as *Co32*). If you are working in a document with more than one section, the section number is displayed too. At your discretion, Word will even show how many lines into the current page your cursor is. The second of the above examples, *P3 S2 L17 C54*, represents "Page 3, Section 2, Line 17, Column 54."

TIP FOR WORD VETERANS

In earlier versions of Word, styles were applied to text by holding down the Alt key and typing a one-character or two-character key code. Beginning with Word 5.5, you accomplish the same thing by holding down the Ctrl key and pressing the Y key, and then typing the key code. Or you hold down the Shift and Ctrl keys simultaneously and type the key code. (This method won't work if you have macros assigned to identical Shift+Ctrl key combinations.) These alternatives to using the Style list box in the ribbon are discussed in the next chapter.

Word updates page numbers continuously (provided you have not used the Utilities Customize command to cancel Background Pagination). This doesn't imply that Word necessarily will include the page numbers in a printed version of the document; getting page numbers to print is a matter of formatting, explored in Chapter 15.

{My....eas} The curly brackets, { }, are Word's *scrap brackets*. Inside them, Word shows whatever is in the word processor's temporary memory, the *scrap*.

In the preceding example, the words "My dog has fleas" have been placed in the scrap. Note that the beginning and the end of the passage are shown, but the middle is indicated by an ellipsis (...). Also, the spaces between words are indicated by tiny dots, smaller and higher than periods. Uses of the scrap are explained in Chapter 10, in the discussions of the Cut, Copy, and Paste commands.

<F1=Help> The *<F1=Help>* symbol is both a reminder for keyboard users and a "hot spot" for mouse users. It reminds that you can get online help with Word by pressing the F1 key. Pointing with the mouse at the *<F1=Help>* spot and clicking the left mouse button accomplishes the same thing: It gives you online help.

Word's help is *context sensitive,* which means that it tries to display information relevant to the task you are performing.

SAVE The *SAVE* indicator comes on when, as a result of editing changes you've made, only 60 percent of Word's available memory remains. The *SAVE* indicator begins to flash when only 40 percent of memory remains. Either save your document or risk losing your work. You can, of course, save more frequently—a good habit. A feature called *Autosave* can back up your documents and other files as frequently as you specify. Although this helps protect against such perils as power failures, it does not free up Word's memory in the same way that deliberately saving a document does. So use the File Save command frequently.

Special modes When any of 12 special conditions, or *modes,* is turned on, letter pairs appear on the right half of the status bar. For some of these modes, a key or combination of keys functions as an on/off switch; other modes are turned on and off with commands.

Figure 4-6 lists these 12 modes, their status-bar abbreviation, the key or keys that activate them, and a brief description. Later chapters describe each mode in detail.

TIP FOR WORD VETERANS

If you use the Utilities Customize command to tell Word to use Word 5.0 function keys, the extend-selection key becomes F6 rather F8. It does not, however, behave identically to the F6 key in earlier versions of Word. Rather, it retains the functionality of the F8 key in Word 5.5. For example, pressing the extend-selection key twice in a row in version 5.5 will highlight a word rather than simply turn Extend Selection mode on and off.

CHAPTER FOUR: The Screen

Mode	Abbreviation	Key	Description
*View Layout	LY	AH+VL	Indicates active View Layout command
Caps Lock	CL	CapsLock	Generates capital letters
*Line Draw	LD	Alt+UL†	Indicates active Line Draw command
Num Lock	NL	Numlock	Prevents cursor movement by keypad
*Maximize	MX	Ctrl+F10‡	Maximizes the active window
Scroll Lock	SL	Scroll Lock	Fixes cursor in place
Extend Selection	EX	F8†	Extends the cursor to select text
Column Select	CS	Ctrl+Shift+F8†	Extends the selection by column
*Revision Marks	RM	Alt+UM, Spacebar, Enter	Reflects additions to and deletions from text
Overtype	OT	Alt+F5/Ins	Types new characters over old
*Macro Record	MR	Ctrl+F3	Records keystrokes as macros
Step	ST	Alt+MR, Alt+S, Enter	Lets you review macros one step at a time

*Dominant mode   †Press Esc to turn off this mode   ‡Press Ctrl+FS to turn off Maximize

Figure 4-6. *Special modes reflected in the status bar.*

NOTE: *Although 12 modes exist, the letter pairs representing them share only 6 positions. For example, the letter pairs LY and CL share a spot on the status bar; if both modes are on, LY rather than CL appears. In Figure 4-6, an asterisk (*) appears before the dominant member of such pairs. Neither EX or CS is dominant; either overrides the other.*

Microsoft Word/Document1/Move/Size/Running Macro Although the right side of the status bar usually displays *Microsoft Word*, it does, on occasion, display other information:

- If Word's window borders are turned off and if the document window is maximized (that is, if Maximize mode is on), the name of the active document appears. If the document has not yet been named, the name *Document*x appears (where *x* is a number).
- If you are using online help with borders turned off and Maximize mode on, the word *Help* appears. (If you are using MasterWord Help, the comprehensive replacement for Word's help file, the word *MasterWord* appears instead.)
- If you are using the Window Move command, the word *MOVE* appears.
- If you are using the Window Size command, the word *SIZE* appears.
- If you are running a macro, the message *Running Macro* appears.

The Message Bar

Below the menu area is the *message bar*. Here Word tells you what a highlighted command does, gives advice, or explains problems by offering such prompts as *Edit document or press Alt to choose commands*, a message that tells you either to write ("edit") or to press the Alt key so that you can use the menu to choose a command. The line displays any of several hundred messages.

We've looked at the top and bottom of the Word screen. Now let's examine the middle of the screen, where documents are displayed.

DOCUMENT WINDOWS

The focus of your work with Word is inside a document window, which, if you have only one open, typically occupies most of the screen. In it, you can read, write, or edit a document. You can open up to 9 document windows at a time and split any of these in two, allowing what is—in effect—18 windows on one screen. In addition, you can add another window for viewing online help. Only one window at a time is active, but you can switch from one window to another in moments.

Before we review the major features of Word's document windows, let's take a brief look at a minor feature—the small diamond that appears on the first line of every new document. It is called the *endmark,* and it signifies the end of the file. When a file is new and empty, its beginning and end are synonymous, which is why the diamond is on the first line. As you add contents, the endmark moves down.

The endmark is not a real character: Although the cursor might appear under the endmark, you can't select (highlight) the endmark. You can't print the endmark either, nor would you want to. In essence, the only things you can do with the endmark are type text at its location, or ignore it.

Window Borders and Title Bar

Normally, a document window is surrounded by borders. The top border doubles as a *title bar*, the place where Word usually centers the title of the document that is contained in the window.

To give your screen as clean a look as possible, you might want to turn off window borders. You do this by choosing the View Preferences command (Alt+VE), moving to the Window Borders field, pressing and releasing the Spacebar to place an X in the check box, and pressing Enter. You can accomplish the same thing by pressing Alt+B before pressing Enter or by pointing and clicking the left mouse button.

Even though you turn window borders off, they won't actually disappear unless you are running Word in Maximize mode. To activate Maximize mode, use the Window Maximize command (Alt+WX) or, as noted above, click on the title bar's window maximize icon. Borders will reappear if you display multiple windows.

When borders and the title bar are not displayed, the name of a document no longer appears in the title bar, of course. Instead, it appears on the right side of the status bar.

TIP FOR MOUSE USERS

In addition to telling you the name of the document contained in the window, the title bar offers three opportunities to mouse users:

- You can move the window around the screen—or even mostly off the right or bottom edge of the screen—by pointing with the mouse at the title bar and holding down the left mouse button. (The leftmost or topmost portion of the title bar remains visible while the window is active.)
- You can close a window by clicking the left mouse button while pointing the mouse at the leftmost character in the title bar, the square *window close icon*.
- You can maximize the window (or restore the window if it is already maximized) by clicking the left mouse button while pointing the mouse at the two-headed up-and-down arrow, which is the rightmost character in the title bar. This character is called the *window maximize icon*.

The Ruler

Any document can have a ruler displayed across the top of its window. Here is how the ruler typically looks, when it spans the only document window that is open on the screen:

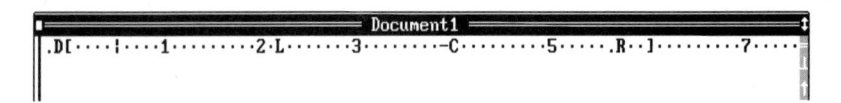

```
================================ Document1 ================================
.D[····¦····1·········2·L······3·········-C·········5·····.R··]·········7····
```

Like the ribbon, the ruler shows you formatting characteristics of selected text or of text that contains the cursor. But whereas the ribbon reflects character formatting and style names, the ruler reflects specific attributes of paragraph formatting: It shows you the width and indentations of lines and the placement of various kinds of tab stops.

As shown in the sample ruler, the [indicates the left indentation of the currently selected paragraph, and the] indicates the right indentation; the ¦ indicates special indentation for the first line of the paragraph. The L reveals the presence of a tab stop that is left aligned; the -C reveals a tab stop that is center aligned, and it has a hyphen leader character. The .R indicates a right-aligned tab stop that has a period leader character. As you'll learn in Chapter 13, you can modify formatting by directly manipulating the ruler with the keyboard or the mouse. For instance, you can click on the ruler with the left mouse button to create a tab stop. In the sample, the .D immediately to the left of the ruler indicates that the next tab stop created with a mouse click will be decimal aligned and have a period leader character.

You can turn the ruler on and off with the View Ruler command (Alt+VR) or by clicking the left mouse button when the mouse is pointing at the ⊥ symbol at the right edge of the screen. If you hold down the Ctrl and Shift keys simultaneously and press the F10 key, the ruler will appear temporarily even if it is turned off with the View Ruler command. Pressing Ctrl+Shift+F10 also moves you to the ruler so that you can make formatting changes to the selected paragraph or paragraphs.

> NOTE: *The ruler is a feature of a given document window, not of the screen. Accordingly, each window can have its own ruler. Contrast this with that other formatting tool, the ribbon, which appears—if at all—only once, near the top of the Word screen.*

If a document window with a ruler is split, the new window will have a ruler.

Scroll Bars

Scroll bars indicate where you are in a document, and they provide an easy way to use a mouse to move (or scroll) through a document. Scroll bars in dialog boxes were introduced briefly earlier in this chapter, at the end of the discussion of the ribbon. Scroll bars in document windows are used in the same general way.

CHAPTER FOUR: The Screen

Scroll bars need not be displayed. You can turn off the vertical scroll bar, the horizontal scroll bar, or both by using Word's View Preferences command. You'll probably want at least the vertical scroll bar on most if not all of the time.

This is the way a small document window can look when both vertical and horizontal scroll bars are displayed:

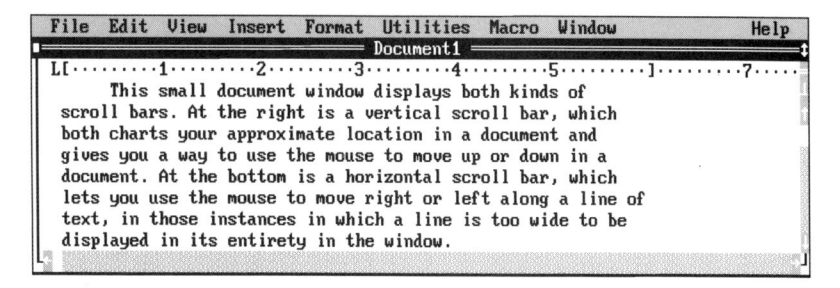

```
 File  Edit  View  Insert  Format  Utilities  Macro  Window            Help
                              Document1
 L[········1·········2·········3·········4·········5·········]·········7·····
         This small document window displays both kinds of
       scroll bars. At the right is a vertical scroll bar, which
       both charts your approximate location in a document and
       gives you a way to use the mouse to move up or down in a
       document. At the bottom is a horizontal scroll bar, which
       lets you use the mouse to move right or left along a line of
       text, in those instances in which a line is too wide to be
       displayed in its entirety in the window.
```

The vertical scroll bar

The vertical scroll bar is the shaded column at the right side of the document window. At the bottom of the document window's scroll bar is a down arrow, and at the top of the scroll bar is an up arrow. This shaded column represents the span of your document, from beginning (top) to end (bottom). Somewhere within the scroll bar is a contrasting rectangle, called the scroll box, which reflects your relative position within the document. In the previous illustration, the scroll box is near the top of the vertical scroll bar, indicating that the text displayed in the window is near the beginning of the document. If you scroll down through the document, the scroll box moves down too.

You can scroll by clicking the left mouse button when the mouse points at the scroll bar's down arrow or up arrow. Clicking on the down arrow moves you toward the bottom of the document, which means text scrolls up the screen. Clicking on the up arrow moves you toward the top of the document, which means text scrolls down the screen. (Similarly, when you press the PgDn key to scroll down in your document, text moves up. And the PgUp key moves text down.)

A faster way to scroll with the mouse is to click not on the arrows but on the scroll bar. If you click on the bar at any location above the scroll box, you will scroll one screen up toward the beginning of the document. If you click on the scroll bar at any location below the scroll box, you will scroll one screen down toward the end of the document.

So far, the scroll box has indicated position. But it also can be an interactive tool, letting you jump to any region of your document. Position the mouse pointer on the scroll box itself, and then hold down the left mouse button while you drag the scroll box to a new location in the scroll bar. When you release the mouse button, your relative position in the document will have changed to match the new relative position of the scroll box.

The horizontal scroll bar

When it is displayed, the horizontal scroll bar spans the bottom of a document window. Like the vertical scroll bar, it has arrows and a scroll box. Unlike the vertical scroll bar, which charts your relative position in a document, the horizontal scroll bar charts your relative position on a line. This has little meaning except when a window is narrower than the lines of text it is displaying.

To scroll one character at a time to the left or right, click on the left or the right arrow at the ends of the horizontal scroll bar. To scroll by larger amounts, click on the scroll bar to the left or right of the scroll box. To move horizontally rapidly, drag the scroll box to a new position by pointing at it and holding down the left button while you move the mouse pointer.

The Selection Bar

On the opposite side of a document window from the vertical scroll bar, inside the left vertical border and immediately to the left of the text, is a blank vertical band, two characters wide, that runs from the top to the bottom of the window. It is the *selection bar*.

If you place the mouse pointer in the selection bar, you can make selections easily:

- To select a line, click the left mouse button.
- To select a paragraph, click the right mouse button, or click the left mouse button twice in fast succession.
- To select an entire document, click both mouse buttons, or hold down the Ctrl key and click the left mouse button.
- To select multiple lines, hold down the left mouse button (without pressing the Ctrl key) and drag the mouse pointer up or down inside the bar.

The mouse pointer changes shape or color when it enters the selection bar. If your computer has graphics capabilities and you're using them, you see the mouse pointer tilt to the right. If you are not using graphics but have a color monitor, the mouse cursor becomes a darker hue.

If you switch to outline mode, descriptive characters are displayed in the selection bar. See the discussion of outline mode, later in this chapter.

The Style Bar

You were introduced to the idea of styles and style sheets in the earlier discussion of the ribbon. Recall that the ribbon's Style list box lets you see the name and key code of whichever style (if any) governs the formatting of the currently selected paragraph. The Style list box also lets you change the style.

An alternative or supplementary way to view styles is with the *style bar*, an optional two-column-wide band that runs vertically to the left of the selection bar (which runs vertically to the left of the text of a document window and cannot be turned off).

The beginning of a document formatted with a style sheet designed for correspondence might look like this:

CHAPTER FOUR: The Screen

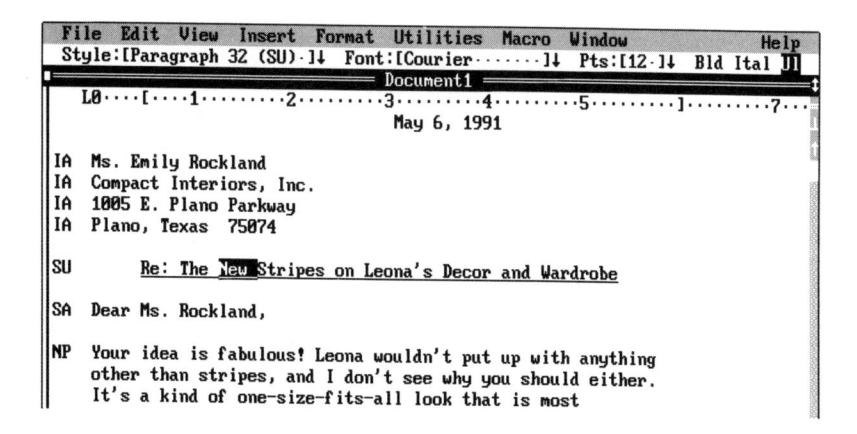

```
 File  Edit  View  Insert  Format  Utilities  Macro  Window              Help
 Style:[Paragraph 32 (SU)·]↓  Font:[Courier······]↓  Pts:[12·]↓  Bld Ital Ul
══════════════════════════════ Document1 ══════════════════════════════
 L0····[····1·········2·········3·········4·········5·········]·········7···
                              May 6, 1991

IA  Ms. Emily Rockland
IA  Compact Interiors, Inc.
IA  1005 E. Plano Parkway
IA  Plano, Texas  75074

SU       Re: The New Stripes on Leona's Decor and Wardrobe

SA  Dear Ms. Rockland,

NP  Your idea is fabulous! Leona wouldn't put up with anything
    other than stripes, and I don't see why you should either.
    It's a kind of one-size-fits-all look that is most
```

The pairs of letters down the left edge of the document window are key codes displayed in the style bar. Each key code is on the first line of a paragraph and tells you which style governs the formatting of the paragraph.

For example, *DA* is the key code for the *date* style. In the particular style sheet used here, the date style formats the date to appear two characters to the right of the center of the page. Below the date is the letter's *inside address,* formatted with a style that has the key code *IA*. Farther down the screen, paragraphs are formatted with styles that have as key codes *SU* for "subject," *SA* for "salutation," and *NP* for "normal paragraph."

In the sample document, *New* is selected. Pressing the Delete key now would delete *New* from the subject-line paragraph. The paragraph is formatted with a style that has as its key code the letters *SU*, a fact noted both in the style bar to the left of the paragraph and in the Style field of the ribbon. Also note that at the far right of the ribbon the letters *Ul* are emphasized. This means that the selected text is underlined.

Viewing Outlines

There is more than one way to look at most things, and documents on your Microsoft Word screen are no exception. Although what you write might not change in any inherent sense, it can take on different appearances depending on your preferences and what you are trying to accomplish.

For example, Word's outline mode provides a dramatically different way to examine a document. It lets you transform a document into an outline of itself and then examine and manipulate the underlying structure of what you have written. When viewed in outline form, a document appears on the screen hierarchically, with subordinate ideas indented or *collapsed*—removed temporarily from the screen so that the only lines that appear are the document's headings, expressing important ideas or the structure of your document. Nothing inherent to the document changes when you view it as an outline. You simply see a different view of the same thing.

For example, as I write this chapter (using Word 5.5) I periodically switch to outline view to observe the organization of my headings. Figure 4-7 shows what I see.

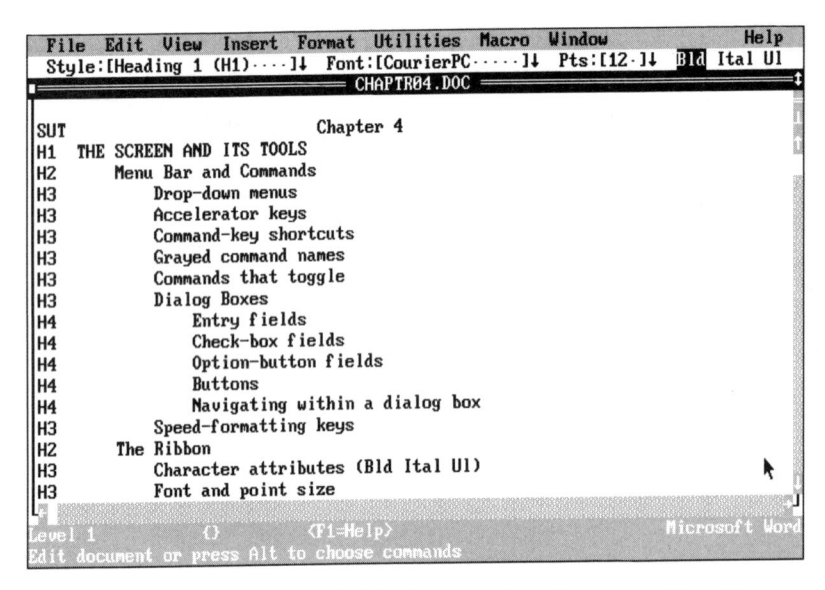

```
File  Edit  View  Insert  Format  Utilities  Macro  Window                Help
Style:[Heading 1 (H1)····]↕ Font:[CourierPC·····]↕ Pts:[12·]↕ Bld Ital Ul
═══════════════════════════════ CHAPTR04.DOC ═══════════════════════════════
SUT                      Chapter 4
H1    THE SCREEN AND ITS TOOLS
H2        Menu Bar and Commands
H3            Drop-down menus
H3            Accelerator keys
H3            Command-key shortcuts
H3            Grayed command names
H3            Commands that toggle
H3            Dialog Boxes
H4                Entry fields
H4                Check-box fields
H4                Option-button fields
H4                Buttons
H4                Navigating within a dialog box
H3            Speed-formatting keys
H2        The Ribbon
H3            Character attributes (Bld Ital Ul)
H3            Font and point size

Level 1          {}          <F1=Help>                    Microsoft Word
Edit document or press Alt to choose commands
```

Figure 4-7. *The beginning of this chapter, viewed as an outline. To turn outlining on or off, use the View Outline command.*

Only headings are displayed because body text has been collapsed. Headings are indented according to their relative levels. First-level headings, such as "THE SCREEN AND ITS TOOLS," are not indented at all. Second-level headings, such as "Menu Bar and Commands" and "The Ribbon," are indented one level. Third-level headings, such as "Drop-down menus," are indented yet another level, and so forth.

I switch in and out of this view by pressing a couple of keys. I move rapidly to any part of the document by switching into outline view, moving the cursor or mouse to a desired heading, and leaving outline view at the new location. I move a whole section of my document from one place to another, simply by moving the section's heading within my outline. And you can do these things too.

You can tell outlining is on if there is a dot to the left of the word *Outline* on the View menu. To turn outlining on or off, use the View Outline command (Alt+VO). Alternatively, press Shift+F2. When you use outlining, Word replaces page-number and column-number information in the status bar with notations such as *Level 2*, *Text*, and *ORGANIZE*.

The first time you enter outline view you might be disappointed because an outline of your document might not appear immediately. You have to help Word along by creating headings. To use outlining most effectively, you probably want to format your documents with a style sheet that contains *Heading* styles. You also need to know how to *expand* and *collapse* text. For information, see Chapters 24 and 26.

In the sample screen, the numbers that appear to the left of the heading lines (in the style bar) show the key codes of the style formatting for the heading. For example, "Drop-down menus," a third-level heading, is marked with *H3*. The key code *H1* was used for the Heading 1 style, and so on.

Viewing Layouts and Previews

Word has two other modes, both of which increase the accuracy with which your document is displayed on the screen. These are not modes in which you are likely to want to work constantly, but they are useful for getting periodic verification of your formatting.

Both of these modes, one called layout and the other called print preview, are introduced in Chapter 7.

Splitting a Window in Two

A document window can be split into two *panes,* each showing the same document. You can scroll independently in each pane so that different parts of the document are displayed in each. You can even view your document in outline or layout mode in one pane and have a normal view of it in the other pane.

The split between two panes in a window is always horizontal and can be created with either the keyboard or the mouse.

Splitting with a keyboard

1. Choose the Window Split command (Alt+WT).
2. Use the Up and the Down direction keys to position the split where you want it. Here's how the top of a blank document window looks with a window pane that is not yet fixed in position.

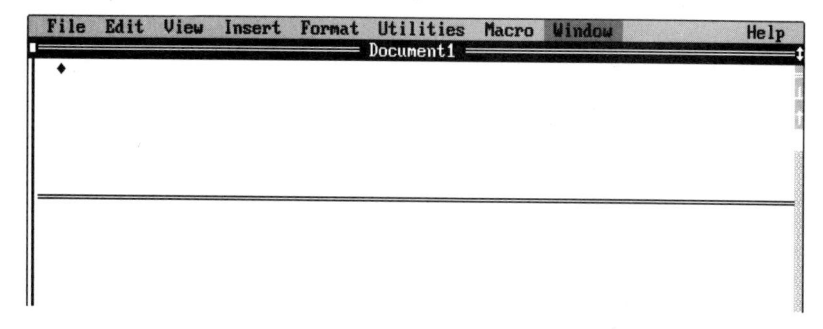

```
┌──────────────────────────────────────────────────────────────────┐
│ File  Edit  View  Insert  Format  Utilities  Macro  Window  Help │
├══════════════════════════ Document1 ═════════════════════════════┤
│ ♦                                                                │
│                                                                  │
│                                                                  │
│                                                                  │
│                                                                  │
│──────────────────────────────────────────────────────────────────│
│                                                                  │
│                                                                  │
└──────────────────────────────────────────────────────────────────┘
```

3. To fix a pane to a position, press Enter.

To close an unneeded pane, choose the Window Split command again, and use the Up or the Down direction key to slide the split either up and off the top or down and off the bottom of the screen. For instance, if you want to get rid of the lower of two panes, move the split downward until it reaches the bottom of the window, and then press Enter, thereby permitting the remaining pane to fill all of the document window.

Splitting with a mouse

1. Point the mouse at the short double-line icon above the up arrow in the vertical scroll bar. This symbol, which looks something like an overlong equal sign, represents the window split.
2. Click the left mouse button twice in succession to split the window into two panes of approximately equal size. Or hold down the left mouse button, and pull the mouse pointer down toward the middle or bottom of the screen. A split will appear and move with the mouse pointer. The split will remain at this location when you release the mouse button.

To use a mouse to close an unneeded pane, double-click on the window split icon again, or hold the left mouse button down and drag the split up or down until it no longer divides the window into separate views.

During the positioning phase, the split will appear as a double horizontal line (or a ruler if the window from which the pane was split has its ruler displayed).

To move between two panes, press the F6 key.

Multiple Windows

Splitting a document window is not the same as dividing the screen into multiple document windows.

Word lets you open as many as nine document windows at a time, displaying some or all of them on the screen simultaneously. Each window can contain a different document (or style sheet, as you'll learn in Chapter 6). If you prefer, the same document can appear in several windows, but a window can never display more than one document. This idea was introduced in Concept 11 of Chapter 2.

Adding still more flexibility, each window can be split, as previously noted.

Of course, you probably won't want to have nine documents open. In particular, you probably won't want to see two views of each of nine different documents. But you might be surprised at how useful multiple windows can be. Recall that you can maximize your document windows so that the active window takes up the entire text area of the screen. This means you can have up to nine chapters of a report or a book loaded into Word simultaneously, with whichever chapter currently interests you open in a full-size document window. Want to check something in a different document? Simply press Ctrl+F6 as many times as are necessary to move to the window that contains the chapter you want to use.

Perhaps the mouse can be used to best advantage in opening and manipulating windows. Any windowing task can be accomplished through commands, which can be executed with either the keyboard or the mouse. But alternative techniques are available for the mouse for many of these tasks, particularly those involving pointing at or moving objects.

Recall from Chapter 3 the document MEMO.DOC, which is shown here in a document window that uses the entire text area.

CHAPTER FOUR: The Screen

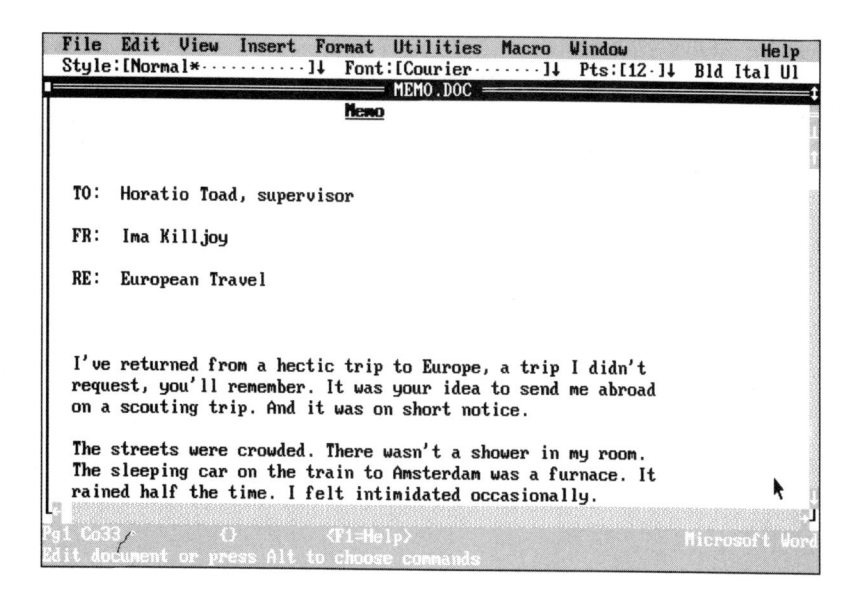

```
 File  Edit  View  Insert  Format  Utilities  Macro  Window           Help
 Style:[Normal*··········]↓  Font:[Courier······]↓  Pts:[12·]↓  Bld Ital Ul
╔══════════════════════════════ MEMO.DOC ══════════════════════════════╗
║                              Memo                                    ║
║                                                                      ║
║                                                                      ║
║   TO:  Horatio Toad, supervisor                                      ║
║                                                                      ║
║   FR:  Ima Killjoy                                                   ║
║                                                                      ║
║   RE:  European Travel                                               ║
║                                                                      ║
║                                                                      ║
║   I've returned from a hectic trip to Europe, a trip I didn't        ║
║   request, you'll remember. It was your idea to send me abroad       ║
║   on a scouting trip. And it was on short notice.                    ║
║                                                                      ║
║   The streets were crowded. There wasn't a shower in my room.        ║
║   The sleeping car on the train to Amsterdam was a furnace. It       ║
║   rained half the time. I felt intimidated occasionally.        ▲    ║
╚══════════════════════════════════════════════════════════════════════╝
Pg1 Co33          {}         <F1=Help>                    Microsoft Word
Edit document or press Alt to choose commands
```

Note that the title bar is a double line. This indicates that the document is active.

To open a second document and display it on top of this document, first choose the File Open command (press Alt+FO, or click with the mouse on the menu bar's File command and then click on the File menu's Open command). Type the name of the desired document (or choose it from the dialog box's list of available documents), and press Enter or click on the OK button in the dialog box.

For example, we can open the document CHAPTR04.DOC, to which you were introduced in outline form a few pages ago:

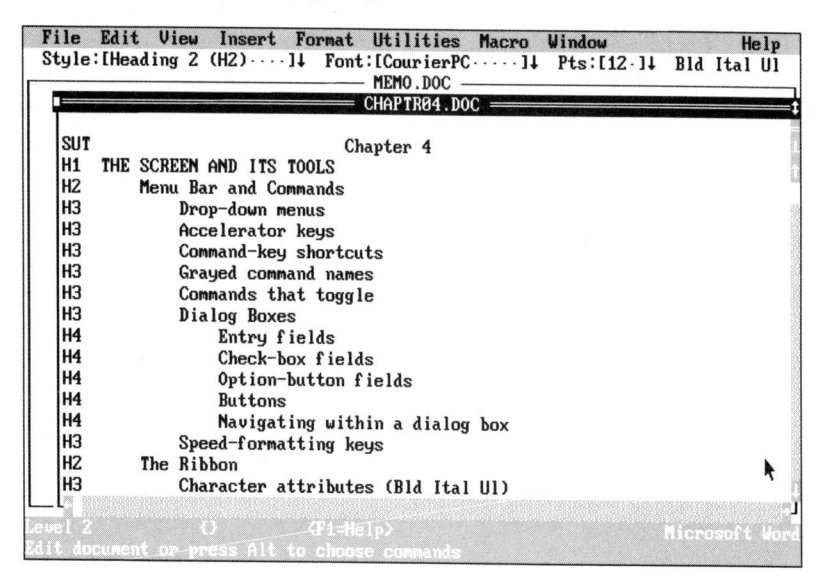

```
 File  Edit  View  Insert  Format  Utilities  Macro  Window           Help
 Style:[Heading 2 (H2)····]↓ Font:[CourierPC·····]↓ Pts:[12·]↓ Bld Ital Ul
┌────────────────────────────── MEMO.DOC ──────────────────────────────┐
╔════════════════════════════ CHAPTR04.DOC ════════════════════════════╗
║ SUT                    Chapter 4                                     ║
║ H1    THE SCREEN AND ITS TOOLS                                       ║
║ H2        Menu Bar and Commands                                      ║
║ H3            Drop-down menus                                        ║
║ H3            Accelerator keys                                       ║
║ H3            Command-key shortcuts                                  ║
║ H3            Grayed command names                                   ║
║ H3            Commands that toggle                                   ║
║ H3            Dialog Boxes                                           ║
║ H4                Entry fields                                       ║
║ H4                Check-box fields                                   ║
║ H4                Option-button fields                               ║
║ H4                Buttons                                            ║
║ H4                Navigating within a dialog box                     ║
║ H3            Speed-formatting keys                                  ║
║ H2        The Ribbon                                                 ║
║ H3            Character attributes (Bld Ital Ul)                ▲    ║
╚══════════════════════════════════════════════════════════════════════╝
Level 2           {}         <F1=Help>                    Microsoft Word
Edit document or press Alt to choose commands
```

The new document is displayed in its own window, one line lower and three spaces to the right of the previous document. You can see the title bar and a little bit of the left side of the document MEMO.DOC, which appears to be underneath CHAPTR04.DOC. The title bar of the new document now has the double line, indicating that it is the active document. Meanwhile, MEMO.DOC has lost its double line because it is inactive.

At this point, if you press Alt+WX to execute the Window Maximize command, the uppermost document takes over the entire window area of the screen. You lose sight of MEMO.DOC entirely. This doesn't mean that MEMO.DOC has been closed. It is simply underneath CHAPTR04.DOC, which is using all the available room. In this case, you can bring MEMO.DOC to the top of the pile by pressing Ctrl+F6—the key combination that makes the next window active.

If you press Alt+WA to run the Window Arrange All command, both documents appear on the screen with their windows tiled (sized and arranged so that all are completely visible) rather than overlapping.

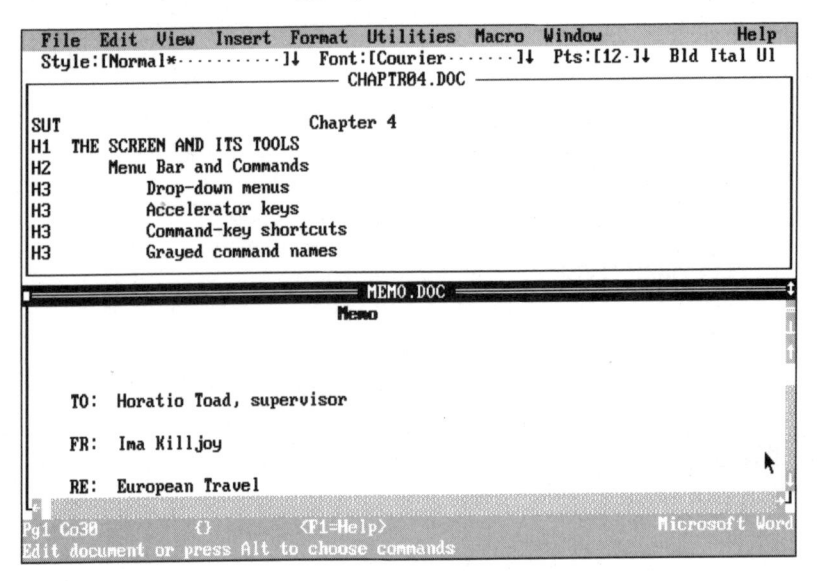

```
File   Edit   View   Insert   Format   Utilities   Macro   Window              Help
Style:[Normal*·········]↕  Font:[Courier········]↕ Pts:[12·]↕ Bld Ital Ul
─────────────────────────── CHAPTR04.DOC ───────────────────────────

SUT                    Chapter 4
H1    THE SCREEN AND ITS TOOLS
H2        Menu Bar and Commands
H3            Drop-down menus
H3            Accelerator keys
H3            Command-key shortcuts
H3            Grayed command names

═══════════════════════════ MEMO.DOC ═══════════════════════════
                              Memo


        TO:  Horatio Toad, supervisor

        FR:  Ima Killjoy

        RE:  European Travel

Pg1 Co38              {}           <F1=Help>            Microsoft Word
Edit document or press Alt to choose commands
```

In this case, there happen to be only two tiles because there are only two document windows. However, if you had the maximum of nine document windows open and used the Window Arrange All command, the screen would be tiled with an array of small windows three wide and three deep.

To close a window, use the Window Close command (Alt+WC), or point with the mouse to the window close icon—the small square at the left end of the title bar—and then click the left mouse button. In the preceding illustration, the title bar for MEMO.DOC has a window close icon, but the title bar for CHAPTR04.DOC does not. This is because MEMO.DOC is in the active window, and only the active window's

CHAPTER FOUR: The Screen

title bar contains the window close icon. To close a window that is not active, you must first make it active (by pressing Ctrl+F6 one or more times or by clicking somewhere inside the window with the mouse).

The Help Window

Regardless of how many document windows you have open, you can open a single help window for online assistance with Word. The window displays a special reference file (Help file) on the screen. You can size the window to suit your needs, display it alongside a document on which you are working, or hide the help window behind your document so that you can jump back and forth to it without losing your place in either window.

When you choose Help from the menu bar, you see this drop-down menu:

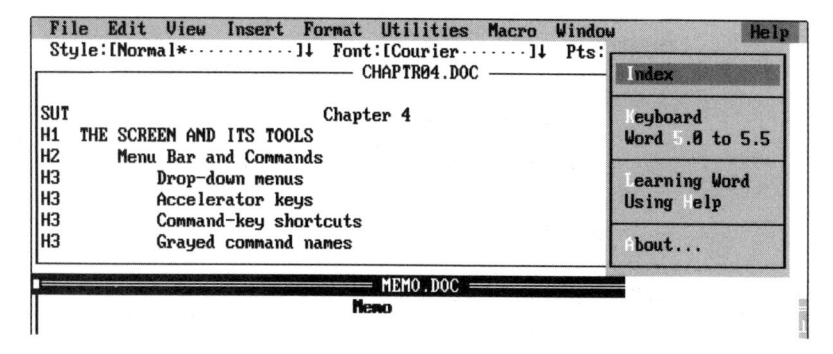

```
File  Edit  View  Insert  Format  Utilities  Macro  Window            Help
  Style:[Normal*··········]↓  Font:[Courier········]↓  Pts:
─────────────────────────── CHAPTR04.DOC ──────────────── Index
 SUT                                                     
 H1    THE SCREEN AND ITS TOOLS          Chapter 4        eyboard
 H2        Menu Bar and Commands                          Word  .0 to 5.5
 H3            Drop-down menus                           
 H3            Accelerator keys                           earning Word
 H3            Command-key shortcuts                      Using  elp
 H3            Grayed command names                      
                                                          bout...
═══════════════════════════ MEMO.DOC ════════════════════
                          Memo
```

Chapter 17 describes how to use this menu and the help screens you can reach from it.

CHAPTER FIVE

Using the Keyboard and Mouse

Working with Word is a conversation of sorts: You tell it what to do, and it tells you what's going on and what's possible. You give instructions with the keyboard or the mouse; Word talks back by showing symbols and messages, and it lets you watch your work take form on the screen.

You already know a good deal about conversing with Word. In Chapter 4 you became acquainted with how Word displays information on the screen and were introduced to the rudiments of giving commands and certain other kinds of instructions.

In this chapter we turn in greater detail to how you use the keyboard and the mouse to give Word instructions. In a sense, when you've finished this chapter you will know how to use the program. After that, it is just a matter of getting to know parts of Word better—and you're the one who decides which parts to explore.

The chapter is divided into three broad sections:

- Keyboard. The first section describes the use of the keyboard, including the general purposes of several keys.
- Mouse. The second section outlines ways you can use the mouse as an alternative to the keyboard.
- Tasks. The final section takes an opposite tack, describing categories of tasks and then giving examples of how you can use the keyboard and the mouse to accomplish them.

THE KEYBOARD

Your keyboard might be one of several designs. Many computers or computer dealers offer a choice. The text and graphics in this book refer to the enhanced 101-key model (Figure 5-1) offered with most personal computers, from IBMs to Apple Macintoshes. Unlike the original IBM PC keyboard layout (Figure 5-2), the enhanced keyboard is arranged to more closely resemble a Selectric typewriter. The Esc key is in the upper left corner, next to the function keys, which are increased in number from 10 to 12 and are placed across the top of the keyboard instead of in pairs to the left. Direction keys (also called cursor keys or arrow keys) are separate from the calculator-style numeric keypad, as are the Insert, Page Up, and other keys directly above them.

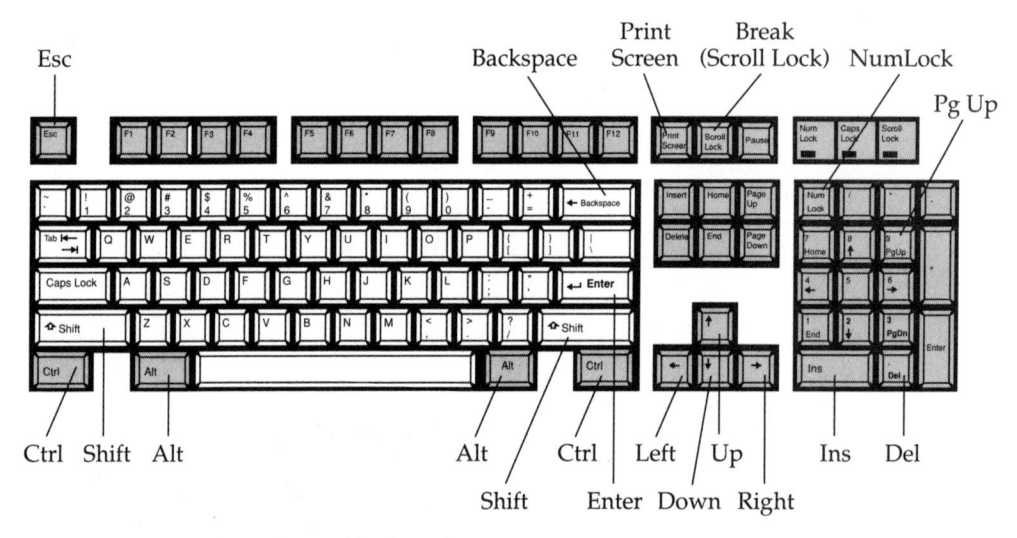

Figure 5-1. The 101-key enhanced keyboard.

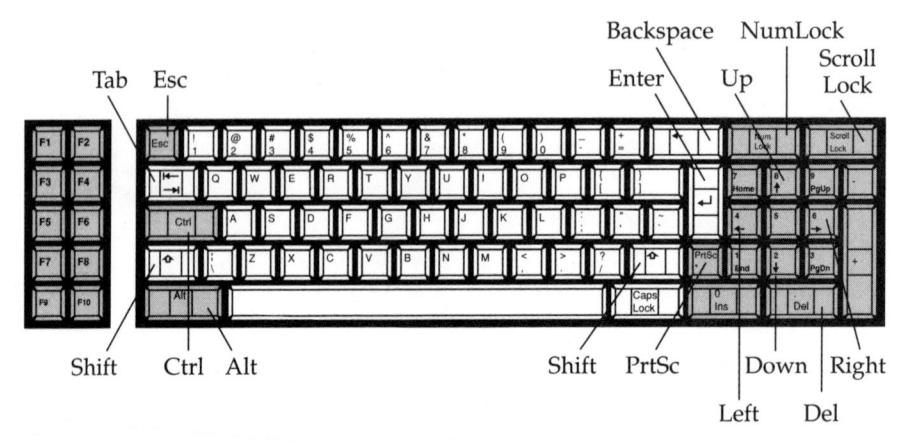

Figure 5-2. The original IBM PC keyboard.

CHAPTER FIVE: Using the Keyboard and Mouse   91

Don't assume, however, that the keyboard is better than the original simply because it is "enhanced" and has more keys. Many people prefer the original keyboard layout, with its 10 function keys on the left. In recent years, some manufacturers have taken to producing hybrid models that offer 12 function keys but keep them on the left.

Keys That Shift Other Keys

In many ways, a computer keyboard is like a typewriter keyboard. You can use keys individually, or you can use them in combination with others. Three keys—Shift, Ctrl, and Alt—expand the capabilities of your keyboard by providing alternative meanings for certain keys. They are known as *shift keys*.

The Shift key

The Shift key capitalizes printable characters, of course. (If the Caps Lock key is on, making capitalization the norm, the Shift key causes letters to be lowercase.) Basically, the Shift key changes the case of letters that you type. (To change the case of letters that already have been typed—from lowercase to initial cap to all caps—select the characters and press Shift+F3 one or more times until the desired effect is achieved.)

When you hold down the Shift key, the keys that normally move the cursor cause the cursor to extend—to highlight more than a single character or space on the screen.

When used with certain function keys, the Shift key moves Word into a different mode or causes a task to be performed:

- Shift+F3 toggles the case of selected text.
- Shift+F4 tells Word to continue searching a document for a particular word or group of characters that you've previously specified.
- Shift+F10 extends the selection to encompass the entire document.

The Ctrl key

As its name implies, the Ctrl key gives you a lot of control. It lets you format, run macros, and change the way in which Word performs. It's almost as if you have two

---

IDENTIFYING SHIFT KEYS

In this book, shift keys are followed by a plus sign.

Keys	Meaning
Shift+F3	Hold down the Shift key and press the F3 key.
Ctrl+AC	Hold down the Ctrl key and press A followed by C.
Alt+FC	Hold down the Alt key and press F followed by C.

In the case of using Alt to access a menu, you needn't hold the key down—you can simply press and release it.

keyboards: In one the Ctrl key is not depressed and all the keys have "usual" meanings, whereas in the other the Ctrl key is depressed and other keys take on new purposes.

The Ctrl key lets you give predefined formatting instructions to your computer. It is the trigger for speed-formatting keys, which were introduced in Chapters 3 and 4. Pressing Ctrl+C, for example, centers the lines of a paragraph. Word has 27 such built-in formats, listed near the beginning of Chapter 3 and in Appendix B. The Ctrl key also can be used to run a macro or insert text from a glossary entry.

Two final notes on the Ctrl key:

- Like the Shift key, the Ctrl key can be used with function keys. For example, Ctrl+F9 is one way to turn on Word's print preview feature.
- If you are running Microsoft Word as a non-Windows application under Microsoft Windows 3.0, you can press Ctrl+Esc to reach the Windows task list. This lets you move to other running applications, whether or not they are in visible windows.

The Alt key

The Alt key is your gateway to Word's commands and accelerator keys. Press the Alt key followed by a letter to make a choice. For example, if you want to save all documents and other files to disk, you can use the File Save All command: Press Alt+FE.

If you are running Microsoft Word as a non-Windows application under Microsoft Windows 3.0, you can press Alt+Tab or Alt+Esc to reach the Windows environment and other programs you might be running there.

Function Keys

Function keys, which have the names F1 through F10 or F1 through F12, give you the means to accomplish tasks quickly. The effective number of function keys is substantially greater than 10 or 12 because combining a function key such as F2 with a shift key creates, in essence, an entirely new function key. For example:

- F5 is a shortcut for the Edit Go To command.
- Shift+F5 switches between two modes of outline view.
- Alt+F5 toggles overtype mode on and off.
- Ctrl+F5 restores a document window to its original size.
- Shift+Ctrl+F5 inserts a bookmark.

See Appendix B for a complete list of function keys.

Emulating Word 5.0's Keys

In the transition from Word 5.5, the function of several keys underwent change. If you are a veteran Word user who prefers the old key assignments, you can use the Utilities Customize command to tell Word to use them, as described in the following sections.

CHAPTER FIVE: Using the Keyboard and Mouse

NOTE: *This book (as well as the Word 5.5 documentation) assumes that you are using the new function-key assignments. If you're a Word novice, start right in using the new assignments; if you're a Word veteran, you might want to begin using the new ones anyway because macros could be incompatible with the old function-key assignments.*

Function keys

Appendix B contains a complete list of Word's function keys and their purposes in both Word 5.0 and Word 5.5. If you decide you want to use Word 5.0 function, simply choose the Utilities Customize command and place an X in the *Use Word 5.0 Function Keys* check box. Press Enter to carry out the command. The command-key shortcuts listed in the menus will change accordingly, as shown in Figure 5-3.

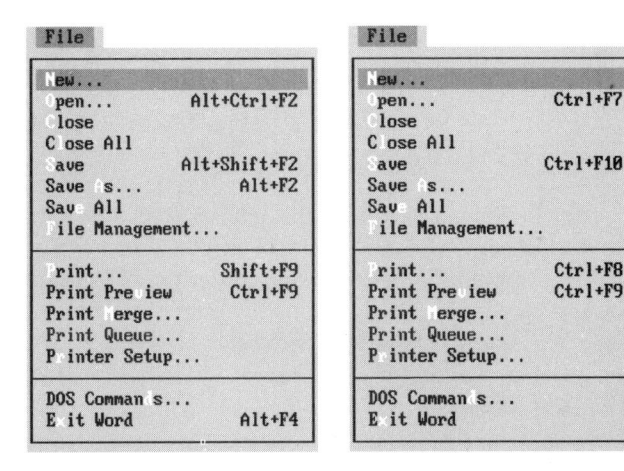

Figure 5-3. Word 5.5's File menu usually looks like the example on the left. But turning off the Utilities Customize command's Use Word 5.0 Function Keys *check box results in new assignments to most function keys, one result being the changes shown in the example to the right.*

The Ins and Del keys

In Word 5.5, you get to dictate the purpose of the Ins key. To do this, you choose the Utilities Customize command and use the *Use INS for Overtype Key* check box:

- To use the Ins key as a toggle for Overtype and Insert modes, place an X in the check box. (Word 5.5 uses this as the standard.)
- To use the Ins key to insert text into your document from the scrap (the Word 5.0 standard), delete the X from the check box.

The command-key shortcuts listed in the menus will reflect your choice, as shown in Figure 5-4.

Even if you decide to use Ins as a toggle, you can still use it (in conjunction with the Del key) to insert from or delete to the scrap: Simply hold down the Shift key as you press Ins or Del.

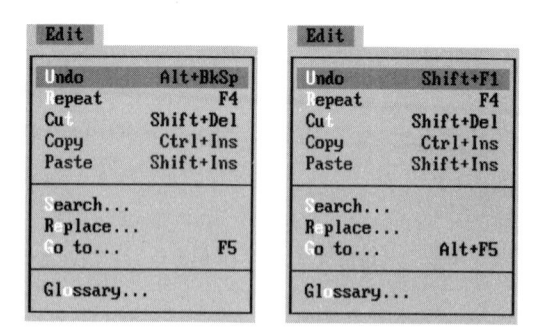

Figure 5-4. Word 5.5's Edit menu looks like the example on the left if you leave the Utilities Customize command's Use INS for Overtype Key check box set to on. If you turn the check box off, it changes to match the example on the right.

THE MOUSE

The mouse is an extension of the keyboard and provides you with an alternative way to give instructions to your computer. The mouse rests on ball bearings or Teflon skids, and you roll it on your desktop a few inches in one direction or another to move a special pointer around the screen. Generally, the mouse pointer appears as an arrow (if your computer is equipped with a graphics-display card) or as a bright or colored rectangle (if your computer is not equipped for graphics or if you choose to run Word in a text mode rather than a graphics mode).

Moving the mouse pointer around the screen does nothing by itself. To make something happen, you press either or both of the buttons on the mouse. Sometimes you hold down the left or right button as you move ("drag") the mouse pointer, but more often you quickly press and release ("click") one or both of the mouse buttons.

Which is the left button and which is the right? Put your palm over the mouse so that a finger rests on each of the buttons. Now the meanings of the instructions "click the right mouse button" and "click the left mouse button" are clear.

Double-Clicking in Word 5.5

Beginning with Word 5.5, you often click a mouse button twice in rapid succession; this *double-click* technique will be familiar to users of the Apple Macintosh and Microsoft Windows, but it is new to PC Word users. Generally, double-clicking involves the left button rather than the right one, and it is more powerful than single clicking. For instance, if you are using the File Open command to choose a file to load into Word, clicking once on a name in the list box highlights the name. But double-clicking on the name doesn't simply highlight the name—it loads the file too. This saves you the trouble of clicking on the OK button or pressing Enter.

If you don't have a mouse, fear not. The keyboard can do 99 percent of what the mouse can, although sometimes not as quickly or efficiently. (And be aware that many actions, such as recording a series of instructions as a macro, simply can't be done with a mouse.) You can even mix and match keystrokes and mouse actions with good results. Before long, many Word users are no more conscious of using a mouse when writing than they are of steering when driving.

Much hoopla is made over the simplicity a mouse brings to learning and using computers. The truth is that many people prefer the keyboard to the mouse and, with a little practice, find that the keyboard is faster for performing such tasks as selecting a word or choosing a command. Even experienced mouse users often find themselves continuing to rely on the keyboard for certain editing functions but using the mouse for other tasks. This is as it should be; every tool has its own uses.

Highest productivity generally comes when you use the keyboard and the mouse together. For example, you might select a lengthy block of text with the mouse but use the keyboard to choose a command to act upon the text. With time, you'll develop your own favorite ways to use the mouse.

Most uses of the mouse involve describing something to the computer by pointing. The mouse proves its worth when the same instruction would require considerably more effort to describe in keystrokes. It is especially helpful when you select large passages of text; move the highlight a considerable distance on the screen; use multiple windows; copy content, formatting, or both from one place to another; manipulate tabular material; or scroll without moving the highlight.

Various icons and regions on the screen are sensitive to the click of a mouse. Chapter 4 covered some of these as part of its description of the screen, and the upcoming third section of this chapter ("Tasks") catalogs other ways to use the mouse. The following page contains a summary of some of these, in table form.

The mouse offers many other opportunities, some of which don't distill well into a table. For example, you can select a section of text with the mouse by placing the mouse cursor at the beginning (or end) of the text to be selected, holding down the left button, dragging the mouse to the other end of the text, and releasing the button.

TIP FOR WORD VETERANS

If you've been using Word with a mouse for a long time, you might be surprised at the differences in Word 5.5. Numerous commands and approaches have changed as Microsoft aligns Word for DOS with the worlds of Microsoft Windows and the Macintosh.

It might help to think of the double-click as a replacement for the right-button click. The Macintosh mouse has a single button, which performs different tasks depending on whether you click it just once or twice in quick succession.

Doing this:	At this location:	Does this:
Clicking left button	On name in menu bar	Displays a drop-down menu of commands
Clicking left button	In scroll bar	Scrolls the document
Clicking left button	<F1=Help> button at bottom of screen	Provides online help
Clicking left button	■ in upper left corner of a document window	Closes the window
Dragging up or down	γ at the top of the vertical scroll bar	Splits the window into two panes and lets you choose a size for each pane
Clicking left button	↕ in the upper right corner of a document window	Enlarges (maximizes) the window to fill the entire text area, or restores the window to its previous size
Clicking left button	⊥ near the top of the vertical scroll bar	Turns the ruler on or off
Clicking right button	= near the top of the vertical scroll bar	Turns the ribbon on or off
Clicking left button	In ribbon	Permits you to choose a paragraph style and character formatting
Clicking left button	In vertical selection bar at left edge of a document window	Selects a line
Double-clicking left button	In vertical selection bar at left edge of a document window	Selects a paragraph
Clicking right button	In vertical selection bar at left edge of a document window	Selects a paragraph
Clicking left button while holding down Ctrl key	In vertical selection bar at left edge of a document window	Selects entire document
Clicking left button	While pointing at a character in a document	Selects the character
Double-clicking left button	While pointing anywhere within a word	Selects the word
Clicking right button	While pointing anywhere within a word	Selects a word
Clicking left button while holding down Ctrl key	While pointing anywhere within a sentence	Selects the sentence

Trivia and Tips

Let's end this introduction to the mouse with a collection of trivia and tips. When used with Word, the Microsoft Mouse

- Moves in units called *mickeys*. A mickey is approximately 1/200 of an inch.
- Comes in serial and bus versions, which behave identically, although their means of connection to a computer differ. The serial version plugs into a serial port. The bus version connects by means of a printed circuit card. The Inport version of the mouse is a bus mouse.
- Needs little rolling space on a desktop. Using the mouse with its default settings, you can move the mouse pointer anywhere on the Word screen by rolling the mouse in a desktop area roughly two inches on a side. If you alter the mouse's sensitivity with its control-panel program, you can increase or decrease the amount of space needed to move the mouse pointer across the screen.
- Runs at two speeds, regardless of the sensitivity you specify with the control-panel program. Rolling the mouse quickly moves the pointer twice as far on the screen as does rolling the mouse slowly the same distance. "If you're moving the mouse fast, chances are you want to go somewhere far away, so we get you there a little faster," explained one of Word's designers.
- Is used in the most unusual ways by unguided newcomers, who have been known to pick one up and roll it around the face of a computer screen...or use grand sweeps of their arms, instead of slow motions of a fraction of an inch...or, not realizing they can lift the mouse and set it down elsewhere to continue a motion, roll the mouse to the edge of the desk and wonder what to do...or lift the keyboard with one hand and roll the mouse under it with the other....

TASKS

The tasks you can perform with the keyboard or the mouse can be lumped into various categories. What follows is an introduction to and notes about these categories rather than a comprehensive list of every possible instruction you can give Word. For greater detail on the specifics of using the keyboard to accomplish these kinds of tasks, see Appendix B.

Turning Modes On and Off

Chapter 4 introduced you to the status bar, a line near the bottom of the screen that contains information about the scrap and about Word's modes. You use the keyboard to tell Word to turn these modes on and off.

To turn this mode on or off:	Press:
Extend Selection (turn it on/off)	F8/Esc
Column Selection	Ctrl+Shift+F8
Overtype	Alt+F5
Macro Record	Ctrl+F3
Line Draw (turn it on/off)	Alt+UL/Esc

Entering and Editing Text

The keyboard gives you ways to type printable text as well as various kinds of nonprinting spacing characters—from Spacebar spaces to paragraph marks. For example, you can force Word to begin a new line by pressing Shift+Enter to insert a newline character into your document.

You can also use foreign, mathematical, and graphics characters in your document, provided that your printer supports these characters and you know what their ASCII codes are. To use any of these *extended characters,* turn on the NumLock key if it is not on already, and then hold down the Alt key while typing the code *on the numeric keypad.* For example, if you are using a PostScript printer and want to place a long dash in a document, be sure the NumLock key is on and then hold down the Alt key while you type *234* on the keypad. The symbol on your screen will not be a long dash because the screen uses a somewhat different character set than does a PostScript printer. Nonetheless, when you print your document on a Postscript printer, you will have the dash.

Text in your document can be deleted. If you delete it to the scrap instead of deleting it outright, you can then insert it elsewhere in the same document or a different document. This is one way to move text from one location to another. You delete text with the Del key (or the Cut command) and insert it with the Ins key (or the Paste command). As discussed earlier in this chapter, you might or might not have to use the Shift key in conjunction with the Del and Ins keys, depending on what choice you make in the Utilities Customize command's *Use INS for Overtype Key* field.

Scrolling, Moving, and Selecting

Keys and the mouse are your means to moving around in a document. This moving around takes various forms but never directly involves changing content. To move, you can

- ♦ *Scroll,* which means you move up and down (or in some cases left and right) in your document, changing whatever parts of the document appear on the screen. Scrolling with the mouse was described in Chapter 4 as part of the discussion of the scroll bars, and scrolling with the keyboard is covered in Appendix B.

- *Move the cursor*, which sometimes results incidentally in scrolling but more often merely involves getting the cursor to the right character. In other words, you might scroll a document to get a desired paragraph displayed and then move the cursor to a particular spot within the paragraph.
- *Select*, which extends the cursor into a highlighted region that varies in size from one character to the length of the entire document.

The basic way to select a section of text with the mouse is to place the mouse cursor at the beginning (or end) of the text to be selected, hold down the left mouse button, drag the mouse to the other end of the text, and release the button.

Selecting with the mouse was covered earlier in this chapter. What follows is an abbreviated version of a chart from Appendix B, listing ways to use the keyboard to select text.

To select:	Press:
A word	Alt+F6
A sentence	Alt+F8
A paragraph	Alt+F10
A column	Ctrl+Shift+F8; then use direction keys
An entire document	Ctrl+5 (on numeric keypad) or Shift+F10
Everything to the next character x	F8; then x (where x is a letter or symbol)
Forward from cursor, character by character	Shift+Right direction key
Backward from cursor, character by character	Shift+Left direction key
Forward from cursor, word by word	Ctrl+Shift+Right direction key
Backward from cursor, word by word	Ctrl+Shift+Left direction key
Forward from cursor, paragraph by paragraph	Ctrl+Shift+Down direction key
Backward from cursor, paragraph by paragraph	Ctrl+Shift+Up direction key

Using Commands

Instructions for using Word commands fall into two categories: general techniques and rules that apply to all commands, such as how to fill in a dialog box, and keystrokes relevant only to a specific command. Here we review briefly the general rules for using commands, recapping information presented in Chapter 4. In Appendix B you'll find a catalog of specific keystrokes for use with particular commands.

Three kinds of shortcut keys

To choose a command, you can use any of three kinds of keyboard shortcuts, all of which you've been introduced to already: accelerator keys, command keys, and speed-formatting keys.

Accelerator keys These help you navigate through menus and dialog boxes. Accelerator keys are bright white, a color such as red, or highlighted (depending on your computer and on the settings you made in the View Preferences dialog box). For example, when the menu bar is active but no menus are dropped down, each name in the menu bar has one letter emphasized: **F**ile, **E**dit, **V**iew, **I**nsert F**o**rmat, **U**tilities, **M**acro, **W**indow, and **H**elp. If you press one of these letters, Word takes you directly to its associated drop-down menu.

Command keys If you leaf back a couple of pages to the picture of the Utilities menu, you see that the notation *Shift+F7* appears next to the word *Thesaurus*. This is a *command-key shortcut*, a reminder that you can execute the Utilities Thesaurus command without using the menu, by holding down the Shift key and pressing the F7 key.

Speed-formatting keys You've read a lot about these keys by now, early in this chapter and in previous ones. To make various common formatting choices, you hold down the Ctrl key and press a letter—a *speed-formatting key*. The keys were introduced in Chapter 3 and are listed in Appendix B.

Choosing commands

1. To choose a command, press Alt or F10 to activate the menu bar.
2. Press the accelerator key for the family of commands you want to use.

Using keys in dialog boxes

- To move to a choice within a dialog box, hold down the Alt key and press an accelerator key.
- To turn a check box on or off, press the Spacebar or click the left mouse button.
- To make a selection from a group of option buttons, click the left mouse button or press the Spacebar until the desired option is selected.
- To use a text-box field, either type in the desired information or make a selection from the associated lists of choices, if available. (Sometimes these lists are in a separate box, and sometimes they are in a drop-down list that appears only if you press Alt+Down.)
- To use a command button, simply press the accelerator key or click the left mouse button. To select OK, simply press Return; to cancel a command, press Esc.

CHAPTER FIVE: Using the Keyboard and Mouse   101

Keys for Microsoft Windows

If you run Microsoft Word as a non-Windows application under Microsoft Windows 3.0, certain key combinations let you move between Word and the Windows environment.

To switch to:	Press:
Next application (program) or minimized icon	Alt+Esc
Next application, restoring applications that are running as icons	Alt+Tab
The Windows Task List so that you can choose among all programs currently running	Ctrl+Esc

Although these Windows key combinations are not, strictly speaking, part of Word, they belong here because you use them while you are in Word—so that you can leave Word temporarily to work with a different program. Be sure not to confuse them with Word's family of Window commands, such as Window New Window or Window Move, which you use to control the document windows that are a part of Microsoft Word 5.5.

CHAPTER SIX

Introducing Styles and Macros

Word has a wealth of features, but that doesn't mean it does exactly what you want.

Imagine you're working in the middle of a long document and you decide the page needs three centered headings to break up the text. You want the headings formatted identically, and you suspect 14-point TMSRMN bold is a good choice.

Word offers you plenty of general-purpose formatting commands and several built-in formats but none that instruct Word specifically to "Center this line in 14-point TMSRMN bold."

You might use a combination of Word's Format Character and Format Paragraph commands to format each of the headings. This isn't much trouble for three headings. But it could prove to be a chore if you add headings on other pages and particularly if you change your mind after the fact and decide to switch the headings from TMSRMN to HELV.

Now imagine you've finished formatting the three headings and you want to print the page to see how it looks. But no single command tells Word to "Print only this page." Instead, either you print the entire document, which is easy but a waste of time and paper, or you follow a small series of steps—verifying that page numbering is up-to-date, noting the number of the desired page, adjusting Word to print only that page number, actually printing, and readjusting Word afterward so that next time you don't simply print the same page over again. The steps are not difficult, but you must attend to them whenever you print less than an entire document.

These examples demonstrate the obvious: Word's commands can't meet the individual needs of everyone all the time. But Word does the next-best thing. It provides tools that permit you or someone working on your behalf to customize the word processor to meet your specific needs. The primary tools Word supplies for this are *styles* and *macros*.

- A style is a description of formatting, stored with a name and a code. You could, for example, create a style for headings that is formatted as centered, 14-point TMSRMN bold. You can then use the name and code to apply the style to any text you desire. A document's styles are stored in a *style sheet,* which might better be called a *style file.* Although you can have more than one style sheet, a particular document uses only one.
- A macro, on the other hand, is a script that tells Word to perform a series of steps on your behalf. You could, for example, create a macro that asks you what pages you want to print and then instructs Word to print only those pages. Macros are stored in a *glossary file,* which you can think of as a macro file. Contrary to the impression the name might give, a glossary does not contain definitions.

For now, let's get started with styles and macros. This chapter explains what they are and how they differ from each other. It walks you through the creation of a simple style, and it does the same thing for a simple macro. The chapter also demonstrates what it is like to use a powerful macro, the page-printing macro. Finally, the chapter explains the role of Word's NORMAL style sheets and glossary files and what the program does when different NORMAL files exist on different disks or directories.

Before continuing, you might review Concept 10 in Chapter 2, which helps provide a framework for understanding styles. Styles were also addressed in some detail as part of the discussion of the ribbon early in Chapter 4.

STYLES VS. MACROS

Even experienced Word users can be confused by the distinctions between macros and styles. This is understandable: Both are shortcuts that let you press a couple of keys to accomplish substantial work. Furthermore, both macros and styles can be used to format text. But the differences are actually greater than the similarities.

- You can think of a style as an adjective and a macro as a verb. Whereas a style describes and controls the formatting of text, a macro takes an action. By analogy, a style describes and defines how a bell sounds, and a macro rings the bell.
- Text is always linked to its style: If you change the style, the formatting of the text changes accordingly. For example, a style might dictate that text should be underlined. If you later change the style's formatting from underlining to italic, all text formatted with the style changes from underlined to italic.
- On the other hand, text is linked to a macro only as long as the macro is executing. When the steps of the macro are complete, the macro's connection to the document vanishes. Changing the macro, even deleting the macro, has no effect on actions that the macro already has completed.

CHAPTER SIX: Introducing Styles and Macros

- Styles dictate formatting; macros can do many things other than format. You can create macros that open windows, set up tables, insert text into a document, or even tell you the correct local time of day in Tokyo.

If you're getting more confused rather than less, read on. The confusion should lift as you work through the rest of the chapter.

If you followed the tutorial in Chapter 3, you created a simple memo that was formatted with the speed-formatting keys. The memo had a heading that you formatted to be centered, with an extra blank line above it, as well as underlined and bold. Each step was easy because it was accomplished with a speed-formatting key: First you used Ctrl+O to create open line spacing for the entire document, and then you used Ctrl+C to center the heading, Ctrl+U to underline it, and Ctrl+B to boldface it.

This time we want headings to be centered and bold, as in Chapter 3, but instead of underlined we want them in a special font, TMSRMN, and in a somewhat-larger-than-normal size, 14 point. No built-in speed-formatting key will do this for you. You've got to select the characters in every heading and format them individually with the help of the ribbon or the Format Character command. Doing this more than a few times will be time-consuming and possibly quite tedious. So we'll do it only once and then record the resulting combination of formats as a style which we then can use to format other headings.

NOTE: *What follows is a tutorial in the basics of recording styles and using a style sheet to format. Nothing in it is difficult, but you might assimilate the details best by following along at your computer.*

TIP

If you didn't perform the tutorial in Chapter 3 or if you didn't save MEMO.DOC on disk, follow these steps to create a practice document for this discussion of styles:

1. Choose File New.
2. Type *Memo* on the first line.
3. Press F8 twice to select the word.
4. Press Ctrl+O for open spacing.
5. Press Ctrl+C for centered alignment.
6. Press Ctrl+U for underlining.
7. Press Ctrl+B for bold formatting.
8. Press the Down direction key to move to the next paragraph.
9. Type the first few lines of the memo shown on page 40.
10. Save the document as *MEMO.DOC*.

1. Use the File Open command to load the document MEMO.DOC from your disk. Put the cursor in the word *Memo* on the first line, and press the F8 key twice to select (highlight) all the characters in the word.
2. Press Ctrl+F two or more times, until the character dialog box appears. You'll be in the first field of the dialog box, a text box called Font.
3. Press Alt+Down direction key, or click on the Font text box's down arrow, to see a list of the fonts available on your printer. Then press the Down direction key until the TMSRMN font is highlighted, or else scroll with the mouse until the desired font is highlighted. (If TMSRMN is not available, make a different choice.)
4. With the font highlighted, press Tab. Or, if you're using a mouse, release the mouse button. The text box will show your font choice, and the drop-down list will disappear.
5. Use the Tab key to move to the Point Size field, which is another list box. Press Alt+Down direction key to see the sizes available for the font you chose.
6. Highlight the point size you want, which in our example is 14.
7. Press Alt+U to turn off underlining. Or, if you are using a mouse, click in the Underline check box. (The word *Memo* was underlined to begin with, but we no longer want it underlined, which is why we take this step.)
8. Press Enter to carry out the command, or click with the mouse on the OK button.

At this point, the word *Memo* should be formatted with open paragraph spacing and centering in 14-point TMSRMN bold. Because this is an example of the formatting we want for headings, it is time to record it as a style.

Recording a Style

When you record a style, you take text that is selected (highlighted) on the screen and record its formatting while ignoring its content. The resulting element, a style, is stored in a style sheet, which can contain as few as 1 or as many as 125 different styles.

Detaching the old style sheet

When you record a style, it is added to whichever style sheet is currently in use. So, before continuing with this practice session, be sure you don't already have a style sheet in use. To check, choose the Format Attach Style Sheet command (Alt+TA), which produces the Attach Style Sheet dialog box.

The style sheet name listed here is NORMAL.STY, a style sheet about which you will learn more later in the chapter. You might not see the name NORMAL.STY in your dialog box, but if you see this or any other name, press the Del key to get rid of it, and then press Enter or click on the OK button to carry out the Format Attach Style Sheet command. If no style-sheet name is listed, simply press Enter or click OK.

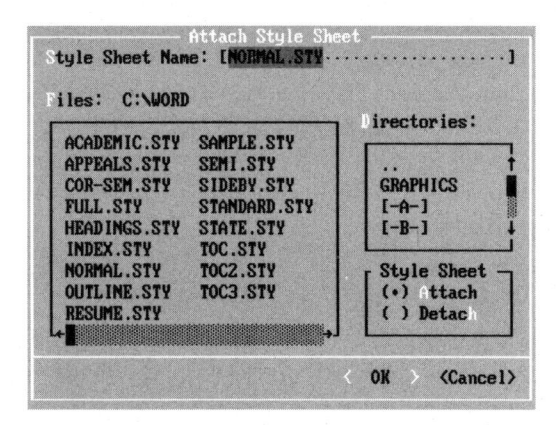

CHAPTER SIX: Introducing Styles and Macros

```
┌──────────── Attach Style Sheet ────────────┐
│ Style Sheet Name: [NORMAL.STY............] │
│                                            │
│ Files: C:\WORD                             │
│                           Directories:     │
│   ┌──────────────────┐  ┌──────────────┐   │
│   │ ACADEMIC.STY  SAMPLE.STY   │  │ ..           ↑│   │
│   │ APPEALS.STY   SEMI.STY     │  │ GRAPHICS     │   │
│   │ COR-SEM.STY   SIDEBY.STY   │  │ [-A-]        │   │
│   │ FULL.STY      STANDARD.STY │  │ [-B-]        ↓│   │
│   │ HEADINGS.STY  STATE.STY    │  └──────────────┘   │
│   │ INDEX.STY     TOC.STY      │  ┌─ Style Sheet ─┐  │
│   │ NORMAL.STY    TOC2.STY     │  │ (•) Attach    │  │
│   │ OUTLINE.STY   TOC3.STY     │  │ ( ) Detach    │  │
│   │ RESUME.STY                 │  └───────────────┘  │
│   └──────────────────┘                     │
│                                            │
│                          < OK >  <Cancel>  │
└────────────────────────────────────────────┘
```

When you delete the name of a style sheet in the above dialog box, you don't delete the style sheet itself. You merely break the link between the style sheet and the active document. Word responds with this message:

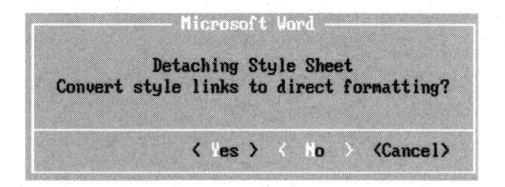

```
┌─────────── Microsoft Word ───────────┐
│                                      │
│         Detaching Style Sheet        │
│  Convert style links to direct formatting? │
│                                      │
│       < Yes >  < No >  <Cancel>      │
└──────────────────────────────────────┘
```

This tells you that you are removing the style sheet from your document, or "detaching style sheet." In some cases, when you detach a style sheet you might be removing a great deal of formatting information from the document. For this reason, Word asks *Convert style links to direct formatting?* If this question doesn't make sense at first, recall from Concept 10 in Chapter 2 that a style sheet provides a document with indirect formatting rather than direct formatting. Word is asking whether you want the document to retain its formatting even though the style sheet is being removed.

TIP FOR WORD VETERANS

Prior to version 5.5, when you detached a style sheet from your document, Word didn't give you the opportunity to convert its indirect formatting to direct formatting. This new feature of Word 5.5 means you can design a document with the assistance of a style sheet and then free the document from the style sheet without losing any of the formatting. This is useful if you need to give a document to someone else in disk form and that person doesn't understand style sheets. It is also valuable when you want the convenience of a style sheet when it comes to formatting but don't want to have to worry about the style sheet later.

In the case of our practice memo document, the style sheet (if any) wasn't doing any formatting of your memo anyway. So you can press N (for "No").

Disconnecting the active style sheet from your document is not something you'll routinely do before recording a style. On the contrary, you might want to build a library of recorded styles for various formatting tasks, with all styles stored in a single style sheet. We disconnected the style sheet in this case to ensure that what you see on your screen and what you read about in the next few pages will be identical or nearly so. As soon as you record a style, you'll start to build a fresh style sheet from scratch.

Using the ribbon to record a style

1. With the word *Memo* still highlighted, press Ctrl+S to activate the Style text box in the ribbon. You'll see the word *Normal** displayed there:

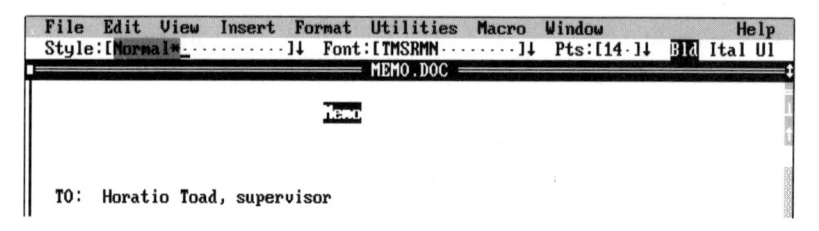

   The ribbon's Style box tells you the name of the style that is formatting the selected text. *Normal* is Word's default style, which it applies to paragraphs that are not dedicated to special purposes (such as footnotes) and that are not specially formatted. The asterisk following *Normal* indicates that the selected text isn't really formatted with any style at all, in the sense that there is no style in the style sheet.

2. Hold down the Alt key and press the Down direction key, or click on the Style box's down arrow, to see a drop-down list of other style names.

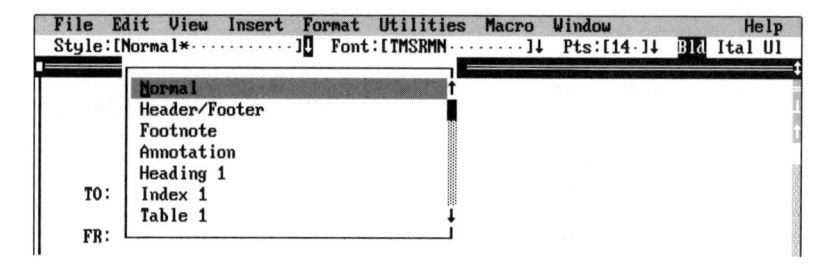

Our immediate mission is to choose which kind of paragraph style you want to record. The choices are

- *Normal.* There can be only one normal paragraph style; Word applies it to paragraphs that don't fall into any of the following categories. Typically, a document has far more paragraphs styled with *Normal* than with any other style.

- *Header/Footer.* A paragraph that will be used as a header or a footer (running head)—text that appears at the top (header) or the bottom (footer) of the pages in a document. Chapter and book titles are elements that are often contained in a header or footer paragraph.

- *Footnote.* Text that appears in paragraph form at the bottom of a page or at the end of a document. A footnote paragraph is always linked to a footnote reference mark in the main body of the document's text.

- *Annotation.* A special-purpose footnote used to list the comments or notes of one or more reviewers of a manuscript or other document.

- *Heading.* A heading within a document, which in Word automatically becomes an element in the outline of the document. Seven heading styles are potentially available in a single style sheet, allowing hierarchical organization of a document's content.

- *Index.* A paragraph contained within a document's index. Word provides up to four index styles so that an index can be arranged hierarchically.

- *Table.* A paragraph contained within a document's table of contents. Word provides up to four table styles, making it easy to format a table of contents with various levels of heading.

- *Paragraph.* Any other paragraph not dedicated by Word to a specific purpose can be formatted with one of 55 other paragraph styles. These styles are numbered rather than named.

3. We want to record the existing formatting as a heading style, so press the Down direction key until the designation *Heading 1* is highlighted, or click on the designation with the mouse.

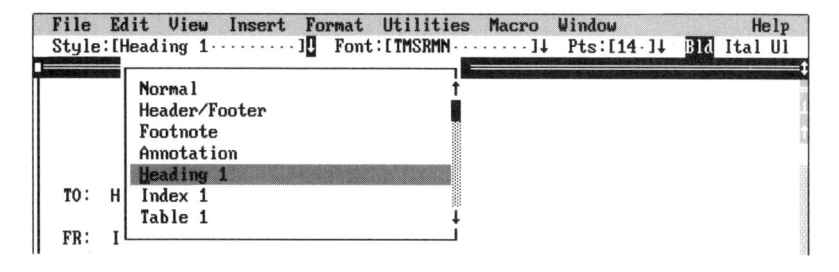

```
File   Edit   View   Insert   Format   Utilities   Macro   Window           Help
Style:[Heading 1·········]  Font:[TMSRMN········]  Pts:[14·]  Bld  Ital  Ul

              Normal
              Header/Footer
              Footnote
              Annotation
              Heading 1
       TO:  H  Index 1
              Table 1
       FR:  I
```

When you choose Heading 1 (by pressing Enter, if necessary), Word takes you to the Record Style dialog box. You can reach the same dialog box by choosing the Format Record Style command (Alt+TR).

```
┌─────────────────────── Record Style ───────────────────────┐
│  Key Code:   [...]  Style Type: [Paragraph ]↓              │
│  Remark:     [............................]               │
│  Style I.D.: [Heading 1...................]↓              │
│                                                            │
│ ─Style to Record─────────────────────────────────────────  │
│  TMSRMN 14/12 Bold. Centered, space before 1 li.           │
│                                                            │
│                                                            │
│                                                            │
│                                                            │
│  <Define Styles...>           <  OK  >   <Cancel>          │
└────────────────────────────────────────────────────────────┘
```

Spend a moment looking at this dialog box. Note in particular, under the label *Style to Record,* the description of the existing formatting of the selected text (in this case, the word *Memo*). This is the formatting that will be recorded as a style.

— The first part of the formatting description, up to the first period, identifies the character formatting of the selected text: The font is TMSRMN, 14 points in size, and bold.

— The second part describes the paragraph formatting of the selected text: It is centered between the page margins and has a blank line of space before it (the so-called "open spacing").

— One final element of paragraph formatting, the spacing between lines, is indicated along with the font size in the first part of the description: *14/12.* This means that the 14-point typeface will be printed in a paragraph that allows 12 points of space between lines. Ordinarily this would suggest that the paragraph's lines will be squished together but not in this case because headings typically consist of only one line, and the paragraph formatting provides for an extra line of "space before."

Near the top of the dialog box is an empty text box labeled *Key Code.* Here you type a one- or two-character code for your style. You'll use the code later, when you are formatting text with the style.

4. If you're not already in the Key Code text box, click on it with the mouse or press Alt+K to move to it. Type *HE* in the box, indicating that you want your heading style to have the key code HE.

To the right is a text box called *Style Type.* You can choose from among three types of styles: Paragraph, Character, and Section. These correspond to the three types of formatting that Word allows. (Paragraph styles are by far the most common.) Word has preselected the

CHAPTER SIX: Introducing Styles and Macros

paragraph type of style, guessing, correctly, that we want to record the formatting of the selected document text as a paragraph style (as opposed to a character style or a section style).

The next text box is labeled *Remark*. Here you can type a brief comment about the purpose and use of the style you are about to record. Having remarks is handy after you have accumulated enough styles that you have trouble recalling which style does what. In this case, since there is but one style, we won't type a remark.

5. The final text box is labeled *Style I.D.* Here you assign the style a real identity. Word has tentatively assigned the I.D. *Heading 1* because this is what you chose a short while ago in the ribbon's Style text box.

In this case, *Heading 1* is the correct I.D., so press Enter or click on the OK button.

After pressing Enter or clicking on OK to finish with the Record Style dialog box, you find yourself back in your document. But now there is a difference. The ribbon (if it is turned on) shows that the selected text is formatted with a style—the style *Heading 1.* And it shows that the style has the key code HE.

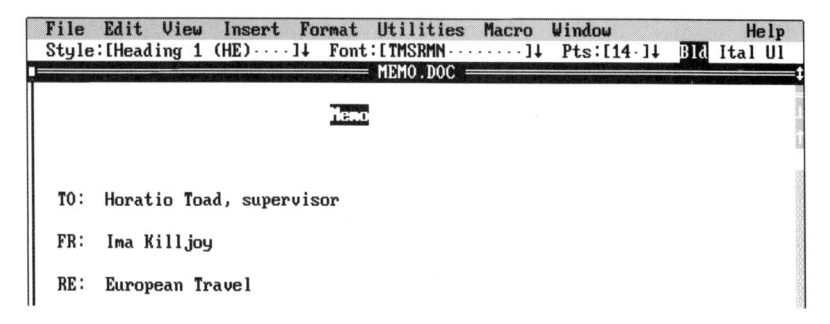

NOTE: *Recall from Chapter 4 that there is another way, besides the ribbon, to see on the screen the key codes of paragraph styles (as well as the key codes of section styles, which the ribbon doesn't show). To see key codes listed just inside the left border of your document window, use the View Preferences command (Alt+VE) to turn on the style bar.*

Applying a Style

You've got a style sheet now! It has only one style, a heading style with the key code HE, but you can instantly turn any paragraph into a heading by formatting it with the style from your style sheet.

Word offers you several different ways to apply your style to text. You can use the ribbon, a command called Format Apply Style, or the key code of the style. The one thing all the methods have in common is that before applying the style you must select the paragraph that is to be formatted. Simply move the cursor anywhere into the desired paragraph. (Before you give formatting with a style a try, be sure to move your cursor to a new paragraph, one that is not already formatted with your style sheet's HE style.)

Using the ribbon to apply a style

1. To apply a style with the ribbon, select the text to be formatted and press Ctrl+S to activate the ribbon's Style text box. Press Alt+Down direction key to see the styles in your style sheet.

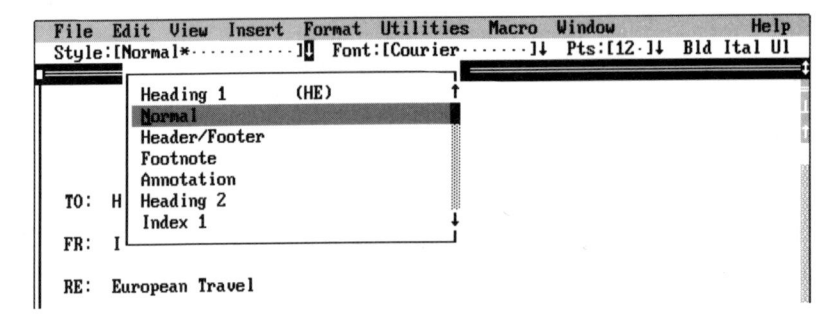

```
File   Edit   View   Insert   Format   Utilities   Macro   Window              Help
Style:[Normal*·········]   Font:[Courier·······]   Pts:[12·]   Bld Ital Ul

              Heading 1        (HE)
              Normal
              Header/Footer
              Footnote
              Annotation
    TO:  H   Heading 2
              Index 1
    FR:  I

    RE:  European Travel
```

   In this illustration, the Style I.D. Normal is highlighted because the text selected beforehand was not formatted with a style. Observe that the first style listed in the ribbon's drop-down list is the heading style you just recorded. In the ribbon's list of styles, Word places the names of styles assigned ahead of names of styles that are available but not yet assigned.

2. To apply the HE style to the selected text, simply use the mouse or the Up direction key to move the highlight from the I.D. Normal to the I.D Heading 1 and press Enter.

   (For a more detailed introduction to this approach, see Chapter 4's discussion of the ribbon. For an alternative way to use the ribbon to apply a style, read on.)

Using the Format Apply Style command

Another way to apply a style to text is to use the Format Apply Style command. You can do this in two ways:

- Hold down the Alt key and press TY (for "Forma*t* Apply St*y*le").
- Use the ribbon's Style box, pressing Ctrl+S twice until the Apply Style dialog box appears.

Regardless of which route you use to get to the Apply Style dialog box, this is what you see when you get there:

```
┌──────────── Apply Style ────────────┐
│ Key Code:   [_..]  Style Type: [Paragraph ]↕│
│ Style I.D.: [.........................]     │
│ ┌─────────────────────────────────────┐ ↑   │
│ │ Normal                              │ ▓   │
│ │ Heading 1        (HE)               │ ▓   │
│ │                                     │ ↓   │
│ └─────────────────────────────────────┘     │
│ ─Style to Apply─────────────────────         │
│                                              │
│ <Define Styles...>        < OK >  <Cancel>  │
└──────────────────────────────────────────────┘
```

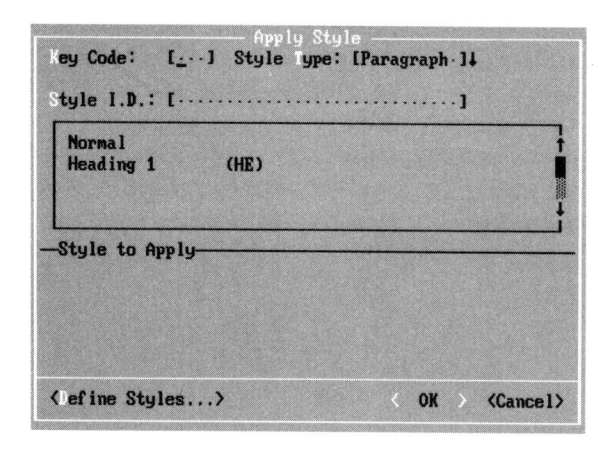

Unlike the example presented in Chapter 4, which showed how this dialog box looks when a style sheet that has a lot of styles is installed, this time the only style the dialog box lists (other than Normal) is the HE style you recorded. Normally you use the direction keys to choose the style you want, but in this case you don't really have a choice. Simply highlight the Heading 1 style, and press Enter or click on OK.

Using a key code to apply a style

The final approach is the fastest way to apply a style to text: Simply select the text and type the code. That's it. You can supply the code in two ways:

- ♦ The preferred method is to hold down the Ctrl key while you press the Y key and then type the code. This causes whatever text is selected at the time to become formatted by the style. For example, you could apply the HE style to a selected heading by pressing Ctrl+YHE.
- ♦ A second method is to hold down the Shift and Ctrl keys and type the style's key code (Shift+Ctrl+HE in our example). This works, but it creates competition with macros, which also can be run by holding down the Ctrl and Shift keys simultaneously.

The Ctrl+Y method always works—and besides, Microsoft has found that touch typists who often use styles work faster with the Ctrl+YHE method than with the Shift+Ctrl+HE method.

Your Style Sheet

To see your style sheet in its own window, where the content and format of any style can be viewed or modified, use the Format Define Styles command (Alt+TD). This displays the style sheet that is in use with your current document. Alternatively, you can use the File Open command (Alt+FO), choose the Style Sheets option button by pressing Alt+S, and highlight or type the name of any style sheet you want to load, regardless of whether it is in current use with a document or not.

If you choose the Format Define Styles command after recording the heading style (code HE), the style sheet appears in its own window, overlapping the document window:

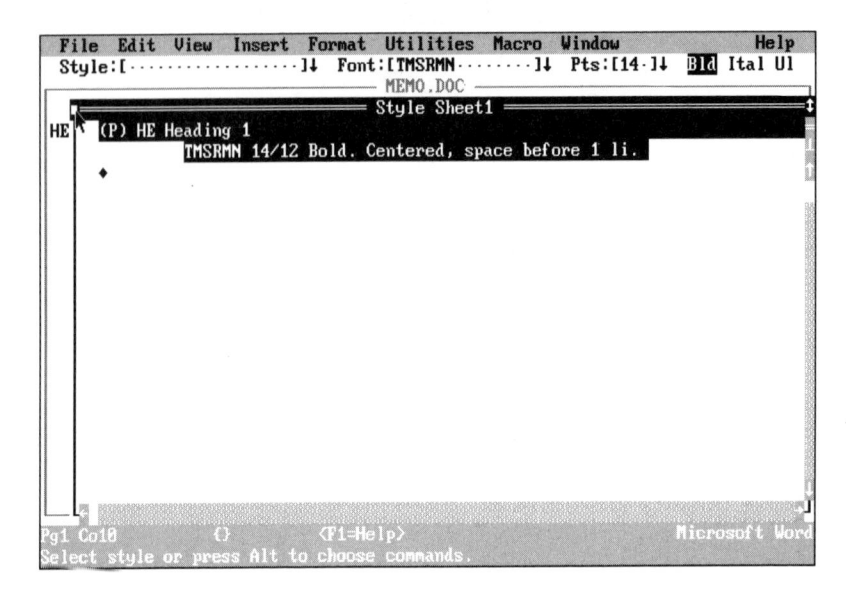

```
File   Edit   View   Insert   Format   Utilities   Macro   Window                Help
Style:[················]↓  Font:[TMSRMN········]↓  Pts:[14·]↓  Bld  Ital  Ul
─────────────────────────────── MEMO.DOC ───────────────────────────────
                           ══════ Style Sheet1 ══════
HE   (P) HE Heading 1
         TMSRMN 14/12 Bold. Centered, space before 1 li.
     ◆











Pg1 Co10          {}          <F1=Help>                       Microsoft Word
Select style or press Alt to choose commands.
```

Because the style sheet has only one style so far, the window contains only one description. The style sheet has no name yet, so the window has *Style Sheet 1* in its title bar. The title bar for your document window is visible, and to the left of the style sheet window are visible the first few characters of the document window beneath it. All you can see is the key code HE in the document window's style bar.

In the description of the HE style in the style-sheet window, the first line identifies the style and the second line indicates its formatting. If the formatting contained such elements as tab stops, its description might stretch to two or more lines.

The style's identity

The identification line of the style is short in our example, containing just three elements. The first, *(P)*, indicates that this is a paragraph style. This element would be *(C)* for a character style or *(S)* for a section style. The second element, *HE*, is the key code for the style. The third element, the words *Heading 1*, is the Style I.D.

There is room for a fourth element, a remark, on the identification line. We didn't specify a remark when we recorded the style, but we can add one now. Press Alt+E to drop down the Edit menu, and move to its last choice, Rename Style. This is a menu choice that isn't available when your active window contains a document; Word tailors the menu differently for style sheets, eliminating many commands, adding a few others such as Rename Style, and changing the purposes of certain other commands that have familiar names.

CHAPTER SIX: Introducing Styles and Macros 115

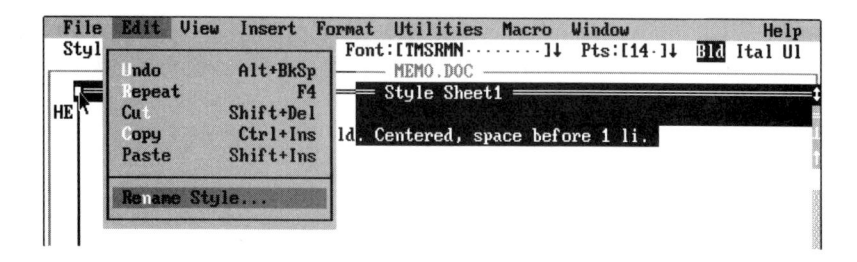

Choose the command, and you are taken to the Rename Style dialog box, where you can change the key code, remark, or Style I.D. of the selected style. We want to add a remark, so move to the Remark text box and type a remark, such as *Your witty remark here*.

Press Enter or click the OK button to add the remark to the identification line of the style. (To see how the remark appears in the description of the style, look at the next screen illustration.)

The style's formatting

You can modify the formatting of a style, just as you can modify its identity. Be sure the style is highlighted in the style-sheet window, and drop down the Format menu by pressing Alt+T or clicking with the mouse on Format. Like the Edit menu, the Format menu is shorter for style sheets than it is for documents:

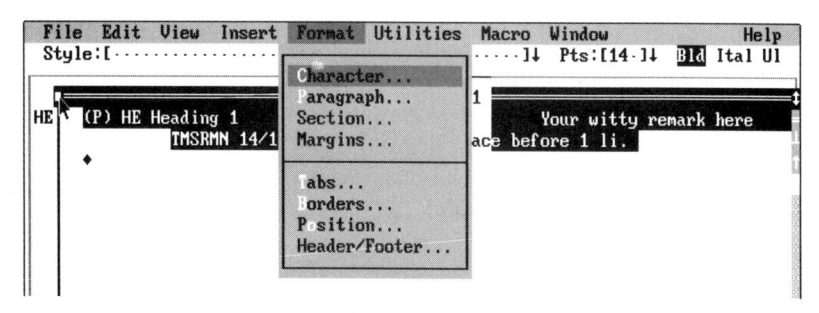

If you choose Character from the Format menu, you are taken to the Character dialog box. The box displays the character formatting of the style. You can make changes. For example, if you press Alt+I you turn on the Italic check box.

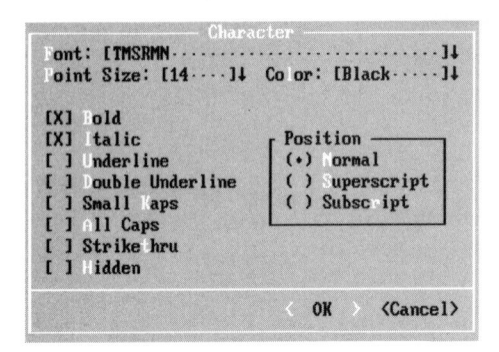

```
┌─ Character ──────────────────────────────┐
│ Font: [TMSRMN·····················]↓     │
│ Point Size: [14···]↓  Color: [Black····]↓│
│                                          │
│ [X] Bold                                 │
│ [X] Italic           ┌─ Position ─────┐  │
│ [ ] Underline        │ (•) Normal     │  │
│ [ ] Double Underline │ ( ) Superscript│  │
│ [ ] Small Caps       │ ( ) Subscript  │  │
│ [ ] All Caps         └────────────────┘  │
│ [ ] Strike thru                          │
│ [ ] Hidden                               │
│                                          │
│             <  OK  >   <Cancel>          │
└──────────────────────────────────────────┘
```

When you press Enter, the formatting change or changes you made are reflected in the description of the style. Here, for instance, the Heading 1 style has been updated to show that the TMSRMN font is italic as well as bold.

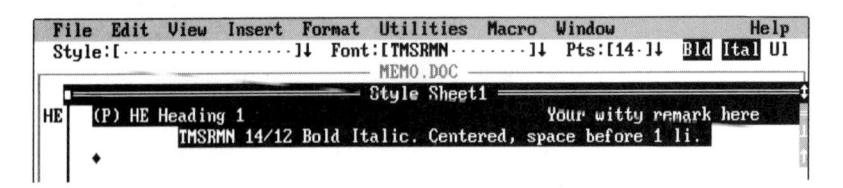

```
┌─ File  Edit  View  Insert  Format  Utilities  Macro  Window        Help ─┐
│ Style:[················]↓ Font:[TMSRMN········]↓ Pts:[14·]↓ Bld Ital Ul │
│ ─────────────────────────── MEMO.DOC ───────────────────────────────────│
│ ═══════════════════════════ Style Sheet1 ═══════════════════════════════│
│ HE  (P) HE Heading 1                            Your witty remark here  │
│         TMSRMN 14/12 Bold Italic. Centered, space before 1 li.          │
│  ♦                                                                       │
└──────────────────────────────────────────────────────────────────────────┘
```

So far, you've created a style sheet containing one style, and you've used that style to format highlighted text. But one thing you haven't done, at least so far in this book, is actually save your style sheet.

Saving a style sheet

After recording a style or otherwise modifying a style sheet, save your work on disk. Unless you do this, the work will be lost when you quit Word.

1. To save a style sheet, first be sure a style-sheet window is displayed and active. If it is not displayed, use the Format Define Styles command (Alt+TD) or the File Open command (Alt+TO) to load your style sheet into a window. These commands were described in the previous section.

2. With the style sheet displayed, choose the File Save command (Alt+FS). If the style sheet has not been saved before and hence has no name, Word will take you to the Save As dialog box, where you can type a name for the style sheet. If the style sheet has been saved before, choosing the File Save command saves the style sheet without delay. In other words, Word lets you save style sheets the same way you save documents, a topic covered near the end of Chapter 3. One difference is that

Word adds the .DOC extension to document files and the .STY extension to style-sheet files. For this reason, when specifying a name for either kind of file, you should type at most eight letters and let Word add the three-letter extension it wants.

In choosing a name for a style sheet, pay attention to the name NORMAL. If you choose the name NORMAL, Word will use the style sheet automatically for any new document that you create in the same directory as the style sheet, unless you deliberately attach a different style sheet to the document or deliberately detach the NORMAL style sheet. It is possible to have different NORMAL style sheets in different directories so that different formatting is available for different documents. You'll learn more about NORMAL style sheets at the end of this chapter.

3. To close the style-sheet window after saving your style sheet, use the Window Close command (Alt+WC).

Attaching a different style sheet

One of the beauties of Word 5.5's style-sheet feature is that you can switch a document from one style sheet to another even after the document is written. Of course, you must have more than one style sheet in order to do this.

To attach a new style sheet to a document, use the Format Attach Style Sheet command (Alt+TA). You already got some experience with this command if you detached an old style sheet earlier in this tutorial. The difference is that to attach a different style sheet to a document, you type the name of a style sheet or choose it from the list of style sheets rather than pressing the Del key to eliminate the name of the current style sheet.

In Chapter 24, you'll learn more about how to create and use style sheets that are fully interchangeable. With such a system of style sheets at your disposal, you can achieve maximum performance with Word's style-sheet feature.

MACROS

Knowing a little goes a long way when it comes to Word's macro feature. In time, you might use the program's macro language to write small scripts that tell Word how to accomplish sophisticated tasks. But for now, as you step into the world of Word, you'll be glad to know at least a few things about macros because they can make your day-to-day work more enjoyable and easier.

To the uninitiated, even the term *macro* might seem a little intimidating, possibly because it suggests bigness and little else. But in fact, macros have everything to do with making Word easier to use and almost nothing to do with making it more difficult.

There's nothing to fear here. Macros are simply another tool, and a useful one. Chapter 23 offers hints and techniques on using macros in conjunction with other features; this chapter prepares you to take advantage of the opportunities.

Often a macro is a script composed solely of keystrokes that you've recorded. For instance, the next time you open a new, blank document and type your name into it at the top, you might record the steps and save them as a macro. Anytime in the future that you want to start a fresh document labeled with your name at the top, you can replay the macro. Word executes the steps of a macro much faster than you can, making this a real time-saver.

Another way to create a macro is to write it as if it were a short document. You write the macro using a macro language based on English; then you store it and give it a code. This approach has advantages:

- By writing a macro you can lay out its text in a way that is easier to read and understand. (For example, you can place each instruction on a separate line instead of running instructions together as in a recorded macro.)
- Written macros can include comments that document their use and design. These comments do not affect the operation of the macro; they only explain it.
- Written macros can include special instructions and other elements that add power by giving the macro the seeming ability to make simple decisions. These embellishments are unavailable in recorded macros.

Writing a macro is more challenging than recording one, so in this chapter we'll look only at the recording method. But when you become more proficient, you might want to read Chapter 23 to learn more about writing macros.

After a macro exists, you have more than one way to tell Word to run it (that is, to tell Word to follow the steps in the script). The most common is to type the macro's *control code*. For instance, a macro that instructs Word to save a document and close its window might have the code Shift+Ctrl+SC (for "Save and Close"). To use this code to tell Word to run the macro, you would hold down Shift and Ctrl and press SC.

The uses to which you can put macros are endless. At first you might want only to automate some common operations. For example, you might create a macro that types your name and address...or sets the margins on a document...or attaches a particular style sheet to a document...or turns the style bar at the left side of a document window on or off. Sophisticated macros can do more substantial tasks, such as printing addresses on envelopes and assisting you in the indexing of a document. Nor do you have to create a macro yourself in order to use one successfully and happily. Word 5.5 comes with a collection of macros (stored in a glossary file called MACROS.GLY), and my add-in software product, MasterWord, includes an extensive collection of macros that do such things as build multicolumn tables. After you have a macro, whether you created it yourself or not, you can use it—today, tomorrow, or next year—exactly as if it were a command built into Word.

CHAPTER SIX: Introducing Styles and Macros   119

The tasks macros can perform fall into several categories, including

- Automating common procedures to save time.
- Recording a series of steps that are difficult to remember or that are complex and demand exactitude. (A macro *always* remembers and is, by nature, exact.) This saves you a lot of fooling around each time you perform the task, although you might have to experiment a bit at the beginning to get the macro perfected.
- Borrowing or lending expertise. Suppose there is a task you want to perform and might do frequently, but you don't know how to do it. Rather than learn it, you can ask someone more knowledgeable to lend you his or her expertise by writing a macro that performs the task for you. This is a perfect use for a macro because it lets you concentrate on your real work. Conversely, you might want to lend some of your expertise to someone else. Perhaps you want to teach your mother how to use two windows. Write a macro that does it, and show her how to use the macro rather than asking her to learn Word's window feature.

The list goes on, but the point is clear: Word's macro feature is worthy of your attention.

Recording a Macro

You can create your first macro in less than a minute by recording it. In the following example, we'll create one that opens a new document window and arranges all your windows so that at least part of each of them displays on the screen. With Word running and the cursor visible in a text window, follow these steps:

1. Choose the Macro Record command by pressing Alt+MC or Ctrl+F3. (Don't make the mistake of pressing Alt+MR, which is the Macro Run command.)
2. Choosing Macro Record causes the Macro Record dialog box to appear. The first field is a text box labeled *Macro Name*.

    In this box, type the descriptive name you want the macro to have. For this example, we'll type the name *ND.newDocumentArrange*.

```
┌─────────── Record Macro ───────────┐
│ Macro Name:                        │
│ [ND.newDocumentArrange_·········]  │
│                                    │
│ Macro Keys:                        │
│ [··················]               │
│                                    │
│         <  OK  >   <Cancel>        │
└────────────────────────────────────┘
```

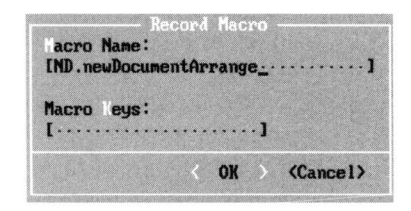

—The ND (for "New Document") at the beginning of the name is the control code we intend to give the macro. You needn't begin the name of the macro with its control code, but by doing so you ensure that all of your macros will be arranged alphabetically by code when you use the Macro Run or Macro Edit command.

—The period simply separates the control code from the words that follow. A disadvantage of periods, however, is that each period uses up one of the 30 characters allowed in the name—and as we'll learn in a moment, there really aren't any characters to waste. An alternative way to separate words or other elements in a macro name is to use capitalization: Simply capitalize the first letter of every new word. In this sample name the letters *D* and *A* were capitalized for this reason.

3. The only other field in the dialog box is labeled *Macro Keys*. In this box you officially declare what the macro's control code will be. We've decided on ND, and because this book suggests starting all macros with control codes beginning with Shift+Ctrl, the full control code will be Shift+Ctrl+ND. You don't need to type all of this in, however.

    Merely hold down the Shift and Ctrl keys and press N, the first letter of the code. Then release the Shift and Ctrl keys and press D, the second letter of the code. Word responds by filling in the Macro Keys field the following way:

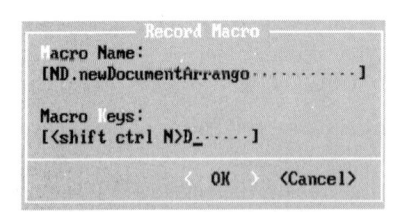

```
┌─────── Record Macro ───────┐
│ acro Name:                 │
│ [ND.newDocumentArrango····]│
│                            │
│ Macro  eys:                │
│ [<shift ctrl N>D_·····]    │
│                            │
│        < OK >  <Cancel>    │
└────────────────────────────┘
```

4. Now press Enter or click the OK button. You expect to start recording the macro, but in this case you get an alert message instead:

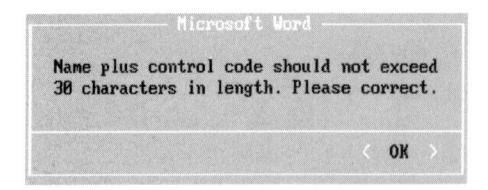

```
┌─────── Microsoft Word ───────┐
│ Name plus control code should not exceed │
│ 30 characters in length. Please correct. │
│                                          │
│                          < OK >          │
└──────────────────────────────────────────┘
```

You see this message because the combination of Macro Name and Macro Key that you typed is longer than 30 characters. This is the one drawback to using Shift+Ctrl instead of Ctrl for macro names; it uses up more of the 30 characters.

When you press Enter or click the OK button to cancel the alert message, the Record Macro dialog box returns, with the excess number of characters highlighted.

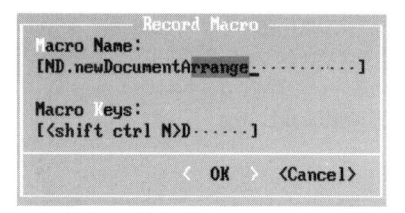

CHAPTER SIX: Introducing Styles and Macros

```
 ─── Record Macro ───
Macro Name:
[ND.newDocumentArrange         ]

Macro Keys:
[<shift ctrl N>D     ]

          <  OK  >   <Cancel>
```

5. If you press the Del key at this point, your macro name and code will be truncated to 30 characters, and you'll be able to begin recording your macro. However, let's edit the name of the macro rather than simply lopping off the end of it.

    Use the direction keys to move within the name, and press the Del key whenever you are on a letter you want to edit out. After you pare the name down, the dialog box might look like this:

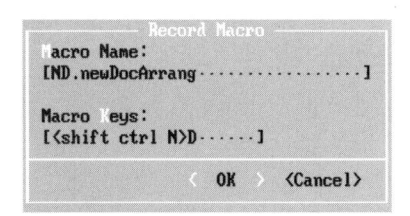

```
 ─── Record Macro ───
Macro Name:
[ND.newDocArrang           ]

Macro Keys:
[<shift ctrl N>D     ]

          <  OK  >   <Cancel>
```

As soon as you press Enter and the dialog box vanishes, the macro recorder is on. You might notice the letters MR (Macro Recorder) on the right end of the status line near the bottom of the screen. Everything you type—until you use the Macro Stop Recorder command (Alt+MC)—will be stored in a macro with the name *ND.newDocArrang* and the code Shift+Ctrl+ND.

We want the macro to open a new, blank document and then arrange all windows so that at least part of each shows. This is quite straightforward, but be sure you take all steps with the keyboard rather than the mouse because a macro can't store mouse actions.

6. To open a new document, press Alt+FN to choose the File New command. When the New dialog box appears on the screen, press Enter without making any changes. The new document will appear, but it will probably overlap or even conceal your existing window.

7. To arrange all windows so that a part of each appears on the screen and none overlap, press Alt+WA to run the Window Arrange All command. Your screen will be divided, with the new, blank document on top and your original document on the bottom.

8. You've completed the steps you want to record, so press Alt+MC to run the Macro Stop Recorder command. If you press Alt+M and pause before pressing the C, you'll see that the Macro menu's first choice is Stop Recorder and that the new and old windows are arranged to display equally:

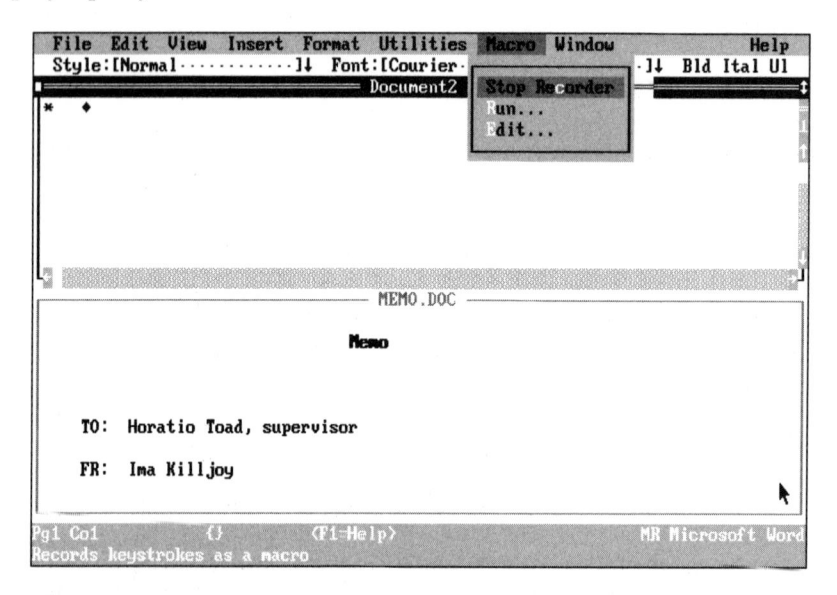

However, as soon as you have stopped recording, the Stop Recorder command is replaced by the Macro Record command.

Playing Back a Macro

Storing a macro isn't enough. You must be able to use a macro after it's stored. Using a macro is called "playing it back" or "running it." These phrases mean the same thing—you put the macro to work, letting it perform its intended task. The following sections describe three ways to run a macro.

Running a macro with a code

The fastest way to play back a macro is to type its control code. Do this by holding down the Shift key and the Ctrl key simultaneously and typing the one-character or two-character code. For example, to run the macro you just recorded—the one that has ND as its code—you press Shift+Ctrl+ND.

CHAPTER SIX: Introducing Styles and Macros

After running the macro, you'll find you have one more window than you did before. You can run the macro several times in a row, until you have nine windows, the maximum number Word allows.

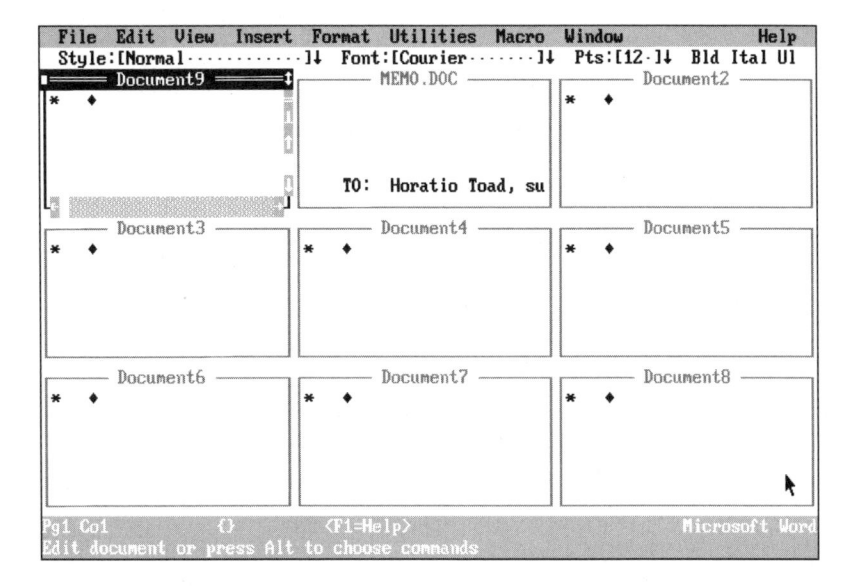

Of course, with nine windows all arranged to display in part, the working area in any of them is pretty small. But this process is an interesting demonstration of both the speed of Word's macros and the flexibility of its windows.

Keep in mind that some macros might have control codes that begin with Ctrl rather than Shift+Ctrl. As noted already in several chapters, macros that use Ctrl without Shift tend to conflict with Word's speed-formatting keys.

Running a macro with a command

Word's Macro Run command offers the advantage of letting you choose your macro from a list of all macros currently stored in Word's glossary. Press Alt+MR, and Word displays the Run Macro dialog box.

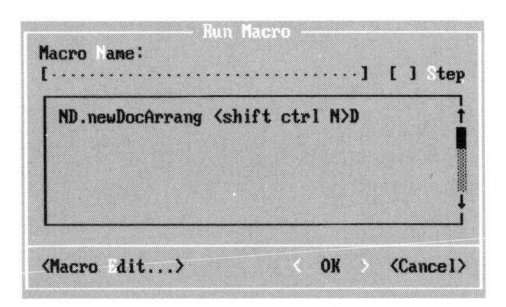

In this case, only the one macro is stored in the glossary, and so its name is the only one displayed. It is possible to have numerous macros, in which case you can scroll through their names in the list box contained within this dialog box.

To choose a specific macro from the Run Macro box, highlight its name and press Enter or click the OK button.

Running a macro with the F3 key

Yet another way to run a macro is to type its name and press the F3 key. When you type the name, do not type its code. In the case of our sample macro, you would type *ND.newDocArrang* and press F3. Capitalization doesn't matter.

This method is a little awkward for most macros, unless you keep names very short. For that reason, it is best suited for people who have only a small number of macros, the names of which are brief and easily remembered.

Step mode

Regardless of how you play back a macro, you might find *Step mode* handy now and then. It lets you run a macro a step at a time, controlling how quickly it executes. In Step mode, Word waits for you to press the Spacebar or another key before it executes each step of the macro. You simply tap your way through a macro, watching the effect each step has.

Step mode was designed to let you debug macros, and it is invaluable in that role. If a macro is not performing as you expect it to, switch into Step mode to monitor what it is doing.

Step mode is also valuable as a means of racing through some parts of a macro and slowing down for other parts. When Step mode is on, holding the Spacebar down causes the macro to move forward through its steps at high speed. But as soon as you stop pressing the Spacebar, the macro stops executing. Each time you press the Spacebar (or almost any other key), another step in the macro executes.

To turn on Step mode, choose the Macro Run command (Alt+MR), and turn on the Step check box. One way to turn the box on or off is to press its accelerator key, Alt+S.

You can also turn Step mode off by using the Macro Run command.

Saving a Macro

If you record a macro, it will be preserved in memory only as long as Word is running. However, if you save the macro on disk, you can reload it during a later Word session and use it again.

Macros are stored in the *glossary*, a special area of Word's memory. When you save the contents of the glossary on disk, you create or update a *glossary file*. To load a previously created macro into Word, you load the glossary file that contains the macro. One implication of this is that you cannot save an individual macro on disk nor load an individual macro from disk unless the macro is the only thing in the glossary or the glossary file. This means that to save a macro, you must save the current contents of the whole glossary file.

To save the glossary file, first press Alt+ME to choose the Macro Edit command, which takes you to the Edit Macro dialog box. Then choose the Save Glossary button by clicking on it or by pressing the accelerator key Alt+S. This takes you to the Save Glossary dialog box, which will look something like this if you have no glossary files in your current directory:

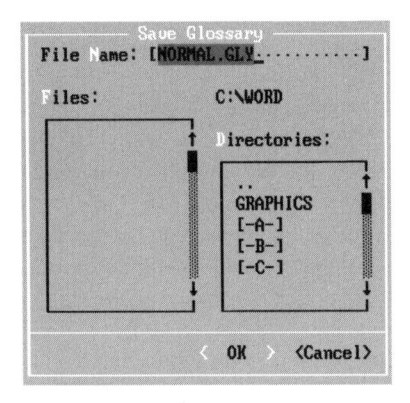

```
                    ─── Save Glossary ───
        File Name: [NORMAL.GLY.........]

        Files:           C:\WORD
        ┌──────────────┐ Directories:
        │              │ ┌──────────────┐
        │              │ │ ..           │
        │              │ │ GRAPHICS     │
        │              │ │ [-A-]        │
        │              │ │ [-B-]        │
        │              │ │ [-C-]        │
        │              │ │              │
        └──────────────┘ └──────────────┘

                   <   OK   >   <Cancel>
```

The proposed name for the glossary file is NORMAL.GLY because no other glossary file has been loaded. If you use the name NORMAL, the macro will be reloaded each time you start Word from the directory that contains the file. This is convenient because you don't have to deliberately load the macro into Word to have it available for your use. Later in this chapter you'll learn more about the NORMAL.GLY file; in Chapters 12, 17, 22, and 23 you'll learn more about macros generally and about the relationship of macros to other contents of glossary files.

Experiencing the Page-Printing Macro

To round out your introduction to Word 5.5's macro language, the next couple of pages show you what it is like to use a macro that prints pages for you. The macro is included with MasterWord, and instructions for creating it are contained in Chapter 23. For now, simply get a sense of what it can do so that you get a sense of sophisticated macros.

Imagine you're editing an essay. You want to print the page you are working on or a series of pages from the middle of the document, but you don't want to print the entire thing. There's the conventional way, which doesn't use a macro, and then there's a new way, which does.

The conventional approach, without a macro

To print a single page without using a macro, take the following steps, which are listed not so that you'll follow them but so that you'll see the dimension of the task.

First, you repaginate the document to be sure page numbering is up-to-date and so that you can note the number of the page you want to print.

Second, you choose the File Print command, note how its Page Range and Pages fields are set, and then set each of the two fields so that Word will print only the desired page.

Third, you carry out the command to print.

Fourth, after printing is complete, you'll probably want to choose the File Print command again and switch its Page Range and Pages fields back to whatever they were originally (they probably were set to print all pages). Resetting these fields requires a little trickery because Word won't accept the changes unless you actually carry out the File Print command—and you're not interested in printing again, and especially not with the original settings. You just want to reset the fields to their original values. One way to trick Word is to change the settings and carry out the File Print command and then press Esc right away. A second way is to tell Word to print to a nonexistent printer port. A third method is to leave the fields set as they are and remember to reset them the next time you actually print. The third method is easiest, but half the time you'll forget to reset the fields and end up printing just the one page all over again.

The unconventional approach, with a macro

The other approach is to run the Print Page macro, which has Shift+Ctrl+PP as its control code. You can run it by choosing the Macro Run command and choosing its name from a list, but why not simply hold down the Shift and Ctrl keys and press PP?

However you start the macro, it immediately repaginates your document if necessary and then displays a message in a dialog box:

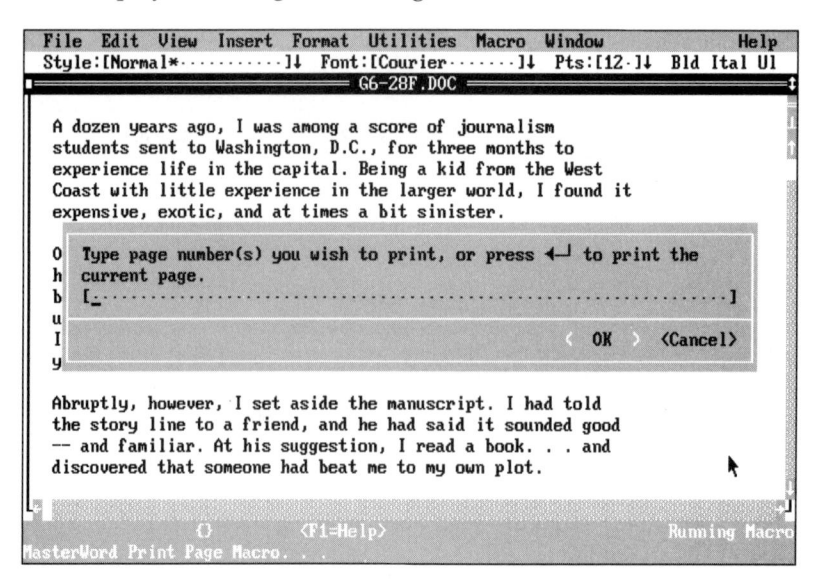

```
 File   Edit   View   Insert   Format   Utilities   Macro   Window            Help
Style:[Normal*············]↓  Font:[Courier·········]↓  Pts:[12·]↓  Bld Ital Ul
═══════════════════════════════ G6-28F.DOC ═══════════════════════════════
A dozen years ago, I was among a score of journalism
students sent to Washington, D.C., for three months to
experience life in the capital. Being a kid from the West
Coast with little experience in the larger world, I found it
expensive, exotic, and at times a bit sinister.

O  ┌──────────────────────────────────────────────────────────────┐
h  │ Type page number(s) you wish to print, or press ↵ to print the│
b  │ current page.                                                 │
   │ [_············································································]│
u  │                                                               │
I  │                              < OK >    <Cancel>               │
y  └──────────────────────────────────────────────────────────────┘

Abruptly, however, I set aside the manuscript. I had told
the story line to a friend, and he had said it sounded good
-- and familiar. At his suggestion, I read a book. . . and
discovered that someone had beat me to my own plot.        ▸

                   {}        <F1=Help>                  Running Macro
MasterWord Print Page Macro. . .
```

Note that the last line of the screen, the message bar, displays the name of the macro and three dots. The next line up shows the message *Running Macro* on the right. In the box in the middle of the screen is the message (a *prompt*) asking you to either

CHAPTER SIX: Introducing Styles and Macros

type the numbers of the pages you want printed or press the Enter key if you want the current page printed. You could type *3,4,12* if you wanted pages 3, 4, and 12 to be printed, or *10-16* if you wanted pages 10 through 16 to be printed. In this case, you want to print the current page, and so you simply press Enter (or click on the OK button).

The message at the bottom of the screen changes briefly to tell you that the macro is "checking settings."

> MasterWord Print Page Macro. . . checking settings

During the moment this message is displayed, the macro is recording current print settings and determining whether Word is set to print in normal mode or in high-speed (and sometimes lower-quality) draft mode. If Word has been set for draft mode, the macro would have asked whether that was really what you wanted. In this case, however, Word is not set to draft mode, and so a moment later the Print dialog box appears and the message at the bottom of the screen tells you that Word is "now printing."

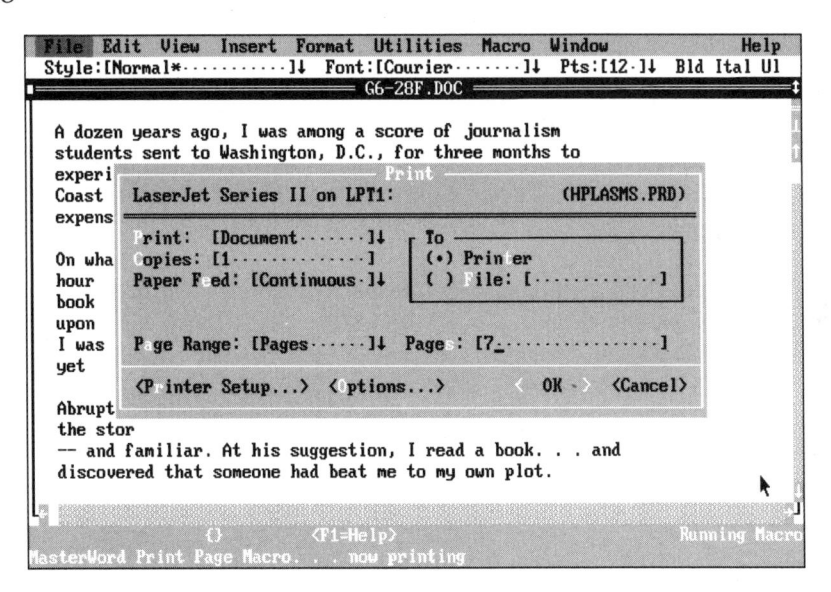

The dialog box's Pages field shows you which page or pages are being printed—in this case, page 7. The dialog box remains on the screen until the document has been sent to the printer or to the computer's print spooler and then vanishes.

Next the macro restores Word's original printing settings, using a technique that is described in Chapter 23. Again, the message bar tells you what is going on.

> MasterWord Print Page Macro. . . restoring settings

When the macro finishes its work, it tells you so:

`MasterWord Print Page Macro... done`

And think—to accomplish all this, you simply press the Enter key or click on the OK button when the dialog box asks you which pages you want to print. The rest of the process, from calculating current pagination to setting and then resetting the printing options, is done for you—all in a matter of seconds.

That's the power a macro provides: the power to add new "commands" to Word.

UNDERSTANDING WHAT'S NORMAL

Despite the names, Word's NORMAL files—NORMAL.STY and NORMAL.GLY— are "normal" in the sense that you normally use them. They give you special powers to configure Word to suit your specific needs or tastes. They can be slightly confusing until you understand them, in part because a computer system can have many copies of each. It's important to grasp what these NORMAL files do and how Word decides when to use one.

Style-Sheet File NORMAL.STY

NORMAL.STY is a name you can give a style sheet. When NORMAL.STY exists, Word will attach it to every new document, making its formatting styles available during the current editing session as well as future ones. The styles will remain available unless or until you deliberately remove the style sheet or attach a different one. This means the styles in NORMAL.STY are custom-formatting tools that are normally available for your use in any document.

You can take this idea of normal formatting a step further by creating, within NORMAL.STY, styles dedicated to particular purposes. Microsoft calls these "automatic styles," and Word applies them to what it believes is appropriate text unless you deliberately format that text a different way. This means that in addition to making a set of styles available for your use, a NORMAL style sheet causes Word to apply the automatic styles to text without your having to do a thing.

For example, if you use a paragraph style called Normal, Word will employ its formatting as the default for both the line layout and font (typeface, such as Courier or TMSRMN) of any paragraph that is not formatted a different way. Similarly, the style called Normal Section sets up a default page layout, including margins, number of columns, and whether or not page numbers are printed. (Don't confuse the individual automatic styles Normal and Normal Section with NORMAL.STY style sheets, which are collections of individual styles.) Other automatic styles format such elements as footnotes, indexes, and tables of contents.

Word attaches the style sheet NORMAL.STY to a document when the document is first created. You create a new document whenever you start Word (provided that you do not start it by typing *word /l*, which loads the last document that was displayed on the screen, or by typing *word* followed by a space and the name of an existing file). You also can create a new document by choosing the File New command.

Glossary File NORMAL.GLY

NORMAL.GLY, on the other hand, is a name you can give a glossary file. When NORMAL.GLY exists, Word loads the file's text entries and macros into the active glossary whenever you start the program. This means that the tools in NORMAL.GLY are available for use all the time, whatever you are working on, unless you use the Open Glossary dialog box to load a different glossary file. To reach the Open Glossary dialog box, choose either the Edit Glossary command (Alt+EO) or the Macro Edit command (Alt+ME), and choose the Open Glossary button.

If you give a macro the name AUTOEXEC and store it in the NORMAL.GLY glossary file, Word will carry out the instructions in the macro whenever you start Word. This gives you considerable power to configure your system. For example, you could create an AUTOEXEC macro that tells Word to open two windows and load a particular document into one of them. Or the AUTOEXEC macro could create a greeting that meets you whenever you start Word: *Hello, Emily. I am your humble servant, a mere computer. What is your command?*

Which NORMAL File?

More than one NORMAL.STY style sheet and more than one NORMAL.GLY glossary file can be stored on your computer at a time—a fact that makes the tools more powerful but sometimes more confusing.

Word follows rules when it chooses which NORMAL file to use:

- Word uses NORMAL.STY if it finds a style sheet by that name either in the current document directory or in the Word program directory.
- If Word finds a NORMAL.STY in both locations, it uses the version in the document directory and ignores the other.

The same rules apply for a NORMAL.GLY file: Word looks first to the current document directory, and if it does not find a NORMAL.GLY file, it then looks for one in the program directory.

You can take advantage of this arrangement by placing in the Word directory the NORMAL files that reflect your general word processing needs and by placing special-purpose NORMAL files in those directories in which you keep specialized kinds of documents. For example, you could keep a master NORMAL.STY style sheet in your Word program directory. Word would routinely attach this style sheet to documents in all directories—all, that is, except those that had a NORMAL.STY of their own.

WHAT'S NORMAL ON A NETWORK?

If you are using Word on a network, Word will look for NORMAL.STY and NORMAL.GLY files first in the current document directory, next in the Word directory on your workstation, and then in the Word directory on the server (the main computer that contains the Word program and links the various workstations). This three-tiered approach allows NORMAL files on the server to function as defaults for all workstations but also allows the user of a workstation to override these defaults (for his or her own workstation only) by creating alternative NORMAL files.

CHAPTER SEVEN

Introducing Graphics and Layout

Some people want their documents to look as if they were produced by a typewriter. Perhaps they write business letters, legal briefs, or manuscripts. Other people want their documents to look as if they came from a typesetting machine or even from the art department of a design house or an advertising agency. Perhaps they produce reports, contracts, or brochures. Still other people want to produce both kinds of documents—those with unadorned prose and those with design and graphical elements.

Whatever the mix of your needs, from "typewritten" memos to moderately sophisticated desktop publishing, Word should please you. Even when you are tapping Word's more advanced features, a modest amount of practice and experimentation will go a long way. There are limits to Word's powers, of course, but the average person isn't likely to reach them often.

When it comes to graphics and sophisticated document design, Word is potent. With an appropriate printer, generally a laser printer, you can produce documents that look almost as good as typeset ones. You can use hidden-text instructions to incorporate photographs, drawings, charts, spreadsheets, and other images. You can box text and shade it with gray. You can change the number of columns in the middle of the page, create adjacent columns of different widths, and tell Word that text should flow around boxes, headlines, or graphics that you have positioned in fixed locations on a page. You can see an image of the printed page on the screen before you print the document.

You can do all of this and more, and yet Word doesn't impose these features on you. This is part of the program's charm. Word stays out of your way. If you type and print a letter, Word will seem as simple and streamlined as the best of the basic word processors. But when you ask for features, you've got them.

The problem, sometimes, is knowing how to ask or what to ask for. Precisely because Word keeps its features out of the way, some of its graphics powers are not obvious.

Sometimes it seems that Word has magic buttons. If you can find the right button or the right combination of buttons, you can do anything. This chapter discusses important concepts and approaches, showing you where to find the buttons you push to create handsome documents. It is not, however, a detailed guide to the ins and outs of creating sophisticated documents. For that, turn to Chapter 30.

WHAT ARE "GRAPHICS"?

The term "graphics" is a hot one in personal computing. But what do we mean when we say that Word has "graphics capabilities"?

The term has at least four different meanings, each of which can be posed as a question.

- How closely do you want the image on the screen to resemble the document as it will print? Some word processors, such as Microsoft Word for Windows and Microsoft Word for the Macintosh, always or almost always display on the screen an image that closely resembles what will print. Other word processors give you, at best, a rough estimate and, at worst, no clue at all as to what a document will look like when printed. Word 5.5 lets you look at documents in a variety of ways.

- How do you lay out a document to make it handsome or at least visually interesting? If you are a writer, you might do virtually no formatting. Journalists, for example, usually need only get their words in the proper order because editors take care of visual presentation. At the other extreme, a designer producing a brochure cares a lot about such issues as typefaces (called *fonts* by Word), charts and illustrations, columns, lines, boxes, and shading.

- How do you bring data, text, and images from other programs into Word? A Word 5.5 document can incorporate outside images and sources of information. You can tell Word to bring in, or *import,* text from a file, data from a spreadsheet, or charts, drawings, photos, or screen images created with other programs.

- How do you get your printer to produce the finished image? For documents of sophisticated design, you probably need to use a laser printer. But because preparing a laser printer to handle sophisticated tasks can be a chore, many people underutilize their laser printers. Helping you more fully tap the potential of your printer is one objective of this book, although the information presented here is, of necessity, rather general.

To begin, let's look more deeply at the first of these four aspects of graphics.

ON THE SCREEN

When it comes to seeing the relationship of text on the screen to text on the printed page, Word provides a spectrum of options.

Why provide a spectrum? Because different people have different needs, and your own needs might vary from those of someone else. When you are writing, on-screen formatting might be more of a distraction than a help. Your object is getting appropriate words in order, and it is nice to have a word processor that is fast and does little to get in your way. Word can be that word processor. On the other hand, when you are trying to fashion a handsome page, or even when you simply want to set up a table of side-by-side columns of text, it's good to have a word processor that tells you a lot about how your printed work will look. Word can be that word processor too.

To change Word's on-screen personality, you generally take advantage of the View Preferences, View Layout, and File Print Preview commands. You use the View Preferences command to choose a video display mode. You also use it, sometimes in conjunction with the Utilities Customize command, to choose between two ways to display line breaks. You use the View Layout command to specify whether side-by-side columns and other elements that print adjacent to each other will appear that way on the screen. And you use the File Print Preview command to turn on Word's page-preview feature, where you get a realistic (albeit small) image of how your document will look when printed.

Let's look at each of these commands.

Graphics and Text Display Modes

Word's screen can be presented in any of several video modes, some of which are known as *graphics modes* and others as *text modes*:

- In a graphics mode, italicized characters look italicized, superscripted characters are smaller than other characters and are raised slightly above the rest of the line, and the mouse pointer is an arrow.
- In a text mode, all characters generally look the same: Italicized and superscripted characters are the same size and shape as normal characters, but they are underlined or appear in a color. The mouse pointer is a bright rectangle.

Word runs a little more slowly in a graphics mode than it does in a text mode. Scrolling is slightly less speedy, for example. For that reason, you might prefer text mode for writing, particularly if your computer lacks a hard disk or is on the poky side. Also, with certain systems you get better on-screen resolution in text modes.

If your objective is to see—on the screen—text that most closely resembles what will print, you'll find graphics modes attractive. (However, if you are creating documents that look typewritten, you might have little need for graphics modes. A text mode probably will show your document much as it will print because "typewritten" documents don't contain much character formatting.)

To choose a mode, use the View Preferences command (Alt+VE) and move to the Display Mode field (Alt+D). The identity of the current mode will be listed and highlighted. If you press the Up or Down direction key at this point, you will move through the available video modes. If you want a drop-down menu of choices, press Alt+Down direction key.

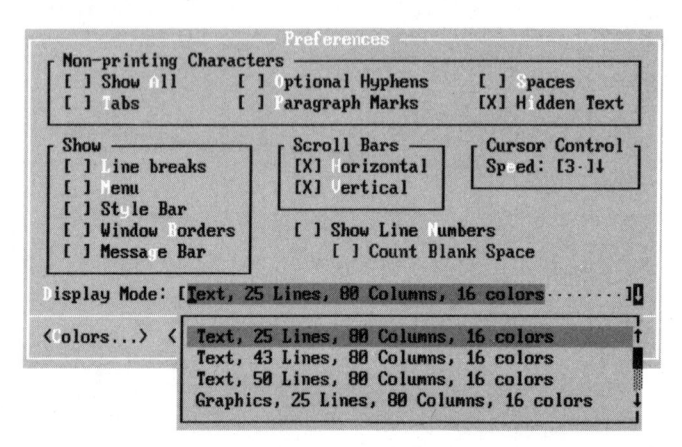

```
┌─────────────────────────── Preferences ───────────────────────────┐
│ ┌─ Non-printing Characters ─────────────────────────────────────┐ │
│ │ [ ] Show All         [ ] Optional Hyphens    [ ] Spaces       │ │
│ │ [ ] Tabs             [ ] Paragraph Marks     [X] Hidden Text  │ │
│ └───────────────────────────────────────────────────────────────┘ │
│ ┌─ Show ──────────────┐ ┌─ Scroll Bars ──┐ ┌─ Cursor Control ──┐ │
│ │ [ ] Line breaks     │ │ [X] Horizontal │ │ Speed: [3-1]      │ │
│ │ [ ] Menu            │ │ [X] Vertical   │ └───────────────────┘ │
│ │ [ ] Style Bar       │ └────────────────┘                       │
│ │ [ ] Window Borders  │ [ ] Show Line Numbers                    │
│ │ [ ] Message Bar     │     [ ] Count Blank Space                │
│ └─────────────────────┘                                          │
│ Display Mode: [Text, 25 Lines, 80 Columns, 16 colors········]    │
│ <Colors...>  < Text, 25 Lines, 80 Columns, 16 colors     ↑       │
│                Text, 43 Lines, 80 Columns, 16 colors             │
│                Text, 50 Lines, 80 Columns, 16 colors             │
│                Graphics, 25 Lines, 80 Columns, 16 colors ↓       │
└───────────────────────────────────────────────────────────────────┘
```

Although the drop-down box shows only four choices at a time, others might be available. You can reach all modes by scrolling. For example, if you have a VGA card in your computer, your choices will be Text in 25-, 43-, and 50-line modes, and Graphics in 25-, 30-, 34-, 43-, and 60-line modes.

NOTE: *If Word's list of available display modes shows only one or two items, and they are text mode only, either your computer is not equipped to display Word's graphics characters or you have not properly run SETUP, described in Appendix A.*

Line Breaks and Measurements

The practical choice you often face when deciding how Word will display a document is between ease of reading and the accuracy of on-screen layout. For example, how should Word display a paragraph that contains proportional fonts or two different font sizes? Word lets you decide the answer to this question by setting two elements—the Line Breaks check box of the View Preferences command and the Measure field of the Utilities Customize command.

First, a little background. When you use Word to write or edit, all characters are the same width on the screen. This presents a fundamental conflict between screen and printer when two or more different type sizes are mixed or when you are using a proportional typeface—that is, a typeface with characters that vary in width. Proportional fonts such as TMSRMN and HELV have a much wider capital M than small i, for example, yet the M and the i take up the same amount of space on the Word screen. Consequently, when your document contains a proportional font or a mixture of fonts, a compromise is necessary.

CHAPTER SEVEN: Introducing Graphics and Layout   135

The View Preferences command's Line Breaks check box lets you control whether Word should, when breaking a line on screen and starting a new one, break at the same spot it will when printing the document. If you mark the check box with an *X*, Word will show you the correct content of each line, even if it causes the line lengths to be irregular on screen or even if it causes lines to be wider than the screen. If you leave the check box off, Word will break lines wherever it needs to in order to preserve an on-screen format that superficially resembles the layout that will print. Leaving the box off also keeps lines shorter than the width of the screen, so you generally can read a whole line without having to scroll horizontally.

The Utilities Customize command's Measure field lets you tell Word the unit of measure to use when expressing distances and measurements. The choices are inches (*In*), centimeters (*Cm*), 10-pitch characters (*P10*), 12-pitch characters (*P12*), and points (*Pt*). If you're in the United States, you probably will want to keep the field set to *In*. But there might be times when you might want other settings, especially if you are using a monospace elite-size font (a font that emulates an elite typewriter). The setting you choose can affect the on-screen appearance of your document.

Showing the Layout

The View Layout command lets you tell Word whether documents that are multi-column or that have other adjacent elements such as side-by-side paragraphs should be displayed on screen much as they will print. This is an example of choosing between ease of reading and editing on one hand and accuracy of on-screen layout on the other.

When View Layout is off, which is Word's usual condition, text appears as a continuous series of paragraphs. For example, Word displays a two-column layout as a single, narrower column. If you're working on the content of your document, having View Layout off is probably better because it lets you concentrate on getting your ideas in order.

In contrast, when View Layout is on, the screen shows an approximation of the document's actual printed layout. It usually isn't exact because of screen limitations, but multiple columns and other special text and graphics elements are represented in their proper locations. Actual graphics images do not appear, but boxes made of dotted lines reserve room for graphics at their appropriate locations. The ruler is reduced in length, spanning only that portion of the top of the screen that aligns with whatever element of the document is highlighted. For example, if you are working in the second column of a two-column layout, the ruler appears only over the second column. Microsoft calls this a "sliding ruler," and it is necessary because in a multicolumn environment a paragraph's tab stops must be measured from the left edge of a column rather than from the left edge of the screen.

Turning View Layout on lets you examine and change the interplay of your document's content and layout. One disadvantage is that some Word operations run more slowly. Also, it is more difficult to navigate within a document. To move from one on-screen element (such as a column) to another, first be sure Num Lock is off. Then hold down the Alt key while you press the 5 key (either on the numeric keypad or on the top row of typing keys). Then release the Alt key and press either the Left direction key (to move to the previous element) or the Right direction key (to move to the next element). In a way, it is almost as if you have a number of separate smaller documents on the screen, each with its own ruler, and you must hop from one to another with Alt+5 and then Left direction key or Alt+5 and then Right direction key.

View Layout mode is unusual in three other respects: Revision marks are displayed only for the leftmost column; whether hidden text is displayed depends on the setting of the Hidden check box in the Print Options dialog box of the File Print command, not the Hidden Text check box of the View Preferences command; and headers and footers ("running heads") are not displayed.

When the View Layout feature is on, a dot appears to the left of the word *Layout* on the drop-down View menu, and the letters *LY* appear in the status bar near the bottom of the screen.

Previewing Printing

Word's print preview feature lets you look at an image of either one page or two pages of the document on screen. This image shows the page much as it will be printed, including graphics. You can't really read the text, nor can you make any changes to a document when it is in this mode. Still, it is a highly useful tool when you are creating a document in which formatting matters. You can make a change to the document, switch to print preview mode to see the effect, and then switch back to the document. This technique is much faster than printing pages, even on a laser printer, and it should contribute to your productivity.

To switch to print preview mode, press Alt+FV to choose the File Print Preview command. To exit the mode, press Esc. You also can switch in or out of print preview mode by holding down the Ctrl key while you press F9.

Try the preview feature now. Press Ctrl+F9 to see what your current document will look like when printed. Depending on the speed of your computer and the complexity of your page layout and the graphics you are incorporating in your document, it might take a few seconds for the image to appear. You can even use this feature when a style sheet is in a window, to see how the style sheet would look if printed.

Because print preview displays what will be printed, settings in the Print Options and Printer Setup dialog boxes affect the screen image. If you choose the File Print command (Alt+FP) and press the Options command button to reach the Printer Options dialog box, you can select the Draft check box. In draft mode, Word omits graphics images when displaying the page preview image, although the page layout is depicted accurately (including appropriate room for the graphics). Putting an X in the Draft check box also tells Word to omit graphics when printing the document, so take the X out of the field before printing, unless you want a quick printout of the document that omits not only graphics but formatting such as correct fonts and proportional spacing.

To see how a different printer changes the look of your document, install a different printer file in the Printer File field of the Printer Setup command.

When a preview image is showing, a special abbreviated menu is available at top of the screen. The commands reached through the menu let you print your document (File Print command) and change your printer's setup (File Printer Setup command), jump to any page in your document (Edit Go To command), choose whether the image of one page or two pages will be displayed (View commands), or use macros (Macro commands). As you can see, the menu really doesn't let you do much more than look at your document; no editing is allowed in print preview mode. To return to editing, press Esc to exit preview.

Certain graphics images stored in PostScript format cannot be previewed. Word can send this kind of file to a printer and can print the image in a Word document in the correct location and in the correct size, but it cannot display on the screen what the image will look like when printed. Word does offer previews of *encapsulated* PostScript files that contain a Tagged Image File Format, or TIFF, version of the image. This is a common form of PostScript on the PC, so it is possible or even probable that you will be able to preview PostScript graphics.

For more details on print preview mode, see Chapters 11 and 31.

CREATING A LAYOUT

Formatting to achieve a graphical look—a *desktop publishing* look, one that you can't achieve with a typewriter—potentially involves many considerations. A document might have more than one column and might contain a variety of typefaces and type sizes, including large ones for headlines. It might contain blocks of text, situated at specific places on the page and boxed. And it might contain drawings, photographs, or other graphics images.

When we use a personal computer to write and design a document that will be reproduced, and when the document comes off the printer with all or most of its various elements already in position, we say we are engaging in desktop publishing. Word 5.5 lacks some of the sophisticated features of dedicated desktop publishing packages such as Aldus PageMaker and Ventura Publisher, but it is much easier to use in general, and it contains most of the desktop publishing features that most people need most of the time. It might be all that you need.

To achieve basic desktop publishing with Word, you use a mixture of formatting tools. Some of these, such as the Format Character and Format Paragraph commands, are also used to create conventional, "typewritten" documents. Look to Chapter 13 for extensive information on these commands and techniques. Other formatting tools are in the province of desktop publishing. To use these specialized tools successfully, you should understand the general approach Word offers for producing layouts.

A key element is that, when you lay out a document, Word lets you fix some items in specific positions but lets other items float or flow around the fixed items. For example, you can box a narrow paragraph of text and position it 3 inches from the top of the page. Other text that is not positioned will flow around the box, changing line lengths as necessary to avoid the fixed text. Similarly, if you position a graphics image at the center of a page or at the top of the right column of a two-column layout, the graphic will remain anchored there while other text flows around it—with no additional work on your part.

A paragraph that is fixed in a certain position is said to be *absolutely positioned*, meaning that it is placed or measured not in relation to other paragraphs but rather in relation to an absolute position on the page or in a column.

Commands for Layout

The main commands you use for sophisticated layout are

- Format Margins, to control the size of the paper and the size of its margins
- Format Section, to control the number of columns
- Format Paragraph, to control the left and right indents and space after and space before paragraphs
- Insert Picture, to import and control the size of graphics created outside of Word so that Word treats them as paragraphs
- Format Position, to fix certain text or graphics paragraphs to particular places on the page and to control the width of those paragraphs

Actually, the Format Position command controls the overall width of the invisible *frame* that surrounds the paragraph, rather than the width of the paragraph's printable content. The invisible frame is an important concept and not a difficult one to grasp. Each paragraph in a Word document has such a frame, which is like armor, a protective shield that stops other text from overlapping it. It carves space out of a document, reserving it for the paragraph. The actual content of the paragraph can be text or a graphic or both and does not have to use all of the frame.

In Chapter 30, we'll return to the idea of frames because understanding it is vital for making the most of Word's layout powers. For now, let's learn how to use the Format Section command (Alt+TS) to create multiple columns, because columns are an important element in layouts of many kinds, including sophisticated ones.

Multiple Columns

There are two main ways to create multiple columns in Word: one simple, the other challenging. Fortunately, the simple technique is so powerful that it might be all you ever need. For now, we will confine ourselves to this easier approach, which involves the Format Section command and, sometimes, section marks.

A *section* is a portion of a document, typically but not always a sequence of pages, that has consistent general layout characteristics. For example, if the first part of a document has two columns per page and the second part has three columns per page, we say that the document has two sections. The barrier between these two sections is called a *section mark*. Although in certain situations Word inserts a section mark for you, generally you must do it yourself by using the Insert Break command (Alt+IB) and choosing the Section option button (Alt+S).

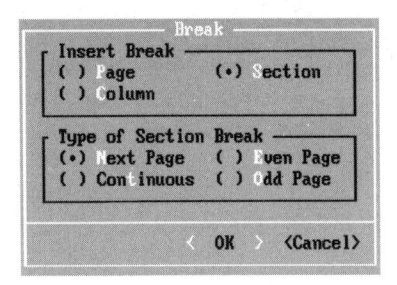

CHAPTER SEVEN: Introducing Graphics and Layout

If an entire document has a single layout—the number of columns never changes, for instance—the document has only one section and doesn't need any section marks.

NOTE: *If a single-section document uses Word's default section formatting or relies on the Normal section style of a style sheet, no section mark is likely to appear anywhere in the document. However, when you add section formatting, a section mark appears at the end of the document.*

When a section mark exists, you can select one or more characters on one side of it and use the various Format commands (or a section style from a style sheet) to control the layout characteristics of all the text on that side. Then you can select text on the other side of the section mark and use the Format Section and Format Margins commands (or a section style) to set up a different layout. When a document has multiple section marks, you can change the layout several times.

The section mark is really only a single character, but it appears on the screen as a series of colons stretching like a boundary across a window or column from left to right. In the following example, a section mark divides the first part of a document, which has two columns, from the latter part, which has three columns.

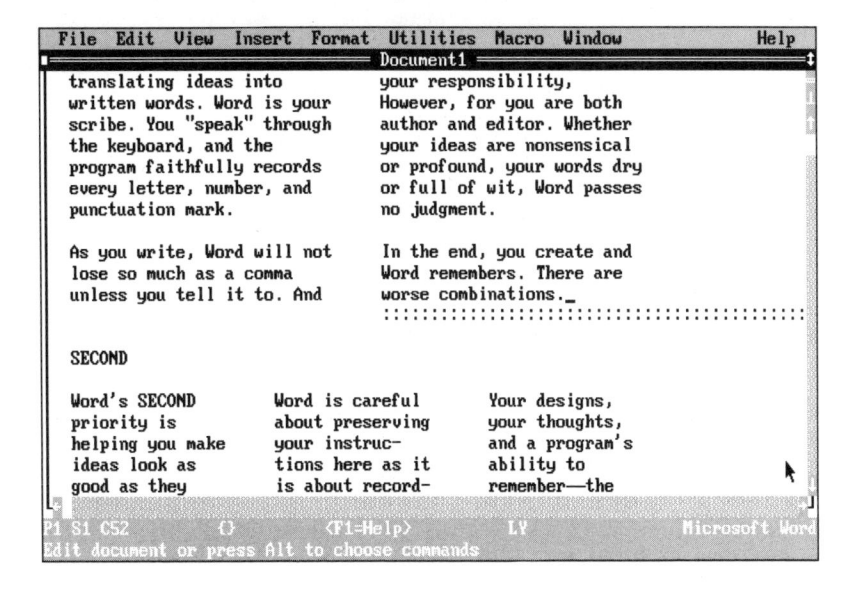

To achieve this image on your screen, you must turn on the View Layout command, which was discussed earlier in this chapter. Otherwise, Word does not show adjacent columns as adjacent.

The formatting of each section of a document can be controlled individually. You accomplish this with the Format Section and Format Margins commands and with the dialog boxes you reach by choosing those commands. For the purposes of creating multiple columns, the relevant command is Format Section, which offers choices on several issues:

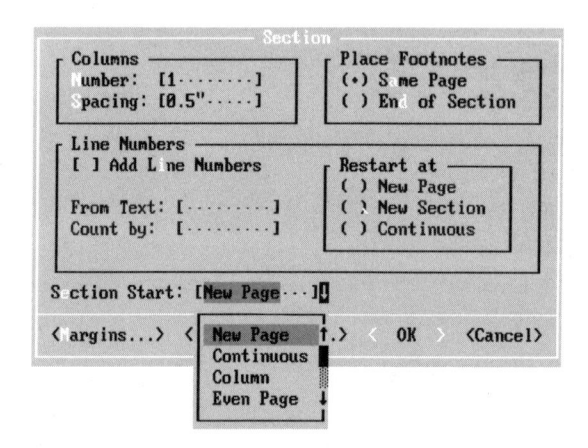

```
┌─────────────────────── Section ───────────────────────┐
│ ┌─ Columns ─────────────┐  ┌─ Place Footnotes ─────┐ │
│ │  Number: [1········]  │  │  (•) Same Page         │ │
│ │  Spacing: [0.5"·····] │  │  ( ) End of Section    │ │
│ └───────────────────────┘  └────────────────────────┘ │
│ ┌─ Line Numbers ────────────┐  ┌─ Restart at ──────┐ │
│ │  [ ] Add Line Numbers     │  │  ( ) New Page      │ │
│ │                           │  │  (•) New Section   │ │
│ │  From Text: [·········]   │  │  ( ) Continuous    │ │
│ │  Count by:  [·········]   │  └────────────────────┘ │
│ └───────────────────────────┘                         │
│                                                       │
│  Section Start: [New Page···]↓                        │
│                                                       │
│      <Margins...>  < New Page  ↑.>  < OK >  <Cancel> │
│                     Continuous                        │
│                     Column                            │
│                     Even Page  ↓                      │
└───────────────────────────────────────────────────────┘
```

We're going to ignore for now the fields in the Line Numbers grouping including the Restart Alt choices because they aren't relevant to page layout. However, the other fields in the Section dialog box are worth examining.

The first two fields, grouped under the Columns heading, control the number of columns across the page and the spacing between them. The Number text box normally is set to 1, meaning that text stretches from the left page margin to the right page margin. If you set the field to 2, there will be two columns of equal width divided by a vertical blank space that is as wide as the distance specified in the Spacing field.

To the right of the Columns grouping are two option buttons under a Place Footnotes heading. Choose Same Page if you want each footnote to print at the bottom of the same page as its text reference. Choose End of Section if you want footnotes to print together at the end of the section (which also is the end of the document in many cases).

The Section Start text box is your way of telling Word what it should do when it encounters the mark that starts the section you are formatting. Should it change formatting immediately, or wait for a convenient spot in the text? At first, you might think that Word should always change layout as soon as it encounters a section mark. But that can be inconvenient. Sometimes you don't want layout—including such things as page margins or the number of columns on the page—to change abruptly. You want the layout to change at the same time the page or column changes. If you move to the Section Start field, and press Alt+Down direction key , you see a dropdown list of five choices (four of which fit in the drop-down list at a time). These five choices let you control where the formatting of a new section will begin in relation to the section mark: New Page, Continuous, Column, Even Page, and Odd Page.

If you choose New Page, Word will start a new page at the location of the section break. The layout of the new page (and those that follow it) will be governed by your use of formatting commands or styles *after* the location of the section mark.

If you choose Column, the section will begin a new column and use the new formatting for that column.

Choosing Even Page has an effect similar to choosing Page, except that Word starts the section on the next even-numbered page. This means that if the section mark is on an even-numbered page, Word stops printing the page at the section mark, leaves the rest of that page and all of the next page blank, and resumes printing (with the new layout) at the top of the even page that follows.

Choosing Odd Page is equivalent to choosing Even, except that Word starts the section on the next odd-numbered page.

The most interesting option is Continuous. If you choose it, most attributes of the new section begin immediately, without beginning a new page or column. The new formatting starts at the section mark and controls the left and right margins, number of columns, and whether line numbers print. The bottom-margin formatting doesn't change until the next page. When a section contains footnotes or annotations, Word ignores the Continuous setting and starts a new page. When the number of columns changes, Word divides the page horizontally, squaring off the upper columns so that all columns that are the same width also are the same length. This is the setting you use to switch from two columns to three in the middle of the page or to place a banner headline across a page (in a single column) and then switch to a multiple-column layout for text.

IMPORTING GRAPHICS

Word can incorporate graphics of various kinds into a document and print them. The graphics can come from numerous sources, including leading software packages that you can use to create graphics. For example, you can print as part of a Word document graphs created with Microsoft Excel or Lotus 1-2-3, charts from Microsoft Chart or Harvard Graphics, drawings or other images from Microsoft Windows applications, photographs or artwork digitized with a scanner, or images captured and cropped from your computer screen.

The first step is to create a file on disk that contains the image you want to incorporate into your document. You can use almost any program that stores graphics images on disk as separate files. Or you can capture images from the screen, using the Capture program, which comes with Word. (For the particulars of using Capture, see Chapter 30.)

The next step is to incorporate the image into your Word document. You accomplish this by using the Insert Picture command (Alt+IP), which takes you to the Picture dialog box, where you fill in information that Word will use to insert an instruction line into your document. The instruction line includes information on the name and location of the graphics file that is to be printed as part of the document, the size in which it is to be printed, and the graphics file format in which it is stored. The first part of the instruction line is formatted to be hidden, which means you won't see the graphic code unless you use the View Preferences command and turn on the Hidden Text check box. However, you really don't need to read the hidden-text instruction line because the same information is displayed in the fields of the Picture dialog box.

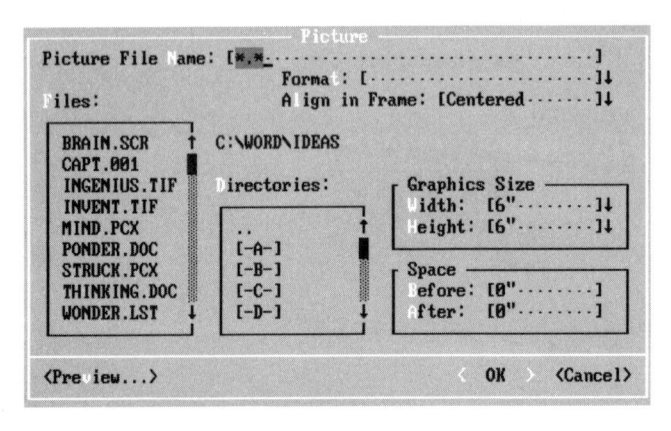

```
┌─────────────────────── Picture ───────────────────────┐
│  Picture File  ame: [*.*............................] │
│                    Forma  : [....................]↕   │
│     iles:          A  ign in Frame: [Centered.....]↕  │
│  ┌─────────────┐                                      │
│  │ BRAIN.SCR  ↑│ C:\WORD\IDEAS                        │
│  │ CAPT.001    │                                      │
│  │ INGENIUS.TIF│  irectories:    ┌─ Graphics Size ──┐ │
│  │ INVENT.TIF  │ ┌───────────┐   │  idth:  [6"....]↕│ │
│  │ MIND.PCX    │ │    ..   ↑ │   │  eight: [6"....]↕│ │
│  │ PONDER.DOC  │ │ [-A-]     │   └──────────────────┘ │
│  │ STRUCK.PCX  │ │ [-B-]     │   ┌─ Space ──────────┐ │
│  │ THINKING.DOC│ │ [-C-]     │   │  efore: [0"...] │ │
│  │ WONDER.LST ↓│ │ [-D-]   ↓ │   │  fter:  [0"...] │ │
│  └─────────────┘ └───────────┘   └──────────────────┘ │
│                                                       │
│  <Pre iew...>                    <  OK  >  <Cancel>   │
└───────────────────────────────────────────────────────┘
```

In the Picture File Name text box, you type the name of the file that contains the image you want to transfer, or *import*. Include the filename extension, such as .TIF.

Instead of typing a name, you can press Alt+F to move to the list of files on the left side of the dialog box. Unless you narrow the possibilities by first typing an entry other than *.* in the Picture File Name text box, the list of files will show every file in the directory, not just graphics files. You need to know which are graphics files.

If the file you want is in a different directory or on a different disk, you can press Alt+D to move to the Directories list, which is near the center of the dialog box. In this list, drives are indicated by [ ] brackets, whereas directories are shown without brackets. Highlight the .. entry when you want to move "up" a level to a "parent" directory on the current drive. For example, if you are working in the IDEAS subdirectory of the WORD subdirectory of the C drive, the current path is C:\WORD\IDEAS. If you want to import a graphic from the C:\WORD subdirectory, you highlight the double dot (..) entry and press Enter, which takes you up one level to C:\WORD. From that position, you can choose a file or continue navigating through your directories, possibly choosing .. again, to move to the root-level directory at the "top" of the C drive. (Techniques for choosing directories and files from such a Directories list are discussed in more detail in Chapter 10.)

The remaining fields of the Picture dialog box tell Word what file format the graphics file is stored in, how the image should be aligned within the paragraph's frame, how wide and how tall the image will be when printed, and whether the paragraph containing the graphic should have any special spacing above or below it.

The only remaining step is to position the graphic on the page, which you accomplish by using the Format Position command. Details on using the Insert Picture and Format Position commands are in Chapter 30.

CHAPTER SEVEN: Introducing Graphics and Layout 143

PRINTING THE IMAGE

For Word to print a graphics document successfully, several elements have to be in place.

- The document must be correctly formatted. You can use the File Print Preview command to verify the general layout of a document before printing it.
- If you are incorporating graphics images from other programs, the files containing the graphics must be available.
- An appropriate printer file (.PRD file) must be installed. This makes it possible not only to print the document, but also to view images of its pages in advance with the File Print Preview command. To install a printer file, run the SETUP program that comes with Word or use the File Printer Setup command.
- If you are using downloadable fonts, as you might do with a laser printer, the fonts must be available on disk. These fonts generally must be purchased, and you might have to run a font-manager program that comes with the fonts, to generate a version that meets your specific needs and those of your printer and Word.
- If you are using downloadable fonts, a .DAT file that matches your printer file must be available on disk. This file contains data that enables Word and your printer to use the downloadable fonts that are referenced in the printer file.
- If you are using a PostScript printer, the file POSTSCRP.INI must be available in the same directory as the POSTSCRP.PRD printer file.

NOTE: *Hundreds of printer files are available for Word, but the SETUP program copies to your hard disk (and decompresses) only those for the printer(s) you specify. Microsoft publishes several disks of supplemental printer files and lets dealers give away copies to Word owners. In addition, the Microsoft Forum on the CompuServe electronic bulletin board offers updated and new printer files so that subscribers can download them by telephone and modem. (There is no charge, but you pay for your connect time to CompuServe.) You also can modify or create printer files, using the MAKEPRD and MERGEPRD programs that come with Word. These tasks are more challenging than routine uses of Word.*

For details on using Word's Print commands, see Chapters 11 and 31.

THE POSSIBILITIES

The interplay of graphics and format commands provides a wealth of opportunities, as well as ways to get confused. For now, it is enough to know that these commands exist and generally how you can use them. With time and additional chapters of this book, you can become proficient—and excited by the possibilities.

CHAPTER EIGHT

Keep in Mind

As you leave Part I, you embark on a journey—the itinerary of which you can design for yourself—through the commands and features of Word. It is an odyssey of many rewards. But until you know Word well, you might find yourself puzzled occasionally.

This chapter is a collection of tips. Some will help you cope with situations that might confuse or trouble you; others can help you use Word more effectively by showing you what's going on behind the scenes. If you get lost during your exploration of Word, refer to this chapter to see if one of its pointers helps you.

Tip 1: Make Paragraph Marks Visible

Paragraph marks normally are invisible on the screen, and yet seeing them can be particularly important to a relative newcomer to Word. By using the View Preferences command (Alt+VE) and turning on the Paragraph Marks check box, you can reduce your chances of making irritating little mistakes.

A visible paragraph mark looks like this: ¶. A paragraph mark appears at the end of each paragraph, cluttering the screen somewhat—which is why Word lets you turn paragraph marks off.

But out of sight shouldn't be out of mind, because the mark is the storage place for paragraph formatting. And until you're experienced with Word, it's easy to inadvertently delete a paragraph mark that you can't see.

What happens when you delete a paragraph mark? The paragraphs immediately preceding and following the mark merge into a single paragraph. This merging poses little problem if the two paragraphs were formatted identically. But if they were not, eliminating the mark causes a sudden change in text appearance as the newly combined paragraph takes on the format of the original second paragraph. If you encounter this problem, try the Edit Undo command (Alt+Backspace). Better to avoid the problem altogether, though, by keeping paragraph marks visible so that you won't delete them unless you really want to.

Tip 2: Move Away from the Final Section Mark

A line of colons (::::::::::) that extends across the width of the text window (or column) is a *section mark*, which contains page-layout information for the text preceding it. You can change this formatting with the Format Section and Format Margins commands or by applying a section style from a style sheet. If you select any part of a section mark, the whole line of dots is highlighted. That's because—wide as the section mark is on the screen—Word considers it a single character.

Sometimes a section mark appears at the end of a document, just before the diamond-shaped endmark. Adding text at the location of a section mark can be unnerving to newcomers. If you don't want to bump into the mark, select it and press the Enter key several times to push the mark down and away from the area where you want to work.

NOTE: *When a document ends in a section mark, write and edit above the mark only. The mark controls the page layout of the paragraphs above it, so any writing you do below the section mark will not have the same section (page) formatting.*

Tip 3: Distinguish Between Margins and Indents

- A left or right *margin* is part of section formatting. Margins help shape page design, and you control them with the Format Margins command.
- An *indent* is part of paragraph formatting; hence you can change indents at will from paragraph to paragraph. Use indents when you want to insert more space to the left or right of a paragraph than section formatting provides.

Indents are of three types—left, right, and first-line—and you control them with the Format Paragraph command. (Left and right indents apply to every line of a paragraph; the first-line indent affects only a paragraph's first line.)

If you let the differences between margins and indents become fuzzy in your mind, or if you think of margins when you mean indents, you might use the wrong command to format your text, or you might do more work than you need to. Pay special attention if you're coming to Word from a word processor that doesn't distinguish between margins and indents. With some programs you must change margins even when you want only a single paragraph indented. Word is conceptually different—and much more flexible.

Tip 4: Tabbing and Spacing in Tables

When you are using type that is proportionally spaced, justified, or of more than one pitch (width), characters all appear on the screen as if they were the same width, even when they aren't. If you create a table using Spacebar spaces, it can look well ordered on the screen yet be a ragged mess when it's printed. Avoid such disasters by lining up tabular text using the Tab key and the Format Tabs command (or, better yet, a style-sheet paragraph style).

Tip 5: Default Margins

Chapter 3 described Word's built-in section format, which governs the page size and margins of any document that isn't formatted in some other way. You can change these default settings in either of two ways:

- You can use the Format Margins command (Alt+TM) to specify new top and side margins and then turn on the Use as Default check box. From that point forward, and even in future sessions with Word, these margins will be used for all documents—unless you establish other margins for a document deliberately or use a style sheet that has a Normal Section style.
- You can use a Normal Section style. As explained at the end of Chapter 6, when a style sheet named NORMAL.STY exists in a directory, it is automatically attached to any new document created in the directory. In turn, if the NORMAL.STY style sheet contains a Normal Section style, the formatting associated with the style is automatically applied to any documents.

Tip 6: Managing Memory

Word will use just about as much memory as you choose to give it. The program requires 384 KB to run. If you install 640 KB, it runs better, especially when performing such memory-intensive operations as compiling an index or sorting paragraphs into alphabetic or numeric order. Word even takes advantage of expanded memory if you have it, to break through MS-DOS's 640-KB memory limit. Using expanded memory noticeably improves the performance of Word 5.5.

Because earlier versions of Word don't manage memory as capably as Word 5.0 and 5.5 do, if you have an earlier version it is to your advantage to know how to manage Word's memory yourself.

First, a little background. All versions of Word use memory to store a variety of information, including

- Document names and information about footnotes and paragraph formatting.
- The selected printer file (PRD file). The whole printer file, not its name only, is stored. This can take a considerable amount of memory, especially when the printer file is for a laser printer or a PostScript device.
- Style sheets for all documents in all windows (although Word uses no extra memory when the same style sheet is in use for more than one document).
- The name of each entry in the current glossary. The amount of memory used by the glossary depends on the number and length of the glossary names, not on the length of the glossary entries themselves. (However, the amount of disk space used by a glossary file is determined primarily by the number and length of the glossary entries.)

- The most recently typed (but unsaved) characters and formatting information for your document(s).
- The *piece table*, which keeps track of the location of all parts of a document.

The piece table is the largest potential user of memory. If you start Word and load a document from disk, the piece table is very small because all of the document exists in one place. If you add text in the middle of a line, the new text is stored in memory, and the piece table keeps track of the point of insertion and the location in memory of the new text. The screen makes it look as if the text has been incorporated into the document, but that is only illusion until you actually save the document. After you have typed about 1000 characters of text, Word shifts the new text from memory to the scratch file. Each time you move the cursor to a different location in a document and make a change, the piece table records what you've done. When you save the document, the piece table is the map that lets Word put the elements of the document together as a cohesive unit on disk. If you wait a long time before saving, the piece table grows large because it is coordinating so much.

Regardless of what version of Word you have and how much memory is installed, you should periodically save to protect your work and to reduce the size of the piece table. It is particularly important to save your document before using commands that require a lot of memory, such as the Utilities Sort, Insert Table of Contents, Insert Index, and Edit Replace commands.

The fastest way to chew up memory is to use the Utilities Sort command, because Word must hold lots of information in memory while it alphabetizes. The Edit Replace command can use up a lot too, and it's easy to understand why. Let's say you replace the name *Suzi* with the name *Suki* throughout a document. Each substitution of a *k* for a *z* is an edit that breaks the document into three pieces as far as the piece table is concerned. Before the substitution, the piece table didn't have to pay much attention to the word *Suzi* at all. But with the new letter inserted, the table must remember that the *Su* is at one place, the *k* is in memory (and later, in the scratch file), and the *i* is at yet another location.

If you include commands such as Replace in a Word macro, a reserved variable named SAVE can be employed to help the macro determine when memory is getting low. Whenever it gets low, the macro can execute a command such as File Save All, which should free considerable memory. See Chapter 23 for details on the SAVE reserved variable.

Finally, keep in mind that both Word 5.0 and 5.5 run under OS/2 as well as under DOS. You don't need a new version of Word; the same version works under both operating systems. If you happen to have OS/2 on your machine and you need to perform a memory-intensive operation, such as indexing a large document, you should run under OS/2, not DOS. In many circumstances, you'll find a dramatic improvement in Word's capacity to perform operations that consume memory.

CHAPTER EIGHT: Keep in Mind

Tip 7: The Virtues of Autosave

Word's autosave feature periodically saves the work you are doing, protecting it in case you lose power, reboot without saving a document, or have other difficulties that cause Word to stop operating. Autosave is a clever feature, but it isn't what you might think it is.

I've long been an opponent of word processing programs that automatically save documents every few minutes (or every few keystrokes). The reason is that sometimes the editing you do is tentative. You edit, you read what you've done, and then you save the changes only if you want them. A program that records everything on disk more or less as you type it can be a real nuisance because it undermines your ability to discard editing you decide you don't like.

Word strikes an elegant balance. Its autosave feature gives you the protection of saving on disk but doesn't interfere with your ability to discard editing. You continue to use the File Save command, as always. You save only when you want to. But, if you use the autosave feature, Word will do a different kind of save as often as you like. An autosave is different because it stores your changes to documents, style sheets, and glossaries in special temporary files. These files are deleted whenever you quit Word. But if you don't quit Word—if instead you lose power, for example—the temporary files are still on disk. When you restart Word, the program detects the presence of the autosave files and asks whether you want your files on disk updated to reflect the changes that were recorded in the autosave files. This scheme gives you all the comfort of frequent, automatic saving, with none of the headaches of having the wrong material saved.

For specifics on using the autosave feature, see the discussion of the Utilities Customize command in Chapter 16. Be aware, however, that using autosave might slow down the operation of Word slightly. This might or might not be a problem for you, depending on your computer and your tastes.

Tip 8: Word's Built-In Virus Detection

If you try to start Word but you get a message saying you can't, cross your fingers and hope for the best. Word 5.5's virus-detection feature might have discovered a virus.

Word doesn't look for viruses in general; it simply alerts you (and refuses to start) if it discovers that it has been tampered with by another program. If this situation happens to you, contact Microsoft product support or run a general-purpose virus-detection program.

Tip 9: What Word Remembers

When it comes to your preferences, Word 5.5 has a terrific memory. It keeps track of more than 100 choices you can make about how the program operates and how it appears on the screen. Whenever you quit Word, these choices are stored on disk in a file called MW.INI. (If you are working on a network, Word creates a different MW.INI file for each workstation because in a network environment Word allows different defaults for different users.)

Word stores the following information in the MW.INI file:

- The on/off status of the ribbon, ruler, status bar, message bar, style bar, and screen borders.
- Whether Layout mode is on, whether line breaks are set to be accurate in content or in layout, and whether Print Preview is set to show one page, two pages, or facing pages.
- Whether Word is set to display hidden text and nonprinting symbols.
- Which display mode Word is using and which colors have been selected for screen elements such as borders and menus. In addition, Word remembers the background color of the first document window.
- All fields of the Utilities Customize command, including current settings for measure, background pagination, autosave, cursor speed, line-draw character, location of the spell-checking file, and whether function keys and the Ins key are using the Word 5.0 or 5.5 conventions.
- All printer setup options, including printer model name, printer file name, printer resolution, and whether queued printing is on.
- Printing options, including whether draft and duplex printing are on, whether a summary sheet should be printed with your document, and whether hidden text should be included.
- Miscellaneous spelling options, file-management options, annotation options, and alignment settings for headers and footers.
- Several additional settings that are controlled through command-line switches or cannot be controlled at all directly through Word. (For example, MW.INI remembers how far you want the screen to scroll when you type to the bottom line of the screen. And if Word is set up with alternative rules for tab stops, this is recorded in MW.INI too—even though Word gives you no direct way to change this setting.)
- The name of the last document you were working on and the location of the selection (highlight) within the document. However, Word will reuse this particular information only if you type *word/l* (rather than *word*) when you start the program.

Each document (rather than MW.INI) stores information such as the name of the style sheet (if any) that was attached to it and choices you have made regarding revision marks.

Some of these settings are easily changed with Word, others less so. Word Set, a separate program that lets you directly adjust all of these settings, comes with the product MasterWord. The program recognizes whether the MW.INI file is for Word 5.0 or 5.5 and gives instructions and options accordingly.

Tip 10: Don't Overlook Word's Powers

One key to success with Word is to avoid taking on too many challenges at one time. If you try to learn everything at once, you might be courting frustration. Word offers a great deal to users at all skill levels, and you needn't explore the far reaches of the program to profit.

On the other hand, as you become comfortable with Word's fundamentals, don't be too cautious or contented. Features such as outlining, style sheets, macros, and multiple windows offer great opportunities and needn't take much time to learn.

Unless you at least try these and other features, you might not know what you are missing. Take your time learning the program, but don't overlook Word's powers.

PART II
Using

CHAPTER NINE

Introducing Commands

Much of Word's flexibility comes from the diversity of its commands. In Part I, you learned the rules and techniques of using commands generally. Here, in Part II, you learn the ins and outs of each specific command.

Across the top of your screen are the names of nine drop-down menus: File, Edit, View, Insert, Format, Utilities, Macro, Window, and Help. Each of these represents an entire family of related commands. And each family is the object of at least one chapter here in Part II.

The File menu offers such a broad range of capabilities that it is divided into two chapters: Chapter 10 describes File commands that manage files; Chapter 11 focuses on File commands for printing.

COMMAND MENUS IN PERSPECTIVE

In a grocery store, you needn't remember exactly where the oranges are located as long as you know generally where to find fruit. Similarly, you needn't remember the exact shelf where cottage cheese is displayed provided you recall that cottage cheese is a dairy product and that dairy products are stored in a case against a certain wall.

Similarly, when using Word you needn't remember where every command or option is located as long as you have a sense of how functions are grouped on each menu. When you want to do something but you don't know how to go about it, thinking about how the tasks fit into the menus might lead you to the proper menu and the proper command.

To this end, let's briefly consider each of the nine menus and the kinds of opportunities they offer.

File menu If you want to read or write a file on disk, chances are you need a File command. Similarly, if you want to print a file, look to this menu. Word itself is a file, and if you want to exit it you move to the bottom of this menu.

Edit menu To manipulate the content of your document, use the commands of the Edit menu. Actions tend to be simple, common, and useful, such as copying text from one location to another.

View menu To control how information is presented on the screen, look to the commands of the View menu.

Insert menu When you want to add a new element to your document, such as page numbers or an index, try the Insert menu.

Format menu Whereas the Edit menu gives you control over document content, the Format menu gives you say about document format—not what a document says, but how it looks.

Utilities menu Tools that help you get more out of Word but that are not necessarily central to the basic task of writing a document are collected on the Utilities menu.

Macro menu As its name implies, the Macro menu contains commands that let you record, write, modify, save, and run macros.

Window menu The Window menu is dedicated to letting you look at more than one thing at a time or to letting you choose between possibilities. In addition, the Window menu lists the names of all open windows.

Help menu When you want assistance right on your screen, the Help menu provides it. You can access Word's original Help or, if you purchase it separately, you can use the expanded replacement, MasterWord Help.

USING MENUS AND DIALOG BOXES

Although Word is a reasonably predictable tool, the following summary of menu and dialog-box conventions might prove helpful.

Using Menus

```
File  Edit  View  Insert  Format  Utilities  Macro  Window          Help
================================ Document1 ================================
```

To drop down a menu

- Point to the menu name with a mouse, and click the left mouse button.
- Press Alt or F10 to activate the menu bar. Then use either the accelerator keys or the direction keys to select and display a menu.

Each command on a drop down menu has accelerator keys too, as shown in this illustration of the View menu.

CHAPTER NINE: Introducing Commands   157

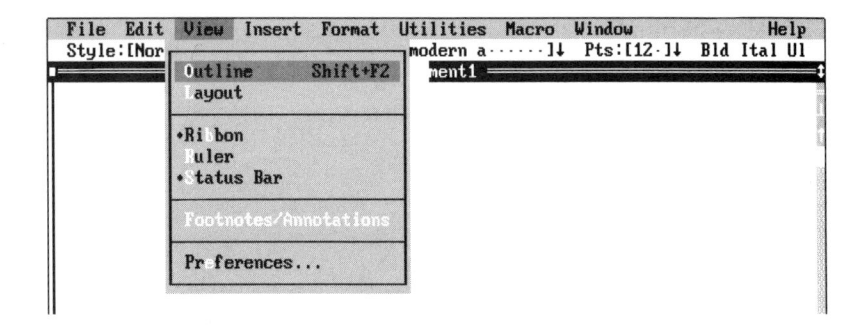

```
 File  Edit  View  Insert  Format  Utilities  Macro  Window         Help
 Style:[Nor                         modern a······]↓ Pts:[12·]↓ Bld Ital Ul
              Outline     Shift+F2  ment1
              Layout

             •Ribbon
              Ruler
             •Status Bar

              Footnotes/Annotations

              Preferences...
```

Note that the accelerator keys in the menu bar are not visible after a drop-down menu has appeared. This reminds you that any letters you press now will be treated as accelerator keys for choices from the drop-down menu, not for the main menu bar.

To select a command from a drop-down menu

- Point to the command name with a mouse, and click the left mouse button.
- Use the direction keys to highlight a command, and then press Enter to select it.
- Use a command-key shortcut if available.

Things to remember

- If a command is grayed or a different color than other names on the menu, it is considered "dimmed", and it isn't available for use.
- An ellipsis (...) following a command name indicates that the command leads to a dialog box.
- Some commands toggle a condition on and off. If a condition is on, a dot appears to the left of the command name. For example, in the illustration of the View menu, a dot appears beside the names *Ribbon* and *Status Bar*. This indicates that the ribbon and status bar are on (displayed on the screen). To turn them off, you simply choose either of these commands.

Using Dialog Boxes

Dialog boxes let you refine how powerful commands operate. You make your choices, and then you choose OK to put the command into effect. With a mouse, you choose OK by clicking on the OK button. With the keyboard, you typically press the Enter key.

Six kinds of choices in dialog boxes

Choices in dialog boxes are presented as a series of *fields,* which fall into six categories. Five of the six categories are exemplified by choices in the dialog box of the File Open command.

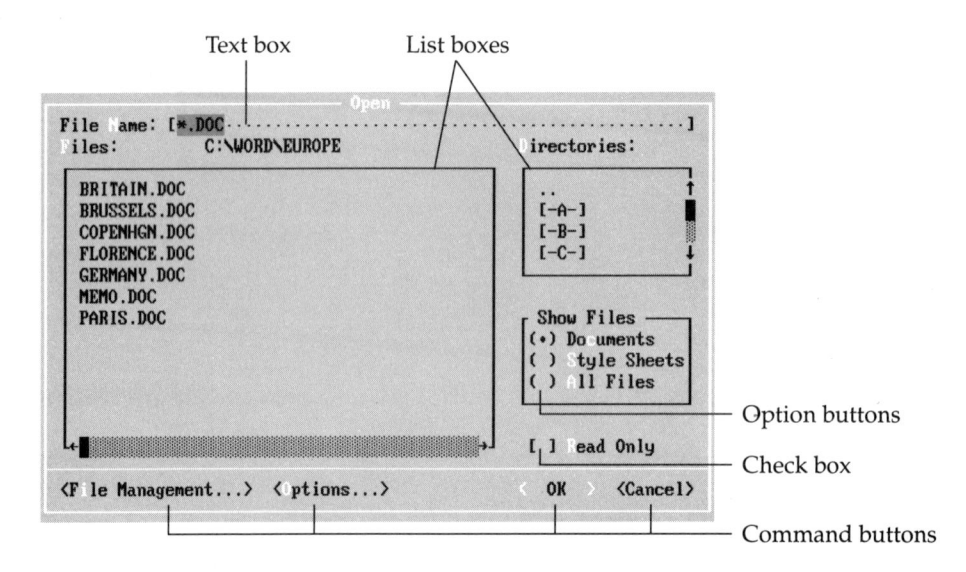

```
                    Text box        List boxes
                       │             │
                ┌──────┴──── Open ───┴──────────────────────┐
      File  ame: [*.DOC·····················................]
      F iles:        C:\WORD\EUROPE        D irectories:
                ┌───────────────────────┐  ┌──────────────┐
                │ BRITAIN.DOC           │  │ ..         ↑ │
                │ BRUSSELS.DOC          │  │ [-A-]        │
                │ COPENHGN.DOC          │  │ [-B-]        │
                │ FLORENCE.DOC          │  │ [-C-]      ↓ │
                │ GERMANY.DOC           │  └──────────────┘
                │ MEMO.DOC              │  ┌ Show Files ──┐
                │ PARIS.DOC             │  │ (•) Do uments│
                │                       │  │ ( ) S tyle Sheets
                │                       │  │ ( )  ll Files│
                │                       │  └──────────────┘ ──── Option buttons
                │                       │  [ ] R ead Only
                └←──────────────────→───┘                   ──── Check box
                <F ile Management...>  < ptions...>    <  OK  >  <Cancel>
                                                                          ──── Command buttons
```

An example of the sixth variety of field, the drop-down list, is contained in the File Print command's dialog box:

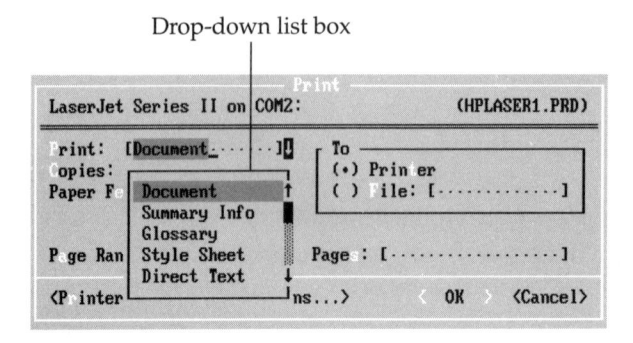

```
                  Drop-down list box
                           │
                ┌──────────┴─── Print ──────────────────────┐
                │ LaserJet Series II on COM2:    (HPLASER1.PRD)│
                │  P rint: [Document_·····]│ ┌ To ──────────┐ │
                │  C opies:                │ │ (•) Prin ter │ │
                │  Paper F┌──────────────┐ │ │ ( )  F ile: [............] │
                │         │ Document   ↑ │ │ └──────────────┘ │
                │         │ Summary Info │ │                  │
                │         │ Glossary     │ │                  │
                │  P ge Ran│ Style Sheet │ │ Page : [................] │
                │         │ Direct Text↓ │ │                  │
                │ <P inter└──────────────┘ ns...>  <  OK  > <Cancel> │
                └──────────────────────────────────────────┘
```

Here is a brief rundown on each of the six kinds of fields:

Text boxes You can type a choice into a text box. For example, you type a number into the Copies text box of the File Print command. Sometimes a text box is linked to a list box, so any choice made in the list box is automatically entered by Word into the text box. An example of this is the relationship between the File Name text box and the Files list box of the File Open dialog box.

List boxes A list box lets you make a choice from a finite group of alternatives. As just noted, a choice in a list box is sometimes also expressed in a text box. In other instances, choices made in list boxes are reflected only in the list box itself. An example is in the Printer Name list box of the File Printer Setup dialog box.

Drop-down list boxes This is a hybrid—part text box and part list box—that can be distinguished by the down arrow at its right end. You can type a choice into a drop-down list box, but only appropriate choices are accepted by Word. Alternatively, you can press the Up or the Down direction key to scroll through the list of acceptable choices. To see the list, you hold down the Alt key and press the Down direction key, which drops down the list. Or, with a mouse, click on the down arrow, and then click on your choice from the resulting list.

Option buttons When there are a few mutually exclusive choices, Word often presents them as a box filled with option buttons. To make a choice, either Tab to the box containing the option buttons and press the Spacebar until the one you want is selected or hold down the Alt key and press the accelerator key of the choice.

Check boxes Binary choices (yes/no or on/off) are made in check boxes. If the box has an X in it, it is set to "yes," or "on." To change the setting of a check box, press the Tab key to move to it, and then press the Spacebar. Or hold down the Alt key, and press the accelerator key of the choice.

Command buttons At the bottom of each dialog box are its command buttons. The OK button carries out the command in accordance with the choices made in the dialog box, and the Cancel button cancels the command. In addition, there might be other command buttons, their names followed by an ellipsis (...). Choosing one of these buttons takes you to another dialog box, where related choices are made. Sometimes, though not often, command buttons take you to the main dialog box of another command.

In this book, when a command button is to be pressed, its name is enclosed in parentheses. For example, File Open (Options) indicates that you should choose the Options command button in the File Open dialog box.

TIP

If you have a mouse, you can move freely among fields of a dialog box. Simply point and click.

If you use the keyboard, as I often do, press the Tab key to move from field to field. To move backwards, press Shift+Tab. To move directly to a field, hold down the Alt key and press the accelerator key of your choice.

Do not use the direction keys to move from choice to choice in a dialog box: You might inadvertently change a setting. If you do so by accident, simply press the Esc key to cancel the command and start again.

CHAPTER TEN

File Commands

After you've created a document or style sheet, what do you do with it? Give it a name, save it on disk, print it, or possibly delete it. For these and similar actions, you employ the commands of the File menu.

The File menu places commands into three groups, separated by horizontal lines.

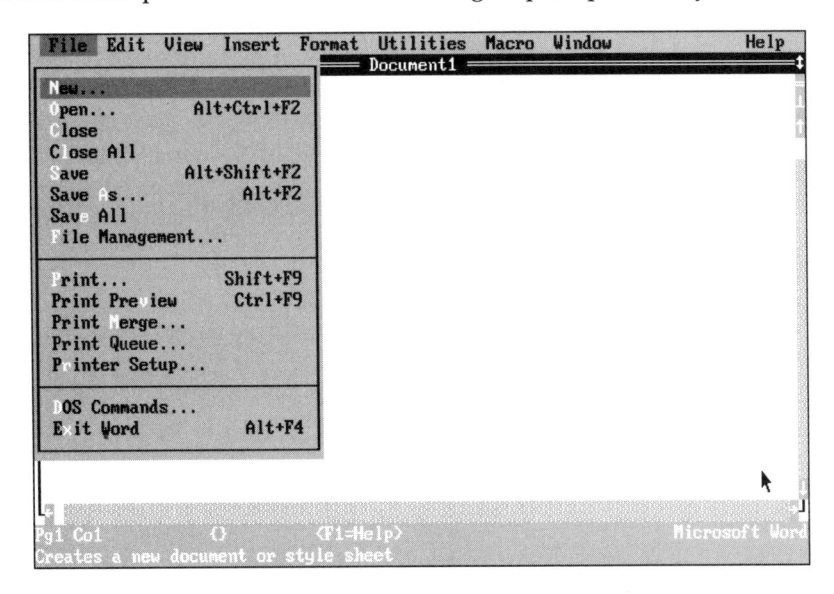

The eight commands of the first group, beginning with File New and ending with File File Management, permit you to transfer information between disk storage and your computer's active memory. You create, open, close, save, and find files through these commands, which are described in this chapter.

The second group has six commands—beginning with File Print and ending with File Printer Setup—that give you various ways to print your work or to see on screen how the work will appear after it is printed. These print commands are covered in the next chapter.

The third group has only two commands, File DOS Commands and File Exit Word. These commands let you suspend the operation of Word, either by setting the program aside in memory temporarily or by exiting altogether. (If you are running Word under the OS/2 operating system rather than under DOS, the command name that appears in the drop-down menu is File OS/2 Commands rather than File DOS Commands.) These two commands are covered in this chapter.

INTRODUCTION TO FILE COMMANDS

In summary form, here is what each File command covered in this chapter permits you to do:

File New—Creates a new document or style sheet and opens a new window to accommodate it.

File Open—Opens an existing document or style sheet.

File Close—Closes an existing window, including the document or style sheet it contains.

File Close All—Closes all windows and files.

File Save—Saves the current document or style sheet. If the file you propose to save does not have a name, Word switches you to the File Save As dialog box.

File Save As—Saves the current document or style sheet, pausing so that you can give it a name.

File Save All—Saves all documents and other files on disk, protecting them against loss and potentially freeing some memory.

File File Management—Creates a list of documents that meet criteria you specify. Permits you to open documents.

File DOS Commands—Lets you run an operating system command (such as Dir or Copy) or, if memory permits, another program—without actually exiting Word. If you are running Word under OS/2 instead of under DOS, this command will appear as FILE OS/2 Commands rather than as FILE DOS Commands.

File Exit Word—Quits Word. If documents or other files have been edited or changed but not saved on disk, Word alerts you with a message.

FILE NEW COMMAND

To start a new document or style sheet, use the File New command to create a blank window. The only time you needn't use the command to create a new document is when you start Word; a blank document window is placed on the screen whenever Word is started.

Run the command by pressing Alt+FN or simply Alt+F followed by Enter. The File New dialog box appears.

CHAPTER TEN: File Commands

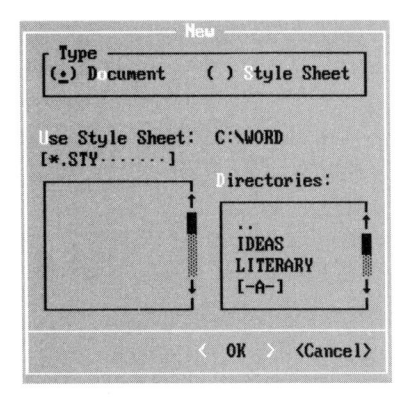

```
┌──────────────── New ────────────────┐
│ ┌─ Type ──────────────────────────┐ │
│ │ (•) Document    ( ) Style Sheet │ │
│ └─────────────────────────────────┘ │
│                                     │
│  Use Style Sheet:  C:\WORD          │
│  [*.STY······]                      │
│  ┌──────────┐  Directories:         │
│  │         ↑│  ┌──────────┐         │
│  │          │  │ ..      ↑│         │
│  │          │  │ IDEAS    │         │
│  │          │  │ LITERARY │         │
│  │         ↓│  │ [-A-]   ↓│         │
│  └──────────┘  └──────────┘         │
│                                     │
│           <  OK  >   <Cancel>       │
└─────────────────────────────────────┘
```

If you press Enter without making any choices in the dialog box, a blank document window is created that has no style sheet attached to it (other than the NORMAL style sheet). This might suit you most of the time.

Fields of the File New Dialog Box

The File New dialog box has four fields in addition to the OK and Cancel command buttons:

Type (option buttons) The choices are Document and Style Sheet, representing the two kinds of files that can be created with this command.

- **Document**—This is the default setting and will create a text file you can save in ASCII or RTF file format, as well as the Word document file format.
- **Style Sheet**—If you choose this option, the new file will be a style sheet, and the remaining three fields of the command—which are specific to new documents—will be irrelevant.

Use Style Sheet (text box) If you choose *Document* in the first field, you can use the Use Style Sheet field to indicate which style you want attached to the new document. The default choice is NORMAL.

Use Style Sheet (list box) The style sheets contained in the current directory are listed here.

Directories (list box) You can use this list box to choose a new current directory. For details on this dialog box, see the discussion near the end of this chapter.

NOTE: *For an exploration of the relationship of documents to windows, see both Concept 11 in Chapter 2 and the beginning of Chapter 4.*

FILE OPEN COMMAND

Use the File Open command to load an existing document, a style sheet, or another file from a disk. The command opens a new window, containing the desired file. If you want to replace an existing document (or another file) on screen with one from disk, first use the File Close or the Window Close command to remove the existing file, and then use File Open.

The command can also be used to change which directory is current.

Run the File Open command by pressing Alt+FO or Alt+Ctrl+F2 or Ctrl+F12. This dialog box appears:

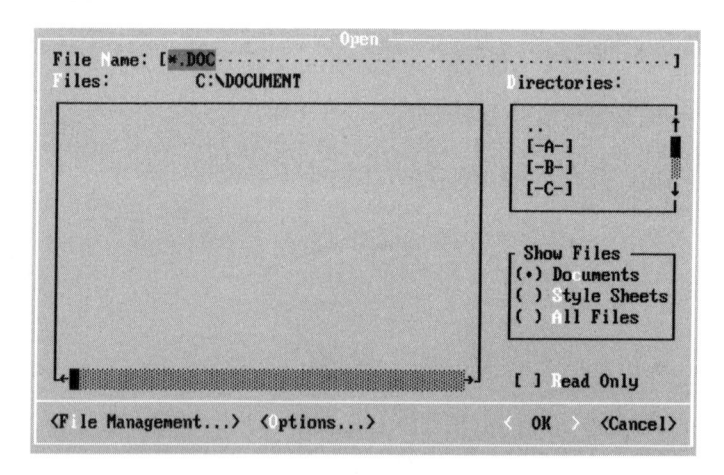

```
┌─────────────────────────── Open ───────────────────────────┐
│ File Name: [*.DOC.........................................]│
│ Files:         C:\DOCUMENT              Directories:       │
│ ┌─────────────────────────────────┐   ┌──────────────┐    │
│ │                                 │   │ ..        ↑  │    │
│ │                                 │   │ [-A-]        │    │
│ │                                 │   │ [-B-]        │    │
│ │                                 │   │ [-C-]     ↓  │    │
│ │                                 │   └──────────────┘    │
│ │                                 │                        │
│ │                                 │   ┌─ Show Files ──┐   │
│ │                                 │   │ (•) Documents │   │
│ │                                 │   │ ( ) Style Sheets│ │
│ │                                 │   │ ( ) All Files │   │
│ │                                 │   └───────────────┘   │
│ └─────────────────────────────────┘                        │
│                                         [ ] Read Only      │
│  <File Management...>  <Options...>    <  OK  >  <Cancel>  │
└────────────────────────────────────────────────────────────┘
```

NOTE: *You can load a document without using this dialog box, but only at the time you start Word. Type* word, *followed by a drive and pathname if appropriate, and the name of the document. For example, at the A or C prompt, you could type* word park *or* word letters\park *to load a document called PARK. To start Word and simultaneously load the document that was in use when you quit the previous editing session, type* word/l.

Fields of the File Open Dialog Box

The File Open dialog box has seven fields in addition to its OK and Cancel command buttons:

File Name (text box) Type the name of a document, a style sheet, or other file you want to open. Word will load the file from the current directory, which is the directory listed on the line below the File Name field. To open a file from a directory other than the current one, type its pathname as well as its filename. (In other words, if you want to load the file called BREAD.DOC from the BAKERY directory of the C drive, type *C:\BAKERY\BREAD*, and press Enter.) You do not need to type the filename extension .DOC, provided the Show Files field is set to Documents.

If you type a full pathname in this way, the identity of the current directory will not change. On the other hand, if you type a pathname without typing the name of a specific file, pressing Enter (or choosing OK) changes the current directory. The contents of the new directory then appear in the Files list box.

Whether you type a pathname or rely exclusively on files in the current directory, you can always use the wildcard characters ? and * in the File Name text box. This is a simple system of pattern matching, in which the question mark represents any single character, and the asterisk represents a series of one or more characters. For example, if you type *L?V**, you might see the filenames LOVE.DOC, LOVE.BAK, LIVING.DOC, and LIVING.BAK because in each the first letter is L, the second letter is any character, the third letter is V, and the remaining characters can be anything. If you type *L?V*.DOC*, you would see only the files LOVE.DOC and LIVING.DOC. If you type *?IV*.DOC*, you might see GIVE.DOC and JIVEMAN.DOC as well as LIVING.DOC.

If you're loading a file that does not have an extension, type a period after the filename.

Files (list box) A list of all files that meet the specifications of the File Name text box are presented in this list box. To choose one, highlight its name and press Enter, or double-click on its name with the mouse.

Directories (list box) Use this list box to choose a new current directory. For details on this dialog box, see the discussion at the end of the chapter.

Show Files (option buttons) This field lets you set the contents of the Files list box:

- **Documents**—List only files that have the extension .DOC
- **Style Sheets**—List only files that have the extension .STY
- **All Files**—List all files, regardless of extension

Read Only (check box) Turning on the Read Only option (placing an X in the Read Only check box) protects the file you open from any changes. This prevents you from accidentally changing a document or style sheet that you want only to read or that you want to save with a different name if you do modify it.

When you load a read-only file, you can edit it as much as you want, but Word will not allow you to save the changed version under the original filename. To save the changed document, type a new filename in the File Name text box of the File Save As dialog box.

> NOTE: *Word also considers files to be read only if they are currently in use by someone else on a network or if the DOS file attribute called* Read Only *has been set to* Yes *for the file.*

File Management (command button) This button takes you to the File Management dialog box. This is equivalent to choosing the File File Management command. See the description of the File File Management command later in this chapter.

Options (command button) This button takes you to the File Options dialog box, which stores the name of a directory and gives you an easy way to use documents or other files from that directory. The directory is remembered from one editing session to another (because it is stored in Word's MW.INI file) and is not changed by actions you take with other commands.

Most significantly, you can force Word to always treat the directory listed in this dialog box as Word's default (current) directory. (This is particularly useful for users who are accustomed to earlier versions of Word, because in these earlier incarnations Word was as reticent to change directories as it is now eager.) If you want Word to stick with a certain directory, simply specify it in this dialog box and check the Always Use as Default check box.

The File Options dialog box looks like this:

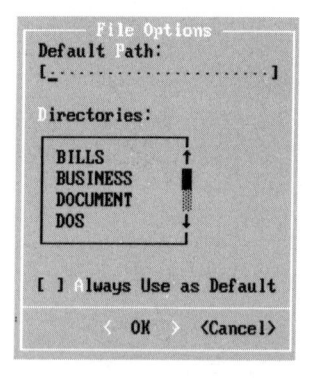

```
┌─────── File Options ────────┐
│ Default Path:               │
│ [_.......................]  │
│                             │
│ Directories:                │
│  ┌──────────────┐           │
│  │ BILLS      ↑ │           │
│  │ BUSINESS   ▓ │           │
│  │ DOCUMENT   ▒ │           │
│  │ DOS        ↓ │           │
│  └──────────────┘           │
│                             │
│ [ ] Always Use as Default   │
│                             │
│      < OK >    <Cancel>     │
└─────────────────────────────┘
```

Let's consider the elements in this dialog box one at a time.

Default Path (text box) Although the text box is labeled *Default path*, it is guaranteed to be the default only if the Always Use as Default check box is checked. This text box is, however, where you specify the directory that you want remembered.

To change the default drive or directory, type the letter of the drive you want, followed by a colon, followed by the pathname (if appropriate) in the Default Path field. Alternatively, use the Directories list box to choose a directory.

Directories (list box) In this instance, the Directories list box does not necessarily change which directory is current. Rather, this Directories list box gives you a way to specify which directory will appear in the Default Path text box, discussed above.

Always Use as Default (check box) This check box lets you indicate whether you want the directory listed in the Default Path text field to, in fact, be the default (current) directory.

There are at least three useful ways to employ the File Options dialog box.

The first is to store in it the name of a directory that you frequently use to save documents. We might call this your favorite directory. Whenever you want to make your favorite directory the current directory, merely choose the File Options dialog box and press Enter, or click on the OK button.

A second way to use the File Options dialog box is to choose it and immediately press the Del key, thereby eliminating from the Default Path list box the name of whichever directory was listed in it. Then, when you press Enter or choose OK, Word removes the dialog box from the screen and (although unseen by you) fills in its Default Path text box with the name of Word's *start-up directory*—the directory that was current at the time Word was started. (An exception is noted in the next paragraph.) This gives you a way, with only a few keystrokes, to get back to the directory in which you started working with Word.

NETWORK NOTE: *If you are running Word on a network or for another reason have stored a directory name in an environment variable called MSWNET55, Word behaves a little differently. Rather than filling in the Default Path text box with the name of your start-up directory, Word will fill it in with the name of whichever directory is listed in the MSWNET55 environment variable. Typically, this directory is the one dedicated to Word files on your local workstation (as opposed to the Word program directory on the network server).*

A third way to use the File Options dialog box is to choose a single directory from which you want to work, type it into the Default Path text box, and then turn on its Always Use as Default check box. Having done this, Word will keep it the current directory regardless of other actions you might take.

FILE CLOSE COMMAND

Use this command to close a document and its window.

To choose the File Close command, press Alt+FC. The command is carried out immediately; no dialog box appears. Alternatively, you can click with a mouse on the window close icon, which is the solid box at the left end of a window's title bar.

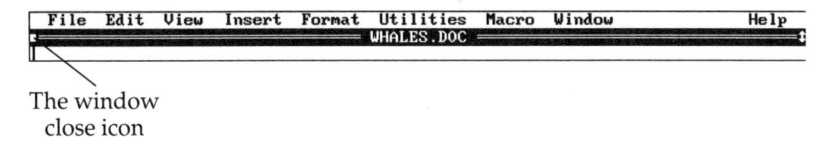

```
 File   Edit   View   Insert   Format   Utilities   Macro   Window              Help
                                      WHALES.DOC
```

The window
   close icon

Unlike earlier versions of Word, which allowed you to clear a window and then load a new document into it, Word 5.5 considers a document and the window containing the document almost inseparable conceptually. You cannot remove a file from a window; you can only close the window. (See Concept 11 in Chapter 2.)

For most purposes, the File Close and Window Close commands are identical. The difference comes when you have the same document or other file open in two windows simultaneously; the File Close command closes both windows at the same time, whereas the Window Close command closes only the active window.

When you use the File Close command, you might encounter the message, *Do you want to save changes to* filename? (Word supplies the name of a file in place of *filename*.)

This indicates there are unsaved editing changes to the file. Any change to a document since it was last saved will cause Word to display this warning. Even printing the document is considered an editing change if it involves a repagination. Choose Yes to save the editing changes and complete the command, No to lose the changes and complete the command, or Cancel (or press Esc) to cancel the command.

The same message appears if you have made changes to a document's style sheet. The message is not necessarily displayed when you close the window containing the style sheet; instead, it might appear when you close the document that is formatted by the style sheet or when you close the help window.

FILE CLOSE ALL COMMAND

This command gives you a fresh start. It closes all text and style sheet windows and removes from memory all style sheets or glossaries except those named NORMAL. It is equivalent to quitting Word and starting it again, except that restarting Word causes a blank Document 1 to be displayed in a window; the Close All command displays no window.

To run the command, press Alt+FL. It executes immediately; no dialog box appears. If there are unsaved editing changes in any files, the command gives you a chance to save the changes on disk. (See the discussion of the message for the File Close command.)

FILE SAVE COMMAND

The File Save command lets you store an updated copy of a document on disk. Unless you're using the autosave feature of the Utilities Customize command to protect your work periodically, you should use File Save frequently—at least every half hour or so. And even if you do use autosave, you're better off doing a conventional save because it frees memory in a way that an autosave cannot.

Choose the File Save command by pressing Alt+FS or Alt+Shift+F2 or Shift+F12. If the document or other file has been saved before and thus has a name, the command executes immediately. Otherwise, Word transfers you to the File Save As command so that you can choose a name and format for the new file.

When you save a document, Word does the following behind the scenes: deletes any existing backup (.BAK) version of the document; renames the existing .DOC version on disk, making it the backup (with the extension .BAK); and saves the newly edited version of the document, giving it the extension .DOC. In this way, the .DOC version is the most recently modified, and the .BAK version is the most recent backup.

The only messages you are likely to encounter with the File Save command relate to disks that are full or files that are marked *read only*. If a disk is full, use the File File Management command's Delete button to remove unneeded files. If a file is marked *read only*, use the File Save As command and save it under a different name, thereby leaving the read-only version in its original form.

FILE SAVE AS COMMAND

The first time you save a document or other file, you must give it a name and choose a file format for it. Optionally, you can also fill in summary information, in which you describe the document in one or more ways. Storing a file for the first time, choosing a name and a format for it, and filling in summary information for it are all tasks accomplished with the File Save As command.

Choose the command by pressing Alt+FA, Alt+F2, or F12. If a file has never been saved before, use the File Save command (Alt+FS, Alt+Shift+F2, or Shift+F12), which also takes you to the File Save As dialog box, shown here:

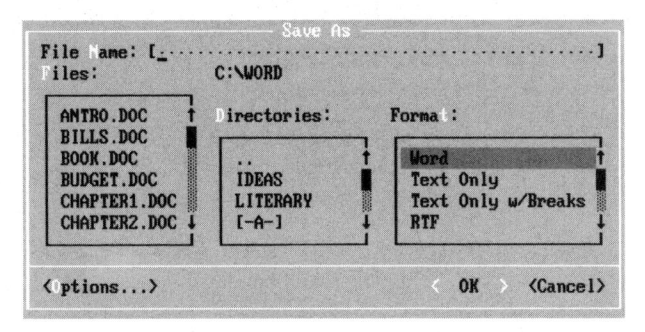

```
─────────────────────── Save As ───────────────────────
File Name: [_·················································]
Files:         C:\WORD

ANTRO.DOC    ↑  Directories:    Format:
BILLS.DOC
BOOK.DOC                         Word              ↑
BUDGET.DOC      ..          ↑    Text Only
CHAPTER1.DOC    IDEAS            Text Only w/Breaks
CHAPTER2.DOC ↓  LITERARY    ↓    RTF
                [-A-]

< Options...>                       <  OK  >  <Cancel>
```

Most of the time, you will simply type a name for the file and press the Enter key, thereby saving the document or style sheet in the current directory in Word format. (To save the third kind of Word file, a glossary file, you use the Save command buttons of the Edit Glossary or Macro Edit command.)

Generally this command is used only once for each document—the first time it is saved. Subsequently, you use the File Save command. However, the File Save As command is one means of creating a duplicate copy of a file. Use the command to save a file under a new name; the original version remains on disk with its original name and contents. This is helpful if you have a letter or another document that you use repeatedly in different forms. You can save it any number of times with different names and modify the individual copies as needed.

Fields of the File Save As Dialog Box

The File Save As dialog box has five fields in addition to the OK and Cancel command buttons.

File Name (text box) Type in a name of up to eight letters, and press the Enter key. Optionally, you can add a period and a filename extension of your own, but this isn't recommended. (Include a filename extension when you want Word to use an extension other than .DOC for a document or .STY for a style sheet.) You can type the name of an existing file that's saved on disk if you want; Word will overwrite the file on disk with the new one.

NOTE: *If you want to store the file somewhere other than in the current directory, type a pathname for your file. (The identity of the current directory is listed on the line just below the File Name field.)*

Files (list box) This field lists the existing files in the directory. To give a new file the same name as an existing file, thereby overwriting the existing version, highlight the name and press Enter, or double-click on the name with the mouse.

Directories (list box) You can use this list box to choose a new current directory. For details, see the discussion at the end of the chapter.

Format (list box) Word lets you save a document in any of four formats: Word, Text Only, Text Only w/Breaks, and RTF. Generally, you'll want to stick with the default format (Word). However, on occasion you might want to use the other formats, described in the next section.

Options (command button) This button takes you to the File Options dialog box, where you can choose a new current directory. For details, see the discussion earlier in this chapter regarding the Options button in the File Open dialog box.

Choosing a File Format

When you save a document, it generally is stored in Word format, a proprietary code that combines information about content and format. A fair amount of Word's power, including its ability to do such things as let you instantly center every line of a 200-page document, stems from its file format and specifically from the way that information about document formatting is stored.

If you want to see what this format looks like when unfiltered by Word, use the DOS Type command: At the DOS prompt, type the command *Type* followed by the full name of a Word file, including the .DOC extension, and press Enter. The document will scroll by the screen—first a short section that contains overview information and then the text of the document followed by the coding that stores all the document's formatting.

Word format is ideal when you are storing and retrieving documents, but sometimes programs other than Word must read files you save with Word. For these occasions, you can use three additional file formats: Text Only, Text Only w/Breaks, and RTF.

Text Only The Text Only format enables you to save a Word document as an unformatted ASCII file. ASCII, an acronym for American Standard Code for Information Interchange, is a coding scheme that assigns standardized values to alphabetic and numeric characters, punctuation marks, and certain other keys (such as Tab). Virtually all microcomputer programs can read and write ASCII files, making this format nearly universal in terms of giving portability to your files.

ASCII has drawbacks, however. Precisely because it is such a generic coding scheme, there is much it cannot communicate. Sophisticated programs rely on more than *ABC* and *123* to give form to their files. Word, for example, adds formatting information to a document—invisible coding that tells it when to italicize a word, indent a paragraph, and so on. Such coding tends to be program-specific: Word understands its own code for italics, but another word processor might not. In preparing a Word file for use with another program, one must know whether the program can accept the file. By choosing to store and transmit your document as an ASCII file, you virtually guarantee that the content will be communicated ("It's a beautiful day"). But you lose the formatting ("It's a *beautiful* day").

By choosing the Text Only format, you create a file containing only the printable characters of your document plus the carriage return and line feed that end each paragraph. This format works well if your paragraphs are less than a line long or if the program with which you are going to use the file doesn't need the ends of lines specifically indicated. For example, you might employ Text Only to store files you intend to transmit as messages on certain electronic mail systems or for computer programs.

Using Text Only retains tab characters rather than converting them to spaces; but paragraph indents, side-by-side and column layouts, and running-head formatting disappear, making all paragraphs plain text. Because Word does not insert a line break at the end of each line, a file saved with the Text Only option is easier to clean up and reformat as a word-processing file than is a Text Only w/Breaks file.

Text Only w/Breaks This, too, is an ASCII file, but it includes a line feed and carriage return (the two components of a paragraph mark) at the end of each line. It also transforms each tab character and paragraph indent into an equivalent number of Spacebar spaces; in essence, your document becomes a space-by-space, character-by-character image of the original. It's useful in producing a copy with more or less the same layout as the original document but without formatting.

Because of the way Word adds line breaks to a file, the Text Only w/Breaks option preserves the layout of documents you format for multiple columns with the Format Section command but does not preserve the layout of multiple columns created with side-by-side paragraph formatting.

Before saving a file in the Text Only w/Breaks format, you might need to ensure that lines in your document are of an acceptable width. You can decrease the page's line width by decreasing the Format Margin command's Width field, increasing its Left and Right fields, or both. Conversely, you can increase line width by increasing the setting in the Width field or decreasing the settings in the Left and Right fields. If you stick with Word's default page width of 8.5 inches and left and right margins of 1.25 inches each, the result is a printable line width of 6 inches, which translates to 60 characters in the default 10-characters-to-the-inch font size.

If you use Save As with Format set to Text Only w/Breaks and discover an unwanted paragraph mark (or other symbol) at the end of every line, use File Save with Format set to Text Only instead.

If you don't know which ASCII format the receiving program expects, you might try saving your Word file both ways. Bear in mind that certain features—such as automatically numbered footnote reference marks and the glossary entries *Page,*

Dateprint, and *Timeprint*—do not carry over into the ASCII version as you might expect. In Text Only format, they remain in your document as solid rectangles, happy faces, hearts, or other such characters. In Text Only w/Breaks, footnote references are carried over; *Page, Dateprint,* and *Timeprint* are converted to the current page number, date, or time and then saved.

> NOTE: *If you're using a telecommunications program to send a Word document by telephone or through a network to a receiving computer that doesn't use Word, the software at the receiving end—not the telecommunications software—determines what form the Word file needs to take.*

RTF The final choice is RTF. This is a hybrid format in that it is an ASCII file and yet preserves all document formatting (including references to a style sheet). It accomplishes this by translating Word's coding into equivalent ASCII codes that can be read and interpreted by any other program designed to understand RTF. Virtually every Microsoft word processor, and some other word processors, read and write RTF. You, however, might not understand an RTF file because a document containing much formatting is typically cluttered with coding.

Filling in Summary Information

Unless you've turned off the Prompt for Summary Info check box of the Utilities Customize command, Word displays a summary sheet each time you save a Word document or a style sheet. This is what a blank summary sheet looks like for a document named *WINDTIME*:

```
──────────── Summary for WINDTIME.DOC ────────────
 itle:      [................................................]
 uthor:     [................................................]
 perator:   [................................................]
 eywords:   [................................................]
 omments:   [................................................]

 ersion Number: [..........]
 Date C eated:   [05/07/1991·]
 Date  aved:     [05/07/1991·]

                              <  OK  >    <Cancel>
```

The dates are filled in by Word, although you can change them. After you fill in some or all of these fields and press OK (or Enter), summary information is attached to your document.

Fields of summary information

To fill in the text-box fields of a file's summary sheet, you press Tab to move from one text box to another, or you click on a desired field with the mouse. These are the fields:

Title *(text box)* Type a title for your document in this field. This provides an easy way to identify the contents of a document more fully than you can with a filename.

CHAPTER TEN: File Commands

You can use up to 40 characters, including spaces and punctuation. For example, if a filename is WINDTIME, the title in the summary information could be *Wind Direction and Airline Travel Time*. Or, if the document is one of several that will be combined to create a larger document, you might want to identify it as something such as *Watershed Dam Proposal; Sect. 6, Equip*. The title is for your convenience rather than Word's because it is not one of the fields you can search by using the File File Management command and then choosing the Search button.

Author (text box) Identify the author(s) of the document in this field. Because the limit is 40 characters, you can include more than an author's name; for example, *Milton (sect 1-4) Eliot (sect 5-9)*. Even though you include such extra information, Word can manage to find any author's name in a search.

Operator (text box) If documents are word processed or handled by someone other than the author, identify the person in this field. The limit is 40 characters.

Keywords (text box) Type as many keywords as you want in this field, up to 80 characters. You can separate keywords with spaces or with punctuation marks such as commas or semicolons.

Comments (text box) Type your comments in this field. Word accepts up to 256 characters. As with the Keywords field, when you reach the limit, Word simply stops responding to your keystrokes. If you run out of space, edit what you have written or press Enter to cause Word to record your first 256 characters.

Version number (text box) Type up to 10 characters to distinguish between the first and subsequent versions of a document.

Date Created (text box) Word always records the date of creation, even if you have the Prompt for Summary Info check box of the Utilities Customize command turned off. If the check box is on and you save a new document or style sheet, Word proposes the current date as the date of creation and uses whatever date format you specified with the Utilities Customize command. If you must type a date—for example, because your computer does not keep the date current—use the same format Word is using. You can separate elements with hyphens instead of slashes, and you can omit the zero in front of single-digit month numbers, but otherwise you must follow Word's lead. Thus, if Word displayed May 7, 1991, as *05/07/91*, you could type the date as *5/7/91* or *5-7-91* but not as *5/7/1991, 7/5/91* or *7 May 91*.

Date Saved (text box) Just as it automatically logs the date of creation, Word always changes the date of revision whenever you resave an existing document. When you save a new document, the revision date Word displays is the same as the creation date. Type a different date if necessary, but follow the format Word uses.

Here is an example of a completed summary sheet:

```
┌─ Summary for WINDTIME.DOC ─────────────────┐
│  Title:    [Wind Direction and Airline Travel Time···] │
│  Author:   [Anne Ribardiere······················]     │
│  Operator: [Z. Frenchy···························]     │
│  Keywords: [navigation,training,OAG,speed········]     │
│  Comments: [for Travel Time Today magazine·······]     │
│                                                         │
│  Version Number: [1··········]                          │
│  Date Created:   [05/07/1991·]                          │
│  Date Saved:     [05/09/1991·]                          │
│                                                         │
│                              < OK >   <Cancel>          │
└─────────────────────────────────────────────────────────┘

When you press the Enter key or click the mouse on OK to complete the save, Word stores the summary information on disk with the file and, as part of its routine, records the number of text characters in the document. You see this number whenever you print, update, or view summary information with the File File Management command. (The number of characters Word reports is a more accurate indicator of apparent document size than the number of bytes of file size reported by your operating system, because Word's count excludes formatting characters and other codes as well as any bytes of disk space that are reserved for but not used by the file.)

## FILE SAVE ALL COMMAND

As its name implies, the File Save All command saves all current files on disk. This means you can, in one step, save a document, its style sheet, and your glossary.

Choose the command by pressing Alt+FE. Word carries out the command immediately, displaying the message *Saving...* followed by the path and filename of each file (document, style sheet, or glossary) that contains unsaved changes.

If the document you are saving has not yet been given a filename, Word displays the File Save As dialog box to request a filename. Unless they've been saved under a different name, style sheets are saved to NORMAL.STY, and glossaries are saved to NORMAL.GLY.

This is a convenient command, but be wary of it when you've made provisional changes to several documents or when you've made provisional or temporary changes to the glossary. File Save All saves *everything* in its current form, erasing the former versions on disk. (Versions of documents on disk become backup files, however, with the .BAK extension.)

## FILE FILE MANAGEMENT COMMAND

In some senses, Word's File File Management command is a sophisticated version of the File Open command. Either command can open a document on your screen; the difference is in how much preliminary assistance the File File Management command can give you in locating the file you want to open.

Word compiles a small database of information about each document; this database is called a *summary sheet* or *summary information*.
```

CHAPTER TEN: File Commands

The database contains one record of summary information for each document you create. Each record has several fields, and although Word fills in the creation date and most-recent save date of the document, you fill in the other fields yourself. You can fill in a document's title, author, word-processing operator, keywords, and comments. Word lets you search based on any of these criteria and will build a list of qualifying documents and style sheets. Word can search for files that meet combination tests, such as those written by a certain author and after a certain date. You can even exclude certain documents that would otherwise match your criteria. Although you don't word your request so conversationally, you can say "Show me the names of all documents written by Nguyen and Juarez except those related to farm policies." You can tell Word to list only those documents that match this *or* that, this *and* that, or this *but not* that—or only those documents created or modified *earlier than* or *later than* a given date.

Earlier versions of Word called this feature *document retrieval*, whereas Word 5.5 gives it the somewhat more encompassing title of *file management*. Either way, the main purpose is to give you a broad spectrum of ways to locate and open desired files.

With file management, you can also

- Mark a group of files for a subsequent action.
- Copy a file or a group of marked files to a different disk or directory. At your option, Word will check the documents for the names of their style sheets and copy the style sheets too.
- Delete a group of files. (When used with the copy feature, this amounts to a Move command because that's what you accomplish by copying a group of files to a new location and then deleting them from their original location.)

Despite these bonuses, the main feature remains document retrieval. The role of file management is often clearer if you think of your documents as books in a library and summary sheets as cards in the library's catalog.

To find something in a library, you either browse or systematically search for a particular title or topic. Indeed, browsing is what most people do with their directories of Word documents; they look through the lists of titles, recalling with greater or lesser precision the location of files. In a library, a card catalog (or its electronic equivalent) is the way you move beyond browsing to purposeful, effective searching; with Word, you use the File File Management command to achieve the same result.

The Word-based equivalent of an individual card in the catalog is a document's summary information.

Filling in Summary Information

The first step is filling in summary information, a process described in the chapter's discussion of the File Save As command. It's good to get in the habit of providing at least a little bit of information whenever you use the File Save As command. The payoff comes as soon as you want to find a file.

If you can persuade yourself to provide thorough information, so much the better. This is especially true when documents must be shared among people on a network. In such circumstances, an effective system of file tracking is particularly valuable.

Suppose, for example, you often share document files with coworkers, and you prefer to save typing time by using your first and last initials to identify yourself as the author of a document. That's fine, unless someone else uses the same initials for the same purpose. By ensuring that everyone uses a unique name, you enhance Word's ability to compile a list of all your documents.

Uniqueness is useful in keywords, too. If you call your company *ABC* and someone else calls it *Aardvark Bedding Corporation,* you'll have to check for both names whenever you search for documents relating to the company.

Where version numbers are concerned, think not only about how you want to number (and date) revisions but about where you want to indicate that a document has been revised. Should the reviser's name replace the author's in the summary information? Should the version number be changed as well as the revision date? Or should revision information be limited to the date (which Word updates when an existing document is resaved), with a descriptive comment added to the summary information?

Let's assume that you've accumulated documents that have summary information and that you're ready to try out Word's document-retrieval and other file-management capabilities. You begin by choosing the File File Management command (Alt+FF), which causes a large dialog box to appear:

```
┌─────────────────────── File Management ───────────────────────┐
 Sorted by: Directory      View: Short         [ ] Open as Read Only
   Path(s): C:\DOCS C:\BILLS
 Files:
    ┌──────────────────────────────────────────────────────────┐
    │ C:\BILLS\DOCTOR.DOC          C:\DOCS\CHAPTER3.DOC        │
    │ C:\BILLS\PAPER.DOC          *C:\DOCS\COWORKER.DOC        │
    │*C:\BILLS\TOO_MANY.DOC        C:\DOCS\DISKLIST.DOC        │
    │ C:\BILLS\TRAVEL.DOC          C:\DOCS\DOCUMENT.DOC        │
    │ C:\DOCS\ANTRO.DOC            C:\DOCS\DOLPHINS.DOC        │
    │ C:\DOCS\BILLS.DOC           *C:\DOCS\EXCUSE.DOC          │
    │ C:\DOCS\BOOK.DOC            *C:\DOCS\FRIENDS.DOC         │
    │*C:\DOCS\BUDGET.DOC           C:\DOCS\JOBS.DOC            │
    │ C:\DOCS\CHAPTER1.DOC         C:\DOCS\LAWYER.DOC          │
    │ C:\DOCS\CHAPTER2.DOC         C:\DOCS\LIST.DOC            │
    └──────────────────────────────────────────────────────────┘
   <Search...>   <Options...>  <Delete...>  <Copy...>
   <Summary...>  <Print...>    <Rename...>  <Open>        <Close>
```

The files displayed initially are those in a list created the last time you used the File File Management command. This list might be composed of files from more than one directory, as in the example screen. If you have not used the command before, the files displayed are documents from your current directory.

Word generally lists the files it finds in the two columns in the main portion of the screen. In the case of the example screen, the line at the top of the dialog box indicates

CHAPTER TEN: File Commands 177

that the files are sorted first by directory, meaning that all the files of one directory are listed before the files of the next directory. The line also says that the view is *Short*, meaning that little information is given about each listed document. The next line down, labeled *Path(s)*, shows the directory or directories containing the files listed in the large list box. All of these values can be changed through the collection of command buttons at the bottom of the screen.

Marking Files from the List

Before examining each command button, let's consider the two other fields contained in the File File Management's main dialog box.

Open as Read Only (check box) Check this box if you want to limit any documents you open to read-only status, meaning you cannot make any changes to them. You might choose this if you want to guarantee you will not make accidental changes or if you want to leave the file available for someone else on a network to open.

Files (list box) This list names each file that met the criteria of the last search conducted by the File File Management command in this or a previous Word session. If the command has never been used or if the MW.INI file has been deleted, the Files list box contains the names of all documents from the current directory. (The MW.INI file is Word's "memory" between editing sessions. If deleted, Word reverts to its default settings.)

A singular feature of this Files list box is that you can use it to mark files, thereby narrowing the list of places that Word searches.

To mark or unmark a file, highlight its name and press the Spacebar. To mark or unmark all files at the same time, press Ctrl+Spacebar. When a file is marked, an asterisk appears before its name. (The sample illustration on the next page includes several marked files.)

> NOTE: *Marking a file has no effect unless the Selected Files Only check box in the Search dialog box of the File File Management command is checked.*

How do you use file marking to your advantage?

Imagine you are looking for a particular document but can't remember its name. You ask Word to list documents that meet certain general criteria so that you can conduct a more thorough examination of each. But when you see the list, you recognize several that you know are not the one you seek. Rather than having Word search through all of them anyway, you mark the ones that you want Word to search and then turn on the Search dialog box's Selected Files Only check box. All unmarked files are ignored in any subsequent searches.

Making Choices with Buttons

Across the bottom of the File File Management dialog box are a series of buttons, all but three of which lead to other dialog boxes. Through these buttons and from these dialog boxes, you can exert the most control over Word's file-management feature.

The buttons that lead to dialog boxes each have an ellipsis (...) after their names and are titled Search, Summary, Options, Print, Rename, and Copy. Two of the remaining three buttons are Open and Close—although they don't refer to opening and closing the same thing: The Open button tells Word to open the selected document, the Close button means close this dialog box. The third button is Delete, which has an ellipsis but doesn't really take you to a dialog box; instead, it uses a message box and asks you to confirm that you want to delete the selected file(s).

Search dialog box

Use the Search dialog box to tell Word what to search for and where to search.

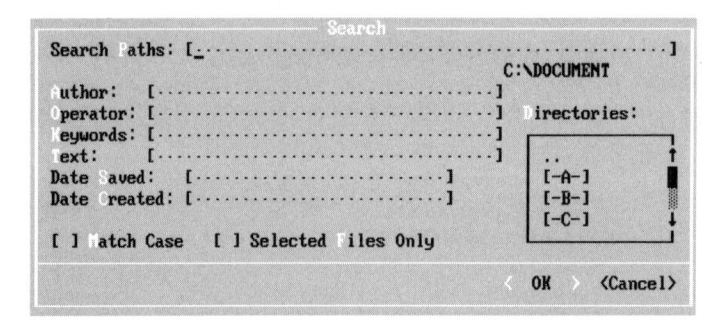

```
┌─────────────────────────── Search ───────────────────────────┐
│  Search Paths: [_····················································]│
│                                          C:\DOCUMENT         │
│  Author:    [·····························]                  │
│  Operator:  [·····························] Directories:     │
│  Keywords:  [·····························] ┌──────────────┐ │
│  Text:      [·····························] │ ..         ↑ │ │
│  Date Saved:   [······················]     │ [-A-]        │ │
│  Date Created: [······················]     │ [-B-]        │ │
│                                              │ [-C-]      ↓ │ │
│  [ ] Match Case   [ ] Selected Files Only   └──────────────┘ │
│                                                              │
│                                        <  OK  >  <Cancel>    │
└──────────────────────────────────────────────────────────────┘
```

The Search dialog box has 10 fields.

Search Paths (text box) Use this field to specify the drives and directories Word is to search. Type one or more paths, separating them with spaces or commas, up to 128 characters. For example, type *c:\proj,c:\biz\91* to search documents that appear in the PROJ directory of the C drive or in the 91 subdirectory of the BIZ directory of the C drive.

If you have a mouse, clicking on the name of the current directory (displayed above the Directories list box) causes it to be appended to the list of directories on the search path.

Word searches only those documents stored on disk. It does not search documents that contain unsaved changes; consequently, you must save any documents that are open if you want them to be searched.

Nor will Word search any directories other than those you explicitly specify. However, the utility MasterWord Seek will search any or all directories of a hard disk to find Word documents or other files that meet your criteria, and if you want, it will feed its results directly to the Search Paths list box. (MasterWord Seek is one part of MasterWord, optional companion programs to Microsoft Word and this book.)

Author, Operator, Keywords, Date Saved, and Date Created (text boxes) These five text boxes correspond to entries in the summary information. By filling in values for any combination of these fields, you tell Word what to look for in the summary information. To further refine the search, you can use wildcards or enter more than one item per field, provided you separate each with a logical operator.

CHAPTER TEN: File Commands 179

The five logical operators are summarized in the following table:

Operator	Name	Meaning
,	OR	"This *or* that"; for example, *Anders,Anderson,Andersen* would mean "Match Anders or Anderson or Andersen"—that is, at least one of these.
&	AND	"This *and* that"; for example, *Anders&Anderson&Andersen* would mean "Match Anders and Anderson and Andersen"—that is, all of these.
~	NOT	"This *not* that"; for example, *Anders~Anderson~Andersen* would mean "Match Anders but not Anderson or Andersen."
<	LESS THAN	"Earlier than" and used only for dates; for example, *<8/13/91* would mean "Before August 13, 1991."
>	GREATER THAN	"Later than" and used only for dates; for example, *>8/13/91* would mean "After August 13, 1991."

Text (text box) Use this field to search for specific text within both Word and non-Word files. As with the text boxes decribed above, your search text for this field can contain wildcards and logical operators (except, of course, the greater-than and less-than symbols). Text searches are relatively slow, so you might not want to use them often. On the other hand, this tool can do in a minute what might otherwise take hours. You can shorten the search time in two ways: Focus the search by filling in as many of the other search fields as possible, and specify the shortest possible string of characters that will still be unique to the text you want to find.

Word searches the text of files located in directories explicitly listed in the Search Paths field. MasterWord Seek, however, can search the text of Word or non-Word files across an entire disk drive and compile a list of files or directories which are then imported directly into the fields of this command.

Match Case (check box) This field relates to the Text field. Check the box when you want Word to pay attention to case when it is searching files for the text you typed in the Text field.

Selected Files Only (check box) As explained in the discussion of the Files list box, by checking this box you can limit searches to files you've marked in advance.

Directories (list box) Use this list box to choose a new current directory. The name of the current directory appears above the list box. Choices made in this list box do not directly affect the content of the Search Paths text box. However, you can append the name of a directory listed in the box to the end of the search path by using a mouse

WILDCARDS AND LOGICAL OPERATORS

You can use the wildcards ? and * in place of specific characters in any text box in the Search dialog box, except for Date Saved and Date Created. If you are familiar with wildcards and system commands, you know that ? can represent any single character and that * can represent multiple characters. Thus, *b?y* can indicate *boy*, *bay*, or *buy*, whereas *bo** can represent anything from *boy* to *box* to *botulism*. Wildcards were introduced in the earlier discussion of the File Name text box of the File Open command.

In the Search dialog box, you can use wildcards to save typing time, to search for files with extensions other than .DOC, or to finesse your way through a spelling you're not sure of. You might, for example, use the file specification *.* as part of the path to indicate all files, whether or not they have the .DOC extension. Or you might type an author's name as *Anders?n* if you're not certain whether the spelling is Anderson or Andersen. If you use wildcards in the Keywords or Text field and you are searching for text that itself contains either a question mark or an asterisk, type a caret (^) first: *Is this a dagger which I see before me, The handle toward my hand ^?*

Even more powerful than wildcards are *logical operators*. Example: You go to an ice-cream parlor and tell yourself, "I'll have chocolate or strawberry." The word *or* in this example is a logical operator, representing that either of two alternatives is acceptable.

Word offers three such operators for use in the text boxes of the Search dialog box:

- The tilde (~) means *NOT*.
- The ampersand (&) or the space character means *AND*.
- The comma (,) means *OR*.

To refine a search, you can use these operators alone or in combinations in any of the dialog box's text boxes except Search Paths and the two date fields.

Because these operators—including the space character—have special meanings for Word, you must enclose them in quotation marks (" ") if you want them to be interpreted literally. Thus, for example, the keyword specification *Alki Software Corporation* tells Word to search for each of the three words without regard to whether they are adjacent, because the spaces between the words are interpreted as AND logical operators. In contrast, using quotation marks around the words as in *"Alki Software Cor-*

poration" tells Word to treat the three as a single string of text that must be located in its entirety.

If you're searching for text that already includes quotation marks, put extra quotation marks around the existing quotation marks and surround the entire string of text in a third set of quotation marks: *""""The time has come," " the Walrus said."*

To use more than one operator and to indicate how the operators are to be evaluated, you can use parentheses much as you do when telling Word how to evaluate a mathematical expression. For example, typing author names as *(Juarez, Nguyen)&Green* tells Word to find documents written by Juarez and Green, by Nguyen and Green, or by Juarez, Nguyen, and Green, but not those written by Juarez and Nguyen.

Notice that no spaces appear between the names in this example because Word interprets a space as the logical operator AND, just as it interprets an ampersand. If the parentheses were moved to encompass the last two names, the expression would be *Juarez,(Nguyen&Green)*. In this case, Word would find documents written by Juarez, by both Nguyen and Green, or by all three.

When more than one logical operator is present and parentheses do not indicate which part Word should evaluate first, Word gives the tilde (~) top priority followed by the ampersand (&) or space; Word gives the comma the lowest priority. So Word evaluates the expressions *Juarez,Nguyen&Green* and *Juarez,(Nguyen&Green)* with identical results.

Word has two additional logical operators, although you can use them only in the Date Created and Date Saved text boxes:

- The less-than symbol (<) means *earlier than*.
- The greater-than symbol (>) means *later than*.

When searching for documents created or revised on or about a certain date, use the logical operators < and > either alone, in combination, or with another operator, such as &. For example, to find all documents created after (not on) November 11 1991, you would specify *<11/11/91* in the Date Created field. To find all documents revised between December 7, 1990, and December 14, 1990, inclusive, you would type *>12/6/90&<12/15/90* in the Date Saved field. (Use the ampersand in such expressions; the space character does not work.)

and clicking on the name of the directory or by using the direction keys to highlight a directory and then pressing Enter.

For details on choosing a current directory and using this list box, see the discussion near the end of the chapter.

Summary dialog box

Choose the Summary button to review or modify the summary information on a document or style sheet. This dialog box was illustrated earlier in the chapter with the discussion of the File Save As command.

```
┌─────────────────────── Summary ───────────────────────┐
│ File Name: BEHAVIOR.DOC        Size: 11014 characters │
│ Directory: C:\DOCUMENT                                │
│                                                       │
│ Title:    [10 Years of Behavioral Observations······] │
│ Author:   [P. Catadon·······························] │
│ Operator: [E. Robustus······························] │
│ Keywords: [whales,behavior,reproduction,feeding·····] │
│ Comments: [Manuscript for publication···············] │
│                                                       │
│ Version Number: [9.2········]                         │
│ Date Created:   [06/01/1991·]                         │
│ Date Saved:     [08/21/1991·]                         │
│                                                       │
│                              < OK >    <Cancel>       │
└───────────────────────────────────────────────────────┘
```

You'll notice that the fields of summary information are nearly identical to those of the Search dialog box just discussed.

Word does some of the work for you, updating the summary sheet's date of revision (called *Date Saved*) and the character count whenever you load and resave the document. Word does not, however, change the contents of any other field of summary information.

Options dialog box

The Options dialog box lets you control how the list of retrieved files is displayed on the screen and generally how much information you see about each file on the list. In addition, it enables you to organize the files by any of several criteria.

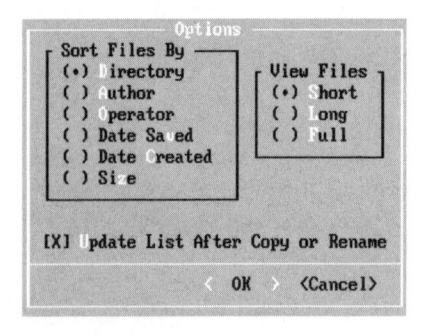

```
┌──────────────── Options ────────────────┐
│ ┌─ Sort Files By ──┐                    │
│ │ (•) Directory    │  ┌─ View Files ─┐  │
│ │ ( ) Author       │  │ (•) Short    │  │
│ │ ( ) Operator     │  │ ( ) Long     │  │
│ │ ( ) Date Saved   │  │ ( ) Full     │  │
│ │ ( ) Date Created │  └──────────────┘  │
│ │ ( ) Size         │                    │
│ └──────────────────┘                    │
│                                         │
│ [X] Update List After Copy or Rename    │
│                                         │
│          < OK >    <Cancel>             │
└─────────────────────────────────────────┘
```

CHAPTER TEN: File Commands 183

The dialog box has three fields, two of which offer several option buttons:

Sort Files By (option buttons) Choose a button to determine the order in which Word will display the names of files it finds after a requested search:

- **Directory**—(Default) Sorts files alphabetically, first by directory (in the event that files from more than one directory are present) and then by filename.
- **Author**—Sorts files alphabetically by the name of the author.
- **Operator**—Sorts files alphabetically by the name of the operator.
- **Date Saved**—Sorts letters by the date on which they were most recently saved on disk, with the earliest date appearing first.
- **Date Created**—Sorts letters by the date on which they first were recorded on disk as Word files, with the earliest date coming first on the list.
- **Size**—Sorts files according to their size, with the smallest file coming first on the list.

View Files (option buttons) The first time you use the File Management command, the list that comes to the screen is in a two-column format of filenames preceded by pathnames (the identity of the drive and directory containing the file). The display will stay in this *Short* mode unless you change it to *Long* or *Full* by altering the View Files field of the Options dialog box:

- **Short**—This is the default mode, in which files are listed by drive and pathname in two-column format. If any are too long to fit, Word displays the beginning and end of the path and filename, replacing the missing middle with an ellipsis (...).
- **Long**—This view provides one line of information about each file: the path and filename and, from the summary information, the title and one other field, such as *author*. (The field displayed is determined by the Sort Files By option buttons.)
- **Full**—This is the most detailed view, offering all summary information about each document. To see information about a specific file, highlight its name in the list in the upper portion of the File File Management dialog box.

Update List After Copy or Rename (check box) Check this box if you want the file list to show changes caused by the Rename function described below. Deselecting this box will speed up Rename operations ever so slightly, but it might also cause confusion because files that you rename will not appear in the file list. Contrary to what the title of this check box implies, the results of Copy operations are always reflected by the file list, even when this box is not checked.

Print dialog box

Use this command to print a document whose filename is highlighted in the File File Management dialog box. The Print button takes you to the Print dialog box, which is covered in the discussion of the File Print command in the next chapter.

Note, however, that the Print field of the dialog box permits you to print summary information instead of full documents. And the Options dialog box permits you to specify that a document's summary information will always be printed when its document is.

Note, too, that you can control the font or other character formatting of summary information before printing by formatting the document with a style sheet that includes a *Summary Info* character style. Whatever character formatting you assign to the style will be used in the summary information. (For details, see Chapter 24.)

Delete button

You can delete a file from your disk, providing it isn't open in Word, by either selecting or marking it in the File File Management dialog box and then choosing the Delete button. Word responds with the question: *Delete selected file?*

If you choose Yes, either the file is deleted or else Word displays another message: *Word cannot delete this file.* This means that the file is open or that it cannot be found on the disk, or that it cannot be deleted either because it is marked Read Only or because the disk has a write-protect tab or is otherwise physically locked against writing.

Rename dialog box

Use this dialog box to rename a file. You can rename files when they are open or closed. (This is a notable departure from earlier versions of Word, in which a document had to be open in order for you to rename it.)

The dialog box offers three fields.

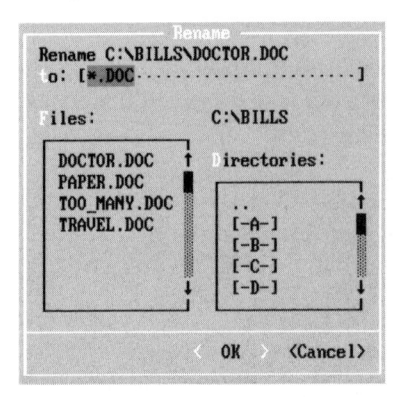

```
┌─────────────── Rename ───────────────┐
│ Rename C:\BILLS\DOCTOR.DOC           │
│     to: [*.DOC·····················] │
│                                      │
│  Files:            C:\BILLS          │
│                                      │
│   DOCTOR.DOC  ↑   Directories:       │
│   PAPER.DOC                          │
│   TOO_MANY.DOC      ..          ↑    │
│   TRAVEL.DOC        [-A-]            │
│                     [-B-]            │
│                     [-C-]            │
│               ↓     [-D-]       ↓    │
│                                      │
│            <  OK  >   <Cancel>       │
└──────────────────────────────────────┘
```

If you use Word on a hard disk with multiple subdirectories, the Rename feature is of even greater value because it enables you to move a file to a different directory on the same drive, as well as rename it.

CHAPTER TEN: File Commands

Rename* pathname *to (text box) Type the new name you want the file to have. If you want to move the file to another directory on the same drive, precede the name with a pathname.

Files (list box) Use this list of files in the current directory to see whether the new name you intend to use for the file is already in use by a different file. If you specify a name that's already in use, Word will ask: *Do you want to overwrite the existing file?*

Directories To choose a directory other than the current one, use this list box. A choice here does not affect which directory Word considers current.

Copy dialog box

Copy a selected file or one or more marked files to a different directory with the four fields of the Copy dialog box:

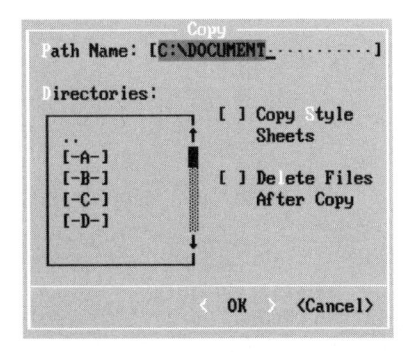

```
                    Copy
Path Name: [C:\DOCUMENT_ · · · · · · · · · ·]

Directories:
                         [ ] Copy Style
      ..                     Sheets
      [-A-]
      [-B-]              [ ] Delete Files
      [-C-]                  After Copy
      [-D-]

                  < OK >   <Cancel>
```

After you've used the Search dialog box to generate a list containing the files you want to copy, go to the File Management dialog box, and highlight or mark the specific files of interest. Then choose the Copy button, make choices in the four fields of the Copy dialog box, and carry out the command.

Path Name (text box) Be sure that this text box holds the name of the directory to which you want to copy the selected or marked files.

Directories (list box) This list box can be used to help locate the directory to which you want to copy the selected or marked files. Choices you make in it have no general effect on which directory Word considers current.

Copy Style Sheets (check box) Check this box if you want Word to copy the style sheets associated with the files you are copying. This is convenient because it saves you the trouble of remembering to copy them along with the documents they format.

Unfortunately, Word does not copy graphics files that are referenced in Word documents. However, the MasterWord program FULLCOPY copies graphics files as well as style sheets when you use it to copy a Word document from one location to another.

Delete Files After Copy (check box) Check this box if you want to delete the files from the original drive and directory after they have been copied. This creates a de facto way to move a file or files from one location to another, by copying them to a new location and then deleting them from the old location. It is a good idea to leave this box unchecked until you are certain of how the Copy feature works.

NOTE: *If you are using Word on a network, any locked files you specify cannot be copied. They do, however, remain marked until you either copy or unmark them.*

Open button

To open the selected document, choose the Open button. You can also open documents with a mouse by double-clicking on a document name or with the keyboard by selecting a document and pressing Enter.

Close dialog box

To close the File File Management dialog box, press Esc or choose the Close button.

The file-management feature is handy and fast but quite literal. It does what you ask and nothing more. When you seek documents or other files with this feature, be sure your requests are unambiguous.

FILE DOS COMMANDS COMMAND

You can run other programs or use system-level commands by putting Word temporarily on hold with the File DOS Commands command. Your computer must have sufficient memory for both the operating system and Word.

NOTE: *If you are running the OS/2 operating system, this command is called the File OS/2 Commands command.*

The first time you choose the File DOS Commands command, Word proposes *COMMAND* if you use DOS and *CMD* if you use OS/2. Press Enter when you see either of these proposed responses to take you to the operating system's prompt (such as C>). From the prompt, you can use system commands, such as Format or Dir.

When you've finished with the other program or programs, type *exit*, and Word will display the message *Press a key to resume Word*. When you press a key, the Word screen returns, exactly as you left it when you chose the File DOS Commands command.

When you choose the File DOS Commands command, you don't need to choose OK (or press Enter) when Word proposes *COMMAND* or *CMD*. Instead, you can type the name of a program or command you want to run. The program or command will execute as if Word were not running. And when you quit the other program, or the command finishes its work, you don't need to type *exit* because you'll be taken straight to the *Press a key to resume Word* message. The next time you choose the command, the choice you typed previously is proposed again. (In versions prior to 5.0, you must enter the program name or command name each time you run it.)

On a floppy-disk system, each time you leave or return to Word with the File DOS Commands command, Word instructs you to enter Y when the Program disk is ready. This is your opportunity to switch disks to put a needed program in place. You needn't switch disks if the software you need is already on the Word Program disk or disks.

Even if your computer doesn't have enough spare memory to run major programs through the DOS Commands command, you can use system commands to good effect. For instance, you can format a disk without leaving Word, which can be a big help on a floppy-disk system if you have a full Program disk. And the MasterWord Seek program lets you find what you want on a hard disk without exiting Word.

NOTE: *It is dangerous to run memory-resident (TSR) programs for the first time through the File DOS Commands command because the random-access memory (RAM) these programs set aside interferes with Word's ability to function when you want to resume word processing. For instance, although you might be able to load Sidekick before starting Word, don't load it through Word's File DOS Commands command. However, you can* use *Sidekick or another resident program after you load it and start Word.)*

FILE EXIT WORD COMMAND

Use the File Exit Word command to end a session with Word and return to operating-system level (the DOS prompt). If no information will be lost as a result of quitting immediately, quits.

If there are any unsaved editing changes to a document, style sheet, or glossary file, Word poses the question *Do you want to save changes to* [filename]? If the document, style sheet, or glossary file named *filename* has been saved before, choosing Yes causes it to be saved again, in updated form, under the same filename. If the file has never been saved or if it has been saved only under a temporary name by Word's autosave feature, choosing Yes causes Word to display the File Save As dialog box.

If, however, you are working with a document or style sheet that has been marked Read Only (on a network, for example, where many people can have access to the same file, but only one person at a time has both read and write privileges), Word will not allow you to save changes unless you give the file a new filename.

You can tell whether a file is Read Only from the way Word displays its name in the title bar: The name of a read-only file is always preceded by an asterisk. For example, the filename DRAFT.DOC would indicate a file you could freely edit; the filename *DRAFT.DOC would represent a file you could read but not change.

Whether the file displayed on screen is read only or not, you can always decide to throw away the editing changes and quit. To do this, choose No.

If you decide not to exit Word after all, choose Cancel or press the Esc key.

HOW WORD USES DIRECTORIES

Until you know the rules it follows, it isn't always clear how Word 5.5 chooses which directory to display. For example, you might wonder how Word picks the directory that will appear when you use the File Open command. Or you might question what really happens when you select a file from a directory other than the current one.

As you probably know, a *directory* is a portion of a hard disk or, sometimes, a high-capacity floppy disk. To use an analogy from the Macintosh world, a disk is like a file drawer, and a directory is like a folder within the drawer. Typically, you dedicate individual directories to specific programs or functions; for example, your Word directory stores the actual Word program and related files, whereas other directories contain documents. If hard-disk C has a directory called *contracts*, which in turn has a subdirectory called *1991*, this final subdirectory is expressed as *c:\contracts\1991*.

The Word program itself is always conscious of the identity of several directories, including: the *start-up directory*, which is the directory that was active when you started the Word program; the *current directory*, which is the directory that Word considers the normal one for storing or retrieving documents; and the *program directory*, which is the directory that contains the actual Word program (WORD.EXE).

In previous versions of Word, the start-up directory and the current directory were usually identical because unless you gave Word instructions to the contrary, it would work from the directory that was active at the time the program was started. However, Word 5.5 uses a different approach: The current directory might be the same as the start-up directory at first, but the relationship often changes (and possibly when you don't want it to).

The path, and the program and start-up directories

If Word is correctly installed on your system, you can run it regardless of which directory is current at the time. This is because the Word program is in one of the directories that is listed in your DOS path—a list of directories the computer searches when

---

MACROS AND DIRECTORIES

Word's macro language gives you the means to monitor the identity of the start-up directory, current directory, and program directory. Three reserved variables, named *StartupDir*, *CurrentDir*, and *ProgramDir* can be used to provide the identity of any of the three directories. For example, a macro consisting of the following text will, when you run it, tell you the identity of each of the three directories:

«PAUSE The start-up directory is «Startupdir». Press Enter.»
«PAUSE The program directory is «Programdir». Press Enter.»
«PAUSE The current directory is «Currentdir». Press Enter.»

For information on these and other reserved variables as well as on macros in general, see Chapter 23.

trying to find a program that corresponds to a name you typed at the DOS prompt. When you type *word*, your computer searches the directories of the path until it finds the Word program, called WORD.EXE, which it then starts up. You are better off if you avoid storing documents in the Word program directory, because it soon becomes cluttered. Rather, create a separate directory for documents or, for greatest convenience and best organization of your work, create a collection of directories, each dedicated to a category of documents.

If you are in a directory called PAPERS when you type *word* to start the program, your computer will run WORD.EXE from its separate directory, which might be called WORD55. In this case, PAPERS would be your start-up directory, and WORD55 would be your program directory. Depending on how Word's options are set, PAPERS probably would be your current directory as well. The current directory is the one in which Word looks for documents when you use a command such as File Open.

Changing the Current Directory

You might on occasion want to change the current directory. For example, perhaps you have finished work on documents in the PAPERS directory and now want to work from the CONTRACT directory. Changing the current directory can be accomplished in at least four ways.

In considering each of these four ways of changing directories, keep in mind that changes you attempt to make using any of the first three methods can be overridden by decisions you make with the fourth (the File Options dialog box).

> NOTE: *If you use OS/2, keep in mind that these four methods, like this entire discussion of directories, pertains specifically to Word when it is being run under DOS or through Windows. If you are running Word under OS/2, you might notice some differences in the way Word determines and treats the current directory.*

Typing a new pathname

If you type a new pathname when a command such as File Open requests the name of a file, the directory at the end of the pathname will become the current one when you press Enter. For example, if you are in the PAPERS directory and you choose the File Open command and type the pathname *c:\contract* in the File Name text box of the command's dialog box, the current directory will switch from PAPERS to CONTRACT as soon as you press Enter. This works only if you omit the name of a file. If you include the name of a file at the end of the pathname, the File Open command will load the file from the specified directory without causing the directory to become the new current one.

Using the operating system

If you use the File DOS Commands command (or File OS/2 Commands) to temporarily suspend Word so that you can return to your operating system, Word will remember any change in directory you make from the DOS (or OS/2) prompt when you return to Word. For example, if the current directory is called CONTRACTS and you use the File DOS Commands command to switch to a directory called MODEM to run a program, when you type *exit* to return to Word, you will find that MODEM has become Word's current directory.

Using a Directories list box

An obvious way to change directories is to use the Directories list box, which appears in the dialog boxes of five File commands and six other commands. The Directories list box lets you press direction keys and the Enter key to navigate across disks and through directories to reach the directory you want to work in.

Using a File Options dialog box

A fourth way to change the current directory is to use the File Options dialog box, which is reached through the dialog box of either the File Open command or the File Save As command.

The File Directories List Box

Several commands have, in their dialog boxes, list boxes labeled *Directories*. Each of these commands offers you an opportunity to specify a file of one kind or another, and the Directories list box is a way to indicate which directory contains the file you want.

But that's only part of the story. For many commands, making a choice in a Directories box also changes which directory is current. As soon as you press Enter or double-click the left mouse button inside a Directories list box, the disk drive and/or directory highlighted at the moment becomes the current one.

This is desirable if you will soon want to look for other files in the same directory; it is less desirable if it effectively moved you out of a directory in which you wanted to continue working.

To use a Directories list box, first choose the File Open command.

From within the dialog box that appears, move to the list box either by pressing the Tab key one or more times or by holding down the Alt key and pressing D. (D is the accelerator key for the Directories list box; it is emphasized, as shown in the following example.)

Regardless of how you get to the Directories list box, when you are there your cursor will be on the first item in the vertical list box. However, the first item will not be highlighted, so neither it nor anything else in the list box will be selected yet. To highlight the first item, press the Down direction key once, as shown here:

```
Directories:
..                    ↑
IDEAS
LITERARY
[-A-]                 ↓
```

CHAPTER TEN: File Commands

In this example, the two highlighted dots (..) represent the *parent* directory of the current directory. (The name of the current directory is listed somewhere in each dialog box that contains a Directories list box.) For instance, if the current directory is called *1991* and is located at the end of the pathname *C:\DOC\1991*, the parent directory of *1991* is *DOCS*.

If you press the Down direction key again, you will highlight the first of two subdirectories of the *1991* subdirectory. In this case, it is the *IDEAS* subdirectory, the full pathname of which is *C:\DOCS\1991\IDEAS*. (If you were to press Enter at this point, *IDEAS* would become the current directory, and the Directories list box would be updated, perhaps like this:

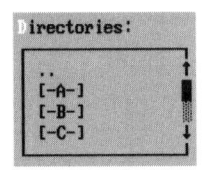

```
Directories:
..
[-A-]
[-B-]
[-C-]
```

Now the parent directory, represented by the two dots, is *1991* because the current directory has become *IDEAS*.

You can navigate from directory to directory and from disk to disk in this way. Simply highlight a directory or disk name, and press Enter or double-click the mouse button. You can only move directly from one directory to another if one directory is the parent of the other. Moving to a directory that is somewhat removed from the current directory requires multiple steps.

Commands that offer Directories list boxes

The following commands each contain a Directories list box that controls which directory is current: File New, File Open, File Save As, Insert File, and Format Attach Style Sheet.

In addition, three of the dialog boxes reached through the File Management command also contain Directories list boxes, although they are used only to select a directory for the purposes of the specific command, not to change which directory is current. These commands are File Management (Search), File Management (Rename), and File Management (Copy). Similarly, the File Options dialog box, which is reached through either the File Open or the File Save As command, displays a Directories list box that is used only to pick a directory for limited purposes.

The dialog boxes of the Edit Glossary (Open), Edit Glossary (Save), Macro Edit (Open), and Macro Edit (Save) commands list the directory that was last used to load a glossary file into Word. Their Directories list boxes can be used to change the directory that is displayed without changing the current directory.

In addition, the File Printer Setup command's dialog box contains a Directories list box that controls which directory Word looks in for printer drivers (.PRD files). A choice made in this list box is remembered, even between editing sessions, but it does not affect which directory is considered current.

Similarly, the dialog boxes of the Insert Picture command and the Utilities Customize command contain Directories list boxes that control which directory Word looks in for graphics and the spelling dictionary, respectively. Choices made in these list boxes have no effect elsewhere.

CHAPTER ELEVEN

File Commands for Printing

When it comes to printing paper copies of your work, Word offers a rich array of options. But most of the time, you'll use a simple procedure to print your document: Choose the File Print command, and press Enter or click the OK button.

For those times when you want something other than a complete printed copy of your document, read on.

The File menu includes five commands devoted to printing. In summary form,

File Print—Prints the current document, summary sheet, style sheet, or glossary contents.

File Print Preview—Displays graphically how pages of your document will appear after being printed by your particular printer. Shows all aspects of page layout, including headers, footers, multiple columns, and graphics.

File Print Merge—Lets you merge data from a separate (data) file into the document displayed in the active window, thereby creating a form letter or other hybrid document. You can store the resulting document on disk or send it to a printer.

File Print Queue—Lets you stop and start the printing of documents queued up to be printed "in the background"—that is, while you continue using Word for other tasks.

File Printer Setup—Lets you tell Word about your printer and ensures that the other File Print commands are carried out according to your needs.

Although these commands are part of the File menu, they are grouped here in a separate chapter because they form a cohesive collection and because such a grouping allows for easy reference.

FILE PRINT COMMAND

Think of this command as Word's print button. Run the command by pressing Alt+FP or Shift+F9. Word responds by displaying the File Print dialog box, which names on its first line the kind of printer to which it believes it will be printing and the name of the installed printer driver. (Printer drivers have the filename extension .PRD—with names such as HPLASMS.PRD and POSTSCRP.PRD—and contain information Word needs in order to communicate with a specific printer.)

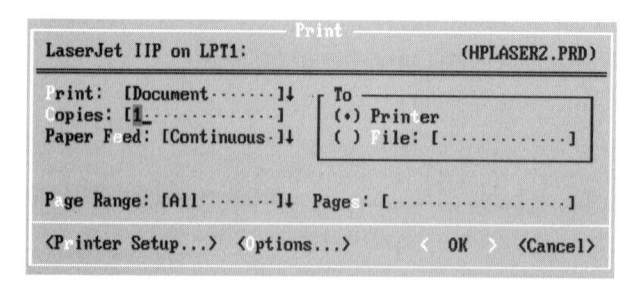

```
───────────────────── Print ─────────────────────
 LaserJet IIP on LPT1:                (HPLASER2.PRD)

  Print: [Document······]↓  ┌To─────────────────┐
  Copies: [1·············]  │(•) Printer        │
  Paper Feed: [Continuous·]↓│( ) File: [········]│
                            └───────────────────┘

  Page Range: [All········]↓ Page : [···········]

  <Printer Setup...> <Options...>     < OK >  <Cancel>
```

Word looks for specific printing instructions (type of printer, number of copies, and so on) in the fields of this dialog box as well as in the fields of the File Printer Setup dialog box. If these fields are set to your satisfaction, click OK or press Enter.

Fields of the File Print Dialog Box

Besides the OK and Cancel command buttons, the Print dialog box has nine fields.

Print (drop-down list box) Choose which of five things you want to print:

- **Document**—Prints the active document (the document in the window that is active when the File Print command is chosen). This is the default choice if a document is in the active window.
- **Summary Info**—Prints the summary information for the current document or style sheet.
- **Glossary**—Prints the current contents of the glossary—both text entries and macros. Entries are printed alphabetically by name, with the content of each entry indented and printed immediately after its name. Only the names and entries in the glossary at the time you choose the command are printed. To print a specific glossary file, first load it either by choosing the Edit Glossary command and then the Open Glossary button or by choosing the Macro Edit command and then the Open Glossary button.
- **Style Sheet**—Prints the active style sheet, which is either the style sheet in the active window or the style sheet attached to the document in the active window. This is the default choice when a style sheet is in the active window.
- **Direct Text**—Sends your keystrokes directly to the printer, without any real word processing taking place. Causes the Print Direct Text dialog box to appear.

Copies (text box) How many copies do you want printed? If you request more than one copy of a multiple-page document, Word "collates" by printing the entire

CHAPTER ELEVEN: File Commands for Printing   195

document and then repeating. Remember to reset the Copies text box to 1 when you complete the printing, unless you want to print the same number of copies of the next document you print.

Paper Feed (drop-down list box) Tell Word how paper is fed to your printer, or press Alt+Down to see a list of the possibilities available on your printer, which might include the following:

- **Continuous**—For printers using fanfold paper or for laser printers or other printers that don't require manual feeding. With Continuous, Word doesn't pause between pages.
- **Manual**—For printers that require paper to be fed in a sheet at a time by hand.
- **Bin 1**—If your printer has a cut-sheet feeder with one or more bins of paper, this choice indicates that paper will be fed from the first bin.
- **Bin 2**—Like Bin 1, except that it specifies paper will be fed from the second bin.
- **Envelope**—Lets you use an envelope feeder on certain printers, such as the HP Laserjet IIP.
- **Mixed**—Lets you print the first page of a document from Bin 1 and the remaining pages from Bin 2. This setting is handy if, for example, you have letterhead stationery in the first bin and nonletterhead paper in the second bin.

To (option buttons) Normally you think of printing a document to a printer, but you can print to a file instead.

- **Printer**—The default; causes the document or other file to be sent to the printer.
- **File**—Sends the document or other file to a disk, not in document form but in a form that can be interpreted by your printer.

File (text box) If you choose the File option button in the To field, you can use this text box to tell Word what to name the resulting file.

Page Range (drop-down list box) By making a choice from this drop-down list, you indicate how much of a file is to be printed:

- **All**—Prints the entire document
- **Pages**—Prints only those page numbers specified in the Pages text box
- **Selection**—Prints only text that is selected (highlighted)

If you typically print only a portion of your document rather than the whole, you might want to use the page-printing macro described in Chapter 6. Instructions on how to create it appear in Chapter 23.

Pages (text box) If you chose *Pages* in the Page Range field, type into this text box the page numbers you want printed. Use commas (*2, 4, 6, 8*) to separate individual page numbers, and use a hyphen (*3-6*) or a colon (*3:6*) to indicate a range of pages to print. (You can also combine the methods: *3-6, 8*.) To print to the end of a document when you don't know the final page number, choose a number substantially higher than the final number. If you want to print a range of page numbers in a document that has more than one section, type *S* and a section number after the page number. For instance, *3S1-5S2* tells Word to print all the pages from the third page of the first section to the fifth page of the second section. (If you're using a comma to represent the decimal character, you must use semicolons instead of commas to separate page numbers.)

Word ignores entries in this text box if the Page Range drop-down list box is not set to *Pages*.

Printer Setup (command button) Choosing this button takes you to the Printer Setup dialog box, which is described later in this chapter under the File Printer Setup command.

Options (command button) Choosing this button takes you to the Print Options dialog box.

Print Options dialog box

The Print Options dialog box is really nothing more than an extension of the File Print dialog box; it contains some of the less popular printing choices.

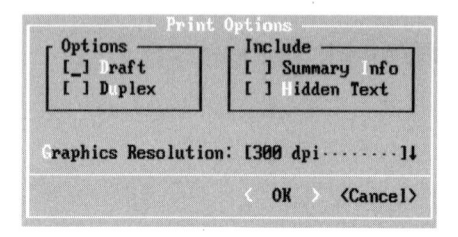

```
┌─────────────── Print Options ───────────────┐
│ ┌─ Options ──────┐  ┌─ Include ───────────┐ │
│ │ [_] Draft      │  │ [ ] Summary Info    │ │
│ │ [ ] Duplex     │  │ [ ] Hidden Text     │ │
│ └────────────────┘  └─────────────────────┘ │
│                                              │
│   Graphics Resolution: [300 dpi········]↓   │
│                                              │
│                    < OK >   <Cancel>         │
└──────────────────────────────────────────────┘
```

The dialog box has four check boxes and one drop-down list box.

Draft (check box) Check this box to cause Word to print in a high-speed draft mode that shows page and line placement but not unusual character formatting and that prints blanks instead of graphics. Also check this box when you want to print a justified document without microspace justification.

Duplex (check box) If your printer can print on both sides of the page without your intervention, check this box for two-sided printing.

Summary Info (check box) If you want a document's summary information to be printed when the document is printed, check this box.

CHAPTER ELEVEN: File Commands for Printing

Hidden Text (check box) Do you want Word to print hidden text? In most cases, you don't. For example, you won't want to print field markers and other elements used for forms. Nor will you want to print the special hidden-text codes Word puts before and after tables, indexes, or imported spreadsheet data or graphics. But if you want to print notes formatted as hidden text or if you want to review hidden indexing and table codes, check this box. When the box is checked, Word prints all hidden text even if it's not visible on the screen and displays hidden text on the screen (if the View Layout command is on). When View Layout is off, this check box doesn't dictate whether hidden text is displayed on the screen; the display of hidden text on the screen is governed by the View Preferences command.

Graphics Resolution (drop-down list box) How fine a resolution do you want Word to use when printing graphics? Resolution is measured in dots per inch, displayed in the Graphics Resolution field as a number followed by the letters *dpi*. The higher the number, the finer (more detailed) the resolution becomes because the dots constituting the graphic are printed more closely together. The resolution Word proposes and the choices available in the list box depend on the capabilities of your printer, as described to Word by the printer file (.PRD file) listed in the Files and Printer Name fields of the File Printer Setup command.

The resolution choices for Epson printers in the FX series, for example, are 60 dpi, 120 dpi, and 240 dpi. The choices for the Hewlett-Packard LaserJet Series II are 75 dpi, 150 dpi, and 300 dpi.

If your printer has considerable memory (1 MB or more) or if the graphics images you want to print are small, you might want to set the field to 300 dpi for the sake of higher resolution. However, higher-resolution printing takes longer.

Print Direct Text dialog box

When you choose Direct Text in the Print drop-down list box of the File Print command and then choose OK, Word presents you with this simple dialog box:

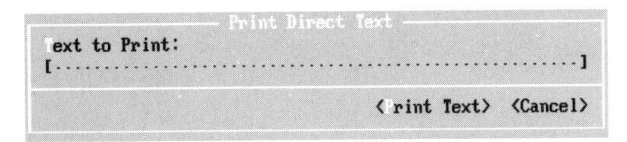

```
┌─────────────── Print Direct Text ───────────────┐
│ Text to Print:                                  │
│ [..........................................]   │
├─────────────────────────────────────────────────┤
│                      <Print Text>  <Cancel>     │
└─────────────────────────────────────────────────┘
```

This dialog box is as close as Word comes to a manual typewriter; no real word processing takes place when you use it, except that you can employ the Backspace key when typing in the first of the two fields.

Text to Print (text box) Type the text you want sent to the printer. You can type more characters than you think—the text will scroll to the left if necessary.

Print Text (command button) This is equivalent to the carriage return of a typewriter. Press it when you want to finish a line. Or better yet, skip this button and simply press Enter; it does the same thing.

If you have a laser printer (such as a LaserJet II), take it off line and press the form-feed or manual-feed button or both to get the printed sheet to print.

The Direct Text option is useful for such tasks as addressing one envelope. Daisy-wheel printers use whatever wheel is mounted when the command is issued; dot-matrix and laser printers use their normal characters.

FILE PRINT PREVIEW COMMAND

Today most computers have graphics capabilities; if yours does, you can use the File Print Preview command to see an on-screen image of how the pages of your document will look printed. The image you see depends on the formatting of your document, of course, but it also depends on which printer driver is installed. If no driver is installed, the preview feature will not work because Word won't know how to display an accurate representation of your printed pages.

Run the command by pressing Alt+FV or Ctrl+F9. Word shows one or two pages at a time, like this:

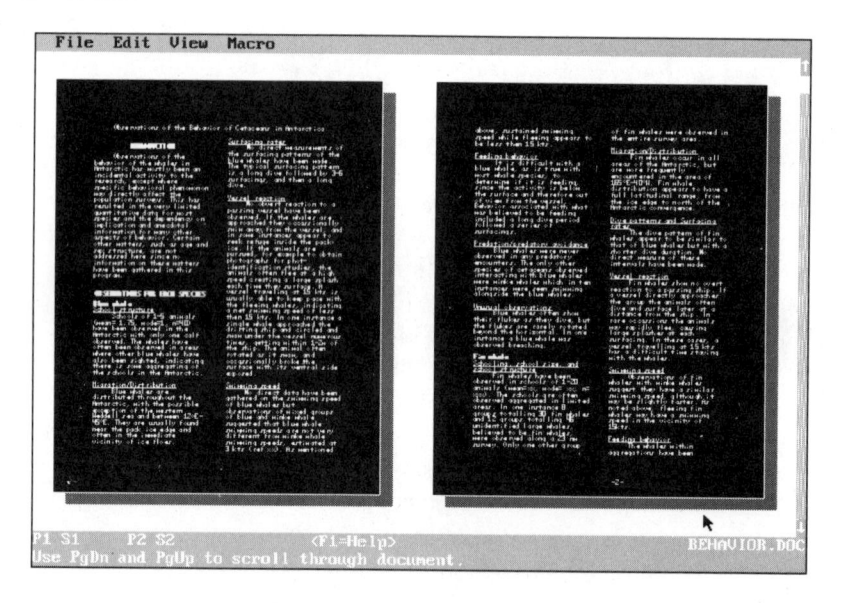

Graphics will be displayed, as will text. Fonts are displayed in a rough approximation. All the elements of the page are properly displayed, however. You see the relative position of such elements as headers and footers, headings, captions, page numbers, columns and side-by-side paragraphs, graphics, borders, footnotes, line numbers, and revision marks.

Commands in Print Preview Mode

While you are in print preview mode, the menu bar at the top of the screen changes: Few of Word's regular commands are available in print preview mode. Others function differently, as noted in the following discussion:

The File menu

Of the three commands that appear on the File menu, both File Print and File Printer Setup are identical to commands from the main File menu. The third command, File Exit Preview, simply returns you to your normal document window, closing the preview. Pressing the Esc key does the same thing.

The Edit menu

This menu has only one choice, the Edit Go To command, which lets you preview a specific page that you designate by number or by footnote, annotation, or bookmark. The use of the regular Edit Go To command is explained in the next chapter.

If you've used bookmarks to tag the captions on graphics, either as navigation aids or as cross-referencing tools, you can use the Edit Go To command to jump to these bookmarks—in essence, to easily review the graphics images in order.

The View menu

The View menu offers three choices:

- **1-page**—Causes Word to display the current page (the page that contains the highlight or cursor at the time you choose the File Print Preview command) in the center of the screen.
- **2-page**—The default, causes Word to display the current page at the left side of the screen and the following page at the right side of the screen. This lets you look at the page you are editing plus the next page. If the document is one page long, this option causes Word to display the page at the left side of the screen.
- **Facing-pages**—Also displays two pages on the screen. This time, however, it displays an even-numbered page at the left side and an odd-numbered page at the right side. This is similar to the 2-page option except that it displays facing pages, much like a book.

The Macro menu

All three Macro commands are available in print preview mode. The use of these commands is discussed in Chapter 17.

Tips on Using Print Preview Mode

Print preview mode is straightforward and not very complex. Basically, it lets you look at images of your document's pages. However, a few tips might prove useful.

- The Edit Go To command is not the only way to move around in a document that is displayed in print preview mode. You can scroll by pressing the PgUp or the PgDn key. Scrolling is fastest when the view is set to Facing-pages because you move two pages at a time instead of one. In addition, you can move to the top of your document by pressing Ctrl+Home or to the end by pressing Ctrl+End.
- Although print preview mode does not have a zoom feature that lets you get a close-up preview of your printed pages, MasterWord includes a macro that generates a close-up, full-screen view of any graphics image included in your document.
- The View Layout command provides an alternative to the File Print Preview command. See Chapter 13 for a discussion of this feature, which has some advantages—and disadvantages—compared with the preview feature.
- If, when trying to leave print preview mode, you encounter the message *There is not enough memory to return to the original display mode*, use the File Save All command to free memory before resuming your work.

FILE PRINT MERGE COMMAND

The dialog boxes of the File Print Merge command cover a wealth of possibilities related to producing customized form letters and other multiple-version documents.

The merge procedure involves combining information from two sources to create the finished document. This section introduces the merge feature and describes the dialog-box choices. Chapter 25 discusses the merge feature in greater detail.

The File Print Merge command merges text or information such as names and addresses from one file (called the *data document*) into specific places in another file (called the *main document* or *master document*). The result is a third document or series of documents, which can be either printed to paper or created on disk.

If you use two windows (one for the main document and one for the data document), be sure that the selection is in the main document when you choose the File Print Merge command; otherwise, merge will not work.

To run the File Print Merge command, press Alt+FM. Word responds with this small dialog box:

```
┌──────── Print Merge ────────┐
│ (•) All:                     │
│ ( ) Records: [............] │
│  <Print...>  <New Document...>  <Cancel>  │
└──────────────────────────────┘
```

The dialog box has four fields in addition to the Cancel button.

All/Records (option buttons) If you don't want to use all records in the data document, this is your opportunity to limit the merge operation to certain records.

CHAPTER ELEVEN: File Commands for Printing

- **All**—Use all data records, generally creating as many merge documents as there are data records.
- **Records**—Limit the creation of merge documents to those based on the data of certain records.

Records (text box) If you have chosen the Records option button, type into this text box the numbers of the records you want to merge. Use commas to separate numbers (for example, *6,21* to merge only records 6 and 21); use colons or hyphens to indicate ranges of numbers (for example, *6:21* or *6-21* to merge records 6 through 21); or use a combination of commas and colons or hyphens (for example, *6-21,25* to merge records 6 through 21, plus record 25).

Using the Record text box is a bit more difficult when you want to use a record from the middle of a long data document and don't know its number. One solution is to set up your data document to include a field for record numbers and to number the records consecutively. If you do this, you can simply type the record number in the Records field of the File Print Merge command.

Print (command button) Choose this button to print paper copies of your merged document or documents. You'll be taken to the File Print dialog box, described in the earlier discussion of the File Print command.

New Document (command button) You choose this button when you want to record your merge document or documents on disk as a single file rather than printing them immediately on paper. In other words, use this command when you want to merge the main and data documents to create a single long document on disk instead of a series of printed documents. Within the document, form letters are separated by page breaks. You can edit, save, or print this document as you would any other. The button takes you to the Print Merge to Document dialog box, in which you can name the merged document.

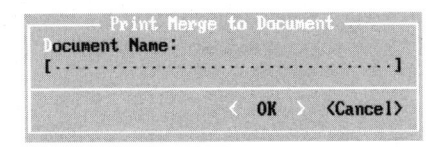

```
       ──── Print Merge to Document ────
       Document Name:
       [..................................]

                    <  OK  >    <Cancel>
```

The dialog box has only one field, a text box labeled *Document Name*. Type the name you want for the file on disk. Later you will be able to edit or print this new file.

Regardless of whether you send your merge documents to the printer or to a file, Word creates one merge document for every record in the data document unless you choose the Records option button to limit the merge to certain records.

For details on creating main documents and data documents and on how to deal with common messages you might encounter while using the Print Merge command, see Chapter 25.

FILE PRINT QUEUE COMMAND

"Queued printing" refers to printing one or more documents while you keep Word available for other uses.

You start the process of queued printing by checking the Use Print Queue check box of the File Printer Setup dialog box and then using the File Print command to print a document. The document is sent to the printer, but first it is "printed" to a file on disk. More than one document can exist in this file; even when only one exists, the document is said to be in the print queue, either printing or waiting to print. While you continue to use the word processor, Word transfers data from this print queue file to the printer. This is how Word achieves "background" printing.

The File Print Queue command lets you control the printing process after you have selected the File Print command.

To run the File Print Queue command, press Alt+FQ while queued printing is in progress. The Print Queue dialog box will appear.

CHOOSING A PRINTER FILE

Most likely, you chose a printer file during Word's original setup procedure, and you don't need to change it. But in case you decide to, here are a few pointers.

- The printer file (also called *printer driver,* or *.PRD file*) must match your printer. To ensure that it does, you can run the Word Setup program again, letting it install a new printer driver as appropriate.
- If a printer file for your printer is not included on the disks that come with Word, check with Microsoft Product Support to see if a driver is included on supplemental printer disks. You can obtain printer files free from your Word dealer, for a small charge from Microsoft, or for the cost of connect charges through the Microsoft Forum on CompuServe.
- One function of a printer file is to notify Word of which fonts and type sizes a particular printer can handle. The lists in the Format Character command's Font and Point Size fields vary according to the printer file installed. Theoretically, Word can accommodate 64 different fonts at a time in many sizes. The program thinks of the fonts in generic terms such as modern a, modern b, decor e, and roman i.

When you install a particular printer file, it tells Word which of the 64 font types are available on the printer and in which sizes. For example, the generic modern a is Pica on an Epson FX-85

CHAPTER ELEVEN: File Commands for Printing

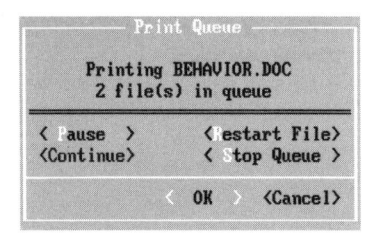

```
┌─────── Print Queue ────────┐
│    Printing BEHAVIOR.DOC   │
│      2 file(s) in queue    │
├────────────────────────────┤
│  < Pause  >    < Restart File>
│  <Continue>    < Stop Queue >
│                            │
│           <  OK  >  <Cancel>
└────────────────────────────┘
```

Fields of the File Print Queue Command

The File Print Queue dialog box has four command buttons in addition to the usual OK and Cancel buttons:

Pause (command button) Temporarily suspends queued printing. Of course, queued printing is not slowed down in Pause mode—it's completely halted!

printer but Courier on an HP LaserJet printer, depending on which font cartridge or downloadable fonts you are using. If you format characters as Pica when the Epson printer file is installed, Word considers the characters to be modern a. It displays the font name as *Pica* for your convenience as long as it thinks you'll be printing the document on an Epson printer. But if you install a LaserJet printer file such as HPLASER1.PRD, Word starts calling the Pica characters and printing them as *Courier*, the LaserJet's modern a font. If you prefer, you can type the generic font names (modern a, modern b, and so on) instead of Pica, Courier, or whatever, in the Font field of the Format Character command or the ribbon. The font used will depend on the printer file and on the printer you choose with the Print Options command.

- Generally, you change the printer file when you change from one printer to another or switch cartridges on a laser printer.
- Although Word 5.0 cannot use printer files designed for Word 5.5, the opposite is not true. Word 5.5 can use the printer files of version 5.0. However, Word 5.5 performs better with up-to-date printer files.
- If you have several printers connected to your computer, you should be able to switch among them without leaving Word, simply by making the appropriate changes in the Files, Printer Name, Connect To, and Paper Feed fields.

Continue (command button) Resumes queued printing that was suspended.

Restart File (command button) Restarts the printing of the document, repeating pages already printed.

Stop Queue (command button) Cancels queued printing, erasing the temporary disk file in which the queue is stored.

The File Print Queue command is frequently grayed on the File menu; it becomes available only when the Use Print Queue check box from the File Printer Setup command is checked.

FILE PRINTER SETUP COMMAND

This command, which can be reached either from the main File menu or through a command button in the File Print command, lets you tell Word what printer you have, which port of your computer it is connected to, and how you want to use it. Most often these choices are made by Word's Setup program; they can, however, be adjusted with this command too.

You can choose the command by pressing Alt+FR. The File Printer Setup dialog box will appear.

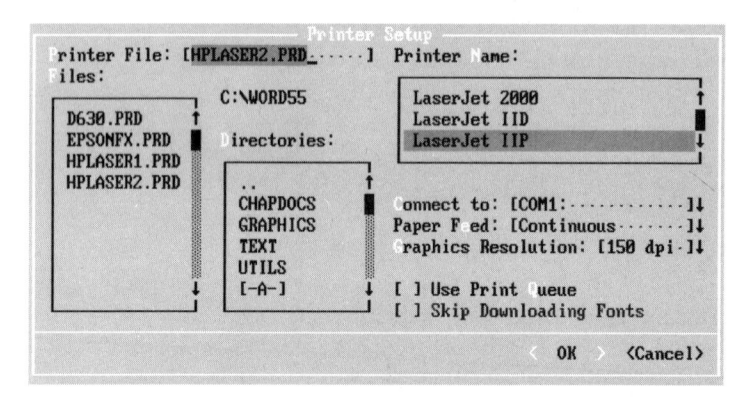

Fields of the File Printer Setup Dialog Box

In addition to the OK and Cancel command buttons, the File Printer Setup dialog box has nine fields.

Printer File (text box) Type a name for the printer file (.PRD file) you intend to use. Most often, you will let Word fill in this text box for you, reflecting your choice in the Files list box. (See the discussion, "Choosing a Printer File.")

Files (list box) All printer files in the printer directory are listed here; if you select a name, Word places it in the Printer File text box.

CHAPTER ELEVEN: File Commands for Printing   205

Directories (list box) Choose a printer directory here. Unlike the choices in the Directories list boxes of many other commands, a choice here has no effect on which directory is considered current.

Printer Name (list box) If the printer driver you choose supports more than one printer or model, this list box contains the various choices. Select the one that best reflects your equipment. The model information you give helps Word handle such features as line drawing, color, printing on two sides of a page (duplex), downloadable fonts, and unprintable regions. Word remembers your choice in the MW.INI file and uses it until you specify a different printer.

Connect to (drop-down list box) Tell Word which port your printer is connected to. Word allows eight possibilities, although DOS typically allows only five of these; indeed, all five might not be available on your computer.

If you have a parallel printer, the possibilities typically allowed by DOS are *LPT1:*, *LPT2:*, and *LPT3:*. Word also offers *LPT4:* if your computer and DOS support it.

If you have a serial printer, the possibilities generally allowed by DOS are *COM1:* and *COM2:*, although Word also lists *COM3:* and *COM4:* because some computer systems allow them. (With any of these serial choices, you must also tell DOS that a printer is connected to the port; if you haven't already done so, use the Mode command as described in your DOS manual.) Be sure to include the colon if you type the name of one of these settings instead of choosing it from the drop-down list.

Paper Feed (drop-down list box) See the File Print Options dialog box for a description of this field.

Graphics Resolution (drop-down list box) See the File Print Options dialog box for a description of this field.

Use Print Queue (check box) After you have turned on queued printing by checking this field, executing the File Print command transfers the current document to a special queue that resides on and is then printed from the Word Program disk or directory. While Word formats the file and transfers it to the queue, you cannot use the program. But when the transfer is complete and printing begins, you can again use Word. The queue file is erased at the end of printing, but in the meantime, Word needs ample free space on the program disk or in the program directory.

You can queue as many documents as the disk can hold. Transferring the document to disk in printer-ready form takes a few seconds per page. While the printer is printing from the queue, Word's performance might be slow when you edit. After queued printing begins, you control it with the Print Queue command.

Skip Downloading Fonts (check box) Check this box if you don't want Word to download fonts to the printer, even though your document calls for downloaded fonts.

There are at least two instances when you might want to skip downloading fonts:

- If you want to speed up printing and you don't care about the document's format.

- If you already printed the document once and don't want to waste time downloading fonts again. (Word will download the fonts every time you print the document unless you check this box. Your printer typically doesn't need fonts to be downloaded more than once unless you have turned the printer off in the interim.)

CHAPTER TWELVE

Edit Commands

Word is a tool for editing, and in that sense most of its menu choices could be called editing commands. But Edit menu commands are distinguished by their focus on the content of your documents.

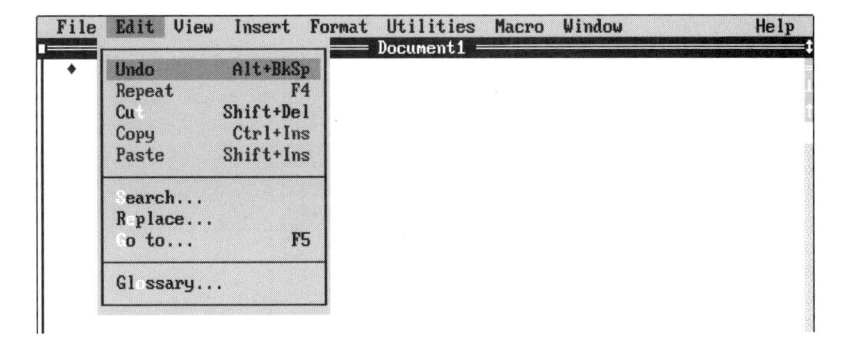

```
 File  Edit  View  Insert  Format  Utilities  Macro  Window         Help
                           Document1
        Undo       Alt+BkSp
        Repeat          F4
        Cut      Shift+Del
        Copy      Ctrl+Ins
        Paste    Shift+Ins

        Search...
        Replace...
        Go to...        F5

        Glossary...
```

You use the Edit commands when you want to move within a document or change its content:

Edit Undo—Reverses the effect of a deletion or virtually any other editing action. This command and the next one (Edit Repeat) also affect formatting. (Pressing Alt+Backspace produces the same result.)

Edit Repeat—Repeats your last editing or formatting action. (Pressing F4 produces the same result.)

Edit Cut—Deletes the selected text to the *scrap*, a storage area represented by two braces { } at the bottom of the screen.

Edit Copy—Copies the selected text to the scrap, leaving your document unchanged.

Edit Paste—Inserts text from the scrap into your document at the cursor location.

Edit Search—Searches for specific text or specific formatting. Also a fast way to move around in your document.

Edit Replace—Searches for and replaces specific text or formatting.

Edit Go To—Moves the cursor to a specific page, electronic bookmark, footnote, or annotation.

Edit Glossary—Offers a variety of choices and lets you store and retrieve passages of text.

EDIT UNDO COMMAND

The Edit Undo command reverses (undoes) your last editing action. It is the functional complement of the Edit Repeat command (F4), which repeats your last editing action. To use Edit Undo, press Alt+EU (or simply Alt+E and then Enter), or press Alt+Backspace. No dialog box appears; the command executes immediately.

If you accidentally delete some text—from a single letter to an entire document—the Edit Undo command will restore it. Or, if you type in a continuous string of text characters and decide you don't want them after all, the Edit Undo command eliminates them. Furthermore, if you make any formatting change and then change your mind, you can undo that formatting.

You can even undo the Edit Undo command by using it twice in succession. This lets you change your mind again or do a before-and-after comparison.

There's another clever wrinkle. If you delete text and then type new text at the same location, Word remembers both the deletion and the insertion, and the Edit Undo command reverses the combination. For instance, if you select the word *tomboy*, delete it all at one time (not a character at a time), and type in the words *lively little girl*, using the Edit Undo command would eliminate the phrase *lively little girl* and reinstate the word *tomboy*.

However, if you invert the process, inserting text (*lively little girl*) in your document and then deleting the original text (*tomboy*), only your last editing act—the deletion—can be reversed with the Edit Undo command.

Finally, the command will undo a global change to a document, provided that the change was the result of a single command used only once. For example, the Edit Undo command will take out all hyphens placed in a document with one use of the Utilities Hyphenate command, or it will revoke any number of replacements made with one use of the Edit Replace command.

You can predict how much the Edit Undo command will do (or rather, undo) if you remember the following rules:

♦ The command reverses only editing acts—actions that change the content or format of a document. For example, it will reverse the deletion of a Format command but will not do the same for the Utilities Customize command or one of the File commands.

♦ The command reverses only the last editing act. Word begins a new editing act whenever you change the location of the selection without changing the content of the document. For example, suppose you type a few words, move the cursor a few spaces with the direction keys or the mouse, and then type a few more words. At this point, the Edit Undo command can affect only the words typed after you moved the highlight, because that move signaled the start of a new editing act.

- There is an exception to the "last editing act" limitation: As in the earlier *tomboy* example, Edit Undo works if you have deleted and replaced text in the same location.
- You can undo (erase) a drawing made in Line Draw mode, but all text in the entire document will be highlighted as a result. This means, unfortunately, that you lose your place because the cursor vanishes.

The name *Edit Undo* on the Edit menu is grayed when your most recent action cannot be reversed. If you press Alt+Backspace to attempt to reverse the irreversible, the following message appears: *There is no edit to undo.*

EDIT REPEAT COMMAND

Use the Edit Repeat command when you want to repeat your last editing act. To use the command, press Alt+ER or the F4 key. No dialog box appears; the command executes immediately.

The Edit Repeat command is closely associated with the Edit Undo command. To understand which actions can be repeated, review the above discussion of the Edit Undo command, which outlines the rules Word follows.

EDIT CUT COMMAND

The Edit Cut command is most commonly used to eliminate selected text from a document or, when used with the Edit Paste command, to move text from one location to another. Edit Cut has no dialog box; the command executes immediately.

Cutting Text to the Scrap

When text is cut from a document, it is stored in the scrap, a special area of Word's memory. The scrap, which was introduced in Chapter 3, is represented by two brackets {} on the screen's status line. The first and last characters of the scrap text appear between these brackets.

If no text is selected, the Edit Cut command cuts the character at the cursor location and places it in the scrap. After being stored in the scrap, text can be inserted in any document with the Edit Paste command.

The scrap can hold anything from a single character to a long document. If you cut or copy to the scrap from a style sheet, the scrap can hold one or more styles. However, only one passage or group of styles can reside in the scrap at a time: When you cut or copy a second item to it, the first is replaced. Consequently, if you move text to the scrap with the idea of pasting it elsewhere in a document, you should do so quickly. If you perform other editing first, you might inadvertently replace the scrap contents.

It is possible to cut text to the scrap without using the Edit Cut command. The shortcut key you use to accomplish this depends on whether or not the Utilities Customize command's Use INS for Overtype Key check box is checked.

- If the box is checked, you can cut text to the scrap by pressing Shift+Del. Pressing Del in this case cuts the text but does not send it to the scrap; it simply deletes it.
- If the box is not checked, you can cut text to the scrap by pressing the Del key. In this case, pressing Shift+Del deletes the text without sending it to the scrap.

NOTE: *You can insert text from the scrap by pressing Shift+Ins, regardless of whether the Use INS for Overtype Key check box is checked. However, if the box is not checked, you also can insert from the scrap by pressing Ins.*

THE USE INS FOR OVERTYPE KEY CHECK BOX

This check box, tucked away in the dialog box of the Utilities Customize command, has significant implications for the way you use the keyboard with the Edit Cut and Edit Paste commands. (If you use the mouse for these operations, the check box is of little significance and it, as well as the following discussion, can be ignored.)

This check box really asks, "When moving text through the scrap, do you want Word 5.5 to behave like older versions of Word or like Word for Windows?" Figure 12-1 summarizes your options.

Keystroke(s)	Checked (functions like Word for Windows)	Not checked (functions like Word 5.0)
Del	Deletes text	Deletes text to the scrap
Shift+Del	Deletes text to the scrap	Deletes text
Ins	Toggles between insert and overtype modes	Inserts text from the scrap

Figure 12-1. The effect of keystrokes on text, depending on whether the Utilities Customize command's Use INS for Overtype Key check box is checked.

EDIT COPY COMMAND

To copy selected text into the scrap so that it can be pasted elsewhere in a document, use the Edit Copy command by pressing either Alt+EC or Ctrl+Ins. No dialog box appears; the command executes immediately.

The Edit Copy command is similar to the Edit Cut command but differs in three respects:

- The Edit Copy command doesn't disturb the selected text while making a copy of it for the scrap, whereas the Edit Cut command deletes the selection from the text.
- The Edit Copy command is grayed on the menu unless text is selected. The Edit Cut command is always available.
- The Edit Copy command is always available through the shortcut key combination Ctrl+Ins.

To illustrate applications of the Edit Cut and Edit Copy commands, let's play around with the word *ballistocardiograph*—a word no one would want to type twice.

- To eliminate *ballistocardiograph* from a document, select it and then use the Edit Cut command to send it temporarily to the scrap.
- To move *ballistocardiograph* to a different location, select it, cut it to the scrap, select the new location, and then paste it with the Edit Paste command or by pressing Shift+Ins. You can move the word between documents in the same way.
- To reuse *ballistocardiograph* repeatedly without retyping it, use the Edit Copy command to copy it to the scrap, move to the location or locations at which you want the word to appear, and use the Edit Paste command or press Shift+Ins. If you want to use the word *ballistocardiograph* over a period of time, use the Edit Glossary command to give it a glossary name, such as *bal*. That way, each time you want to reuse the word, you need only type *bal* and press the F3 key.

The Edit Glossary command is described later in this chapter.

EDIT PASTE COMMAND

Most of what can be said about the Edit Cut and Edit Copy commands can be said about the Edit Paste command.

The command, which executes immediately without displaying a dialog box, lets you paste text from the scrap into your document. To run the command, press Alt+EP or Shift+Ins. If the Use INS for Overtype Key check box of the Utilities Customize command is checked, you also can paste from the scrap by pressing the Ins key.

You cannot paste text from the scrap into a style sheet, nor can you paste styles from the scrap into a document.

EDIT SEARCH COMMAND

The Edit Search command quickly scans a document for specified text or for specified character or paragraph formatting (including styles). A closely related command, Edit Replace, goes one step further, both searching for and replacing specified text or formatting.

The Edit Search command highlights the text being sought or text that is formatted as sought. It finds hidden text only if it has been made visible with the View Preferences command.

To search for additional occurrences of the same text, hold down the Shift key and press the F4 key. This method works even if you've done other editing since you last used the Edit Search command.

Choose the Edit Search command by pressing Alt+ES. The Edit Search dialog box appears:

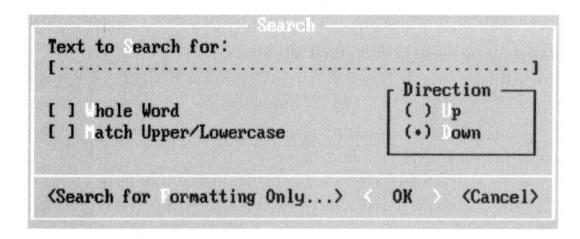

```
┌─────────────────────── Search ───────────────────────┐
│ Text to Search for:                                  │
│ [......................................]            │
│                              ┌─ Direction ─┐         │
│   [ ] Whole Word             │ ( ) Up      │         │
│   [ ] Match Upper/Lowercase  │ (•) Down    │         │
│                              └─────────────┘         │
│                                                      │
│   <Search for Formatting Only...>  < OK >  <Cancel>  │
└──────────────────────────────────────────────────────┘
```

Fields of the Edit Search Dialog Box

The Edit Search dialog box has five fields in addition to the OK and Cancel command buttons:

Text to Search For (text box) Enter the word, words, or characters you want to replace. Word can search for up to 255 characters, including numbers, spaces, and punctuation marks; the fewer the characters, the faster the search.

You can use a question mark (?) as a wildcard to represent any character. For example, entering *fo?l* causes Word to find such character combinations as *foil, fool, foul, foal,* and *fowl*. Similarly, typing *I love ??* will cause Word to find *I love NY, I love LA, I love it,* and so on. The asterisk (*) cannot be used as a wildcard in text searches.

The ^ symbol (the shifted 6 key on IBM and compatible keyboards) tells Word that the next character is one of the following special symbols:

- ^?—Represents a question mark. (Word interprets ? without the ^ as a wildcard.)
- ^^—Represents a caret. (The first caret tells Word to treat the next one as the caret symbol.)
- ^-(hyphen)—Represents an optional (nonrequired) hyphen. (You can insert an optional hyphen with the Utilities Hyphenate command or by using the Ctrl+hyphen key combination.) An optional hyphen is one you use only if the word must be broken at the end of a line. Such a hyphen,

CHAPTER TWELVE: Edit Commands   213

if not at the end of a line, is visible only if either the Show All or the Optional Hyphens check box of the View Preferences command is checked. Visible or not, however, to Word an optional hyphen is a character like any other, so you must specify it in the text field if you have inserted it in a word you are searching for.

- ^c—Represents a new-column character, which you insert into a document by using the Insert Break command.
- ^d—Represents either a section mark or a new-page mark, both formatting characters.
- ^n—Represents a new-line character (which you insert into a document by pressing Shift+Enter), which forces a new line to begin within a paragraph.
- ^p—Represents a paragraph mark, which you insert into a document with the Enter key.
- ^s—Represents a nonbreaking space, which you place between two words or elements by pressing Shift+Ctrl+Spacebar when you want to ensure that a new line won't begin between the words.
- ^t—Represents the tab character, which you create with the Tab key.
- ^w—Represents any and all spaces and spacing characters in your document, including Spacebar spaces, tab characters, paragraph marks, new-line characters, section marks, new-page marks, and nonbreaking spaces.

This field is relevant only if you are searching for text, not formatting.

Whole Word (check box) If you check this box, Word stops only at matching text it interprets as a whole word (that is, a collection of characters with spaces or punctuation marks at both ends).

If you do not check the box, Word finds the characters you specify even if they are fragments of other words. For example, if you specified *valid* in the Text to Search For field and did not check the Whole Word box, Word would display not only the word *valid* but the same letters in the words *invalid* and *validity* as well.

This field is relevant only if you are searching for text.

Match Upper/Lowercase (check box) If you check this box, Word considers capitalization when searching for a match. In other words, if you type *Dog*, Word ignores *dog* in its search.

If you do not check this box, Word ignores case during the search (finding both *Dog* and *dog*, regardless of how you typed the word in the Text to Search For field).

This field is relevant only if you are searching for text.

Direction (option buttons) You can search either up or down in a document, relative to the position of the selection:

- **Up**—Searches up, toward the beginning of the document. When the search reaches the top of the document, Word asks if you want to continue the search from the bottom.

- **Down**—Searches down, toward the end of the document. This is the default choice. When the search reaches the bottom of the document, Word asks if you want to continue the search from the top.

This field is relevant for any kind of search, whether for text or formatting.

Search for Formatting Only (command button) This button takes you to the first of a short series of dialog boxes, permitting you to search for instances of formatting rather than of text.

Searching for Formatting

At your request, Word will search for instances of specific character or paragraph formatting in your document or for instances in which styles have been used for formatting. When the formatting you seek has been created with a style, the only successful way to search for it is to specify the key code of the style.

When you choose the Search for Formatting Only button of the Edit Search command, you are taken to the Edit Search for Formatting dialog box, which offers three additional buttons, representing Character, Paragraph, and Style formatting:

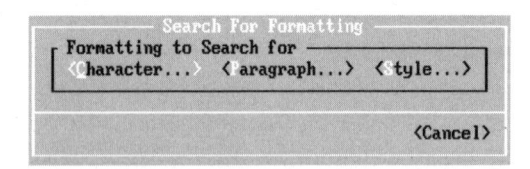

```
┌─────────── Search For Formatting ───────────┐
│ ┌─ Formatting to Search for ──────────────┐ │
│ │  <Character...>  <Paragraph...>  <Style...>  │ │
│ └─────────────────────────────────────────┘ │
│                                             │
│                                   <Cancel>  │
└─────────────────────────────────────────────┘
```

Character button and dialog box

Choosing the Character button in the Search for Formatting dialog box takes you to yet another dialog box—the Search for Character dialog box:

```
┌──────────── Search For Character ─────────────┐
│ Font: [_............................]↕        │
│ Point Size: [......]↕  Color: [..........]↕  │
│                                                │
│ [-] Bold                                       │
│ [-] Italic         ┌─ Position ──────┐        │
│ [-] Underline      │ ( ) Normal       │        │
│ [-] Double Underline│ ( ) Superscript │        │
│ [-] Small Caps     │ ( ) Subscript    │        │
│ [-] All Caps       └──────────────────┘        │
│ [-] Strike thru                                │
│ [-] Hidden                                     │
│                                                │
│                      <  OK  >   <Cancel>       │
└────────────────────────────────────────────────┘
```

The choices in this dialog box are similar to those in the Format Character command's dialog box. (See Chapter 15 for details about Format Character.) The Search for Character dialog box, however, locates examples of text formatted in the specified way; it doesn't format them.

CHAPTER TWELVE: Edit Commands

Paragraph button and dialog box
Choosing the Paragraph button takes you to the Search for Paragraph dialog box:

```
─────────────── Search For Paragraph ───────────────
┌ Alignment ──────────────────────────────────────┐
│ (_) Left   ( ) Center   ( ) Right   ( ) Justified│
└──────────────────────────────────────────────────┘
┌ Indents ─────────────────┐┌ Spacing ────────────┐
│ From Left:  [·········]  ││ Before: [·········] │
│ First Line: [·········]  ││ After:  [·········] │
│ From Right: [·········]  ││ Line:   [·········]↓│
└──────────────────────────┘└─────────────────────┘
┌ Keep Paragraph ──────────────────────────────────┐
│ [-] Together                [-] Side by Side     │
│ [-] With Next                                    │
└──────────────────────────────────────────────────┘
                                  < OK >  <Cancel>
```

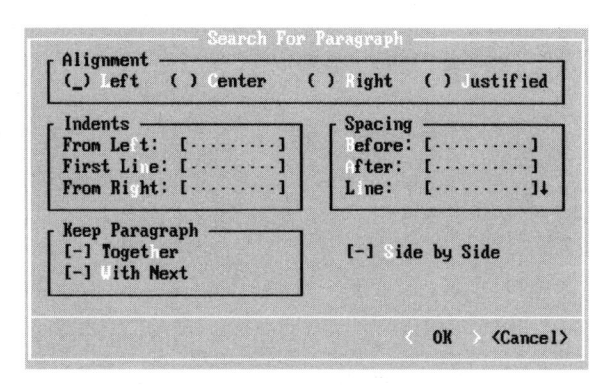

The choices in this dialog box are identical to those in the Format Paragraph command's dialog box. (See Chapter 15 for details about Format Paragraph.) The Search for Paragraph dialog box, however, locates examples of paragraphs formatted in the specified way; it doesn't format them.

Style button and dialog box
Choosing the Style button in the Search for Formatting dialog box brings up the Search for Style dialog box:

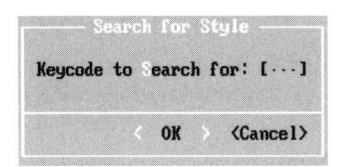

```
────── Search for Style ──────
Keycode to Search for: [···]

           < OK >  <Cancel>
```

In addition to buttons, the dialog box has one field, Keycode to Search for, wherein you type the key code of a character, paragraph, or section style. The key code you type must exist in the style sheet currently attached to the document.

EDIT REPLACE COMMAND

The Edit Replace command lets you substitute new characters or formats for old. If the cursor is on a single character on the screen, the Edit Replace command makes all appropriate substitutions from there to the document's end. If you expand the cursor to highlight a passage, Edit Replace makes substitutions only within the highlighted region.

When the Edit Replace command is complete (or when you stop it by pressing the Esc key), Word indicates the number of replacements made. If, after you use the Edit Replace command, you decide that you prefer the document's original form, use the Edit Undo command.

Choose the Edit Replace command by pressing Alt+EE. The Edit Replace dialog box appears:

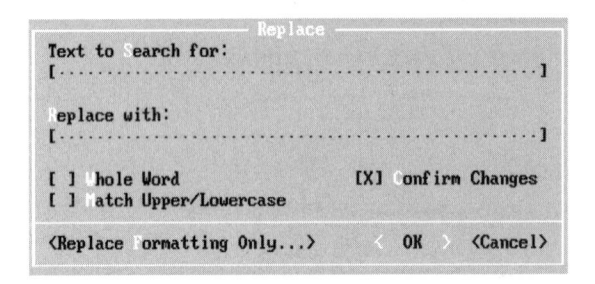

```
                        Replace
Text to Search for:
[................................................]

Replace with:
[................................................]

[ ] Whole Word                    [X] Confirm Changes
[ ] Match Upper/Lowercase

<Replace Formatting Only...>      <  OK  >  <Cancel>
```

Fields of the Edit Replace Dialog Box

The Edit Replace dialog box has six fields in addition to the OK and Cancel command buttons:

Text to Search For (text box) This is identical to the Edit Search command's text box of the same name.

Replace With (text box) Enter the word, words, or characters that you want to substitute for instances of the material specified in the text field. As with the Text to Search For text box, you can specify up to 255 characters, and you can use the same list of ^ symbols, except that ^w won't give you the same result. (In this field, ^w produces the letter *w*.) The question mark is treated as a question mark, not as a wildcard.

Whole Word (check box) This field was explained in reference to the Edit Search command. It is relevant only if you are replacing text.

Match Upper/Lowercase (check box) If this box is checked, Word ignores all but exact matches, both of text and case, when searching. When a match is found, Word replaces it with the exact contents of the Replace With text box.

If this box is not checked, Word ignores case during the search (finding both *Dog* and *dog*). When a match is found, Word mimics the capitalization of the text being replaced—it replaces *Dog* with *Cat*, *dog* with *cat*, *DOG* with *CAT*, and so on. In other words, if the box is not checked, it doesn't matter what capitalization you used in the Replace With text box because Word uses the same capitalization it finds in the document.

Confirm Changes (check box) Do you want Word to ask you to confirm each replacement? If this box is checked, Word stops each time it finds a potential replacement, highlights it, and asks *Do you want to replace the selection?* If you choose Yes, Word replaces the text and continues searching. If you choose No, Word leaves the original text unchanged and continues searching. If you choose Cancel, you both reject the proposed replacement and cancel the Edit Replace command.

CHAPTER TWELVE: Edit Commands

Each time Word poses the question, it also presents the Confirm Changes check box. If you uncheck this box, Word verifies your intention by presenting you with the question *Edit Replace All?* If you choose Yes, Word continues replacing text without confirming each substitution with you.

If the Confirm Changes box is not checked in the first place, Word makes all (and reports the number of) replacements.

Replace Formatting Only (command button) Pressing this button takes you to the first of a series of dialog boxes, permitting you to substitute one kind of formatting for another.

Replacing Formatting

If you choose the Replace Formatting Only button, Word offers you the opportunity to substitute throughout some or all of your document one kind of character formatting for another, one kind of paragraph formatting for another, or one style for another. Initially, you decide which of these three kinds of substitutions you want to accomplish. Word presents the choices in a dialog box:

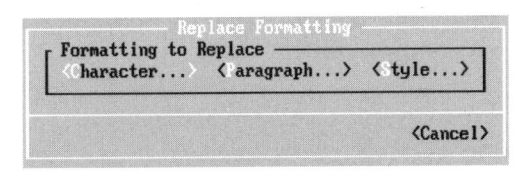

```
┌─────────── Replace Formatting ───────────┐
│ ┌─ Formatting to Replace ─────────────┐  │
│ │  <Character...>  <Paragraph...>  <Style...>  │
│ └─────────────────────────────────────┘  │
│                                          │
│                                <Cancel>  │
└──────────────────────────────────────────┘
```

Character

By choosing the Character button, you move to the Replace Character Formatting dialog box:

```
┌─────────── Replace Character Formatting ───────────┐
│ Font: [........................................]↓  │
│ Point Size: [......]↓  Color: [........]↓          │
│                                                    │
│ [-] Bold                                           │
│ [-] Italic           ┌─ Position ──────┐           │
│ [-] Underline        │ ( ) Normal      │           │
│ [-] Double Underline │ ( ) Superscript │           │
│ [-] Small Caps       │ ( ) Subscript   │           │
│ [-] All Caps         └─────────────────┘           │
│ [-] Strike Thru                                    │
│ [-] Hidden                                         │
│                                                    │
│           <Replace With...>  <Cancel>              │
└────────────────────────────────────────────────────┘
```

This dialog box is similar to the Search for Character dialog box. Use the Replace Character Formatting dialog box to describe the character formatting you want to replace in your document. After you have made the choices, press the Replace With command button. This takes you to another dialog box, called Replace With Character Formatting. Use this dialog box to describe the replacement formatting.

Paragraph

As with the Character button, choosing the Paragraph button will take you to another dialog box—the Replace Paragraph Formatting dialog box:

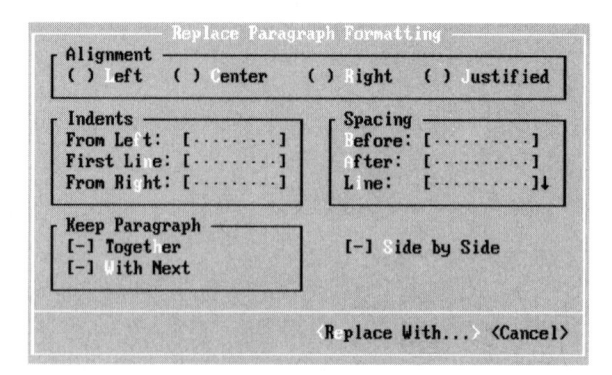

```
─────────── Replace Paragraph Formatting ───────────
┌ Alignment ──────────────────────────────────────┐
│  ( ) Left    ( ) Center    ( ) Right    ( ) Justified │
└─────────────────────────────────────────────────┘
┌ Indents ──────────────┐  ┌ Spacing ──────────────┐
│  From Left:  [........] │  │  Before: [........]   │
│  First Line: [........] │  │  After:  [........]   │
│  From Right: [........] │  │  Line:   [........]↓  │
└───────────────────────┘  └───────────────────────┘
┌ Keep Paragraph ───────┐
│  [-] Together         │     [-] Side by Side
│  [-] With Next        │
└───────────────────────┘

                              <Replace With...>  <Cancel>
```

This dialog box also has a Replace With button, which takes you to the Replace With Paragraph Formatting dialog box. Both of these dialog boxes are virtually identical to the Format Paragraph command's dialog box, described in Chapter 15.

Style

By choosing the Style button, you move to the Replace Style dialog box:

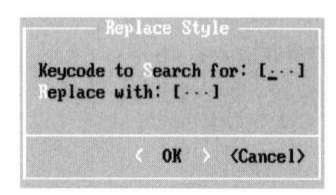

```
──────── Replace Style ────────
 Keycode to Search for: [_..]
 Replace with: [...]

        <  OK  >   <Cancel>
```

Use this simple dialog box to tell Word the key code of the style you want to replace and the key code of the replacement style.

EDIT GO TO COMMAND

The Edit Go To command quickly gets you where you want to go. You can jump

- To a page, a section, or a page in a section
- To footnote reference marks or between footnote reference marks and corresponding footnote text
- Between annotation marks and annotation text
- To a specific passage of text that you've previously labeled with a bookmark

Choose the command by pressing Alt+EG, pressing F5, or double-clicking the mouse on the status bar anywhere outside the Help button. The Edit Go To dialog box appears.

CHAPTER TWELVE: Edit Commands

```
┌─────────────── Go To ───────────────┐
│ Go To: [..................................]│
│             Bookmark Name:              │
│                                         │
│  (•) Page         ┌─────────────┐  ↑   │
│  ( ) Bookmark     │             │  ▓   │
│  ( ) Footnote     │             │  ▓   │
│  ( ) Annotation   │             │  ↓   │
│                   └─────────────┘      │
│                                         │
│              <  OK  >   <Cancel>        │
└─────────────────────────────────────────┘
```

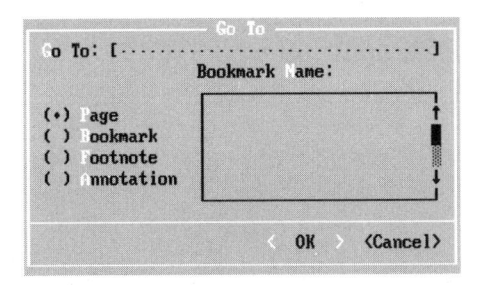

Fields of the Edit Go To Dialog Box

The Edit Go To dialog box has three fields in addition to the OK and Cancel command buttons:

Go To (text box) Tell Word where you want to go. Type the number of the page, footnote, or annotation or the name of the bookmark.

Page, Bookmark, Footnote, Annotation (option buttons) Use these option buttons to tell Word whether you want to go to a page, a bookmark, a footnote, or an annotation.

- **Page**—This is the default setting, and it takes you to a specified page.
- **Bookmark**—If your document contains bookmarks, choose this setting and use the Bookmark Name list box to select the name of the one you want to go to.
- **Footnote**—If your document contains footnotes, choose this option button to take you to the next footnote reference mark. If you are on a footnote reference mark, it takes you to the associated footnote text. If you are in the text of a footnote, it takes you back to the mark in the document.
- **Annotation**—If your document contains annotations, this takes you to the next annotation reference mark. If you are on an annotation reference mark, it takes you to the associated annotation text. If you are in the text of an annotation, it takes you back to the mark in the document.

These choices are described in greater detail below:

Bookmark Name (list box) The names of all bookmarks in your document are listed here. To jump to one of them, select its name and then choose the Bookmark option button.

Going to a page

The Edit Go To Page command moves the cursor to the first character of the first column of the page you specify. It works only after Word has calculated breaks between pages for a document. The tips on the following page might prove useful.

- In multisection documents, a particular page number might appear more than once. Word moves to the next page that has the number you specify. To move to a particular page in a particular section, follow the page number with *S* and the number of the section. For instance, if you type 3S2, Word moves to the third page of the second section. If you omit the page number, Word moves to the first page of the specified section.
- If you specify a page number higher than any in the document, Word jumps to the beginning of the last page.
- Word jumps to the next-higher page number if the page number you specify is no longer in the document because its new-page mark was deleted and background pagination is not on. It's possible to inadvertently delete new-page marks because each is tied to the final character of the preceding page. If this final character is visible or if it is a spacing character, deleting it can cause the new-page mark to vanish too. Furthermore, the Edit Undo command will not restore the new-page mark: Either repaginate the document and then retry the Edit Go To command, or jump instead to the next-higher page number and scroll back to the desired position.

NOTE: *You can force Word to calculate page breaks by using the Utilities Repaginate Now command (Alt+UP). This shouldn't be necessary, however, if you check (turn on) the Utilities Customize command's Background Pagination check box. When this feature is on, Word keeps page numbering current. Even when automatic repagination is off, several other commands cause Word to update page numbering. These commands include File Print, File Print Preview, View Layout, and Insert Index and Insert Table of Contents.*

Going to a bookmark

Choosing Edit Go To and selecting Bookmark enables you to move directly to a section of text that has been previously marked and given a bookmark name. To give selected text a bookmark name, use the Insert Bookmark command (Alt+IM).

Together, Insert Bookmark and Edit Go To with the Bookmark option let you skip from place to place in a long document. For example, suppose you write a report broken into a number of major and minor discussions, such as Introduction, Scope, Methods and Procedures, Budget, and so on. Select each discussion in turn, and use the Insert Bookmark command to give it a bookmark name. That way, you can quickly move to any discussion regardless of its page number or section number, if the section you want to see is part of the current document. For details on creating bookmarks, see Chapter 14.

When you use the Edit Go To command, the Bookmark Name list box displays the names of existing bookmarks. Select one, choose the Bookmark option button, and press Enter or choose OK to execute the command. Word immediately jumps to the bookmarked text and highlights all of it, from the first character (beginning anchor) to the last character (ending anchor).

As described in Chapter 21, bookmarks also provide a means of automatically cross-referencing a document at print time. If you use bookmarks to mark tables or figures to be sequentially numbered by Word, using Edit Go To with the Bookmark option is an ideal way to review the finished document for missing or incomplete bookmarks before you print it.

Going to a footnote

Choosing Footnote gives fast results, but what those results are depends on where the cursor is when you use the Edit Go To command.

- If a footnote reference mark is the first character of the selection or if the cursor is at the footnote reference mark, the command takes you to the corresponding footnote text.
- If a footnote/annotation window is open, the selection moves to it. Otherwise, Word instantly scrolls to where footnote and annotation text is stored at the end of the document.
- Conversely, if footnote text contains the cursor, the Edit Go To command takes you to the corresponding reference mark in the main text.
- If no reference marks are selected, if the cursor is not a reference mark, and if the cursor is not in footnote text, the command takes you to the next existing reference mark in the document.
- When more than one character is selected and one of them (but not the first one) is a reference mark, Edit Go To with the Footnote option reduces the size of the selection to the character or characters that form the reference mark.

Going to an annotation

The Edit Go To command with the Annotation option works like Edit Go To with the Footnote option but with annotations rather than ordinary footnotes.

Annotations, which really are simply a special kind of footnote, are created with the Insert Annotation command. (See Chapter 14.) Annotations are useful as means of inserting comments, remarks, suggestions, and the like into a document. Whereas traditional footnotes are generally numbered or identified by special marks, you can use initials, group identifications, even first and last names as annotation marks; and you can tell Word to label each annotation with the date and time of its insertion.

EDIT GLOSSARY COMMAND

When it comes to storing and retrieving text, you can think of the glossary as a virtually endless collection of scraps—each a location to which you can copy or delete text and from which you can restore text that you have cut or copied from your document, and from which you can insert passages. Unlike the scrap, however, information you store in the glossary is not overwritten the next time you store something else; indeed, you can have any number of entries in your glossary and save them for as long as you want.

Understanding the distinctions between a few similar-sounding terms and ideas will help you make the most of the glossary:

- The glossary is a storage area in computer memory. It holds any number of passages of text that you might reuse.
- The glossary can hold any number of *macros*. (A macro is a series of instructions for Word.)
- A stored passage or macro is a *glossary entry*. You create a text-only glossary entry by selecting text and then storing it in the glossary with the Edit Glossary command. You create a macro by writing or recording it and then storing it in the glossary with the Macro Edit command.
- You insert a text-only glossary entry from the glossary into a document with the Insert Glossary command, or by typing the name of the glossary entry into your document and pressing the F3 key, or by pressing the control code.
- You can store the entire contents of the glossary on disk in a special *glossary file*. You create and name the file by using either the Edit Glossary command and the Save Glossary button or the Macro Edit command and the Save Glossary button. Word assigns it the filename extension .GLY. These files can be whole collections of glossary entries—special-purpose ones, for example, that contain names, boilerplate text, and even related macros for use with a particular kind of document, such as a report or letter.
- During an editing session, you can load a stored glossary file into the glossary to make its glossary entries available for use.
- You can use a special glossary file called NORMAL.GLY to save glossary entries you use frequently. Word loads this file into the glossary when you start a session, so its glossary entries are always available for use. Different document disks (and directories on a hard disk) can have different glossary files named NORMAL.GLY. This makes it easy to dedicate disks (or directories) to different purposes and always have the appropriate glossary entries instantly available for each.

This chapter focuses on text glossary entries, not macros. For a discussion of the Macro Edit command, which is a direct counterpart of the Edit Glossary command, see Chapter 17.

Preparing to Use the Glossary

Before you use the Edit Glossary command, you need to prepare in one of two ways:

- If you intend to define a passage of text as a glossary entry, first select (highlight) the passage.
- If you intend to insert text from the glossary, first position your cursor at the location in the document where you want the insertion to occur.

CHAPTER TWELVE: Edit Commands

After you have prepared accordingly, you choose the Edit Glossary command by pressing Alt+EO. Word responds by showing you the main Edit Glossary dialog box:

```
┌─────────────────────────── Glossary ───────────────────────────┐
│ Glossary Name:                    Optional Keys:               │
│ [...........................]     [...................]       │
│ Names:                                                         │
│  ┌──────────────────────────────────────────────────────────┐  │
│  │  date                         Office                     │  │
│  │  dateprint                    page                       │  │
│  │  footnote                     Section1                   │  │
│  │  Friends <shift ctrl F>S      time                       │  │
│  │  nextpage                     timeprint                  │  │
│  └──────────────────────────────────────────────────────────┘  │
│ Selection:                        Glossary File: NORMAL.GLY    │
│  Balaenoptera·acutorostrata¶                                   │
│                                                                │
│  <Define>  < Delete >  < Open Glossary...>                     │
│  <Insert>  < Clear All> < Save Glossary...> <Merge...> <Close> │
└────────────────────────────────────────────────────────────────┘
```

Observe that, below the list of glossary entries in the center of the dialog box, a line shows you some or all of the document text that is selected at the moment. This is the text that will become a new glossary entry if you decide to define it as that. When no text is selected, the line says *(No Selection)*.

This dialog box will become familiar to you as you use Word because it is Word's response to two different commands—Edit Glossary and Macro Edit. The only difference between these commands, other than three or four words of labeling near the top of the screen, is that the Edit Glossary command lists only text entries from the glossary file passages, whereas the Macro Edit command lists only macro entries from the glossary file.

Fields of the Edit Glossary Dialog Box

The Edit Glossary dialog box has 10 fields, in addition to the Close command button:

Glossary Name (text box) Type a name for the glossary entry you want to define, delete, insert, edit, or otherwise affect. If you use the Names list box, the Glossary Name text box will be filled in automatically.

Glossary names can have up to 31 characters. No spaces are allowed, although for ease of reading you can separate words in a name by capitalizing the first letter of each. You can also insert a hyphen, a period, or the underline character between the words in a name, provided the name begins and ends with at least one alphabetic or numeric character. (For example, the name *name-1* is acceptable, but *name1-* and *-name1* are not.) Keep the names of glossary entries short, even to a few letters or a word, so that you can type them quickly.

Optional Keys (text box) When you are preparing to define a macro, you can create a *control code* for it. This one-letter or two-letter code becomes a shortcut way to later insert the glossary entry's content into a document. For example, if you give a macro the control code *Shift+Ctrl+ID*, you can press that combination of keys while in a document to insert the text of the glossary entry.

Names (list box) Word examines your glossary and lists in this box all entries that are not macros. If you select a name in this list box, it will appear in the Glossary Name text box. The name also is shown below the Names list box, followed by up to the first 54 characters of the glossary text.

Define (command button) Choose this button after you fill in the Glossary Name and possibly the Optional Keys text boxes. The Define button actually copies the selected text into the glossary, thereby creating a new glossary entry.

Insert (command button) To insert the text of the named glossary entry into a document, choose this button. It inserts the text of the glossary listed in the Edit Glossary Name text box.

An alternative way to insert the text of a glossary entry is to type its name into a document and press the F3 key. This is a fast method and avoids the Edit Glossary command completely, but it requires that you remember the exact name of the entry.

Delete (command button) To delete the selected or named glossary entry, choose this button. Deleting entries from the active glossary does not affect the contents of a glossary file on disk, unless you save the glossary after deleting some or all of its contents.

If you want to erase entries from a glossary file on disk, load the appropriate glossary file by choosing the Glossary command and the Open Glossary dialog box; eliminate unwanted entries with the Delete button; and use the Save Glossary button to record the amended version back on disk with the same name.

Clear All (command button) To clear all glossary entries, choose this button. Word responds with the message *Do you want to delete all glossary entries now?* If you choose OK, the only entries that will remain will be the reserved glossary names, such as *time* and *date*, which cannot be removed.

Open Glossary (command button) To load a glossary file from disk into Word, thereby displacing the current entries in the glossary, choose this button. It brings to the screen a dialog box:

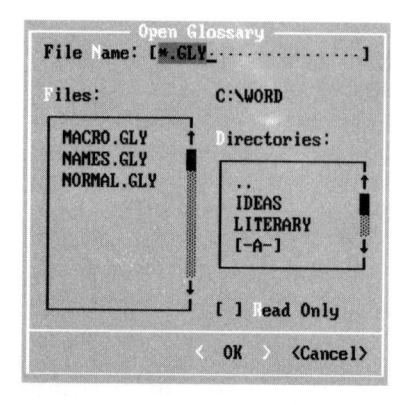

```
──────── Open Glossary ────────
File  ame: [*.GLY................]

 iles:              C:\WORD

 ┌─────────────┐
 │ MACRO.GLY  ↑│  irectories:
 │ NAMES.GLY   │
 │ NORMAL.GLY  │ ┌─────────────┐
 │             │ │ ..        ↑ │
 │             │ │ IDEAS       │
 │             │ │ LITERARY    │
 │             │ │ [-A-]     ↓ │
 │           ↓ │ └─────────────┘
 └─────────────┘
                [ ]  ead Only

          <  OK  >   <Cancel>
```

CHAPTER TWELVE: Edit Commands

This dialog box contains only four fields: a File Name text box, in which you can type the name of the glossary file you want to load; both Files and Directories list boxes, which together provide an alternative way to choose a glossary file; and a Read Only check box, which lets you specify that you want to be able to use the contents of the newly loaded glossary file but that you don't want to be able to change them.

Save Glossary (command button) To save your current glossary as a file, press the Save Glossary button. Word responds by displaying a dialog box that looks virtually identical to the Open Glossary dialog box, except that it does not have a Read Only check box. Use this dialog box to give your glossary file a name, change its name, or simply resave it after making changes.

During any single editing session, new glossary entries exist only in your computer's memory until you save the glossary on disk as a file. When you quit Word without saving, you lose the glossary. If you save your glossary on disk, you can use its entries during different editing sessions, and you can reuse macros, phrases, paragraphs, and even long sections of text again and again without retyping them.

You might save all the glossary entries for a particular report in a glossary file dedicated to the report. Type the name you want for the new glossary file.

Merge (command button) Sometimes you want to load a glossary file from disk into your current glossary, but you don't want to displace the existing glossary entries. In this situation, press the Merge button. It brings to the screen a dialog box that is similar to the Open Glossary dialog box but that does not have a Read Only check box.

If an entry in a glossary file that is being merged has the same name as one already in the glossary, the newly merged entry replaces the existing one.

The permanent glossary names

The entries *page*, *nextpage*, *footnote*, *date*, *dateprint*, *time*, and *timeprint* are permanently recorded in the glossary. (If you're using Word under Microsoft Windows, you'll find the additional permanent glossary name *clipboard*.)

The glossary name *page* causes Word to print the number of the current page. The *page* entry is handy to use with headers or footers at the tops or bottoms of pages, where you might want a page number in a particular position on every printed sheet of paper. When you insert this into text, you see *(page)* on the screen, but the correct page number will be printed.

If you want to precede the page number with the word *Page*—that is, *Page 1* on the first sheet, *Page 2* on the second, and so forth—type the word *Page* in the document before inserting the Glossary entry. For example, if you type the words *Page page* and press the F3 key, you will see *Page (page)* in the header on the screen, but it will print as *Page* followed by the page number.

Word offers a related glossary name, *nextpage*, which prints the number of the page following the current page. For example, if you are working on page 24 of a document and insert the glossary name *nextpage* in the text, it will appear as *(nextpage)* on screen but will be replaced by the number *25* in the printed version of the document. This is useful for people who want the bottom of a page to make reference to the number of the next page or who want to say, as part of a table or a figure, *continued on page (nextpage)*.

The glossary name *footnote* is generally used in one special case: If you accidentally delete the reference mark for an automatically numbered footnote from the footnote text part of a document, typing *footnote* and pressing F3 will restore the special autonumber character. Using the *footnote* glossary name causes the deleted reference mark to reappear as a number on the screen.

The *footnote* glossary name doesn't work if you accidentally delete a footnote reference mark from the main body of a document, because the deletion causes the corresponding footnote text to be deleted too.

The remaining four permanent names in the glossary allow you to put the date and time in your documents.

The glossary name *date* causes Word to insert the current date—or the date your computer believes to be current—into your document. Simply type the word *date*, and press the F3 key. The date appears in your document in the form *April 27, 1991*, if the Date field of the Utilities Customize command is set to the default display of month-day-year (*MDY*). If you change the Date field of the Utilities Customize command to day-month-year (*DMY*), the date will be inserted in this form: *27 April, 1991*.

If you want Word to update the date automatically each time it prints the document, use the glossary name *dateprint* instead of *date*. Type *dateprint*, and press the F3 key. The Word screen will show *(dateprint)*, but your document will be printed with the current date. This is handy for correspondence you send often.

The glossary names *time* and *timeprint* are similar to *date* and *dateprint*, except that they show the time your computer believes it to be in the format (12-hour or 24-hour) specified in the Time field of the Utilities Customize command. With *timeprint*, the screen shows *(timeprint)*, but the document is printed with the actual time. In 12-hour format, you see something like this: *7:57 PM*. In 24-hour format, the same time is expressed as *19:57*.

By using both *dateprint* and *timeprint* in a document that you update and print frequently, you can label all your copies with the date and time they are printed.

By using the *date* and *time* glossary names, you needn't check your office calendar or clock. For instance, if you type the word *time* and press the F3 key, you see the time. You can delete it either by pressing the Backspace key a few times or by using the Undo command (Alt+Backspace) followed by the Del key.

Note that Word relies on the operating system to tell it the correct date and time; those values are correct only if the operating system either gets the time from a built-in clock/calendar or is given the date and time when the computer is started up.

Final Tips

- If you want a reference to the contents of your glossary, use the File Print command and choose Glossary in the Print drop-down list box. Word gives you a paper copy of glossary names, control codes, and the text you have stored as an entry with each name.
- If you are using Word on a network, a glossary file stored in one of the document directories on the network server might already be in use. If

the glossary is a read-only file, you can load it and use it, but if you make changes to it and want to save those changes, you must save the changed glossary under a different filename. If the glossary is not a read-only file, only one person at a time can use it, so Word displays the message *File is in use* and refuses access to it until the other person saves it.

For a better understanding of NORMAL.GLY, refer to the end of Chapter 6. For additional information on text glossaries, see Chapter 22. To learn about macros, see Chapters 6, 17, and 23.

EDIT COMMANDS FOR STYLE SHEETS

When a style sheet is in the active window, the Edit menu is shorter and has one new command.

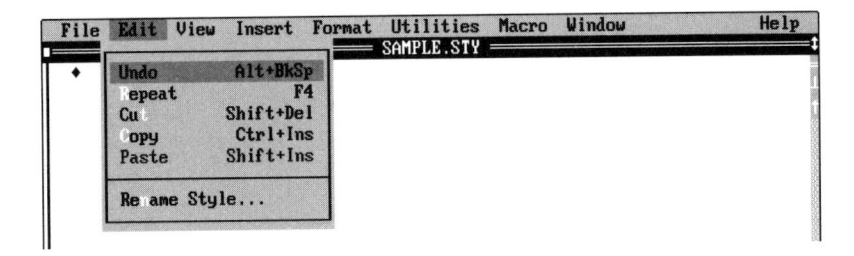

The Edit Undo, Edit Repeat, Edit Cut, Edit Copy, and Edit Paste commands are much the same as they are when a document is active except that the actions you take with them pertain to style sheets. You can cut a selected style or styles from a style sheet and paste them elsewhere in the same or a different style sheet, for example.

The new command is Edit Rename Style.

The Edit Rename Style Command

This command appears on the Edit menu only when a style sheet is active. When you press Alt+EN to choose the command, Word displays the following dialog box:

The choices you make in this dialog box allow you to change the name of a style. For this reason, a style must be selected before the command can be used.

A style's name is composed of four elements—its key code, type, I.D., and remark. The Edit Rename Style dialog box lets you change three of these; the only one you cannot change is the style's type, which remains *paragraph*, *character*, or *section*, depending on what it was when the style was created.

The Edit Rename Style dialog box is virtually identical to the Record Style dialog box, which you access by choosing the Format Record command. The main difference is that the Record Style dialog box lets you specify a type of style—type being the one thing you cannot change with the Edit Rename Style command.

For information on the fields of the Edit Rename Style command, see the discussion of the Format Record Style command in Chapter 15.

CHAPTER THIRTEEN

View Commands

View commands are Word's acknowledgment that there's more than one way to look at almost anything: They let you establish or change the way Word presents information on the screen. You use them when you want to see your document as an outline, change your screen's display mode, or alter the color of your background window. You use them to turn on the ribbon or turn off the ruler, speed up the movement of the cursor, or control the width of lines on screen without changing the width at which they will print. You use them when you want to see paragraphs and tab characters displayed in your document. In short, you use View commands to control how you view your work.

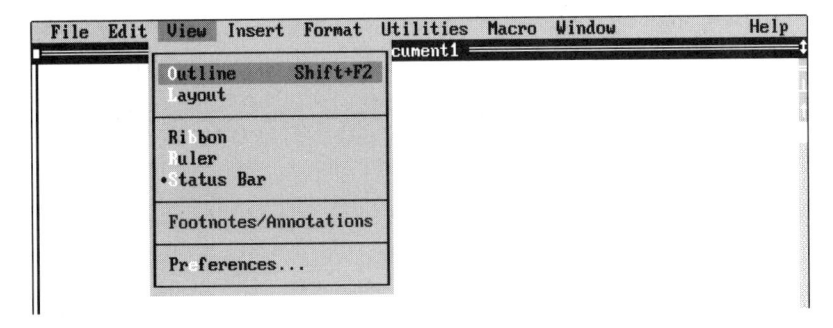

```
 File  Edit  View  Insert  Format  Utilities  Macro  Window          Help
                                   cument1
              Outline    Shift+F2
              Layout

              Ribbon
              Ruler
             •Status Bar

              Footnotes/Annotations

              Preferences...
```

Many of the features controlled by the View menu were introduced in some detail in Chapter 4.

In summary form, here is what each of the View commands permits you to do:

View Outline—Examine or edit a document in an abbreviated, outline form.

View Layout—Edit a document, with the relationship of its columns, graphics, and other elements approximated on screen.

View Ribbon—Turn on or off the *ribbon*, a horizontal bar near the top of the screen that shows—and lets you change—aspects of your document's formatting.

View Ruler—Turn on or off a ruler at the top of a document window.

View Status Bar—Turn on or off the *status bar,* the line near the bottom of the screen that lists the page number and other information about your work with Word.

View Footnotes/Annotations—Open or close a special window pane that lets you view or edit footnotes or annotations.

View Preferences—Make a large number of additional choices about what is displayed on your screen, including the colors assigned to various elements when you use a color monitor.

THREE VIEWS OF A DOCUMENT

When you are editing a Word document, you see it in one of three mutually exclusive views: *document view, outline view,* or *layout view.* Although the content of your document doesn't change when you switch from one view to another, its appearance does.

Document View

Document view is the conventional way of looking at a document. By scrolling the screen, you can see every part of your document; however, the sequence of its elements reflects their position in your document file, not necessarily the layout of the printed page. For example, a page laid out in two columns will appear as a single column in document view. This makes it easier to edit content and preserves a beginning-to-end feeling for your document.

In document view, the left side of the status bar shows *Pg,* followed by the current page number, and *Co,* followed by the current column number. (If the document contains multiple sections or if you have the Show Line Numbers field of the View Preferences command turned on, you see both the current section number and line number.)

Here's how a two-column document with a centered graphic might look on screen in document view:

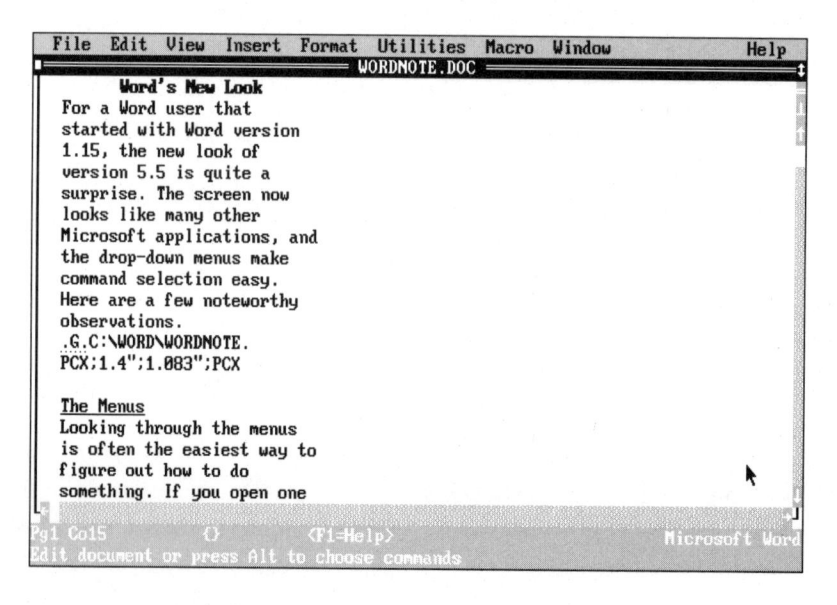

Outline View

Outline view shows a document in outline form, with headings indented to reflect their level. You can choose to see main headings only, main headings plus subheadings down to a certain level, or the headings plus all of the text. You can also show the text associated with one heading at a time so that you can, for example, move around in the outline and expand any heading to see the text that follows it in the document.

To use outline view effectively, you must indicate to Word which paragraphs are headings. This is accomplished for you if you format your documents with style sheets that contain Paragraph Heading styles. If you are not formatting headings with these styles, you must deliberately tell Word which paragraphs to treat as headings for the purposes of outline view. This task is described in Chapter 26.

When you are in outline view, the left side of the status bar shows the word *Text* or the word *Level* followed by the outline level of the currently highlighted paragraph. When in outline view, you can switch into a special mode called *outline organize* by pressing Shift+F5. In outline organize, the lower-left corner of the screen shows the word *ORGANIZE*.

Here's how the document looks in outline view:

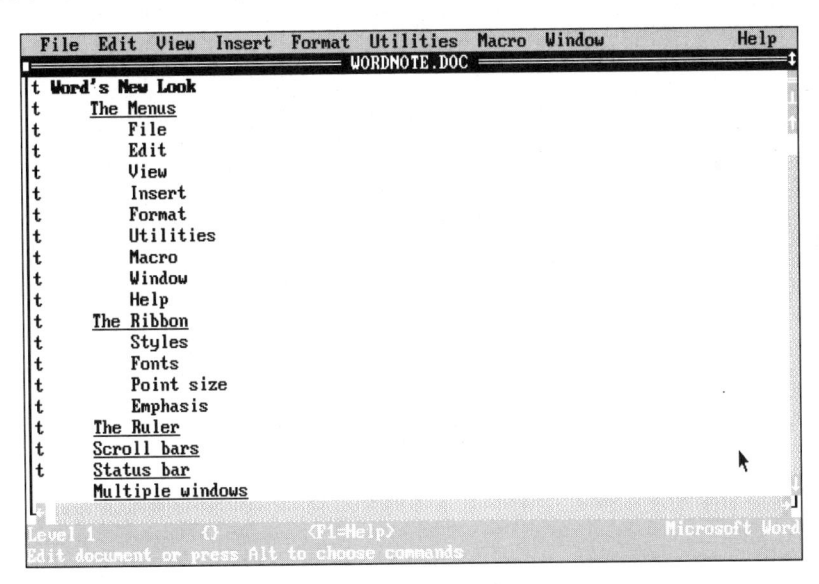

```
 File   Edit  View  Insert  Format  Utilities  Macro  Window           Help
═══════════════════════════ WORDNOTE.DOC ═══════════════════════════
t Word's New Look
t     The Menus
t         File
t         Edit
t         View
t         Insert
t         Format
t         Utilities
t         Macro
t         Window
t         Help
t     The Ribbon
t         Styles
t         Fonts
t         Point size
t         Emphasis
t     The Ruler
t     Scroll bars
t     Status bar
t     Multiple windows

Level 1        {}        <F1=Help>                      Microsoft Word
Edit document or press Alt to choose commands
```

Observe that the headings that appeared on screen in document view (*Word's New Look* and *The Menus*) also appear here but that none of the text is displayed. Observe, too, how much more of the document can be represented on the screen at one time when the body text of the document has been collapsed out of view.

Layout View

Layout view lets you edit a document at the same time that you see its expected layout on the page. Layout view might look no different from document view when your document is as simple as a one-column business letter. However, the layout view of a newsletter containing multiple columns and fixed graphics or text can look quite different from the document view. Layout view reflects the relative positions of multiple columns, side-by-side paragraphs, absolutely positioned paragraphs, and graphics.

NOTE: *To see actual graphics, running heads, and footnotes, you must use the File Print Preview command.*

Here is how the same document looks when presented in layout view:

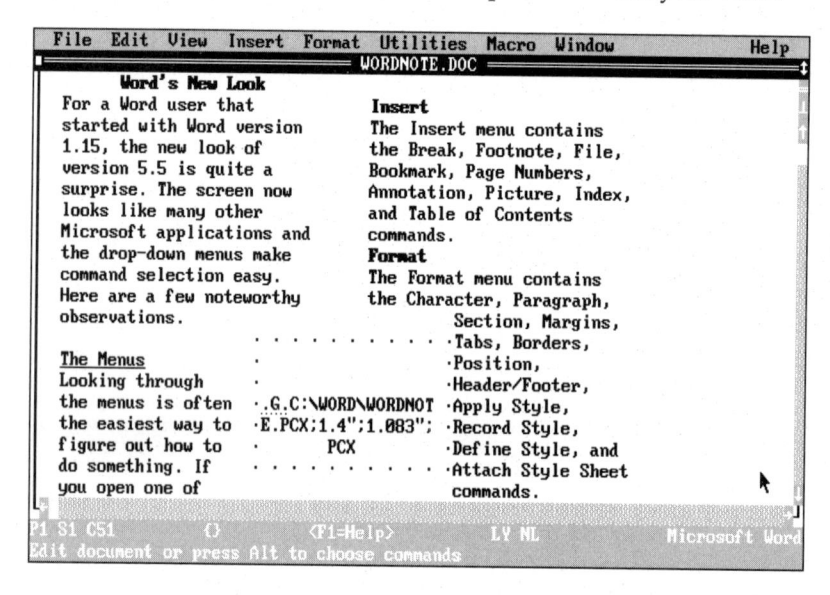

```
 File   Edit   View   Insert   Format   Utilities   Macro   Window              Help
╞═══════════════════════════════ WORDNOTE.DOC ═══════════════════════════════╡
    Word's New Look
    For a Word user that          Insert
    started with Word version     The Insert menu contains
    1.15, the new look of         the Break, Footnote, File,
    version 5.5 is quite a        Bookmark, Page Numbers,
    surprise. The screen now      Annotation, Picture, Index,
    looks like many other         and Table of Contents
    Microsoft applications and    commands.
    the drop-down menus make      Format
    command selection easy.       The Format menu contains
    Here are a few noteworthy     the Character, Paragraph,
    observations.                    Section, Margins,
                        · · · · · · · ·Tabs, Borders,
    The Menus                      ·       ·Position,
    Looking through                ·       ·Header/Footer,
    the menus is often    ·.G.C:\WORD\WORDNOT ·Apply Style,
    the easiest way to    ·E.PCX;1.4";1.083"; ·Record Style,
    figure out how to          PCX          ·Define Style, and
    do something. If    · · · · · · · · · ·Attach Style Sheet
    you open one of                         commands.                  ▸
╘════════════════════════════════════════════════════════════════════════════╛
P1 S1 C51        {}           <F1=Help>          LY NL      Microsoft Word
Edit document or press Alt to choose commands
```

Observe that the columns are displayed side by side and that text flows around the graphic, which is represented by a dotted outline.

You can tell at a glance if you are in layout view, either by looking at the status bar at the bottom of the screen to see if the letters *LY* are displayed there or by choosing the View menu to see if a dot appears to the left of the Layout command's name.

Switching Among the Three Views

The first two commands on the View menu are mutually exclusive toggles: View Outline and View Layout. Word is in the most recent view you turn on—outline if you've most recently used View Outline or layout if you've most recently used View Layout. If both are off, Word is in document view.

VIEW OUTLINE COMMAND

To move in or out of outline view, choose the View Outline command by pressing Alt+VO or by holding down the Shift key and pressing the F2 key. When you are in outline view, a dot appears to the left of the View Outline command's name.

To avoid confusion, turn off outline view when you're not using it. Word doesn't behave the same in outline view as it does in document view.

For details on the use of outline view, see Chapter 26.

VIEW LAYOUT COMMAND

To move in and out of layout view, choose the View Layout command by pressing Alt+VL. When you are in layout view, a dot appears to the left of the View Layout command's name, and the letters *LY* appear in the status bar.

It's a good idea to turn off layout view when you don't need it. Word operates more slowly in layout view, macros might not perform as expected, and some key combinations differ from document view.

> NOTE: *Because layout view reflects your document as it will print, the display of hidden text is controlled by choosing the File Print command, choosing the Options button, and then clicking the Hidden Text check box.*

For details on the use of layout view, see Chapters 7 and 30.

VIEW RIBBON COMMAND

To turn the ribbon on or off, choose the View Ribbon command (Alt+VB). If you have a mouse, you can turn the ribbon on or off by clicking the right mouse button when the mouse pointer is on the ribbon/ruler icon at the top of the vertical scroll bar. The ribbon, described in detail in Chapter 4, is a single line of formatting information that appears near the top of the screen, just below the menu bar and outside any document windows. It lets you monitor and control several aspects of the text. Specifically, you can keep tabs on which paragraph style is in use, as well as which font and font size are in effect, and whether the text is bold, italic, or underlined.

VIEW RULER COMMAND

Use the View Ruler command to turn the ruler at the top of a window on and off. If you have a mouse, you can turn the ruler on or off by clicking the left mouse button when the mouse pointer is on the ribbon/ruler icon at the top of the vertical scroll bar.

Normally, the ruler shows a number for every inch and a mark for every one-tenth of an inch. A left bracket ([) shows the position of the left indent of the paragraph that contains the selection; a vertical bar (¦) indicates the special indentation (if any) of the first line of the paragraph that contains the selection; and a right bracket (]) marks the right indent of the selected paragraph.

If the selected paragraph contains tab stops, they'll show in the ruler too. If more than one paragraph is selected, the tab stops will show only if they are the same in each paragraph. *L* marks a left-aligned tab stop; *C* marks a center-aligned stop; *R* marks a right-aligned stop; *D* marks a decimal-aligned stop; and a vertical line marks the position of a vertical tab stop. A period, a hyphen, or an underline immediately preceding a tab-stop character indicates that the tab stop is formatted with that particular punctuation mark as a leader character. (Tab stops are explained in detail in Chapter 15.)

The ruler is *live*, meaning that it responds to mouse actions; it is *scalable*, meaning that it adjusts its scale to the kinds of characters you use in your document; and it is *slidable*, meaning that it can give you an on-screen approximation of layout.

The Live Ruler

The live ruler gives you an easier, more interactive way to manipulate tab stops and paragraph indents than the Format Tabs and Format Paragraph commands do.

By pointing with the mouse to the ruler and clicking, you can set, clear, and move tab stops, paragraph indents, and first-line indents for paragraphs you've highlighted, without choosing a command. And you can use the ruler, rather than the Format Tabs command, to choose among leader characters and tab alignments. Because you immediately see the results of your formatting in the paragraphs containing the cursor, you can refine your tab stops and indents easily by pointing to the ruler and clicking a mouse button or dragging the mouse. (For a description of how to use the live ruler, see the discussion of the Format Tabs command in Chapter 15.)

The Scalable Ruler

The terms *scalable* and *slidable* are both related to Word's on-screen display of document layout.

Scalable means that Word can expand the distance between inch marks on the ruler. As mentioned earlier, Word's ruler normally shows each character as occupying one-tenth of an inch because 10 pica-size (12-point) characters of nonproportionally spaced type fit in a horizontal inch of printed output. But when you use proportionally spaced fonts, such as Times Roman or Helvetica, or any font in sizes other than 12-point, this standard tenths-of-an-inch ruler no longer represents the number of characters Word will actually print per inch. Proportionally spaced fonts, even printed in 12-point type, don't print one character per one-tenth of an inch because some letters (*i*, for example) occupy much less space than do other letters (such as *W*). Similarly, one inch holds more 8-point characters than it does 12-point characters.

Such programs as Microsoft Word for Windows show characters on the screen in their correct widths, giving you a what-you-see-is-what-you-get view of a document. But Microsoft Word for DOS is a character-based program, meaning that each character takes up the same amount of space on the screen. This gives superior speed and, in many people's judgment, superior readability. But it leaves unsolved the question of how to display the effects of different font sizes and widths. That is where the scalable ruler comes in.

In essence, because Word cannot change the apparent scale of the font, it instead changes the scale of the measuring tool, the ruler. It expands the distance between inch marks so that the correct number of characters of the correct font are displayed in what the ruler shows to be an inch.

As a feature, the scalable ruler is useful, but it has limitations.

First, Word uses it only when you check the Line Breaks field of the View Preferences command. (Word sets Line Breaks to Yes for you when you are in layout view.)

Second, Word uses it only when a tab character is present (and not always then). The scalable ruler is intended to help you align the columns of tables properly on the screen when you are using small fonts. So, if your document doesn't contain tab characters, the ruler won't change in scale, regardless of the font you are using.

Third, the scale of the ruler expands readily, but it doesn't contract. If you format a table in small characters, for example, Word will expand the distance between inch marks on the ruler. But when you move beyond the table, returning to larger characters, the ruler doesn't contract. It continues to show the location of tab stops and paragraph indents relative to the overall width of the paragraph, but it no longer reflects the location of specific characters on each line.

After the scale of the ruler is expanded, it remains expanded as long as the Show Line Breaks field is checked. (To turn this field on or off, press Alt+VEL.)

The Slidable Ruler

And what of the slidable ruler? It comes into play when you have switched to layout view in order to view the layout of a document that contains either multiple columns or absolutely positioned paragraphs. In a document containing either of these elements, saying that the ruler is *slidable* means that it slides from side to side, aligning its left edge with the leftmost element of whichever column or absolutely positioned paragraph currently contains the highlight. For example, the following illustration shows the ruler above the left column of a two-column document:

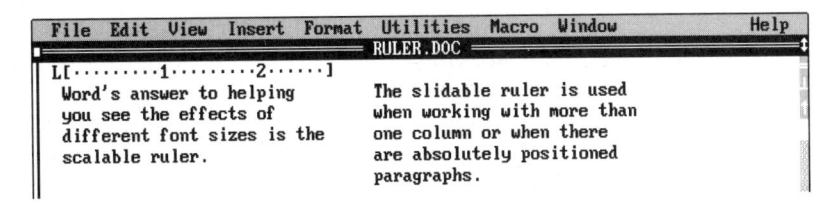

```
 File   Edit  View  Insert  Format  Utilities  Macro  Window          Help
══════════════════════════════ RULER.DOC ══════════════════════════════
 L[·········1·········2······]
 Word's answer to helping     The slidable ruler is used
 you see the effects of       when working with more than
 different font sizes is the  one column or when there
 scalable ruler.              are absolutely positioned
                              paragraphs.
```

When you move the highlight to the right column by turning off Num Lock, pressing Alt+5, and then pressing the Right direction key, the ruler slides to the right like this:

```
 File   Edit  View  Insert  Format  Utilities  Macro  Window          Help
══════════════════════════════ RULER.DOC ══════════════════════════════
                              L[·········1·········2······]
 Word's answer to helping     The slidable ruler is used
 you see the effects of       when working with more than
 different font sizes is the  one column or when there
 scalable ruler.              are absolutely positioned
                              paragraphs.
```

Thus, you don't need to do any mental addition or subtraction to figure out where your tab stops or indents are in relation to the left edge of the column (or of the frame of an absolutely positioned paragraph), and you can immediately see the width of the column or frame, starting from 0.

VIEW STATUS BAR COMMAND

To turn the screen's status bar on or off, press Alt+VS to use the View Status Bar command. The status bar, described in Chapter 4, is the line near the bottom of the screen that reflects the current page number, shows you what is in the scrap, reminds you that pressing the F1 key gives you online help, and so forth.

VIEW FOOTNOTES/ANNOTATIONS COMMAND

This command could have been placed on the Windows menu because it opens or closes a special window pane that lets you view the content of footnotes and annotations. This command is available for use only in documents that contain footnotes or annotations.

When a pane is open, it uses part of the screen space that otherwise would be consumed by the window containing the active document. As you move through your document, causing the reference marks to footnotes and annotations to scroll onto and then off the screen, the corresponding footnote and annotation text also appears and then disappears. This lets you see the text associated with any footnote reference mark or annotation reference mark that is displayed on the screen.

When a footnote/annotation pane is open, you can manipulate it as you would a pane created with the Window Split command, which is described in Chapter 18.

VIEW PREFERENCES COMMAND

The View Preferences command leads to a dialog box crammed with choices regarding how you look at your work with Word. Many of these choices could well have been separate View commands had they not been collected here.

Choose the View Preferences command by pressing Alt+VE. The View Preferences dialog box appears:

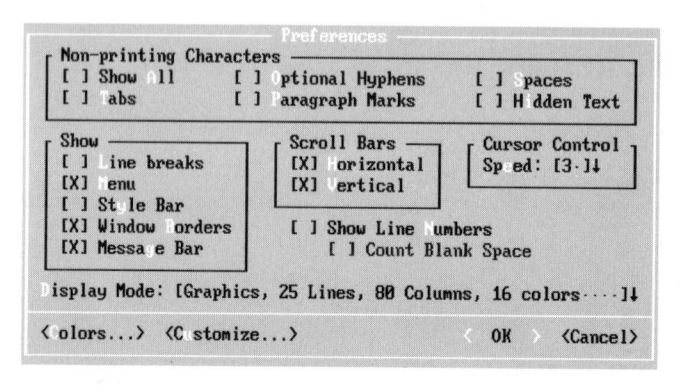

```
┌─────────────────────── Preferences ───────────────────────┐
│ ┌─ Non-printing Characters ─────────────────────────────┐ │
│ │  [ ] Show All      [ ] Optional Hyphens  [ ] Spaces   │ │
│ │  [ ] Tabs          [ ] Paragraph Marks   [ ] Hidden Text │
│ └───────────────────────────────────────────────────────┘ │
│ ┌─ Show ──────────┐ ┌─ Scroll Bars ─┐ ┌─ Cursor Control ─┐│
│ │ [ ] Line breaks │ │ [X] Horizontal│ │ Speed: [3-]↓    ││
│ │ [X] Menu        │ │ [X] Vertical  │ └──────────────────┘│
│ │ [ ] Style Bar   │ └───────────────┘                     │
│ │ [X] Window Borders │  [ ] Show Line Numbers             │
│ │ [X] Message Bar    │  [ ] Count Blank Space             │
│ └────────────────────┘                                    │
│  Display Mode: [Graphics, 25 Lines, 80 Columns, 16 colors····]↓│
│  <Colors...>  <Customize...>           < OK >   <Cancel>  │
└───────────────────────────────────────────────────────────┘
```

CHAPTER THIRTEEN: View Commands

Most of the decisions you make with these commands are stored between editing sessions in Word's MW.INI file. This is the file, introduced in Chapter 8, that stores Word's settings so that the next time you use Word it will be customized as it was when you quit Word last. (To reset all settings to their default values, delete the MW.INI file from the Word program directory before starting Word.)

Fields of the View Preferences Dialog Box

In addition to the usual OK and Cancel command buttons, the View Preferences dialog box has 19 fields, including a button that takes you to the Colors dialog box and a button that leads to the dialog box of the Utilities Customize command, where you have another wealth of choices about how to customize Word.

Nonprinting characters

The first six fields of the View Preferences dialog box are check boxes that control whether certain nonprinting characters used by Word to create various kinds of spaces in a document should be represented on the screen by special characters. Keeping some or all of these characters invisible helps keep the screen uncluttered, but it also can make them easy to forget. And overlooking their existence can lead to such results as the unwitting deletion of paragraph marks, with a consequent sudden change in paragraph formatting.

The first of the six check boxes is called Show All, but we'll get to it last because it makes more sense that way.

Tabs *(check box)* A tab character in a document tells Word to move to the next tab stop. You create a tab character by pressing the Tab key. The tab character is only a single character, but when you select it, a highlighted bar extends from the actual tab character to the location of the tab stop to which it corresponds. Tab characters are represented as arrow symbols when this box is checked.

Optional Hyphens *(check box)* The optional hyphen is a hyphen that is not required to separate two words. The hyphen in *talk-ing*, for example, is optional because you insert it only when the word breaks at the end of a line. Insert optional hyphens by holding down Ctrl and pressing the hyphen key or by using the Utilities Hyphenate command.

Paragraph Marks *(check box)* The paragraph mark indicates the end of a paragraph and stores the paragraph formatting for the preceding text. Insert it by pressing Enter.

The Paragraph Marks check box also governs whether the new-line character will be displayed. The new-line character appears at the end of a line of text and indicates an intentional break to begin a new line. To insert a new-line character, hold down Shift and press Enter. The new-line character does not create a new paragraph (or new paragraph formatting).

Finally, the Paragraph Marks check box influences how hidden text is represented on the screen.

Spaces (check box) A spacebar space (represented by a vertically centered dot) separates words or characters in a document.

Hidden Text (check box) Do you want Word to make characters that have been formatted as "hidden" visible in the text window? Checking this field causes otherwise hidden characters to appear on the screen, with a dotted underline. (If your computer does not have graphics capabilities, or if you're running Word in text mode, the underline is solid or the hidden characters appear in color.)

When the Hidden Text field is not checked but the Paragraph Marks field is checked, the presence of hidden text is not completely ignored on screen. Instead, a double-headed arrow reveals that hidden text exists in the document at that point. The arrow is a single character, which can represent any number of consecutive characters of hidden text.

When you use hidden text, remember that two Hidden Text check boxes exist—one here in the View Preferences dialog box and one in the Options dialog box of the File Print command. The choices you make with these two fields interact:

- If you want both to display and to print hidden text, turn on both check boxes.
- If you want to see but not print hidden text, turn on only the Preferences check box.
- If you want to print but not see hidden text, turn on only the File Print command's check box.
- If you want to preview page breaks or see how your document will print without hidden text, be sure both check boxes are off before using the Utilities Repaginate Now or the File Print Preview command. If you want to see where lines will break before you print, be sure that either layout view or the Line breaks check box of this dialog box is turned on.

Show All (check box) This is an unusual check box. It checks other boxes for you, and it can check itself.

Checking the Show All check box is a shortcut that causes Word to check all five of the previously mentioned check boxes: Tabs, Optional Hyphens, Paragraph Marks, Spaces, and Hidden Text. If you turn on all five of these but not Show All, Word checks the Show All box for you when you press Enter. Turning off this check box does not turn off the other check boxes; you must uncheck each box individually. And when you turn off any of these check boxes, Word turns off the Show All check box if it is still checked.

The Show check boxes

Six of the next seven check boxes let you turn on and off elements of the screen, defining what is displayed and what isn't. The first of them, the Line breaks check box, lets you tell Word whether or not to make it a priority to show exactly where one line ends and the next begins.

Line breaks (check box) A printed line is composed of both contents (characters) and format (appearance). The printed copy properly shows both the contents and the format of each line, and the screen often does too. There are many exceptions on the screen, however, and you use the Line breaks check box to tell Word how to handle each of them.

When your on-screen documents have conventional formats that emulate what a typewriter might produce, Word can usually display each line's content and format on the screen exactly as it will appear when printed. But when you change type sizes within a document or use a proportional font or a nonproportional font in a size other than 10-point or 12-point, Word might be limited to displaying either the exact characters that will be printed on a particular line or the format of that line.

The Line breaks check box asks, in effect, "Do you want the characters in the lines on your screen to match, line for line, the way they'll be printed?"

Checking this box tells Word to show which line each character will print on, even if it means the format of the document will be distorted on the screen. For example, it might cause some justified text to appear unjustified on the screen, even though Word will still print it properly.

Leaving this box unchecked tells Word to forgo accuracy in line content in order to represent paragraph formats accurately. In this case, justified text is justified both on the screen and on the printout, but a particular word might appear in different lines in the two versions.

When you use the Utilities Hyphenate command and set its Confirm field to Yes, Word temporarily switches the Line breaks box to Yes, unless you have already done so. When you enter layout view, Word temporarily sets the Line breaks box to Yes.

If both the ruler and the Line breaks box are on, the ruler can become elastic when documents containing tab characters are formatted for proportionally spaced fonts or font sizes other than 12-point. If your ruler stretches sideways and part of your document runs off the screen to the right, don't worry that Word has suddenly lost its bearings. You are seeing Word's scalable ruler: In an effort to show you the layout of the document, the program is matching the ruler to the font and font size you are using in the document. (For a more detailed description, see the previous discussion of the View Ruler command.)

Menu (check box) Do you want the menu at the top of the screen to be displayed while you are editing a document or style sheet?

Checking this box causes the menu bar to be displayed at all times. If this box is not checked, the menu will appear only when you are using a command. (To signal that you want to use a command, press the Alt or the F10 key.)

Style Bar (check box) Turn the style bar on and off with this check box. The style bar is a vertical band, two spaces wide, that runs from the top to the bottom of the text window, immediately inside the left edge of the window. When a style sheet is attached to a document, the style bar shows you the one-character and two-character key codes of the paragraph styles you assign.

Using the style bar has another benefit, even when a document doesn't have a style sheet. The style bar indicates where paragraphs that you formatted as headers or footers (*running heads* or *feet*) will print: *h* means a header and will print at the top of the page; *f* means a footer and will print at the bottom of the page; *o* means only on odd pages; *e* means only on even pages; and *f* means only on the first page. These letters might appear in combinations. For example, if the letters *he* appear in the style bar to the left of the first line of a paragraph, it means that the paragraph is a header that appears only on even pages.

Window Borders (check box) If you are running Word in its Window Maximize mode, the Window Borders check box lets you decide whether to display the title bar and other borders surrounding a window.

If you are not in Window Maximize mode, Word insists on displaying borders because it must contend with the possibility of displaying more than one window at a time—a situation that makes window borders imperative.

To activate Window Maximize mode, use the Window Maximize command (Alt+WX), or click with the mouse on the title bar's window maximize icon, which is the two-headed arrow at the far right end of the title bar.

When borders are turned off, the name of the document appears in place of the words *Microsoft Word* in the status bar in the lower-right corner of the screen.

Message Bar (check box) Use this check box to turn on or off the message bar on the last line of the screen. You might do this for the same reason you would turn off the menu bar on the screen's top line—to make a little more room to display your work.

Scroll bars

If you don't have a mouse, you might prefer turning off the scroll bars by unchecking the two scroll bar check boxes. On the other hand, even if you don't have a mouse, the scroll bars prove to be handy indicators of your location within a document.

When you turn off the scroll bars, you affect only the display of document windows, not the display of list boxes in the dialog boxes of other commands.

Horizontal (check box) The horizontal scroll bar is the shaded band across the bottom of a document window. It lets you use a mouse to scroll horizontally when a document's lines are wider than your screen can conveniently display. This check box controls whether this scroll bar is displayed or not.

Vertical (check box) The vertical scroll bar is the shaded band at the right side of a document window. It lets you use a mouse to scroll vertically when a document is too long to display all at one time in a window. In addition, its vertical scroll box shows your relative position in a document; the closer the scroll box is to the bottom of the scroll bar, the closer you are to the end of the document.

The remaining fields

Two drop-down list boxes, two check boxes, and two command buttons complete the array of choices in the Preferences dialog box.

CHAPTER THIRTEEN: View Commands 241

(Cursor Control) Speed (drop-down list box) How fast do you want the cursor to move when you press a direction key? You can enter any number from 0 to 9 or choose a number from the drop-down list. The higher the number, the faster the cursor moves. Word's proposed response, *3*, moves the cursor at a pace adjudged moderate by its designers. Setting the cursor speed to *0* slows the cursor to a sedate walk, while setting the speed to *9* sends the cursor zipping across the screen at a rate that will challenge your reflexes.

Show Line Numbers (check box) Do you want Word to display the number of the current line relative to the top of the page? If you check this box, Word displays the current position of the cursor by line number as well as by the ever-present page and column numbers. (If you are working on a document that has not yet been paginated and you check the Show Line Numbers field, Word counts from the first line of the first page and continues sequentially throughout the document to a maximum of 999 lines. To start the numbering from the top of each page, paginate the document with the Utilities Repaginate Now command or turn on background pagination with the Utilities Customize command.)

Word normally counts only lines that have printable characters. If you want it to count all lines, use the Count Blank Space check box.

This check box does not cause Word to print line numbers on the pages of a printed document; to accomplish this, choose the Add Line Numbers check box of the Format Section command.

Count Blank Space (check box) This check box is unavailable and hence grayed unless you have checked the previous field, Show Line Numbers.

The Count Blank Space field tells Word to include in its tally of lines on each page all the blank lines as well as those lines that have printable characters. For example, if your pages have a 1-inch top margin, the first printable line probably will be listed as line 7 if the Count Blank Space check box is checked. That's because the blank lines in the top margin are counted.

Display Mode (drop-down list box) Chances are that your computer is equipped to display the Word screen in a variety of modes. If you have a VGA video card, for example, you have eight modes available. If you have a Hercules or similar monochrome graphics card, you have three distinct modes available. And so forth.

The Display Mode drop-down list box lets you choose from among the modes available on your particular system. Each display mode falls under one of two categories: *text* or *graphics*. Within these categories are variations that depend on the number of lines displayed on the screen.

Text modes rely on colors to communicate character attributes such as italics, boldface, or changes in font size. The mouse pointer is a rectangle when viewed in a text mode. A graphics mode, on the other hand, can show italic and boldface as well as an arrow mouse pointer but does not give any visual clue differentiating font sizes.

If your computer is equipped with a VGA video adapter, you can view your Word screen in 25-line, 43-line, and 50-line text modes or in 25-line, 30-line, 34-line, 43-line, and 60-line graphics modes. If you have an EGA system, you have four choices: 25-line and 43-line modes for both text and graphics. If yours is a Hercules or similar monochrome graphics system, you have 25-line text mode and both 25-line and 43-line graphics modes.

You can move through the choices in the Display field by pressing the Down or Up direction key, but that lets you see only one choice at a time. To see a larger list of the possibilities, hold down the Alt key and press the Down direction key, or else click with the mouse on the down arrow on the right side of the box. Either way, you see the drop-down list of choices.

If you have a monochrome monitor, the list shows black and white as *2 colors*. If you have a color monitor, the list shows the colors Word can display simultaneously (typically, *16 colors*).

With the Display Mode field, you can change the display option whenever and as frequently as you want. Word remembers the last two modes you've used, and you can switch between them by pressing Alt+F9. If you quit and restart Word, it returns you to the last display mode you used.

Colors (command button) Choosing the Colors command button calls up the Colors dialog box, which allows you to select the hues you want on your screen. This dialog box is discussed in detail in the next section.

Customize (command button) Choosing the Customize command button takes you to the Utilities Customize dialog box, which is discussed in Chapter 16.

Choosing Colors

If you use a high-resolution color monitor and a compatible display card such as an EGA or a VGA, Word gives you extensive control over on-screen colors. You can set the color of virtually every element on the screen—not only background and menu colors but the colors of the message bar, status bar, dialog boxes, and even accelerator keys. Furthermore, if you are working in a text mode rather than a graphics mode, you can choose and set colors for different font sizes and character formats, such as italic, underline, and boldface. To reach the Colors dialog box, select the command button of the same name in the Preferences dialog box:

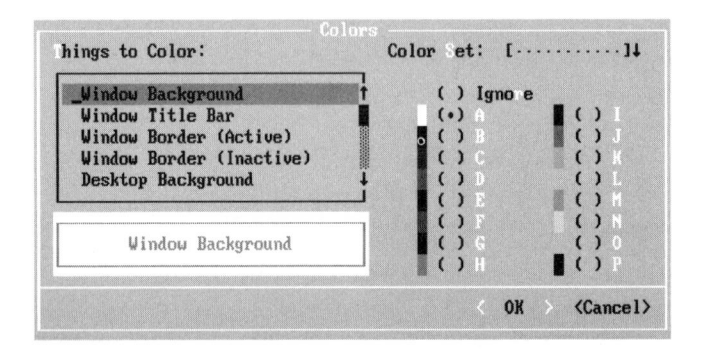

```
┌─────────────────────────── Colors ───────────────────────────┐
│ Things to Color:                  Color Set: [···········]↕  │
│  ┌──────────────────────────┐↑                               │
│  │ Window Background        │   ( ) Ignore                   │
│  │ Window Title Bar         │    (•) A              ( ) I    │
│  │ Window Border (Active)   │    ( ) B              ( ) J    │
│  │ Window Border (Inactive) │    ( ) C              ( ) K    │
│  │ Desktop Background       │↓   ( ) D              ( ) L    │
│  └──────────────────────────┘    ( ) E              ( ) M    │
│                                  ( ) F              ( ) N    │
│  ┌──────────────────────────┐    ( ) G              ( ) O    │
│  │    Window Background     │    ( ) H              ( ) P    │
│  └──────────────────────────┘                                │
│                                       <  OK  >   <Cancel>    │
└──────────────────────────────────────────────────────────────┘
```

Fields of the Colors dialog box

The dialog box has three fields: a list box called Things to Color, a drop-down list box called Color Set, and a series of option buttons that don't really have a collective name but that we might call the *Color Choices,* because they represent the available colors. One color is associated with each option button, and each has an accelerator key with a letter from A through P. In addition, the letter R is the accelerator key for the color choice Ignore, which is explained below.

Things to Color (list box) If you are operating in a graphics display mode, the Things to Color list box contains the names of 21 elements of the Word screen. Character formatting is depicted on the screen (italics are italicized, for instance). You can adjust the color of many on-screen elements, but text will be either white or black, depending on the setting for the window background. If you are in a text mode, the number of elements in the list box grows to 39 because in a text mode color can be used to distinguish between characters that are formatted differently. Consequently, you can assign colors to 18 different kinds and combinations of character formatting— bold text can be red, italic text blue, and bold italics yellow, if you want.

Of all the elements in the list, background color is the only one that can vary from one window to another. You can choose different colors for different windows to give them distinct and immediate visual identities. You can even combine a white background with dark letters for a black-on-white look.

As the first step in assigning a color to a screen element, use the mouse or the Up and Down direction keys to select the desired element name.

Color Choices (option buttons) Each of the letters A through P is associated with a color on screen. The color choice you make is reflected in whatever screen element is selected in the Things to Color list box. For example, if you want to make the window background red, select Window Background in the Things to Color list box, and then press Alt+E to choose the option button for red. If you change your mind, simply select a different color.

Adjust the colors of as many elements as you want, and then press the Enter key to put them all into effect at once. Word will remember your choices for future editing sessions.

Using colors in text mode to reflect formatting is awkward at best, especially when you consider that some characters in a document might qualify for two different colors. In this situation, Word needs to know which color to use. To that end, Word has a priority list—but it is a priority list that you can override by using the Ignore option button.

Normally, the colors you choose for character formatting override the colors you choose for font sizes. For example, if italic characters are blue and small characters are red, and you format some characters to be both italic and small, Word will display them in blue. When Word decides how to display characters that have several formats, it uses the following order: hidden, subscript, superscript, strikethrough, small capitals, uppercase, double underline, bold and italic, bold and underline, italic and underline, italic, underline, bold, and normal. Hidden text is listed first because it is the attribute on which Word places most importance when it comes to deciding which color to use.

For example, you might choose dark blue for uppercase and orange for italics. Normally, Word would display uppercase italic characters in dark blue because uppercase comes before italic on the priority list.

But because you can see uppercase characters on screen anyway, you might choose to suppress the color for uppercase characters (dark blue in this case) in favor of showing the color for italics (orange in this case). To do this, you would choose *Uppercase* in the dialog box and then choose the Ignore (Alt+R) option button. From that point onward, whenever you formatted characters for uppercase italics, Word would display the characters in the italic color (orange) rather than in the uppercase color (dark blue).

In short, the Ignore option button is your means of reestablishing Word's priorities when it comes to assigning colors.

Color Set (drop-down list) Word comes with five complete sets of colors built in. You can choose any of the five by pressing Alt+S to move to the Color Sets drop-down list and then pressing the Down direction key to move through the choices. Unfortunately, it is easy to accidentally move into this field by pressing the direction keys; it is irritating to spend time choosing colors only to accidentally move into this field and have them all be lost in favor of one of the color sets.

On the other hand, the sets are attractive and easy to choose. They are called *Color 1, Color 2, Color 3, Monochrome,* and *LCD*.

- *Color 1* is Word's standard set for color monitors. The window background is dark blue (color B); the title bar is turquoise (color D); menus and dialog boxes are light gray (color H); accelerator keys are bright white (color P); and so on.
- *Color 2* is similar to the first color set. Among the differences, it uses deep red (color E) for accelerator keys.
- *Color 3* uses only black, white, and two shades of gray. It is a striking choice for people who have color monitors but prefer a more monochromatic look.
- *Monochrome* uses only black, white, and gray. It is intended for monochrome systems.
- *LCD* is a color set designed specifically for use on monochromatic laptops, which use liquid-crystal displays (LCDs).

If you use MasterWord, you have additional tools to help you set up screen colors. MasterWord Help contains ACT buttons which will install any of more than a dozen color sets for you. In addition, MasterWord's WordSet utility lets you adjust more than 100 default settings in Word, including all the colors. The advantage of WordSet is that it lets you see a sample Word 5.5 screen with examples of all the elements displayed. As you change settings, you get immediate feedback on what the screen will look like.

CHAPTER FOURTEEN

Insert Commands

You can insert more than text into a document, as the commands of the Insert menu demonstrate.

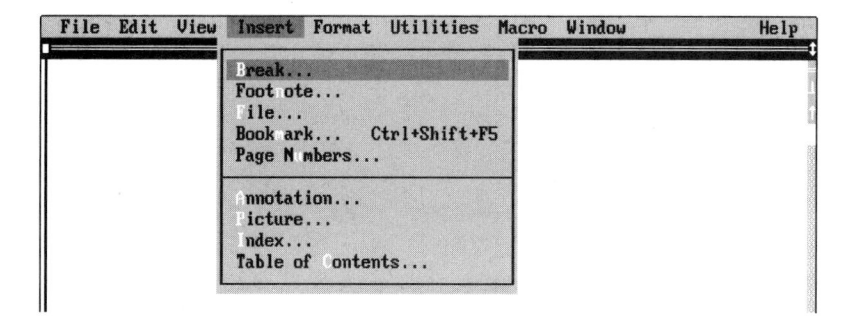

Each Insert command is summarized below:

Insert Break—Inserts a special character indicating that a new page, section, or column is to begin.

Insert Footnote—Inserts a footnote reference mark and then lets you type the text of the corresponding footnote.

Insert File—Inserts some or all of another document or spreadsheet.

Insert Bookmark—Inserts a "bookmark," by labeling selected text with a name of your choice so that you can later return to the location instantly and easily.

Insert Page Numbers—Inserts a page number on each page.

Insert Annotation—Inserts an annotation reference mark and then lets you type the corresponding annotation text.

Insert Picture—Inserts a graphics image into a document.

Insert Index—Inserts an index after compiling it from coding that you do in advance.

Insert Table of Contents—Inserts a table of contents based either on your document's headings or on previous coding.

Part III of this book dedicates chapters to several of the features associated with this powerful collection of tools.

INSERT BREAK COMMAND

To insert a page, section, or column break into a document, press Alt+IB to bring the Insert Break command's dialog box to the screen:

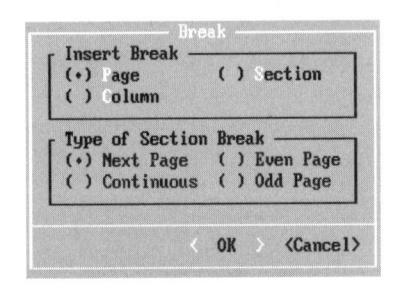

```
┌─ Break ──────────────────────┐
│ ┌─ Insert Break ──────────┐  │
│ │ (•) Page    ( ) Section │  │
│ │ ( ) Column              │  │
│ └─────────────────────────┘  │
│ ┌─ Type of Section Break ─┐  │
│ │ (•) Next Page  ( ) Even Page │
│ │ ( ) Continuous ( ) Odd Page  │
│ └─────────────────────────┘  │
│          < OK >  <Cancel>    │
└──────────────────────────────┘
```

HIDDEN TEXT

Insert commands frequently use hidden coding that you place in a document before you run the command. In some cases, the command itself inserts the hidden coding.

For example, you use hidden-text characters to place coding around words and phrases that you want included in a document's index. Word looks for the hidden text when you use the Insert Index command to compile an index for the document. This command is one that requires hidden text to be in place before it can run.

Perhaps the strongest example of a command that relies on hidden text is the Insert Picture command, which simply places a line of hidden text into your document. The hidden text causes Word to print a graphic as part of the document that contains the hidden coding; but the Insert Picture command actually inserts only the hidden coding, not the graphic.

Hidden-text coding typically consists of a period on either side of a key letter or phrase. For example, .i. signifies an index entry, and .g. indicates the name of a graphics image to be printed as part of a Word document.

To code text as hidden, use the speed-formatting key combination Ctrl+H, or check the Hidden check box of the Format Character command. For maximum flexibility, use a character style that is formatted as hidden. (For information on character styles, see Chapter 24.)

CHAPTER FOURTEEN: Insert Commands

In addition to the Cancel and OK command buttons, the Insert Break dialog box has two fields, both composed of option buttons.

Insert Break (option buttons)

- **Page**—Inserts a new-page character into a document, forcing a new page to begin at that point. You can accomplish the same thing by pressing Shift+Enter. The new-page character, inserted or deleted like any other individual character, is displayed as a row of periods (…………) across the width of the document window. To grasp the differences between a new-page character (……), which you insert into a document, and a new-page mark (. . . . .), which Word inserts into a document, see Chapter 16's discussion of the Utilities Repaginate command.
- **Section**—Inserts a new-section character (a *section mark*) into a document, creating an opportunity to change page formatting without starting a new document. After you choose this option button, the option buttons in the Type of Section Break field become available. Unlike previous versions of Word, Word 5.5 provides no keyboard shortcut for creating a section break (formerly known as a *division break*).
- **Column**—Inserts a new-column character into a document. You can accomplish the same thing by pressing Shift+Ctrl+Enter. A new-column character is identical in appearance to a new-page character (……….) except that it spans only the width of the column of text in which it appears.

Type of Section Break (option buttons) These option buttons are grayed until you choose the Section option button in the Insert Break field. They let you dictate where the new section formatting should begin:

- **Next Page**—Word starts a new page at the page break. The layout of the new page is governed by formatting commands or styles used *after* the section mark.
- **Even Page**—Similar to Next Page except that Word numbers the new page with the next even number that is available, possibly leaving an intervening odd-numbered page blank.
- **Odd Page**—Similar to Next Page except that Word numbers the new page with the next available odd number, possibly leaving an interim even-numbered page blank.
- **Continuous**—Starts most of the section's formatting immediately without beginning a new page or column. The bottom-margin formatting doesn't change until the next page, however, and when a section contains footnotes or annotations, Word treats the section mark as if it were set to Next Page.

NOTE: *Although you make a choice when you insert the section break, you can change your mind at any time by placing the cursor inside the section and using the Format Section command's Section Start drop-down list box.*

For a more thorough introduction to these choices, see the "Multiple Columns" discussion in Chapter 7. For more information on the implications of each of these choices, see the discussion of the Section Start drop-down list box in Chapter 15's examination of the Format Section command. (Note, too, that the Insert Section command's drop-down list box has a fifth choice for Section Start: Column.)

INSERT FOOTNOTE COMMAND

The Insert Footnote command places a footnote reference mark, such as an asterisk (*) or an auto-numbered numeral, at the cursor location. It also allows you to create corresponding footnote text. To use this command, press Alt+IN. Word responds by displaying this simple dialog box:

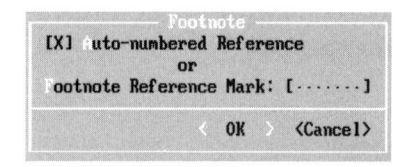

```
┌─ Footnote ──────────────────────┐
│ [X] Auto-numbered Reference     │
│              or                 │
│ Footnote Reference Mark: [·····]│
│                                 │
│        <  OK  >   <Cancel>      │
└─────────────────────────────────┘
```

Most of the time you can ignore the dialog box's two fields and simply press the Enter key or click OK with the mouse. By executing the command immediately in this way, you cause Word to insert an automatically numbered footnote reference mark into the document at the location of the cursor and to insert a matching number at the end of the document, where footnote text is stored. The command leaves you at the reference number at the end of the document so that you can type the footnote text.

Fields of the Insert Footnote Dialog Box

The two fields are interesting, however, if only for the ways they interact.

Auto-numbered Reference (check box) As long as this box is checked, as it is by default, pressing Enter inserts an automatically numbered footnote number into the document. In other words, the first footnote will be assigned the number 1, the next will get the number 2, and so forth. If you move what was originally footnote 4 to the beginning of the document, it becomes footnote 1 and the other footnotes are renumbered as appropriate—all without your intervention.

If you turn off the Auto-numbered Reference check box, Word inserts an asterisk into the other field, the Footnote Reference Mark check box. If you execute the command at this point, the footnote reference mark will be an asterisk rather than an automatically assigned number.

Footnote Reference Mark (text box) You make an entry in this text box only if you want a footnote to have a reference mark other than an automatically assigned number. In other words, if you want to assign a number yourself, you type the number in this text box. As soon as you type the first character, the Auto-numbered Reference check box becomes unchecked.

When you execute the Insert Footnote command, Word immediately moves to the end of the document, where it stores all footnote text. The footnote reference mark appears again, and you can type corresponding footnote text after it. When you are through, you can use the Edit Go To command to return to the footnote reference mark in the text. (Conversely, if you are working in the main part of a document and want to see a certain footnote, select the appropriate reference mark and use the Edit Go To command to jump to the text of that footnote.)

> NOTE: *A special kind of footnote, called an annotation, lets you specify the author of comments included in an annotation/footnote and record the time and date the comments are made. See the discussion of the Insert Annotation command later in this chapter.*

Word prints footnotes and annotations either at the bottoms of respective pages or at the end of a document or, if your document is divided into two or more sections, at the end of the current section. Where your footnotes and annotations print depends on how you set the Format Section command's Place Footnotes field.

- If you choose the Same Page option button, Word will print all of the footnote on the same page as the footnote reference if there is room. If there is not enough room, Word will wrap footnote text to successive pages as necessary.
- If you choose the End of Section option button, Word will gather together all footnotes and annotations contained in a section and print them at the end of the section. If you want the footnotes to appear on a page by themselves, insert a new-page character immediately before the section mark, the row of colons (:::::::) at the end of the document. Most documents have only a single section, which means that *End of Section* refers to the end of the document.

Changing and deleting footnote reference marks

You might find the following points helpful as you work with footnotes and annotations:

- If you delete a footnote or annotation reference mark to the scrap or to the glossary, Word deletes the associated footnote text. If you reinsert the reference mark, Word reinserts the footnote text. If you're using automatic footnote numbering, Word renumbers and reorders the footnotes when you move or delete footnote reference marks.
- If you accidentally delete an automatically numbered footnote reference mark from the footnote text, you can use Word's special-purpose, permanent footnote entry in the glossary that restores both the mark and its formatting (such as superscripting and a small font size):

    —1. Place the cursor at the location of the missing reference mark.

    —2. Press the Spacebar once if necessary to add a blank space.

    —3. Type the word *footnote*, and press the F3 key.

    The automatically numbered reference mark will be restored.

- You can also change a footnote reference mark in the body of a document (for example, from an asterisk to a plus sign):
  - —1. Highlight the reference mark you want to change, and choose the Footnote command. Word displays the existing reference mark as its proposed response.
  - —2. Type a different reference mark and press Enter.

    Word changes the reference mark both in the document and in front of the associated footnote text at the end of the document or section. The key to success with this method is to highlight the reference mark rather than to simply position the cursor at the mark.

Footnote Windows and Superscripting

By using the View Footnotes/Annotations command to open a special window pane, you can write, edit, or view footnote text without jumping back and forth to the end of your document. The *footnote/annotation pane* shows the footnote text corresponding to any footnote reference mark displayed in the main window. As reference marks are scrolled on and off the screen in the main window, the corresponding footnote text appears in and disappears from the footnote/annotation pane.

While the pane is open, you can get to it by pressing the F6 key, by clicking in it with the mouse, or by highlighting a footnote or annotation mark in the document and using the Edit Go To command to jump to the corresponding footnote or annotation text in the pane. While working in the pane, you can scroll up or down to see the text of any footnote or annotation mark, provided its reference mark is visible in the document window. You cannot, however, scroll to a footnote or annotation whose corresponding reference mark is not displayed in the document window.

To visually set off footnote or annotation reference marks from your text, you can superscript them. To do so, select the reference mark and then use either the Format Character command or the built-in superscript character format (hold down the Ctrl key and press the + key). For greatest convenience, you can superscript footnote references automatically by using a style sheet that has a Footnote ref character style.

Footnote Limitations

Although Word's footnoting capabilities are impressive, you should be aware of three limitations:

- Automatic numbering restarts with the number 1 at every section mark. If you want sequential footnote numbering across two or more sections (parts of a report, for example), you must type the footnote numbers in all but the first section. On the other hand, if you want automatically numbered footnotes reset to 1 in the middle of a document, a new-section mark will do the job.

- The counter for automatic numbering counts every footnote and annotation, regardless of its reference mark. If you use an asterisk as the reference mark of your first footnote and an auto-numbered reference mark for your second footnote, Word will assign the number 2 to the second footnote. Also, Word does not distinguish between footnotes and annotations. If you have three annotations and then a footnote, Word will assign the number 4 to the footnote.
- Word's Format Section command won't allow you to collect and print all footnotes at the end of a multisection document. If you choose the End of Section option button in the Place Footnotes field of the Format Section command, Word prints the footnotes at the end of the section, not the end of the document. To overcome this limitation, wait until you've finished writing a document, and then copy the footnotes from the end of each section to the end of the main document or into a separate document. If you've used automatically numbered footnotes in the document, the footnote reference numbers for all but the first section will change; you can correct them manually.

INSERT FILE COMMAND

Use the Insert File command to insert into your main document some or all of a different document, all of a plain ASCII text file, or some or all of a spreadsheet. If you want, you can link your main document to the source of the inserted information so that subsequent changes to the source can be reflected in your document at the press of a few keystrokes.

Insert File is one of Word's most powerful commands and is often overlooked by people who don't see its possibilities. For example, you might want to incorporate into a document information from a spreadsheet and then periodically update the document to reflect changes in the spreadsheet. Perhaps you do a weekly sales report based on numbers from a Lotus 1-2-3, Multiplan, Microsoft Excel, or Microsoft Works spreadsheet or from a spreadsheet program compatible with a recent version of one of these four programs. You can use the Insert File command to import the desired data, being sure to tell Word you want to link the document to the spreadsheet. When Word inserts the data into the main document, it also inserts hidden text that notes the location and name of the spreadsheet and the location of the desired information within the spreadsheet. With this hidden coding in place, updating the main document to reflect changes in the spreadsheet can be as simple as highlighting some or all of the document and pressing the F9 key.

The Insert File command doesn't combine documents or documents and spreadsheets in the sense that files lose their individual identities. The command copies information from the source file on disk and places it in the main document on the screen, leaving the source file unaffected.

Whatever you import is inserted into the document in your text window at the current location of the cursor.

Choose the Insert File command by pressing Alt+IF. The Insert File dialog box appears:

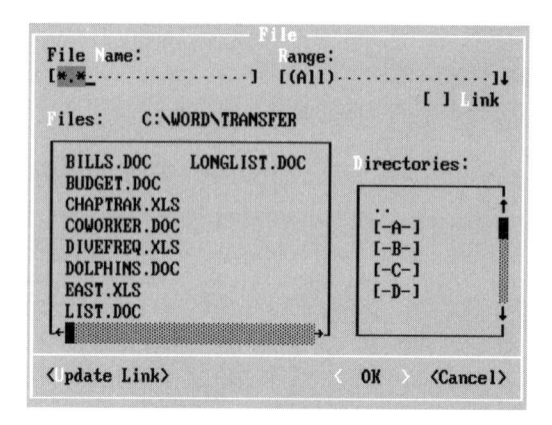

```
┌─────────────────────── File ───────────────────────┐
│  File Name:              Range:                    │
│  [*.*            ]     [(All)           ]↓         │
│                                      [ ] Link      │
│  Files:    C:\WORD\TRANSFER                        │
│  ┌──────────────────────────┐  Directories:        │
│  │ BILLS.DOC    LONGLIST.DOC│  ┌──────────┐        │
│  │ BUDGET.DOC               │  │ ..       │↑       │
│  │ CHAPTRAK.XLS             │  │          │        │
│  │ COWORKER.DOC             │  │ [-A-]    │        │
│  │ DIVEFREQ.XLS             │  │ [-B-]    │        │
│  │ DOLPHINS.DOC             │  │ [-C-]    │        │
│  │ EAST.XLS                 │  │ [-D-]    │        │
│  │ LIST.DOC                 │  │          │        │
│  └──────────────────────────┘  └──────────┘↓       │
│                                                    │
│  <Update Link>        < OK >    <Cancel>           │
└────────────────────────────────────────────────────┘
```

Fields of the Insert File Dialog Box

In addition to the OK and Cancel buttons, the Insert File dialog box has six fields:

File Name (text box) Enter the drive, path, and filename of the Word document, plain ASCII file, or spreadsheet that contains the information you want to insert into your main document. By main document, we mean the document in which you are using the Insert File command. Be sure to include the filename extension, such as .DOC for documents.

Range (drop-down list box) Tell Word what part of the spreadsheet or document you want to import.

The default choice is All, which is the only choice available if the filename you specified in the previous field was for a plain ASCII file rather than for a spreadsheet file or a Word document. (An ASCII file is an unformatted text file that can be created by a variety of programs.) Also choose All if you want to import all of a Word document (stored in Word format) or all of a spreadsheet.

To import a portion of a Word document, you must label the text to be imported with a bookmark name. Type the name of the bookmark in this Range field. If you press Alt+Down direction key or click with the mouse on the down arrow, a list will drop down containing the name of any bookmark in the source document. (Of course, in order for Word to list the bookmarked name, the name of the source file must be entered in the File Name field.)

To import a portion of a spreadsheet, you can type the name of a cell, a range of cells, or a name previously assigned to a range of cells. For example, if you want to import the cell at column C and row 6 of a Microsoft Works spreadsheet, you type *C6*. If you want to import the cells in the range A3 through D5 of a Lotus 1-2-3 spreadsheet, you type *A3-D5*. (To specify a range of cells, you determine which rectangle of cells contains the information you want and type the coordinates of the upper left cell followed by the coordinates of the lower right cell.)

Instead of typing a range of cells into the Range field, you can use your spreadsheet program to assign a name to a group of cells. This is accomplished with the Lotus 1-2-3 Range Name Create command, the Microsoft Excel Formula Define Name command, the Multiplan Name command, or the Microsoft Works Edit Range Name command. After the range is named, it will appear in the drop-down list box of the Range field; to see the list, press Alt+Down direction key or click with the mouse on the down arrow.

Link (check box) Turn this check box on to establish an ongoing link between your document and the source of the information you are inserting.

The link takes the form of hidden-text coding that Word will insert into your main document before and after the inserted data. The coding that appears before inserted document text begins with .D., followed by the drive, path, and filename of the source and the name of the bookmark you have imported. The coding at the end is a simple .D., which identifies the end of the inserted document text. The coding before inserted spreadsheet data begins with .L., followed by the drive, path, and filename of the source and the cells you have imported. An .L. is at the end of the spreadsheet data.

Besides establishing a link, which you can exploit later by pressing the Update link command button, hidden coding documents the source of the inserted information. Because the coding is formatted as hidden text, it appears on screen only if you turn on the View Preferences command's Hidden Text check box, and it prints (or appears in screen layout view) only if you turn on the Hidden Text check box in the Options dialog box of the File Printer command.

Files (list box) To choose a file from the current directory, you can highlight its name and then press Enter, or you can double-click on its name with the mouse. Word puts your choice in the File Name text box.

Directories (list box) You can use this list box to specify a new directory as current. For details on this list box, see the discussion near the beginning of Chapter 10.

Update Link (command button) Select this button to update the link between your main document and the file that is the source for information you previously inserted into the main document with the Insert File command. Of course, you can update the link only if the link exists—a choice you made with the Link check box when you originally inserted the file contents.

When you update a link, you cause Word to delete the previous insertion and replace it with a fresh insertion from the same source as the original. In this way, you can keep your main document up to date with ongoing changes in the source files that contribute to it.

To update a link, follow these steps:

1. Highlight the inserted data.
2. Choose the Insert File command.

3. Press the Update Link command button (or press the F9 key, which does the same thing).

If you want to update multiple links, highlight them all before choosing the command or pressing F9. If you want to update every link in your main document, highlight the entire document.

Word pauses at each highlighted link and asks *Do you want to update this link? Choose YES to update or NO to go on.* Press Y to update the information, N to skip updating this information, or Esc to cancel the command.

Tips on Using the Insert File Command

Here are a few pointers that might help you understand and use the Insert File command:

- When you insert a plain text file into your main document, Word might first present you with the following message, to which you can answer Yes: *Word does not recognize the format of that file. Do you still want to insert the file?*
- If the region of a spreadsheet that you want to import into a Word document is password protected, Word asks you to type the password. The password will not appear on your screen.
- Spreadsheet data is imported into your Word document as a single paragraph. Word separates columns with tab characters and ends each row of cells with a new-line character. Because your data represents one paragraph, you can quickly adjust the spacing of lines with the Format Paragraph command and do the same for columns by using the Format Tabs command or by changing the Default Tab text box of the Utilities Customize command. Use care if you change the default tab width because this can also affect other tab stops in your document.
- When importing spreadsheet data, be sure the decimal character specified in the Decimal text box of the Utilities Customize command matches the decimal character (and currency format) used in the spreadsheet. Word uses the currency format defined by the COUNTRY command in your operating system's CONFIG.SYS file. If the spreadsheet you import uses a different currency format, change the *COUNTRY=* statement in the DOS CONFIG.SYS file. (Your operating system's manual tells you how to do this.)
- The Insert File command in Word 5.5 performs the functions that Word 5.0 divided among three commands: Transfer Merge, Library Link Document, and Library Link Spreadsheet.
- Closely related to the Insert File command is the Insert Picture command, discussed later in the chapter.

CHAPTER FOURTEEN: Insert Commands   255

INSERT BOOKMARK COMMAND

Have you ever wished you could jump from place to place in an on-screen document in much the same way you can shuffle through pages on a desk? Or, perhaps, have you wanted to bracket some text—from a few characters to several pages—that you knew you would later want to include in a different document or move?

Word offers a command that lets you mark the text you want, find it again instantly, and move it anywhere: the Insert Bookmark command.

When you use the Insert Bookmark command, you begin by highlighting the text you want to mark. In practical terms, there isn't much of a limit on the amount you can highlight—anything from a single character to whole sections of a document. (However, Word will not let you attach a bookmark to a column of text selected with the column-select key combination Shift+Ctrl+F8.)

Choose the command by pressing Alt+IM or Shift+Ctrl+F5. The Insert Bookmark dialog box will appear:

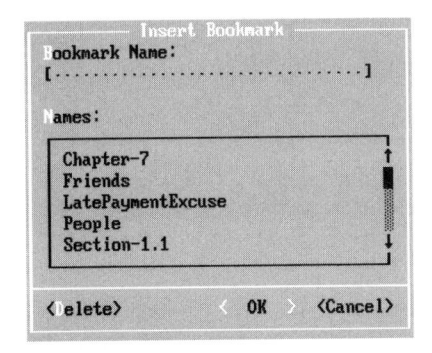

```
┌─────────── Insert Bookmark ───────────┐
│ Bookmark Name:                         │
│ [.................................]   │
│                                        │
│ Names:                                 │
│  ┌──────────────────────────────┐↑    │
│  │ Chapter-7                    │     │
│  │ Friends                      │     │
│  │ LatePaymentExcuse            │     │
│  │ People                       │     │
│  │ Section-1.1                  │↓    │
│  └──────────────────────────────┘     │
│                                        │
│  <Delete>        < OK >   <Cancel>     │
└────────────────────────────────────────┘
```

Fields of the Insert Bookmark Dialog Box

In addition to the OK and Cancel command buttons, the Insert Bookmark dialog box has three fields:

Bookmark Name (text box) Type a name for your bookmark. Like a glossary name, a bookmark name can be up to 31 characters long; spaces are not allowed, but you can separate words with hyphens, periods, or underlines, provided that you do not use any of those three characters at the beginning of the name. Make the name descriptive enough to remind you of the text with which it is associated. If you type a name that already exists, Word asks *Do you want to replace the existing bookmark?*

Names (list box) Existing bookmarks in the current document are listed here.

Delete (command button) To delete a bookmark, type its name in the Bookmark Name text box, or highlight its name in the Names list box and then press the Delete command button.

When you press Enter to carry out the Insert Bookmark command, Word creates the bookmark and identifies the first and last characters of its text as invisible "anchors" that define its beginning and end.

After you have created a bookmark, you can return to it at any time by using the Edit Go To command. Press Alt+EG or simply press F5, and then type the bookmark name or choose it from the Bookmark Name list box, and press Enter. Word immediately moves to the text you want, highlighting everything from the beginning anchor to the ending anchor.

You can use the Insert File command to include, in one document, text that is bookmarked in another document. Highlight the place in the one document where you want to incorporate the text, choose the File command by pressing Alt+IF, type in the File Name field the name of the file containing the bookmarked text, and in the Range drop-down list box type the name of the bookmark. To drop down a list of available bookmarks, press Alt+Down direction key. What you see in this list depends on which file you have entered into the File Name field.

You can edit, move, or delete the contents of bookmarked text as follows:

- You can insert text anywhere between the beginning and ending anchor characters; the new text will be associated with the bookmark.
- You can delete text anywhere between the anchors without affecting the bookmark.
- You can delete an anchor; Word will assign a new character to be the replacement anchor. The character will be the closest one to the deleted character, provided that it was part of the original bookmark.
- You can move bookmarked text by deleting it to the scrap and inserting it elsewhere. You can even insert it in a different document, provided the same bookmark name does not exist in the new document. Note, however, that you must move all text associated with the bookmark, including both anchors, in order to retain the bookmark name.
- You can copy bookmarked text to another part of the same document. If you do this, however, only the originally marked text remains associated with the bookmark name because a single bookmark cannot refer to two places in the same document.

NOTE: *In addition to letting you move quickly to specific text, the Insert Bookmark command helps Word cross-reference a document when you print it. Cross-referencing is described in detail in Chapter 21.*

INSERT PAGE NUMBERS COMMAND

To turn on the printing of page numbers in your document, use either the Insert Page Numbers command or the reserved glossary name *page*.

To use the Insert Page Numbers command, first place the cursor inside the section of the document in which you want page numbers to print. If your document has more

CHAPTER FOURTEEN: Insert Commands

than one section, extend the selection to all sections in which you want page numbers to print. Then use the command by pressing Alt+IU and making choices in the Insert Page Numbers dialog box:

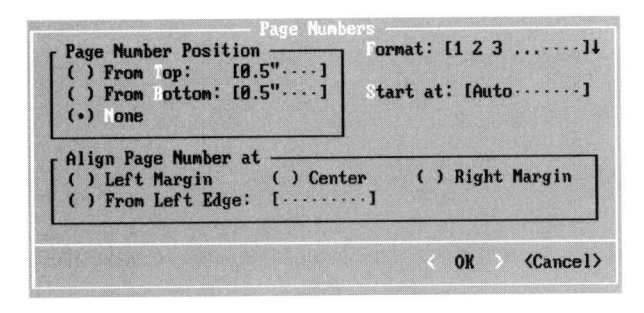

```
┌─────────────────────── Page Numbers ───────────────────────┐
│ ┌─ Page Number Position ──┐   Format: [1 2 3 ......]↓     │
│ │ ( ) From Top:    [0.5"..]│                               │
│ │ ( ) From Bottom: [0.5"..]│   Start at: [Auto.....]      │
│ │ (•) None                 │                               │
│ └──────────────────────────┘                               │
│ ┌─ Align Page Number at ─────────────────────────────┐    │
│ │ ( ) Left Margin    ( ) Center    ( ) Right Margin │    │
│ │ ( ) From Left Edge: [........]                    │    │
│ └────────────────────────────────────────────────────┘    │
│                                     <  OK  >   <Cancel>    │
└────────────────────────────────────────────────────────────┘
```

You can also reach this dialog box by choosing the Page Numbers command button in the Format Section dialog box.

Fields of the Insert Page Numbers Dialog Box

Use the Tab key or the accelerator keys to move from field to field of the Insert Page Numbers dialog box. The first three fields control the vertical placement of page numbers, the next two control the numbering scheme, and the final two control the horizontal placement of the numbers.

Page Number Position (option buttons) Indicate the vertical placement of the page numbers or whether you want them to appear.

- **From Top**—Choose this button if you want page numbers to print near the tops of pages; then fill in the associated From Top text box.
- **From Bottom**—Choose this button if you want page numbers to print near the bottoms of pages; then fill in the associated From Top text box.
- **None**—This is the default setting. Choose it if you don't want page numbers to print or if you want them to print but want to insert them through the use of the *page* reserved glossary entry rather than by using the Insert Page Numbers command.

From Top (text box) Indicate how far from the top of the page you want numbers to print. Use any of the accepted units of measure. The proposed distance is 0.5 inch. The distance expressed in this text box is used by Word when you select the From Top option button.

From Bottom (text box) Indicate how far from the bottom of the page you want numbers to print. Use any of the accepted units of measure. The proposed distance is 0.5 inch. The distance expressed in this text box is used by Word when you select the From Bottom option button.

Format (drop-down list) Page numbers are printed in one of five formats, as represented in this drop-down list:

- **1 2 3**—Arabic numerals (Word's default)
- **a b c**—Lowercase alphabetic lettering
- **A B C**—Uppercase alphabetic lettering
- **i ii iii**—Lowercase Roman numerals
- **I II III**—Uppercase Roman numerals

Your choice in this drop-down list box also controls the format of numbering resulting from the use of the reserved glossary entry *page*.

Yet another kind of format applies to page numbers: the character formatting associated with the printed number. For page numbers created through the Insert Page Numbers command, character formatting is governed by the formatting of the Character Page Number style of the style sheet attached to the document. In the event there is no Character Page Number style, the formatting is governed by the character-formatting portion of the Paragraph Normal style. In the event no style sheet is attached to the document, the formatting of the Paragraph Normal style is identical to Word's default formatting. For more on style sheets, see Chapters 15 and 24.

Start At (text box) Type the number you want on the first page of the document. If you have a multisection document and have not selected all sections before using the command, type the number you want on the first page of the first of the selected sections. The default choice is *Auto*, which causes Word to number the pages of a document sequentially, usually starting with 1. To choose *Auto*, you can either type the word or leave the field blank. Except for the word *Auto*, Word accepts only Arabic numerals in this field. If you choose lettering or Roman numerals in the Format field, you nonetheless must type an Arabic number in the Start At field. For example, if you have chosen uppercase letters for your format and you want to start with the fifth letter of the alphabet, E, type 5 for the fifth letter. The Start At text box also controls numbering printed with the special glossary entry *page*.

Align Page Number At (option buttons) Control the horizontal placement of page numbers on the printed page with these option buttons and the related From Left Edge text box. These option buttons are available only if your choice in the Page Number Position field is From Top or From Bottom.

- **Left Margin**—Aligns the page number with the left margin
- **Center**—Puts the page number in the center of the page, between the two margins
- **Right Margin**—Aligns the number with the right margin
- **From Left Edge**—Positions the number at the horizontal position of your choice, as defined in the text box of the same name

CHAPTER FOURTEEN: Insert Commands 259

NOTE: *If you want to print a page number outside the normal margins of the page, use the reserved glossary entry* page *and set the Align At field of the Format Header/Footer command to Edge of Paper.*

From Left Edge (text box) If the Left Edge option button is selected, use this text box to enter the distance from the left edge of the page at which you want the number to be printed. Use any accepted unit of measure. Word proposes 7.25 inches.

Using the *Page* Reserved Glossary Name

A more flexible alternative to the Insert Page Numbers command is the reserved glossary entry *page*. Most often, this glossary name is typed into a header or footer, and it can be given a label or other accompanying text, such as the word *Page*.

No matter which method you use, you establish the starting number and its printed form (Arabic, Roman, or alphabetic) with the fields of the Insert Page Numbers command.

The word *page* actually represents a special character stored permanently in the glossary. You can insert it into the text at any time by typing *page* and pressing F3. It is represented as *(page)* on the screen, but the current page number is printed on paper.

The *Character Page Number* style in a style sheet does not affect the formatting of page numbers printed with *(page)*. Instead, you format it using conventional commands, including paragraph and character styles.

In addition, a *(nextpage)* character, also stored in the glossary, lets you print the number of the next page. For example, at the bottom of a page you can use the phrase *Continued on page (nextpage)*.

INSERT ANNOTATION COMMAND

Word enables any user to annotate a document. This feature is useful when you want to insert notes to yourself or when a document is passed by disk or network to several reviewers.

If you know how to use footnotes, you also know how to use annotations. To Word, annotations are simply glamorized footnotes. In fact, an annotation *is* an automatically numbered footnote—one that lets you add your initials or other reference characters before the number. It also lets you tell Word to stamp the date, the time, or both on each annotation. And Word remembers whatever characters you use as well as whether you want the date and time stamp. It even remembers your preferences between editing sessions.

To insert an annotation into a document, choose the Insert Annotation command by pressing Alt+IA. The Insert Annotation dialog box appears:

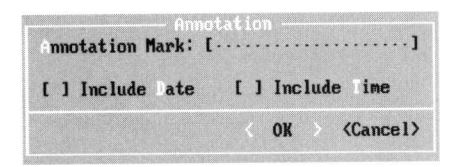

```
┌─────────────── Annotation ───────────────┐
│ Annotation Mark: [·····················] │
│                                          │
│ [ ] Include Date     [ ] Include Time    │
│                                          │
│               <  OK  >   <Cancel>        │
└──────────────────────────────────────────┘
```

Fields of the Insert Annotation Dialog Box

In addition to the OK and Cancel command buttons, the Insert Annotation dialog box contains three fields:

Annotation Mark (text box) The first field is called Annotation Mark, but this is a bit of a misnomer. Actually, Word always assigns the mark, giving it an automatically assigned footnote number. This text box lets you add a label immediately after the mark. The label—your initials, perhaps, or someone's name—can be up to 28 characters long including spaces and punctuation marks. If you and several people are annotating the same document, make your label unique. The next time you choose Insert Annotation, Word will display the last annotation mark you typed as its proposed response in the command field.

Include Date (check box) Check this field if you want Word to insert the date as part of the annotation mark.

Include Time (check box) Check this field if you want Word to insert the time as part of the annotation mark.

After you press Enter or select the OK button, Word jumps to the footnotes and annotations at the end of the document, and lets you type the text of your new annotation. If you insert more than one annotation or footnote in a document, Word numbers the annotations sequentially as, for example, *1LTG, 2LTG, 3LTG,* and so on. If footnotes are mixed in with annotations, the numbering is applied to both, such as *1* (a footnote), *2LTG* (an annotation), *3* (a footnote), and so on.

To move between annotation marks and annotation text, use the Edit Go To command, described in Chapter 12.

ANNOTATIONS AND FOOTNOTES TOGETHER

Because the Insert Annotation command really is the same feature as the Insert Footnote command but in a slightly different guise, a practical problem arises when you want to use both features at the same time. Word uses the same numbering sequence for both footnotes and annotations. So if a footnote is assigned the number 1 and is followed by an annotation, the annotation will have the number 2.

This means that if you want to print a document that contains both footnotes and annotations and you don't want the annotations to print, gaps will occur in the numbering of the footnotes. You can get around this by removing the annotations before printing—but you might not want to lose them. A workaround solution is to save a second copy of the document, remove the annotations from that copy, and then print it.

CHAPTER FOURTEEN: Insert Commands

To change an annotation mark, highlight the mark you want to change, choose the Insert Annotation command, type the new mark, and press Enter. To delete an annotation, highlight the annotation mark in text and use the Del key or the Delete command.

A special character style is reserved for annotation reference marks, and a special paragraph style is reserved for the text of annotations. These are separate from styles that are reserved for ordinary footnote reference marks and text. The availability of these four styles makes distinctive formatting of annotations and footnotes easy for users of style sheets.

For additional information on annotations, see this chapter's earlier discussion of the Insert Footnote command.

INSERT PICTURE COMMAND

Use the Insert Picture command to incorporate a graphics image into a Word document and to control its printed size. The graphic itself is not stored in the document; rather, the document contains a reference to the name of a separate file containing the image. The beginning of this reference is hidden text. Sometimes it helps to think of this single-line paragraph of text as being the graphic, because whatever you do to the paragraph (such as centering it) will affect the printing of the graphics image.

> NOTE: *You might want to review the rudiments of the Insert Picture command, which were discussed in the "Importing Graphics" section of Chapter 7, before reading further. In addition, you might want to refer to Chapter 30, which covers the Picture command in considerable detail.*

Word can incorporate graphics stored in a variety of graphics formats, including Microsoft Paintbrush .PCX files, Lotus 1-2-3 .PIC files, Hewlett-Packard HPGL plotter files, TIFF (Tag Image File Format) scanner files, and PostScript files. Graphics from Microsoft Windows applications can be imported if they were converted to .PCX format. If the graphic you want to import cannot be saved in one of these formats, you can bring it into Word as a print file (described in Chapter 11) or by taking a snapshot of it on screen with the Capture program.

When you execute the Picture command after filling in the appropriate fields, Word adds a line of coded text to your document at the current location of the cursor. The line, beginning with the code .G. in hidden text, contains the path and filename of the graphics file, the width and height of the graphic, and the type (format) of the file. For example, the following code reflects a graphic that is on drive C, in the PBRUSH directory, as a file named ICON.PCX. The graphic is 2 inches wide and 2.4 inches high and is in .PCX format:

```
.G.C:\PBRUSH\ICON.PCX;2";2.4";PCX
```

To see this tag, turn on the View Preferences command's Hidden Text check box. To see both the tag and a dotted border showing the positioning of the graphic relative to nearby text, turn on the View Layout command. To see a representation of the graphic itself, use the File Print Preview command or simply choose the Insert Picture command's Preview button.

To choose the Insert Picture command, press Alt+IP. The Insert Picture dialog box appears:

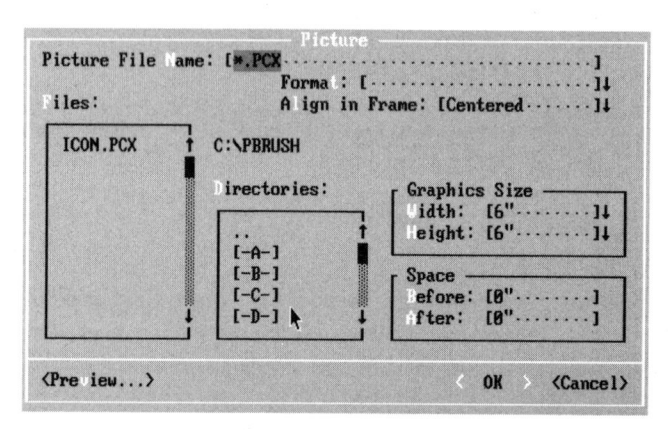

```
┌─────────────────────────── Picture ───────────────────────────┐
│  Picture File Name: [*.PCX·················]                  │
│                    Format: [···············]↓                 │
│     Files:         Align in Frame: [Centered·······]↓         │
│  ┌──────────────┐                                             │
│  │ ICON.PCX   ↑ │  C:\PBRUSH                                  │
│  │              │                                             │
│  │              │  Directories:     ┌─ Graphics Size ──────┐  │
│  │              │  ┌────────────┐   │  Width:  [6"······]↓ │  │
│  │              │  │  ..       ↑│   │  Height: [6"······]↓ │  │
│  │              │  │  [-A-]     │   └──────────────────────┘  │
│  │              │  │  [-B-]     │   ┌─ Space ──────────────┐  │
│  │              │  │  [-C-]     │   │  Before: [0"······]  │  │
│  │            ↓ │  │  [-D-] ▸   │   │  After:  [0"······]  │  │
│  └──────────────┘  └────────────┘   └──────────────────────┘  │
│                                                               │
│   <Preview...>                       <  OK  >    <Cancel>     │
└───────────────────────────────────────────────────────────────┘
```

Fields of the Insert Picture Dialog Box

In addition to the OK and Cancel command buttons, the Insert Picture dialog box has ten fields:

Picture File Name (text box) Type the name of the graphics file you want to import, including the extension, or use the Files list box to select a name.

Files (list box) Rather than type an entry in the File Name text box, you can choose a filename from the directory that is current for the command. The identity of this directory, which can be changed with the Directories field, is shown immediately to the right of the Files list box. The sample dialog box shown lists the current directory as PBRUSH.

Directories (list box) Use this field to change the directory that is current for the command. This is not necessarily the same directory that is current for the majority of Word's operations. For example, if you keep all your graphics images in a particular directory, you can make this the current directory for the Picture command without it being the current directory for other commands.

Format (drop-down list) If the file you specify is stored in a format Word recognizes, Word fills in this field for you. However, if this field is blank even though a graphics file has been named in the Picture File Name text box, press Alt+Down direction key or click on the down arrow to see a list of file formats that Word recognizes; choose the one that is appropriate.

Align in Frame (drop-down list) Each graphic you import is positioned within the *frame* of the paragraph. The frame is an invisible boundary that defines the width and

CHAPTER FOURTEEN: Insert Commands

height of the paragraph that contains the graphic; it protects and defines the area that a graphic potentially can fill. Word proposes to center the graphic within its frame. If you want the graphic positioned toward either the left or the right edge of the frame, enter the alignment or press Alt+Down direction key to choose from a list that contains the choices *Left*, *Centered*, and *Right*. The field has meaning only if the graphic, as specified in the next field, the Graphic Size Width drop-down list, is narrower than the width of the frame.

Width (drop-down list) How wide do you want the graphic to be? Word proposes the width of the frame, but you can type a different width or press Alt+Down to choose from a list.

Height (drop-down list) How tall do you want the graphic to be? Word proposes a height that will maintain the proportions of the original graphic. As you did for the width of the graphic, type a value or press Alt+Down direction key to choose from a list. You should maintain the width/height ratio of the original graphic to avoid distorting the image.

Before (text box) Do you want extra space above the graphic? If so, specify the amount here. If you type a value, such as 2, Word adds the equivalent number of blank lines above the graphic. You can, however, specify units of measure, such as inches (*0.5"*) or points (*12 pt*). This field adds extra space above the content (graphic) of the paragraph but within the invisible paragraph frame surrounding it.

After (text box) Do you want extra space below the graphic? Fill in this text box using considerations similar to those you use for the Before text box, typing a number, which represents that number of lines, or a number followed by a unit of measure.

Preview... (command button) Choosing this button switches you to Word's preview mode, as if you had chosen the File Print Preview command.

INSERT INDEX COMMAND

Three stages are involved in using Word's automatic indexing feature:

- You use hidden text throughout the document to mark the entries you want indexed.
- You run the Insert Index command, which compiles the entries.
- Optionally, you format the compiled index so that its appearance better reflects your tastes and needs.

Chapter 27 covers all the indexing particulars, but for now you should know what form the hidden-text marking of entries generally takes. You can type this hidden text yourself, or you can use a macro to do it.

To code a phrase for inclusion as a main heading in an index, type the characters *.i.* (or *.I.*) immediately before the phrase, and format the characters as hidden. At the end of the word or phrase, type a semicolon (;), also formatted as hidden. The text between the hidden *.i.* and the hidden *;* is marked as an index entry. Because the coding is hidden, it will not print. Because the word or phrase within the coded area is not in hidden text, it will print. When you choose the Insert Index command, Word will note the entry and its page number and include them in the index.

To code a phrase for inclusion as a subheading rather than as a main entry, follow the hidden *.i.* with the name of the main heading under which you want the subheading to appear, and follow that with a colon. Put this all in hidden text.

After you have prepared a document for indexing, you can use the Insert Index command to compile the index. Word will place it at the end of the document, separated from the rest of the text by a section mark (:::::::::) across the width of the text window. Because the index is in its own section, you can use the Format Margins command (or a section style) to format the pages of the index differently from those of the main body of the document.

An index created with the Insert Index command is an alphabetized list of all the previously designated index entries from the document, complete with page numbers. When the same index entry appears on more than one page of your document, Word eliminates duplicate listings from the index and combines page numbers.

The Insert Index command will create an index with up to five levels of entry—the main entry and four sublevels. You can do rudimentary formatting of the levels with the Insert Index command, or you can do sophisticated formatting by telling the command to use a style sheet.

Before using the Insert Index command, be sure the Hidden Text check box of the File Print command's Options dialog box is not checked. Printable hidden text affects pagination, and you don't want page numbers in your index to be wrong.

Word assembles an index that begins with a line of hidden text that says *.Begin Index.*, and ends with a similar line that says *.End Index.* You can delete these lines, but generally there's little reason to because they won't be printed—that is, they won't be printed unless you've checked the Hidden Text field of the File Print command's Options dialog box.

If the *.Begin Index.* and *.End Index.* lines are in the document when you execute the Index command, Word replaces the old index with the new one. However, before making this substitution, Word displays the message *Do you want to replace the existing index?*, giving you a chance to change your mind.

To choose the Insert Index command, press Alt+II. This dialog box appears:

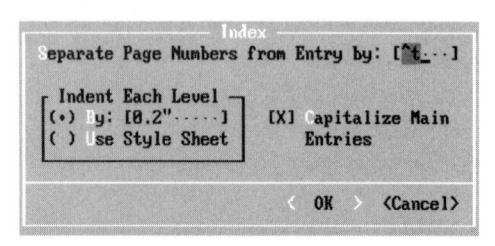

CHAPTER FOURTEEN: Insert Commands   265

Fields of the Insert Index Dialog Box

In addition to the OK and Close command buttons, the Insert Index dialog box has four fields:

Separate Page Numbers from Entry By (text box) Unless you change the setting in this text box, Word will insert a tab character between the index entry and the first of its page numbers. You can, if you prefer, change this setting to a single space, multiple spaces, or characters such as hyphens. Although the text box appears to be only four characters long, you can type as many as 256 characters in it.

Indent Each Level (option buttons) This field, in conjunction with the next one, controls how Word indents subentries in an index.

- **By**—If you choose this option button, Word directly formats each subheading to be indented a certain distance relative to the next-higher index level preceding it. The amount of this indentation is governed by the By text box adjacent to the option button. Word ignores any style sheet attached to the document when it carries out the paragraph formatting of the index.
- **Use Style Sheet**—This option button causes Word to disregard the By text box of the Insert Index command and to format the index according to the style sheet attached to the document. If the style sheet contains the styles Index 1, Index 2, Index 3, and Index 4, Word follows the formatting of the appropriate style when formatting the various levels of the index. If any of these index styles is not in the style sheet, Word substitutes the formatting of the Normal Paragraph style for the missing style(s). If you add the missing index style(s) later, Word updates the format of the index at that time to reflect the dictates of the style(s).

Word can accommodate five levels of index entry, but the style sheet contains only four index styles. If you create an index with five levels, entries on the fifth level are formatted with the Normal Paragraph style—unless you later change the formatting by applying a different style manually or by using direct formatting.

If you choose Use Style Sheet and no style sheet is attached to the document, the levels of entry in the index will not have relative levels of indentation until an appropriate style sheet is attached.

Indent Each Level By (text box) If the By option button is selected, this text box governs the relative indentation of index entries. The default setting is *0.2"*, which corresponds to two spaces of pica-size (10-pitch or 12-point) typewriter type. This means that a first-level index entry will not be indented (unless you format it later) but that a second-level index entry will be indented 0.2 inches, a third-level entry will be indented another 0.2 inches, and so forth. If you want each level indented three pica-size (p10) spaces instead of two, change the field from *0.2"* to *0.3"*. If you want two elite-size (p12 or 10-point) characters, change the field to *0.17"* (or *2 p12*), and if you want three elite-size characters, change it to *0.25"* (or *3 p12*).

Capitalize Main Entries (check box) Do you want Word to capitalize the first word of each main (first-level) entry in the index? Generally you'll want to leave this field checked, although for some scientific and other indexes lowercase letters are preferred, in which case you should uncheck the box.

INSERT TABLE OF CONTENTS COMMAND

To compile a table of contents in the easiest way possible, choose the Insert Table of Contents command (Alt+IC) and then press O, which chooses an option button called Outline. This tells Word to identify every heading in the document as an entry for the table of contents. When you press Enter to carry out the command, Word creates the table of contents for you. That's all there is to it...but there is a catch. In order for this to work, the headings must be formatted with Paragraph Heading styles from a style sheet so that Word knows they are headings.

If your document has no headings or if the headings aren't the only elements you want to include in your table of contents, you can code the desired elements yourself, using hidden text, and then rely on the Insert Table of Contents command to compile the results.

When you do the hidden-text coding yourself (or with the help of a macro), the Insert Table of Contents command can generate not only a table of contents but a table of figures, photographs, or any other element in the document. You can use the command successive times to create several different tables. Tables can have relatively sophisticated formats, including any number of levels of subheadings, each indented from the preceding level. You can do rudimentary formatting of the levels with fields of the Insert Table of Contents command, and you can do sophisticated formatting of the first four levels (which is more than most people need) by instructing the Insert Table of Contents command to consult a style sheet.

Creating a table of contents is much like creating an index except that the task of manually coding entries often can be omitted. The Insert Table of Contents command arranges the references it compiles according to page number, from first to last. In contrast, the Insert Index command arranges references in alphabetic order, from A to Z, and combines duplicates into single entries followed by multiple page numbers.

If you elect to code your document for purposes of using the Insert Table of Contents command, you should consult Chapter 28 for full details. But in brief, the coding consists of the following series of elements, formatted as hidden:

1. The characters .c. or .C., formatted as hidden and placed immediately before the text that you want to include as an entry in your table of contents.
2. Optionally, following the .c. but before the actual text of the entry, up to three colons, formatted as hidden. One colon indicates that the text following it is to be a second-level entry (indented one level, for example). Two colons indicate that the text following them is to be a third-level entry (indented two levels, perhaps). Three colons indicate a fourth-level entry. The following code, for example, would precede a fourth-level table-of-contents entry: .c.:::

3. The entry. Most often this is a heading from a document, but it needn't be. In any case, this portion of the instruction is not in hidden text.
4. Optionally, following the entry, a semicolon formatted as hidden or a paragraph mark.

Here is the first of two sample entries:

```
.c.Types of newspapers;
```

Here is a second sample, which is marked as a second-level entry:

```
.c.:Daily tabloids;
```

After coding is complete, choose the Insert Table of Contents command by pressing Alt+IC. The Insert Table of Contents dialog box appears:

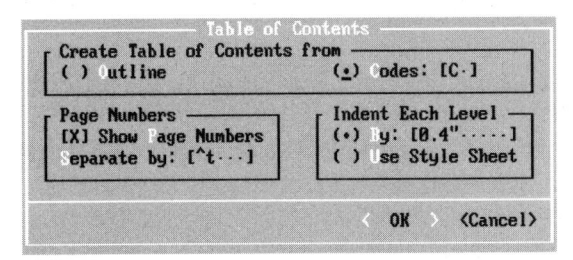

```
┌─────────────────── Table of Contents ───────────────────┐
│ ┌─ Create Table of Contents from ──────────────────────┐│
│ │ ( ) Outline               (•) Codes: [C.]            ││
│ └──────────────────────────────────────────────────────┘│
│ ┌─ Page Numbers ──────────┐ ┌─ Indent Each Level ─────┐│
│ │ [X] Show Page Numbers   │ │ (•) By: [0.4"......]    ││
│ │ Separate by: [^t...]    │ │ ( ) Use Style Sheet     ││
│ └─────────────────────────┘ └─────────────────────────┘│
│                                   < OK >   <Cancel>    │
└─────────────────────────────────────────────────────────┘
```

Fields of the Insert Table of Contents Dialog Box

In addition to the OK and Cancel command buttons, the Insert Table of Contents dialog box has six fields:

Create Table of Contents from (option buttons)

- **Outline**—If you choose this option, Word creates a table of contents from the headings of your document. These headings must be formatted with Paragraph Heading styles from a style sheet. You can preview which elements will appear in the table of contents by using the View Outline command to enter outline view. Those headings that appear in outline view will be included by Word in the table of contents. This gives you an opportunity to fine-tune which headings will appear in your table, by expanding or collapsing headings in outline view. (For details on expanding and collapsing headings, see Chapter 26.)
- **Codes**—If you want to create a table based on hidden-text coding, choose this option and then fill in the Codes text box.

Create Table of Contents from Codes (text box) If the Codes option button is selected, this text box governs which code will be used to search through the document for table entries. The default entry in this text box is *C*. This stands for *Contents*, but you can use any letter. To avoid complicating matters, avoid using letters you or Word have reserved for other uses—for example, I for indexes (the Insert Index command) or D, G, or L for information imported from documents, graphics files, or spreadsheets (the Insert File command). Unlike the Insert Index command, which always looks for the hidden text *.i.* to identify index entries in the text, the Insert Table of Contents command will seek any letter of your choice that is set off between periods. You might use *.F.* (for *Figure*) to compile a list of drawings in a document, for instance. And because you can run the command several times, using a different letter to compile each different set of entries, you can incorporate a variety of tables in a single document.

Page Numbers

- **Show Page Numbers (check box)**—If you don't want Word to put page numbers in the table, turn off this check box.
- **Separate by (text box)**—The default setting in this field is ^t, the tab character. It causes the command to place a tab character between the name of each table entry and the corresponding page number. The command also incorporates a right-aligned tab stop into the table's paragraph formatting. This combination of the tab character and right-aligned tab stop causes table entries to print on the left, with indentation as appropriate, and the page number for each entry to print on the right.

You can type something else, such as a few spaces, or a comma and a few spaces. If you do not include a ^t in the field, Word will not add a right-aligned tab stop to the table.

And, despite appearances, Word will accept as many as 256 characters in this field.

Indent Each Level (option buttons) This field, in conjunction with the next one, controls how Word indents subentries from main headings in a table of contents.

- **By**—If you choose this option button, Word directly formats each heading to be indented a certain distance relative to the next-higher table of contents level preceding it. For example, a second-level heading will be indented a set distance relative to the first-level heading that falls somewhere above it in the table of contents. The amount of this indentation is governed by the By text box adjacent to the option button. Word ignores any style sheet attached to the document when it carries out the paragraph formatting of the table of contents.
- **Use Style Sheet**—This option button causes Word to disregard the command's By text box and to format the table of contents according to the style sheet attached to the document. If the style sheet contains the styles

Table 1, Table 2, Table 3, and Table 4, Word follows the appropriate style when formatting the various levels of the table of contents. If any of these table styles is not in the style sheet, Word substitutes the formatting of the Normal Paragraph style for the missing style(s). If you add the missing table style(s) later, Word updates the format of the table of contents at that time to reflect the dictates of the style(s).

Word can accommodate more than a dozen levels of table indentation, and only four table styles exist, so if a table contains more than four levels of entry, Word will initially format the additional levels with the Normal Paragraph style.

Indent Each Level By (text box) If the By option button is selected, this text box governs the relative indentation of headings in the table of contents. The default setting is *0.4"*, which corresponds to four spaces of pica-size (10-pitch) typewriter type. This means that a first-level table entry will not be indented (unless you format it later) but that a subentry under it (a second-level table entry) will be indented 0.4 inches, a third-level entry will be indented another 0.4 inches, and so forth. Word will accommodate virtually any number of levels of entry, each indented more than the level above it by the amount specified in the By text box. If you want each level indented five pica-size (p10) spaces instead of four, change the value in the text box from *0.4"* to *0.5"*. If you want four elite-size (p12) characters, change the field to *0.33"* (or *4 p12*), and if you want five elite-size characters, change it to *0.42"* (or *5 p12*).

Like the Insert Index command, the Insert Table of Contents command places its compilations at the end of the document, separating each table from the other text with a section mark (:::::::). After the section mark, Word starts a table with a line of hidden text that says *.Begin Table.* and ends it with a similar line that says *.End Table.* If you keep these hidden lines in your document, any new table you create with the Insert Table of Contents command will replace or be appended to the existing table. If a table already exists when you choose the command, Word displays the message *Do you want to replace the existing table? Choose yes to replace or no to append the new table.*

After you've compiled a table, you can change its location in the document. However, be aware that moving the table can change the pagination of the document. Often this is not a problem because the tables in the front of a book or other formal document frequently are on pages numbered separately (typically in lowercase Roman numerals) from the main pages of the text (typically numbered with Arabic numerals). For tips on how to move tables while keeping pagination consistent, see Chapter 28.

NOTE: *You can use Word's cross-referencing feature to automatically number cross-references or groups of similar items, such as tables and figures. If cross-references are coded as table entries, Word includes and correctly numbers them in a table, adding the number of the page on which they appear. For details on creating cross-references, refer to Chapter 21.*

INSERT COMMANDS FOR STYLE SHEETS

When a style sheet is in the active window, the Insert menu consists of two special commands:

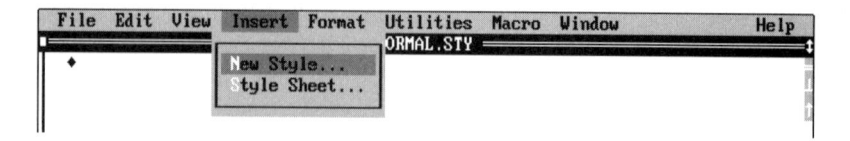

```
 File  Edit  View  Insert  Format  Utilities  Macro  Window              Help
                                   ORMAL.STY
                          ew Style...
                          tyle Sheet...
```

The two commands are Insert New Style, which adds a new style to a style sheet, and Insert Style Sheet, which merges the contents of a different style sheet into the style sheet displayed in the window.

The Insert New Style Command

When you press Alt+IN to choose the Insert New Style command, Word displays the following dialog box:

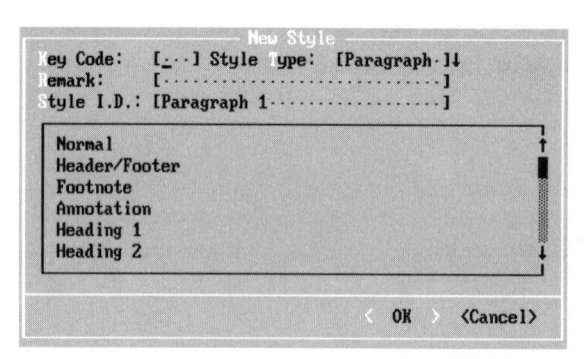

```
                           ─ New Style ─
  ey Code:    [ _ ] Style  ype:  [Paragraph ]↓
  emark:      [............................]
  tyle I.D.:  [Paragraph 1.................]

  ┌──────────────────────────────────────┐
  │ Normal                              ↑│
  │ Header/Footer                        │
  │ Footnote                             │
  │ Annotation                           │
  │ Heading 1                            │
  │ Heading 2                           ↓│
  └──────────────────────────────────────┘

                        <  OK  >   <Cancel>
```

The choices you make in this dialog box allow you to create a new style and give it a name. A style's name is composed of four elements: key code, type, I.D., and remark. The Insert New Style dialog box lets you specify any of these.

The Insert New Style dialog box is virtually identical to the Record Style dialog box, which you access by choosing the Format Record Style command. The difference is that the Format Record Style command lets you create a style, saving it to the active style sheet while you are working within your document. In contrast, the Insert New Style command lets you do the same thing, but while you are working in the style sheet itself.

For information on the fields of the Insert New Style command, see the discussion of the Format Record Style command in Chapter 15.

CHAPTER FOURTEEN: Insert Commands

The Insert Style Sheet command

Use this command to insert a copy of a style sheet into the style sheet that is displayed in the active window. The dialog box you reach has only three fields:

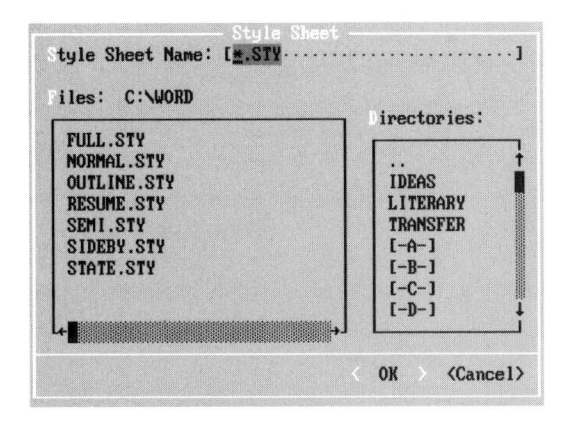

```
                    ─── Style Sheet ───
  Style Sheet Name: [*.STY·······················]

  Files:  C:\WORD
  ┌──────────────────────────┐  Directories:
  │ FULL.STY                 │  ┌──────────────┐
  │ NORMAL.STY               │  │ ..         ↑ │
  │ OUTLINE.STY              │  │ IDEAS      ■ │
  │ RESUME.STY               │  │ LITERARY     │
  │ SEMI.STY                 │  │ TRANSFER     │
  │ SIDEBY.STY               │  │ [-A-]        │
  │ STATE.STY                │  │ [-B-]        │
  │                          │  │ [-C-]        │
  │                          │  │ [-D-]      ↓ │
  └──────────────────────────┘  └──────────────┘

                              <  OK  >   <Cancel>
```

Style Sheet Name (text box) Specify the name of the style sheet you want to insert into your current style sheet.

Files (list box) As an alternative to typing the name of a style sheet, you can review available names in the current directory— and select one from this list.

Directories (list box) To change the identity of current directory, choose the name of a drive/directory from this list.

CHAPTER FIFTEEN

Format Commands

Word can help you shape and reshape the appearance of your document, both before and after you've written it, through the use of *formatting*. You can do this shaping at any time because Word draws a clear distinction between content and format. Thus, you can make even dramatic changes to either one without affecting the other.

Word offers several approaches to formatting:

- Speed-formatting keys, described in Chapter 3, give you quick access to widely used formats, such as centering and underlining, that are built into Word.
- The ribbon and ruler, described in Chapter 4, provide a graphical approach to formatting that is especially popular with mouse users.
- Format commands let you govern the appearance and placement of printed text and graphics, giving you control over everything from the layout of your document's pages to the format of footnotes, page numbers, and even the typeface and size of a single character. You describe your desires by making choices in dialog boxes. In this chapter you'll become acquainted with the Format commands in detail.

A fourth approach to formatting a style sheet offers the most flexible and in many respects the most efficient method of formatting. A style sheet combines the ease of the speed-formatting keys and the ribbon with the design options offered by the Format commands and then gives you the ability to save formats and recall them at will. See Chapter 24 for a complete introduction to style sheets.

> NOTE: *Before beginning this chapter, you might benefit from reviewing Chapter 5's discussion of the Ctrl key and its guidelines for using Ctrl for speed-formatting, Ctrl+Y for styles, and Shift+Ctrl for macros.*

INTRODUCTION TO FORMAT COMMANDS

The first eight Format commands are available regardless of whether your active window contains a document or a style sheet. They allow you to change the formatting of the selected text or styles. Using the Format commands on text is known as *direct formatting* because you act on the text itself. Formatting with a style is called *indirect formatting* because you format the style and then use the style to format text.

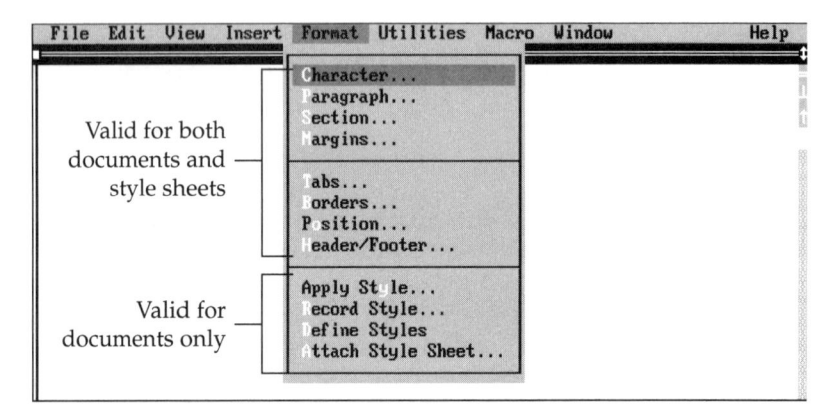

```
File  Edit  View  Insert  Format  Utilities  Macro  Window          Help
                          Character...
                          Paragraph...
Valid for both            Section...
documents and             Margins...
style sheets
                          Tabs...
                          Borders...
                          Position...
                          Header/Footer...

Valid for                 Apply Style...
documents only            Record Style...
                          Define Styles
                          Attach Style Sheet...
```

Format Character—Controls the appearance of printed characters, including their font and size.

Format Paragraph—Controls the appearance of a paragraph, including indentations and horizontal alignment.

Format Section—Offers broad control of page formatting, including the number of columns and the footnote location.

Format Margins—Governs page margins.

Format Tabs—Inserts or removes tab stops.

Format Borders—Places lines around one or more sides of a paragraph and lets you shade a paragraph.

Format Position—Fixes a paragraph of text or a graphic to a specific location on the page. Other text will flow around an object positioned with this command.

Format Header/Footer—Formats a paragraph as a *header* or *footer*—text that prints on successive pages of a document. Commonly includes page numbers, dates, document titles, names of intended recipients, or other information.

The final four commands on the Format menu pertain to formatting a document with the assistance of a style sheet. You use them when a document window is active:

Format Apply Style—Lets you format using prearranged combinations of formatting. Each formatting combination is called a *style*, and a file containing a set of related styles is called a *style sheet*.

Format Record Style—Lets you create a style from your document window without opening a style-sheet window.

Format Define Style—Opens a style-sheet window containing the style sheet that is formatting the active document. This is the only Format command that does not lead to a dialog box.

Format Attach Style Sheet—Lets you choose a style sheet to format the active document.

NOTE: *For simplicity, most discussions in this chapter assume you are formatting text in a document window rather than styles in a style-sheet window. However, the first eight commands on the Format menu can all be used to format styles as easily as they are used to format text. Simply highlight what you want to format, and carry out the command.*

FORMAT CHARACTER COMMAND

The Format Character command lets you control the look of the text within your document. Use it to choose a font and size and to control such character attributes as underlining, boldfacing, and italicizing. The command also lets you specify color if you have a color printer, and it lets you hide text. If text is selected (highlighted), the Format Character command formats it. If no text is selected, the Format Character command acts on the text you type next, unless you move the cursor before typing.

The command is also used in a style-sheet window, to impose formatting on the highlighted character style.

If you don't specify character formatting in the Format Character command fields (or through built-in formats or with a style), characters are printed in whatever font and size are "normal" for your printer, and they have no special attributes. On many dot-matrix printers, normal characters are printed in 12-point Pica (generally 10-pitch) type; on many laser printers, normal characters are printed in 12-point Courier.

Whether or not you can see character formatting on your screen depends on the capabilities of your computer and screen.

- If you use Word in text (nongraphics) mode with a monochrome display, certain character attributes (italics, for example) are probably underlined or treated in a distinctive way.
- If you use Word in text mode with a color display, character attributes are reflected by color as specified in the Colors dialog box of the View Preferences command (discussed in Chapter 13).

Regardless of the way character formatting is displayed, however, it will print as you intend if your printer can reproduce it. If your printer cannot handle a particular character size or attribute, Word makes an appropriate substitution or, as a last resort, omits the formatting and uses normal characters.

If you later print the same document on a printer with sufficient capabilities, all character formatting will be reproduced. Word won't forget character formatting, even if your computer and screen can't show it or your printer can't print it.

To choose the Format Character command, press Alt+TC. When you choose the Format Character command, the Format Character dialog box appears.

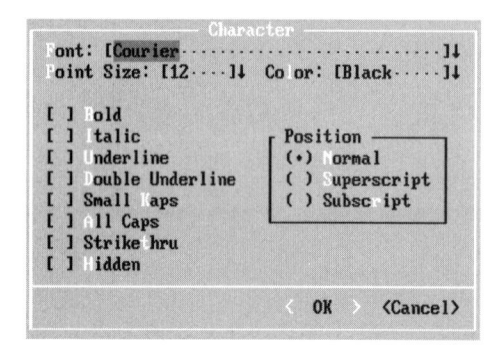

```
┌──────────────── Character ────────────────┐
│ Font: [Courier·····························]↓
│ Point Size: [12····]↓  Color: [Black·····]↓
│
│ [ ] Bold
│ [ ] Italic           ┌─ Position ─────┐
│ [ ] Underline        │ (•) Normal     │
│ [ ] Double Underline │ ( ) Superscript│
│ [ ] Small Caps       │ ( ) Subscript  │
│ [ ] All Caps         └────────────────┘
│ [ ] Strike Thru
│ [ ] Hidden
│
│                     <  OK  >   <Cancel>
└───────────────────────────────────────────┘
```

UNITS OF MEASURE

The dialog boxes of many Format commands allow you to specify a location for text in terms of some unit of measure. Word understands six units of measure: inches, centimeters, 10-pitch and 12-pitch characters, points (1/72 inch), and lines (1/6 inch). These units can be used interchangeably, and fractional units are permitted when expressed as decimals (not ½ or ¾, but .5 or .75).

The U.S. version of Word is shipped with inches set as the standard unit of measure. (To choose a different standard, use the Utilities Customize command.) For the most part, Word assumes that all numbers you enter in the fields of Format dialog boxes are in the standard unit of measure. But

- You can use any unit of measure you want in a field, provided you type in its abbreviation when specifying a measurement. That is, even if you specify centimeters in the Utilities Customize command's Measure drop-down list box, you can still express a measurement as an inch (1") in a particular command field, and Word will convert it to 2.54 centimeters.

- Vertical measurements in the Format Paragraph command's Spacing text boxes always are presumed to be in lines, unless you specify a different unit. One line is 1/6 inch, or 12 points. Because six lines to an inch is the usual line-space setting on typewriters and typewriter-like printers, the number of lines is a conve-

CHAPTER FIFTEEN: Format Commands

An alternative way to reach this dialog box is to press Ctrl+FF or Ctrl+PP while working in your document or style-sheet window. This method, which relies on the ribbon, was introduced near the beginning of Chapter 4.

Fields of the Format Character Dialog Box

In addition to the Cancel and OK command buttons, the Format Character dialog box has 12 fields:

Font (drop-down list box) What font (shape of type) do you want for the selected text? You can either enter a font name or press the Down direction key to scroll through the choices on a list. (To see more than one choice at a time from the list, press Alt+Down direction key.) The list of choices is dictated by the printer (.PRD) file that is installed. You can change which printer file is installed by choosing the File Printer Setup command.

> nient way to specify vertical measurements in the Format Paragraph command fields. Although vertical measurements are usually specified in inches or lines, using points provides potentially greater flexibility as well as conformity with professional printing terminology. For instance, if you want eight lines to an inch instead of six, type *9 pt* in the Line field of the Format Paragraph command.
>
> ♦ If a paragraph contains characters of different sizes—for example, a combination of 10-point and 14-point characters—you can choose the line-spacing option called Auto in the Line field of the Format Paragraph Command. This choice tells Word to adjust the spacing between the lines of a single-spaced paragraph so that the tallest characters in any line do not bump against the characters in the line above.
>
> ♦ If you are accustomed to using the typographic unit of measure called a *pica*—12 points, or roughly ⅙ inch—you can use lines instead. The abbreviation is *li*, so if you want a 7-pica left margin for a brochure, type *7 li* in the Left field of the Format Margins command.
>
> ♦ MasterWord includes a macro that permits you to enter fractions into dialog boxes. For example, using the macro, you can type *1 7/8* rather than first converting it to *1.875*.

Point Size (drop-down list box) After choosing a font name, you can choose a font size (height of type). You specify the font size in points, and you can press Alt+Down to choose from a list, exactly as you did for Font. The Point Size list, however, varies according to which sizes are available on your printer for the font you've specified.

Font size is measured in points during formatting, but for daisy-wheel and certain other printers it is expressed in pitch during printing. A printer that emulates a typewriter probably uses pica type, which is 10 pitch and 12 point (10 characters to the inch, using characters that normally need a vertical space 12 points high), or elite type, which is 12 pitch and 10 point (12 characters to the inch, using characters that normally need a vertical space 10 points high). This means that if you format characters as Pica 12 and print them on a daisy-wheel printer, when Word instructs you to mount the proper daisy wheel, it will request *Pica 10*. The distinction can be confusing at first.

For a table showing the conversion of points to pitch, see Chapter 31.

Color (drop-down list box) What color will be used to print the selected text? The colors or shades appearing in the drop-down list will vary according to information provided by the installed printer file.

The only choice you will see is Black, unless your printer supports color printing or you use certain other printers or downloadable font packages that use this field for printing type in shades of gray or with other effects. For example, if you use a PostScript printer (with the printer file POSTSCRP.PRD installed), you have the choices Black, Dark, Medium, Light, or White. This last choice, White, lets you print white letters against a black background. To obtain a black background, set Background Shading to 100 in the dialog box of the Format Border command.

Bold (check box) Do you want the selected text (or the next text you type) to be in boldface? On some daisy-wheel and dot-matrix printers, boldfacing is created by printing each character twice.

Italic (check box) Do you want the selected text (or the next text you type) to be in italics? If you check this box, Word instructs your printer to italicize if it can. If you have a daisy-wheel printer, Word stops printing and asks you to mount an italic font.

Underline (check box) Do you want the selected text (or the next text you type) to be underlined? Think a moment about this one. Choosing this means Word will underline blank spaces too. If you want only the words to be underlined, first select and underline one word. Then select the next word, and underline it by pressing the F4 key (which repeats the last editing act). Continue in the same way, moving from word to word and underlining each individually with the F4 key until you have finished. (MasterWord includes a macro you can use to underline words but not the spaces between them.)

Double Underline (check box) Do you want the selected text (or the next text you type) to have two underlines, one below the other? (Sometimes this yields an extra-heavy single underline instead of two thin underlines.)

CHAPTER FIFTEEN: Format Commands   279

Small Kaps (check box) Do you want the selected text (or the next text you type) to be displayed and printed as smaller-than-normal capital letters?

All Caps (check box) Do you want the selected text (or the next text you type) to be displayed and printed in all capital letters?

Notice that when you check this box, Word displays and prints characters as uppercase without actually *changing* them to uppercase. If this box is not checked, Word displays characters as they were typed.

You can also change the case of letters by toggling them with Shift+F3. This is equivalent to retyping characters—but vastly faster:

- If you do not select a character before pressing Shift+F3, Word changes the case of the entire word containing the cursor.
- If you select a single character and press Shift+F3, the case of that character will change.
- If you select multiple characters—such as a word or sentence—and press Shift+F3, the feature is more sophisticated. If the selection begins with a lowercase letter, all the letters become uppercase. If the selection is composed entirely of uppercase letters, they become lowercase with the first letter of each word uppercase. If the selection contains lowercase letters but begins with an uppercase letter, they all become lowercase.

The following is a simplified, but practical, illustration of the effects of pressing Shift+F3:

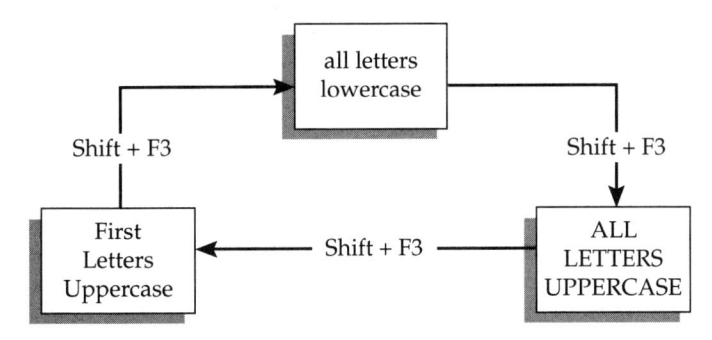

```
                    ┌─────────────┐
                    │ all letters │
           ┌───────▶│  lowercase  │───────┐
           │        └─────────────┘       │
           │                              ▼
       Shift + F3                     Shift + F3
           │                              │
  ┌─────────────┐                  ┌─────────────┐
  │    First    │                  │     ALL     │
  │   Letters   │◀── Shift + F3 ──│   LETTERS   │
  │  Uppercase  │                  │  UPPERCASE  │
  └─────────────┘                  └─────────────┘
```

Strikethru (check box) Do you want the selected text (or the next text you type) to have a horizontal line struck through it? This attribute is useful for showing proposed deletions—for example, in legal documents.

Hidden (check box) Do you want the selected text (or the next text you type) to be formatted as hidden? If you so choose, Word will give the text formatting that enables you to make it visible and invisible at will, either on the screen or on paper. When hidden text is displayed on the screen, a string of tiny dots forms an underline beneath it if you are running Word in a graphics mode.

Position (option buttons) Do you want the selected text (or the next text you type) to be positioned normally or printed slightly above^{abc} or below$_{xyz}$ the line? Superscript is useful in footnote references, and both superscript and subscript are used in scientific and mathematical notation.

What Is Hidden Text?

Except in the diversity of its purposes, hidden text is little different from italicized, boldfaced, or underlined text. "Hidden" is a character format. You can apply it to highlighted text, or turn it on and off while typing, exactly as you do the italic, bold, and underline character formats. But instead of causing characters to print in a special format, the hidden-text format causes them seemingly to disappear.

Working with hidden text might surprise you at first. If you type with hidden characters, you won't be able to see what you are typing unless the Hidden Text field of the View Preferences command is checked. Nor will hidden characters print on a printer, unless you check the Hidden Text field of the Options dialog box for the File Print command. However, if the View Layout command is turned on, the on-screen display of hidden text is governed not by the View Preferences command but by the Options dialog box of the File Print command because the purpose of layout view is to approximate your page as it will print.

Hidden text lets you place hidden instructions in a document—instructions that command Word to perform a task or that label parts of a document as special. If you want to, you can type some of these special instructions yourself, using hidden text. But certain Word commands will do much or all of this typing for you. For example, when you use an Insert command to incorporate a graphic or data from a spreadsheet into a document, Word places the necessary hidden-text coding in the document in the appropriate location.

You type hidden text exactly as you do any other text, formatting it as hidden either as you type or afterwards. To format as you type, take any of the following steps just before you type. To format existing type, take any of the same approaches, but after first selecting (highlighting) the text you want to format.

- Use the Format Character command, and check the Hidden box.
- Use the built-in format for hidden text, which has the speed-formatting key combination Ctrl+H.
- If a macro that has a control code beginning with Ctrl+H is in the glossary, use the aforementioned built-in format by pressing Ctrl+AH.
- If a style sheet is attached to your document and it contains a character style expressly for hidden text, use the key code for that style. For instance, the key code for a hidden-text style might be HC (for "Hidden Character"). You would apply this style by pressing Ctrl+Y (for "stYle") followed by HC.

The fastest way to return hidden text to normal text is to select it and press Ctrl+Spacebar. This causes all character formatting (including character styles) to be discarded. If the hidden text has other character formatting you want to preserve, the Ctrl+Spacebar technique is too powerful. Instead, use Format Character to turn off the Hidden check box.

For a discussion of how hidden text is displayed on the screen, refer to the View Preferences command in Chapter 13.

FORMAT PARAGRAPH COMMAND

The Format Paragraph command lets you specify such line formatting as indentation, spacing, and alignment. The command acts on as many paragraphs or styles as you have selected in whole or in part.

On screen, paragraph formats generally look much as they'll print, although representational accuracy decreases when you format characters in more than one size because in Word's normal mode, the screen shows all characters as the same size.

Remember that Word somewhat redefines the meaning of the word "paragraph." As writers, we're accustomed to thinking of a paragraph in terms of content—as a cohesive block of text devoted to a single theme or point. But Word manipulates format as well as content, so to Word a paragraph is also a cohesive unit of formatting. Word considers a paragraph to be whatever lies between two paragraph marks. Because any paragraph can be formatted distinctively, you can start a new paragraph for formatting reasons as well as for content. For example,

- ♦ To center a single line, make it a separate paragraph and then format it to be centered. The same goes for titles and headers and footers, if you want to center them.
- ♦ To construct a form or a table in which different lines have different tab stops, make each line a separate paragraph.

In some senses, the Format Paragraph command could be called the Format Line command because you can give any single line a distinctive design simply by making it a paragraph in itself. And, because your readers never see paragraph marks, they need never know that two (or more) consecutive lines are, to Word, consecutive paragraphs with different paragraph formatting.

Assuming no style sheet is in use, Word's "normal" (built-in) paragraph format is flush-left, ragged-right alignment, with single spacing, no indentations, and with no extra blank lines before or after the paragraph. Additionally, there are no restrictions on where normal paragraphs split from one page to the next during printing, except that Word never strands a single line by itself at the top of a page unless it is a one-line paragraph. (However, you can turn off this widow/orphan control by using the Utilities Customize command.)

Paragraphs are "normal" until you change them by making choices in the Format Paragraph dialog box or by using built-in paragraph formats or paragraph styles from a style sheet. You can redefine what is "normal" paragraph formatting by designating a Paragraph Normal style in a style sheet.

The Paragraph Mark

Understanding the role of the paragraph mark is crucial to understanding paragraph formatting. Whenever you press the Enter key during writing or editing, a paragraph ends and several things happen:

- Word marks the end of the paragraph with a paragraph mark (¶). Although it is not printed, this mark is as much a real character as is any letter, number, or punctuation mark, so you can select, copy, or delete it.

- Within the paragraph mark, Word stores the formatting instructions for the paragraph that the mark ends. Technically, the formatting for each paragraph mark is stored near the end of a Word document. But conceptually, you can think of formatting as being stored "inside" the paragraph mark: If you delete the mark, any special formatting the paragraph had will vanish.

- Word moves you to a new line and begins a fresh paragraph, giving it the same formatting as the preceding paragraph. This paragraph formatting prevails unless you change it.

How does this affect you? Imagine you've written two paragraphs and have formatted each differently. During editing you inadvertently delete the mark that ends the first paragraph. You've just deleted the first paragraph's identity as a separate paragraph. The result? The two paragraphs join at the position where the mark used to be, and the formatting instructions for the second paragraph take control of the newly unified paragraph. The formatting of the first paragraph disappeared with its paragraph mark. Annoying? Confusing? Quite possibly, if you don't understand. All is not lost, of course; there is always Edit Undo. (Or, if the two paragraphs had the same formatting to begin with, you could simply press Enter to insert a new paragraph mark that breaks them apart again.)

The Paragraph Frame

Each paragraph is surrounded by an invisible frame. The frame is like a protective shield that stops the text of other paragraphs from intruding on the space reserved inside it.

When you indent one or both sides of a paragraph, you are indenting from the edges of the frame—leaving the frame size unaffected. This is worth keeping in mind if you experiment with the interactions of the Format Paragraph command and other commands such as Format Position.

For a full discussion of paragraph frames, see Chapter 30.

Besides the Format Paragraph command, paragraph formatting can be employed through the use of speed-formatting keys, the ruler, and the Style text box of the ribbon. In addition, MasterWord users can employ the format box, which adds to Word some of the interactive formatting features of the Word for Windows ruler. The paragraph box lets you use the keyboard or mouse to manipulate icons that control the line spacing, space before, alignment, and first-line indentation. Choose the Format Paragraph command by pressing Alt+TP. The Format Paragraph dialog box appears.

CHAPTER FIFTEEN: Format Commands

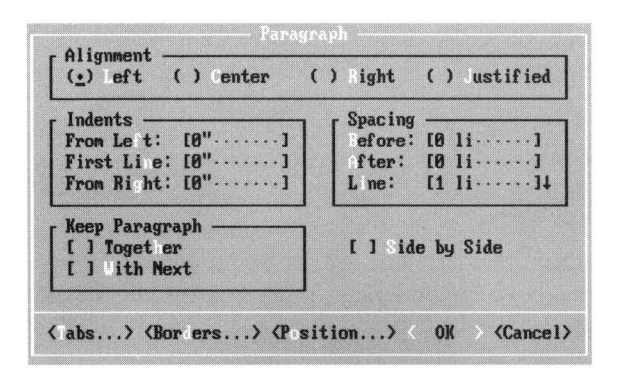

```
┌─────────────────────── Paragraph ───────────────────────┐
│ ┌─ Alignment ─────────────────────────────────────────┐ │
│ │ (•) Left    ( ) Center    ( ) Right    ( ) Justified│ │
│ └─────────────────────────────────────────────────────┘ │
│ ┌─ Indents ──────────────────┐ ┌─ Spacing ───────────┐ │
│ │ From Left:  [0"·······]    │ │ Before: [0 li······]│ │
│ │ First Line: [0"·······]    │ │ After:  [0 li······]│ │
│ │ From Right: [0"·······]    │ │ Line:   [1 li······]│ │
│ └────────────────────────────┘ └─────────────────────┘ │
│ ┌─ Keep Paragraph ───────────┐                          │
│ │ [ ] Together               │    [ ] Side by Side      │
│ │ [ ] With Next              │                          │
│ └────────────────────────────┘                          │
│                                                         │
│  <Tabs...> <Borders...> <Position...>  < OK > <Cancel> │
└─────────────────────────────────────────────────────────┘
```

Fields of the Format Paragraph Dialog Box

In addition to the OK and Cancel command buttons, the Format Paragraph dialog box has thirteen fields. Four of these fields govern the horizontal placement of lines, three govern the vertical placement of lines; three control the relationship of a paragraph to those surrounding it, and three are buttons leading you to related dialog boxes.

Controlling horizontal placement

The first field in the Format Paragraph command's dialog box is a set of option buttons that permit you to control the overall alignment of a paragraph. The next three fields, all text boxes, control a paragraph's indentations.

Alignment (option buttons) The following option buttons let you specify how to lay out the individual lines of a paragraph:

- **Left**—The default is a typewriter-like format, in which the left margin is flush and the right margin is ragged. Left alignment is common in correspondence because, with a letter-quality printer and a fixed-pitch font such as Courier or Pica, it has a more personalized typewritten look than the obviously computer-generated or typeset appearance of text that is justified on both the left and right. Often the first line of a left-aligned paragraph is indented. This book is set with "Left" alignment—also called "ragged right."
- **Center**—This causes every line of a paragraph to be centered between the paragraph's left and right indentations, if any. Centering is useful where the paragraph consists of a single distinctive line—an element such as a title, a heading, or banner text—or consists of text that is boxed or bordered or that is "glued" to an absolute position on the page with the Format Position command. When using center alignment, you probably want to set the first-line indent to 0 to avoid offsetting the line to the right of center.
- **Right**—Not surprisingly, this is the opposite of Left. It makes lines align flush right, with a ragged left margin—an uncommon formatting choice.

♦ **Justified**—This makes each line fill all available space between the left and right edges of the paragraph's frame; in other words, the left and right edges of the text align vertically. Only the final line of a justified paragraph doesn't need to align on the right. Newspapers and many magazines and books have justified type. As a further refinement, with most printers, Word automatically uses microspacing (that is, finely adjusted spacing between letters and words when printing justified paragraphs) even though microspacing does not show on the screen. Type fonts that are proportionally spaced automatically print with microspace justification if the printer is capable of it and if the alignment field is set to Justified. When you are printing fixed-pitch (nonproportional) fonts, you can avoid microspace justification by choosing Draft in the Options dialog box of the File Print command.

Three indent fields control to what extent, if any, a paragraph or its first line is indented inside the paragraph's frame. The First Line indent gives you a way to indent the beginning of a paragraph without pressing the Spacebar or using the Tab key. The From Left and From Right fields let you put additional blank space to the left or right of a paragraph—such as when you want a quoted passage to be printed in lines shorter than those of surrounding text.

The ruler, which you can turn on and off with the View Ruler command or by clicking the left mouse button on the ribbon/ruler icon at the top of the vertical scroll bar, is displayed across the top of the window. It shows the location of indents and tab stops for whatever paragraph is selected. Left and right indents are indicated by square brackets ([ ]), and a first-line indent is indicated by a broken vertical bar (┆).

From Left (text box) How far from the left side of the selected paragraph's frame do you want the selected paragraph or paragraphs to be positioned? The normal setting, 0, aligns the left edge of the text with the left side of the frame. In single-column documents that have no fancy formatting, the left and right sides of the paragraph frames are essentially synonymous with the left and right page margins.

First Line (text box) How far in from the paragraph's left indent do you want the first line to begin? A popular setting is 0.5, which indents the first line an additional half inch from the left edge of the other lines of the paragraph. The 0.5-inch setting provides five blank spaces of pica-size type at the beginning of the paragraph. If you're using smaller, elite-size type and you want a five-space indentation, specify .42" or *5 p12* instead.

Negative settings (such as −0.5") are allowed, so you can combine a positive left indent with a negative first-line indent to create a hanging-indented paragraph.

Hanging indents are valuable for, among other things, paragraphs in an outline—where the first line is farther to the left than the rest of the paragraph (to accommodate the numeral or letter that precedes the outline entry).

From Right (text box) How far from the right page margin do you want the selected paragraph or paragraphs to be indented? The normal setting, 0, means that a full-length text line reaches the right margin.

CHAPTER FIFTEEN: Format Commands

Controlling vertical placement

Vertical spacing between the lines of a paragraph and between paragraphs is established in three fields: Before, After, and Line. Word's ability to show line spacing on the screen is limited, but it will print fractional line settings, such as 1.5 lines, to the best ability of the printer.

Before (text box) How much extra vertical space, if any, do you want Word to place immediately above the paragraph?

After (text box) How much extra vertical space, if any, do you want Word to place immediately below the paragraph?

Remember that the extra space between two paragraphs is the sum of the space after of the first paragraph and the space before the second. When you add spaces between paragraphs, it's advisable to consistently create any blank lines with either Before or After but not both. This standardizes your formatting and minimizes the possibility of inadvertently "stacking" extra spaces—as when a paragraph with space after is followed by a paragraph with space before. Consider standardizing with Before, the same convention used in Word's built-in format (Alt-O) for open paragraph spacing and the convention used in MasterWord style sheets.

Line (drop-down list box) How much space do you want between the lines of a paragraph? The normal setting is one line. If you specify 2, the lines will be double-spaced. Although Word assumes six 12-point lines to an inch, measures other than lines are permitted. So, for example, you could increase the space between lines slightly by specifying *13 pt* in the Line drop-down list.

You also can choose Auto from the Line drop-down list. This causes Word to adjust line spacing on a line-by-line basis so that lines of small type are closer together than lines of large type. The rule Word follows is that line spacing will be sufficient to comfortably accommodate the point size of the largest type on a line.

Controlling the relationship of paragraphs

Three check boxes offer control over the relationship of paragraphs to each other on the printed page. They are the Together, With Next, and Side by Side fields.

Word generally follows this rule when breaking a paragraph across two pages during printing: Unless a paragraph consists of a single line, Word never prints only one line of it at either the bottom of the page or the top of the next page. Instead, Word arranges pages so there are at least two lines of the paragraph on each. You can override the rule by turning off the Widow/Orphan Control check box of the Utilities Customize command, or you can strengthen and supplement the rule with Format Paragraph commands Together and With Next fields.

Together (check box) If a paragraph falls near the end of a page, do you want Word to print the entire paragraph on one page or, in the case of multicolumn pages, in the same column? If you choose this field, Word moves the whole paragraph to the next page or column rather than splitting it. Among the uses of this setting is keeping all of a table together.

***With Next** (check box)* Do you want Word to lay out the page so that the last line of the paragraph is printed on the same page as the first two lines of the next paragraph? Turning this check box on for a paragraph that is a heading ensures that it prints on the same page as the beginning of the text to which it refers. Checking this box for the last paragraph in the body of a letter guarantees that at least the final portion of the body of the letter is printed on the same page as the letter's complimentary closing.

To ensure that all of two consecutive paragraphs are printed on the same page, check both Together and With Next for the first paragraph and Together for the second paragraph.

***Side by Side** (check box)* Do you want paragraphs to be printed beside each other on the page? Word lets you print paragraphs of text next to each other in two or more columns, provided that each of the paragraphs involved has been formatted with the Side by Side field checked and that the paragraphs would not overlap each other if they were printed on the same lines.

Side-by-side paragraphs are a handy way to format and visually set off any paragraphs within a document that benefit from a side-by-side presentation—lists, perhaps, or point-by-point comparisons. Side-by-side paragraphs are also useful in creating multiple-column tables, as described in Chapter 29.

To print two paragraphs beside each other, you might format the first one with a wide right indent, format the second one with a wide left indent, and check Side by Side for both paragraphs. Specifically, if a page is 8.5 inches wide and the right and left margins are 1.25 inches each, you have 6 inches of printable width. You could set the Paragraph command's From Right field to 3.5" for the first paragraph and its From Left field to 3.5" for the second paragraph. Provided that Side by Side was on for both, they would print beside each other with a 1-inch space between them.

If, instead, you wanted to print a series of five paragraphs beside five other paragraphs, you would turn on Side by Side for each of them and format the left series with a wide right indent and the right series with a wide left indent. When printing, Word would put each paragraph on the appropriate side, positioning it as high in the column as possible. The same technique can be used to print three or more columns side by side on the same page.

On screen, Word positions side-by-side paragraphs appropriately, in that left-side paragraphs are at the left side of the screen and right-side paragraphs are at the right.

If you are in layout view (in which case the characters *LY* appear on the status line), Word shows the paragraphs next to one another. You can toggle View Layout mode with the View Layout command.

If you use View Layout, bear in mind that Word's display, because it shows a fixed number of characters per line on the screen, does not necessarily match the layout of your lines on the printed page. Because of this, words or lines in your side-by-side paragraphs might be truncated on the screen. The words and lines will, however, print correctly.

CHAPTER FIFTEEN: Format Commands 287

If you are not in layout view, Word staggers the paragraphs on the screen like this:

```
This is the left
paragraph of a pair of
paragraphs formatted for
side-by-side printing.
                            This is the right
                            paragraph of the pair
                            formatted for side-by-
                            side printing.
```

On paper, however, the paragraphs print as you would expect.

If your computer display has graphics capability, the best way to see side-by-side paragraphs before printing is with File Print Preview.

When you format side-by-side paragraphs, always begin with the leftmost paragraph(s) and work your way toward the right side of the page. Word neither thinks nor scans ahead when it lays out your document. Thus, if it encounters a left-side paragraph after a right-side paragraph, Word doesn't print the right-side paragraph and then back up and insert the left-side paragraph where it belongs. It simply forges ahead, and the result is this:

```
                            Here the right paragraph
                            precedes the left
                            paragraph.
    The result is not what
    you might expect to see
    on the printout.
```

instead of this:

```
    Now the left paragraph    And the result is just
    comes first.              the way you want it.
```

For more extensive multiple-column formatting of the type you see in newspapers and magazines, refer to the discussion of Format Section later in this chapter.

Command buttons offer related choices

Not all of Word's paragraph-formatting choices are in the dialog box of the Paragraph command. In fact, four of the other commands of the Format menu are devoted to paragraph formatting. These commands, which are grouped together between horizontal lines in the middle of the menu, are Format Tabs, Format Border, Format Position, and Format Header/Footer. In addition to being available on Word's menus, the first three of the these commands can be reached by way of command buttons at the bottom of the Format Paragraph dialog box.

Tabs (command button) Choosing this button takes you to the dialog box of the Format Tabs command, discussed later in this chapter.

Borders (command button) Choosing this button takes you to the dialog box of the Format Borders command, discussed later in this chapter.

Position (command button) Choosing this button takes you to the dialog box of the Format Position command, discussed later in this chapter.

FORMAT SECTION COMMAND

Section formatting, which until version 5.5 was called *division formatting*, permits you to design the layout of pages. You can change this formatting as often as you want within a document, thereby creating sections that are formatted differently—hence the name *section formatting*.

Three commands control section formatting: Format Section, Format Margins, and Insert Page Numbers. A fourth command, Format Header/Footer, also controls an aspect of section formatting but only if you use the command's Options button to specify page placement for headers or footers.

If a document has but a single section, you can use one or more of these commands to set up page design throughout. If the document has two or more sections, you can use the commands to format the pages of each section differently.

These commands can be used directly on text, or they can be used to format a section style that in turn can be used to format text. To use a style to format text, you can use Format Apply Style or a key code. (Key codes are discussed in Chapters 6 and 24.)

Within a document, the boundary between two sections is indicated by a section mark. A section mark appears immediately above the end mark when you execute the Format Section, Format Margins, Insert Page Numbers, or Format Header/Footer (Options) command or when you manually start a new section by inserting a section break with the Section button of the Insert Break command. Technically, the section mark is a single character, even though it displays on the screen as a series of colons (::::::::::) that stretches the width of the column or text window.

Remember that the mark contains the section formatting for the text that precedes it, not the text that follows. The first time you use a section-formatting command, a section mark appears at the end of the document. The section mark, like the end mark, can be puzzling to newcomers who try to write or format at or below its position, so it's best not to do any text entry or any character or paragraph formatting when the section mark is highlighted.

Normal Section Formatting

When you create a new document, its section formatting will be normal until you change it or unless you are using a style sheet that redefines the normal section style.

CHAPTER FIFTEEN: Format Commands

Normal or default section formatting can be changed, but as Word is shipped from Microsoft to the U.S. market it gives you a single-column, 8.5-by-11-inch page, with 1-inch margins at the top and bottom and 1.25-inch left and right margins. If you choose to print page numbers, they are consecutive Arabic numerals, beginning with 1, printed 0.5 inch from the top and 7.25 inches from the left edge of the page. Footnotes, if any, are printed at the bottom of the page, and running heads, if any, are 0.5 inch from the top or bottom of the page, depending on whether they are headers or footers. Line numbers, if you choose to print them, are consecutive, right-aligned Arabic numerals printed 0.4 inch from the left edge of the text.

This 8.5-by-11-inch page size is the default in the United States but is relatively uncommon elsewhere. If you have a European version of Word, the normal section formatting likely will be for A4 paper, which is 8.268 inches wide and 11.69 inches tall.

If you use MasterWord WordSet, its Default Page Size dialog box lets you redefine the normal page size to any of the following common choices:

Paper type	Width	Height
U.S. letter	8.5"	11"
U.S. legal	8.5"	14"
U.S. executive	7.25"	10.5"
Tabloid	11"	17"
A3	11.69"	16.53"
A4	8.27"	11.69"
A5	5.83"	8.27"
B4	10.11"	14.33"
B5	6.93"	9.84"

You can accomplish the same thing by using the Format Margins command to fill in the Width and Height text boxes with the dimensions of the desired paper, using this chart as a guide. Change margins at the same time if you want and then check the Use as Default check box to make the setting the new normal section format for Word. (See the discussion of the Format Margins command later in this chapter for additional information.)

Beyond redefining Word's overall default section formatting, you can use a style sheet to impose its version of normal section formatting on a document. You do this by employing an existing style sheet or by creating one. Either way, the style sheet's Section Normal style will govern page layout unless you deliberately use a different section style or use the Format Section or Format Margins command directly on the document. In addition, if the style sheet has the name NORMAL.STY, Word will attach it to all documents that you don't deliberately format with a different style sheet. You can create a series of different directories, each for a different kind of document and each with its own NORMAL.STY style sheet, with each of these in turn containing a distinctive Section Normal style.

Dividing the Responsibility Among Commands

For your convenience, section-formatting responsibilities are divided among several commands. Early versions of Word lumped all section-formatting features into a single command called Format Division. It offered an almost bewildering number of choices, which is why Microsoft has divided it in recent years.

Here is the division of labor for Word 5.5:

- **Format Section**—Controls the overall "look" of pages, including the number of columns, whether footnotes appear at page bottoms or at the end of the section, how the transition from the formatting of one section to the next is handled, and whether and how line numbers are printed on pages.
- **Format Margins**—Controls the size of paper and the four margins of the page, including whether special allowances are made in margins for binding documents. In addition, the Format Margins command lets you redefine Word's default section formatting, as described earlier.
- **Insert Page Numbers**—Controls the location and format of page numbers, except for those page numbers created by formatting a paragraph to be a header or footer. This command can be reached from the Insert menu or by pressing the Page Numbers command button of the Format Section command.
- **Format Header/Footer**—This is primarily a paragraph-formatting command in that it turns a paragraph into a *running head*—a header or footer. But when you choose the command's Options button, the resulting dialog box lets you control how far from the top of the page headers are to print and how far from the bottom of the page footers are to print. This is section formatting.

You choose the first of these commands, Format Section, by pressing Alt+TS. The Format Section dialog box appears.

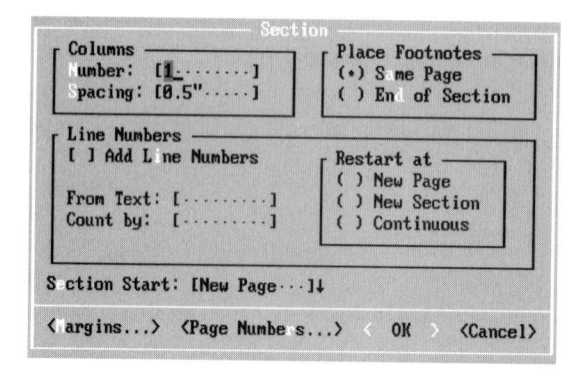

```
┌─────────────────────── Section ───────────────────────┐
│ ┌─ Columns ──────────────┐ ┌─ Place Footnotes ──────┐ │
│ │  Number:  [1......]    │ │ (•) Same Page          │ │
│ │  Spacing: [0.5"....]   │ │ ( ) End of Section     │ │
│ └────────────────────────┘ └────────────────────────┘ │
│ ┌─ Line Numbers ─────────────────────────────────────┐│
│ │ [ ] Add Line Numbers      ┌─ Restart at ─────────┐ ││
│ │                           │ ( ) New Page         │ ││
│ │ From Text: [........]     │ ( ) New Section      │ ││
│ │ Count by:  [........]     │ ( ) Continuous       │ ││
│ └───────────────────────────┴──────────────────────┴─┘│
│                                                       │
│ Section Start: [New Page...]↓                         │
│                                                       │
│ <Margins...>  <Page Numbers...>  < OK >  <Cancel>     │
└───────────────────────────────────────────────────────┘
```

CHAPTER FIFTEEN: Format Commands

Fields of the Format Section Dialog Box

In addition to the OK and Cancel command buttons, the Format Section dialog box contains ten fields. The first two permit you to control the number of columns on the page, the next one stipulates where footnotes shall print, the next four govern line numbering, and the last three lead to additional choices, including how formatting is to change between sections of a document.

Controlling columns and footnotes

Word offers a variety of ways in which you can achieve multiple columns on a page. For example, you can use side-by-side paragraphs or paragraphs that are absolutely positioned on the page. For greatest ease in managing those cases in which you want columns to be the same width, you can use the method described here—the two Columns fields of the Format Section command.

Number (text box) Word proposes 1, and that's all you want on a single page of a typical document, such as a business letter. If you want more than one column on a page, type in the number of columns you need. The text will print as you instruct, but on the screen normally you'll see a single, narrower column of type, adjusted to fit within the margins specified with the Format Margins command and allowing for the space between columns specified in the Spacing field.

You can also change to a different number of columns on a single page as follows: Place the highlight where you want the number of columns to change and press Alt+IBS, followed by Enter. This starts a new section. Move the highlight anywhere below the row of colons (::::::::) that marks the section break, and choose the Format Section command. Specify the number of columns you want, specify the space between columns if necessary, and finally choose Continuous in the Section Start field (described below).

Spacing (text box) When there are several columns on a page as a result of section formatting, how much blank space do you want between any two of them? Word proposes 0.5 inch.

You can see multiple-column layouts on screen by choosing the View Layout command. Although this does not necessarily show you complete lines (because of the shape and size of the characters Word displays), it does give you a way to preview page and column breaks before printing. To break a page at a particular location, press Ctrl+Enter to insert a manual page break; to break a column at a particular place, press Shift+Ctrl+Enter, or use Insert Break.

Place Footnotes (option buttons) Choose where you want footnotes and annotations to be collected for printing: at the bottoms of pages or at the ends of sections.

- **Same Page**—Footnotes and annotations are placed at the bottom of the page on which the footnote reference mark or annotation reference mark appears.
- **End of Section**—Footnotes and annotations appear at the end of the section.

Controlling line numbering

Word can print line numbers next to text, a feature of particular interest to the legal profession and to people who want to number lines in a computer program or an annotated manuscript. The line numbers do not appear on the screen, but if you turn on the Show Line Numbers check box of the View Preferences command, the status bar will display the number of the line containing the cursor.

Add Line Numbers (check box) Choose this check box if you want line numbers printed in your document. Unless the box is checked, all other related fields are unavailable and hence grayed.

Word shows some wisdom in adding line numbers. It does not count any text—such as in headers, footers, and footnotes—that is outside the main body of the document. Nor does it count blank space between lines or blank space added with the Before or After field of the Format Paragraph command. It does, however, count any blank lines you add to a document by pressing the Enter key. If a document is formatted with side-by-side paragraphs, Word ignores the number of columns they create and instead numbers each matched set of lines as a single line. In contrast, when you have a document that has multiple columns created with section formatting, Word numbers each line of each column separately.

From Text (text box) How far from the left edge of the line do you want the number printed? Word proposes 0.4 inch—enough to make the numbers clearly visible, even if you use revision marks or paragraph borders to add vertical lines to the left of the text. You can, however, specify any distance from the text, provided it is less than the width of the left margin. In multiple-column documents, be careful to set the From Text field to a value that is less than the space between columns.

Word prints line numbers as right aligned. If there is not enough room to print the entire number, it eliminates digits, beginning with the one farthest to the left. Thus, on long documents, be sure to allow enough room for however many digits will be in the largest line number. To allow for more white space on a crowded page or to match the font and size of line numbers with the rest of the document, you can use a Character Line Number style and format it as you please. (For more on styles, see Chapter 24.)

Count by (text box) Do you want the lines numbered *1, 2, 3, 4, 5,* and so on, or do you prefer a different increment, such as 5 (making it *5, 10, 15,* and so on)? Specify the increment if you do not want Word's default of *1*.

Restart at (option buttons) Do you want printed numbering to reflect the number of lines since the beginning of the page, the section, or the document?

- **New Page**—Word starts numbering anew at the beginning of each page in the section.
- **New Section**—Word starts numbering at the beginning of the section, with line numbers increasing until the end of the section.
- **Continuous**—Word numbers lines continuously through a document containing multiple sections.

CHAPTER FIFTEEN: Format Commands

Additional formatting choices

Near the bottom of the dialog box is one of Word's most interesting controls. It is the Section Start drop-down list, which lets you decide how you want Word to handle the transition between the differing formats of two sections of a document. The only other fields at the bottom of the box are buttons that take you to related commands.

Section Start (drop-down list box) This field controls what Word does when it encounters a section mark. To use it, position the cursor somewhere in the text *following* the section mark before you choose the Format Section command.

- **New Page**—The section mark is treated as if it were a page break, and the formatting of the new section goes into effect on this new page. This is the default choice.
- **Continuous**—Starts most aspects of the section's formatting immediately, without beginning a new page or column. But the bottom-margin formatting doesn't change until the next page. This setting is useful because it is one way to print different numbers of columns on one page; Word balances the length of the columns in the first section before changing to the new number of columns in the middle of the page. When a section contains footnotes or annotations, Word treats the section mark as if it were set to New Page.
- **Column**—Starts printing the new section at the top of the next column. If there is only one column to a page, Column begins a new page.
- **Even Page**—Similar to New Page, but the new page is given the next available even number, inserting a blank odd-numbered page if necessary. This ensures that the new section will begin at the top of a left-side page if printing is double-sided.
- **Odd Page**—Similar to New Page, but the new page is given the next available odd number, inserting a blank even-numbered page if necessary. This ensures that the new section will begin at the top of a right-side page if printing is double-sided.

Four of these same choices are available in a set of option buttons when you use the Insert Break command to create a section break. The buttons give you a fast way to create a new section and stipulate how its formatting is to start. The Section Start list box gives you a way to change your mind later, to impose formatting on a section you did not deliberately create, or to use the Column choice, which is not available in the Insert Break command's dialog box.

To see where page breaks will occur, use File Print Preview or View Layout.

Margins (command button) Choosing this button takes you to the dialog box of the Format Margins command, discussed on the following page.

Page Numbers (command button) Choosing this button takes you to the dialog box of the Insert Page Numbers command, discussed in Chapter 14.

FORMAT MARGINS COMMAND

Page margins are bands of blank space along the four edges of your paper. The inner edges of the page margins are the out-of-bounds lines for ordinary text. You can adjust each of the four margins individually. The only elements that Word will print in a margin are a header, a footer, a paragraph that you have deliberately positioned in the margin by using the Format Position command, line numbers, and revision marks. Often paragraphs positioned in this way will contain graphics images.

Understanding the distinction between page margins and paragraph indents is important. The margins govern the whole page; paragraph indents pertain to specific paragraphs. To compute how far a paragraph's lines will print from the left edge of the page, add the left page margin and the left paragraph indent. By having both margins and indents, Word gives you the flexibility to change the horizontal placement of lines on a paragraph-by-paragraph basis.

The Format Margins command is one of several devoted to section formatting, a topic introduced with the previous command, Format Section.

Choose the Format Margins command by pressing Alt+TM. The Format Section Margins dialog box appears.

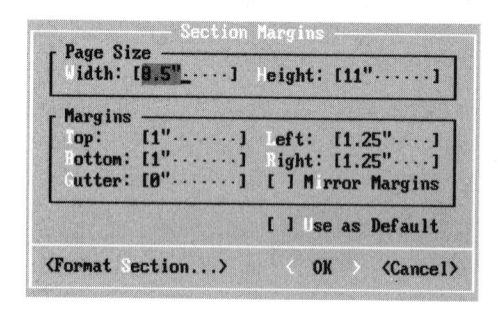

```
┌─────────────── Section Margins ───────────────┐
│ ┌─ Page Size ─────────────────────────────┐   │
│ │  Width: [0.5"    ]  Height: [11"     ]  │   │
│ └─────────────────────────────────────────┘   │
│ ┌─ Margins ───────────────────────────────┐   │
│ │  Top:     [1"    ]  Left:  [1.25"   ]   │   │
│ │  Bottom:  [1"    ]  Right: [1.25"   ]   │   │
│ │  Gutter:  [0"    ]  [ ] Mirror Margins  │   │
│ └─────────────────────────────────────────┘   │
│                         [ ] Use as Default    │
│  <Format Section...>     < OK >   <Cancel>    │
└───────────────────────────────────────────────┘
```

You can also reach this dialog box by choosing the Margins command button in the Format Section dialog box.

Fields of the Format Section Margins Dialog Box

In addition to the OK and Cancel command buttons, the Format Section Margins dialog box contains ten fields. Two of these relate to page size and six to page margins. Of the two remaining fields, one permits you to impose a new normal (default) section format on your Word documents, and the other is a button that takes you directly to the Format Section dialog box.

Setting a paper size

Choose a size of paper for your document and indicate its dimensions in the Width and Height text boxes. A chart of common sizes was included in this chapter's earlier discussion of the Format Section command.

Width (text box) Enter the width of your paper, using any of Word's accepted units of measure. Pica-size characters (P10) are equivalent to tenths of an inch; elite-size characters (P12) are equivalent to twelfths of an inch. The proposed width typically is 8.5 inches; the maximum permitted is 22 inches or 254 characters, whichever is narrower.

Height (text box) Enter the length of your paper in inches ("), centimeters (cm), points (pt), or lines (li). The proposed height typically is 11 inches; the maximum is 22 inches.

Establishing page margins

Word provides a rich assortment of controls for page margins.

Top (text box) Enter a measurement in any accepted unit of measure for the distance from the top of each page to the first line of ordinary text. Word proposes 1 inch, which allows room for a modest header. If you use a header that doesn't fit in the top margin you have allowed, Word will increase the margin as needed. To prevent Word from making this adjustment, express the top margin as a negative number. For example, if you want the top of the page to begin printing at 1 inch even if a header intrudes into the top two inches of the page, type –1" in the Top field. The header might print on top of the body text in this case.

Bottom (text box) Enter a similar measurement for the distance from the end of a page's text to the bottom edge of the paper. Word proposes 1 inch. If you place a footer that would interfere with the body text on the page, Word will increase the bottom margin sufficiently to avoid conflict. However, if you express the bottom margin as a negative number, Word will follow your instruction even if it causes the body text and the footer to print on the same line or lines.

> NOTE: *If you feed paper into your printer a sheet at a time, the top margin of your printed page might come out about five lines too deep and the bottom margin about five lines too shallow. To adjust the top and bottom fields, try reducing the top margin by 0.83 inch and increasing the bottom margin by the same amount. (You can set up a section style in a style sheet to take care of this for you.)*

Gutter (text box) When formatting pages that will be reproduced on both sides of the paper and bound, specify a gutter (extra margin) allowance for the binding. A gutter of 0.5 inch typically is suitable for pages that are to be inserted into three-ring notebooks. Word puts this extra space on the left side of odd-numbered pages and on the right side of even-numbered pages. If pages are to be printed on only one side, leave the gutter margin at 0 and add to the left margin any additional width required for binding.

Left (text box) Enter a measurement for the left margin—the distance from the left edge of the paper to the left edge of text. Typically, Word proposes 1.25 inches. Some nonlaser printers are considerably slower when a page has a left margin of 1.25 inches because the 0.05 portion of the measurement requires microspacing. If this affects your printer, try changing the margin to 1.2, 1.3, or another multiple of 0.1. Also keep in mind that if a left indent is specified in paragraph formatting, text will be as far from the left edge of the paper as the combined total of the left indent and the left margin measurement.

Right (text box) This is the same as for Left, but measured from the right edge of the paper to the rightmost edge of text.

Mirror Margins (check box) You can use the Mirror Margins check box to create "mirror-image" left and right margins of different widths on two facing pages. This is the type of design you see when you open a book in which the left and right pages have wide margins on the outer edges and narrower margins on the inner edges (near the binding), or vice versa.

To create mirror margins, check this field and specify different left and right margin widths. Word alternates the left and right margins when it prints, using the specified margin widths for all odd-numbered pages and swapping left and right margins for even-numbered pages.

Additional formatting choices

Two fields remain in the Format Section Margins dialog box. The first is an important choice that has far-reaching implications; the second is a button that takes you to the Format Section command.

Use as Default (check box) Turn on this check box if you want to adopt the settings expressed in the other fields of the dialog box as Word's new defaults for page size and margins. This is your way to redefine what Word considers normal section formatting—a concept introduced near the beginning of the discussion of the Format Section command. As noted before, Word will disregard this normal section formatting if you use a style sheet that contains a normal section style or if you deliberately apply section formatting to your document.

The Use as Default check box is peculiar because it doesn't remain checked even though its settings remain in effect. For example, if you choose a new page size and check this box, Word will accept the page as normal for the remainder of this and all future editing sessions, but when you return to look at the field it will not be checked. This means you don't have a ready way to know whether the default section formatting has been changed, except by deducing it from Word's behavior or by using a separate utility such as MasterWord WordSet.

Format Section (command button) Choosing this button takes you to the dialog box of the Format Section command, discussed earlier.

FORMAT TABS COMMAND

Normally, Word presets a tab stop every half inch: Press the Tab key, and the highlight moves half an inch to the next predetermined stop. This built-in formatting meets many basic needs, and it requires no work on your part. But when you're ready to set your own tabs, Word offers a formidable array of tab features.

Using Word's tab features, you can

- Change the distance between preset tab stops by altering the setting of the Default Tab text box of the Utilities Customize command.
- Choose a different type of alignment for each tab stop and, if you want, define a leader character that fills the blank space leading to the tab stop with dots, hyphens, or underlines.
- Use the ruler to set, move, and clear tab stops, whether with the keyboard or a mouse.

These techniques work whether you are formatting a paragraph directly or whether you are formatting a style that you will, in turn, use to format paragraphs. Of all the methods, the ruler is perhaps easiest—especially if you use a mouse.

Before delving into the particulars of these techniques, let's cover a little background to help you understand and use tabs correctly.

Content vs. Format

Recall the distinction between a document's content and its format. When setting and using tabs, bear in mind that a tab *character* is content, but a tab *stop* is format.

When you press the Tab key, Word inserts a tab *character* into the text at the location of the highlight. The tab character keeps blank the space between its insertion point and the location of the next tab stop in the same line. Although it can blank out many consecutive spaces, the tab character is a single character and is selected, deleted, and copied like any other single character.

If this concept seems a bit fuzzy, try displaying a few tab characters on the screen. Choose the View Preferences command, and check the Tabs field. Now press the Tab key a few times. Each time you press it, a small, right-pointing arrow (→) followed by some blank space appears. The arrow and the space together represent a single tab character. Thus, if you select one of these arrows, the highlight encompasses both the arrow and the space following it. Likewise, if you press the Del key, you remove both the arrow and the space.

On the other hand, when you use the Format Tabs command or the ruler, you create formatting—a tab *stop* containing instructions on how any tab character that comes in contact with it will affect the appearance of the document.

A tab stop is part of paragraph formatting, although you apply it with the Format Tabs command rather than with the Format Paragraph command. You can vary tab stops between paragraphs. One way to create tab stops that apply throughout a document is to select the entire document before using the Format Tabs command.

However, unless you use tab stops only occasionally, you are almost always better off to insert the tab stops into a paragraph style and then use the style to format text. Setting up tab stops can be a little more complicated than most formatting; do it once in a style and you save yourself the trouble of repeating the steps for each paragraph that is to have the same stops. Simply apply the style to the paragraph.

Choose the Format Tabs command by pressing Alt+TT. The Format Tabs dialog box appears.

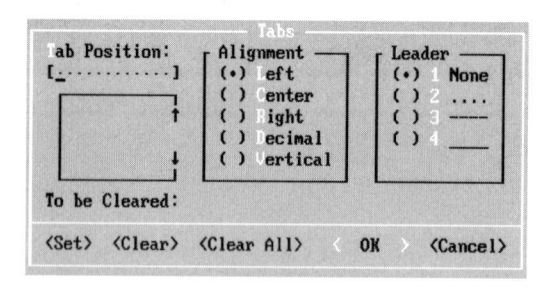

```
┌─────────────────── Tabs ───────────────────┐
│ ┌ Tab Position: ┐ ┌─ Alignment ─┐ ┌─ Leader ──┐│
│ │ [_..........] │ │ (•) Left    │ │ (•) 1 None││
│ │               │ │ ( ) Center  │ │ ( ) 2 ....││
│ │        ↑      │ │ ( ) Right   │ │ ( ) 3 ----││
│ │               │ │ ( ) Decimal │ │ ( ) 4 ____││
│ │        ↓      │ │ ( ) Vertical│ └───────────┘│
│ └───────────────┘ └─────────────┘             │
│ To be Cleared:                                │
│                                               │
│ <Set>  <Clear>  <Clear All>   <  OK  >  <Cancel>│
└───────────────────────────────────────────────┘
```

You can also reach this dialog box by choosing the Tabs button in the Format Paragraph dialog box. Tab stops are part of a paragraph's formatting.

Fields of the Format Tabs Dialog Box

In addition to the Close and OK command buttons, the Format Tabs dialog box has seven fields, three of which are buttons you use in conjunction with the other fields.

Tab Position (text box) How far from the left side of the paragraph's frame do you want the tab stop to be located? You can use any of Word's units of measure, or simply type a number if you want to use the default unit of measure defined in the Measure field of the Utilities Customize command.

After you have typed a number in this text box, you can act on it with any of the three buttons—Set, Clear, and Clear All. Pressing one of these buttons lets you make a tentative choice before carrying out the command.

Tab Position (list box) As tab stops are tentatively set (with the Set button), they are listed here. When the command is finally executed, the tab stops listed in the box are imposed upon the selected paragraph or style.

Alignment (option buttons) What part of the text do you want lined up with the tab stop?

- **Left**—Aligns text flush left at the tab stop.
- **Centered**—Centers text at the tab stop.
- **Right**—Aligns text flush right at the tab stop.
- **Decimal**—Aligns the decimal points of numbers at the tab stop. Percentages are aligned at their % signs.
- **Vertical**—This is not so much a tab stop as it is a method of drawing a vertical line down through a paragraph at the position you specify. Use it for separating columns in a table or for dividing a large box on a form into smaller boxes.

Note the tab-stop information in the ruler above the text in these examples of left, center, right, and decimal alignment.

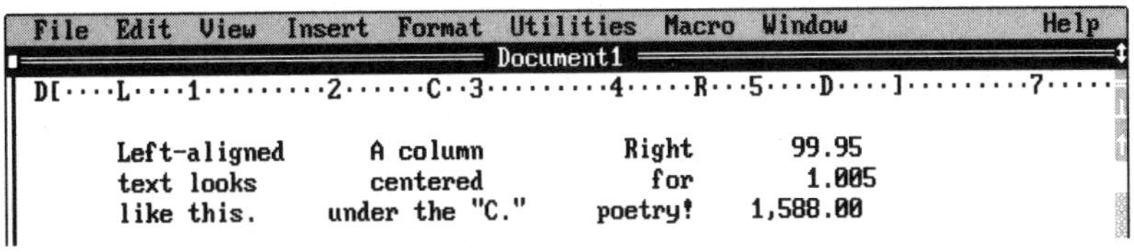

CHAPTER FIFTEEN: Format Commands   299

```
 File  Edit  View  Insert  Format  Utilities  Macro  Window          Help
═══════════════════════════ Document1 ═══════════════════════════
 D[····L····1·········2·····C··3··········4·····R···5····D····]·········7····

        Left-aligned    A column       Right         99.95
        text looks      centered        for           1.005
        like this.      under the "C."  poetry!   1,588.00
```

And here is an example of a vertical tab stop:

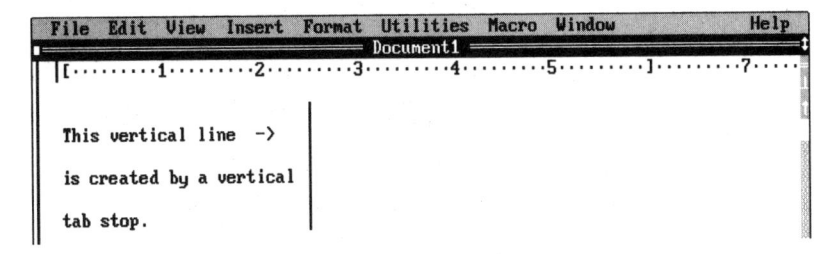

```
 File  Edit  View  Insert  Format  Utilities  Macro  Window          Help
═══════════════════════════ Document1 ═══════════════════════════
 |[·········1·········2·········3·········4·········5·········]·········7····


    This vertical line  ->  |

    is created by a vertical|

    tab stop.               |
```

Leader (option buttons) Which leader character, if any, do you want displayed in the otherwise blank space leading to the tab stop? (Leaders are often used in tables of contents.)

1 **None**   The default choice is no leader character.

2 .....   A dotted underline.

3 ----   A series of hyphens, or dashes.

4 __   A solid underline.

In this example of the three kinds of leader characters, note how information is displayed in the ruler:

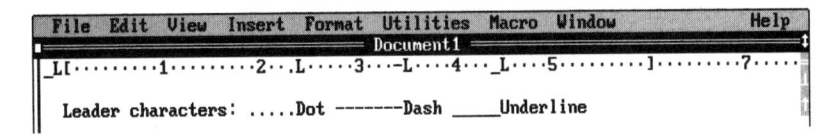

```
 File  Edit  View  Insert  Format  Utilities  Macro  Window          Help
═══════════════════════════ Document1 ═══════════════════════════
 _L[·········1·········2··.L·····3····-L····4····_L····5·········]·········7····

      Leader characters: .....Dot -------Dash ____Underline
```

NOTE: *Leader characters do not apply to tab stops with vertical alignment.*

Set (command button) After you enter a measurement in the Tab Position text box, you can add it to a tentative list of tab stops by pressing the Set button.

Clear (command button) If you highlight a tab stop in the Tab Position list box and press this button, the stop will vanish from the list box and appear instead in the dialog box after the To be Cleared message. If you clear several tab stops from the list box using the Clear button, each will appear in the To be Cleared list.

Clear All (command button) Eliminates all tab stops at one time, thereby restoring the preset tab stops.

When you finally choose OK (Enter) to carry out the command, the tentative tab stops appearing in the Tab Position list box are imposed on paragraphs that are selected in whole or in part or on selected styles in a style sheet window.

Word is limited to 19 tab stops per paragraph.

Using the Keyboard with the Ruler

The ruler shows the location, alignment, and leader characters (if any) of tab stops for the selected paragraph(s). By using the direction keys or a mouse in conjunction with the ruler, you can create or change tab stops without using the Format Tabs command at all.

To activate the ruler for use with the keyboard, press Shift+Ctrl+F10. Then use any of these keys when the cursor is in the ruler:

Key(s)	Result
Right direction	Moves the cursor to the right.
Left direction	Moves the cursor to the left.
Ctrl+Right direction	Moves the tab stop currently under the cursor to the right.
Ctrl+Left direction	Moves the tab stop currently under the cursor to the left.
Down direction	Jumps the cursor to the next existing tab stop to the right.
Up direction	Jumps the cursor to the next existing tab stop to the left.
L	Inserts a left-aligned tab stop at the location of the cursor.
R	Inserts a right-aligned tab stop at the location of the cursor.
C	Inserts a center-aligned tab stop at the location of the cursor.
D	Inserts a decimal-aligned tab stop at the location of the cursor.
V	Inserts a vertical tab stop at the location of the cursor.
Ins	Inserts another tab stop that has the same alignment as the previous one.
. (Period)	Gives the tab stop currently under the cursor, or the next tab stop to be inserted, a period (....) leader character.

(continued)

CHAPTER FIFTEEN: Format Commands   301

Continued.

Key(s)	Result
- (Hyphen)	Gives the tab stop currently under the cursor, or the next tab stop to be inserted, a hyphen (----) leader character.
_ (Underscore)	Gives the tab stop currently under the cursor, or the next tab stop to be inserted, an underline (___) leader character.
Space	Gives the tab stop currently under the cursor, or the next tab stop to be inserted, a blank leader character.
Del	Deletes the tab stop currently under the cursor.
Ctrl+Del	Deletes the tab stop currently under the cursor, along with any tab stops to the right of the cursor.
Enter	Returns the cursor to the document, saving changes made to the paragraph or to the style's tab stops. Until you press Enter, all other actions you make with the keyboard in the ruler are merely tentative.
Esc	Returns the cursor to the document, without making any changes to the tab stops of the paragraph or the style.

The ruler displays the current status of its tab stops, using the same descriptive letters you use to impose the formatting. For example, it shows a left-aligned tab stop that has a period leader character as .L—the exception being that vertical tab stops are represented with a vertical line rather than the letter V.

Using the Mouse with the Ruler

One of the most powerful, intuitive features of the mouse is the ease it brings to setting, changing, and deleting tab stops. To set a tab stop without using a command, move the mouse pointer to the top of the window. If the ruler is not displayed, move the pointer to the ribbon/ruler icon at the top of the vertical scroll bar, and click the left mouse button.

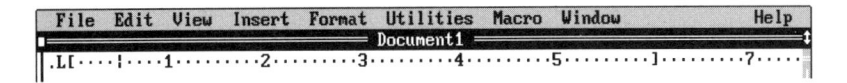

```
 File  Edit  View  Insert  Format  Utilities  Macro  Window          Help
============================= Document1 =================================
.L[····|····1·········2·········3·········4·········5·········]·········7····
```

When the ruler is displayed, you can click anywhere on it with the mouse to insert a tab stop at that location. To move a tab stop, drag it along the ruler. (That is, point at it with the mouse and hold down the left mouse key while moving the pointer.) To delete a tab stop, point at it with the mouse and drag it down one line toward the bottom of the screen.

To adjust the kind of tab stop you insert with the mouse, first move the mouse pointer to the left end of the ruler. Here you will find the letter L, C, R, or D or a vertical line the height of a single character. This letter or line represents the alignment of the next tab stop that will be inserted. Click on this space as many times as is necessary to rotate through the five possible types of alignments. Stop when you reach the alignment you want.

From this point, merely move the mouse pointer one character to the left if you want to adjust the kind of leader character that will be inserted the next time you click on the ruler. The choices are a period (.), a hyphen (-), an underscore (_), and a blank. Click on this space until the character you want is displayed. Then, to actually insert the tab character, simply move to the desired location on the ruler, and click the left mouse button.

To clear a tab stop, click both mouse buttons.

The ruler also lets you use the mouse to move paragraph and first-line indents (signified on the ruler by [for the left indent,] for the right, and ¦ for the first line). Point to the indent marker you want to move, press and hold down the right mouse button, and drag the marker to its new location. When you finish, any selected paragraph or paragraphs will have the new indents you chose.

The same shortcuts work in the style-sheet window, provided that a paragraph style is currently selected.

FORMAT BORDERS COMMAND

Use the Format Borders command to place lines on some or all four sides of a paragraph. The paragraph can contain either a graphic or text.

Like first-line indents or double-spacing, borders are a form of paragraph formatting. You use the Format Borders command to specify which if any of the four lines (top, bottom, left, or right) is to be drawn around a paragraph. You use the Format Paragraph command to govern the location of the lines relative to the content of the paragraph:

- A left border is drawn at the paragraph's left indent.
- A right border is drawn at the paragraph's right indent.
- A top border runs between the paragraph's left and right indents; space above it is controlled by the Before field of the Format Paragraph command.
- A bottom border runs between a paragraph's left and right indents; space below it is controlled by the Format Paragraph command's After field.
- Vertical spacing between top and bottom borders is governed by the Line field of the Format Paragraph command. To create additional blank space between the top and bottom borders, add blank lines to the paragraph by pressing the Shift+Enter key combination.

Whether you select a paragraph and then put a border around it or create a border and then type text into it, Word adjusts the size of the border to fit the text within it.

Because borders are a part of paragraph formatting, you create a new set of borders whenever you press the Enter key. If the Before and After fields of the Format Paragraph command are set to *0 li* and successive paragraphs have the same left and right indents, Word gives neighboring paragraphs with the same type of border lines a common border, like this:

```
This is the first of two paragraphs formatted with a box
border. Both have the same left and right indents and have
no extra space before or space after.¶

This is the second of the two paragraphs. Notice the
shared horizontal line between the two.¶
```

Otherwise, each paragraph is given its own borders.

One way to print multiple paragraphs in a single box is to make the text all one large "paragraph." You can create what seem to be new paragraphs by forging new lines with the Shift+Enter (new-line) key combination instead of with the Enter key. Here is an example:

```
     To Word, this example is a single paragraph because
there is a paragraph mark only at the very end. On screen
and on paper, however, these lines can look like a series
of paragraphs enclosed in a box.↓
↓
     To create this look, give the paragraph a box border
with the Format Border command. For breaks between
"paragraphs," press Shift-Enter (indicated by the
downward-pointing arrows in this illustration). Press the
Tab key to create a "first line indent" for each
"paragraph." Word's default tab width of 0.5" was used
here.¶
```

Whenever possible, Word prints all of a boxed paragraph on a single page. If the box is less than one page long but will not fit in the space remaining on the current page, Word prints the entire box on the next page. If the box is more than one page long, Word prints as much as it can and then completes printing on the next page. Word does not draw the bottom border of the box until it reaches the end of the paragraph.

Another way to print a succession of paragraphs in a single box is to give all the paragraphs left and right borders, give the first paragraph a top border, and give the last paragraph a bottom border.

You can preview page breaks with the Utilities Repaginate Now command or, if your system displays graphics, with the File Print Preview command.

For practical examples of ways to use the Border command, see Chapter 29.

Choose the Format Borders command by pressing Alt+TB. The Format Paragraph Borders dialog box appears.

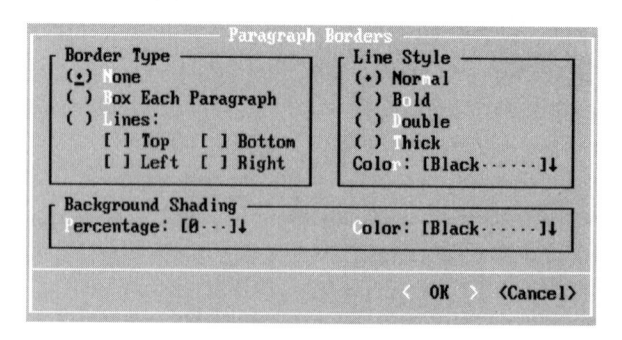

```
┌─ Paragraph Borders ──────────────────────────┐
│ ┌─ Border Type ──────────┐ ┌─ Line Style ──────┐ │
│ │ (·) None               │ │ (•) Normal        │ │
│ │ ( ) Box Each Paragraph │ │ ( ) Bold          │ │
│ │ ( ) Lines:             │ │ ( ) Double        │ │
│ │     [ ] Top  [ ] Bottom│ │ ( ) Thick         │ │
│ │     [ ] Left [ ] Right │ │ Color: [Black   ]↓│ │
│ └────────────────────────┘ └───────────────────┘ │
│ ┌─ Background Shading ────────────────────────┐ │
│ │ Percentage: [0   ]↓      Color: [Black   ]↓ │ │
│ └──────────────────────────────────────────────┘ │
│                              < OK >  <Cancel>   │
└──────────────────────────────────────────────────┘
```

You also reach this dialog box by choosing the Borders command button in the Format Paragraph dialog box.

Fields of the Format Paragraph Borders Dialog Box

In addition to the OK and Close buttons, the Format Paragraph Borders dialog box contains nine fields:

Border Type (option buttons) Do you want the paragraph or style formatted with a border and, if so, on all sides or only some?

- **None**—The default choice; the paragraph has no borders. Also used to remove borders from an existing paragraph.
- **Box Each Paragraph**—Puts lines on all four sides of the paragraph, creating a box.
- **Lines**—Puts lines on only those sides of the paragraph that are indicated in the four check boxes below. Unless this option button is chosen, the check boxes are grayed and unavailable.

Top (check box) Do you want a line above the paragraph?

Bottom (check box) Do you want a line below the paragraph?

Left (check box) Do you want a line to the left of the paragraph?

Right (check box) Do you want a line to the right of the paragraph?

Choosing all four of the check boxes is the equivalent of telling Word to draw a box around the selected paragraph or paragraphs. Word does not attempt to keep the bordered paragraphs on a single page; if it reaches the end of a page when printing or repaginating, it breaks the box across successive pages.

CHAPTER FIFTEEN: Format Commands

Line Style (option buttons) What type of border do you want? If your printer supports the IBM extended character set, the list shows the following four choices. If it doesn't support IBM graphics characters, the choices are limited to Normal and Bold.

- **Normal**—Gives a single line, like the ones in the illustrations on page 303. This is the default.
- **Bold**—Renders a boldfaced, single-line border.
- **Double**—Results in a double-line border.
- **Thick**—Offers a broad-lined border.

Color [of lines] (drop-down list box) In what color do you want to print the border? You can choose a printing color if you have a color printer and have specified it in the File Printer Setup command. Type the name of a color, or press Alt+Down direction key to see a list of those you can use. If you do not have a color printer, you generally see only one choice: black. However, on PostScript or similar printers you might see the choices Black, Dark, Medium, Light, and White.

Percentage (drop-down list box) If your printer supports the IBM extended character set, you can choose background shading at intensity levels from 0 (none) through 100 (solid). On an IBM graphics printer, for example, a value of 10 gives light shading, a value of 40 gives medium shading, and a value of 70 gives dark shading. You can either type in a value or press the Down direction key to see a list of choices. If your printer does not support background shading, Word displays 0.

Color [of shading] (drop-down list box) If your printer supports the IBM extended character set *and* can print in different colors, you can use this field to specify the color of whatever background shading you choose in the Percentage field. On PostScript or similar printers, you might also have choices of black-and-white patterns. The colors or patterns that are available depend on the make and model of your printer; press Alt+Down direction key to see a list.

FORMAT POSITION COMMAND

The Format Position command enables you to tell Word exactly where on the page you want one or more paragraphs to be printed. This capability, known as *absolute positioning*, works with both text and graphics and is built around the concept of a *paragraph frame*. This portion of the chapter briefly describes these concepts and the way you use the Format Position command. For more detailed descriptions of absolute positioning, refer to Chapter 30.

Recall that Word "sees" a document as being composed of two parts, content and format, and that it generally distinguishes quite clearly between the two. Think, now, of a paragraph you type. Its content is text; but, excluding the character formatting of the text itself, a paragraph's format in large part is defined by white space: left, right, and first-line indents; space before; and space after, aligned with the margins or edges of the page. This white space, although it contains no text, occupies the page exactly as the text does, and it ends at an invisible boundary, the paragraph's frame.

Word has no problem seeing this invisible frame and treating it as a unit that can be positioned anywhere on the page. Because the frame is separate from the paragraph formatting itself, it encompasses not only text or graphics but line borders drawn with the Format Borders command. Furthermore, you can control the amount of white space surrounding the text with the Distance from Text field of the Format Position command and with the alignment, indents, and spacing fields of the Format Paragraph command.

Normally, Word treats the paragraphs you type as a sequence of frames, which it prints neatly, one after the other, in one or more columns, as you specify. If you specify Together in the Format Paragraph dialog box, Word attempts to keep all of a paragraph frame and contents on a single page; if you specify With Next, it places the paragraph frame on the same page as the frame of the succeeding paragraph. No two paragraph frames occupy the same space, nor is any paragraph frame (except a header or footer) destined for a particular part of the page. Not, at least, unless you use the Format Position command to reserve a particular (*absolute*) position on the page for the paragraph. The Format Position command can position normal body paragraphs and headers/footers, as well as paragraphs that contain graphics.

When you give a paragraph an absolute position on the page, you define the size of its frame and reserve a location for it. Because this location is set aside, Word adjusts page layout so that the text of other paragraphs flows around the reserved area.

Choose the Format Position command by pressing Alt+TO. The Format Position dialog box appears.

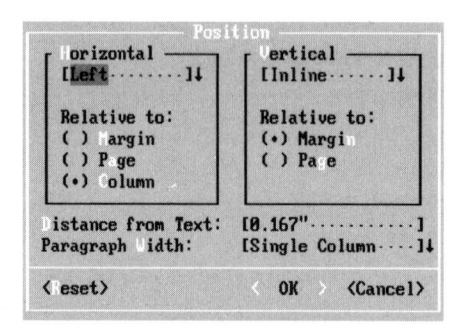

```
┌─ Position ──────────────────────────┐
│ ┌─ Horizontal ──┐  ┌─ Vertical ──┐  │
│ │ [Left·····]↓  │  │ [Inline··]↓ │  │
│ │               │  │             │  │
│ │ Relative to:  │  │ Relative to:│  │
│ │ ( ) Margin    │  │ (•) Margin  │  │
│ │ ( ) Page      │  │ ( ) Page    │  │
│ │ (•) Column    │  │             │  │
│ └───────────────┘  └─────────────┘  │
│                                     │
│ Distance from Text: [0.167"······]  │
│ Paragraph Width:    [Single Column]↓│
│                                     │
│ <Reset>      <  OK  >   <Cancel>    │
└─────────────────────────────────────┘
```

You can also reach this dialog box by choosing the Position command button in the Format Paragraph dialog box.

Fields of the Format Position Dialog Box

In addition to the OK and Cancel command buttons, the Format Position dialog box has seven fields:

Horizontal (drop-down list box) How do you want the frame of the paragraph to be positioned horizontally (left to right)? You can type a measurement for the distance between the left edge of the frame and the left edge of the column, margin, or page (whichever you choose in the adjoining Relative To field). You can use any unit of

CHAPTER FIFTEEN: Format Commands

measure Word understands, but if you use one (such as centimeters) that differs from the setting in the Measure field of the Utilities Customize command, include the abbreviation for the unit of measure you use. For placing frames exactly, using points (*Pt*) gives you control to about 1/72 of an inch.

Instead of typing a measurement, you can choose one of five relative options from the drop-down list:

- **Left**—This is Word's proposed response. It pushes the frame to the left relative to the column, margins, or page.
- **Centered**—Centers the frame relative to the column, margins, or page.
- **Right**—Pushes the frame to the right, relative to the column, margins, or page.
- **Inside**—Positions the frame to the left on odd-numbered pages and to the right on even-numbered pages.
- **Outside**—Positions the frame to the right on odd-numbered pages and to the left on even-numbered pages.

Relative To [Horizontal] (option buttons) Do you want to position the frame horizontally in relation to the column, margins, or edges of the page?

- **Margin**—The frame is positioned horizontally relative to the page margins.
- **Page**—The frame is positioned horizontally relative to the edges of the page.
- **Column**—The frame is positioned horizontally relative to the column. This is the default. If the page has only one column, this choice has the same effect as Format Margins.

NOTE: *If you position a frame within the left or right margin, test print a page or use the File Print Preview command to ensure that your text, borders, or text and borders print completely. The horizontal frame position might be pushed toward the edge of the page by the value you specify in the Horizontal field. If it moves too close to the edge, part of the paragraph might be cut off.*

Vertical (drop-down list box) How do you want the frame positioned vertically (top to bottom) on the page? The choice you make here is a key to success with absolute positioning. You can also type a distance, which is measured relative to the top of the page or the top margin, depending on the setting of the associated Relative To field:

- **Inline**—Word's proposed response. Choosing this causes the paragraph to be normal—in other words, printed immediately after the paragraph that precedes it in text.
- **Top**—Positions the paragraph frame at the top margin or top of page.

- **Centered**—Positions the frame vertically at the center of the page, relative to the top and bottom margins or top and bottom of the page.
- **Bottom**—Positions the paragraph frame at the bottom margin or bottom of the page.

Relative To [Vertical] (option buttons) Do you want to position the frame vertically in relation to the page margins or in relation to the edges of the page?

- **Margin**—The frame is positioned vertically in relation to the page margins.
- **Page**—The frame is positioned vertically in relation to the top and bottom edges of the page.

Distance From Text (text box) How far do you want the edge of the frame (not the edge of the text within the frame) to be from the surrounding text, on the top, bottom, left, and right? Word proposes 0.167 inch, which is equal to one normal line. Adjust this amount as needed. You might, for example, want more space if the absolutely positioned paragraph has a thick line or double lines for a border.

The Distance From Text field has an effect only in certain circumstances, based on choices you make in other fields of the Format Position command. See the "Distance From Text" discussion in Chapter 30.

Paragraph Width (drop-down list box) How wide do you want the paragraph frame to be? You can type a value for the width, or you can press the down arrow key to see your choices:

- **Single Column**—The width of the column, which in the case of a one-column layout is the width of the page.
- **Width of Graphic**—Matches the paragraph frame's width to that of the graphic it contains.
- **Double Column**—Twice the width of a column. Available only when the current section contains more than one column.
- **Between Margins**—The width of the printed page between the left and right margins. Available only when the current section contains more than one column.

For each of these choices in the drop-down list, the actual measurement is listed in parentheses. For example, Between Margins might read *Between Margins (6")*.

Reset (command button) This button clears any changes you have made to the position formatting of the selected paragraph or style. Pressing it returns all values in the Position dialog box to their default settings: The frame is positioned to the left horizontally relative to the column, is positioned inline vertically relative to the page margins, and is the width of the column plus .167 inches (⅙ inch) from surrounding text.

CHAPTER FIFTEEN: Format Commands

FORMAT HEADER/FOOTER COMMAND

A header or a footer (called a *running head* in earlier versions of Word) is one or more lines of text printed in the margin at the top or bottom of one or more pages. A title, for example, often is printed at the top of each page of a chapter or report, and a page number or other element might appear at the top or bottom of each page. Sometimes different headers or footers appear on odd-numbered and even-numbered pages, and often headers or footers are omitted on the first page of a document or the first page of a section.

You can accommodate all these situations and more with the Format Header/Footer command, which turns any paragraph in which it is executed into a header or footer and lets you choose generally where it will be printed. Simply select the paragraph, choose the command, fill in the fields of its dialog box as desired, and execute the command.

The command is unusual in that it controls aspects of both paragraph and section formatting. The relation to paragraph formatting is fairly obvious: The paragraph in which the command is executed is converted into a header or footer or converted from a header or footer back into a normal paragraph. The section formatting is less apparent because it is hidden behind the dialog box's Options button. Choosing the button takes you to another dialog box, where you choose the position on the page for all headers or footers appearing in the section.

Choose the command by pressing Alt+TH. The Format Header/Footer dialog box appears.

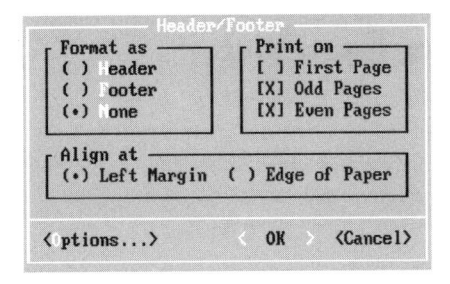

```
┌─ Header/Footer ─────────────────────┐
│ ┌─ Format as ──┐  ┌─ Print on ──────┐│
│ │ ( ) Header   │  │ [ ] First Page  ││
│ │ ( ) Footer   │  │ [X] Odd Pages   ││
│ │ (•) None     │  │ [X] Even Pages  ││
│ └──────────────┘  └─────────────────┘│
│ ┌─ Align at ──────────────────────┐  │
│ │ (•) Left Margin  ( ) Edge of Paper │
│ └─────────────────────────────────┘  │
│                                      │
│ <Options...>     < OK >   <Cancel>   │
└──────────────────────────────────────┘
```

Fields of the Format Header/Footer Dialog Box

In addition to the OK and Cancel command buttons, the Format Header/Footer dialog box contains six fields:

Format as (option buttons)
- **Header**—Turns the paragraph into a header.
- **Footer**—Turns the paragraph into a footer.
- **None**—If the paragraph is a header or footer, this choice transforms it into normal text. This is the default and, when chosen, causes all other fields except the command buttons to be irrelevant and unavailable.

First Page (check box) Do you want this header (or footer) to be printed on the first page of the section? Often you do not, because headers usually don't appear on title or cover pages. If you check this box, make the header the first paragraph in the section.

Odd Pages (check box) Do you want the header or footer printed on odd-numbered (right) pages? Generally you do unless you are using a different header on odd-numbered from the header you use on even-numbered pages.

Even Pages (check box) Do you want the header or footer printed on even-numbered (left) pages? Most often you do, unless you are using different headers on even-numbered and on odd-numbered pages.

Align At (option buttons) Do you want the header or footer aligned horizontally in reference to the left margin, as Word proposes, or with the edge of the paper (extending into the left margin)?

- **Left Margin.**
- **Edge of Paper**—This setting is useful when you want a header to be exempt from the left and right margins you set with the Format Margins command. This setting means your header or footer can print to the left or right of ordinary text, unconstrained by page margins.

Prior to Word version 5.0, all headers and footers were oriented to the edge of the paper, and you deliberately gave them a left indent if you wanted them to align with the page margin that governed the rest of the document. You can still use the Paragraph command's Left field to indent a header, but it is easier to set the Align At field to Left Margin and leave the paragraph's left indent set to 0.

NOTE: *If you are an experienced user of versions of Word prior to 5.0, bear in mind that you do not need to specify a left indent with the Format Paragraph command in order to align headers and footers. If you do specify a left indent when the Align At field is set to Left Margin, your header or footer will be indented the distance of the left margin plus the left indent.*

Options (command button) Choosing this button causes the Header/Footer Options dialog box to appear. This is where you specify the position of the header or footer relative to the top and bottom of the page.

The Format Header/Footer Options Dialog Box

The vertical placement of headers or footers on a page is controlled by two text boxes in the Format Header/Footer Options dialog box: Header Position from Top and Footer Position from Bottom.

Inserting measurements into these fields does not obligate you to have headers or footers. Like the default section settings, they simply indicate how far from the top or bottom of the page Word will print headers or footers if you use them. Headers are printed in the margins of a document and are repeated page after page.

Header Position from Top How far from the top of the page do you want headers to be printed? This field applies only when you have a header formatted to appear in the top margin of a page. Word proposes 0.5 inch, but printers into which you hand-feed paper might not be able to print a header that close to the top of the page.

Footer Position from Bottom How far from the bottom of the page do you want footers to be printed when Footer is specified with the Format Header/Footer command? Word proposes 0.5 inch, but some laser printers might not be able to print that close to the bottom of a page.

Understanding Headers and Footers

Headers and footers print from the page at which the Format Header/Footer command is put into effect until the end of the section in which they appear or until Word encounters another header or footer with the same combination of position, odd pages, even pages, and first page. To keep a header or footer from printing beyond a particular page, either create a new section or replace the header paragraph with another one—even if the new one is a paragraph that has no printable characters in it (some spaces and a paragraph mark, for instance).

If you want a header or footer to print on the same page on which it exists in the text, it must be the first paragraph on the page. Word adjusts top and bottom margins to accommodate headers that are deeper than the page margin, and it wraps the lines of a header to fit the page.

Format Header/Footer and other commands

You use the Format Header/Footer command in conjunction with the Format Margins, Format Paragraph, and sometimes the Format Character, Format Tabs, and Format Position commands. Jointly, they provide remarkable flexibility, but their interactions can be relatively complex. Understanding how the commands relate to each other is a key to success:

- The Format Header/Footer command turns a selected paragraph into a header or footer and specifies where and on what pages it is printed. It does not control the appearance of the header or the exact vertical position of it on the page.
- The Options button of the Format Header/Footer command takes you to a dialog box in which you can specify the exact vertical positions reserved for headers at the tops of pages and footers at the bottoms of pages. But specifying these positions has no effect unless a paragraph is formatted to be a header or footer. (Remember, you convert paragraphs into running heads with the Format Header/Footer command.)
- The Format Paragraph command controls the layout of the line or lines that make up the header or footer. The Align At field of the Format Header/Footer command also provides control over horizontal placement.

- The Format Character command can be used to boldface, underline, or otherwise format the characters within the header or footer.
- The Format Position command can be used to give a header or footer a fixed, or absolute, position on the page—useful in designing complex or nonstandard layouts. This lets you put a header literally anywhere on the page, and if used with the Insert Picture command, it lets you put a picture or image in the same place on multiple pages.
- The Format Tabs command is often used to create tab stops in headers because headers frequently contain words or phrases separated by tab characters. For example, the header for a report might have a title printed flush left and a page number printed flush right, courtesy of a tab character and a right-aligned tab stop. (In any version of Word, tab stops are another way to produce formatting. For example, if you want the page numbers always on the outside and the titles always on the inside of double-sided pages, use different headers for odd-numbered and for even-numbered pages.)

Header and footer symbols

On screen, headers and footers are identified in a document by a caret (^) and a symbol that appears to the immediate left of the first line of the paragraph. The symbols consist of one or two lowercase letters. They indicate where in the document the adjacent header or footer will print.

Symbol	Header/Footer location
h	Header, top of both even-numbered and odd-numbered pages
f	Footer, bottoms of all pages
ho	Header, odd pages only
he	Header, even pages only
hf	Header, first page only
fo	Footer, odd pages only
fe	Footer, even pages only
ff	Footer, first page only

Page numbers

Word's automatic page numbering can be activated in headers or footers, either with the glossary entry *page* or with the Insert Page Numbers command. Both techniques are described as part of Chapter 14's discussion of the Insert Page Numbers command.

FORMAT APPLY STYLE COMMAND

Each of the twelve commands on the Format menu can be used in a way that relates to Word's most powerful formatting tool, the style sheet. The first eight commands, discussed in the earlier pages of this chapter, all are used to apply formatting either to text or to a style. After the style is formatted as desired, it is used to format text.

The remaining four commands on the Format menu are devoted exclusively to helping you use style sheets. Unlike the earlier commands, which provide you with tools to define specifics of a style's formatting, these last commands let you manage style sheets.

Each of the commands, beginning with Format Apply Style and ending with Format Attach Style Sheet, was introduced in the first half of Chapter 6. You might want to review that chapter for an overview and refer to this chapter for specifics.

The first of the four, Format Apply Style, lets you apply the formatting of a style to whatever text is selected (highlighted). It does not create or modify style sheets.

A variety of alternative ways to apply a style to text exist after you have selected the text. You can

- Press Ctrl+Y followed by the key code of the desired style.
- Hold down Shift+Ctrl and press the key code of the style. This method is flawed because it creates a conflict between a macro and a style that happen to share the same Shift+Ctrl code. A macro always wins such disputes.
- Press Ctrl+S to apply a paragraph style directly from the ribbon.

When you use the Format Apply Style command's dialog box to accomplish this task, you do so either by choosing the command (press Alt+TY) or by pressing Ctrl+S twice to activate the ribbon's Style text box.

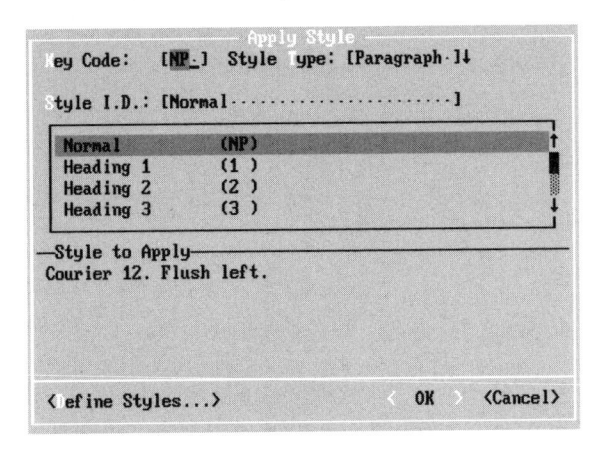

Fields of the Format Apply Style Dialog Box

In addition to the OK and Close command buttons, the Format Apply Style dialog box has five fields that let you describe a style to Word.

Key Code (text box) Type the one-character or two-character key code of the style that you want to use to format the selected text. It is possible the style does not have a key code, in which case you must identify it to Word exclusively through a combination of its style type and style I.D..

Style Type (drop-down list box) Which of the three types of formatting does the desired style control?

- Choose Paragraph if it is a paragraph style.
- Choose Character if it is a character style.
- Choose Section if it is a section style.

When you choose the command, the command field shows the name of the paragraph style of the selection, provided that the entire selection has the same style. The Style Type drop-down list is blank if the document selection contains more than one paragraph style or if it contains any direct paragraph formatting, accomplished with the Format Paragraph command or a built-in format.

Style I.D. (text box) If you have not identified the style from its key code, you can type the style's I.D. code here. The style I.D. is the name Word uses to identify a style (such as Normal or Section 2). To choose from a list of the available styles, press the Down direction key to move from the text box to the list box.

Style I.D. (list box) The names (I.D.s) of all styles in the active style sheet are listed in this box. To apply one, you highlight its name with your cursor or mouse. The characteristics of the style are shown in the Style to Apply section of the dialog box.

Define Styles (command button) Choosing this button opens a style-sheet window containing the active style sheet. Pressing the button has the same effect as choosing the Format Define Styles command (Alt+TD).

FORMAT RECORD STYLE COMMAND

When working on a document, you might want to record an existing example of formatting as a style so that it can be reused easily later. The Format Record Style command lets you save formats from your documents as styles without requiring you to enter the style-sheet window. This is Word's "style by example" feature, an efficient means of creating or modifying a style sheet. You can record styles either from an existing, formatted document or from a document you are formatting as you write and edit.

To use the Format Record Style command to save existing character, paragraph, or section formatting, first select the text that has the formatting you want to copy. Be

CHAPTER FIFTEEN: Format Commands

cautious here. If the text you highlight contains mixed formatting—character, paragraph, or section—Word records some, but not all, of the formatting it encounters. The formatting of a sentence containing normal and italic words, for example, might be translated into either a normal or an italic character style, based on the formatting of the first character in the selection. In the case of paragraphs or sections with mixed formatting, Word records the formatting of the first paragraph or the first section and ignores the rest.

When the text is selected and formatted as you want, choose the Format Record Style command (Alt+TR) and fill in the fields.

```
┌─────────────────── Record Style ───────────────────┐
│ Key Code:   [...] Style Type: [Paragraph ]↓        │
│ Remark:     [........................]             │
│ Style I.D.: [........................]↓            │
│                                                     │
│ ─Style to Record─────────────────────────           │
│ Courier 12. Flush left.                            │
│                                                     │
│                                                     │
│                                                     │
│ <Define Styles...>         <  OK  >   <Cancel>     │
└─────────────────────────────────────────────────────┘
```

Fields of the Format Record Style Dialog Box

In addition to the OK and Close command buttons, the Format Record Style dialog box has five fields, at least three of which you must fill out before you begin recording the keystrokes of your macro.

Key Code (text box) Type a one-character or two-character key code of your choice. A two-character key code is preferable because it gives you more flexibility and is more likely to suggest the type of style it represents. Avoid beginning a key code with the letter A.

Style Type (drop-down list box) As noted for the previous command, Format Apply Style, Word 5.5 uses three broad types of styles, corresponding to the three types of formatting.

- Choose Paragraph if you want to record a paragraph style containing both line-formatting and character-formatting information.
- Choose Character if you want to record a style that affects only text.
- Choose Section if you want to record the document's page size, margins, and other layout characteristics.

Remark (text box). A remark is optional, but it's a good way to describe a style for future reference. It can be up to 28 characters long, including spaces. Some people use all-capital letters for remarks to make them stand out when either printed or displayed in the style-sheet window.

Style I.D. (text box) An I.D. is the name that distinguishes one style from another within a type, as your first name distinguishes you from other family members with the same last name. Type the name or number you want to assign, or choose one from the list box.

Style I.D. (list box) If you select an I.D. from the list box, avoid choosing any potential I.D.s that are followed by parentheses enclosing a key code. Such codes already are in use within the style sheet.

Define Styles (command button) Choosing this button opens a style-sheet window containing the active style sheet. Pressing the button has the same effect as choosing the Format Define Styles command (Alt+TD).

After you fill in the fields of the Format Record Styles command, press Enter to create the style. If you enter the style-sheet window (by choosing Format Define Styles), you'll see the style displayed there. To save the styles you have recorded, use the File Save or File Save As command. If you save the style sheet as NORMAL.STY, Word will use it whenever you work from the drive or directory in which the style sheet has been saved.

FORMAT DEFINE STYLE COMMAND

This command is a doorway through which you pass when moving from a document window to a style-sheet window. By making the move to the new window, you can see and modify the styles of the style sheet attached to the active window.

Unlike the other commands on the Format menu, Format Define Style does not have a dialog box. It executes promptly. The command takes you to a new window containing a style sheet, exactly as if you had used the File Open command to place the new style sheet on the screen.

When in the style-sheet window, you use commands from the main Word menu to modify the formatting of the styles or other characteristics of the file.

For additional information on the style-sheet window, see Chapter 24.

FORMAT ATTACH STYLE SHEET COMMAND

Use the Format Attach Style Sheet command to look at the name of the style sheet (if any) attached to the current document, or use it to assign or switch a document's style sheet. Because more than one style sheet can be applied to a document (although not at the same time), you can dramatically change the appearance of a document simply by swapping one style sheet for another.

Step by step, this is how you attach a different style sheet to a document:

1. Choose the Format Attach Style Sheet command.
2. When the name of the presently attached style sheet, if any, is displayed in the Style Sheet Name field, type in the name of a different style sheet if you know its name and (if appropriate) which drive or directory it's

CHAPTER FIFTEEN: Format Commands

in. (You can omit the .STY extension.) If you're not certain of the style sheet's name or location, use the Files and Directories list boxes to locate it. If the name appears, highlight it.

3. Execute the command. The new style sheet will replace the former one, and the appearance of the document will immediately reflect the new style-sheet formats.

When you press Alt+TA to choose the command, you see this dialog box:

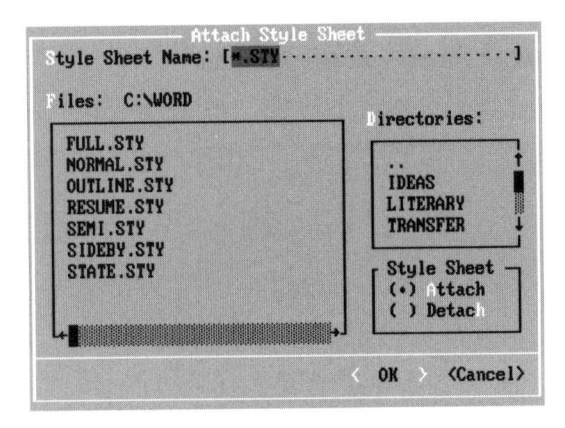

```
┌─────────────────── Attach Style Sheet ───────────────────┐
│ Style Sheet Name: [*.STY........................]        │
│                                                          │
│ Files:  C:\WORD                                          │
│                                 Directories:             │
│  ┌─────────────────┐           ┌─────────────┐           │
│  │ FULL.STY        │           │ ..          │           │
│  │ NORMAL.STY      │           │             │           │
│  │ OUTLINE.STY     │           │ IDEAS       │           │
│  │ RESUME.STY      │           │ LITERARY    │           │
│  │ SEMI.STY        │           │ TRANSFER    │           │
│  │ SIDEBY.STY      │           └─────────────┘           │
│  │ STATE.STY       │           ┌ Style Sheet ┐           │
│  │                 │           │ (•) Attach  │           │
│  │                 │           │ ( ) Detach  │           │
│  └─────────────────┘           └─────────────┘           │
│                                                          │
│                        <  OK  >    <Cancel>              │
└──────────────────────────────────────────────────────────┘
```

Fields of the Format Attach Style Sheet Dialog Box

In addition to the OK and Close command buttons, the Format Attach Style Sheet dialog box contains four fields:

Style Sheet Name (text box) The name of the style sheet you are attaching.

Files (list box) Highlight the name of an existing style sheet, if you want.

Directories (list box) Choose a new directory (and drive, if necessary), to find the file you want to load.

Style Sheet (option buttons) You can either attach a new style sheet or remove an existing one:

- **Attach**—This is the default setting.
- **Detach**—Choose Detach if you want to break the formatting link between an existing a style sheet and the document. Word will ask whether you want to convert the formatting from the style sheet to direct formatting within the document. Choose Yes if you want the document to maintain the formatting of the style sheet even after the style sheet is detached, or No if you want to be rid of the formatting altogether.

Pressing the Del key when the Style Sheet Name text box is highlighted has the same effect as choosing the Detach option button; it breaks the link between the document and the style sheet.

CHAPTER SIXTEEN

Utilities Commands

You can check spelling, hyphenate the words in a document, find a synonym, sort and renumber lists, and customize a variety of Word features and characteristics—all with the commands from the Utilities menu. You can also keep track of tentative editing changes, count words, draw lines, perform arithmetic, and update page numbering. Each of the 11 commands enhances Word's power and flexibility.

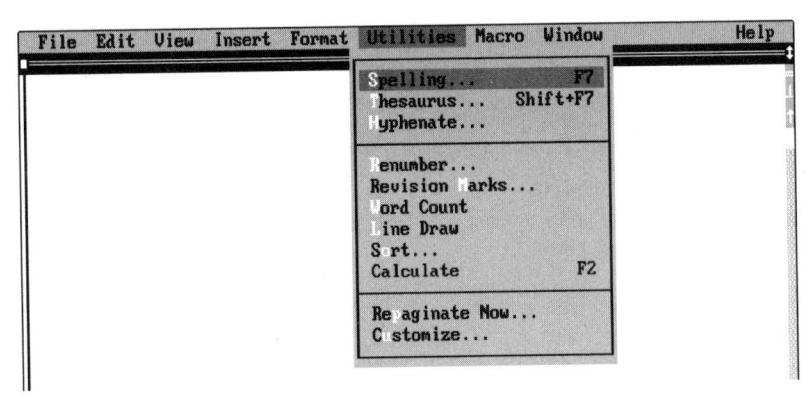

```
File  Edit  View  Insert  Format  Utilities  Macro  Window              Help

                                  Spelling...        F7
                                  Thesaurus...   Shift+F7
                                  Hyphenate...

                                  Renumber...
                                  Revision Marks...
                                  Word Count
                                  Line Draw
                                  Sort...
                                  Calculate          F2

                                  Repaginate Now...
                                  Customize...
```

In summary form, here is what each of the Utilities commands covered in this chapter permits you to do:

Utilities Spelling—Checks the spelling of your entire document or of just the word or words that are highlighted. Checking is normally in American English, although a variety of other languages are available.

Utilities Thesaurus—Offers synonyms for a highlighted word.

Utilities Hyphenate—Hyphenates a multisyllabic word so that part of it prints at the end of a line and the rest of it prints at the beginning of the following line.

Utilities Renumber—Numbers, renumbers, or removes numbers from paragraphs.

Utilities Revision Marks—Controls *redlining,* the feature that lets you mark new editing in a document with strikethroughs and underlines. Later you can accept or reject these tentative changes.

Utilities Word Count—Counts the words in a document.

Utilities Line Draw—Turns Word's line-drawing feature on and off (used in conjunction with the Customize command and Format Character).

Utilities Sort—Places paragraphs or lines in alphabetic or numeric order.

Utilities Calculate—Performs simple arithmetic, using the numbers from the selected text.

Utilities Repaginate Now—Updates the page breaks in a document. (Using this command is unnecessary if you use the Utilities Customize command to turn on the Background Pagination check box.)

Utilities Customize—Lets you tailor Word to suit your special needs.

The Utilities Customize command is similar to View Preferences. Each offers a dialog box filled with choices about Word's behavior, and each includes a command button that takes you to the other command's dialog box. The difference is that View Preferences is devoted to controlling the way Word displays information on the screen, whereas Utilities Customize refines Word's performance with a variety of other commands and features.

UTILITIES SPELLING COMMAND

Checking spelling can be a simple or a somewhat complicated affair, depending on how demanding you are. For most people most of the time, the following steps are all that are required:

Step 1. If you want to check the spelling of a single word or of a portion of your document, select (highlight) the text you want to check. If you want to check the entire document, do not select any text.

Step 2. Choose the Utilities Spelling command (Alt+US or F7). Word responds by displaying the Utilities Spelling dialog box in the bottom of the screen and your document in the upper part of the screen.

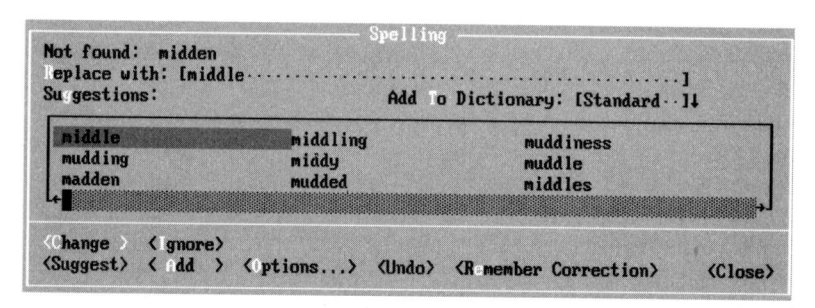

```
┌─────────────────────────── Spelling ───────────────────────────┐
│ Not found:  midden                                             │
│ Replace with: [middle······································]   │
│ Suggestions:              Add To Dictionary: [Standard··]↓    │
│  ┌──────────────────────────────────────────────────────────┐ │
│  │ middle           middling          muddiness             │ │
│  │ mudding          middy             muddle                │ │
│  │ madden           mudded            middles               │ │
│  └──────────────────────────────────────────────────────────┘ │
│                                                                │
│ <Change>   <Ignore>                                            │
│ <Suggest>  <Add>   <Options...>  <Undo>  <Remember Correction>  <Close> │
└────────────────────────────────────────────────────────────────┘
```

Immediately, Word begins searching for words it doesn't recognize—those not contained in the dictionary it consults.

Step 3. When an unrecognized word is highlighted in the document (upper) part of the screen, you can respond in any of several ways:

- Press Alt+I if you want to ignore the word and leave the document unchanged.
- Press Alt+C to make the change (if any) proposed by Word in the dialog box.
- Press Alt+R to replace the unrecognized word with a new word. Type the name of the new word, and then press either Enter or Alt+C. If Word doesn't recognize what you have typed, it displays this message: *The new spelling is not in the dictionary. Do you want to accept it?* If you're sure the spelling is correct, choose Yes (Enter).
- Press Alt+G to choose from among the list of suggestions that Word might display. Use the direction keys to highlight your choice, and then press Enter to carry out the substitution. Alternatively, point to your choice on the list with the mouse and double-click.

Although these three steps should be sufficient to deal with most of your needs, a wide variety of options is available. Let's take a look at the various kinds of dictionaries Word can consult. Then we'll examine the opportunities offered in the fields of the Utilities Spelling dialog box.

Word's Standard Dictionary

Like spell-checker programs in general, the Utilities Spelling command compares the words in your document with entries in an electronic dictionary and offers you a chance to review those words in the document that are not in the dictionary. Such unrecognized terms might be misspellings, or they might be legitimate words that aren't in the dictionary. They might be proper names, plurals, foreign terms, technical or discipline-specific jargon, or slang. Word also spots words that appear twice in a row and words that are capitalized in unorthodox ways.

Word's comprehensive list of correctly spelled words is called the *standard dictionary*. It is stored in a form you cannot read in a file named SPELL-XX.LEX. The XX stands for a two-letter code that indicates the language, country, or discipline for which the dictionary was created. In the United States, for example, the dictionary is SPELL-AM.LEX. The other choices are

SPELL-LG.LEX	American English plus legal terms
SPELL-MD.LEX	American English plus medical terms
SPELL-BR.LEX	British English
SPELL-FR.LEX	French

SPELL-GE.LEX	German
SPELL-SP.LEX	Spanish
SPELL-IT.LEX	Italian
SPELL-SW.LEX	Swedish
SPELL-NL.LEX	Dutch (The Netherlands)

The legal and medical dictionaries each contain all of the words from the American English dictionary plus more than 20,000 terms peculiar to the legal or medical profession. The remaining dictionaries are used by Microsoft in its foreign-language versions of Word.

Whichever standard dictionary you use, Word normally stores it in the Word program directory. The location of the standard dictionary is reflected in the Speller Name drop-down list box of the Utilities Customize command. (The list box lets you switch among the various standard dictionaries if you have more than one.)

The standard dictionaries typically have more than 125,000 words. Nonetheless, they usually do not contain every possible spelling of every word in a given language. Such a dictionary would be too unwieldy for Word to use quickly and could mask errors by including obscure words that match your misspellings. For example, if you meant to type *buttering*, *father*, and *sleepiness*, but you actually typed *butterine*, *fother*, and *steepiness*, such a dictionary wouldn't catch the typos because it would recognize the spellings as legitimate words. So to balance thoroughness and practicality, the spell checker's American English standard dictionary contains most of the words used in everyday writing.

You can add words to the standard dictionary by choosing the spell checker's Add command and specifying Standard in the Add to Dictionary drop-down list box. When you add to the standard dictionary, the word goes into a supplementary file that the spell checker treats, to a certain extent, as part of the standard dictionary. This supplementary file is given the name UPDAT-*XX*.CMP. (Again, the *XX* represents the language, country code, or discipline.)

Word treats terms in the standard dictionary differently from those in the supplementary (UPDAT-*XX*.CMP) file. Whereas the standard dictionary is compressed and indexed for extremely fast searches, the supplementary dictionary is not. Accordingly, every word added to the UPDAT-*XX*.CMP file slows down the overall spell-checking operation slightly. Consequently, you probably don't want to let this supplementary list grow beyond a few hundred words at most. In addition, when a term is not recognized by the spell checker, Word can propose alternative spellings from the standard dictionary, but it cannot propose spellings from the supplementary dictionary.

User and Document Dictionaries

In addition to the standard dictionary and its supplement, Word lets you create and modify two special dictionaries: *user* dictionaries and *document* dictionaries.

- A user dictionary is one in which you place words that are not in the standard dictionary but that you use frequently or use for particular types of documents. If you work with engineering terminology, for example, you might create a user dictionary that contains mathematical and construction words that are normal to your work but are too specialized for the standard dictionary.

  Word reserves the name SPECIALS.CMP for one user dictionary, but you can create others as well. For example, you might create one for accounting documents and another for the company newsletter.

- A document dictionary is an even more specialized list of words. You use it to check the spelling of words in a particular document. For example, if you are writing a letter to someone with an unusual name, you might want the name to be listed in the document's own dictionary. That way, the name won't keep popping up every time you run the spell checker. (Of course, you could add the name to a standard or user dictionary, but this wouldn't make sense unless you write the name periodically in a variety of documents.)

You can add any unrecognized word in a document to the document's dictionary by choosing the Add command from the Utilities Spelling dialog box and choosing Document from the Add to Dictionary drop-down list box. When you press the Enter key, Word adds the word to the document dictionary. If a document dictionary doesn't exist for the document, Word creates one.

To begin spell checking, press F7 or Alt+US.

Fields of the Utilities Spelling Dialog Box

In addition to the Close command button, which makes the dialog box disappear, the Utilities Spelling dialog box contains 10 fields:

Replace With (text box) Type the correct spelling or capitalization here if the unrecognized word is, in fact, incorrect. If Word has proposed a correct version of the word, it appears in this text box by default and you need type nothing. If you type another word that Word doesn't recognize, the program displays the message: *The new spelling is not in the dictionary. Do you want to accept it?* To accept it, choose Yes (Enter).

Suggestions (list box) When Word finds a misspelled word and presents a list of possible alternatives, it places the first word in the list into the Replace With text box. To substitute a different word from the list of proposals, move to the Suggestions list box and choose the word you want.

Add To Dictionary (drop-down list box) Choose which dictionary you want Word to add the unrecognized word to when you use the Add button. (These dictionaries were described in greater detail earlier in the chapter.)

- **Standard**—A supplement to the standard dictionary. Use it for words that are likely to appear with some frequency in your work or in the work of others who use your copy of Word. The spell checker always refers to words in this dictionary.
- **User**—A dictionary intended for use with a certain class of documents, such as all documents on one topic or all documents edited by a particular person (user). The spell checker refers to words in this dictionary only when the dictionary has been associated with a particular document. The default user dictionary is SPECIALS.CMP, which is associated with all documents until the name of a different user dictionary is substituted. Use the Options button to reach the Spelling Options dialog box, where you indicate which user dictionary should be associated with the active document.
- **Document**—A dictionary used for only a single document. A document dictionary has the same name as the document but with the extension .CMP instead of .DOC.

Change (command button) Press this button to accept the proposed change to the unrecognized word.

Suggest (command button) Choose this button when you want Word to propose alternative spellings for the unrecognized word. The alternatives will appear in the Suggestions list box. The Suggest button is irrelevant, and hence grayed, if the Always Suggest check box of the Spelling Options dialog box is turned on.

Ignore (command button) Choose Ignore if the spell checker highlights a word and you want it to skip the word and continue checking the rest of the document. The spell checker will ignore that particular spelling throughout the document. If the word is one that you use regularly in your documents, you might consider adding it to a dictionary or even telling Word to remember the correction.

Add (command button) If the word is correct and you want Word to remember that it is correct, press this button to add it to one of Word's dictionaries. The dictionary that it is added to is controlled by the Add To Dictionary drop-down list box. Word carries out the Add instruction immediately.

NOTE: *If you try to add a word to a document dictionary when the active document is new and has not yet been named, Word causes your computer to beep and then displays the following message:* Word cannot add to the dictionary of a document that has never been saved. *If this happens, close the Utilities Spelling dialog box, use File Save As to give the document a name and save it, and try again.*

Options (command button) Choosing this button takes you to the Spelling Options dialog box, which is discussed in detail in the next section.

Undo (command button) Choose this to undo the last correction. Word restores the original spelling and highlights it so that you can redo the correction.

NOTE: *You can undo all corrections made during a spell-checking session by exiting the spell checker and using the Undo command. You must, however, use Undo immediately after returning to your document and before you perform any other editing act.*

Remember Correction (command button) Choose the Remember Correction button if you want Word to remember both the misspelled word and the way you corrected it. Word will remember the spelling from one session to the next and will make the appropriate correction in any document whenever you check your spelling. This field can be particularly useful for checking and correcting those spellings that pose a chronic problem for you.

This command has a downside. After you have told Word to remember a correction, it remembers it even if you use the Undo command to change your mind. Imagine, for example, that you use the Remember Correction button to change the word *Hubble* to *humble*. You immediately realize, however, that the discussion was of the Hubble space telescope and that you didn't want to make the substitution. So you use the Undo button, which returns the spelling to *Hubble*. Although everything seems fine, it really isn't because from now on, whether later in the same document or three months from now in a different document, the word *Hubble* will be transformed into *humble* whenever the spell checker encounters it. And Word won't ask you to verify this change; it will simply do it.

To make Word forget the substitution, you must edit or delete a file named REMEM-AM.COR. (If you are using a non-American English version of Word, the *-AM* portion of the name will differ.) This file contains all of the corrections you have asked Word to remember. In the case of our example, you could edit the file by removing the line that says *Hubble -> humble* and its trailing paragraph mark. If you do this in Word, use File Save As to save the file, being sure it is in Text Only format.

The REMEM-AM.COR file is stored in the same directory as the standard dictionary, usually the Word program directory. If you are using Word on a network, your workstation will have its own REMEM-AM.COR file, stored in the local Word directory, which is the directory specified in the MSWNET55 environment variable. (See Chapter 8 for more on the environment variable.)

The Spelling Options dialog box

To enter the Spelling Options dialog box, choose the Options button in the Utilities Spelling dialog box.

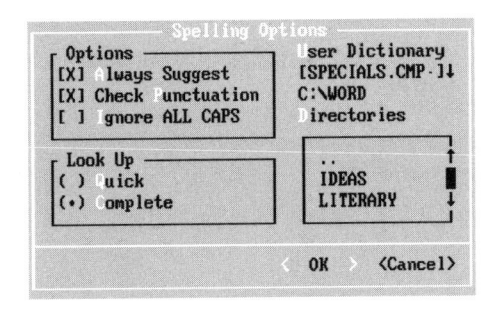

```
┌─ Spelling Options ─────────────────────┐
│ ┌─Options──────────────┐ ┌User Dictionary│
│ │ [X] Always Suggest   │ │[SPECIALS.CMP-]│
│ │ [X] Check Punctuation│ │C:\WORD        │
│ │ [ ] Ignore ALL CAPS  │ │Directories    │
│ └──────────────────────┘ │               │
│ ┌─Look Up──────────────┐ │ ..          ↑ │
│ │ ( ) Quick            │ │ IDEAS       ▓ │
│ │ (•) Complete         │ │ LITERARY    ↓ │
│ └──────────────────────┘ └───────────────┘
│              < OK >   <Cancel>           │
└──────────────────────────────────────────┘
```

The Spelling Options dialog box contains six fields:

Always Suggest (check box) Check this box if you want Word to provide a list of alternatives whenever it finds a word it does not recognize. If you do not check this box, you can still see a list by choosing the Suggest button from the main Utilities Spelling dialog box.

Check Punctuation (check box) Check this box if you want Word to consider the location of punctuation marks in its checking. This setting causes Word to highlight certain patterns of punctuation marks that are frequently incorrect. Word's copyediting abilities in this area are, however, somewhat limited.

Ignore ALL CAPS (check box) Do not check this box if you want Word to examine all words in your document. Check it if you want the spell checker to ignore words composed entirely of capital letters—for example, IBM, UNICEF, and NATO.

User Dictionary (drop-down list box) Specify the name of the user dictionary you want Word to consult, or type the name of a new user dictionary you want to create.

Directories (list box) This list box gives you an easy way to change the directory in which you are storing or looking for a user dictionary. Use the field in conjunction with the previous one, using the techniques described early in Chapter 10.

Look Up (option buttons)

- **Quick**—With this setting, Word assumes that the first two letters of the unknown word are correct and presents alternatives beginning with those letters.
- **Complete**—With this setting, Word does not assume that the first two letters of an unrecognized word are correct. The result is a more thorough search for alternative spellings, which takes longer. This is the default setting for Word's spell checker.

UTILITIES THESAURUS COMMAND

Word includes a modest thesaurus that you use to find synonyms for words in your document. Select a word or place the cursor anywhere on the word or immediately to its right, and choose the Utilities Thesaurus command or hold down the Shift key and press F7.

Word responds by displaying the Utilities Thesaurus dialog box. In most cases it also scrolls your document slightly so that the highlighted word you are looking up is displayed, in the context of your document, above the dialog box.

CHAPTER SIXTEEN: Utilities Commands 327

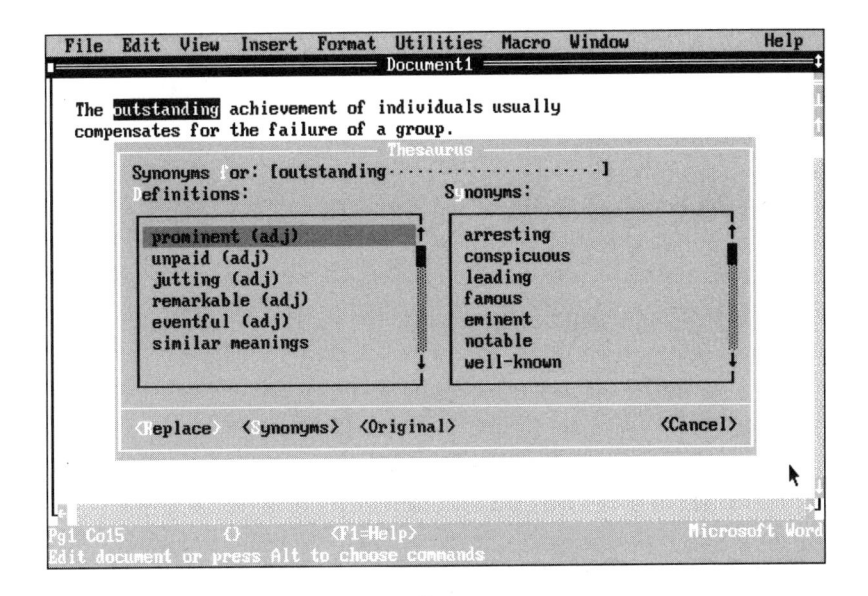

In addition to the Close button, the Utilities Thesaurus dialog box has seven fields, although you see only four or six of them at a time. The preceding illustration shows six fields because Word found synonyms for the highlighted word in the document. When no synonyms are found, as in the following illustration, only four fields appear.

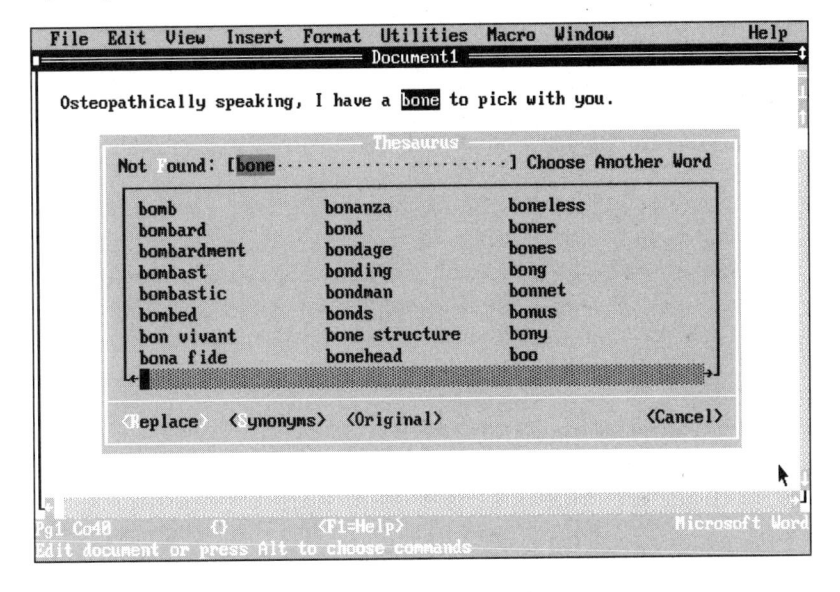

The fields of the Utilities Thesaurus dialog box are as follows:

Synonyms For (text box) This text box contains the word for which you are seeking a synonym (if the word is in the thesaurus).

Definitions (list box) Rather than display all synonyms for a word in one window, Word offers a synonym list for each of a word's meanings. The meanings are grouped by part of speech (noun, verb, and so on). Highlight in the Definitions list box the meaning that best suits your needs; the Synonyms list box will then present a more-refined list of actual synonyms.

Synonyms (list box) Here's where you see the actual synonyms. If you see one that suits you, you can choose Cancel (Esc) to return to work on your document, or you can use either the Replace or the Synonyms command button.

Not Found (text box) This text box contains the word for which you are seeking a synonym if the word is not in the thesaurus. A large list box beneath this field contains words with letters similar to those of the word you seek. Each of these words has a synonym. To replace the word in the text file with a word from the list box, simply highlight your choice and choose the Replace button.

Replace (command button) Press this button to replace the selected word in your document with the highlighted word from any list box.

Synonyms (command button) Press this button to look up synonyms of the word that is highlighted in any list box.

Original (command button) If you have asked for synonyms of synonyms, pressing this button returns you to your original list of alternatives.

UTILITIES HYPHENATE COMMAND

For manuscripts, screenplays, and certain other documents, hyphenation generally isn't very important. On the other hand, for justified text or narrow columns, hyphenation is desirable because it increases the average number of characters per line, thereby reducing unnecessary white space between words and letters. Use the Utilities Hyphenate command to have Word hyphenate any amount of text, from a single word to a whole document.

Word recognizes three types of hyphens. On the printed page, these hyphens are indistinguishable from one another. To Word, however, they serve different purposes:

- A *normal* hyphen is the type you use to hyphenate compound words or words with hyphenated prefixes, such as *blow-dry* and *un-American*. You create these hyphens by pressing the hyphen key, and you always insert them manually, as part of the word.

CHAPTER SIXTEEN: Utilities Commands

- A *nonbreaking* hyphen is like a normal hyphen, but you enter it by pressing Ctrl+Shift+hyphen. This key combination tells Word never to split a compound word at the end of a printed line. For example, suppose you insert a nonbreaking hyphen in the name *Morley-Chan*. If Word does not have enough room to print the entire name at the end of a line, it will move both parts to the beginning of the next line, rather than printing *Morley-* at the end of one line and *Chan* at the beginning of the next.
- An *optional* hyphen is one that Word uses only when it is needed to break a word at the end of a line. This is the type of hyphen that evens out line breaks, especially in justified or in multiple-column text. You can insert optional hyphens manually by pressing Ctrl+hyphen. Or you can have Word insert any that you need by choosing the Utilities Hyphenate command.

Hyphens inserted with the Utilities Hyphenate command are of the *optional* or nonrequired variety, so they are displayed and printed only if a word needs to break at the end of a line. When such a hyphen is not at the end of the line, Word displays it only if the Optional Hyphens field of the View Preferences command is checked. If you are not displaying nonprinting symbols and you press the Left or Right direction key to move your cursor across a word containing an invisible optional hyphen, the cursor seems to pause rather than move when it reaches the hyphen. This is because the cursor is on the invisible character. If you press the Del key at this point, you will delete the optional hyphen.

At your option, the Utilities Hyphenate command either inserts hyphens on its own or shows you where each hyphen would be placed and lets you accept or change the suggestions individually. Word finds the correct places to hyphenate multisyllabic words by using a sophisticated formula and a substantial amount of data from the file named HYPH.DAT, which the Setup program copies to your Program disk or directory (or, if you are using 360-KB disks, to your data disk). Word does not place a hyphen at every possible break between syllables: It ignores words that already contain hyphens, and it ignores words in which the addition of an optional hyphen won't affect the present layout of the document. In the following example, a sentence is repeated twice, the second time hyphenated. Observe that in the unhyphenated version, the word *seating* is at the beginning of the second line, and some space exists at the end of the preceding line. In the hyphenated version, the first syllable of *seating* has been moved up to use the space.

```
The early purchase of season tickets provides the best
seating in the house.

The early purchase of season tickets provides the best seat-
ing in the house.
```

What Does Word Hyphenate?

You can choose to hyphenate a word, sentence, paragraph, or section of a document by selecting the appropriate text before executing the Utilities Hyphenate command. The command follows the same rules as the Edit Replace command:

- If no text is selected, all words from that point forward are candidates for hyphenation, provided they don't already contain hyphens. You also have the option of continuing hyphenating from the beginning of the document.

- If text is selected, hyphenation is confined to words that are partially or totally selected.

Removing Existing Optional Hyphens

Word won't look for a new hyphenation point in any word that already contains a hyphen. Consequently, to achieve the most effective hyphenation, first remove existing optional hyphens with the Edit Replace command: Type ^- (Shift+6, followed by the hyphen key) in the Edit Replace command's Text to Search for field, tab past the Replace with field, and to save time, turn off the Confirm Changes check box. If you leave the Confirm Changes box checked, you should first set View Preferences to display optional hyphens.

Inserting or deleting a large number of hyphens uses up a lot of computer memory, so for best performance on large jobs, use File Save immediately before and after inserting hyphens with the Utilities Hyphenate command or after removing hyphens with Edit Replace.

When it has completed the Utilities Hyphenate command, Word tells you the number of words hyphenated.

If used immediately, Edit Undo removes all hyphens inserted with the Utilities Hyphenate command. Because you can execute Edit Undo repeatedly, you can compare the hyphenated and the unhyphenated versions of the document. For an accurate reflection of how the document will look when printed, check the View Preferences command's Line breaks field before comparing the two versions of a single-column document, or choose View Layout before comparing two versions of a multiple-column document. If your computer has graphics capability, you can also preview the hyphenated version with File Print Preview and still use the Edit Undo command, provided that you perform no other editing acts in between.

Choose the Utilities Hyphenate command by pressing Alt+UH. The Utilities Hyphenate dialog box appears.

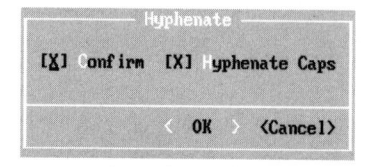

```
────── Hyphenate ──────
[X] Confirm  [X] Hyphenate Caps

       < OK >   <Cancel>
```

Fields of the Utilities Hyphenate Dialog Box

In one sense there are two fields in the Utilities Hyphenate dialog box, and in another sense there are five. Initially you see only two, as in the preceding illustration. However, if you ask Word to confirm each potential hyphenation point, it does so by presenting you with this version of the dialog box:

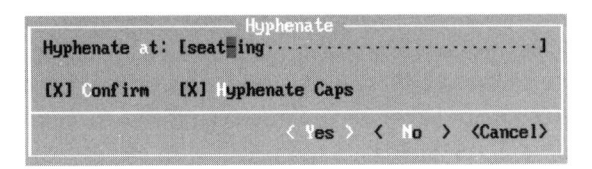

```
┌─────────────────── Hyphenate ───────────────────┐
│ Hyphenate at: [seat=ing·························]│
│ [X] Confirm    [X] Hyphenate Caps                │
│                    < Yes >  < No >  <Cancel>     │
└──────────────────────────────────────────────────┘
```

Confirm (check box) Turning this box off causes Word to execute the command without asking you to confirm each hyphenation point, resulting in fast execution of the command.

HYPHENATING IN OTHER LANGUAGES

In choosing hyphenation points, Word relies on a sophisticated formula. For American English, this formula is stored in a file about 25 KB long, called HYPH.DAT.

You do not want to use this version of HYPH.DAT if you are writing in a different language, however, because each language has its own distinctive rules of hyphenation. Consequently, each Microsoft spell-checker dictionary comes with its own HYPH.DAT file. This lets you check spellings and hyphenate in British English, French, German, Swedish, Dutch, Italian, and Spanish.

Unfortunately, the hyphenation files for each of these languages is called HYPH.DAT. Consequently, you cannot switch from one to another by making a choice in a dialog box as you can when switching among spell-checker dictionaries. This means that if you want to hyphenate in more than one language, you must rename the hyphenation files so that the version you want to use at a given moment—and only that one version—is named HYPH.DAT and stored in the Word program directory.

You can accomplish this in several ways. One is to rename each version of HYPH.DAT so that all the files can exist together in the Word program directory. For example, the French version could be renamed HYPH-FR.DAT and the American version HYPH-AM.DAT. Then, to install the French version, you would type at the DOS prompt (before starting Word) *COPY HYPH-FR.DAT HYPH.DAT* and press Enter. Later, to reinstall the American version, you could type *COPY HYPH-AM.DAT HYPH.DAT*.

On the other hand, if you keep this box checked you maintain greater quality control. Word temporarily turns on the Line breaks check box of the View Preferences command so that the screen shows the lengths and content of lines as they will be printed. This mode gives you the information you need to review potential hyphenation points intelligently. (If you set Line breaks to No before executing the Utilities Hyphenate command, Word turns it on during the hyphenation and then turns it back off.) Word then searches for potential hyphenation points. Each time it finds one, it displays the five-field version of the dialog box and asks you to make a choice in its Hyphenate At text box.

If you begin hyphenating with the Confirm box checked, you can change your mind (have Word hyphenate automatically) by unchecking the box any time Word asks you to make a confirmation.

Hyphenate Caps (check box) When this box is checked, as it is by default, Word considers words that start with a capital letter to be fair game for hyphenation. For example, it will examine a word such as IBM or UNICEF. If you uncheck this box, Word does not consider words that are entirely capitalized.

Hyphenate At (text box) When Word asks you to confirm a hyphenation point in a word, the word appears in this text box with hyphens between its syllables. The proposed hyphenation point is indicated with a rectangle. You can move the hyphenation point to the left one letter at a time by pressing the Left direction key or one syllable at a time by pressing the Up direction key; you can move the hyphenation point to the right one character at a time by pressing the Right direction key or one syllable at a time by pressing the Down direction key. Word will insert an optional hyphen at whichever point you choose. (You make this choice by choosing Yes.)

NOTE: *If you insert an optional hyphen to the right of the proposed hyphenation point, the hyphenation possibly won't affect the layout of the lines because Word can't fit more of the word into a line than the line's length allows.*

Yes (command button) To accept a tentative hyphenation point, as described in the Hyphenate At text box, choose Yes (Enter).

No (command button) To tell Word not to hyphenate a word, choose No.

UTILITIES RENUMBER COMMAND

Use the Utilities Renumber command to renumber lists, paragraphs, headings, or subheadings. The command, which recognizes and updates a variety of numbering (and lettering) schemes, can also remove numbering. The command affects only text that is selected; when no text is selected, the entire document is subject to the command.

With the exception of numbering performed when Word is in outline mode, elements that are not numbered (or lettered) before the Utilities Renumber command is executed will not be numbered or lettered by the command. In other words, Word renumbers or removes numbering but doesn't add numbering on its own to unnumbered elements (except in outline mode).

In some senses, the Utilities Renumber command is related to the Utilities Sort command. For instance, you can use either command to update a series of numbered paragraphs in which the numbers are out of sequence. But Utilities Sort rearranges whole paragraphs so that their numbers are in order, whereas the Utilities Renumber command updates the numbers but leaves the paragraphs in their original order.

Word recognizes several kinds of characters as "numbers" and can update any of the following:

- Arabic numerals (1, 2, 3)
- Roman numerals (I, II, III)
- Lowercase Roman numerals (i, ii, iii)
- Capital letters (A, B, C)
- Lowercase letters (a, b, c)
- Double numeration (1, 1.1, 1.2, 1.3)

Word recognizes and updates a number or letter provided it is followed by a period or a close parenthesis that is in turn followed by a space or tab character and some text. The Utilities Renumber command won't update a number that isn't followed by punctuation and text. Also, the number or letter must begin a paragraph, except that it can be preceded by spaces, tab characters, an open parenthesis, or all of these characters.

As examples, Word recognizes and updates all of these: 4.4), (4), IV., IV), (IV), iv., iv), (iv), A., A), (A), a., a), (a), 2.3, 2.3), and (2.3).

Word renumbers by using the numbering scheme (such as Roman or Arabic) and punctuation that it first encounters. A number that Word puts at the beginning of a paragraph has the same character formatting (font type and size plus attributes such as underlining) as the first printable character in the paragraph.

When you want to renumber several lists within the same document, you can select each set of elements to be renumbered and execute the Utilities Renumber command once for each list. In this way, you can number different lists using different schemes—for instance, Arabic numerals for one list and Roman numerals for another.

But Word can handle several renumbering tasks simultaneously with a single execution of the Utilities Renumber command, as long as the different lists are at discrete levels of indentation in a document. The best example of a document with suitable levels of indentation is an outline whether it is viewed in Word's outline mode or not. Each level of heading in an outline is indented a different amount, and each can have a separate numbering scheme. Subheads that are indented one level could be in Arabic numerals, and main headings could be in Roman numerals, with each numbered independently. This works only when the indentation has been created with paragraph formatting, such as the indent fields of the Format Paragraph command, the built-in format Ctrl+N, or paragraph styles from a style sheet. (When apparent indentation has been achieved by pressing the Spacebar or the Tab key, the indented effect reflects the *content* of the document rather than its formatting. Word ignores such indentations for purposes of renumbering because the Utilities Renumber command disregards spaces or tab characters that precede a number.)

Two notes on renumbering outlines:

- For each level of heading that is indented farther to the right than the level that preceded it, Word restarts its renumbering (from I or 1 or A or a) so that subheadings are numbered in relation to the heading they follow. In other words, the Utilities Renumber command is smart enough not simply to continue counting at each level of indentation; in any level of heading, it starts counting all over again when the structure of the outline suggests that this is appropriate.

- When Word is in outline mode, the Utilities Renumber command will *number* as well as *renumber* an outline's levels of heading. In document mode, Word won't do this (even for a document that has levels of indentation and appears to be an outline) because the program can't assume that you want every paragraph numbered. But in outline mode, Word knows it is dealing with an outline, and it assigns an appropriate number to each paragraph. By default, Word assigns a standard system of outline numbering, following this pattern: I., A., 1., a), (1), (a), i). You can alter this pattern of numbering, or you can have Word assign a double numeration system (1.1, 1.2, 1.3, and so on) to an outline. For details, see Chapter 26.

Also note that the double numeration system works differently in Word's normal document mode from the way it does in outline mode. Normally, the Utilities Renumber command uses double numeration by updating the digits to the right of the final decimal point. For instance, if a list begins with 1.1, the successive numbers assigned by Word will be 1.2, 1.3, 1.4, and so on. However, in outline mode the double numeration system is considerably more powerful: Word updates each digit and assigns new digits as it encounters changes in levels of indentation.

If you don't like the consequences of the Utilities Renumber command, use Edit Undo immediately.

Choose the command by pressing Alt+UR. The Utilities Renumber dialog box appears.

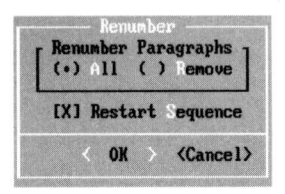

```
┌─────── Renumber ───────┐
│ ┌ Renumber Paragraphs ┐ │
│ │ (•) All  ( ) Remove │ │
│ └                     ┘ │
│    [X] Restart Sequence │
│      < OK >  <Cancel>   │
└─────────────────────────┘
```

CHAPTER SIXTEEN: Utilities Commands

Fields of the Utilities Renumber Dialog Box

Although the Utilities Renumber command has great flexibility, it takes many of its cues as to how to renumber by mimicking what it already finds in a document. Consequently, the dialog box has only two fields in which you give it explicit instructions:

Renumber Paragraphs (option buttons)

- **All**—Use this setting unless you want to remove all the numbers, letters, or both numbers and letters that start paragraphs in a document or a section of a document.
- **Remove**—This setting eliminates the numbers at the beginnings of paragraphs. This is handy when you want to convert an outline into a document that no longer has paragraph numbering or when you want to eliminate numbers you have temporarily added to the beginnings of paragraphs.

Restart Sequence (check box) Do you want renumbering to begin at 1 (or I or i or A or a)? Word will number the selection starting with the first number or letter in the numbering system you specify. If this field is not checked, Word accepts the first number in the selection (or in the document, if only a single character is selected) and continues the sequence upward.

UTILITIES REVISION MARKS COMMAND

We usually think of editing as a one-stage process: We make a change, and that's it—the change is made. But Word's manuscript-revision feature lets you break editing into a two-step process. If you turn the feature on, Word considers all the additions or deletions you make to be tentative. At your option, Word will show all the changes you've made. This is the first stage. When you're sure of what you want, you're ready for the second stage: telling Word to accept or reject the changes. The Utilities Revision Marks command lets you accomplish this too. This manuscript-revision feature is also known as *redlining*.

In stage one, if you delete a passage, Word "deletes" the original text to the scrap, as usual. But instead of removing the text from the document, it marks the text as deleted by striking it through (with a horizontal line). Similarly, if you insert new material, Word displays it as usual but treats it as provisional—and can mark the provisional addition with underlining, boldfacing, or another format you specify.

To make changes easier to spot, you can also tell Word to place a vertical bar in the margin next to each altered line of text.

In stage two, you decide whether to keep the provisional changes: You accept marked changes and incorporate them into the document by selecting text that includes them and telling Word to remove revision marks so that it becomes normal text. Or you reject a potential change by telling Word to undo the revision.

When the manuscript-revision feature is on, Word guards against undocumented deletions of original text by refusing to remove even a single character from the document without leaving visual evidence of its removal. Thus, although you can freely delete newly inserted text, you can neither overtype any existing text nor backspace over it without first turning off the revision feature. Similarly, if you use the Edit Replace command to replace one word with another, Word marks the old one as deleted rather than simply replacing it.

When manuscript revision is turned on, the letters *RM* appear at the bottom right of the screen, in the status line. If manuscript revision was turned on when you saved a document, Word turns it on again when the document is reloaded.

Choose the command by pressing Alt+UM. The Utilities Mark Revisions dialog box appears at the bottom of the screen.

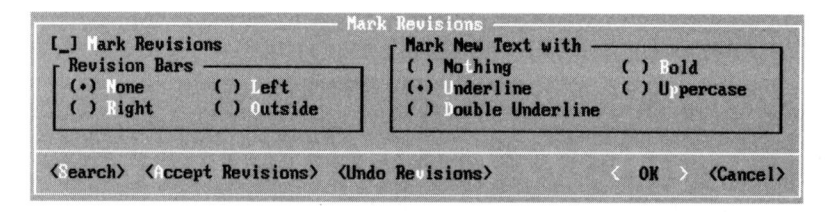

```
┌──────────────────────── Mark Revisions ────────────────────────┐
│ [_] Mark Revisions          ┌─ Mark New Text with ─────────┐   │
│ ┌─ Revision Bars ─────────┐ │ ( ) Nothing      ( ) Bold    │   │
│ │ (•) None     ( ) Left   │ │ (•) Underline    ( ) Uppercase│  │
│ │ ( ) Right    ( ) Outside│ │ ( ) Double Underline         │   │
│ └─────────────────────────┘ └──────────────────────────────┘   │
│                                                                 │
│ <Search>  <Accept Revisions>  <Undo Revisions>    < OK >  <Cancel> │
└─────────────────────────────────────────────────────────────────┘
```

Fields of the Utilities Mark Revisions Dialog Box

In addition to the OK and Cancel command buttons, the Utilities Mark Revisions dialog box has six fields:

Mark Revisions (check box) This is the manuscript-revision feature's on/off switch. If you check this field, Word will consider any new editing to be tentative. It will strike through any characters you delete and will mark insertions and changed lines according to the preferences you express in the next two fields of the command. If you turn off this check box, Word turns off the manuscript-revision feature. Turning off the revision feature does not affect editing you've already completed. Editing that Word considers tentative will remain marked until you use the Undo Revisions command button.

Revision Bars (option buttons) Revision bars appear on both the screen and the printed page and are placed next to changed or inserted body text, running heads, footnotes, and annotations. Which side of the text do you want revision bars to appear and print on?

- **None**—Word's proposed response. Turns off revision bars if they are already visible.
- **Left**—Puts all revision bars in the left margin.
- **Right**—Puts them in the right margin.
- **Outside**—Puts revision bars in the left margin on even-numbered printed pages and in the right margin on odd-numbered printed pages (a good choice for documents printed on both sides of the page).

Mark New Text With (option buttons) Do you want insertions visually distinguished from surrounding text, and if so, what special formatting do you want them to have? Word proposes underlining all insertions, but you can choose boldfacing, uppercasing, or double-underlining if you prefer.

- **Nothing**—With this setting, Word does not mark insertions in any way; that is, whatever you type in looks exactly like the text surrounding it. Be careful when making this choice, because insertions—especially small ones—will not be as easy to spot as they would if they were distinctively formatted. If you do choose Nothing, you probably will want Word to display revision bars in a margin. Remember that if you choose Nothing, even though insertions will look like any other text, Word still considers them to be only tentative changes to the document. Thus, if you later highlight a section of the document and tell Word to undo revisions, Word will eliminate the insertions, and you could inadvertently undo work you did not mean to lose.
- **Underline**—New text appears with an underline, Word's default.
- **Double Underline**—New text appears with a double-underline.
- **Bold**—New text appears in boldface.
- **Uppercase**—New text appears in uppercase.

Search (command button) Choose this button to highlight the next continuous section of revised text. The Mark Revisions dialog box remains on screen so that you can give Word instructions about what to do with the revised text it finds. This means you can change options as well as remove or undo revision marks for the highlighted text, or you can use Search again to move to the next revision.

Accept Revisions (command button) Removes revision marks and makes all indicated revisions to the portion of the document currently highlighted. When you use this command, all struckthrough text is deleted—including any text given strikethrough formatting with the Format Character command, the built-in key code Ctrl+S, or a character style in a style sheet. The command also incorporates all insertions in the selected text and removes revision bars from the margin.

Before choosing the Accept Revisions button, be sure to select the portion of the document from which you want to remove the marks. One way to do this is to use the Search button to highlight an instance of revised text so that you then can accept it (with Accept Revisions) or reject it (with Undo Revisions). If you forget to select text, or if no revisions exist in the highlighted text, Word responds with the message *Word cannot find any revised text*. To remove marks from an entire document, first press Shift+F10 to select all of it.

Word keeps the Search button highlighted to ask if you want to search for the next occurrence of revised text. If you do, choose Search or simply press Enter. Word highlights the next section of revised text, and the dialog box remains on screen so that you can choose and execute another command. If you don't want to search for the next revision, choose either the Cancel (Esc) or the OK (Enter) button. Choose the OK button if you have made any changes to the fields in the Mark Revisions dialog box.

Undo Revisions (command button) Use this button to reject proposed revisions to your document. It has the opposite effect of Accept Revisions: It returns selected text to normal, throwing away the tentative edits that were made with the Revision Marks command.

UTILITIES WORD COUNT COMMAND

To count the words in your document, choose the Utilities Word Count command (Alt+UW). If no text is selected, all the words in your document are counted except for footnote text. If text is selected, only those words partly or completely highlighted are counted.

Writers often pause in the middle of a long document and want to know how many words they have completed, to that point, rather than the total number of words in the document. To make this calculation, extend the selection back to the beginning of the document, and then use Utilities Word Count. Specifically, you can

1. Press F8 to turn on extend-selection mode;
2. Press Ctrl+Home to extend the selection to the beginning of the document;
3. Choose Alt+UW to count the selected words;
4. The number of words will appear in the message box. Press the Right direction key to return to your original location in the document.

Chapter 23 includes the text of a macro that performs a word count for you, giving you both the number of words in the document and the number of words so far.

UTILITIES LINE DRAW COMMAND

Before you use the Utilities Line Draw command, you might want to do two things:

- ♦ Use the Utilities Customize command to choose your Line Draw character (a single line, a double line, or some other character).
- ♦ Use a style sheet (or create one) that contains a character style. The font and other formatting you choose for the Line Draw style is what Word will use to draw the lines. (If you find that lines look fine on the screen but print incorrectly, you need to change the font that is formatting your Line Draw style.)

With these preliminaries behind you, turn on Line Draw mode by choosing the Utilities Line Draw command (Alt+UL). The letters *LD* will appear at the bottom of the screen. In this mode, when you press the direction keys (Left, Right, Up, and Down) you cause lines to appear on the screen. You can turn corners or create junctions of three or four lines; at a junction you'll sometimes need to draw something more than once to get it right. Any lines you create will draw over any other characters, so press the keys with care.

If you make a mistake that you can't fix by retracing the desired pattern, you can turn off Line Draw mode by pressing Esc and then repair the damage. You can use Edit Undo, but this can be annoying because it undoes whatever line drawing you have accomplished and then highlights the entire document. When the document is highlighted in its entirety, you immediately move to the beginning (usually) or end (sometimes) of the document if you press any key.

NOTE: *If you have a mouse, you can avoid moving away from where you want to work. Although the entire document is highlighted, your work location should still be on the screen. If you point to this location with the mouse and click the left button, the highlight disappears and the cursor returns to your work area.*

Line drawing has its limitations. It doesn't always work predictably with proportionally spaced fonts or with paragraphs that have either unusual line spacing or blank lines created with the Before or After field of the Format Paragraph command.

UTILITIES SORT COMMAND

The Utilities Sort command sorts lists and columns of words and numbers either alphabetically or numerically. Word will sort in either ascending (1, 2, 3... or a, b, c...) or descending (9, 8, 7... or z, y, x...) sequence.

Before choosing the Utilities Sort command, you must select (highlight) the text to be sorted. The selection can be sequences that span whole paragraphs, or it can simply be a column in a table. Generally, Word reorders the selected text according to the letters or numbers that begin each paragraph, but if you select a column of characters and mark the Sort Column Only check box, Word sorts by individual lines instead of by paragraphs.

If you complete a sort and decide you made a mistake, immediately use the Edit Undo command to restore the selected text to the form it had before you sorted it.

To run the command, choose Utilities Sort (Alt+UO). The Utilities Sort dialog box appears.

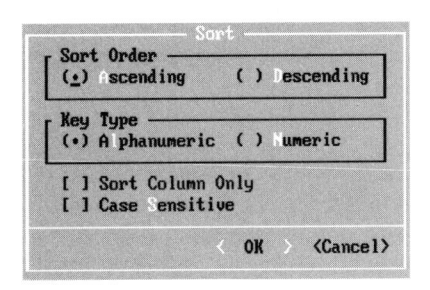

```
┌─────────────── Sort ───────────────┐
│ ┌─ Sort Order ──────────────────┐  │
│ │ (•) Ascending    ( ) Descending│  │
│ └───────────────────────────────┘  │
│ ┌─ Key Type ────────────────────┐  │
│ │ (•) Alphanumeric ( ) Numeric  │  │
│ └───────────────────────────────┘  │
│    [ ] Sort Column Only            │
│    [ ] Case Sensitive              │
│                                    │
│           <  OK  >    <Cancel>     │
└────────────────────────────────────┘
```

Fields of the Utilities Sort Dialog Box

In addition to the OK and Cancel command buttons, the Utilities Sort dialog box has four fields:

Sort Order (option buttons)

- **Ascending**—This causes Word to alphabetize from *A* to *Z* and to number from *0* to *9*.
- **Descending**—This causes Word to sort from *Z* to *A* and from *9* to *0*. In an alphanumeric sort with the Set Order field set to Descending, paragraphs starting with special characters (such as & or #) come last instead of first.

Key Type (option buttons) Do you want Word to put the selected elements in alphanumeric order or in numeric order?

- **Alphanumeric**—With this choice, Word alphabetizes the paragraphs or lines, putting special characters (such as @ and #) first, followed by numbers and then letters. The sort ignores accent marks in letters such as *ú* and *á*; the character *ć* is treated as *c*.
- **Numeric**—With this choice, Word orders the elements by numeric value. It recognizes only numerals 0 through 9 and the following characters: decimal point (.), dollar sign ($), percent sign (%), minus sign (–), comma (,), and open and close parentheses ().

Sort Column Only (check box) This field lets you sort the elements in one column of a table without affecting the order of the other columns. To understand the sorting of individual columns, recall that you can select individual columns of text using Word's Column Selection mode. You turn this mode on by pressing Shift+Ctrl+F8. The Sort Column Only check box is grayed unless Column Selection mode is on.

After you select a column in a table, you can sort the elements in it with the Utilities Sort command. The question becomes whether you want to apply the new order only to the selected column or to the entire table. For instance, if you are sorting a table that contains last names in one column and addresses and phone numbers in another column, you probably do not want Word to reorganize the order of the names without also reorganizing the order of the corresponding addresses and phone numbers. In this case, do not choose Sort Column Only, because you want all the columns to be reordered.

If you want to sort a table by more than one column, you do so consecutively, sorting first by the least important column (the *secondary sort*) and last by the most important column (*the primary sort*). For example, if you want to alphabetize a table of people by the city in which they live and then by family names within the various cities, you first sort the column containing family names and then sort the column of city names. The city names in this case are the objects of the primary sort, and the family names are the objects of a secondary sort.

Case Sensitive (check box) Check this box to instruct Word to list words beginning with capital letters ahead of words beginning with lowercase letters when performing an alphanumeric sort. (For example, it would list *Armageddon* and *Atlanta* before *alligator*, *artichoke*, and *attention*.)

SORTING: ALPHANUMERIC VS. NUMERIC

An example of the difference between alphanumeric and numeric sorting is instructive. If you select a column of numbers that contains 12, 2, 112, and 0.12, you obtain different results by sorting it alphanumerically from those you would obtain by sorting it numerically. An alphanumeric sort considers the digits in a number from left to right, as if it were alphabetizing a word. So it returns the numbers in this order: 0.12, 112, 12, and 2. The first number is 0.12 not because it is the smallest number, but because it starts with a special character, in this case a decimal point. (Word ignores the 0.) The number 2 comes last because its first digit has a higher value than the first digit of any of the other numbers. In contrast, the numeric sort looks at all the digits in a number at the same time and assigns the number a priority dependent on its overall numeric value. So it returns the numbers in lowest-to-highest order: 0.12, 2, 12, 112.

A valuable use of a numeric sort is to reorganize a document by numbering its paragraphs according to the order in which you want them to appear. Selecting the document (or portion of a document) and executing the Utilities Sort command with the Key Type field set to Numeric causes the document to be restructured in the numbered order. Because a numeric sort recognizes decimals, you can give a paragraph a number between two existing numbers. For instance, if you want to put a paragraph between two paragraphs already numbered 7 and 8, you can give the paragraph to be inserted the number 7.5. You must type these numbers at the beginnings of the paragraphs. You can remove them later by selecting the whole document (or the relevant portion), setting the Utilities Renumber Paragraphs field of the Utilities Renumber command to Remove, and executing the command.

UTILITIES CALCULATE COMMAND

Inserting Mathematical Answers

Word performs simple mathematical operations: addition (+), subtraction (–), multiplication (*), and division (/). Conveniently, you needn't retype numbers because Word can perform math on numbers that are already on the screen regardless of whether the figures are arranged horizontally or in a column. Simply select the numbers, and then use Utilities Calculate (Alt+UC or F2).

- To select a horizontal row of numbers, drag with the mouse, or press the F8 key and extend the highlight with the direction keys. Alternatively, you can hold down the Shift key while you extend the highlight with the direction keys.

- To select a column of numbers, first move the cursor to one corner of the rectangular area that makes up the column. (If the numbers are aligned on the right or on the decimal point, be sure to allow enough space for the largest number in the column to be completely selected.) Next hold down the Shift and Ctrl keys, and press the F8 key. This will activate Word's Column Selection mode, and the letters *CS* will appear on the bottom line of the screen. Extending the highlight (with the direction keys or with the mouse) causes a rectangular shape to be highlighted on the screen.

After you've selected the numbers you want calculated, press the F2 key. Word performs the desired operation on the highlighted numbers. The answer appears in the scrap so that you can insert it into a document with Edit Paste. If you want to perform a calculation but don't want to lose the previous contents of the scrap, use Edit Undo immediately after pressing the F2 key.

NOTE: *Word adds numbers by default. It performs other operations only when it encounters a number preceded by a minus sign or enclosed in parentheses (both indicate that the value must be subtracted), an asterisk (indicating multiplication), a slash (indicating division), or a percent sign. Thus, you can simply highlight a row or column of figures, press the F2 key, and see the total in the scrap.*

If the figures are separated by text, don't worry: Word ignores all other letters and characters except the percent sign (%), which causes it to divide by 100 the number preceding the symbol. For example, pressing F2 when the following is selected causes the result *254* to appear both in the message bar and in the scrap:

| he had 157 but then he got 97 more

Selecting either *157 + 97* or *157 97* would have the same effect because Word always adds numbers unless instructed otherwise.

The following operators prompt Word to perform other calculations—multiplication, division, and percentages.

- A minus sign preceding a number or parentheses enclosing a number indicates subtraction or a negative number; for example, both 10 − 5 and 10(5) equal 5.
- An asterisk indicates multiplication; for example, 10*5 equals 50.
- A forward slash indicates division; for example, 10/5 equals 2.
- A percent sign indicates percentages. Note, however, that the percent sign simply tells Word to divide the preceding value by 100.

To use more than two numbers in a calculation, you must understand the order in which Word performs operations. Here are the rules Word follows:

1. When parentheses surround two or more numbers, Word executes the operator or operators that are inside the parentheses before it executes any operators outside the parentheses. The effect is to reduce the expression inside parentheses to a single number and then to use that number for subsequent calculations. For example, Word calculates *2*(5–1)* to be 8 because it calculates the *(5–1)* in parentheses first, resulting in 4, and then multiplies the 2 by 4, resulting in 8. On the other hand, if the parentheses were left off, Word would multiply the 2 by 5 and then subtract the *1*, resulting in 9.

2. Word calculates percentages before it adds, subtracts, multiplies, or divides surrounding numbers. The percent sign causes Word to divide the number (or parenthetical expression) immediately preceding it by 100. For example, *50%* is calculated to be 0.5, and *(2 * 50)%* is calculated to be 1.

3. Word performs multiplication and division before addition and subtraction. For example, the expression *1 + 2 * 3* is calculated to be 7 because the multiplication of the *2* and *3* is performed first, and then the *1* is added. (Multiplication and division are equivalent operations and are given equal priority. Similarly, addition and subtraction are equivalent.)

4. Except as noted in the previous three rules, Word performs calculations from left to right and from top to bottom. You can think of Word as sweeping across your highlighted expression to perform each multiplication or division as it is encountered and then making a second pass to perform each addition or subtraction as it is encountered. For example, the expression *1 * 2 + 3 * 4 + 5* is calculated as 19, because Word multiplies the *1* by the *2* for a result of 2 and then the *3* by the *4* for a result of 12 and then adds the remaining numbers together *(2 + 12 + 5 = 19)*.

Here are several points to keep in mind when you are using Word's math functions:

- To calculate a certain percentage of a number or parenthetical expression, multiply the number or parenthetical expression by the percentage and add the percent sign. For example, to calculate 60 percent of 50, highlight the expression *50 * 60%*, and press F2. The result is 30.

- The answer Word gives has at least as many decimal places to the right of the decimal point as does the number in the selection that has the most decimal places. If no decimals are specified, Word displays up to two decimals (for example, displaying the result of ⅓ as 0.33). If the answer contains more decimal places than any of the values you selected, Word rounds the result. This means that dividing 5 by 6 gives 0.83 because Word displays decimal fractions to two places. Similarly, dividing 5.00 by 6 gives the answer 0.83 because 5.00 has two decimal places. But dividing 5.0 by 6 gives the answer 0.8 because by using 5.0 (instead of 5 or 5.00), you indicate that you want the answer to have a single decimal place.
- Decimal points will be expressed.
- Results of up to 15 characters including the decimal point are placed in the scrap. If an answer is longer than this, the message *The result exceeds 14 digits* appears. However, Word can perform calculations that have intermediate results greater than 14 digits, provided that the calculated final result has no more than 14 digits (plus the decimal point).
- Your result will contain commas as separators if at least one of the numbers in the selection contains a comma. However, your answer will not contain a dollar sign ($) even if one of the selected numbers is expressed in dollars. You must add dollar signs manually.
- Provided that the Use INS for Overtype Key check box of the Utilities Customize command is off, you can replace a series of selected numbers with the result that appears in the scrap by holding down the Shift key and pressing the Ins key. For example, if you select *3+4* and press the F2 key, the result 7 appears in the scrap. But the *3+4* remains selected. Holding down the Shift key and pressing the Ins key causes the selected numbers to be deleted and replaced with the contents of the scrap—in this case, the number 7.
- To substantially increase Word's math powers, you can use the MasterWord calculator macro. The calculator macro makes available all the dozens of financial and math functions included in Microsoft Excel 2.0. It does this by passing your math arguments to a separate program, MasterWord Calc, and then bringing the result back into your Word document. This lets you do such things as calculate mortgage payments. To use the calculator, hold down the Shift and Ctrl keys and then press CA.

As a final example of how Word calculates a highlighted expression when you press the F2 key, look at the following expression, which calculates how much sales tax is due on a total of three items when the tax rate is 8.1 percent:

(29.95 19.95 3.00) * 8.1%

Word first adds the numbers that are in parentheses. (Word always adds numbers that are not separated by an operator.) The sum is 52.90. Next Word divides 8.1 by 100 (because of the percent sign), with a result of 0.081. Note that this result has three decimal places. Finally, it multiplies 52.90 by 0.081 for a result of 4.285—corresponding to tax of $4.29 on purchases totaling $52.90. Note that although the numbers have only one or two decimal places, the result has three decimal places. This is because Word sees percentages as their decimal equivalents: 8.1% is viewed as .081, which contains three decimal places.

UTILITIES REPAGINATE NOW COMMAND

A document can come to be paginated in several ways. For example, page breaks are calculated when you print the document by using the File Print command or when you use either the Insert Index command or the Insert Table of Contents command. In these and similar situations, the pagination is a by-product of the main operation of a command.

In contrast, the Utilities Repaginate Now command causes pagination for its own sake. It calculates where the breaks between pages would fall if the document were printed in its current form.

If you turn on the Utilities Customize command's Background Pagination check box, Word keeps pagination up-to-date in most circumstances, rendering the Utilities Repaginate Now command largely unnecessary.

After a document is paginated, by whatever means, page breaks are indicated by a loosely spaced dotted line across the screen. This line, called a *new-page mark*, shows you where a new page begins.

To choose the command, press Alt+UP. The Utilities Repaginate Now dialog box appears.

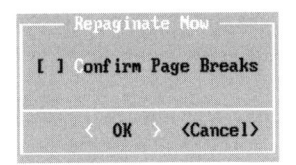

```
┌─ Repaginate Now ──────┐
│                       │
│  [ ] Confirm Page Breaks │
│                       │
│    <  OK  >   <Cancel> │
└───────────────────────┘
```

In addition to the OK and Cancel command buttons, the Utilities Repaginate Now dialog box has only one field:

Confirm Page Breaks (check box) If you do not check this box, Word repaginates your document from top to bottom without delay. If you do check the box, Word pauses each time it reaches what it calculates as a page-break location. At the pause, Word displays the tentative position of the new-page mark and displays this message asking you to confirm or change the choice: *Press Enter to confirm page break or use direction keys to reposition it.* If you accept the proposed location by pressing Enter, Word displays the new-page mark at that location and continues the pagination. Alternatively, you can press the Up direction key to choose a point higher on the page. You can't choose a point lower than that proposed by Word, but you can use the Down direction key to move the break back down after moving it up. When you've found the line at which you want the break to occur, press Enter. If it differs from the one Word proposed, Word inserts a new-page character (a row of dots) at that point and continues repaginating the document.

If new-page characters are already in a document when you choose Utilities Repaginate Now, they remain in effect unless you remove them. To pass individual judgment on whether to retain these new-page characters, check the Confirm Page Breaks field. Word will stop at each one and prompt you to press *Enter to confirm the page break or Del to remove it*. In this situation, this message will alternate, perhaps irregularly, with the message asking you to press Enter or use a direction key to accept a proposed new page break.

A new-page character also can be inserted manually by pressing Ctrl+Enter or using the Insert Break command. A new-page character is similar to the page-break mark that Word adds during repagination in that it is displayed as a series of dots across the text window (although it does not print). But there is a big difference: A new-page character forces Word to begin a new page. It is part of the content of a document, just as a paragraph mark is. It will remain forever, causing a new page at its location, unless you remove it. A page-break mark, on the other hand, is simply an indication of where pages happen to break during the current pagination.

A new-page character really is a single character, even though it is displayed as a fence across the window, like this:

∥ ·· ∥

Notice that the dots are closely spaced. A new-page mark, on the other hand, consists of more widely spaced dots and isn't a character at all—it's simply an indicator on the screen, and it looks like this:

∥ · ∥

A freshly repaginated document lets you see how the pages will break when printed, but don't jump to the conclusion that you need to use Utilities Repaginate Now frequently—or at all. As already mentioned, you can also choose Background Pagination in the Utilities Customize dialog box when you start a new document, and Word will display page breaks at the appropriate locations as your document grows. With any version of Word, wise use of the Together and With Next fields of the Format Paragraph command helps ensure that text will not break across pages in visually undesirable ways. And even if you never choose to paginate a document you are creating, Word paginates it correctly when you print.

Furthermore, you might encounter a circumstance in which a fresh repagination of a document can be undesirable. If you print a long document that is heavily marked with deletions and insertions, you'll probably want to turn off background repagination and not repaginate manually until you've finished incorporating all of your changes into the on-screen version. As long as the document is not repaginated, the on-screen page numbers will match the printed page numbers, making Edit Go To a handy way to jump to a particular page. A repagination undertaken part of the way through the correction process will render the paper copy's pages out of sync with the screen version's pages.

UTILITIES CUSTOMIZE COMMAND

A wide range of options regarding how Word functions are gathered together in the dialog box of the Utilities Customize command (Alt+UU).

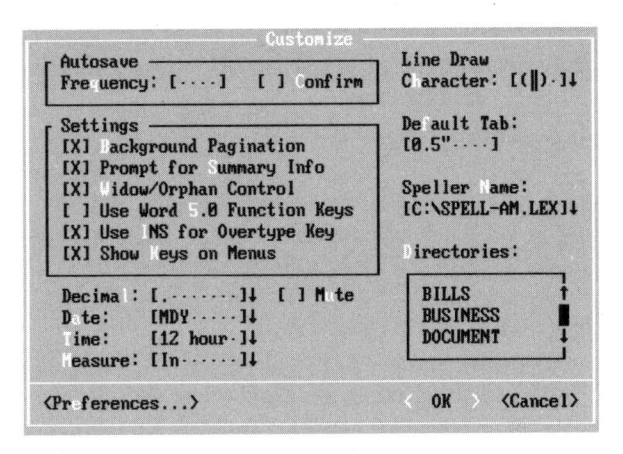

```
┌─────────────────── Customize ───────────────────┐
│ ┌Autosave─────────────────┐  Line Draw          │
│ │ Frequency: [····]  [ ] Confirm  Character: [(|)·]↓ │
│ ┌Settings─────────────────┐  Default Tab:       │
│ │ [X] Background Pagination   [0.5"····]        │
│ │ [X] Prompt for Summary Info                   │
│ │ [X] Widow/Orphan Control    Speller Name:     │
│ │ [ ] Use Word 5.0 Function Keys  [C:\SPELL-AM.LEX]↓ │
│ │ [X] Use MS for Overtype Key                   │
│ │ [X] Show Keys on Menus      Directories:      │
│                                                 │
│   Decimal: [········]↓  [ ] Mute   BILLS     ↑  │
│   Date:    [MDY·····]↓              BUSINESS █  │
│   Time:    [12 hour·]↓              DOCUMENT ↓  │
│   Measure: [In······]↓                          │
│                                                 │
│   <Preferences...>           <  OK  >  <Cancel> │
└─────────────────────────────────────────────────┘
```

You can also reach this dialog box by choosing the Customize button in the dialog box of the View Preferences command. Similarly, the Customize dialog box includes a Preferences button that takes you to the Preferences dialog box. This makes sense because the two commands have a great deal of apparent similarity. The chief difference, as noted early in this chapter, is that the Utilities Customize command controls aspects of Word's behavior, whereas the View Preferences command controls aspects of Word's appearance.

NOTE: *Customize is the only command from the Utilities menu that is available for use in style sheet windows as well as in document windows.*

Fields of the Utilities Customize Dialog Box

In addition to the OK and Cancel command buttons, the Utilities Customize dialog box contains 18 fields.

The autosave fields

You can tell Word to save your work periodically in a special backup file, called an *autosave* file.

When you save your documents with File Save, or when you exit Word, the program cleans up behind itself, leaving no trace of the autosave backups it made. The only exception to this rule, and a welcome one, occurs if you do not go through the normal save-exit-shutdown procedure when ending a Word session. For example, suppose your Word session is terminated abruptly by a power failure. If the autosave feature was in effect, the next time you start Word it will tell you that autosave backup files exist and ask you to press Y to recover them. After they are recovered, the files are given the extension .DOC, .STY, or .GLY, thus making whatever data they contain available. Although these recovered files will not contain any editing changes you made after the last backup, you can save a substantial amount of work.

For an overview of the feature, particularly the difference between an autosave backup file and a conventional backup file, refer to Tip 7 in Chapter 8.

Frequency (text box) Specify the interval, in minutes, you want Word to use between autosaves. A reasonable number is *10* or *15*, but you might want a shorter interval. To turn autosave off, type *0*.

When autosave is turned on, Word briefly interrupts your work at the specified intervals, informing you that it is saving your latest editing changes in a temporary backup file on disk. The backup is *not* the regular .DOC or .BAK file, which also exists on disk. Instead the autosave backup file for a document always has the extension .SVD. If you are working on a new, as yet unnamed file, Word saves your work as UNTITLED.SVD. (If more than one unnamed file is open, Word will save the active file as UNTITLEX.SVD, where X is a number, such as 1, 2, or 3.) If the document has previously been saved with File Save, Word saves the interim version with the assigned filename but again, with the .SVD extension. Backup files for style sheets have the extension .SVS, and backup files for glossaries have the extension .SVG.

If, during an intense session, you want Word to save your work periodically but not at inopportune moments, consider setting the next field, the Confirm check box, to No.

Confirm (check box) This field indicates whether Word should notify you before it saves an autosave backup file. If you do not check this box, Word displays the message *Saving [DRIVE:\PATH\FILENAME.SVD]* whenever your computer's clock indicates that it is time to create a backup of your work.

When this box is checked and it is time for an autosave, Word displays the message *Do you want to back up changes with autosave now?*, asking for permission to temporarily disrupt your work while it saves recent editing changes on disk. If you don't want to be bothered—whether because you are in a frenzy of creation or because you haven't written anything worthwhile since the last save—press Esc.

As a practical matter, the amount of time Word takes to make an autosave is so small, onto a hard disk at least, that answering the Confirm message might be more bothersome than waiting a moment for the autosave to complete.

Settings check boxes

Six check boxes, gathered together under the heading *Settings*, each provide you with a significant option regarding the operation of Word.

Background Pagination (check box) If this box is checked, Word paginates a document as you create it, inserting a page break (represented by a widely spaced dotted line across the screen) whenever your document overflows onto a new page. Because Word is paginating as you go, it displays the number of the current page at the lower left corner of your screen. (Without automatic pagination, the page number remains 1 until you use a command that causes pagination to occur.)

Word is clever about automatic pagination: It monitors and updates page breaks as your document takes shape. For example, if you return to a section that has already been paginated and perform some editing (such as making a deletion or an insertion) that affects pagination, Word recalculates all succeeding page breaks and moves them, if necessary, to reflect their new positions.

If you turn this option off, Word does not paginate the document until you print it (with File Print), repaginate it (with Utilities Repaginate Now), preview it (with File Print Preview), or tell Word to compile an index or table of contents for it (with Insert Index or Insert Table of Contents).

Prompt for Summary Info (check box) Do you want Word to offer you a chance to fill in summary information whenever you save a document for the first time?

Summary information, as its name implies, is a collection of text fields about a document: author, date of creation, key words and phrases, comments, and so on. Having summary information for your documents makes it practical to use the File File Management command to seek and load desired documents.

If you check the Prompt for Summary Info box, Word presents you with the blank fields of a summary sheet whenever you save a document for the first time.

Widow/Orphan Control (check box) This field lets you decide whether Word will permit a document to be paginated in such a way that single lines of text are not stranded at the tops or bottoms of pages. A widow is created when the final line of a paragraph is printed by itself at the top of a new page; an orphan is created when the first line of a paragraph is printed by itself on the bottom of a page, with the remainder of the paragraph printed on the next page. Widows and orphans (in text, that is) are generally considered unattractive.

If you leave the Widow/Orphan Control box checked, Word will readjust the lengths of specific pages as needed to eliminate widow lines and orphan lines. If you turn off the check box, Word will always print as many lines on a page as the page's formatting allows, regardless of whether this results in widows and orphans.

As long as the box is checked, you can extend your control even further over how page length is adjusted to keep blocks of text on the same page. See the Together and the With Next check boxes of the Format Paragraph command, described in Chapter 15.

Use Word 5.0 Function Keys (check box) If you turn on this check box, Word 5.5 will for the most part give the function keys F1 through F12 the same assignments they had in Word 5.0. However, the Help key remains F1 regardless of how you set this field, and although F6 becomes the extend-selection key as it was in Word 5.0, it actually functions like the F8 key in Word 5.5 rather than like the Word 5.0 F6 key.

Use INS for Overtype Key (check box) At issue here is what purposes the Ins and Del keys should have, alone and in combination with other keys (principally the Shift key). The differences are summarized in the following table, which was explained in greater detail early in Chapter 5:

To do this:	Press (Ins check box checked):	Press (Ins check box unchecked):
Delete to scrap (Cut)	Shift+Del	Del
Delete completely (not to scrap)	Del	Shift+Del
Insert from scrap (Paste)	Shift+Ins	Ins
Toggle between insert and overtype modes	Ins *or* Alt+F5	Alt+F5

Show Keys on Menus (check box) Do you want command-key shortcuts to appear in menus? For example, do you want the words *Alt+BkSp* to appear to the right of the Undo command in the drop-down Edit menu?

The remaining fields

The remaining fields influence Word's behavior in a wide variety of ways.

Line Draw Character (drop-down list box) What character do you want Word to use when you draw lines and boxes? Initially, Word proposes a single line, although if you change the setting Word will remember your new preference.

If you press the Down direction key, you scroll through 12 choices. If you press Alt+Down direction key, three of those choices at a time are displayed in the small drop-down list box. However, you are not limited to the 12 characters. You can type any one of these characters or any other character into the field.

After you have chosen the character you want to use to draw lines, use Utilities Line Draw to actually draw the lines.

Default Tab (text box) Word comes from Microsoft with a default tab width of half an inch (0.5"). Word assumes you want tab characters to be half an inch apart, which gives five spaces between stops with pica-size type (10-pitch, meaning 10 characters to the inch). You can, however, change this to a different default tab width. For example, if you write computer programs you might want to set a tab width of 0.8 inch. A drawback to using these built-in tab stops is that they must be evenly spaced, left-aligned, and without leader characters. For a greater range of options, use Format Tabs or the ruler.

Speller Name (drop-down list box) Where should Word look for its standard spell dictionary when you use Utilities Spelling to check spelling in a document? If you are using Word on a hard disk and have installed the spell checker during the setup procedure, Word assumes it should look in the program directory.

You can have more than one standard dictionary and switch from one to another by changing the name of the file in this drop-down list box. For example, you might have Microsoft's Spanish dictionary, SPELL-SP.LEX, and the medical version of the American English dictionary, SPELL-MD.LEX. You could switch back and forth by choosing the name of the desired dictionary from the list.

Directories (list box) Use this list box to make it easier to choose a directory containing a standard spell dictionary. The use of Directories list boxes was explained in Chapter 10.

Decimal (drop-down list box) Do you want a decimal point to be represented as a period or as a comma?

- A period is the decimal point used in many places, including the United States and Canada.
- The comma is the decimal point used in many other places, including much of Europe.

If you change the decimal character to a comma, Word will no longer recognize the comma as a separator of entries in lists, so you must use semicolons instead. For example, data files and header paragraphs in form-letter documents to be merge printed will require semicolons instead of commas.

Date (drop-down list box) What format shall Word use when you use the *date* or *dateprint* glossary entry to insert a date into a document?

- **MDY**—Leaving this field set to *MDY* causes Word to insert the date in the month-day-year format (for example, *June 15, 1991*).
- **DMY**—Changing the setting to *DMY* causes Word to use the day-month-year format (for example, *15 June, 1991*).

Time (drop-down list box) Should Word use a 12-hour clock or a 24-hour clock when you use the *time* or *timeprint* glossary entry?

- **12 hour**—This setting causes Word to use the hours of the day 1 through 12 and append *am* or *pm* as needed.
- **24 hour**—This setting causes Word to use the hours of the day 1 through 24, so *3:05 pm* becomes *15:05*.

Measure (drop-down list box) Which unit of measure do you want Word to use to express distances and measurements in the fields of various Format command dialog boxes?

- **In**—Inches.
- **Cm**—Centimeters, of which there are 2.54 to the inch.
- **P10**—10-pitch characters, of which there are 10 to the inch.
- **P12**—12-pitch characters, of which there are 12 to the inch.
- **Pt**—Points, of which there are 72 to the inch. Word can accept instructions as exact as $1/20$ point—$1/1440$ inch—a degree of precision that is necessary if Word is driving typesetting equipment.

The following diagram shows you the relationships among these units of measure:

```
Centimeters   Inches   Pica(P10)   Elite(P12)   Points
   2.54 ─┐     1 ─┐     10 ─┐       12 ─┐        72 ─┐
    2  ─┤                              10 ─┤        60 ─┤
         │      3/4 ─┤                                  48 ─┤
   1.5 ─┤                   5 ─┤                        
    1  ─┤      1/2 ─┤                 5 ─┤        36 ─┤
    .5 ─┤                                          24 ─┤
         │      1/4 ─┤                                  12 ─┤
    0  ─┘
         └───────────────────┘       └──────────────────┘
         Displays pica characters     Displays elite characters
           accurately on screen          accurately on screen
```

By way of example, let's see how these units of measure are reflected in the Format Paragraph command. First, let's assume the Measure field of the Customize command is set to *In*, Word's default value. Your From Left field might read *1"*. Set the Measure field to *Cm*, and, for the same paragraph, the same field reads *2.54 cm*. Set Measure to *P10*, and the field's value changes to *10 p10*. Choose *P12*, and the field displays *12 p12*. Or choose *Pt*, and you see *72 pt*. In each example, the measurement stayed the same—they were simply expressed in different units.

One final note: You probably think in terms of inches or centimeters. Don't worry about needing to convert them to Word's other units of measure. Enter your measurement in inches (*1"*, *2"*, and so on) or in centimeters (*2.54 cm*, *5.0 cm*), and when you execute the Format commands, Word will convert your measurement to whatever unit you have specified in the Customize measure field.

Mute (check box) Do you want to hear about it when you attempt the impossible? Word sounds a beeping alarm as a reminder when you try something not allowed, such as scrolling up when you've already reached the top of a document. Turn off the alarm by checking this box.

Preferences (command button) Choosing this button takes you to the View Preferences dialog box, discussed in Chapter 13.

CHAPTER SEVENTEEN

Macro Commands

The Macro menu is Word's shortest menu: It has only three commands. Yet these commands, and the capabilities they provide, are potentially among the most powerful, useful, and entertaining aspects of Microsoft Word.

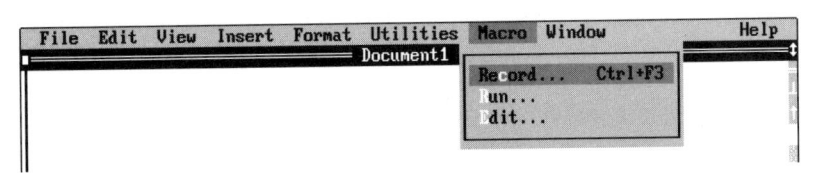

In summary form, here are the three commands and the opportunities they permit:

Macro Record—Lets you record a series of keystrokes so that you can "replay" them later. The replaying of keystrokes is known as *running a macro*.

Macro Run—Lets you replay an existing macro whether it was recorded from keystrokes or written in the macro recording language.

Macro Edit—Converts written macro instructions into actual macros or deletes macros from the glossary file. Like the Edit Glossary command, it lets you save, merge, or clear the glossary file.

These commands are available in both document and style sheet windows.

All macros are stored in the *glossary*, a special area of memory. This is the same glossary that stores passages of text, although you aren't necessarily conscious of this as you use the Macro commands.

Chapter 6 provided an introduction and tutorials to most of the fundamental uses of the Macro commands. You might want to review that chapter as well as the discussion of the Edit Glossary command in Chapter 12, before continuing with this chapter.

MACRO RECORD COMMAND

Choose the Macro Record command to begin recording keystrokes as a macro. When the recording commences, the Macro Record command vanishes from the Macro menu and is replaced by the Macro Stop Recorder command. This command in turn vanishes when you use it to end recording the macro.

Choose the Macro Record command from the Macro menu (Alt+MC), or press Ctrl+F3. The Record Macro dialog box appears.

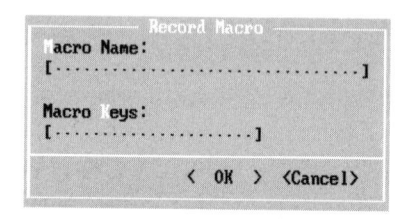

```
┌─── Record Macro ───┐
│ Macro Name:        │
│ [................] │
│                    │
│ Macro Keys:        │
│ [..........]       │
│                    │
│   < OK >  <Cancel> │
└────────────────────┘
```

Fields of the Record Macro Dialog Box

In addition to the OK and Cancel command buttons, the Record Macro dialog box has two fields:

Macro Name (text box) Type a name for the macro you are about to record. As noted in Chapter 12, a macro or other glossary entry can have a name of up to 31 characters in length (including the control code). No spaces are permitted in a name, although you can break up a long name with mixed capitalization, hyphens, periods, and underlines.

Macro Keys (text box) If you want the macro you are about to record to have a control code so that you can run the macro by holding down the Shift and Ctrl keys (or only the Ctrl key) and pressing the one-character or two-character code, type the code here.

In the tutorial in Chapter 6, a macro was given the control code Shift+Ctrl+ND. To tell Word you want to use that code, highlight the Macro Keys text box, and hold down both the Shift and Ctrl keys while pressing the N key; then release the Shift and Ctrl keys, and press the D key. Word records this code in the Macro Keys text box as *<Shift Ctrl N>D*.

MACRO RUN COMMAND

You can run a macro in a variety of ways:

- Type the macro's name into a document, and press the F3 key.
- Press the macro's control code, such as Shift+Ctrl+RB (if your macro has the code RB).
- Use the Macro Run command, and choose the macro from those listed in the glossary.

CHAPTER SEVENTEEN: Macro Commands

These methods were introduced in Chapter 6 and are easy to understand. The Macro Run command has a little more to it than the other approaches because it provides an extra opportunity—Step mode.

To use the Macro Run command, press Alt+MR. The Run Macro dialog box appears.

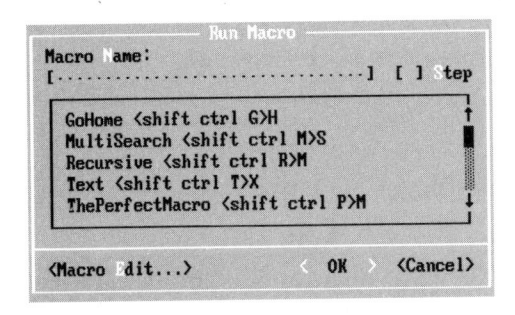

```
┌─────────────────── Run Macro ───────────────────┐
│ Macro Name:                                     │
│ [.............................] [ ] Step       │
│  ┌──────────────────────────────────┐ ↑         │
│  │ GoHome       <shift ctrl G>H     │ ▓         │
│  │ MultiSearch  <shift ctrl M>S     │ ▓         │
│  │ Recursive    <shift ctrl R>M     │ ▓         │
│  │ Text         <shift ctrl T>X     │ ▓         │
│  │ ThePerfectMacro <shift ctrl P>M  │ ↓         │
│  └──────────────────────────────────┘           │
│                                                 │
│  <Macro Edit...>        < OK >   <Cancel>       │
└─────────────────────────────────────────────────┘
```

Fields of the Run Macro Dialog Box

In addition to the OK and Cancel command buttons, the Run Macro dialog box has four fields.

Macro Name (text box) Type the name of the macro you want to run, if you know its exact name.

Macro Name (drop-down list box) Choose the name of the macro you want to run. As you move through the list of available macros, the currently selected name appears in the Macro Name text box.

Step (check box) Checking this check box causes Word to run a macro one instruction at a time. This lets you closely study the operation of a macro that is not working properly or a macro that you do not understand.

In Step mode, Word waits for you to press the Spacebar or another key before it executes each step of the macro. You simply work your way through a macro, watching the effect each step has. When Step mode is active, the letters *ST* appear on the status line near the bottom of the screen.

Step mode is also valuable as a means of racing through some parts of a macro and slowing down for other parts. When Step mode is on, holding down the Spacebar causes the macro to move forward through its steps at high speed. But as soon as you stop pressing the Spacebar, the macro stops executing.

To turn Step mode on and off—even if you are not running or are not about to run a macro—choose the Macro Run command, change the setting of the Step check box, and then execute the command without specifying a macro name in the Macro Name text box.

You also can turn Step mode on or off in the middle of executing a macro. Simply press Esc, which brings the following message to the screen: *The macro was interrupted.*

Do you want to continue running? Below this message is the Single Step check box. You can use this box to turn Step mode on or off and then choose OK (Enter) to resume the operation of the macro.

MACRO EDIT COMMAND

The Macro Edit command is, from most standpoints, virtually identical to the Edit Glossary command. Both commands let you add and delete entries from the active glossary as well as save or clear the glossary or load or merge a file into the glossary. Consequently, you might want to review the discussion of the Edit Glossary command in Chapter 12.

Preparing to Use Macro Edit

As with the Edit Glossary command, you might want to prepare before using the Macro Edit command. If you intend store a passage of text as a macro, you must first select (highlight) the passage. On the other hand, if you intend to insert the text of a macro into a document, you probably want to open a new document.

After you have prepared in one of these ways, you choose the Macro Edit command by pressing Alt+ME. Word responds by showing you the main Edit Macro dialog box.

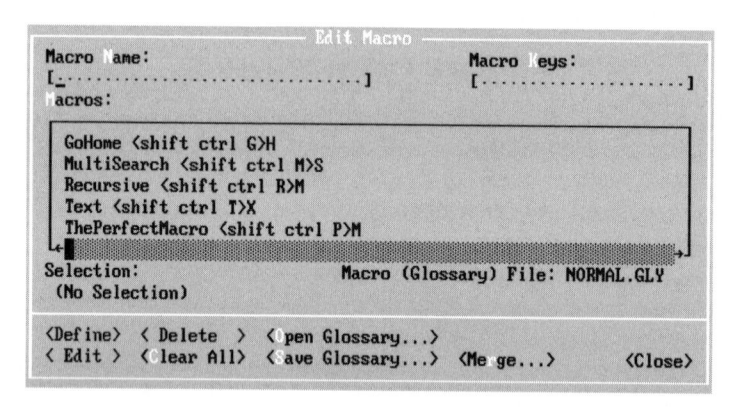

```
┌─────────────────────── Edit Macro ───────────────────────┐
│ Macro Name:                      Macro Keys:             │
│ [..............................]  [....................] │
│ Macros:                                                  │
│   ┌──────────────────────────────────────────────────┐   │
│   │ GoHome  <shift ctrl G>H                          │   │
│   │ MultiSearch  <shift ctrl M>S                     │   │
│   │ Recursive  <shift ctrl R>M                       │   │
│   │ Text  <shift ctrl T>X                            │   │
│   │ ThePerfectMacro  <shift ctrl P>M                 │   │
│   └──────────────────────────────────────────────────┘   │
│ Selection:                                               │
│ (No Selection)       Macro (Glossary) File: NORMAL.GLY   │
│                                                          │
│ <Define>  < Delete  >  <Open Glossary...>                │
│ < Edit >  <Clear All>  <Save Glossary...> <Merge...>  <Close> │
└──────────────────────────────────────────────────────────┘
```

As with the Glossary Edit dialog box, observe that a line right below the list of macros in the center of the dialog box shows you some or all of the document text selected at the moment. This is the text that will become a new macro should you decide to define it as such. When no text is selected, the line says *(No Selection)*.

Fields of the Edit Macro Dialog Box

In addition to the Close command button, the Edit Macro dialog box contains 10 fields:

Macro Name (text box) Type a name for the existing or new macro entry you want to work with. If you prefer, use the Macros list box to choose an existing name.

CHAPTER SEVENTEEN: Macro Commands

Macro Keys (text box) When you are preparing to define a macro, you can create a *control code* for it. This one-character or two-character code becomes a shortcut to inserting the glossary entry's content into a document later. For example, if you give a macro the control code Shift+Ctrl+ID, you can press that combination of keys in a document to insert the text of the glossary entry into your document—as if you had typed it, although much more quickly.

Unfortunately, you cannot use this field to modify the control code of a macro after it is defined. If you want to change a control code, insert the text of the macro into a document, delete the macro from the glossary if you want, and then define the macro all over again—this time giving it a different control code.

In general, it is an excellent idea to give a macro a control code starting with Shift+Ctrl rather than only Ctrl because—as noted elsewhere in the book—the Ctrl key by itself is used by Word for a wide variety of formatting chores.

Macros (list box) Word lists here all the entries from the current glossary that are macros rather than text entries. Text entries are displayed separately, in the Edit Glossary command's dialog box. You can highlight a name from the Macros list box; Word will display it in the Macro Name text box too.

Define (command button) Choose this button when you are ready to create a new macro or redefine an existing one. The Define button is what actually copies the selected text into the glossary, thereby creating the macro. If you are redefining an existing macro, Word will ask you to confirm that you want to replace the existing version of the macro with the new version.

Edit (command button) Choose this button to insert the text of an existing macro into the active document. Word loads the macro into your document in text form, with nonletter key names inside angle brackets. (For example, the Insert key is represented as <*Ins*>, and the Ctrl+Esc combination as <*ctrl esc*>.) The particulars of editing macros are described in Chapter 23.

Delete (command button) This button deletes from the active glossary the macro named in the Macro Name text box. Deleting a macro from the glossary does not affect the contents of any glossary file on disk unless you save the glossary on disk after deleting some or all of its contents.

Clear All (command button) To clear all macros from the glossary file, choose this button. Word responds with the following message: *Do you want to delete all macros now?* If you choose OK (Enter), the only entries that will remain will be text glossary entries, which can't be viewed in the Edit Macro dialog box in any case. (To see, use, or delete text glossary entries, use the Edit Glossary command.)

Open Glossary (command button) To load a glossary file from disk into Word, thereby displacing the current entries in the glossary, choose this button. It brings to the screen the Open Glossary dialog box.

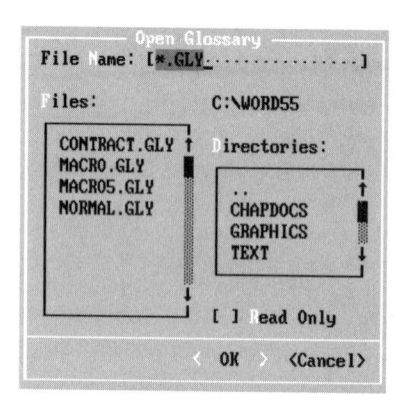

```
┌─ Open Glossary ──────────────────┐
│  File Name: [*.GLY................]          │
│                                                │
│  Files:           C:\WORD55                    │
│  ┌─────────────┐                               │
│  │CONTRACT.GLY↑│ Directories:                  │
│  │MACRO.GLY    │ ┌─────────────┐               │
│  │MACRO5.GLY   │ │..         ↑ │               │
│  │NORMAL.GLY   │ │CHAPDOCS    ▌│               │
│  │             │ │GRAPHICS    ▌│               │
│  │             │ │TEXT       ↓ │               │
│  │            ↓│ └─────────────┘               │
│  └─────────────┘                               │
│                  [ ] Read Only                 │
│                                                │
│              < OK >   <Cancel>                 │
└────────────────────────────────────────────────┘
```

This dialog box contains only four fields: a File Name text box, in which you can type the name of the glossary file you want to load; both Files and Directories list boxes, which together provide an alternative way to choose a glossary file; and a Read Only check box, which lets you specify that you want to be able to use the contents of the newly loaded glossary file but don't want to be able to change them.

When you open a new glossary file, Word discards existing glossary entries. Most often, this is what you want. However, in some cases you might want to add the entries that are stored in the file on disk to the entries already in the glossary. You can accomplish this with the Merge Glossary button.

Save Glossary (command button) Word remembers macros and other glossary entries only until you quit the program. Then it forgets them unless you save the current collection of entries on disk as a glossary file. To keep a macro indefinitely, use the Save Glossary button. Using this button saves all the current macros and other glossary entries on disk.

When you ask Word to save a glossary file, it might propose a name. Often the name it proposes is NORMAL.GLY, the normal glossary file. You can accept the name Word proposes, or you can type a different name. Word adds the filename extension .GLY, so you do not have to type it yourself.

If the name you type is a new one, Word creates a glossary file by that name. If you type the name of an existing glossary file, Word asks if you want to replace the file. Remember: When you replace a file on disk, the earlier version is gone.

You might decide to store macros in a variety of glossary files, each dedicated to a different task. Because the only glossary file that Word loads when you start the program is called NORMAL.GLY, you must deliberately load any other glossary file that contains macros you want to use. You can accomplish this with either of two commands—Open Glossary or Merge. Like Save Glossary, both of these commands are reached through the Macro Edit command (or the Edit Glossary command). You choose one of these commands and then type the name of the desired glossary file (or select it from the list box), and then you press Enter. The two commands are nearly identical, but Open Glossary eliminates existing glossary entries before loading the new ones, whereas Merge adds the new file's entries but retains the existing ones.

CHAPTER SEVENTEEN: Macro Commands

Merge (command button) When you want to combine a glossary file on disk with the current glossary file, choose this button. It lets you specify the name of the glossary file you want to merge into the active glossary file.

If an entry in a glossary file that is being merged has the same name as one already in the glossary, the newly merged entry replaces the existing one.

CHAPTER EIGHTEEN

Window Commands

In its windowing capability, as in so many other ways, Word has power to spare. By allowing you to see up to nine windows at one time (more than you'll typically need), Word puts the power of easy organization at your fingertips. In fact, perhaps the improvement of Word 5.5 over earlier versions is nowhere more apparent than with multiple windows. The ease with which you can open and manipulate windows is a source of convenience and even pleasure.

Although you can use the keyboard to gain access to the Window commands, you can perform almost every function related to using multiple windows more quickly and easily with a mouse: Simply reach out and do to the screen what you want done. You want to move a window? Grab the top border and slide it to wherever you want it—even if it's positioned mostly off the edge of the screen. You want to make a window smaller or larger? Grab its lower-right corner, and slide it until the window assumes the size and shape you want. You want to close a window? Simply click with the mouse pointer on the window close icon, the small rectangle (■) that appears in the upper-left corner of every Word window.

In summary form, here is what each of the Window commands permits you to do:

Window New Window—Opens a new window containing another copy of the existing document, allowing you to move between parts of a document or to see two pages simultaneously.

Window Arrange All—Arranges all windows, including the help window, so that none overlap.

Window Maximize—Expands the active window so that it takes up all of the screen (except the area consumed by such fixtures as the menu, status bar, and scroll bars). The maximize feature was called *zoom* in previous versions of Word.

Window Restore—Reverses the effect of the Window Maximize command, returning a maximized window to its previous size.

Window Move—Moves the active window around on the screen.

Window Size—Changes the size of the active window.

Window Split—Splits a window into two *panes,* each of which can be used independently to provide multiple views of a single document.

Window Close—Closes a window.

Window Filenames—At the end of the Window menu appear the names of open documents and style sheets. To make one of these active, simply choose it.

All Window commands are available in both style sheet windows and document windows. As a matter of fact, you can have multiple style sheet windows, just as you can have multiple document windows.

Another of the joys of the Window commands is their simplicity, as you'll see in the following descriptions.

WINDOW NEW WINDOW COMMAND

Use this command to open a second window containing the active document or style sheet. Or use it to open a third, fourth, or fifth window on the same file. If your original version of a document is JILLY.DOC, the second view of the same document will be labeled *JILLY.DOC:2,* the third will be *JILLY.DOC:4,* and so forth.

Though similar to the File Open command, the Window New Window command doesn't require you to specify the name of an existing file.

To execute the command, press Alt+WN.

WINDOW ARRANGE ALL COMMAND

Here's how a screen can look that has nine open windows, all in the positions given them by Word at the time they were opened. Note that the windows overlap.

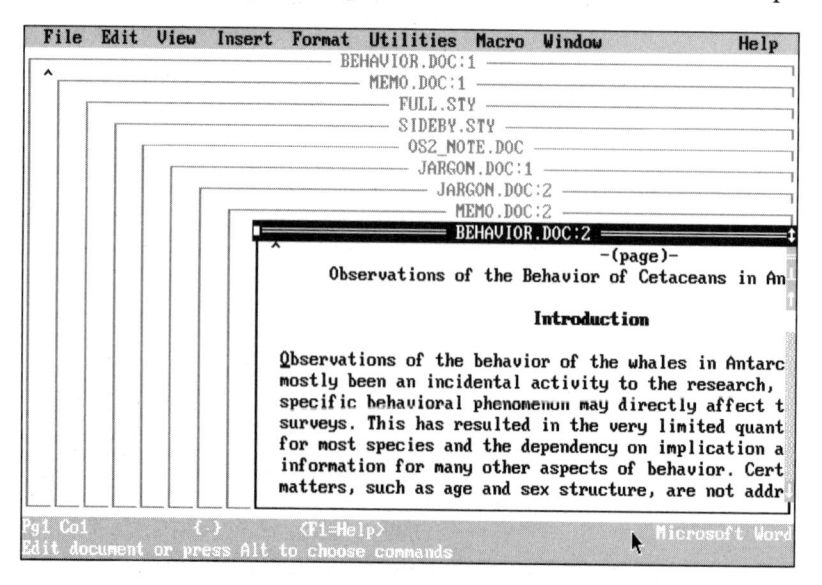

CHAPTER EIGHTEEN: Window Commands

Now look at the same screen after the Window Arrange All command has been used. It divides the screen into windows of roughly equal size and arranges them like tiles, so none overlap.

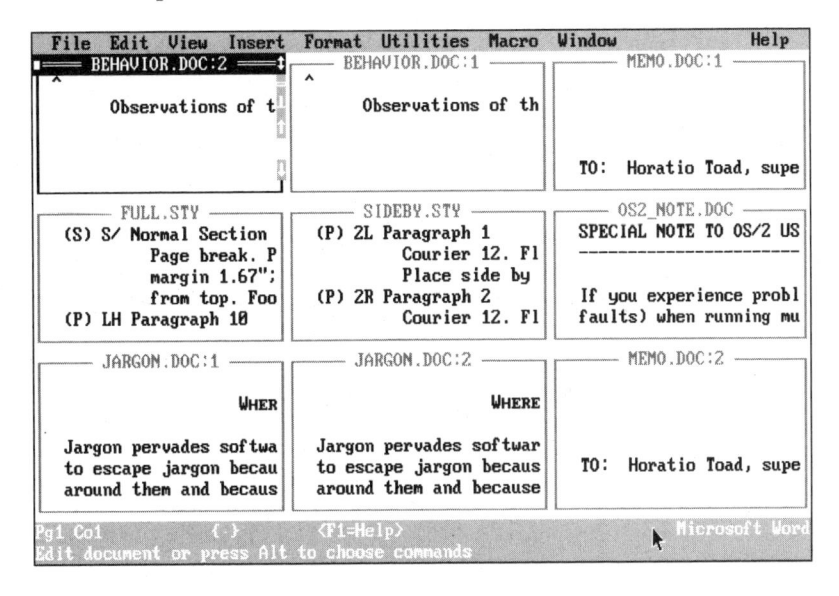

```
 File  Edit  View  Insert  Format  Utilities  Macro  Window              Help
├─── BEHAVIOR.DOC:2 ───┤├─── BEHAVIOR.DOC:1 ───┤├─── MEMO.DOC:1 ──────┤
│                       ││                       ││                      │
│   Observations of t   ││   Observations of th  ││                      │
│                       ││                       ││ TO:  Horatio Toad, supe│
├───── FULL.STY ───────┤├───── SIDEBY.STY ─────┤├──── OS2_NOTE.DOC ────┤
│(S) S/ Normal Section  ││(P) 2L Paragraph 1    ││SPECIAL NOTE TO OS/2 US│
│       Page break. P   ││       Courier 12. Fl ││─────────────────────│
│       margin 1.67";   ││       Place side by  ││                      │
│       from top. Foo   ││(P) 2R Paragraph 2    ││If you experience probl│
│(P) LH Paragraph 10    ││       Courier 12. Fl ││faults) when running mu│
├──── JARGON.DOC:1 ────┤├──── JARGON.DOC:2 ────┤├──── MEMO.DOC:2 ──────┤
│                       ││                       ││                      │
│          WHER         ││          WHERE        ││                      │
│                       ││                       ││                      │
│ Jargon pervades softwa││ Jargon pervades softwar││ TO:  Horatio Toad, supe│
│ to escape jargon becau││ to escape jargon becaus││                      │
│ around them and becaus││ around them and because││                      │
Pg1 Col            { }          <F1=Help>                    Microsoft Word
Edit document or press Alt to choose commands
```

This is a pretty extreme example, but it demonstrates the difference between Word's standard overlapping windows and the tiled windows provided by the Window Arrange All command.

To use the command, press Alt+WA.

WINDOW MAXIMIZE COMMAND

A maximized window looks like a normal Word window that is using all of the document portion of the screen.

But what makes a maximized window special is what you can't see—the one or more other windows hidden behind it, out of sight but quickly available. (To bring another window to the front, either press Ctrl+F6 or pick the name of a document or style sheet from the bottom of the Window menu.)

To maximize your windows so that one at a time consumes all available screen space, do one of three things:

- Hold down the Ctrl key and press F10.
- Choose the Window Maximize command (Alt+WX).
- Click the mouse on the maximize icon (↕) in the upper-right corner of the window.

You can use Window Maximize with Window Arrange All to control multiple windows. With several windows open, use the Window Arrange All command so that each window occupies the same amount of space as the others, and then use the

Window Maximize command on the window in which you want to work. To switch to a different window, use the Window Restore command, and then maximize a different window.

WINDOW RESTORE COMMAND

After maximizing your windows, you can use the Window Restore command to return each window to its previous size. To run the command, press Alt+WR or Ctrl+F5.

You can reduce the size of a maximized window without using the Window Restore command by resizing the window with the mouse or with the Window Size command.

The Window Restore command is gray and unavailable if windows are not maximized.

TIPS FOR MANAGING WINDOWS

Examine and experiment with the following approaches to window management. One (or more) of them might help you use available screen space to best advantage:

- Use multiple windows much as Word presents them to you—as large overlapping work spaces that can be shuffled so that the one you want comes to the top without causing others to go away.
- Maximize windows so that you always get a full work space.
- Resize windows freely, making the active window of ample size to suit your needs and keeping other windows close at hand for easy reference.
- Reformat documents temporarily so that they fit in smaller windows: Increase the margin size or decrease the page-width size, for example. Be sure to reformat the margins before you print the document.
- Get in the habit of opening temporary windows to meet specific needs. You can close a temporary window promptly when it's no longer needed.

Deliberately omitted from this list is *horizontal scrolling*, a method that permits you to read lines that are wider than the window. Even with the help of Word's horizontal scroll bar, horizontal

WINDOW MOVE COMMAND

To move a window, use the mouse to grab the title bar and slide the window to a desired position. If you don't have a mouse, the Window Move command is an admirable replacement: Simply choose the command (Alt+WM), and use the direction keys to slide the window around the screen as you want.

Only the upper-left corner of the window must remain within the confines of the screen.

WINDOW SIZE COMMAND

To alter the size of a window, you adjust the positions of its right and bottom edges without affecting the positions of its top and left edges.

To do this with the mouse, grab the lower-right corner of the window, and move it around without affecting the position of the opposite corner.

> scrolling is confusing compared to the preceding approaches because it forces you to shift the window's display back and forth to the right and left.
>
> With any of these techniques, including horizontal scrolling, you might obtain more satisfactory results by adjusting the Line Breaks field of the View Preferences command.
>
> You can also experiment with different display modes (25, 43, or 50 lines per screen in text or graphics mode) by changing the setting in the Display Mode field of the View Preferences command. Or, if you are working with side-by-side paragraphs or multiple-column documents, you can use the View Layout command. This will help eliminate unnecessary distraction, even though it does slow Word's performance somewhat.
>
> Don't overlook the organizational power of multiple windows. Temporary windows are effective for gathering and gradually organizing large amounts of information—a report written in sections, for example. Create a document for each major topic or section. At first, a document might consist of nothing more than a title and a few lines. Over time, and even as you write on other subjects, you can open temporary windows and type ideas, information, and passages into the appropriate documents. In the end, your thoughts and words will be waiting for you, sorted by topic.

To do this with the keyboard, choose the Window Size command (Alt+WS or Ctrl+F8), and press the direction keys. In this mode, the Up and Down direction keys affect the position of only the bottom border of the window, and the Left and Right direction keys affect only the position of the right window border.

Often you must use both the Window Move and Window Size commands to get a window positioned the way you want it on the screen.

WINDOW SPLIT COMMAND

Use the Window Split command to divide a window into two panes so that different parts of the same document can be displayed. For example, you might display a document in one pane and its outline in the other or display the top of a document in one pane and the middle or bottom in another. The new border created by the Window Split command runs from left to right, and the resulting working spaces are called panes rather than windows.

If you have a mouse, you can split a window into two panes by grabbing the window split icon (=) from above the vertical scroll bar and dragging it down to the desired position. To split the window evenly across the middle, simply point to the split icon and double-click. To close the split, double-click the split icon again.

If you don't have a mouse, or if you prefer the keyboard method, choose the Window Split command (Alt+WT), and use the Up and Down direction keys to move the split up and down along the left edge of the screen to where you want the border between the panes to appear. If you try to move the marker too far up or down for a valid window split, Word refuses to move the marker and might beep. When the split is properly positioned, press Enter.

To remove the split, use the Window Split command again. This time, move the split to either the very top or the very bottom of the window, and then press Enter.

Whether you use the keyboard or the mouse to split the window, try to get in the habit of working in the bottom pane rather than in the top one if the split is merely temporary. Word remembers the location of the cursor in the top window but not in the bottom one. Consequently, if you use the bottom pane to scroll to a new location and do some work, and then you close the bottom pane, your cursor will return to the precise location it had before you split the window. If you do your work in the upper pane instead, Word won't remember its presplit location.

WINDOW CLOSE COMMAND

The Window Close command closes the active window. Choose the command by pressing Alt+WC or Ctrl+F4.

If the window you are closing contains unsaved editing changes that will be lost when the window is closed, Word asks if you want to save changes to your document.

To close a window with the mouse, simply click on the close icon (the small square in the upper-left corner of the window).

CHAPTER EIGHTEEN: Window Commands

The Window Close command can be used interchangeably with the File Close command when the window being closed is the only window containing the document or style sheet. However, if the file is displayed simultaneously in more than one window, the File Close command will close all the windows containing the file, whereas the Window Close command will shut only the window that is active when the command is used.

WINDOW *DOCUMENT NAMES* COMMAND

Perhaps the most valuable feature of the Window menu really isn't a command at all. It is the list of numbered windows that appears at the bottom of the menu. Every open window, including the help window, is mentioned in the list.

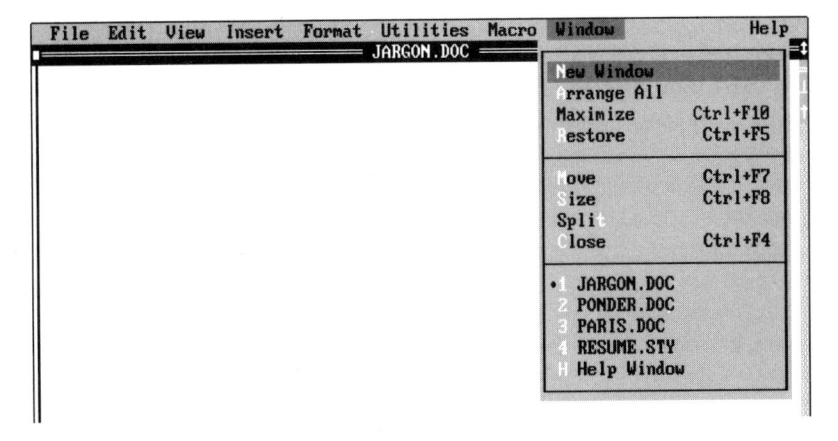

```
 File  Edit  View  Insert  Format  Utilities  Macro  Window          Help
═══════════════════════════════ JARGON.DOC ═══════════╔══════════════════╗
                                                      ║ New Window       ║
                                                      ║ Arrange All      ║
                                                      ║ Maximize  Ctrl+F10║
                                                      ║ Restore   Ctrl+F5 ║
                                                      ║                  ║
                                                      ║ Move      Ctrl+F7 ║
                                                      ║ Size      Ctrl+F8 ║
                                                      ║ Split            ║
                                                      ║ Close     Ctrl+F4 ║
                                                      ║                  ║
                                                      ║•1 JARGON.DOC     ║
                                                      ║ 2 PONDER.DOC     ║
                                                      ║ 3 PARIS.DOC      ║
                                                      ║ 4 RESUME.STY     ║
                                                      ║ H Help Window    ║
                                                      ╚══════════════════╝
```

To activate one of the windows, you either choose its name with the mouse or press its number with the keyboard. If you want to activate the help window (assuming it is open), you press Alt+WH—Alt+W activates the Window menu, and H chooses the help window from the list.

CHAPTER NINETEEN

Help Commands

When you need a fast answer or a quick reminder while working with Word, turn to online help. You can reach help by pressing the F1 key, by clicking with the mouse on the <F1=Help> button on the status bar at the bottom of the screen, or by using the Help menu.

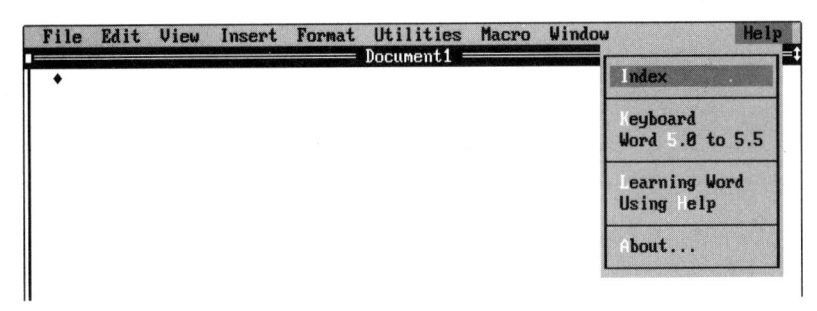

You use the Help menu as a jumping-off point for excursions into the help screens:

Help Index—Provides a simple table of contents that outlines in broad terms the kind of on-screen help that is available.

Help Keyboard—Offers help on the purposes and uses of keys and key combinations.

Help Word 5.0 to 5.5—Tables show Word 5.0 commands and keystrokes and Word 5.5 equivalents. Handy for people familiar with Word 5.0.

Help Learning Word—A gateway to an interactive tutorial in using certain aspects of Word.

Help Using Help—Help with the online help.

Help About—Shows Word's version number, Microsoft's copyright notice, and both the serial number and the identity of the person or company to whom the particular copy of the program is licensed.

If you need assistance with a specific command or command field, don't use the Help command right away. First use the menu to highlight the command or dialog box about which you're seeking information; then, without executing the command, ask for help by pressing F1 or by placing the mouse pointer on the <F1=Help> button in the bottom line of the screen and clicking either mouse button. When used this way, the help feature is *context sensitive*: Word senses the context in which you're working and tries to oblige you.

If you are familiar with the on-screen help Microsoft has supplied in the past with Word, you will find that for Word 5.5 Microsoft improved this on-screen information in two distinct ways:

- Help for Word 5.5 is more than twice as large as in Word 5.0, and it is organized more thoughtfully. The increased information comes at a price, however, because Microsoft eliminated one of the three printed manuals that came with earlier versions of Word. Gone is the reference manual that listed information command by command and described each of Word's messages. Now much of this information is presented in somewhat different form—on screen.
- The Help command in Word 5.5 is dramatically enhanced and now permits resizable windows and hypertext cross-references. The resizable window lets you keep the help window open in one part of your screen while you work in another. The hypertext feature lets you jump between related topics by choosing a button on the screen.

Both of these improvements are reflected in the help index, which you can reach by choosing Help Index:

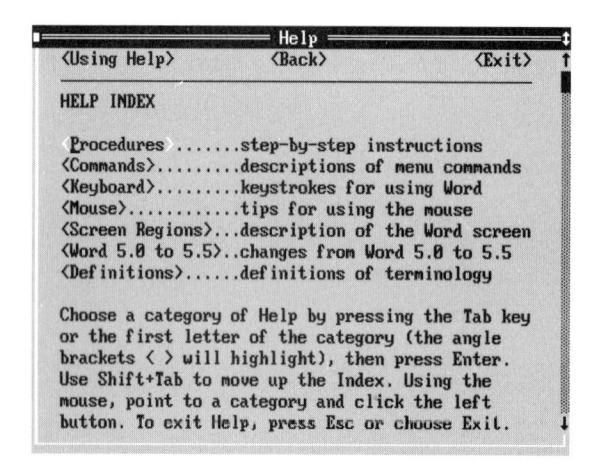

```
═══════════════════════════ Help ═══════════════════════════
 <Using Help>        <Back>                      <Exit>

HELP INDEX

   <Procedures>.......step-by-step instructions
   <Commands>.........descriptions of menu commands
   <Keyboard>.........keystrokes for using Word
   <Mouse>............tips for using the mouse
   <Screen Regions>...description of the Word screen
   <Word 5.0 to 5.5>..changes from Word 5.0 to 5.5
   <Definitions>......definitions of terminology

   Choose a category of Help by pressing the Tab key
   or the first letter of the category (the angle
   brackets < > will highlight), then press Enter.
   Use Shift+Tab to move up the Index. Using the
   mouse, point to a category and click the left
   button. To exit Help, press Esc or choose Exit.
```

As already noted, the help index is not an index. In some ways, it is really an extension of the Help menu, duplicating several choices from the menu and adding five others. The additions are as follows:

Procedures An alphabetic list of 115 topics, each of which leads either to a short menu of additional procedures or to specific instructions for performing a task. When choosing a procedure takes you to a menu of additional procedures, each of those leads to step-by-step instructions. Each set of instructions is typically cross-referenced to a specific command.

Commands A description of each command reached through a menu. The commands are presented as a long list, in the same order as they appear on the menus. Each command cross-references a related procedure.

Mouse A collection of seven short tables that provide guidelines to mouse users. For example, if you choose the Mouse Shortcuts table, you learn that to bring the Format Section dialog box to the screen, you can double-click the left mouse button when the mouse pointer is on a section mark.

Screen Regions A visual representation of the screen, with each major region cross-referenced to a short discussion. The buttons are hidden on this screen; almost everything is a button, however. Simply point to the screen element that interests you and press Enter, or press the Tab key until that element is highlighted and then press Enter to move to a screen that describes the element.

Definitions A glossary of terms, with definitions that appear in small windows. Unfortunately, you cannot jump from these definitions to the related procedures or commands.

THREE TYPES OF HELP

Microsoft's online help takes three forms, depending on your location when you request help:

- Help windows
- Dialog box help
- Message help

Help Windows

If you request help while working in a document or style-sheet window or when you have a menu item highlighted, you are taken to a *help window*. Help windows are scrollable and sizable, and you can browse through their contents or freely change their size.

Dialog Box Help

If you request help when you are in a dialog box, you are taken to another dialog box, one that contains brief information relating to the dialog box with which you are seeking assistance.

Here is what the dialog box help for the Edit Search command looks like:

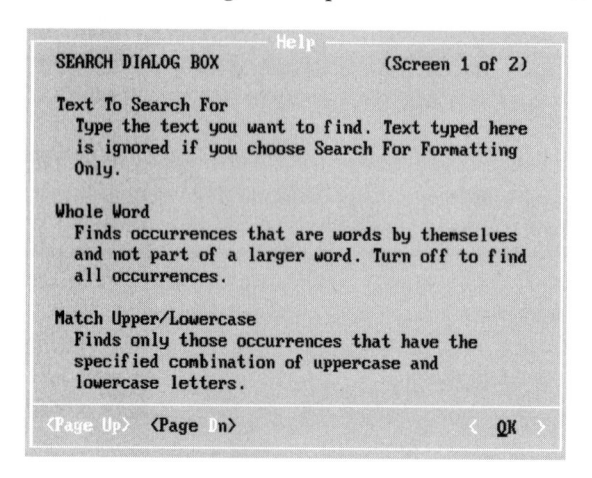

```
┌─────────────────────── Help ───────────────────────┐
│ SEARCH DIALOG BOX              (Screen 1 of 2)     │
│                                                    │
│ Text To Search For                                 │
│   Type the text you want to find. Text typed here  │
│   is ignored if you choose Search For Formatting   │
│   Only.                                            │
│                                                    │
│ Whole Word                                         │
│   Finds occurrences that are words by themselves   │
│   and not part of a larger word. Turn off to find  │
│   all occurrences.                                 │
│                                                    │
│ Match Upper/Lowercase                              │
│   Finds only those occurrences that have the       │
│   specified combination of uppercase and           │
│   lowercase letters.                               │
│                                                    │
│ <Page Up>  <Page Dn>                    <  OK  >   │
└────────────────────────────────────────────────────┘
```

To see a second screen of help, choose the PgDn button.

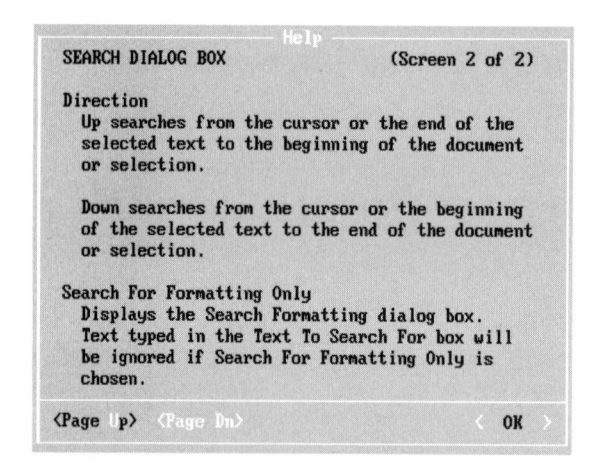

```
┌─────────────────────── Help ───────────────────────┐
│ SEARCH DIALOG BOX              (Screen 2 of 2)     │
│                                                    │
│ Direction                                          │
│   Up searches from the cursor or the end of the    │
│   selected text to the beginning of the document   │
│   or selection.                                    │
│                                                    │
│   Down searches from the cursor or the beginning   │
│   of the selected text to the end of the document  │
│   or selection.                                    │
│                                                    │
│ Search For Formatting Only                         │
│   Displays the Search Formatting dialog box.       │
│   Text typed in the Text To Search For box will    │
│   be ignored if Search For Formatting Only is      │
│   chosen.                                          │
│                                                    │
│ <Page Up>  <Page Dn>                    <  OK  >   │
└────────────────────────────────────────────────────┘
```

To return to the previous screen, choose the PgUp button.

Message Help

If you request help when a message is displayed on the screen, you'll see an explanation of the message and a suggested course of action.

For example, if you try to quit Word or close a window when a document has unsaved editing changes, a message appears.

CHAPTER NINETEEN: Help Commands

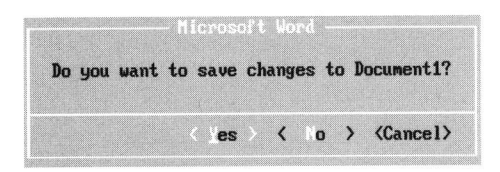

> **Microsoft Word**
> Do you want to save changes to Document1?
> < Yes >   < No >   <Cancel>

Press F1 while the message is displayed, and you get an explanation:

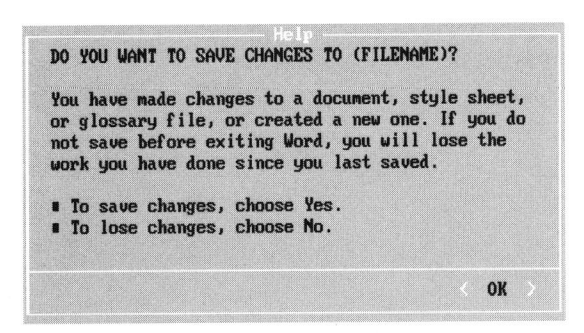

> **Help**
> DO YOU WANT TO SAVE CHANGES TO (FILENAME)?
>
> You have made changes to a document, style sheet, or glossary file, or created a new one. If you do not save before exiting Word, you will lose the work you have done since you last saved.
>
> ■ To save changes, choose Yes.
> ■ To lose changes, choose No.
>
> < OK >

When you are done viewing the explanation, choose OK (Enter).

MESSAGES YOU MIGHT ENCOUNTER

You might encounter the following messages while using help:

No Help is available on this topic. You should not encounter this message when using Microsoft's help, although there is no cause for alarm if you do. The message means you have chosen a button that does not lead anywhere. This might be due to a problem with Word or an omission on the part of the person who wrote the help. If you are using MasterWord Help (an alternative help system described briefly later in the chapter), this message means you have requested help on a topic but during installation of MasterWord chose not to include the topic in the help file. (MasterWord Help allows you to choose the size of your help file by excluding topics of no interest you.)

There are no more Help topics in the backtrack list. You have pressed the Backspace key or chosen the Back button to retrace your path through the cross-referenced help screens, but Word cannot take you back any farther. This typically means one of two things: Either you have returned to the first help screen you viewed during the current editing session or you have already backtracked through 20 screens, which is the limit of Word's memory.

The Help file was not found. Insert the disk containing MW.HLP. Word is unable to find the MW.HLP file, which is where Word gets the information it supplies as on-screen help. If you are using Word on a computer with a hard disk, Word should be able to find MW.HLP without any trouble. If you set up Word to run on a floppy-disk system, however, Word's Setup program might have copied your help (and possibly hyphenation) files to a data disk instead of to the Word Program disk. If you see this message, either insert the disk containing MW.HLP into the disk drive and choose Retry, or press the Esc key to cancel your request for help.

SUMMARY OF KEYSTROKES

Press:	To move to the:
A letter	Button beginning with the letter
A number	Button beginning with the number
Tab	Next button in help screen
Shift+Tab	Previous button in help screen
Backspace	Previous help screen
Esc	Exit

MASTERWORD HELP

MasterWord Help, an alternative to the original Microsoft help file, works hand-in-hand with this book. It is part of a collection of utilities, macros, style sheets, and other resources for Word 5.0 and 5.5.

MasterWord's installation program lets you choose one of three versions of online help:

- **Compact**—A 720-KB help file for people with limited hard-disk space or who use laptops or other computers with only high-capacity floppy disks.
- **Standard**—A 1-MB help file containing complete information on Word and MasterWord. Includes hundreds of ACT buttons, which, when selected, cause Word to perform tasks.
- **Expanded**—A 1.4-MB help file that contains all of the Standard help plus help on such related topics as using a printer, using DOS, researching in a library, and writing and formatting common business documents.

The ACT buttons are unique to MasterWord and allow you to carry out a task with a single keystroke. Here is a partial list of ACT buttons:

```
═══════════ MASTERWORD HELP: MULTIPLE COLUMNS ═══════════
      <1=Index> <2=Tree> <3=Back> <4=Xref> <5=Exit>  <?>

ACT Buttons for Multiple Columns        ▶ Acts on... ◀

Press      To create this multi-column formatting
▶ .01 ◀  =  1 column
▶ .02 ◀  =  2 columns, .25" space between columns
▶ .03 ◀  =  2 columns, .33" space between columns
▶ .04 ◀  =  2 columns, .50" space between columns
▶ .05 ◀  =  2 columns, .75" space between columns
▶ .06 ◀  =  2 columns, 1.0" space between columns
▶ .07 ◀  =  3 columns, .20" space between columns
▶ .08 ◀  =  3 columns, .33" space between columns
▶ .09 ◀  =  3 columns, .50" space between columns
▶ .10 ◀  =  3 columns, .75" space between columns
▶ .11 ◀  =  3 columns, 1.0" space between columns
▶ .12 ◀  =  4 columns, .20" space between columns
```

CHAPTER NINETEEN: Help Commands

The buttons are on the left; each begins with a period, so you can press the period key to move from one ACT button to another. To the right of each ACT button is a phrase that describes what the ACT button does.

In order for the ACT buttons to work, a small collection of macros must be present in the glossary. Each of these macros includes the word *ACT* in its name.

The dialog box help in MasterWord is linked to the main help system. If you find the initial dialog box help to be inadequate, press Shift+F1 to move to the appropriate part of the main help system.

The message help is enhanced, too, with multiscreen discussions of many messages. In addition, you can look up messages in an alphabetic index or see a list of the messages pertaining to each command. This lets you see the same explanatory text you would see if you encountered the message and pressed the F1 key.

All of the keystrokes listed in the summary of keystrokes earlier in this chapter also apply to MasterWord Help. But in addition, you can do the following:

Press:	When you are in MasterWord Help and you want:
<1=Index>	Alphabetic Topic Index
<2=Tree>	Tree of Contents
<3=Back>	Previous help screen
<4=XRef>	A cross-reference screen
<4=Top>	Top of the Tree of Contents
<4=Next>	Next help screen on related topic
<4=More>	More help on the topic
<4=ACTs>	Screen of appropriate ACT buttons
<5=Exit>	To put help window into background
.(period)	Next ACT button (then press Enter to run it)
Shift+F1	To get additional help on a dialog box topic when used in a dialog box. To return to the most recently used help screen when used in a document.

PART III
Mastering

CHAPTER TWENTY

Speed

An accomplished writer I know organizes her manuscripts and magazine articles on toilet paper. White is her favorite color, and inexpensive brands are best because they're not too soft.

When she finishes her research and is ready to put her thoughts and notes in order, she opens a fresh roll of paper and feeds the loose end into her typewriter. Bang, bang, bang—the ideas are pounded out, one to a square. She tears them apart and deals them like cards into piles around the floor. Observations or quotations of similar "suit" are stacked together, possibly off to her left. An intriguing sequence of events might be laid down, like a triumphant poker hand, to her right. Over and over, she shuffles the tissues until she's stacked a winning deck. Only then, when her resources and ideas are lined up from beginning to end, does she begin to write.

More commonly, writers use index cards. Another method is "cut and paste," in which the elements of a document are written in sections, cut apart, rearranged in some new and pleasing order, and pasted or taped back together to form a draft. Whatever the technique, the goals are the same: to work quickly and efficiently.

Computers haven't made paper outlines, index cards, and other conventional writing tools obsolete, any more than typewriters made pencils obsolete. But, like the typewriter, the computer has supplemented the writer's tools in powerful ways. Word's glossary feature, its outlining feature, even its bookmark feature can be used as a fast, modern adaptation of the cut-and-paste technique; you can electronically shuffle dozens of elements in an article or a manuscript without scissors, paste, or tape.

This chapter is the first of 12 on mastering Microsoft Word. In these chapters, you'll find tips that give you finer control of the Microsoft Mouse. You'll explore Word's cross-referencing feature. You'll learn how to use Word's glossary and its Edit Search and Edit Replace commands in powerful ways.

You'll expand your knowledge of macros, and you'll learn how to use special instructions to write macros that can ask you for information and make independent decisions. You'll be introduced to the subtleties of Word's File Print Merge command—including step-by-step instructions on using five popular database and filing programs to create mailing lists that Word can use for personalized form letters and other documents.

You'll learn how to create and modify Word's style sheets. You'll discover how to use Word's outlining feature to organize documents and how to compile indexes and tables of contents. You'll find out how to set up tables and manipulate columns. Finally, you'll see how Word can satisfy everyday desktop publishing needs with its layout and graphics powers and its abilities with printers and downloadable fonts.

From here on, it's presumed you understand the fundamentals of Word and are ready for hints, tips, and strategies. To use an automobile analogy: By now you know how to operate a car and are prepared for suggestions on ways to sharpen your driving skills. We begin at the racetrack, with tips on speed.

Tip #1: Returning to the Previous Help Screen

Even if you've closed your help window, you can return to the last help screen you were reading. Simply press F1 to activate the help screen. Then press Backspace. You can press them almost, but not quite, simultaneously.

This can be quite a timesaver, but it doesn't work if you have exited Word or used the File DOS Commands command (or File OS/2 Commands command) since you last used Help.

Tip #2: Returning to the Last Editing Location

Sometimes you might want to return to the place in a document where you were last adding text or editing. For example, suppose you accidentally select a paragraph and want to return the cursor to where it was before, or suppose you change your mind while quitting Word and decide that you want the selection to resume its previous size and location.

To return to the last place at which you changed content, use the Edit Undo command (Alt+EU) twice in a row, and then press the Right direction key. This will shrink the selection to a single character, positioned immediately after your last insertion or edit of text.

Tip #3: Returning to the Beginning of an Insertion

When you insert a passage with the Edit Paste command, with the Insert File command, or by pressing Shift+Ins, the action finishes with the cursor positioned on the first character following the insertion. To return the cursor to the beginning of the insertion, first use the Edit Undo command twice in a row, as described in Tip #2.

The text you inserted will be selected. Simply type, and the cursor will appear at the beginning of the selected text.

Tip #4: Selecting Single-Sentence Paragraphs

The Alt+F8 key combination selects a sentence; the Alt+F10 key combination selects a paragraph. The distinction is unmistakable—until you select a single-sentence paragraph. At first glance, either operation appears to highlight the sentence/paragraph. But Alt+F10 also selects the paragraph mark at the end. (A similar thing happens if you press the F8 key several times in a paragraph that has only one sentence. After pressing F8 three times you might find that the sentence—but not its paragraph mark—is selected. The next time you press F8, the paragraph mark is added to the selection.) Although the difference might not be obvious, the effects of the difference can be the following:

- Suppose you delete the selection. The whole paragraph disappears if the paragraph mark as well as the sentence is selected, but the paragraph and its formatting remain—though without any text—if the mark is not deleted.
- Suppose you apply character formatting to the selected text. If only the sentence is selected, the character formatting is limited to the visible characters and the spaces between them. But if the entire paragraph is selected, the entire paragraph is formatted, including its paragraph mark. In the latter case, any new writing at the location of the mark—or in a new paragraph formed by pressing the Enter key at the end of the existing paragraph—will have the same character formatting.

Tip #5: Moving Two Passages at the Same Time

To move two unconnected passages at the same time, follow these steps:

1. Copy one of the passages to the glossary, giving it a name (nothing fancy—any unused character or two will do).
2. Now that the passage is stored in the glossary, delete it from the document.
3. Delete the other passage to the scrap.
4. Scroll to the destination for the passage in the scrap, and insert it by pressing Shift+Ins.
5. Scroll to the destination for the passage in the glossary, and insert it by typing its name and pressing the F3 key or by using the Insert command button in the Edit Glossary command's dialog box.

An alternative method uses the mouse:

1. Delete the first passage to the scrap; select the second passage.
2. If necessary, use the mouse in the scroll bar to scroll the document to the destination you intend for the selected passage. Use the mouse to scroll, not the keyboard, so that the scrap passage you intend to move remains selected.

3. Position the mouse pointer where you want to insert the selected passage; hold down the Ctrl key, and click the right mouse button to complete the move.
4. Move the highlight to the new location for the text in the scrap, and insert it.

NOTE: *MasterWord includes a macro called "Move Many" that permits you to move any number of passages from one location to another. If you want to move three passages to different locations, it prompts you to select each passage and then asks you to identify the destination for each.*

Tip #6: One-Step Text Copying with the Mouse

People often overlook using the mouse as a means of copying or moving text from one place to another, particularly from one window to another. Using the mouse is faster than using the scrap or the glossary. This technique also has the advantage of being a single-step editing process, so the Edit Undo command can operate on an entire text movement. Follow these steps:

1. Select the text to be moved or copied.
2. Scroll to the location at which you want the text to appear. Use the mouse and scroll bar so that the selection remains in the location specified in step 1.
3. Move the mouse pointer to the exact destination for the selected text.
4. Hold down the Shift and Ctrl keys, and click the right mouse button. The selected text will be copied.

If you accidentally move the selection to a different window before completing the move, press Alt+Backspace to undo the action. This restores the selection to the previous window.

Tip #7: Keys That Change Case

Have you ever typed something—a heading, a caption, a person's rank or title—only to retype it with different capitalization? Word lets you use the Shift+F3 key combination while editing a document to change the case of selected text. When you press Shift+F3, either once or repeatedly, Word cycles through the following types of capitalization: from lowercase (*major general*), to all capitals (*MAJOR GENERAL*), to first letters capitalized (*Major General*). Thus, if you begin with lowercase, pressing Shift+F3 changes the text to all capitals; pressing Shift+F3 again changes the text to initial capitals. Pressing Shift+F3 twice when the selected text consists of uppercase and lowercase changes the words to lowercase and then to all capitals.

Changing capitalization with Shift+F3 is equivalent to doing so with the Caps Lock key or the Shift key. You can also add or change character formatting, including hidden text, with a style sheet or with the Format Character command.

When you use Shift+F3 to change selected text to initial capitals, remember that Word capitalizes the first letter of *every* word you selected, including *a*, *and*, and *the* and short prepositions, such as *with* and *in*. Because headings and titles often use lowercase for such words, you might need to edit the results.

When the cursor is in a word somewhere but no text is selected, the Shift+F3 key combination causes capitalization to occur as if the entire word were selected.

Tip #8: Formatting a New Paragraph

To create a new paragraph that matches the formatting of a neighboring paragraph, create the new paragraph from the old one, exactly as Word does when you press the Enter key while creating a new document. Use the View Preferences command to make nonprinting characters (including paragraph marks) visible. Then take one of the following two actions:

- Place the cursor on the first character of the existing paragraph, press the Enter key, and then press the Up direction key. This creates a new, similarly formatted paragraph that precedes the existing one.
- Or place the cursor on the paragraph mark at the end of the existing paragraph, and then press the Enter key. This creates a new, similarly formatted paragraph that follows the existing one.

Keep these techniques in mind when you add a paragraph between two existing paragraphs that have different formatting. Choose which paragraph you want the new one to match, and press the Enter key when the cursor is on either its first character or its paragraph mark.

Tip #9: Adding Characters to a Formatted Zone

When adding new characters to the very end of a string of characters that are underlined or otherwise formatted, decide whether you want the new characters to have the same formatting as the existing ones. If you do, position the cursor on the last formatted character, retype it, and then continue typing. Conclude by deleting the character you retyped. If you don't want new characters to be formatted like the others, begin typing at the first space following the formatted characters.

Tip #10: Copying Formatting with the Keyboard

The most powerful way to copy and reapply formatting is by using the Format Record Style command. For temporary use in a single document, all you need do is choose the command; assign the formatting any one-letter or two-letter key code that strikes your fancy; tell Word whether you want to copy character, paragraph, or section formatting; and then let Word worry about choosing and proposing an available variant number.

If you don't use style sheets, you can use the keyboard to copy character, paragraph, or section formatting from one location to another without copying content. You can even copy formatting from one document to another, using several windows. These are the steps:

1. Select some text that is formatted in the desired way. This text can be a single character with the character formatting you want, or it can be part of a paragraph or division that is formatted the way you want.
2. Choose the appropriate Format command and, without making any changes in its command fields, press the Enter key to carry it out. For example, if you want to copy character formatting, choose Format Character and press Enter.
3. Before doing any other editing, select the character(s), paragraph(s), or section(s) you want to format to match the sample. If the text to be formatted is a paragraph or a section, remember that you needn't select all of it.
4. Press the F4 key, which repeats the last editing act. Word applies the formatting from the sample to the selected text.

Tip #11: Monitoring Progress with a Spreadsheet

To track the total number of pages in a manuscript or report, consider using a spreadsheet program. Cells can show the chapter's number of words or illustrations or the projected number of pages (calculated by dividing the number of words by the estimated number of words per page). It can calculate, on an ongoing basis, your total number of words or pages and how close you are to completion.

Recall, too, that you can incorporate the output of a spreadsheet into a Word document with the Insert File command. This is useful if you want to show a table of numbers or if you want to include data from your spreadsheet without retyping it.

Tip #12: Dedicating Your Computer to Word

You can set up your Word disk or hard disk so that whenever you start or reboot your computer, Word starts too. You do this with a special kind of batch file, called *AUTOEXEC.BAT*, that runs whenever your computer is started. For details on *AUTOEXEC.BAT*, see your DOS manual.

If you make *word* the last line in the AUTOEXEC.BAT file, Word will start automatically. If you make the line *word /l*, Word will load the document you were working on when you last quit Word.

Tip #13: The Extended Character Set

You can access any of about 250 characters, including mathematical symbols, foreign letters, and graphics symbols, by turning on your keyboard's NumLock key and then holding down the Alt key and typing on the calculator-style numeric keypad the number of the ASCII character you want.

CHAPTER TWENTY: Speed

You'll find a complete list of ASCII characters in your Word manuals. Here are a few of the more interesting characters and their numbers:

Code	Character	Code	Character	Code	Character	Code	Character
0	(null)	35	#	153	ö	189	╝
1	☺	36	$	154	Ü	190	╜
2	☻	37	%	155	¢	191	┐
3	♥	38	&	156	£	192	└
4	♦	39	'	157	¥	193	┴
5	♣	40	(	158	₧	194	┬
6	♠	41	)	159	ƒ	195	├
7	•	42	*	160	á	196	─
8	◘	43	+	161	í	197	┼
9	(tab)	44	,	162	ó	198	╞
10	(reserved)	128	Ç	163	ú	199	╟
11	(reserved)	129	ü	164	ñ	200	╚
12	(reserved)	130	é	165	Ñ	201	╔
13	(reserved)	131	â	166	ª	202	╩
14	(reserved)	132	ä	167	º	203	╦
15	☼	133	à	168	¿	204	╠
16	►	134	å	169	⌐	205	═
17	◄	135	ç	170	¬	206	╬
18	↕	136	ê	171	½	207	╧
19	‼	137	ë	172	¼	208	╨
20	¶	138	è	173	¡	209	╤
21	§	139	ï	174	«	210	╥
22	▬	140	î	175	»	211	╙
23	↨	141	ì	176	░	212	╘
24	↑	142	Ä	178	▓	213	╒
25	↓	143	Å	179	│	214	╓
26	→	144	É	180	┤	215	╫
27	←	145	æ	181	╡	216	╪
28	∟	146	Æ	182	╢	217	┘
29	↔	147	ô	183	╖	218	┌
30	▲	148	ö	184	╕	219	█
31	(reserved)	149	ò	185	╣	220	▄
32	<space>	150	û	186	║	221	▌
33	!	151	ù	187	╗	222	▐
34	"	152	ÿ	188	╝	223	▀

Tip #14: Don't Ignore Your Brain

Writing with Word and a computer permits you to dash off ideas, store them in computer memory or on disk, shuffle them around in new combinations, and print them in various forms. It's a wonderful augmentation of human creativity and capacity. But it can breed lazy mental habits because it's easy to write before you think and then use the computer to manipulate and revise endlessly. The final product might be good, even very good; but trying out myriad ideas on the screen can take longer than thinking through what you want to say ahead of time. A partial analogy can be found in the pocket calculator, which has reduced some people's ability to manipulate numbers mentally. Do you reach for a calculator to add 213 and 127?

If you find that your written product bears little resemblance to your first draft and that it takes a long time for your ideas to evolve on the screen, you might be relying too heavily on the computer as a writing crutch. Take full advantage of your computer's speed and Word's flexibility, but don't ignore the power of your mind.

CHAPTER TWENTY-ONE

Navigation Aids

If you had all the time in the world, you might not mind searching through a document to locate a desired word, phrase, or topic. If you wanted to find a particular passage but the passage didn't seem to want to be found, you wouldn't grumble. You'd simply keep at it, happily, seeking the elusive words.

Of course, if you had all the time in the world you probably wouldn't be using Word in the first place, because efficiency is Word's raison d'être. No, most likely you are short on time rather than willing to waste it; and so, most likely, you'll want to know about some powerful Word features that sift through a document for you, locate desired elements, and—at your option—make changes. These features let you search for text, basing your search on either its content or its formatting, and replace it if you so desire; they let you label a passage with a name of your choice and then return to that passage merely by asking for it by name. Specifically, these are tasks you can accomplish with the Edit Search and Edit Replace commands and with the combination of the Insert Bookmark and Edit Go To commands.

You're not the only one who might want to skip around in what you have written. Your reader, too, might want to jump from place to place, and (depending on the nature of your topic) you might want to help him or her do it. For this, you can add cross-references to other passages or to tables, figures, or lists. Word will help you mightily by numbering items for you and by updating the numbers and the references to those numbers as you make changes in your document.

For instance, you can include in your document a sentence that says *See Table X on page XX*, and Word will number the table and include the correct page number. If you delete tables, move text to new pages, or even simply repaginate your document, Word will track all the changing page numbers and update the cross-references accordingly.

This chapter describes ways to find your way through the wilderness of words that can sometimes mask the overall shape of a document. You'll see ways to map the terrain as you go and leave markers to show the way for others.

FINDING, MARKING, AND CHANGING TEXT

The Edit Search and Edit Replace commands become familiar aids soon after you begin to use Word. When you want to search a document for a particular word or set of words, you use the Edit Search command. If case or whole words are important, you tell Word so by setting fields of the command. And if the first occurrence Word finds is not the one you seek, you press Shift+F4 to search for the next occurrence. Similarly, you use the Edit Replace command both to find specific text and to replace it with something else. With either command, you don't need to scan the document because Word does it for you.

This chapter assumes you know the basics of these commands, including the use of special ^ characters described in Chapter 12. You also might want to reacquaint yourself with the way the Edit Replace command is used with the Utilities Hyphenate command, as discussed in Chapter 16.

The Edit Search Command

For finding a word or a phrase somewhere in a document, the Edit Search command is your obvious choice. To locate the section on diesel engines in an article about automobiles, for example, you might search for the word *diesel*.

To begin, the following are some tips about using the Edit Search command:

- Move the cursor to the top of the document so that Word will search the entire article. Or move the cursor to the end of the document, and choose the Up option button in the Direction field.
- Consider saving your place in a document by using the Window New Window command and then conducting your search in the new window. When you're done, close the new window and resume your work in the original window. Your cursor will be undisturbed.
- Or save your place in a document by splitting its window and searching or otherwise working in the *lower* of the resulting two panes. You can split the window with the Window Split command, or you can use the mouse to pull down the split icon from the top of the right window border. You want to work in the lower rather than the upper pane because the exact location of your cursor is remembered only in the upper pane. If you search in the upper pane, the original location of your cursor will be lost, but Word will retain its approximate location in the lower pane.
- Hold down the Shift key and press the F4 key to re-execute the Edit Search command if you need to find another occurrence of the same text.

Suppose you're in the midst of editing a document and need to check on a dollar value included in an earlier table. The Edit Search command provides a fast way to skip backward from table to table until you find the entry you need. Set the direction field to Up to cause Word to search backward from your current position in the document. Type *Table* in the Text to Search For field, and execute the command. Word will find and select the last instance in which you used the word, allowing you to see or quickly scroll to the entries under it. If that table is not the one you need, press Shift+F4 and try again until you find the information you seek. Again, you might want to preserve your location in the document by conducting the search in a separate window or a separate pane or by typing a few unique characters to act as placeholders.

Extending the selection

The Edit Search command also lets you extend the selection to include all text between your current location and that of a particular word or phrase. Suppose that, in the automobile article mentioned earlier, you want to delete all text between the present location of the selection and the word *diesel*. Press the F8 key to turn on Extend Selection mode, and then search for the word *diesel*. Word moves to the next occurrence of the word, at the same time selecting all text between its former and new positions. Now press the Del key, and Word removes the selection.

Place markers

The Insert Bookmark command, discussed later in this chapter, provides an excellent means of placing a *bookmark,* a kind of place marker, in a document. However, sometimes you might prefer to simply type a marker consisting of plain text and then use the Edit Search command to return to it later.

In its simplest form, a place marker can be formed from any character or collection of characters unique to a document. Candidates include @, #, $, ;, &, *, +, =, and other symbols, especially in unique combinations.

After you've set a place marker, you can scroll freely through your text. When you're ready to return to your original location, choose Edit Search and type your place marker in the Text to Search For field. Choose the appropriate direction for the search and choose OK (press Enter).

When you execute the Edit Search command, Word moves to the place marker and selects it. Because it is selected, you can remove it immediately by pressing the Del key.

You can use this procedure to place more than one marker in a document. If all the markers are identical, execute the Edit Search command until you reach the marker you want. If the markers are different, you can return to any of them selectively. And you can have the best of both worlds by creating markers that are identical except for one character. For example, *1* could be your first marker, *2* your second, *3* your third, and so on. To find marker number 2, search for *2*. To find any or all markers, search for *?*.

Before printing, you'll probably want to remove all place markers you created in this way. The fastest method is to use the Edit Replace command, replacing *?* with nothing (by leaving the Replace With field blank). If you prefer one last look at each marked passage before removing the markers, leave the Confirm check box turned on, and then choose Yes or No as Word prompts you to confirm each replacement.

Using Edit Search as Edit Replace

The Edit Search command, when used in conjunction with the F3 key and the Shift+F4 key combination, can be used as a slower, but in some cases more powerful, version of the Edit Replace command. It is more powerful because the replacement text inserted from the glossary can have previously assigned character or other formatting.

Similarly, you can search for the first instance of text with the Edit Search command and then delete it and type in the replacement text. If you format this replacement text, do so before you type it. For example, apply the underlining format and then type the text rather than typing the text and then going back and underlining it. The advantage to formatting first is that you can search for subsequent instances of the text by pressing Shift+F4 and then carry out each replacement by pressing F4—the key that repeats the last editing act. The replacement text will be formatted appropriately.

The Edit Replace Command

You're a novelist and you want to change the name of the protagonist throughout your book. The Edit Replace command will do it for you. Type the old name in the Text to Search For field, type the new name in the Replace With field, and execute the command. Or you're an attorney and you've decided to ask for $1 million in damages instead of $12,000. Update your documents by typing the old figure in the Text to Search For field and the new figure in the Replace With field.

The Edit Replace command uses computer memory, so you might find the *SAVE* indicator coming on after you make an appreciable number of replacements. Saving the document after using the Edit Replace command is a good habit, although it's unnecessary when the command makes only a handful of replacements. If you attempt too many replacements at one time, Word will warn you that it has insufficient memory and will complete only the portion of the replacements that it can. Save the document immediately, and then execute the Edit Replace command again to make the remaining replacements. As a practical matter, after you run out of memory, you can do little but save the document.

Changing content for formatting purposes

Sometimes you must change the content of a document so that it will work ideally with Word or another program. Often this means changing some or all of the spacing characters in the document. For example, perhaps a document created with a different word processor or by a less experienced user of Word has paragraph indentations that were formed by typing spaces manually. Or perhaps you've aligned the columns in a table by pressing the Spacebar instead of using tab stops, so you need to substitute one tab character for a large number of Spacebar spaces. Sometimes spacing characters of various kinds—including both paragraph marks and tabs—must be removed. Usually, the Edit Replace command can accomplish what you want, although you might need to be creative.

Eliminating extra paragraph marks

If you want to remove an extra paragraph mark from between paragraphs throughout a document, use the Replace command to change each instance of two successive paragraph marks (^p^p) to one (^p).

```
┌──────────────── Replace ────────────────┐
│ Text to Search for:                      │
│ [^p^p..............................]     │
│                                          │
│ Replace with:                            │
│ [^p_..............................]      │
│                                          │
│ [ ] Whole Word              [ ] Confirm Changes │
│ [ ] Match Upper/Lowercase                │
│                                          │
│ <Replace Formatting Only...>   < OK >   <Cancel> │
└──────────────────────────────────────────┘
```

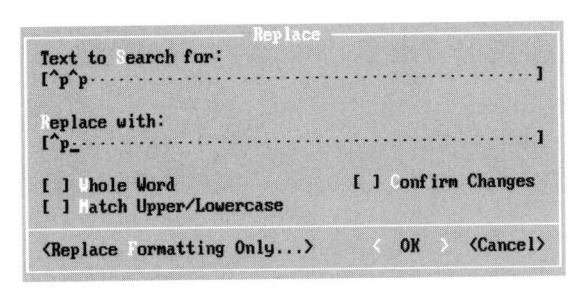

If the document is long, you might want to use the Edit Replace command on only a portion of it at a time—select a section, use the command, save the document, select another section, use the command, and so on. This procedure reduces the possibility of running out of memory.

Indentations

If the first lines of paragraphs have been indented manually with blank spaces (five is common), you can use the Edit Replace command to change every occurrence of five Spacebar spaces to no space. If there are other sets of five Spacebar spaces you don't want to remove, you can replace with a paragraph mark every occurrence of a paragraph mark followed by five blank spaces. (Replace ^p followed by five Spacebar spaces with ^p.) If you want, you then can use the Format Paragraph command to put paragraph indentation back into the document or otherwise correct formatting that might have been fouled up by the Edit Replace command.

Spacing characters

It's a little trickier to eliminate variable numbers of excess blank spaces throughout a document. This need can arise when you're editing a file created with a different word processor or program or when you're editing a file that has been printed to disk with Word's Print File command. Such documents might be riddled with long lines of spaces you want to be rid of. Using the Edit Replace command with the ^w symbol, in combination with other characters, can often solve the problem for you. The ^w symbol represents all kinds of spacing characters in a document: Spacebar spaces and nonbreaking spaces, tab characters, paragraph marks, new-line marks, and section marks. Putting ^w in the Text to Search For field lets you remove everything but printable characters from a document or file.

- To convert every type of space to a Spacebar space, type ^w in the Text to Search For field and a Spacebar space in the Replace With field. This technique is one way to strip out such characters as nonbreaking spaces, which might confuse some typesetting and other computer systems; the other way is to use the Save As command to save a document in the Text Only or Text Only w/Breaks formats.

- To convert every occurrence of more than two Spacebar spaces into a tab character, type two Spacebar spaces followed by ^w in the Text to Search For field, and type ^t in the Replace With field. This is useful when you are changing a table created with Spacebar spaces to one created with tab characters and tab formatting.

- Some databases and other programs write files that contain unwanted lines of blank spaces preceding a quotation mark. This happens when a field enclosed in quotation marks has a set length, but there isn't enough text to fill the field. To eliminate these spaces, type a space, ^w", and then another space in the Text to Search For field; and type a space, ", and another space in the Replace With field. (You don't *need* to include the spaces, but their presence eliminates the possibility that you'll accidentally replace a paragraph mark followed by a quotation mark that starts a new paragraph.)

Multiple-Step Replacements

The Replace command becomes more powerful when you use it for multiple passes over a document. Make a game of coming up with an effective combination of replacements. For example, if you want to remove nonbreaking spaces, tab characters, newline marks, and section marks from a document but you want to maintain paragraph marks, you can use the Replace command several times:

1. Temporarily replace existing paragraph marks (^p) with a special symbol not used elsewhere in the document. In this example, the symbol is @!@. (This causes paragraph formatting information to be lost, but presumably if you're doing major surgery on your document, you plan to format it later anyway.)

```
─────────────── Replace ───────────────
Text to Search for:
[^p·········································]

Replace with:
[@!@_········································]

[ ] Whole Word                    [ ] Confirm Changes
[ ] Match Upper/Lowercase
<Replace Formatting Only...>    <  OK  >  <Cancel>
```

2. Next replace all spacing characters in the document (^w) with a normal Spacebar space.

CHAPTER TWENTY-ONE: Navigation Aids

```
┌──────────────────── Replace ────────────────────┐
  Text to Search for:
  [^w.............................................]

  Replace with:
  [_..............................................]

  [ ] Whole Word                [ ] Confirm Changes
  [ ] Match Upper/Lowercase

  <Replace Formatting Only...>    < OK >   <Cancel>
└─────────────────────────────────────────────────┘
```

3. Finally replace the special symbol (@!@) with paragraph marks (^p) to complete the transformation of the document.

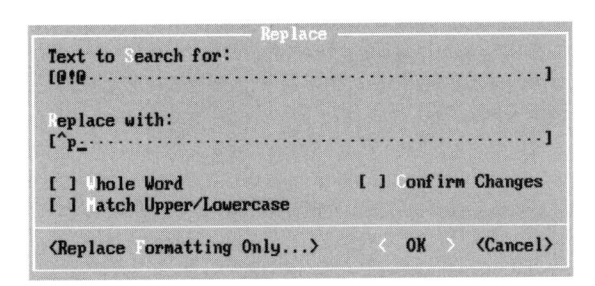

```
┌──────────────────── Replace ────────────────────┐
  Text to Search for:
  [@!@............................................]

  Replace with:
  [^p_............................................]

  [ ] Whole Word                [ ] Confirm Changes
  [ ] Match Upper/Lowercase

  <Replace Formatting Only...>    < OK >   <Cancel>
└─────────────────────────────────────────────────┘
```

Because the letter Q is usually followed by the letter U, it can be valuable when you pair it with a different letter. For instance, you can replace each paragraph mark with the letters *QP* and later replace all instances of *QP* with paragraph marks again. If you used another pair of letters, such as *AP* or *bp*, you'd risk the possibility that the letter pairs would appear naturally in your document (for example, *AP*PLE, su*bp*lot) and would be replaced with paragraph marks.

SEARCHING AND REPLACING FORMATS

Often a single document contains certain elements that appear again and again. Headings and subheadings, multiple-column tables, and itemized lists are examples. For consistency and for the sake of appearance, such items are usually given the same type of formatting. Whether or not you use style sheets, you might sometimes want to check on the formatting you applied to one of these elements—perhaps to be certain you use the same formatting in a similar item. Or you might want to replace one type of formatting with another.

You take the first step toward the search for formatting by choosing the Edit Search command and pressing its Search for Formatting Only command button. You take the first step toward replacing one kind of formatting with another by choosing the Edit Replace command and pressing its Replace Formatting Only button.

As a second step, either of the commands offers three choices: Character, Paragraph, and Style. When you search for or replace formats, Word searches from the current location of the highlight toward the end of the document. To search or replace in an entire document, move the highlight to the beginning by pressing Ctrl+Home.

For specifics on using commands to seek or replace formatting, see Chapter 12. Also, bear in mind that

- If you are not using a style sheet, you use Character or Paragraph, as the situation demands.
- If you are using a style sheet, you use Character or Paragraph to search for or replace formatting you applied with built-in formats or the Format commands, and you use Style to search for or replace formatting applied with styles.

Although the distinction between Character or Paragraph and Style might seem obvious, it is also important because Word will find formatting applied with a style only if you use the Style button. After you press the button, Word asks you to tell it what key code to search for. Thus, if you italicize a few characters with a style and later use the Character option of the Edit Search command to find italic formatting, Word will tell you it couldn't find what you sought. The same happens with Replace Character. The reason is that when you choose Character instead of Style with either command, you tell Word to look for direct formatting applied with built-in formats or with the Format Character command, not formatting applied with a style.

The Shift+F4 key combination repeats the last search for formatting just as it repeats the last search for text. If the same formatting is consistently applied to a particular element in a document, such as an itemized list, you can use the Search command the first time and the Shift+F4 key combination each subsequent time to skip to the next element in the list.

If you prefer, you can also use the Replace command to seek and replace formatting. Press the command's Replace Formatting Only command button, and then specify the type of formatting you want to find followed by what you want to replace it with. You move through several dialog boxes before all choices are specified.

PLACING BOOKMARKS

The Insert Bookmark command is like a highlighting pen, a bookmark, and a cross-referencing tool all rolled into one. It enables you to mark passages of text, graphics, captions, and other such elements. You can use the command as you create a document or when you revise it.

Its companion, the Edit Go To command, enables you to find and highlight a bookmarked passage whenever you need to see it.

A passage you bookmark becomes accessible not only when you're working on that document but also when you're working on any other document. This is because the Insert File command lets you import into a document text that is bookmarked in a different document.

As described in Chapter 14, you use the Insert Bookmark command to assign a unique name to highlighted text. For example, in a document with many tables, you could assign a bookmark name to each table or table caption. To move to a particular table, you would choose the Edit Go To command, choose the Bookmark button, and type the table's bookmark name or choose it from the list of existing names.

CHAPTER TWENTY-ONE: Navigation Aids

As described later in this chapter, bookmarks also are handy for adding cross-references to elements in a document; the cross-references are assigned numbers at the time you print.

Using a Bookmark as a Place Marker

Bookmarks make excellent place markers. They offer three advantages over typing markers into a document and using the Edit Search command to find them: First, you don't need to worry about removing them before you print; second, you can give bookmarks descriptive names; and third, the Edit Go To command with the Bookmark option will return you to the bookmark and highlight the entire passage for you. Creating bookmarks is the best approach when you want to name each passage descriptively; inserting markers and using Edit Search is preferable when you want to use the same marker over and over throughout a document so that you can jump to it successive times by pressing Shift+F4.

You can use the Insert Bookmark command to mark as many passages as you want, and you can give a passage more than one bookmark name. For example, suppose you write fiction and you want to mark the highlights of your story so that you can refer to them easily. You might create bookmark names such as *boy_meets_girl*; *fight_with_Brad*; *fight_with_girl*; *boy_loses_girl*; *fight_with_self*; and *boy_gets_girl*. You could quickly find whatever section of the story you wanted with the Edit Go To command and the appropriate bookmark name.

In a reference work, you might use the same approach to create bookmarks for topics that you want to refer to as you discuss them periodically in the document. Or you might bookmark a questionable passage and then use the Insert Annotation command to add and date a reminder to verify the text.

Reorganizing a Document

You can use bookmarks to rearrange sections of a document. Suppose you are reviewing a document and encounter a passage you want to move, but you're not certain where it should go. Here is one way to mark and move it:

1. If paragraph marks are not set to display, choose the View Preferences command and turn on the Paragraph Marks check box. Doing this prevents accidental loss of paragraph formatting, ensures that whole paragraphs remain whole, and gives you flexibility in adding new text to the end of the bookmarked passage.
2. Select (highlight) the entire passage.
3. Choose the Insert Bookmark command, and type a descriptive name for the selected text.
4. When you find a suitable new location for the passage, highlight the word that will immediately follow the text you are about to move. Use Insert Bookmark to give the word a temporary bookmark name.

5. Choose Edit Go To to jump to the bookmark associated with the text you want to move. This highlights the text.
6. Choose Edit Cut to delete the passage to the scrap.
7. Use Edit Go To to jump to the word you bookmarked—the word that follows the location at which you want to insert the passage you are moving.
8. Choose Edit Paste to insert the bookmarked text from the scrap.

Because the bookmark name remains attached to bookmarked text, you can move the passage as many times as you want until you are satisfied. You can also copy a bookmarked passage or a passage containing a bookmarked section to the scrap (instead of deleting it to the scrap) and insert the text elsewhere. But when you copy a passage, only the original retains the bookmark name, because a bookmark name cannot be duplicated in a document. Thus, the copy you insert from the scrap reverts to plain text, and you cannot use the Edit Go To command either to move to it or to select it. However, if you copy a bookmarked passage to the scrap and insert it in a *different* document, both documents will contain the bookmark and the text.

Bookmarks have another important purpose. They are a vital part of creating cross-references, as we'll now see.

NUMBERING AND CROSS-REFERENCES

Most of this chapter has focused on ways to help you find and change elements in a document. Now let's turn to your audience and to two of the ways in which you can help the reader find passages or elements you refer to in your text:

- If the document contains a series of similar items, such as tables, figures, or sections, you can distinguish among them by numbering the items sequentially. Doing so serves two purposes: It makes clear the relationship between the elements, and it helps the reader find them.
- If you want to refer the reader to another part of the document, you can add *See* or *See also* cross-references—for example, *See Table 3 on page 21; See also Chart 2; Refer to the discussion of colors on page 32.*

Word lets you eliminate the dual chore of numbering parts of a document and adding correctly numbered cross-references. Word can do both for you at print time. Let's begin with the simpler of these procedures: numbering parts.

Numbering Items in a Document

The first step in numbering items in a document is deciding on a *series name* (such as *figure*) that applies to all the items you want numbered. You type this name, followed by a colon, wherever you want an item number to be printed (for example, above or below each figure) and then turn the name into a special code called a *sequence holder* by pressing the F3 key. At print time, whenever Word encounters a sequence holder, it

CHAPTER TWENTY-ONE: Navigation Aids   397

replaces the sequence holder with the appropriate number. When you add, delete, or move sequence holders, Word renumbers the remaining ones—much as it keeps track of and updates footnote numbers.

In terms of what you do and what you see on screen, Word handles sequence holders much as it handles reserved glossary names, such as *page*, which cause the pages of a document to be numbered sequentially. To Word, sequence holders and *page* are different, but there are parallels in how you use them.

Let's assume you've created a document that contains a number of items you want to refer to as figures. They might be charts, diagrams, spreadsheets, or whatever; regardless, you want to call them figures. The following step-by-step procedure describes how you would tell Word to number each figure for you at print time.

1. Decide on a descriptive series name for the items you want numbered. The name can be any valid glossary name and can include the digits 0 through 9.

   In effect, whatever series name you choose becomes a type of "reserved" glossary name (like *page*), but of your own creation. The word *figure* is used in this example.

2. Position the highlight where you want a number to be printed. For a figure number, you might choose a blank paragraph above or below the figure; both are logical places to insert a figure number and, if you want, a caption.

3. You probably want to use a printable word or phrase to identify each numbered item: *Figure 1*, *Figure 2*, *Figure 3*, and so on. Type whatever identifying label you want (such as *figure*), and press the Spacebar—for example,

   ```
   ‖ Figure _                                                        ‖
   ```

4. Now type the series name you've chosen, followed by a colon:

   ```
   ‖ Figure figure:_                                                 ‖
   ```

5. Next press the F3 key. Doing this tells Word to interpret the preceding name and colon as an instruction to print a number at print time. Until you press F3, the name and colon are nothing more than ordinary characters.

6. When you press the F3 key, Word surrounds your series name and the colon with parentheses on screen, like this:

   ```
   ‖ Figure (figure:)█                                               ‖
   ```

The notation *(figure:)* shows you where a number will be printed later, just as the notation *(page)* shows where a page number will appear. At this point, if you hold down the Shift key and press the Left or Right direction key to highlight a single character, the highlight encompasses the entire sequence holder—parentheses, series name, and colon. That's because Word considers it a single character—a number, to be exact—even though it appears on the screen as a distinctive name.

When you print the document, this sequence holder

```
Figure (figure:)
```

becomes

```
Figure 1
```

Although these steps have pointed out similarities to using *page*, don't consider your reference names the exact equivalents of reserved glossary names, such as *page*. There are two major differences:

- Even though you assign a glossary-type name to it, a series name is not a glossary entry, so you cannot use the Edit Glossary command to view it or to choose it from a list as you can with Word's reserved names.
- A series name must be followed by at least one colon (exceptions are noted below). If you don't type a colon, Word won't accept the name.

Like page numbers, the numbers for your references are calculated by Word at print time, so as you edit the document you can move and delete referenced material at will and add any new references you want, all with the assurance that the final numbering will be correct.

Because each set of items you number is identified by a series name, you can tell Word to add sequential numbers to separate sets of items by defining a different series name for each set, to a maximum of 10. You might, for example, want to number figures and tables separately as *Figure 1*, *Table 1*, and so on. To do this, you could use the series name *figure:* for all figures and *table:* for all tables. Even if figures and tables are intermingled in the document, Word numbers them individually.

Numbering items in multiple-part documents

Figures and tables in a multiple-part document are often numbered using a form such as *Figure 1-1* or *Table 3-5*, where the part number precedes the figure or table number. If you want to use this convention, you cannot simply type the reference as something like *Figure 1-figure:* and press the F3 key. Word would interpret the characters *1-figure:* as a complete series name rather than as a *1-* followed by the series name *figure:*. As a result, your caption would be printed as *Figure 1* rather than *Figure 1-1*. You can get around this limitation and include hyphens (or colons) in your numbering scheme, however, by using the following approach:

1. Type the label and series name for each figure or table in the form described earlier; that is, use *Figure figure:*, *Table table:*, or whatever label and name you decided on. Do this throughout the document, even if you intend to change the labels to *Figure 1-*, *Figure 2-*, and so on.

2. When you have numbered all items in the series, return to the beginning of the document by pressing Ctrl+Home.
3. Use the Edit Replace command. Type *Figure*, plus a space, in the Text to Search For field, and type *Figure 1-*, without an ending space, in the Replace With field. (If you type an ending space in this field, your captions will print as *Figure 1-1* instead of *Figure 1-1*.)

If the part number will change (from *Figure 1-* to *Figure 2-*), turn the Confirm Changes check box on so that you can cancel the Edit Replace command when all captions in part one have been changed. Repeat the procedure, making an appropriate change in the Replace With field, for part two, part three, and whatever other parts you need to number.

You can use this same approach for other elements in a document, including sections and numbered headings. To number headings, for example, you could print

1.1 Continents of the World
1.2 Oceans of the World

by typing the series name and text as something like this:

*number: Continents of the World
*number: Oceans of the World

and, after pressing F3 to turn *number:* into a series name, deleting the asterisk and the space following it, and typing in their place the number and punctuation mark desired—for instance, replacing * with *1.* (a number followed by a period) in the preceding example.

Adding flexibility to numbering

Word also accepts two variations for a series name that can add considerable flexibility to your numbering scheme. Suppose you want to include one or more items in a series but do not want the numbers printed out. By ending the series name with a double colon (::) instead of a single colon, you can tell Word to include the item in its count without printing the number on the finished page. For example, if a document contains three figures, of which you want to print numbers for the first and third but not the second, type the series name (let's use *figure* again) for each as follows:

- For the first figure, type *figure:*
- For the second figure (the one that will not be numbered on the printout), type *figure::*
- For the third figure, type *figure:*

On the printout, the first figure will be numbered 1. The second figure will be *counted* as number 2 but will not be identified by a printed number. The third figure will be numbered 3.

In addition, you can end a series name with a double colon, plus a number of your choice, to set the count to a particular value. Again, the sequence holder is counted, but no value is printed in your document. The double colon plus a number can be especially useful if you have divided a document into sections. You can use the same series name throughout, yet you can restart numbering at 1 in each section.

For example, suppose you have a two-part document with figures in both parts. You want to number the figures in part one as *Figure 1-1*, *Figure 1-2*, and so on, and you want to restart numbering in part two as *Figure 2-1*, *Figure 2-2*, and so on. You can do this easily and use the series name *figure* throughout the document by taking advantage of the double colon:

1. Number the figures throughout the document as *Figure (figure:)*, *Figure (figure:)*, and so on. Then use Edit Replace, as described earlier, to change the captions to *Figure 1-(figure:)*, *Figure 2-(figure:)*, and so on. The printed results will be *Figure 1-1*, *Figure 1-2* to *Figure 2-1*, *Figure 2-2*, and so on.

2. Somewhere between the last figure in part one and the first figure in part two, type *figure::0* to create the sequence holder. The point to remember is that this is a nonprinting sequence holder that will simply serve to reset numbering. You might, for example, place this sequence holder immediately after the last "real" figure caption—for example, *Figure 1-(figure:)(figure::0)*.

3. Notice that you type a number (0) that is one less than the next number you want printed (1). This is what you want because Word will give the value *n+1* to the next sequence holder with the same series name. Thus, if you type *(figure::0)*, Word will give the number *1* (0+1) to the next *(figure:)* notation that it encounters—in this example, *Figure 2-(figure:)*.

NOTE: *If you count, but do not print, numbers for items in a series, bear in mind that the sequence holder occupies space on the screen but* not *on the printed page. The double colon at the end of the series name tells Word to include the sequence holder in its count but to replace the sequence holder with nothing on the printed page. Thus, to avoid inadvertently adding extra spaces to your document, be certain to avoid surrounding a count-only sequence holder with extra spaces on the screen. In fact, you might want to consider putting such a sequence holder at the end of a sentence or somewhere else out of the way.*

Cross-Referencing a Document

It's but a short step from telling Word to number series of items in a document to telling Word to add correctly numbered cross-references to those items. You can even use three built-in series names, *page*, *footnote*, and *para-num*, to refer to specific pages, footnotes, even paragraphs in a document—and all without ever worrying about where those tables, footnotes, or references happen to be.

To create a cross-reference, you follow a series name with a colon and a bookmark name. The series name tells Word which group of items to evaluate; the bookmark tells Word which item in the group you want. As you do when telling Word to number items in a series, you press the F3 key—this time to tell Word you are creating a cross-reference.

When you assign a bookmark name to a portion of a document, use a bit of judgment and remember that you are giving Word the location of the "target" of a cross-reference. Word might seem smart about cross-references, but it really doesn't think. If you want to reference a topic by page number, be certain to select the beginning of the topic when you create the bookmark. When a cross-reference is to a page number (or to a footnote or a paragraph), Word prints the number of the page on which a bookmark *starts,* assuming correctly that the reader wants a reference to the beginning, not the middle or end, of a topic.

To refer to a portion of a document, you select the text to be referenced and use the Insert Bookmark command to assign it a descriptive bookmark name. If you then want to reference the page on which this material appears, you type the built-in series name *page,* followed by a colon and the name you gave the bookmark.

Suppose you are writing a section about experimental airplanes and want to refer to a section on rockets that begins on page 24. First, you move to page 24 and give the section on rockets a bookmark name, such as *rockets.* Then, in the section on experimental planes, you refer to the rocket section by typing a reference like *See page page:rockets* and pressing the F3 key. Word will display the reference as (*page:rockets*) but, at print time, it will replace the notation with the number of the page (24) on which the bookmarked text named *rockets* begins. If, after further editing, the section on rockets moves to page 26, Word will accommodate the change and print the correct page number.

On the other hand, if you want to reference one of a series of items, such as a table or figure, identified by a sequence holder, think about what type of reference you want to make before you select the text to be bookmarked.

If you want to refer to the item by number but not by page, you can select text immediately following the sequence holder—the caption, for example—and assign it a bookmark name. For instance, if you were importing a figure into a document:

```
        C:\LOGOS\EMPIX2.PCX;3";2.135";PCX
Figure (figure:). A "scenic" logo.
```

you could select the text *A "scenic" logo.* and give it the bookmark name *scene.* In text, you could refer to the figure, like this:

```
    symbols associated with corporations include initials,
    faces, half-moons, and scenery (see Figure (figure:scene))
```

and Word would print the number of the figure on your output.

On the other hand, if you want to refer to the picture itself, you select the entire figure, including the sequence holder (and caption, if you want). You then type

```
    symbols associated with corporations include initials,
    faces, half-moons, and scenery (see Page (page:scene))
```

and Word prints the number of the page on which the picture *begins*. Whereas this example would probably not break over two pages, a long table might. Choose whether you want to refer to the beginning of the item by page number or to the item itself.

If you want to use one of the other built-in series names *footnote* or *para-num*, bear these points in mind:

- Type a reference to a footnote in the form *footnote:bookmark-name*. The name *footnote* is replaced by the footnote number immediately preceding the first character of the item you designate as *bookmark-name*.
- In a document with numbered paragraphs, use Utilities Sort. Type a paragraph-number reference in the form *para-num:bookmark-name*. The name *para-num* will be replaced by the number of the paragraph containing the first character of *bookmark-name*.

You can include cross-references in index entries or include a table of contents as easily as you can in text, and without worrying about correct referencing.

To see how cross-referencing works, let's consider a sample document. This document, a proposal to study populations of bottom-dwelling marine animals, contains the sections listed below (notice the sequence holders). For your information only, the portion of each line that is shown in italics has been given the bookmark name in parentheses at the end; the "page number" where the item appears follows the bookmark name.

- Introduction
- Part (part:): *Scope of Work* (scope), page 2
- Part (part:): *Methods and Procedures* (how-to), page 15
- Part (part:): *Budget* (budget), page 22
- Part (part:): *Schedule* (schedule), page 25
- Part (part:): *Qualifications and Personnel* (personnel), page 28

Within the proposal are the following figures and tables. Again, sequence holders are shown in parentheses; the italicized portion of each line is bookmarked text identified by the bookmark name in parentheses, and the page number is at the end:

- Figure 1-(figure:). *A map of the study area.* (map), page 3
- Table 1-(table:). *Species to be observed and counted.* (critters), page 9
- Table 3-(table:). *Equipment needs and costs.* (equipment), page 23
- Table 3-(table:). *Personnel costs.* (payroll), page 24
- Table 4-(table:). *Projected schedule.* (timechart), page 27

Here is a concluding paragraph that contains as many cross-references as possible:

CHAPTER TWENTY-ONE: Navigation Aids

```
In conclusion, as shown by the map in Figure 1-(figure:map),
the study area can be seen to be large enough to provide a
representative sampling of bottom-dwelling animals listed in
Table 1-(table:critters) on page (page:critters) yet small
enough to be manageable on the time scheduled, as shown in
Table 4-(table:timechart). Assuming no major problems with
weather and no additions to the personnel listed in Part
(part:personnel), the project should be completed as
outlined in Part (part:schedule) and within the budget
itemized in Part (part:budget), especially in Table 3-
(table:equipment), page (page:equipment) and Table 3-
(table:payroll), page (page:payroll).
```

And the following is the result:

```
In conclusion, as shown by the map in Figure 1-3, the study
area can be seen to be large enough to provide a
representative sampling of bottom-dwelling animals listed in
Table 1-14 on page 9 yet small enough to be manageable on
the time scheduled, as shown in Table 4-2. Assuming no major
problems with weather and no additions to the personnel
listed in Part 5, the project should be completed as
outlined in Part 4 and within the budget itemized in Part 3,
especially in Table 3-5, page 23 and Table 3-7, page 24.
```

CHAPTER TWENTY-TWO

Glossaries

When you first use Word's glossary, it might seem like a quiet presence hovering in the background somewhere like a competent butler. Or it might seem more like a handy repository for text you may or may not want to recycle. Then again, you might never think about the glossary. Maybe you simply use it and leave the details to Word.

Earlier chapters have presented the glossary as a place where you can store both passages of text (text-only glossary entries) and sequences of keystrokes (macros). You've seen that you can insert any word, phrase, or longer passage from the glossary into a document as often as you want. You can use built-in glossary entries, such as *page* and *date*, to paginate or date a document with no fuss. And you can play back any combination of keystrokes and commands by simply storing it in the glossary as a macro and recalling it by typing its name or control code.

In this chapter, we'll explore ways you can derive extra performance from the glossary feature. Specifically, we'll look at the glossary as a tool for organizing information and as a speedy way to format documents. Neither of these are conventional uses for the glossary, but that shouldn't stop you from trying these approaches or other even more inventive ones.

In the next chapter, we'll explore some of the intricacies and opportunities of using the other kind of glossary entry—macros.

A REORGANIZING TOOL

You can use the glossary to reorganize the elements of a document, taking advantage of the glossary's ability to store passages, quotations, and other elements under individual glossary names in a glossary file.

Instead of selecting and moving long passages or scrolling through the pages of a lengthy document to find what you seek, simply insert appropriate glossary entries back into your document when and where they are needed. Or type the glossary names as a list, shuffle them around into the order you want, and then transform each into its corresponding text by placing the cursor after each name and pressing the F3 key. You can even use the glossary names as the elements of a formal outline and then transform the series of names into a document with the F3 key.

Organizing the Document

Imagine that you're writing about pasta. You could be writing a magazine article, a cookbook chapter, or a long letter to a relative. Regardless, pasta is the topic. You've already written passages on a variety of pastas—cannelloni, tortellini, tagliarini, cappelletti, ravioli—and you've typed two or three recipes for each into your computer. You've also written a passage about sauces and a few paragraphs about stuffed pastas. In short, most of the elements have been gathered into a single Word document, which you call PASTA. Now you must organize the elements and add an introduction, a conclusion, and some transitions. This is where the power of the glossary makes it a useful editing tool.

You can delete each element of the document into the glossary and assign it its own descriptive glossary name. After all the pieces are stored, you can start your document fresh, or nearly fresh, and call forth material from the glossary as you need it. If you use Word's outlining feature, as described in Chapter 26, you can sketch the document organization in outline form and then insert appropriate passages into your outline by typing the glossary name and pressing the F3 key.

Whether or not you use outlining, when construction is under way you can insert passages into the document more than once to try them out in various locations. If you change your mind about some of your editing changes, you can delete them and start again from scratch by calling forth the needed elements from the glossary. And if editing takes longer than a single session, you can save the glossary entries as a glossary file and pick up later where you left off.

Preparing the glossary entries

Let's assume you've assembled your material for the document PASTA and you are ready to store the passages in the glossary. The following is a step-by-step example of how you might proceed:

1. Select a passage of text. Make it small enough or complete enough so that you aren't likely to want to break it up later into independent pieces. Depending on your vision of the finished document, you might select the whole section on cannelloni, a smaller section on cannelloni with butter sauces, or a single cannelloni recipe. By segmenting your material and labeling each part descriptively, you allow yourself the luxury of being able to extract tightly focused sections later.
2. Choose the Glossary command from the Edit menu.
3. Think up an appropriate glossary name for the selected text. If it is about cannelloni in general, you might choose an easily remembered name, such as *Cannelloni*. Or you might shorten it to *Can*. Or, for convenience, just *C*. If the selected text is about cannelloni with butter sauce, you

might call it *Cannelloni_Butter* or *CanBut*. For that matter, you could call it *Beethoven* or any other string of up to 31 letters, numbers, and acceptable symbols, but a meaningful name helps you later, when you want to retrieve text from the glossary.
4. Type the name into the Glossary Name text box, and choose the Define command button. The selected text is placed in the glossary under the name you typed.
5. Repeat the process for the other passages.

You're finished when each segment of the document has been defined in the glossary under an appropriate name. If you want to quit Word at this point and leave the reorganizing for another time, you can store all the glossary entries in a file with the Glossary dialog box of the Save Glossary command. Such a file might be called PASTA.GLY. If you do this, when you resume work, use the Glossary dialog box of the Open Glossary command.

Using the glossary entries

Now you're ready to organize. Perhaps you begin your document with a general introduction telling how different areas in Italy have developed regional variations in cuisine. That done, you move on to the main part of your text. Time to mention the different sauces? Call the sauce section from the glossary. The first pasta you want to write about is cannelloni? Call the cannelloni passage back from the glossary.

Type the glossary name at the place in the document where you want the entry to appear, and press the F3 key.

Using Glossary Names as an Outline

Word's outlining feature is more flexible than the glossary in this regard. If you've assigned good, descriptive names to your glossary entries, you can use the names as a means of collecting your thoughts, viewing your planned organization for the document, and when all is in order, inserting segments of text one right after the other. Type each glossary name on a separate line of what can be either a formal or an informal outline. Shuffle the order of the lines as you want, either moving them with the mouse or deleting to and inserting from the scrap. When the names are in the desired order, position the selection after each one in turn; and press the F3 key to insert the text it represents.

After you've inserted all the passages from the glossary back into your text, your document might be close to complete, although you'll probably smooth out the transitions between passages, write a conclusion, and give it a final editing.

Clever use of the glossary lets you redirect the organization of a document with little trouble. In PASTA, for example, you might at first group recipes according to which type of pasta they use. Perhaps you'd insert the glossary entries named *Cannelloni_Butter*, *Cannelloni_Tomato*, and *Cannelloni_Olive_Oil* in succession. But after reading the resulting document, maybe you decide you really want all the tomato-sauce pasta recipes in one place, all the butter-sauce ones in another, and all the olive oil-based ones in yet another. Using the glossary, it's easy. Delete what you've written, or open a new document and start over again. To group the tomato-sauce recipes together this time, you could use the glossary to insert *Cannelloni_Tomato*, followed by *Ravioli_Tomato*, *Manicotti_Tomato*, and so on.

As mentioned, you can use Word's outlining capabilities to organize and reorganize a document or to enhance the use of the glossary described above. You can type a descriptive line for each paragraph or group of related paragraphs and turn the line into a heading. Under each heading, you can insert text from the glossary. Then, by collapsing the text, you can reorder the elements of a document easily in outline mode.

A Variation: Numbers as Names

Sometimes, especially with long documents or those in which paragraphs within major sections require extensive reorganizing, it's difficult to perform on-screen editing and still maintain a feeling for the continuity of the document. Try using numbers as glossary names in such situations. When you use this technique, you make decisions with pencil and paper.

On a printout of the unrevised document, circle or bracket complete passages you want to keep. Number the passages in the order in which you want them to appear in the final document, and mark any passages you want to eliminate altogether.

After you've marked all passages in some fashion, put Word to the task. Working with the on-screen version of the document, dispose of every paragraph or passage you marked by deleting it (to eliminate it) or by putting it in the glossary (to save it). When naming the glossary entries, use the number you gave the passage on paper.

Now comes the snappy part. Move the cursor to the new location of passage 1. Type *1* and press the F3 key. Instantly, the passage you want appears on the screen. Type *2* and press F3. The second passage appears in the document, following the first. Continue until every numbered passage has been inserted. The document will now be organized as you want.

> NOTE: *You can obtain much the same effect by using the Utilities menu's Sort command. Instead of deleting paragraphs to the glossary with numbers as names, number the paragraphs in the order you want them to appear, and then execute the Sort command. You can use the Sort command to reorganize a section of a document provided you number each paragraph in the section. To ensure that no other paragraphs are affected, highlight the numbered ones before choosing the Sort command. The advantage of using the glossary instead of Sort, however, is that you can assign a single number to a passage that extends for several paragraphs or several pages.*

Pulling Information Together

You can also use the glossary to collect material from many different parts of one document or from several documents. For instance, suppose you're an attorney who has hundreds of pages of transcripts in one or more Word documents. Move through the text, copying to the glossary any passages pertaining to a particular subject. You

CHAPTER TWENTY-TWO: Glossaries

can give the glossary entries distinctive names, abbreviated names, or simply numbers. Afterward, you can form a new document on the specific subject in a matter of minutes.

Use the same technique to gather information on a number of topics simultaneously. A student who has amassed a jumble of notes on several subjects can read through them once, copying passages to the glossary. Entries on fish might be named *Fish1*, *Fish2*, and *Fish3*; entries on birds might be named *Ducks* and *Geese*. Later, the student can insert the collected entries in the glossary into new, separate documents on each subject. All of the entries with *Fish* in their names could be one document. *Ducks* and *Geese* could flock together in another.

A SPEEDY WAY TO FORMAT AS YOU WRITE

Character, paragraph, and section formats exist in as little as one character of text. You can copy or delete a formatted character to the glossary, giving it a distinctive name or handy abbreviation, and later insert it into a document as you would any other glossary entry. After you've inserted a formatted character from the glossary, you can treat it like any other formatted character. You can, for instance, continue writing from that point with the benefit of the formatting.

Characters

Character formatting can be stored in a single, blank, space character. Perhaps you use capitalized, boldfaced characters frequently in preparing contracts. Apply that combination of formatting to a single space in the document and store it in the glossary with a suitable name and, if you want, a control code. Perhaps you call the formatting *CapsBold* and give it the control code Shift+Ctrl+CB. To insert this formatted space into a document, either type *CapsBold* and press the F3 key or simply press Shift+Ctrl+CB. Then press the Left direction key once to move the selection into the formatted space so that when you resume typing, the new text will have the character formatting of "CapsBold."

The same technique can be used for hidden-text character formatting.

Paragraphs

Recall that paragraph formatting is stored in paragraph marks. Inserting a formatted paragraph mark (from the glossary) formats the text that precedes the mark, all the way back to the previous mark. You can place several paragraph marks in the glossary, each with a different name and formatting. A paragraph mark that centers text might be given the name *Center*; a mark that double-spaces lines might be called *Double*; and so forth. In addition, both paragraph and character formatting can be stored together in the same paragraph mark. You accomplish this by formatting the mark with both Format menu's Character and Paragraph commands.

Use these formatted marks instead of the Enter key to create new paragraphs that have desired formats already in place. In some cases, this technique rivals the use of style sheets for speedy formatting.

Sections

Section formatting is stored in a Section mark, which you create by pressing Alt+IB and choosing Section, and which appears as a double row of dots across the text window.

If you have a particular page layout you use for certain documents, consider formatting a section mark appropriately and storing it in the glossary. You might call the glossary entry *2col* if it contains a section mark that creates two columns on a page. To format a single-section document with this mark, select the last character of the document, and either type *2col* and press the F3 key or use a control code you've assigned. Word inserts the section mark and causes the section formatting of the document to change. To format one section of a multiple-section document, replace the mark at the end of the section with an appropriately formatted mark from the glossary. If you often use the same formatting characters from the glossary, you can store them as a glossary file.

An Example of Glossary-Based Formatting

To practice applying formatting with glossary entries, use the following instructions as a tutorial. Let's assume you want to use the glossary to make each heading in a report capitalized, underlined, and centered, with two blank spaces preceding it and one following it. This is a combination of character and paragraph formatting. First you place the formatting in the glossary:

1. Select a paragraph mark at the end of a paragraph, and press the Enter key to create a new paragraph mark alone on a line. (You can see the paragraph marks if you've checked the Paragraph Marks field of the View Preferences command.) Then select the new paragraph; one way to do this is to hold down the Shift key and press the Right direction key to cause the paragraph mark to become highlighted.

2. Choose the Format Paragraph command and choose Center in the Alignment field. Type *0* (zero) in each of the three Indents fields, *2* in the Before field, and *1* in the After field. Execute the command.

3. Without moving the selection, choose the Format Character command and check both the Underline and All Caps fields. Carry out the command to complete the formatting.

4. Still without moving the selection, choose the Format Glossary command, and type *Heading* as the glossary name. Choose the Define command button.

A paragraph mark laden with paragraph and character formatting is now stored in the glossary under the name *Heading*. To use it to format a paragraph as a heading, type *Heading*, and then press the F3 key.

There are a couple of different ways to use the glossary entry.

If you are at the end of a paragraph and want the next paragraph to be the heading

1. Press the Enter key at the end of the current paragraph.
2. Type *Heading* (or whatever name you've given the glossary entry), and press the F3 key (or type the control code). This places the formatted paragraph mark in the text but also moves you to the next paragraph.
3. Press the Up direction key to return to the paragraph mark of the heading paragraph.
4. Type the text of the heading.
5. Presumably you want only one heading paragraph at a time, so don't press the Enter key. Instead, press the Down direction key to complete the heading and move to the next paragraph.

To insert a heading paragraph in the midst of other paragraphs

1. Place the cursor at the beginning of the paragraph that will follow the heading you want to insert.
2. Type the name of the glossary entry: *Heading* (no space after the name of the entry) and press the F3 key, or type the control code. This inserts the new paragraph above the one you selected.
4. Press the Up direction key. This moves the cursor to the new heading paragraph.
5. Type the text of the heading.

In general, glossary-based formatting is less practical than using a style sheet as a means of fast formatting, unless you are skilled at using the glossary but are not very familiar with style sheets. A key difference between style sheets and glossary-based formatting is that style sheets control only the formatting of text already in the document, but glossary-based formatting also inserts content—even though it may be only a blank space, a paragraph mark, or a section mark.

A variation of glossary-based formatting can also let you pull preformatted parts of a standard document together with little trouble. For example, how often have you typed and formatted the same parts of a letter, such as the return address, a standard closing paragraph, and the complimentary closing and signature? Type them once, format them once, and save them in the glossary. If you want, save the entire "skeleton" as a single glossary entry with a name such as *Letter*. Insert the glossary entry into a brand-new document, insert the remainder of the letter where you want, print it, and mail it.

You might find it even easier to assign a control code, as well as a name, to each glossary entry that contains a formatting character as its content. This approach takes advantage of the fact that glossary entries and macros are closely related. It lets you use a control code to insert the formatted character much as you use a macro's control code to carry out commands. To assign a control code, you format a character as desired, as described earlier. Then select the character, choose Edit Glossary, give the entry a descriptive name, press Tab to move to the Macro Keys text box, and then hold down the Ctrl key and type the code of your choice. (As with macros, two characters are recommended.) To distinguish formatting characters from other glossary entries, you might want to precede each name with an identifier, such as *format*. For example, you might store italic character formatting under a name such as *format.ital^<Ctrl I>C.*

CHAPTER TWENTY-THREE

Macros

The first time you try out a Word macro, it's a lark, an experiment. Maybe you're simply curious. But soon macros become familiar, and then they seem necessary. Before long, you can't imagine being without them. You're hooked. They simplify word processing, permitting you to be more productive. They make simple tasks more pleasurable and complex ones more feasible.

A Word macro can, for instance, peer into the settings of the View Preferences command or the Utilities Customize command and make decisions based on what it finds. Or it can read information from the screen and take any of several courses of action, depending on what it discovers. For example, a macro can switch back and forth between two different style sheets by first reading the name of the style sheet attached to a document and then attaching the other one. Or a macro can move you between different windows or speed up editing by evaluating text and making decisions based on what it finds.

Macros often are described as a way to record and quickly play back sequences of keystrokes. This definition is true as far as it goes. But a more revealing way to think of a macro is as a method for tailoring a computer program by giving the program a new feature that precisely suits your needs. If you often start letters by attaching a specific style sheet and typing your name and address in a particular way, you can easily create a macro that will do this for you whenever you press a certain key combination. The keys might be Shift+Ctrl+C (for "correspondence") or Shift+Ctrl+LE (for "letter"). If you wanted it to, the same macro could type the correct date and even open other windows, loading them with information you frequently need when writing letters. As you move beyond the rudiments, you will find that a macro is more than simply a string of keystrokes; it is a string of instructions that includes opportunities for the macro to make any of several prearranged decisions.

This chapter shows you how to write, edit, and fix (debug) a macro. It discusses the various elements of the macro programming language and proposes useful conventions that you can follow. It also offers a collection of tips and a couple of sample macros—including one that improves on the word-counting feature of Word and another that lets you easily print a page from the middle of a document.

A macro is a form of glossary entry, so you should be familiar with the contents of Chapters 6, 17, and 22 before jumping into the deeper material of this chapter. Together, these earlier chapters explain how to copy macros and other glossary entries to the glossary and how to retrieve them for use later.

Don't be intimidated. Developing sophisticated macros of your own can be a complex task but not an unfathomable one. It can be exciting, as you conquer challenges. Even if you never learn to write a macro of your own or never even learn to record one, you can certainly use macros created by other people. In other words, you don't need to make a tool in order to use it.

WRITING OR EDITING A MACRO

When a macro is in the glossary, either because you've recorded it or because it was stored on disk during a previous Word session, you can edit it if you want. You do so by inserting the macro into a document in text form and then modifying its text as if it were a normal document (which, in a sense, it is). If you're already working on a document, you'll probably want to open a new window before inserting the macro's text.

On the other hand, you can write a macro from scratch. Simply start a new document, or even write the lines of macro instructions in the middle of a document you're working on and delete them from the screen after storing them in the glossary.

Treating a Macro as Text

To insert a macro into a document in text form, choose the Macro Edit command (Alt+ME). This brings to the screen a list of current glossary entries. Highlight the name of the macro you want to edit, press Alt+E (for "Edit"). Word inserts the macro into your document in text form, with nonletter key names inside angle brackets. (For example, the Insert key is represented as *<ins>* and the Ctrl+F10 combination as *<ctrl f10>*.)

Alternatively, you can insert the text of a macro into a document by typing the macro's name, typing a caret, and then pressing the F3 key. Again, don't forget to type the caret.

For example, you could have in your glossary a macro called *FirstIndent* that adds a first-line indent of half an inch to a paragraph. If you inserted the text of this macro into a document, you would see this or something similar:

<alt T>p<alt N>.5"<enter>

This simple macro reflects only a few keystrokes and no macro programming: *<alt T>* calls the Format menu just as holding down the Alt key and pressing the T key does; *p* chooses the Paragraph command from the Format menu; <*alt N*> is the accelerator key that moves the cursor to the First Line field; .5" is the measurement typed into the field; and <*enter*> is the keystroke that carries out the command, thereby imposing the first-line indent of 0.5 inch on whichever paragraph or paragraphs are selected when the macro is run.

A half-inch indent is fine for a monospaced font, such as 12-point Courier, but if you're working in a proportional font, such as Times Roman or Helvetica, you might want a first-line indent that is only half as long. Consequently, you might want the macro to impose an indent of only 0.25 inch.

To modify the macro, you edit its text, select it, and copy it back into the glossary with its original name. Let's do this one step at a time.

First, edit the text of the macro. In this case, .5" becomes .25".

<alt T>p<alt N>.25"<enter>

Second, select (highlight) the text of the macro. Be sure not to select anything except the text of the macro. Do not select extra spaces, for example, because if you do the macro will interpret the spaces as instructions and try to insert them into a document or take a similarly inappropriate action. (You can, however, select paragraph marks and tab characters because a macro ignores them.)

Third, choose the Macro Edit command, and in its dialog box select the name of the macro, *FirstIndent*.

Fourth, press Alt+D to choose the Define button, telling Word that you want to define the *FirstIndent* macro to contain the selected text, which is the text you edited.

Fifth, when Word asks *Do you want to replace the existing macro?* choose OK (Enter).

Remember that if you want to use your revised macro on some later occasion, you must save it on disk with the Save Glossary command button from the Edit Macro dialog box. Otherwise, the original, unrevised version will remain on disk.

A RUDIMENTARY LANGUAGE

The previous macro was a series of keystrokes, which could have been recorded. But writing a macro has the advantage of letting you add programming instructions. Such instructions are written in a language based on English that resembles Basic.

A Sample Macro: Counting Words

Typically, a listing for a more complex macro will look something like the following, which comes from MasterWord. The macro causes Word to perform two kinds of word counts: one count of the entire document and one of the words between the beginning of the document and the cursor. This second count lets you see how many words you need to put into final form if you are making an editing pass over a finished document or if you are working somewhere other than the end of the document.

```
┌─────────────────────── Document1 ═══════════════════════╗
│ «IF Wordversion <> 5.5»  «COMMENT Check Word version»
│     «QUIT»
│ «ENDIF»
│ «SET Echo = "Off"»       «COMMENT Turn off screen updating»
│ <esc>                    «COMMENT In case extend-selection
│                                    mode is on, turn it off»
│ «SET scrp = Scrap»       «COMMENT Store the scrap's content»
│ «SET length = LEN(Selection)» «COMMENT Note the length of
│                                    selection (highlight)»
│ <F8>                     «COMMENT Turn on extend-selection
│                                    mode»
│ <ctrl home>              «COMMENT Select to top of document»
│ <alt u>w                 «COMMENT Run Utilities Word Count»
│ «SET sofar = Scrap»      «COMMENT Store result of the count»
│ <esc>                    «COMMENT Turn off extend-selection
│                                    mode»
│ <right>                  «COMMENT Reduce selection to a
│                                    single character»
│ <alt u>w                 «COMMENT Run Utilities Word Count»
│ «SET total = Scrap»      «COMMENT Store result of the count»
│ «Set Scrap = scrp»       «COMMENT Restore scrap's content»
│ «REPEAT length»          «COMMENT Attempt to restore the
│                                    selection to its original
│                                    condition»
│     <shift right>
│ «ENDREPEAT»
│ «SET length2 = LEN(Selection)»    «COMMENT Correct size of
│                                    selection to account
│                                    for paragraph marks»
│ «WHILE length2 > length»
│     <shift left>
│     «SET length2 = LEN(Selection)»
│ «ENDWHILE»
│
│ «COMMENT»Report results in a dialog box.«ENDCOMMENT»
│
│ «ASK result = ?There are «sofar» words to this point, and
│ «total» total words in the document. (Press Enter.)»
└─────────────────────────────────────────────────────────┘
```

The macro might look intimidating at first, but from the standpoint of the user it is to the point: To know both how many words you have finished and how many are in a total document, you simply run the macro. Hold down the Shift and Ctrl keys and press a code, such as CW for "Count Words." The macro works for a few seconds and then presents a dialog box such as this:

```
┌─────────────────────────────────────────────────────────┐
│ There are 51 words to this point, and 432 total words in the
│ document. (Press Enter.)
│ [..........................................................]
│
│                                      <  OK  >   <Cancel>
└─────────────────────────────────────────────────────────┘
```

Part of what makes this macro look long and perhaps intimidating are the line breaks, comments, and indentations. If the comments and indentations were removed and the lines were run together to save space, the macro would function the same but would look much shorter:

CHAPTER TWENTY-THREE: Macros

```
«IF Wordversion <> 5.5»«QUIT»«ENDIF»«SET Echo = "Off"»<esc>
«SET scrp = Scrap»«SET length = LEN(Selection)»<F8>
<ctrl home><alt u>w«SET sofar = Scrap»<esc><right><alt u>w
«SET total = Scrap»«Set Scrap = scrp»«REPEAT length»
<shift right>«ENDREPEAT»«SET length2 = LEN(Selection)»
«WHILE length2 > length»<shift left>
«SET length2 = LEN(Selection)»«ENDWHILE»
«ASK result = ?There are «sofar» words to this point, and
«total» total words in the document. (Press Enter.)»
```

If you don't have MasterWord, you'll need to type in this macro as a document if you want to use it. Type the shorter version to save time. Then select the text, and use the Define button in the Edit Macro dialog box to save it as a glossary. To save the glossary on disk, use the Save Glossary button.

Elements of the Sample Macro

You haven't learned yet how to use many of the specific components of a macro, but let's wade into this macro and see how it works. On your first reading, quite possibly you won't follow every particular, but try to gain a sense of how the macro accomplishes its mission.

Characters Word ignores

Before considering what all elements in the macro do, let's consider a couple of elements that don't really do anything—and are valuable for exactly that reason.

In the long version of the macro, each step has been placed on its own line, making it easier to follow the steps and to see which keystrokes relate to each other. Placing each step on its own line necessitates ending each line with a paragraph mark (by pressing Enter) or with a new-line character (by pressing Shift+Enter). You can use these characters freely in a macro because Word ignores them. So if you want to put an extra line or two between different parts of a long macro, press Enter or Shift+Enter.

Word also ignores tab characters. Tab characters let you indent elements, thereby creating horizontal separations on a line without affecting the way the macro operates. In contrast, if you use the Spacebar to separate items on a line, the macro will "play back" the spaces as it does any characters except tabs, paragraph marks, and new-line marks. So, to create horizontal blank space, use the Tab key.

Does this mean you cannot use paragraph marks, new-line marks, or tab characters as elements within a macro? Not at all. But instead of pressing the Enter key to indicate a paragraph mark, you type *<enter>*. Instead of holding down Shift and pressing Enter to create a new-line mark, you type *<shift enter>*. And instead of pressing the Tab key, you type *<tab>*.

The COMMENT instruction

Most lines in the macro end in *comments*. In most cases, tab characters were used to position each *«COMMENT»* to the right of the specific step of the macro to which the comment pertained.

But what is a comment? It is a fourth kind of element that Word ignores when running a macro. Anything contained within the left chevron («, created by holding down Ctrl and pressing [) and the right chevron (», created by holding down Ctrl and pressing]) of a COMMENT instruction is invisible to Word when it runs the macro. But comments aren't invisible to you when you look at a macro in text form. Comments let you place explanations and notes, and even instructions to yourself or to other people, within the body of a macro. They are the easiest macro programming instruction to understand and to use because they don't actually perform any task. A comment simply lets you write or read explanatory information.

You can use chevrons in either of two ways: A single set of chevrons can encompass both the word COMMENT and the explanatory text that follows it; or the word COMMENT can be enclosed in chevrons by itself, with the explanatory text following the right chevron. In the latter case, the instruction ENDCOMMENT, also surrounded by chevrons, must follow the explanatory text. The last comment in the sample macro follows this second form.

Variables

Throughout the macro are words that represent values, such as numbers or words. These words are known as *variables* because the value assigned to each can vary depending on circumstances. Certain variables have preassigned names, which Word understands to have particular meanings. These are known as *reserved variables* because the names are reserved for specific purposes. (A convention used to distinguish between variables and reserved variables is an initial capital letter for a reserved variable name and all lowercase letters for a variable name.)

The element in the macro is the reserved variable *WordVersion*. The value of *WordVersion* is assigned by Word and equals the version number of Word (5.5 when Word 5.5 is running).

Other reserved variables used in the macro are *Echo*, *Scrap*, and *Selection*. The first of these, Echo, has one of two values, *On* or *Off*. It is *On* by default, which means that Word displays (echoes to the screen) the steps of the macro as they are executed. When Echo is set to *Off*, the screen remains impassive until the macro has completed its work or until there is some reason for the screen to be updated, whichever occurs first.

As you might expect from their names, the reserved variable *Scrap* is equal to whatever is contained in the scrap, and the reserved variable *Selection* is equal to whatever text is selected in the document.

In contrast, the variable *scrp* is not reserved. It is an arbitrary word representing whatever the author of the macro wishes it to stand for. In the case of this macro, *scrp* is set to equal *Scrap*; this is a way that the original value of the scrap can be remembered by Word, even when the macro causes the contents of the scrap to be changed. More about this in a minute.

Other variables are *length, sofar, total, length2,* and *result*.

Toward the end of the macro, *Scrap* (the reserved variable) is set to equal *scrp* (the normal variable); in this way, the original contents of the scrap are preserved. The

CHAPTER TWENTY-THREE: Macros

macro preserves them because sometimes you might want to insert the contents of the scrap somewhere in a document and might be annoyed to have a macro that unceremoniously deletes the scrap's contents.

Conditionals

The macro begins with three lines that translate to the following sentence: "If the version of Word that is running is not 5.5, quit the operation of the macro, and return control of Word to the user." This involves the macro instruction IF, which is one of Word's three *conditionals*.

A conditional is an instruction that causes a macro to perform a certain task if (and only if) a given condition is true. In addition to IF, Word's macro language contains the conditionals WHILE and REPEAT. An IF statement says "In the event one thing is true, do some particular thing." A WHILE statement is a variation that says "As long as one thing remains true, do some particular thing." A REPEAT statement says "Do some particular thing so many times, and then go on."

Each IF instruction in a macro must have a matching ENDIF; similarly, each WHILE must have an ENDWHILE, and each REPEAT must have an ENDREPEAT. These END statements signal to Word where the conditional instructions end and the main part of the macro resumes.

> **CONDITIONS AND INDENTATION**
>
> By convention, instructions that are executed conditionally are indented—with a Tab character—to make them easy to discern. In other words, all instructions between an IF statement and its matching ENDIF typically are indented. Similarly, the statements between a WHILE statement and its ENDWHILE or between a REPEAT statement and its ENDREPEAT are usually indented.

Operators

The macro's initial IF instruction compares the reserved variable *WordVersion* with the number 5.5. The comparison is accomplished with an *operator,* specifically the "not equal" operator, which is expressed as <>. If the condition is true (the version of Word is not 5.5), the macro is told to execute the next instruction, which tells it to quit. If the condition is not true (the version of Word *is* 5.5), the macro skips to the ENDIF statement and executes succeeding steps of the macro.

Instructions

IF and WHILE are the only two conditionals in the macro language, but they are not the only two instructions. The sample macro also uses the *SET*, *REPEAT*, and *ASK* instructions, and of course the *COMMENT* instruction.

After determining the version of Word, the macro uses a SET instruction to turn off screen updating. The instruction, «SET Echo = "Off"», relies on the reserved variable *Echo*, which was discussed a few paragraphs back. It tells Word not to bother displaying changes on the screen until the macro has finished its work or until another reason to update the screen occurs. Having Echo off speeds up the execution of a macro and often eliminates the distraction of a screen that reflects the racing activities of a macro.

Similarly, the macro uses SET to record the content of the scrap to the variable *scrp*. As noted, this variable holds a copy of the content of the scrap so that the macro can change the content of the scrap and yet restore it easily.

NOTE: *Formatting information is lost when you store the scrap in a variable.*

Functions

The macro's third SET instruction creates a variable called *length* and assigns to it the length of the selected text. It computes the length through the use of one of Word's four macro functions—each a specialized tool that permits something to be computed or processed. In this case, the function is LEN(x), which computes the length of *x*. Specifically, it is LEN(Selection) that computes how many characters are selected (the selection being represented by the reserved variable named *Selection*). The instruction «SET length = LEN(Selection)» creates the variable named *length* and assigns it a value equal to the number of characters that are selected.

Keystrokes

The macro includes keystrokes, of course: <esc> represents the Escape key; <F8> represents the F8 key; <ctrl home> represents the act of holding down the Ctrl key and pressing the Home key, and so forth.

After recording the length of the selection, the macro uses F8 to turn on extend-selection mode and Ctrl+Home to jump to the top of the document. Because extend-selection mode is on, jumping to the top of the document causes the selection to extend from the original location of the cursor or selection to the top of the document. After this happens, the macro runs the Utilities Word Count command, which places into the scrap the count of the words that are selected. This replaces the original content of the scrap, which is why the macro earlier stored the original content of the scrap.

The next macro instruction is «SET sofar = Scrap». This creates the variable *sofar*, which is set to equal the new value of the scrap (the number of words in the selected portion of the document). Now Word is remembering two values for the scrap: the original, stored as *scrp*, and the new, stored as *sofar*.

Now the macro presses Esc, which turns off the extend-selection mode, followed by the Right direction key, which eliminates the selection and causes the cursor to return to its original location. (If the original location was a selection, the cursor now rests on the first character of the original selection.)

Because there is a cursor now instead of a selection, it's a good time for the macro to compute the total number of words in the document. And it does so, telling Word to run the Utilities Word Count command again. This time Word reports the total number of words in the file, placing the number in the scrap.

The macro creates yet another variable, called *total*, and sets it equal to this third value in the scrap.

Pulling it all together

By now, Word knows the word count from the beginning of the document to the location of the cursor (stored as *sofar*) and the total number of words in the document (stored as *total*). All that remains is to restore the scrap to its original condition, restore the cursor to its original condition, and report the results on the screen.

Restoring the scrap is easy with the instruction «*SET Scrap = scrp*».

Restoring the cursor to its original position isn't always as easy. In general, the next few lines of the macro cause the selection to return to its original size, which was recorded in the *length* variable. If the original size was 0 (indicating a cursor rather than a selection), the cursor is already in the correct location. If the size was 5 characters, the selection needs to extend five characters to the right. The macro accomplishes this with a REPEAT instruction that loops for as many times as characters were recorded in the original selection. Each loop extends the selection one more character to the right. Then the macro compares the actual length of the selection with the recorded length of the original. If necessary, it reduces the size of the new selection to be certain it matches the original. (This final checking and adjusting is accomplished with the macro's lone WHILE instruction and is fruitful only if a paragraph mark was included in the original selection. See the discussion of the LEN function later in this chapter for a description of why a paragraph mark throws off the measurement of the length of the selection.)

The macro's final act is to place on the screen the results of the count. It uses an ASK statement, which traditionally lets the macro request information. In this case, however, the ASK statement allows a message to be placed in a dialog box in the center of the screen. After you respond to the dialog box by pressing Enter or clicking on OK, you're returned to your document—right where you left off—with your scrap seemingly undisturbed.

If you don't quite get it, don't panic. To really understand the macro, you must know some of the information about macro instructions that is presented later in this chapter. But this introduction should have given you at least a taste of the power of macro programming.

> NOTE: *This macro is one of more than 100 included with MasterWord, my software product for Word 5.5. See the front of the book for details or the back of the book for an order card.*

MACRO CONVENTIONS

Before plunging into the actual rules of writing macros, let's consider briefly a few conventions you might choose to follow. These are only suggestions, but adhering to them can make your use of macros more consistent and understandable.

Naming

It's been pointed out several times, but it bears one more mention. When giving macros control codes, use Shift+Ctrl+*two letters* rather than Ctrl+*two letters*. This keeps your control keys free for use as speed-formatting keys. And you won't find conflict between style-sheet key codes and macros if you use Ctrl+Y+*style code* instead of Shift+Ctrl+*style code* when formatting a document with the assistance of styles.

For previous versions of Word, I advised that macro names start with the letter m so that all macros would be grouped together alphabetically within your glossary file. This is no longer necessary because Word segregates macros from the remaining glossary entries, listing them separately in their respective commands (Macro Edit and Edit Glossary).

However, you might consider starting the name of each of your macros with the same two letters that compose its control code. When you follow this convention, you can see at a glance what your control code is.

Here is what the Macro Edit dialog box looks like when your macro follows this naming convention:

```
┌─────────────────────────── Edit Macro ───────────────────────────┐
 Macro Name:                           Macro Keys:
 [....................................] [....................]
 Macros:

   AC.AreaCode      <shift ctrl A>C    CA.Calculate     <shift ctrl C>A
   AM.AdjustMouse   <shift ctrl A>M    CC.CmpileTOC     <Shift Ctrl C>C
   AT.AdjustTable   <Shift Ctrl A>T    CF.CopyToFile    <Shift Ctrl C>F
   BP.BoxParagrphs  <Shift Ctrl B>P    CL.CountLength   <shift ctrl C>L
   BS.SideBySide    <Shift Ctrl B>S    CP.CursorSPeed   <Shift Ctrl C>P

 Selection:                     Macro (Glossary) File: NORMAL.GLY
   (No Selection)

   <Define>   < Delete  >   <Open Glossary...>
   < Edit >   <Clear All>   <Save Glossary...>  <Merge...>      <Close>
```

Try to assign two-letter control codes that are easy to remember. If you use single-letter codes, you limit yourself to a total of 26 control codes that start with letters, whereas if you use two-letter codes, you have a far greater range of possibilities. You might want to assign related macro control codes that start with the same letters. For example, the macros that involve printing might start with P (for instance, Shift+Ctrl+PP for a macro that prints the current page and Shift+Ctrl+PS for a macro that prints the selection).

Capitalization

In most regards, Word is blind when it comes to capitalization. When writing a macro, you can type the COMMENT instruction as «COMMENT» or «comment» or «Comment» or even «cOmMeNt». Word doesn't care, but perhaps you should. Following certain (admittedly arbitrary) guidelines will make it easier to read a macro.

Element	Capitalization	Example
Keystroke names	lowercase (often inside angle brackets)	\<alt e>g5\<enter>
Macro instructions	UPPERCASE (inside chevrons)	«COMMENT»
Functions and operators	UPPERCASE	INT
Variables	lowercase (in or out of chevrons)	«interest»
Reserved variables	initial or other letters capped (inside chevrons)	«Field»
Constants	numbers or uppercase and lowercase (in quotation marks)	18 "Yes"

The chevrons surrounding variables (including reserved variables) often encompass other elements as well. For example, although you would use *«Scrap»* to print the contents of the scrap (with the chevrons surrounding only the reserved variable), you also might use *«SET x = Scrap»* (with the entire phrase inside a single set of chevrons).

To experience the effectiveness of using capitalization deliberately, consider the following line from a macro:

```
«IF result = Selection»<enter>«ENDIF»
```

Looking at capitalization, we know that *IF* and *ENDIF* are instructions, that *result* is a variable, that *Selection* is a reserved variable, and that *<enter>* is a keystroke. This isn't so readily discernible when the same line is presented in all uppercase letters:

```
«IF RESULT = SELECTION»<ENTER>«ENDIF»
```

The Well-Behaved Macro

It is a laudable goal to write a macro that handles potential problems gracefully and cleans up after itself. A macro that works well in the specific situation for which it is written could be considerably less polite if executed in a different situation. For example, a macro designed to delete five characters of text with five presses of the Del key might cause real damage if it were executed in a style-sheet window—where it could delete five styles in a row. Consequently, try to write any macro that will become a part of your permanent collection with an eye toward avoiding potential problems. For example, a macro that deletes five characters could begin with the following steps.

```
<shift ctrl esc>e<up>
«If Field <> "Glossary...»
    <esc>
    «QUIT»
«ENDIF»
<esc>
```

The object of these steps is to verify that the active window is a document window rather than a style-sheet window so that the remaining steps of the macro execute in an appropriate setting. The macro uses <shift ctrl esc> to go to the menu bar, *e* to get to the Edit menu, and presses the Up direction key once, which selects the last item on the menu. If a document window is open, this last item is *Glossary...*; if a style-sheet window is open, the last item is *Rename Style...* instead. The macro's IF statement says, in effect, "If the selected item on the menu does not say *Glossary...*, then escape from the menu and quit running the macro. Otherwise, escape from the menu and continue with the additional steps of the macro (deleting five characters, or whatever)." The result is the elimination of a threat to a style sheet. (The use of <shift ctrl esc> to go to the menu bar is discussed in the next subsection of this chapter, "Keystrokes (Names of Keys).")

The ideal macro is tidy. If it opens a new window, it probably should also close the window at the end. If it changes the settings of fields in commands so that it can accomplish some task, it should set the fields back to the status in which it found them. If it changes what's in the scrap, it should restore the scrap to the way it found it.

Of course, writing farsighted and tidy macros takes longer than writing "quick and dirty" ones, and in many cases the extra care might not be justified. Also, elaborate macros put more demands on computer resources and take longer to run. Try to strike an appropriate balance between fast execution and trouble-free operation.

MACRO RULES

As you've already learned, a macro that you record contains only keystrokes. A macro that you write or edit can also include *constants, variables, array variables, reserved variables, operators, functions,* and *instructions.* Let's take a look at each of these kinds of elements, beginning with keystrokes.

Keystrokes (Names of Keys)

When you are viewing, writing, or editing a macro, letter and number keys are expressed by their own names. Other keys and key combinations are expressed by special macro names, which, as you've already seen, are bracketed inside less-than (<) and greater-than (>) signs. For example, the Enter key is expressed as *<enter>*, and Shift+Ctrl+Enter is expressed as *<shift ctrl enter>*.

Here is a list of keys and their macro names. When one of these keys is to be pressed more than once, the number of times can be included inside the brackets. For instance, instead of typing *<space><space><space>*, you can type *<space 3>*.

CHAPTER TWENTY-THREE: Macros

Key	Macro name
Alt key	<alt>
Ctrl key	<ctrl>
Shift key	<shift>
Esc key	<esc>
Enter key	<enter>
Tab key	<tab>
Del key	<del>
Ins key	<ins>
Home key	<home>
End key	<end>
Left direction key	<left>
Right direction key	<right>
Down direction key	<down>
Up direction key	<up>
PgDn key	<pgdn>
PgUp key	<pgup>
* on numeric keypad	<keypad*>
+ on numeric keypad	<keypad+>
– on numeric keypad	<keypad–>
Spacebar	<space>
Backspace key	<backspace>
Num Lock key	<numlock>
Scroll Lock key	<scrolllock>
Caps Lock key	<capslock>
Function keys F1 through F12	<f1> through <f12>

In addition to these keystrokes, several special-case keys and combinations are useful for the writing of macros. (Some are included in Word 5.5 only because they are identical to key sequences used for similar purposes in Word 5.0; it makes it easier to convert certain macros if you can use the same keystrokes in both versions.)

<menu> The <menu> key signals that the menu is to be activated or deactivated. It is an alternative to <alt> or <f10>, both of which do the same thing.

<ctrl esc> This key combination activates the menu bar even if you are in a dialog box, which it closes. It activates either the main menu bar, which is displayed above a document or style-sheet window, or the print preview menu bar, which is displayed only when File Print Preview is in use.

<shift ctrl esc> This combination resembles the previous one, except that it forces Word to go to the main menu rather than to the print preview menu. It does not, however, distinguish between the main menu displayed when a document is active and the main menu displayed when a style sheet is active.

<shift ctrl esc><esc> This key combination forces the macro to begin in the document or style-sheet window rather than in a menu.

Bracket, chevron, and caret Three characters are considered special by macros and must be paired with a preceding caret when they are representing themselves. The characters are the left angle bracket (<), the left chevron («), and the caret (^). In other words, you can use the left angle bracket as part of a keystroke (such as <alt>), but if you want to search for a left angle bracket you must express it as ^<. Similarly, you can use the left chevron as part of a macro instruction (such as «ENDIF»), but when a left chevron is representing itself it must be expressed as ^«. And when a caret is representing itself, it must be preceded by a caret: ^^.

Constants

Numbers, text and numbers enclosed in quotation marks, and dates are constants. They are of unchanging value. Examples of constants are *99.95, 69, 8/13/61, 6/7/78*, and *"Jill."* Word assumes that numbers arranged in any of the following six month-day-year formats are dates and therefore constants: *mm/dd/yy, mm/dd/yyyy, mm-dd-yy, mm-dd-yyyy, mm.dd.yy*, and *mm.dd.yyyy*.

Constants also can include the same special caret characters that are used with the Edit Search and Edit Replace commands, but the carets must be doubled.

Typing:	Produces:
^^?	A question mark
^^-	A nonrequired (optional) hyphen
^^n	A new-line mark
^^c	A new-column mark
^^d	A section mark or a new-page mark
^^p	A paragraph mark
^^s	Nonbreaking spaces (Ctrl+Spacebar)
^^t	Tab characters
^^w	All spaces and spacing characters

Be careful with the last one; it's powerful.

Variables

In contrast to a constant, a variable can assume one value or a whole series of values during the running of a macro. You create a variable by making up an arbitrary name and then assigning a value to it (or by creating a situation in which the macro assigns a value to it).

The name you assign is symbolic. Choosing a descriptive name, such as *amount* rather than *x*, will make it easier to write and understand the macro. You can use virtually any word or string of characters as the name of a variable. The exceptions are words that Word uses for another purpose—in particular, a collection of special-case names reserved for specific, known variables. (See "Reserved Variables" later in this chapter.)

For example, a macro might ask "How much does the customer owe?" and wait for you to type in an amount. The macro could assign this amount the variable name *owes* and then add a 1 percent service fee and assign the new amount the name *due*.

In this case, both *owes* and *due* would be variables.

Such a macro might look like this:

```
«ASK owes = ?How much does the customer owe?»
«SET due = owes * 1.01»
Well, now he owes «due»!
```

Array Variables

An array variable is much like any other variable, except that it is part of a related series of variables, all of which have related names. For example, a macro that manipulates the salaries of eight employees might use an array variable that has the name *employee* with eight *index* numbers. The first employee would have the array-variable name *employee«1»*, whereas the second employee would have the array-variable name *employee«2»*, and so forth.

This kind of variable is of considerable interest to people with programming experience because it allows flexibility. For example, it is possible to create a series in which the total number of variables can vary each time the macro is run. (In this instance, the macro might ask you to enter a series of numbers, assigning each an array-variable name until you indicate you are finished by pressing Enter without having typed in a number. Then it could add the numbers or perform some other action.)

An array variable has two components. The first is the name of the array, which remains unchanged through the series. In the preceding example, *employee* is the array name. The second component is an index number, which can be either a numeral or, more often, a variable name that represents a number. A macro might contain a loop that processes the array variable several times, each time incrementing the index number by one.

In this example, the macro asks four times for the name of an employee, each time using a number: "What is the name of Employee 1 ?", "What is the name of Employee 2 ?", and so forth. The second half of the macro prints the four names, with a space between them.

```
«SET a = 1»
«WHILE a < 5»
    «ASK employee«a» = ?What is the name of Employee «a» ?»
    «SET a = a + 1»
«ENDWHILE»

«SET a = 1»
«WHILE a < 5»
    «employee«a»»<space>
    «SET a = a + 1»
«ENDWHILE»
```

Keep in mind that Word can accommodate in one macro at most 64 variables of all combined types.

Reserved Variables

Word sets aside certain names for what are called *reserved variables*. You can always read the value of a reserved variable to learn about some current condition of Word. In addition, certain reserved variables are *read-write,* which means that you can set their values as well as read them. When you set the value of a reserved variable, you change the condition of Word. For example, the reserved variable *Window* is read-write. If you read the value of the variable, you learn the number of the window that is active. If you write to the variable, through the use of a SET instruction for example, you cause Word to make active whatever window corresponds to the number you specified.

Although the Microsoft Word manual does not propose the convention, you might find it convenient to capitalize the first letter of the name of a reserved variable to easily differentiate it from other variables.

The following are the reserved variables available in Word 5.5, some of which were introduced briefly early in the chapter.

Read-write reserved variables

Echo You can turn off the updating of the screen, causing Word to run certain macros somewhat faster. This approach also lets you suppress from view distracting activity on the screen. After the macro has finished its work, it updates the screen to reflect the result.

Generally, the *Echo* variable is used in one of two ways: «SET Echo = "Off"» turns off screen updating, and «SET Echo = "On"» turns updating back on. It is possible to turn updating on and off repeatedly during a macro, and a macro can check whether *Echo* is on or off by using the IF instruction: «IF Echo = "Off"»...«ENDIF».

Setting *Echo* to *Off* does not guarantee that Word will not update the screen; rather, doing so tells Word not to update the screen when updating might slow the execution of the macro.

PromptMode The reserved variable *PromptMode* lets a macro convey to Word whether you want prompts to be ignored or whether replies to prompts should be supplied by the macro itself or by the person running the program. (A prompt is a request by Word for information. For example, if you—or a macro—close a window containing a document that has unsaved editing changes, Word will want to know whether you want to save the changes to the document on disk before actually closing the window. Word will ask *Do you want to save changes to (filename)?* This is a prompt.)

The *PromptMode* reserved variable can be set to one of three values: *Macro*, *User*, or *Ignore*.

If you include the instruction «*SET PromptMode = "Macro"*» in your macro, the macro will assume that proper responses to prompts are included at appropriate places in the macro. For example, the macro might close a window and then include an *N* as the next step. With *PromptMode* set to *Macro*, the macro would take the *N* to be a response to the prompt *Do you want to save changes to (filename)?* Leaving out a *PromptMode* statement is like including one that says «*SET PromptMode = "Macro"*».

If you include the instruction «*SET PromptMode = "User"*» in the macro, the macro will pause at each prompt and wait for you to type in your desired response.

If you include the instruction «*SET PromptMode = "Ignore"*» in your macro, Word will roll right over prompts as if they had never appeared. This can result in loss of unsaved editing, for example, but there are circumstances in which you don't want a macro to need to deal with prompts. (In reality, Word has a default answer for every prompt. If you set *PromptMode* to *Ignore*, what really happens is that Word simply takes its default answer, which varies from prompt to prompt.)

Word5Keys Word's Utilities Customize command lets you set up the keyboard to follow the function-key assignments of Word 5.0. This can be handy if you are making the transition from the old Word to the new one. However, it adds a level of complication to macro writing because a macro that uses function keys will have different results depending on whether the Utilities Customize command's Use Word 5.0 Function Keys check box is checked or unchecked.

The *Word5Keys* reserved variable solves this problem by letting you turn the Word 5.0 emulation either on or off for the duration of the macro. If early in your macro you include the instruction «*SET Word5Keys = "Off"*», it forces Word to use the 5.5 function-key map for the duration of the running of the macro. Similarly, if you include the instruction «*SET Word5Keys = "On"*», it forces Word to use the 5.0 function-key map.

A handy little macro can be written using this reserved variable:

```
«SET Word5Keys = "On"»
«PAUSE Use Word 5.0 keys...then press Enter»
```

If you give this macro the control code Shift+Ctrl+W5, you will have access to the Word 5.0 function keys whenever you press the code. You press the code, and the macro turns on Word 5.0 emulation and begins a PAUSE statement that displays the following message on the screen's message bar: *Use Word 5.0 keys...then press Enter*. For the duration of this pause, which lasts until you press Enter, you can press any function keys you want; they will behave as they did in Word 5.0.

For example, if you want to move ahead a word at a time by pressing the F8 key several times, first press Shift+Ctrl+W5, and then press F8 as desired. When you are through, press Enter to end the PAUSE instruction, which, because it is at the end of the macro, also ends the macro. When the macro stops running, the function keys are returned to their previous condition.

InsOvertype This reserved variable is quite similar to *Word5Keys*. But instead of turning on or off emulation of the Word 5.0 function keys, it turns on or off emulation of Word's treatment of the Ins and Del keys. As noted in Chapters 5 and 16, the Use INS for Overtype check box of the Utilities Customize dialog box lets you toggle the functions of these keys: In Word 5.5 mode, the Ins key turns on and off overtype mode, and deleting to the scrap is accomplished by pressing Shift+Del; in Word 5.0 mode, the Ins key inserts text from the scrap, and the Del key deletes text to the scrap.

If early in your macro you include the instruction «SET *InsOvertype* = "On"», Word uses the 5.5 function-key map for the duration of the running of the macro. Similarly, if you include the instruction «SET *InsOvertype* = "Off"», Word uses the 5.0 function-key map for the duration of the macro. In either case, as soon as the macro is finished running, the Ins and Del keys return to the functions specified by the check box in the Utilities Customize command.

Scrap This reserved variable has as its value whatever is contained in the scrap at the time. Word assumes the selection to be text unless any of the following conditions apply: it is numerals only, in which case it is presumed to be a number; or it follows the *mm/dd/yy*, *mm/dd/yyyy*, *mm-dd-yy*, *mm-dd-yyyy*, *mm.dd.yy*, or *mm.dd.yyyy* format, in which case it is assumed to be a date.

Because the *Scrap* reserved variable is read-write, you can set the value of the scrap as well as read it. As noted early in this chapter, being able to set the value of the scrap is useful when you want to save the contents of the scrap, even though a macro needs to put information into the scrap on a temporary basis; simply start the macro by saving the content of the scrap to a variable, and end the macro by setting the scrap back to the value of the variable.

Window This reserved variable "knows" the number of the active window. Because you can have only nine windows plus a help window open at a time, the only possible values are the numbers 1 through 9 (1 through 10 if there is a help window). You can use the number of the active window by using the word *Window* in a macro; or you can check to see how the active window number compares to some other expression (such as «IF *Window* = 3» or «IF *Window* < 5»); or you can move directly to a desired window by using the SET command. («SET *Window* = 1» moves you to the first window, for example.)

Read-only reserved variables

The next fifteen reserved variables are read-only; you can read—but not directly change—their values. The final seven of these reserved variables are not only read-only, but also Boolean.

NOTE: *To change the value of a read-only reserved variable, you must change the aspect of Word that the variable reflects; this is not possible for the* WordVersion *reserved variable, unless you quit Word and start a different version of the program.*

Field This reserved variable has as its value whatever is highlighted in a menu or a dialog box at the time. Again, it can be text, a number, or a date. Word assumes the selection to be text unless it is numerals only, in which case it is presumed to be a number or unless it follows the *mm/dd/yy, mm/dd/yyyy, mm-dd-yy, mm-dd-yyyy, mm.dd.yy,* or *mm.dd.yyyy* format, in which case it is assumed to be a date.

Selection The *Selection* reserved variable has as its value whatever text, number, or date is highlighted inside a document window or style-sheet window. When there is a cursor instead of a selection, the value of the variable is null. As with the *Field* and *Scrap* reserved variables, Word assumes the selection to be text unless it consists of only numerals or follows the pattern of a date.

Page The current page number of the active document is reported by this reserved variable, which is new in Word 5.5.

WordVersion This reserved variable indicates which version of Word is running. For example, in Word 5.5 «*WordVersion*» is 5.5. If you write a macro that runs on 5.5 and you want to be sure no one tries to run it on version 4.0 or 5.0, you can place early in the macro the instruction «IF WordVersion <> 5.5»«QUIT»«ENDIF».

However, be aware that the *WordVersion* variable is sensitive to the setting of the Decimal field of the Utilities Customize command. If the field is set to a comma rather than a period, a macro that includes the instruction «*IF WordVersion <> 5.5*» will fail. Instead, use the «*IF WordVersion <> 5,5*» instruction.

DialogTitle The text displayed in the title of a dialog box is represented by the reserved variable *DialogTitle*. When a dialog box is not displayed, the value of this variable is ""—which is how a macro can check to see if a dialog box is active or not. The text in a help window is not reported by this variable except for help that is itself in a dialog box.

StartupDir The name of the directory that was in use when the Word editing session began is stored as the reserved variable *StartupDir*. If you were in the C:\DIETPOP directory when you started Word, the reserved variable will be equal to C:\DIETPOP for the duration of the editing session. This is handy if your macro needs a place to write information on disk, to look for information, or to return you after switching to a different directory.

ProgramDir The name of the directory containing the Word program (WORD.EXE) is reflected in this reserved variable.

CurrentDir The name of the current directory is reflected in this reserved variable.

NOTE: *Power users might be interested in the subtlety described in this paragraph. Word keeps track of the* boot *directory throughout an editing session. The boot directory and the start-up directory are synonymous, provided that the environment variable MSWNET55 has not been set. Typically, this environment variable is set only when your computer is a workstation on a network; in this event, MSWNET55 stores the pathname of your workstation's local Word directory (the one containing your individual MW.INI file, SCREEN.VID file, and possibly NORMAL.GLY file or NORMAL.STY file). If MSWNET55 has been set, Word treats its directory as the boot directory and pays no heed to the start-up directory. A macro can check for the value of MSWNET55 by comparing the value of* StartupDir *with the value contained in the Default Path text box of the File Options dialog box. To check this dialog box value, the macro must choose the File Open or File Save As command, choose the Options button, be sure the Always Use as Default check box is not checked, delete the existing value from the Default Path check box, choose OK, and then immediately choose the Options button a second time and check the new value of the Default Path text box. If the environment variable MSWNET55 has not been set, the value of the text box will be the same as that of the start-up directory. If the environment variable has been set, the text box will show that directory instead. Of course, the start-up directory and the directory listed in the environment variable are the same if you start Word from that directory.*

Boolean (read-only) reserved variables

The remaining reserved variables are Boolean, meaning they have one of two states: On/1/True or Off/0/False. Boolean variables do not use an explicit operator; the equal sign is the implied operator. This is illustrated in the next paragraph.

   Found *Found* is perhaps the single most important reserved variable for sophisticated macros. It is used subsequent to the Search command to test whether desired text or formatting was found. If the most recent search was successful, *Found* is assigned the value True. Otherwise, it has the value False. For example, a macro might conduct a search and then execute the instruction «IF Found»«QUIT»«ENDIF». This would cause the macro to quit, returning control of Word to you, if (and only if) the Edit Search command had found the desired text. See the discussion of the WHILE instruction for an example of how *Found* is put to practical use.

   Notfound This Boolean variable is identical in almost all respects to *Found* except that it has a value of True if the previous search failed to find the desired text. The instruction «IF Notfound»«QUIT»«ENDIF» would cause the macro to quit if the Edit Search command had not found the desired text.

   Checked The name of this reserved variable is a bit misleading because it seems to suggest an ability to determine whether check boxes in dialog boxes are checked or not. This reserved variable does not do that, although the reserved variable *Field* does.
   Instead, the *Checked* reserved variable indicates whether or not certain items on the View and Window menus have a dot beside them. For example, if you highlight the name of the Outline command on the View menu, the checked variable tells you whether the dot is displayed—that is, whether Word is in outline view or not.

CHAPTER TWENTY-THREE: Macros

If a macro would not work in outline view, you might include among its early steps coding such as this:

```
<shift ctrl esc>v
«IF Checked»
     <enter>
«ELSE»
     <esc>
«ENDIF»
```

Endmark When the cursor is on the end mark (the small diamond at the end of a document or style sheet), the *Endmark* Boolean variable becomes True. This might signal the end of the macro if code such as the following were included in the macro:

```
«IF Endmark»
     «QUIT»
«ENDIF»
```

Maximized This reserved variable has a value of True when Word's windows are maximized. Otherwise, the value is False. If you want to be sure windows are maximized, you can include the instruction *«IF NOT Maximized»<ctrl f10>«ENDIF»*. This says "If Maximized is not equal to True, press Ctrl+F10 to maximize it. Conversely, if you want to be sure Word is not maximized, you can include the instruction *«IF Maximized»<ctrl f5>«ENDIF»*."

Help The *Help* variable is True when the help window is active. This lets you create macros that run only when the help window is displayed or that run only when the help window is not displayed.

Save The *Save* reserved variable remains False until the SAVE indicator appears on the screen, at which time it becomes True. This is a handy variable when you have complex macros or macros that use memory-intensive commands, such as Edit Replace, Utilities Sort, Insert Index, or Insert Table of Contents. These kinds of operations can quickly use up a lot of Word's memory, causing the SAVE indicator to appear. When the SAVE indicator begins to flash, matters are critical—you must save your files or you risk losing data. You can place the following statement at strategic points in a macro, thereby causing the macro to execute the File Save All command whenever it finds that *Save* has become True. The macro statement is *«IF Save»<shift ctrl esc>fe«ENDIF»*. The only drawback to this approach is that in some instances it could save unwanted documents, glossary entries, or style sheets on disk. An alternative is to have the macro statement execute the File Save command rather than File Save All.

Operators

You can use any of several *operators* within a macro instruction. Operators play a variety of roles; their most important is instructing Word to compare two expressions.

An expression can be a constant, a variable of any kind, or a combination of constants and variables. The following are Word's *comparison operators*.

Operator	Description
=	Equal to
<>	Not equal to
<	Less than
<=	Less than or equal to
>	Greater than
>=	Greater than or equal to

These comparison operators are used in the IF and WHILE macro instructions to compare the value of one expression to another. IF and WHILE are called *conditional* instructions because they tell a macro to perform different tasks depending on the outcome of the comparison, or condition. For example, an IF instruction can tell a macro to do one task if two expressions are equal but do a different task if they are unequal. You need the help of an operator in phrasing all IF instructions except those involving the Boolean reserved variables.

In each of the following examples, *task* represents something that a macro will accomplish if the comparison inside the IF instruction is true:

```
«IF x > 5»task«ENDIF»
«IF 5 > x»task«ENDIF»
«IF 5 < x»task«ENDIF»
«IF Field = "No"»task«ENDIF»
«IF number <= 100»task«ENDIF»
«IF Found»task1«ELSE»task2«ENDIF»
«IF Save»task«ENDIF»
```

Other operators play slightly different roles. The following *mathematical operators* let calculations take place inside a macro. Parentheses let you control the order in which the macro performs calculations; a macro acts on operators inside parentheses before it acts on operators outside parentheses.

Operator	Description
+	Add
−	Subtract
×	Multiply
/	Divide
%	Percentage
(	Open parenthesis
)	Close parenthesis

Mathematical expressions can use numeric constants, they can use variables that represent numbers, or they can mix constants and variables. (*Numerical constants* is a fancy way of saying *numbers*.) In the following example, Word will assign the correct value to the variable name *newBalance*, provided you tell it the values of the other two variables (*paycheck* and *bills*) beforehand.

```
«SET newBalance = 1500 + paycheck - bills»
```

And in the following example, Word will compute the value of *total*, provided that it knows the value of *orders*. Note that the parentheses inform Word that it should add 1050 to the value of *orders* and then multiply the result by 2.2.

```
«SET total = 2.2 * (1050 + orders)»
```

The final three operators are *logical operators*, so called because they let you refine Word's logic when it reads macro instructions.

Operator	Description
AND	True if both conditions are true
OR	True if either condition is true
NOT	True if the condition is false

For example, the following is a single IF instruction that is composed of two conditions that are linked by the AND operator. The consequence is that the task will be accomplished if *both* of the comparisons in the IF statement are valid.

```
«IF check <> "Y" AND check <> "Yes"»task«ENDIF«
```

Similarly, using the OR logical operator, you can cause a macro to perform a task if *either* of two comparisons is valid. And using NOT, you can, for example, cause a macro to perform a task in the event the first of two comparisons is valid but the second comparison is invalid. Or you can combine NOT with the reserved variable *Save* and the instruction WHILE to begin a loop that executes until the SAVE indicator appears at the bottom of the screen. The form is «*WHILE NOT(Save)*»…«*ENDWHILE*».

Logical operators are powerful tools, but it might take some practice for you to get the hang of them.

Macro Functions

Word offers four macro functions. One rounds a number down to the next-lower integer, and the other three manipulate *strings* (passages) of text, letting you discover such things as the lengths of words.

You can use these functions together to synergistic effect. For example, you can find the length of a string of text with the LEN function, divide that number in two to find its midpoint, and use the INT function to round the resulting number to a whole number if it is a fraction. Then you can use the MID function to move to the computed midpoint in the text string and read one or more letters from that location.

None of this is hard to do, although it might be a bit intimidating at first.

INT The INT (integer) function rounds a number to the next-lower whole number (or "integer"). The number can be a constant or a variable (positive or negative) or a math expression (including a math expression that uses a different function).

Assuming *number* is the number you start with and *wholeNumber* is the result you seek, the INT function follows this form:

```
«SET wholeNumber = INT(number)»
```

If you want to compute the nearest integer rather than rounding down to the next-lower integer, add 0.5 to *number*. This means that 5.6 becomes 6.1 and then is rounded down to 6—the whole number nearest to 5.6. Specifically, rounding to the nearest integer follows this form:

```
«SET wholeNumber = INT(number + .5)»
```

LEN The LEN function calculates the length of a string of text, where the text or a variable name representing the text is inside parentheses to the right of the letters *LEN*. For example, «*SET length = LEN(Scrap)*» would give the variable named *length* a numeric value equal to the number of characters, including spaces, in the scrap. Instead of *Scrap*, the LEN expression can operate on other reserved variable names, such as *Field* and *Selection*, or on such other variables as might be used in a macro.

Using LEN to measure the length of the selection has one rude twist. LEN counts a paragraph mark as two characters, although a paragraph mark is treated on the screen as if it is a single character. (In truth, a paragraph mark is two characters, a carriage return and a line feed.) This means that the count of characters will be one character too long for each paragraph mark contained in the selection if the selection includes one or more paragraph marks. There are ways to compensate for this; the sample macro at the beginning of this chapter includes such error-correcting steps.

MID The MID function lets you look at one or more characters in a text string. It follows the same basic form as LEN, except that in addition to naming the text string, the parentheses also enclose instructions regarding the specific characters you care about. It follows this form: *MID(string,a,b)*, where *string* is the constant or variable name of the string the macro is to examine, *a* is the number of the first character in the string that is of interest, and *b* is the number of following characters that are of interest.

For example, in the following portion of a macro the user is asked if he or she wants to *(F)ind a name, (A)dd a name, or (P)rint the phone book*. To find a name, the user might type either *F* or *Find*. Regardless, the macro assigns the user's response the variable name *response*, and then the MID function comes into play.

```
«ASK response =? Do you want to (F)ind a name, (A)dd a name,
or (P)rint the phone book?»
«SET response = MID(response,1,1)»
«If response = "F"» «COMMENT Find a name»
```

The SET instruction in this fragment of a macro says "Take the original value of *response* (which could be *F* or *Find*), and look at only its first letter. Now make this first letter (*F* in this case) the new value of the variable named *response*." In this way, the MID function lets you be more flexible in the responses your ASK statements accept.

If you want the MID statement to look at the second, third, and fourth characters of *response*, you can write it this way instead:

```
«SET response = MID(response,2,3)»
```

The 2 indicates that the second letter is the first one of interest, and the 3 indicates that a total of three letters (the second, third, and fourth) are of interest.

Concatenation Rounding out Word's fairly rudimentary string manipulation functions is a concatenation feature. It lets you create a new text string by combining a series of existing strings. For example, if you set the variable «*first*» equal to a first name and the variable «*last*» equal to a last name, you could create a new variable called «*full*» by using the SET instruction in this way:

```
«SET full = first " " last»
```

This actually concatenates three text strings: the first name, a blank space (enclosed in quotation marks), and the last name. If you leave out the space between the quotation marks, the two names run into each other. This is more a feature than an annoyance because it lets you combine parts of words or numbers into single-word or single-number results. So remember to include the space, in quotation marks, when you need one.

You can combine any number of strings, provided the resulting string has fewer than 256 characters. List all the strings to be concatenated to the right of the equal sign, with a blank space between each pair.

Macro Instructions

You can program Word's macros extensively, using the ASK, COMMENT, IF, MESSAGE, PAUSE, QUIT, REPEAT, SET, and WHILE macro instructions. All macro instructions must be enclosed in chevrons. By convention, the names of instructions are capitalized. This is to make it easier for you, not Word; Word doesn't care about capitalization.

ASK The ASK instruction asks a question and awaits your response, to which it assigns a variable name. The generic instruction takes this form:

```
«ASK variable =?prompt»
```

prompt is an optional message of up to 136 characters (the amount that fits, under the best of circumstances, in the dialog box generated by the ASK instruction). The prompt is intended to remind you what the macro is asking. A prompt can include a variable name, provided that it is enclosed within chevrons. This means if a macro has a variable called *day* that represents a day of the week, a prompt can include the expression *«day»*—and the message line will show the value of the variable (*Monday, Tuesday,* or another day of the week) rather than the word *day*.

For example, if we assume that *«day»* happens to be equal to *Monday,* the following ASK instruction

```
«ASK date =?Which date is next «day» ?»
```

would cause Word to display a message that says *Which date is next Monday ?*

When the user answered the question, the response would be stored as a variable with the name *date*.

NOTE: *The SET instruction can be used in the same way as the ASK instruction.*

COMMENT (...ENDCOMMENT) As noted early in this chapter, the COMMENT instruction lets you place explanatory information inside a macro. Word ignores comments, which take one of two forms:

```
«COMMENT This is a comment.»
```

or

```
«COMMENT» This is a comment. «ENDCOMMENT»
```

You must follow one of these schemes exactly. You cannot, for instance, place a colon immediately after the word COMMENT. (If you do, you'll get an error message.)

An advantage to the second method, which uses both a *«COMMENT»* and an *«ENDCOMMENT»* instruction, is that it allows great length and freedom in your explanations. You can, for instance, place a *«COMMENT»* at the top of your macro and follow it with several paragraphs of explanation or instructions. You might indent these instructions by using the Tab key. At the end of one of these comments you must include the *«ENDCOMMENT»* instruction, however.

One hint: If you go on at length in your comments or if you go on at length in your macros in general, use new-line marks (Shift+Enter) rather than paragraph marks (Enter) to end lines. Paragraph marks are Word's repository for paragraph-formatting information, and each takes disk space and memory.

IF (...ELSE)...ENDIF This is one of the workhorses of Word's macro language, a conditional instruction. As you've already seen in this chapter, the IF instruction causes a macro to perform a task *if and only if* a certain condition exists or a test is met. For example, an IF instruction can cause a paragraph to be deleted if it starts with the letter R. Or it can cause a new window to be created in the event there was only one window to begin with. Or it can cause the File Save All command to be executed if more than seven windows are open.

Every IF instruction must be matched with a subsequent ENDIF instruction, which tells the macro that the conditional portion of the macro is finished.

The instruction takes this generic form:

```
«IF condition»result«ENDIF»
```

The *condition* is an expression (a constant or a variable) followed by an operator and another expression. In the instruction

```
«IF Window > 7»<alt f>a«ENDIF»
```

the *condition* is *Window > 7*, with the greater-than sign (>) being the operator. The *result* is the execution of the File Save All command (*<alt f>a*). Note that the IF instruction is matched with an ENDIF instruction.

The IF instruction can take a slightly more complex form:

```
«IF condition»result«ELSE»alternate_result«ENDIF»
```

In this form, if the *condition* is true, the result is executed. Otherwise, the alternative result is executed.

MESSAGE This is a simple macro instruction. It presents a message of your choice on the bottom of the screen when written in this form:

```
«MESSAGE Type up to 80 characters of your choice here.»
```

The message stays on the screen until the macro finishes running or until some other command or instruction triggered by the macro displays a message of its own, which then replaces your message. As a practical matter, this might mean that your message remains on the screen for only about one second and is then replaced. There are at least four ways to keep the message on the screen longer.

One is to use the MESSAGE instruction only in situations in which you know, by the way the macro is written, that no other message will replace it for at least a second or two. (For example, immediately after a MESSAGE instruction you can place a REPEAT instruction in this form: «REPEAT 350»«ENDREPEAT». The macro will perform a do-nothing loop 350 times, giving you a moment to read the message. You can adjust the delay by changing the 350 to another number.)

Another way to be sure you can read a message is to place what you want to be displayed in a PAUSE instruction rather than a MESSAGE instruction. PAUSE displays the message and won't continue until you press the Enter key.

Yet another way, and the one I use most often, is to include the message as a prompt in an ASK instruction. It doesn't matter what variable the ASK statement requests you to give a value for, nor does it matter what you type in response to the ASK statement. What matters is that the ASK statement presents its message in a dialog box across the middle of your screen and waits for you to press Enter. This message is just about impossible to miss, and it is a patient message—it will sit there for as many seconds, minutes, or hours it takes you to press Enter.

A fourth approach, perhaps the most elegant, is to turn Echo on, display the message on the message line, and immediately turn Echo off. The result is that the message will remain on the screen even while the macro continues with other instructions. You'll see an example of this in the sample macro at the end of the chapter.

PAUSE This instruction pauses operation of the macro until you press Enter. Optionally, it displays a prompt. The command takes either of two forms:

```
«PAUSE»
```

or

```
«PAUSE Your message of up to 80 characters goes here.»
```

With a macro paused, you can fill in a dialog box, scroll your document, use the mouse, or do other tasks.

The PAUSE instruction can display messages that appear on the screen until you press Enter. This aspect of PAUSE can be something of a mixed blessing because it is easy to forget to press Enter, in which case the macro remains active—although paused—while you type merrily away, oblivious to the macro. Consequently, it is a good idea to include within the message of a PAUSE instruction the reminder *Press Enter* or *Press ↵*. (The latter approach saves a couple of letters and can be more eye-catching. To type ↵, be sure Num Lock is turned on, and then hold down the Alt key and type *17* on the numeric keypad. Release the Alt key, and then press it again and type *196* on the keypad. Finally, release Alt again, and press it once more, this time typing *217* on the keypad.)

CHAPTER TWENTY-THREE: Macros

QUIT Sometimes you want a macro to stop by itself. For such cases, Microsoft included the QUIT instruction in Word's macro language. When Word encounters the instruction «*QUIT*», it immediately quits running the macro. It does not quit Word.

REPEAT...ENDREPEAT This instruction repeats a portion of the macro a specified number of times. It takes the form

```
«REPEAT x»task«ENDREPEAT»
```

where *x* is a number, either a constant (such as 3 or 12 or 101) or a variable that was previously defined (through an ASK or SET instruction) to have a numeric value.

The following macro uses the REPEAT and ENDREPEAT instructions to display each open window briefly:

```
«SET Window = 8»        «COMMENT Goes to the highest numbered window»
«REPEAT Window»         «COMMENT Repeats the following steps as many
                                 times as there are windows»
    <ctrl f6>           «COMMENT Moves to the next window»
    «REPEAT 100»        «COMMENT Delays while the REPEAT instruction
                                 cycles 100 times»
    «ENDREPEAT»         «COMMENT Matches with the REPEAT instruction
                                 immediately above»
«ENDREPEAT»             «COMMENT Matches with the REPEAT instruction
                                 that cycles through the windows»
```

SET The SET instruction, like the IF instruction, is among the most powerful in Word. You use it to establish the value of any variable (except those reserved variables that cannot have their values changed). The instruction takes this generic form:

```
«SET variable = expression»
```

The expression can be a constant, such as a number or a string of text in quotation marks, or it can be a combination of constants and variables or reserved variables.

Examples of uses of the SET instruction abound in this chapter. SET is necessary to use many other features, such as the functions and several of the reserved variables.

One use of the SET instruction is to initialize the value of a variable. To initialize variables in a macro, you make note of the names of variables that you plan to use during the execution of the macro and set them to a known value (generally 0 or 1 in the case of numeric variables). For example, a macro employing several numeric variables might start out with a series of SET instructions that establish the initial value of each variable as 0. (If the macro has a sufficient number of variables, you might want to use array variables and a loop, a portion of the macro that repeats, to set each variable in turn to 0.) Although not always strictly necessary in Word, initializing is a sound practice.

Word objects with a *This field name is not defined...* message if you attempt to set a variable to equal an expression when the expression contains a variable that has not itself been set to a value.

You can use a characteristic of the SET instruction that is well known to programmers, including Basic programmers, to increment the numeric value of a variable. For example, you can use the instruction «*SET x = x + 1*» as a counter in a loop so that each time the macro reaches the instruction, *x* increases in value by 1. You can also use an IF or a WHILE instruction in the loop to cause the looping to stop when the counter (*x*) reaches a certain number.

You can also use the SET instruction in the same ways you use ASK.

WHILE...ENDWHILE The WHILE instruction performs a looping (repetitive) task as long as a certain condition is met. Every «*WHILE*» statement must have an «*ENDWHILE*», much as every «*IF*» must have an «*ENDIF*». The WHILE instruction uses the following form:

```
«WHILE condition»task(s)«ENDWHILE»
```

Or, when indented it uses the following form:

```
«WHILE conditions»
    task(s)
«ENDWHILE»
```

For a discussion of conditions, see the description of the IF instruction earlier in this chapter.

A key to understanding the WHILE instruction is recognizing that the truth of the condition is tested *before* each repetition of a task or tasks is performed. Then the tasks are repeated as long as the condition remains True—after which the macro moves beyond the ENDWHILE instruction.

For example, this short macro uses a WHILE loop to remove trailing blank spaces from the right end of a line:

```
<end>                      «COMMENT Move to the right end of the line»
<shift left>               «COMMENT Move left one character»
«WHILE Selection = " "»    «COMMENT Loop while the selected character
                                    is a space (" ")»
    <del>                  «COMMENT Delete the space»
    <shift left>           «COMMENT Move selection left one character»
«ENDWHILE»                 «COMMENT Return to the WHILE instruction to
                                    see if it is still true»
```

This is an interesting macro to watch in operation. The cursor works its way from right to left on a line that ends with a lot of extra blank spaces. The cursor chews up these spaces one at a time until it hits a letter or punctuation mark, where it stops. It's vaguely reminiscent of Pac Man.

One useful structure for a macro begins with a search for text, followed by a WHILE FOUND instruction. This is followed by steps that act on the found text. For example, the steps might change the text to something else, or format it in some way. Just before the ENDWHILE instruction, the key combination <shift f4> is placed, which results in the initial search being repeated. The search will only be repeated as long as the FOUND variable remains True, which means that the looping WHILE instruction stops operating as soon as no more instances of the desired text are found.

REMAPPING FUNCTION KEYS

Not every control code needs to involve the Ctrl key. You also can assign function keys as control codes so that using your favorite macros is as convenient as pressing F2, F3, Shift+F9, or Alt+F5. Remapping the effects of function keys in this way lets you design your own word processor, in a small sense. You think that F9 should set the page margins? Fine. Write a macro that lets you adjust margins, and assign F9 as its control code. You think Shift+F1 should move you backward through multiple windows, from Window 4 to Window 3? Okay, change what Shift+F1 does. It's your word processor, after all.

A slight disadvantage to remapping the function keys is that they're pretty handy the way they are now. Each time you create a new purpose for one of them, you make it a bit more awkward to use the key or key combination for its original task.

This is not a serious obstacle, however. If you use the prefix Ctrl+A, you can reach the original purpose of any function key or combination. For example, if you write a macro and assign it to the function-key combination Shift+F8, you still can reach the original purpose of Shift+F8 (which is to shrink the selection) by holding down the Ctrl key and pressing A and then holding down the Shift key and pressing F8.

To assign a function key as a control code, store your macro exactly as you would any other; simply put the appropriate code in the Macro Keys text box of the Macro Record dialog box or the Option Keys text box of the Edit Glossary dialog box.

A couple of implications of remapping function keys need to be mentioned.

First, because Ctrl+A is your means of accessing the original purpose of a function key or key combination, it is important not to use A as the first or only letter of the control code of any macro. If you create a macro that has as its control code Ctrl+A or that begins Ctrl+A (such as Ctrl+AX), you lose your ability to use Ctrl+A to access the original purposes of function keys you've reassigned as the control codes of other macros.

Second, when you write a macro that uses a function key, it's not a bad idea to list <ctrl a> in front of the name of the function key. For example, if the macro uses <f8> twice in a row to highlight a word, the macro could contain the reference <ctrl a><f8 2>. The reference to "Ctrl A" ensures that the macro will run even on a copy of Word containing macros that have remapped the purposes of the function keys. (If you are the only person who uses your macros and you never remap function keys, there's no point in inserting all the <ctrl a> references in your macros.)

DEBUGGING

Frequently, a macro you write won't work correctly at first. You'll have overlooked a detail, failed to understand something, or simply typed something wrong. When this happens, it is time to debug—to get the "bugs" (errors) out of your macro.

This can be painstaking work and usually isn't great fun. Fortunately, Word has features and techniques that can speed the process a bit.

Step Mode

The primary debugging tool is step mode, which you turn on or off with the Step check box of the Macro Run dialog box. Unless a macro is running, Word performs no differently in step mode than it does otherwise. You'll know that step mode is on by the letters *ST* on the status line. But when you run a macro in step mode, Word executes only a single step at a time. Each time you want another step of the macro to execute, you press the Spacebar or almost any other key. This lets you watch the effect of the macro, step by step, and helps you pinpoint the place at which it goes wrong.

If you hold down the Spacebar while in step mode, Word will race forward, executing step after step. The moment you let up, the macro pauses. This lets you vary the speed at which a macro performs its work.

Macros often begin with a series of SET instructions that sets variables to 0 (zero) and performs other initial steps. Consequently, in step mode you might need to press a key quite a number of times before you see any evidence that a macro is running.

It helps, when debugging a macro, to have a copy of the macro's text in front of you, either on the screen or on paper. That way, you can follow along as Word performs the macro's instructions. If a macro is short and its steps don't change windows or otherwise interfere with your ability to read the screen, you might be able to place a copy of the macro text in the window and follow along there as the macro executes. Otherwise, you can use a printed copy.

It's not a bad idea to run a macro in step mode the first time you try it out, even if you expect it to work perfectly. An error in a macro can damage your work in progress or even files on disk (assuming the macro includes instructions that write information on disk). In step mode, you're able to monitor the progress of a macro and cancel it by pressing the Esc key if things take a wrong turn.

To turn step mode off while a macro is running, press the Esc key. This brings to the screen a message asking whether you want to continue running the macro. The message is displayed in a dialog box and contains a Single Step check box that turns step mode on and off. If you press Alt+S, you can toggle step mode on or off at this point. After making the adjustment, press Enter to resume the operation of the macro.

Spies

Sometimes when a macro is malfunctioning, it's difficult to figure out what it is doing at any given moment, even in step mode. In these situations, you might want to place "spies" in your macro—little instructions that don't materially interfere with the macro's operation but that keep you informed of what the macro is doing.

For example, you can litter your macro with temporary MESSAGE or PAUSE instructions, each with a message that identifies its location and that possibly includes the value of a variable. The instruction might be «*PAUSE Bottom of second loop where variable "cost"* is «cost»». This lets you keep close track of what is going on and helps you isolate the place at which things go haywire.

Along the same lines, your "spy" could insert a log of progress into a document. This would have the same general effect as a MESSAGE or PAUSE instruction but would leave behind a more permanent record. Again, the log can contain specific information, such as the value of a particular variable. This kind of data can be quite useful when you're trying to understand what a macro is up to—and what you're up against as you debug it.

Yet another way to pinpoint problems is to highlight a small portion of your macro and copy it to a name in the glossary such as *test*, giving it a control code such as Shift+Ctrl+TE. By running these little test macros, you can find out which sections of your larger macro seem to be healthy and which are ailing.

Missing Chevrons

A common source of problems is missing chevrons. It is easy to omit a chevron by accident, particularly at the end of a line. The consequences are varied. Most troubling are the missing chevrons that cause subtle problems. Occasionally a macro missing a chevron might run without protest, but it might not act quite right. Usually, however, a missing chevron will result in an error message of some kind.

Word 5.5's error messages are pretty good at identifying the source of difficulties because they describe the apparent problem and reproduce in a dialog box the offending portion of the macro text. (Actually, what you see is the text just before the offending text; no matter, it tends to pinpoint the trouble spot.) Sometimes, however, the problem isn't apparent at the location Word identifies. For example, the source of the problem might be a missing right chevron a few lines earlier in the macro, possibly at the end of a COMMENT instruction. Because it didn't encounter a right chevron, Word thinks it is reading a long comment. But when it encounters another left chevron, it realizes something is wrong. Pow! It quits running the macro and displays an error message, but the message shows the wrong line of the macro.

TIPS

Becoming good with macros takes a little time, but the rewards are manifold. Here are a few tips—shortcuts on your path to becoming an expert.

Tabbing in Column Selection Mode

Indenting the lines of a macro to show the relationship of elements and the presence of loops is useful. But it can be bothersome, especially if you want to push each of a whole series of consecutive lines to the right by typing a tab character for each.

Here's a trick that will speed the process. Highlight the first character of the first line you want to indent, and turn on Column Selection mode by pressing

Shift+Ctrl+F8. (You'll see the letters *CS* on the last line of the screen.) Now move the cursor straight down until you have selected the first character of every line you want to indent. Then press Tab. This causes a tab character to be inserted in every line.

You also can use Column Selection mode when you want to reduce the indentation of each consecutive line. Highlight the first character of the top line of the series, turn on Column Selection mode, move the cursor to the bottom line, and then press the Del key. Assuming the lines were indented with tab characters in the first place, Word will remove one tab character from each of them.

The one thing to be cautious about is lines in the macro that are so long they wrap down to the next line. This is fairly common with comments and is particularly true with PAUSE and ASK instructions that use long prompts. You need to be sure that these wrap-over lines are not selected with the Column Selection technique. If you select a wrap-over line as part of a column, you'll add a tab character in the heart of the line when you press the Tab key, or you'll delete a character you don't mean to delete when you press the Del key.

Preliminary Recording

Sometimes the fastest way to create a macro that includes programming instructions is to record portions of it with the Record Macro feature. Let's say you want a macro that has a lot of straightforward keystrokes, but in three places it contains IF instructions. Record the keystrokes from beginning to end, and then go back and add the instructions by editing the macro as text.

To augment this technique, you might want to place a marker in your series of keystrokes to indicate a location at which macro instructions are to be placed during editing. For instance, if you press the 5 key on the numeric keypad while recording a macro, generally all that will happen is that the characters *keypadfive* will be inserted into the sequence of recorded keystrokes. Later, you can replace this with an IF instruction or other programming.

Using Foreign and Graphics Characters

When writing a macro, sometimes you want to place unique markers in the text of a document so that you can use the Search command to return to them later or so that Word will recognize that it has reached a boundary of some sort when it encounters the marker.

One approach is to use a unique string of characters, such as $%#$@# or even *QW* or *QZ*. (Because *Q* normally is not followed by any letter other than *U*, letter pairs such as *QS* are likely to be unique in a document and therefore are suitable as markers.)

But perhaps the best approach is to use single-character markers that employ an ASCII graphics or a foreign-language character. You access these characters by being sure that Num Lock is on and then holding down the Alt key and typing a number between 127 and 255 on the numeric keypad. For example, Alt+200 generates this character: ╚. You can type, delete, or search for these characters as you do for any other character. Many of them are distinctive and are likely to be unique in your document. Because each is only one character long, a macro can move the cursor across a line one character at a time, searching for a boundary with the instruction «*IF Selection = "↵"*».

Running DOS Commands

A macro can execute a DOS command (such as Dir or Copy) or even run a different program (memory permitting and provided that the macro contains instructions that execute File DOS Commands). The macro will resume operation within Word as soon as the DOS command or other program has finished running. (But you still must press a key when the screen message tells you to.)

The same technique works if Word is running under OS/2.

The AUTOEXEC Macro

Recall that a glossary file named NORMAL.GLY loads as part of Word's regular start-up process when you start the program. If you store important macros and other glossary entries in NORMAL.GLY, you might not need to use the Macro Edit (Open) or Macro Edit (Merge) command often, if at all.

This automation of the macro-loading process can be taken one step further. If you have a macro that you want to run every time you start Word, name the macro *AUTOEXEC* and store it in *NORMAL.GLY*. (Do not give it the name *m.AUTOEXEC* or *AUTOEXEC.MAC* or add a control code. Simply call it *AUTOEXEC*.)

If this macro is stored in NORMAL.GLY, it will run whenever you start Word.

You could use it to flash a greeting on the screen, to set up a favored multiwindow configuration, or to use the document-retrieval menu to search for new documents on a network.

Starting Word and a Macro Together

New for Word 5.5 is a command-line switch that lets you specify a macro you want Word to run immediately upon startup. The switch is /*m*, and you use it at the DOS prompt, typing it after you type *word*. Following *m*, type a space and the name of the macro you want to run. For example, if you have a macro called *Monday* that you run first thing every Monday morning, you could start your work week by typing the following and pressing Enter:

```
word /m monday
```

Cutting Down on Paragraph Marks

To keep macros short, use few paragraph marks within them. Instead, use new-line characters. (That is, at the end of each line, press Shift-Enter instead of Enter.) A paragraph mark uses a disproportionate amount of disk space and memory because Word stores a lot of formatting information in each paragraph mark—even if the paragraph mark creates only a blank line.

Searching for Chevrons

When editing the text of a macro, you can jump to the previous right chevron by holding down the Ctrl key and pressing the < key. You can jump to the next right chevron by holding down the Ctrl key and pressing the > key. The Ctrl+> and Ctrl+< combinations were added to Word to let you move quickly through on-screen forms (which also use the right chevron), but they are handy for editing macros too. Pressing the F11 key will also jump you forward to the next right chevron; pressing Shift+F11 will jump you to the previous one.

A SAMPLE MACRO

To inspire you to make macros of your own, here is one that is ready to be typed in and used. It is a macro from MasterWord; its use was previewed in Chapter 6, the introduction to macros. It allows you to print a single page or a series of pages.

When typing it in, be careful not to make any errors. You do not need to type in any of the comments, so the task is not quite as intimidating as it might seem at first.

```
«IF WordVersion <> 5.5»«QUIT»«ENDIF»
«SET InsOvertype = "On"»
«SET Word5Keys = "Off"»
«IF DialogTitle <> ""»«QUIT»«ENDIF»
«SET title = "MasterWord Print Page Macro. . ."»
«MESSAGE «title» repaginating»
«SET Echo = "Off"»
<alt e><up>«IF Field <> "Glossary..."»<esc>«QUIT»«ELSE»<esc>«ENDIF»
<alt v>e<alt g>
«SET msgSave = Field»
«IF Field = "No"»<alt g>«ENDIF»<enter>
<alt u>p<enter>    «COMMENT Repaginate»
«MESSAGE «title»»
«ASK pagetemp = ?Type page number(s) you want to print,
or press ↵ to print current page»
«SET Echo = "On"»
«MESSAGE «title» checking settings»
«SET echo = "Off"»
«IF pagetemp = "q"»
   «QUIT»
«ENDIF»
«IF pagetemp = ""»
   «SET thepage = Page»
«ELSE»
   «SET thepage = pagetemp»
«ENDIF»
<alt f>p  «COMMENT File Print command»
<alt o>   «COMMENT Choose Options»
```

(continued)

CHAPTER TWENTY-THREE: Macros

continued

```
«SET draft = Field»
«IF draft = "Yes"»
    «ASK keepDraft = ?Word is set to print fast, low-
quality Draft mode. Press Enter to keep Draft on,
or press N and then Enter to turn it off.»
    «IF keepDraft = "N"»
        «COMMENT Spacebar space inserted»
    «ENDIF»
«ENDIF»
<enter>    «COMMENT Leave Options»
<alt c>    «COMMENT Go to Copies field»
«SET copy = Field»
«IF copy <> 1»
    «ASK howmany = ?To print 1 copy, press Enter. To print
«copy» copies, press Y and Enter. Or type a number and press Enter.»
    «IF howmany = "Y"»
    «ELSE»
        «IF howmany = ""»
            1
        «ELSE»
            «howmany»
        «ENDIF»
    «ENDIF»
«ENDIF»
<alt a>                    «COMMENT Go to range field»
«SET range = MID(Field,1,1)»«COMMENT Note page range»
p                          «COMMENT Choose Page»
<tab>
«SET pages = Field»        «COMMENT Note current setting»
«thepage»                  «COMMENT Set new page numbers»
«SET PromptMode = "user"»«COMMENT In case of downloads»
«SET Echo = "On"»
«MESSAGE «title» now printing»
«SET Echo = "Off"»
<enter>                    «COMMENT Print»
«SET PromptMode = "macro"»
«SET echo = "On"»
«Message «title» restoring settings»
«SET echo = "Off"»
«SET PromptMode = "ignore"»
<alt f>p                   «COMMENT Choose File Printer command»
<alt c>                    «COMMENT Go to Copies field»
<del>
«copy»                     «COMMENT Set field to its original value»
<alt a>                    «COMMENT Go to Page Range field»
```

(continued)

continued

«MID(range,1,1)»	«COMMENT Set field to equal "range"»
<alt s>	«COMMENT Go to Pages field»
<del>	
«pages»	«COMMENT Set field to equal "pages"»
<alt f>	«COMMENT «Go to File field»
<del>	
NUL	«COMMENT Print to NUL»
<enter>	«COMMENT Carry out the command»

«SET Echo = "On"»
«MESSAGE «title» done»
«SET Echo = "Off"»
«IF msgSave = "Yes"»<alt v>e<alt g><enter>«ENDIF»

CHAPTER TWENTY-FOUR

Style Sheets

For an hour, for a day, or for as long as you use Microsoft Word, style sheets are the key to using the program's ability to remember formats and replay them whenever you want. Before we continue, however, let's consider one question you might have about style sheets: Do you really need them?

Many people use Word seriously, and quite productively, without using style sheets. Word's built-in formats and the family of Format commands are capable and flexible, and the formatting ribbon is especially easy to use. Why, then, learn to create and use style sheets? The answer is "power." Style sheets give you more power, more of what you use Word for. And although you need to grasp the concept underlying style sheets, after you have the idea firmly in mind, the actual use of a preexisting style sheet is easy, especially in relation to what it accomplishes.

A style sheet lets you tailor Word's formatting capabilities to suit a particular kind of document. One style sheet can give a consistent look to many documents of the same type (letters, for example). Conversely, a collection of style sheets can give a single document a variety of looks. After you create a suitable style sheet, you can use it to format a document much more quickly than with any other formatting method.

Imagine you have a second keyboard—a special keyboard for which you can define any number of keys, up to a maximum of 125. The keys of this keyboard are dedicated to formatting: Each applies one format or set of formats to whatever text is selected. One key might center text. Another might underline text. Yet another might center and underline. You can put whatever labels you want on the keys. You can change the formatting associated with any key at will—take away any formats you decide are unnecessary or add new ones whenever you want. You can even change the formatting of all of the keys at one time so that the keyboard takes on an entirely different personality for each new word processing task. Imagine what a powerful tool such a keyboard would be.

Of course, there isn't a special keyboard devoted to formatting. But if you can imagine one, you already understand the concept underlying Word's style sheets.

STYLES: THE BUILDING BLOCKS

Word lets you use your regular keyboard as if it were dedicated to formatting. Word remembers up to 125 different formatting instructions (such as "Make these characters italic" or "Center this paragraph") or combinations of instructions (such as "Center this paragraph, and make its characters italic"). Each of these instructions or combination of instructions is a *style*, a building block for a *style sheet*. Word lets you give each of these styles a one-character or two-character label called a *key code*. When you want to format, instead of pressing up to 125 formatting keys, you hold down Ctrl and press the Y key. Then release the Ctrl key and type one of up to 125 key codes on the regular keyboard. For example, you might press Ctrl+YCI (the key code portion of this is CI) to use a style that both centers and italicizes. Using this approach can be a dramatically faster way to format—and speed is only one advantage to formatting with styles.

A key code can be almost any one or two letters, numbers, or symbols of your choice and is comparable to a label you might stick onto a keyboard key.

As described in Chapter 6, Word organizes the 125 potential styles into three major groups, or families: Character, Paragraph, and Section, corresponding to the three types of formatting.

- Twenty-nine styles are available for *character formatting*. You can use them instead of built-in speed-formatting–key character formats and the Format Character command.
- Seventy-four styles are available for *paragraph formatting*. They can replace the built-in paragraph formats and the Format Paragraph command. For instance, if you have a paragraph style intended for titles, you can define its formatting so that paragraphs controlled by the style will be centered. As a bonus, a paragraph style also lets you specify the character formatting that is considered normal in the paragraphs controlled by the style. So, for example, the paragraph style intended for titles could also specify that the characters in title paragraphs will be boldfaced and underlined. Whenever you apply the style to selected text, that text not only is centered but is boldfaced and underlined too. (You can override the normal character formatting in a paragraph by highlighting its characters and using a character style, a built-in format, or the Format Character command.)
- Twenty-two styles are available to control *section formatting*. The formatting of a section style guides the page design of the document or section of a document in which formatting is executed.

Automatic Styles

To make style sheets easy to use, often you don't need to use key codes to apply specific styles to appropriate parts of a document. Certain styles are dedicated to particular tasks, and if these *automatic* styles are available, Word will use them unless otherwise instructed.

For example, if you create a "normal" paragraph style in a style sheet, Word formats each paragraph with it unless you deliberately apply other formatting. Word lets you create a special Footnote paragraph style for footnote text, and it will also assign appropriate styles to headings used in outlines and to the various elements in an index or a table of contents. In addition, Word gives to page numbers, footnote reference marks, and annotation reference marks whatever character formatting you specify in appropriate character styles.

Similarly, Word will print summary information using the font and size specified in the formatting of the Summary Info character style and will print linedraw characters in the font specified in the formatting of the linedraw character style. Of course, you don't have to create or use any of these automatic styles, and when you do, you can always override them.

Looking at a Style

You can look at pertinent information about the styles contained in a style sheet. Choose Format Define Styles (Alt+TD) to cause Word to open a window containing descriptions of the active style sheet. The style sheet window looks like a document window except that it contains descriptions of styles instead of text; if the window is empty, it means either that no style sheet is attached to your document or that you have a style sheet called NORMAL.GLY but have not yet created any styles for it.

Recall that just as there are three types of formats—section, paragraph, and character—there are three corresponding types of styles. You can work with any of them in the style-sheet window. A section style, for example, controls page layout. Here's what a style-sheet window looks like when it has a style sheet displayed in it. In this case, the style sheet has only one style, a paragraph style.

```
(P) NP Normal                                    NORMAL PARAGRAPH
        modern b 12. Flush left (first line indent 0.5"), space before 1
        li.
```

Here, a section style has been added to the style sheet:

```
(S) SS Normal Section                            STANDARD MARGINS
        Page break. Page length 11"; width 8.5". Page # format Arabic. Top
        margin 1.67"; bottom 1"; left 1.25"; right 1.25". Header at 1"
        from top. Footer at 0.83" from bottom. Footnotes on same page.
(P) NP Normal                                    NORMAL PARAGRAPH
        modern b 12. Flush left (first line indent 0.5"), space before 1
        li.
```

A paragraph style controls paragraph formatting (line layout and spacing) and establishes a "normal" format for the characters in a paragraph.

You can override "normal" character formatting whenever you want by applying a character style to selected text. In the following illustration, an example of a character style has been added to the style sheet:

```
(S) SS Normal Section                       STANDARD MARGINS
        Page break. Page length 11"; width 8.5". Page # format Arabic. Top
        margin 1.67"; bottom 1"; left 1.25"; right 1.25". Header at 1"
        from top. Footer at 0.83" from bottom. Footnotes on same page.
(P) NP Normal                               NORMAL PARAGRAPH
        modern b 12. Flush left (first line indent 0.5"), space before 1
        li.
(C) UC Character 1                          UNDERLINED
        modern b 12 Underlined.
```

To put styles in the style sheet you either

- Record formatting from your document with the Format Record Style command. You can then move to the style sheet window to see an English-language description of the formatting you've recorded.

or

- Create styles directly in the style sheet window, with that window's menu of commands. Specifically, you use the style sheet window's Insert New Style command to create the style and give it a name, and then you select the file and use Format commands to infuse it with the desired combination of formatting.

The Elements of a Style

Regardless of its purpose or the formatting it describes, every style you see in the style sheet window has the same basic structure. Let's look again at the paragraph style illustrated earlier. This time, labels distinguish the different parts of the style:

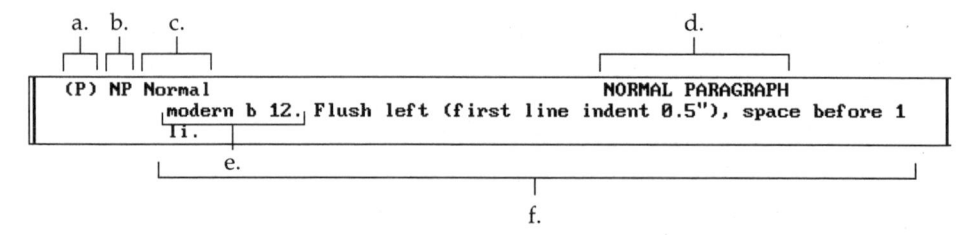

```
  a.  b.   c.                                           d.
  ┌┐  ┌┐  ┌┐                                      ┌──────────┐
┌─┴┴──┴┴──┴┴───────────────────────────────────────┴──────────┴─┐
│ (P) NP Normal                               NORMAL PARAGRAPH  │
│         modern b 12. Flush left (first line indent 0.5"), space before 1 │
│         li.                                                    │
└────────┬─────┬─────────────────────────────────────────────────┘
         └──e.─┘
                              f.
```

At first glance, this collection of names and numbers might seem terse and possibly confusing, so let's use an analogy. The following "style" has similar elements, but it is about something more familiar:

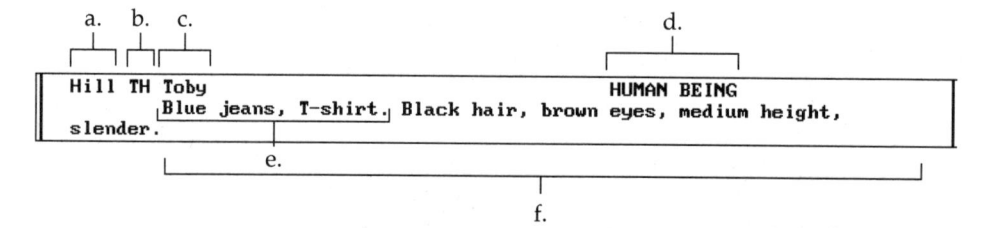

```
  a.  b.   c.                                           d.
  ┌┐  ┌┐  ┌┐                                      ┌──────────┐
┌─┴┴──┴┴──┴┴───────────────────────────────────────┴──────────┴─┐
│ Hill TH Toby                                HUMAN BEING       │
│         Blue jeans, T-shirt. Black hair, brown eyes, medium height, │
│ slender.                                                       │
└────────┬─────┬─────────────────────────────────────────────────┘
         └──e.─┘
                              f.
```

CHAPTER TWENTY-FOUR: Style Sheets   455

Here is a summary of the style:

a: *(P)*. This is a paragraph style, indicated here by the *(P)*. Section styles are indicated with *(S)* and character styles with *(C)*. Think of the type as the style's "family" name (like *Hill*)—the group to which the style belongs.

b: *NP* is the key code assigned to the style. It's a shorthand way of referring to the style (as are the initials *TH*).

c: *Normal*. This is the style's I.D., which when taken in combination with the type uniquely identifies the style among the 125 styles that are possible in any one style sheet. In this case, this Paragraph style is identified as *Normal*. *Normal* (like *Toby*) identifies the member of the family.

d: *NORMAL PARAGRAPH*. This is an optional descriptive remark (as is *HUMAN BEING*). You can add such a remark to any style you create, to remind yourself of its purpose. The remark can be up to 28 characters long; capitals help the remark stand out but are not necessary.

e: *Modern b 12*. This portion of the style's description, up to the period, is devoted to character formatting. It describes the font and type size that will be considered normal for characters in the paragraph. In this case, the font is modern b and the size is 12 point. (If the paragraph were to be double-spaced, the size would be listed as 12/24, indicating 12-point characters in 24 points of vertical space.) A point is ½₂ inch, so 12-point spacing yields 6 lines to an inch. Like Toby's blue jeans and T-shirt, this character formatting is the typical "dress" applied to paragraphs formatted with this style. Changing the character formatting of a paragraph style is easy.

f: *Flush left (first-line indent 0.5"), space before 1 li*. This describes the line layout of the paragraph itself: flush with the left margin, the first line indented ½ inch, and a blank line above the paragraph. It is like saying Toby has black hair, brown eyes, and so on.

Observe that the first line of a style describes its identity ("name") and the second and subsequent lines are devoted to describing its formatting. This reflects the basic division of a style into two parts: name and formatting. Let's take a closer look at each.

Style names

The name portion of a style includes its *style type, key code, style I.D.,* and *remark*.

Type indicates what kind of formatting a style does—character, paragraph, or section. The I.D. distinguishes one style from another within each of the three type groups. In the paragraph style name Normal, Paragraph is the type and Normal is the I.D.

Character styles are named Character 1, Character 2, and so on up to Character 23. There are also six automatic styles, named Page number, Line Number, Footnote Ref, Annotation Ref, Line Draw, and Summary Info. Unlike the Paragraph and Section types, the Character type does not include a "normal" character style. This is because in Word, normal characters in one paragraph can be totally different from normal characters in another. Thus, the definition of a normal character depends on—and corresponds to—the formatting specified in the character-formatting section of the paragraph style. If you alter character formatting in a paragraph, you can change it back at any time to the normal character formatting specified in the paragraph style by selecting (highlighting) the characters and pressing Ctrl+Spacebar.

Paragraph styles are named Paragraph 1, Paragraph 2, and so on, up to Paragraph 55. Additionally, there are *automatic* paragraph styles named Normal, Header/Footer, Footnote, and Annotation, as well as seven for the various levels of heading you might use in a document and four each for indexes and tables of contents. By "automatic," we mean that Word will use the formatting from these styles without any deliberate act on your part when the paragraph you are formatting falls into one of these categories that Word understands. For example, when a paragraph has not been deliberately formatted in some other way, Word gives it the Paragraph Normal style. When a footnote has no other paragraph formatting, it is assigned the Paragraph Footnote style. When you create a header or footer (in other words, a running head) by using the Format Header/Footer command, any formatting you've defined for the Header/Footer style is applied to the text of the header. Assign paragraph and character formatting of your choice to the Normal, Header/Footer, Footnote, and Annotation styles, and these elements of your document assume the look you want.

Section styles are named Section 1, Section 2, and so on, up to Section 21. An additional, automatic section style, named Normal Section, is the style Word uses unless you change the document's section formatting.

A character can be controlled by only one character style, one paragraph style, and one section style at a time. For example, when you attach a paragraph style to a paragraph, that style dislodges whatever paragraph style was previously attached. This is a major feature of style sheets because it enables you to wholly change the formatting of any element in a document by simply replacing one style with another. The following is an organization chart for the potential styles in a style sheet:

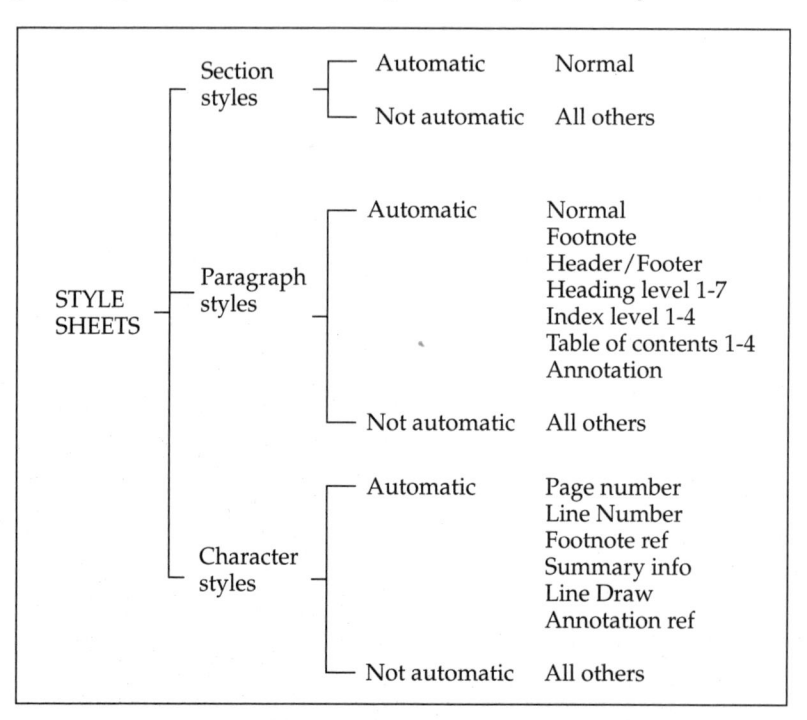

STYLE SHEETS			
	Section styles	Automatic	Normal
		Not automatic	All others
	Paragraph styles	Automatic	Normal Footnote Header/Footer Heading level 1-7 Index level 1-4 Table of contents 1-4 Annotation
		Not automatic	All others
	Character styles	Automatic	Page number Line Number Footnote ref Summary info Line Draw Annotation ref
		Not automatic	All others

Style formatting

A name, such as Normal, is only half of what makes a style a style. The other component is formatting.

Although the names of the 125 styles are fixed, some of their other characteristics are flexible. You can, if you want, change a style's key code to one that is easier to type or to remember. More important, you can freely alter the formatting of any style. That is, you can change the effect it has on the text to which it is applied.

This flexibility means, for example, that you can change formatting of the Character 7 style from underlined to boldfaced italics at any time. All you need to do is redefine the style's formatting from underlined to boldfaced italics. It takes only a few seconds to make the change in a style sheet window, and your entire document, as well as other documents controlled by the same style sheet, reflects the change from beginning to end. Passages still have their characters formatted with the Character 7 style, but the style no longer means underlining; now it means boldfaced italics. (In this example, the key code for Character 7 might have been UC to help you remember "Underlined Character." When you changed the formatting, you could also change the key code to BI or to some other code indicative of "Bold Italic." But you wouldn't have to; you could leave it UC. Word wouldn't get confused.)

Applying a Style to Text

You apply a style to text much as you apply any other formatting instruction. First you select the text to be formatted, and then you actually apply the formatting. As noted in earlier chapters, applying the formatting to the selected text can be accomplished in a variety of ways:

- If the style is an automatic one, you don't need to do anything—except avoid applying some other style or formatting to the text. For example, if you want to format a footnote reference mark as a superscripted version of the font Helvetica, you would format the Footnote Ref character style with Helvetica and superscripting and leave it to Word to apply the style to your footnote reference marks. This would work as long as you didn't select the footnote reference marks, either by themselves or as part of a larger selection, and apply other character formatting.
- If you know the style's key code, you can press Ctrl+Y and then the key code. Be sure to release the Ctrl key before typing the code. This is the best method for touch typists.
- If you are not using macros, you can apply a style by pressing Shift+Ctrl plus the style's key code. The drawback to this method is that Shift+Ctrl also is the best prefix for macro control codes, which sets up potential conflicts. Because a macro takes precedence over a style when both have the same code, it is a conflict the style always will lose. It also can be confusing, because if you remember a key code incorrectly you might find yourself running a macro unintentionally.

- The Format Apply Style command (Alt+TY) can be used in several ways. The first field of the command's dialog box is the Key Code text box, in which you can type the key code of the desired style. This is almost as fast and uses as few keystrokes as the Ctrl+Y or Shift+Ctrl method, and it has the advantage of displaying a list of available styles in a list box in the middle of the screen. If you don't know the key code, you can scroll through the list box until you find the desired style and, while it is highlighted, press OK (Enter). Unless you change it, the list box displays paragraph styles. To change this, use the Style Type drop-down list box, which offers all three choices—Character, Paragraph, and Section.
- One of Word's most exciting features is the ribbon, which was discussed early in Chapter 4. If the ribbon is turned on, it lists in its Style field the name (I.D. and key code) of whichever paragraph style is governing the formatting of the paragraph containing the cursor or selection. In the event the selection extends across paragraphs that are formatted in different ways, the Style text box is blank. If a paragraph has been formatted first with a style and then with a Format command or a speed-formatting key, the hybrid nature of the formatting is indicated in the ribbon by an asterisk. The Style text box will list the name of the style that is contributing to the formatting, followed by an asterisk. Even if the ribbon is not displayed, pressing Ctrl+S activates it and highlights its Style text box. You then can use the Down direction key or Alt+Down direction key or the mouse to scroll through a list of existing paragraph styles and choose one. If you press Ctrl+S a second time, the Apply Style dialog box appears and you can make the same choices you could had you selected Format Apply Style.
- The final method is available only if you use the MasterWord Help system and style sheets. Each of the approximately 75 styles in these style sheets is listed by name in the online help. If you press (or click with the mouse) on the name of the style, a help window appears that tells you the purposes of the style and how to use it. If you press or click next to the name of the style, on a special ACT button, MasterWord applies the style to your text for you.

Styles versus built-in formats

Recall that *direct formatting* is applied with a speed-formatting key (for example, centering is Ctrl+C, boldface is Ctrl+B) or with a Format command, such as Format Character. In addition, all of the features of the ribbon except the Style field let you apply direct formatting.

A style, in contrast, lets you perform *indirect formatting,* so called because the actual formatting instructions remain attributes of the style, not of the document; the document is formatted indirectly by reference to the style sheet. This idea of indirection is discussed in Concept 10 in Chapter 2.

A strong apparent resemblance exists between formatting a document using styles and using a speed-formatting key. Both methods control appearance, and you can put either into effect by holding down the Ctrl key and pressing a key code. Note some practical differences, however:

- Speed formats have unchangeable key codes, such as U for underline, I for italics, and R for right alignment. In contrast, styles can have virtually whatever one-letter or two-letter key codes you choose to give them. If you use a particular style frequently and want to code it with your initials, you can do so.
- Speed-formatting keys are built into Word. They are almost always available. Styles, on the other hand, are available only when you have attached a style sheet containing them to the document on which you are working. Of course, if the style sheet has the name NORMAL.GLY, it is attached automatically to any document that is not deliberately formatted in some other way.
- Speed formats cannot be changed. Style sheets can be changed at will.
- Speed formats can be attached to documents only through the use of key codes, but styles can also be attached with Format Attach Style Sheet.
- Because they cannot be created or modified, using built-in formats requires only a single step: You simply apply them by key code to a selection in a document. Applying a style from an existing style sheet is equally easy, but creating styles and organizing them into usable style sheets can be a comparatively complex task.

I strongly recommend that you use two-letter key codes rather than single-letter key codes for styles. Two letters allow for many more combinations of letters, providing you with more flexibility.

STYLE SHEETS: SETS OF STYLES

A style sheet is a collection of styles, all of which are accessible to you at the same time. By switching from one style sheet to another, you can instantly bring into Word an entirely different group of formatting styles for a document. You attach or switch style sheets with the Format Attach Style Sheet command.

Think again about our imaginary keyboard, mentioned at the beginning of this chapter. We can change the formatting effects of all its keys at once. Changing the style sheet with the Format Attach Style Sheet command is analogous to telling Word "BIZLETTR" when you want all the "keys" (styles) customized for formatting business letters or telling it "REPORT" when you want the "keys" (styles) to assist you in formatting reports. (BIZLETTR and REPORT are hypothetical names for style sheets. You can use any name of up to eight letters for a style sheet.)

After you have put a different style sheet into place with the Format Attach Style Sheet command, the styles that are displayed in the style sheet window change, and your document takes on the appearance specified by the formatting of the new styles.

This means, for example, that any text in the document with a Paragraph 26 style assumes the formatting specified for Paragraph 26 style in the new style sheet. However, any direct formatting remains unchanged because it was applied directly to the text with a built-in format or the Format command. For example, if you underline some characters with the built-in format Ctrl+U, these characters remain underlined and in the same font even if you attach a different paragraph style or style sheet.

(To eliminate direct character formatting, select the characters and press Ctrl+Spacebar. If you don't know whether a document contains direct formatting but you know you don't want it to, you can press Shift+F10 to select the whole document and then press Ctrl+Spacebar.)

If you expect to use style sheets routinely—particularly if you think you will be merging existing styles or blocks of styles to create new style sheets—I strongly advise you to plan ahead and define a systematic method of assigning key codes and I.D.s to your styles. By using the same I.D.s and key codes in all style sheets, you can change the style sheet attached to a document with little worry that the new styles will produce odd or unexpected formatting. You might, for example, reserve *Paragraph 5* only for a double-spaced paragraph style in any style sheet you create. To further simplify matters, you could then reserve the key code ND (Normal Double-spaced) for use only with this type of style.

When you have a system of coherent style sheets, you can write a document with one style sheet attached to it and print it later after you have attached a different style sheet to it. You might write a report draft with a style sheet that double-spaces all the lines but print the final version with a style sheet that formats text to be single-spaced and justified—in keeping with your requirements for a polished document.

MODIFYING AND CREATING STYLE SHEETS

After you've had some experience using existing style sheets, you're ready to modify one or to create some styles on your own. Modifying an existing style sheet is easier, so we'll start there.

As you have seen, a style sheet is a collection of styles you can save on disk with a filename and the extension .STY (for example, REPORT.STY). You can move whole blocks of styles from one style sheet to another by selecting them and passing them through the scrap. You can also alter the name of an individual style with the Edit Rename Style command, which is available only when a style sheet window is active. However, Word will not let you merge into a style sheet any styles that conflict in name or key code with styles already in the style sheet. Consequently, when there is a conflict you should decide in advance which styles will be incorporated into the merged style sheet and which will not, and then you can delete the unwanted ones before attempting to merge the style sheets.

Most often you change a style sheet one style at a time by changing a style's name with the style-sheet window's Edit Rename Style command and the various Format commands.

CHAPTER TWENTY-FOUR: Style Sheets   461

Modifying a Style's Name

When you choose the Edit Rename Style command, you can enter any remark, key code, or I.D. you want. You cannot, however, change a style's type.

To choose a new I.D., you choose from the pool of I.D.s not already assigned to other styles of the same type (Character, Paragraph, or Section). Word proposes the I.D. that the selected style had before you used the Edit Rename Style command. To choose a different I.D., select the Style I.D. drop-down list box and press the Down direction key, press the Alt+Down direction key, or click with the mouse on the down arrow on the right side of the text box. Widely spaced parentheses are displayed next to the name of each I.D. that has already been used. Inside the parentheses are displayed the corresponding key codes, if any.

For example, the list of I.D. choices for Paragraph styles might look like this, assuming that several I.D.s have already been assigned styles and key codes:

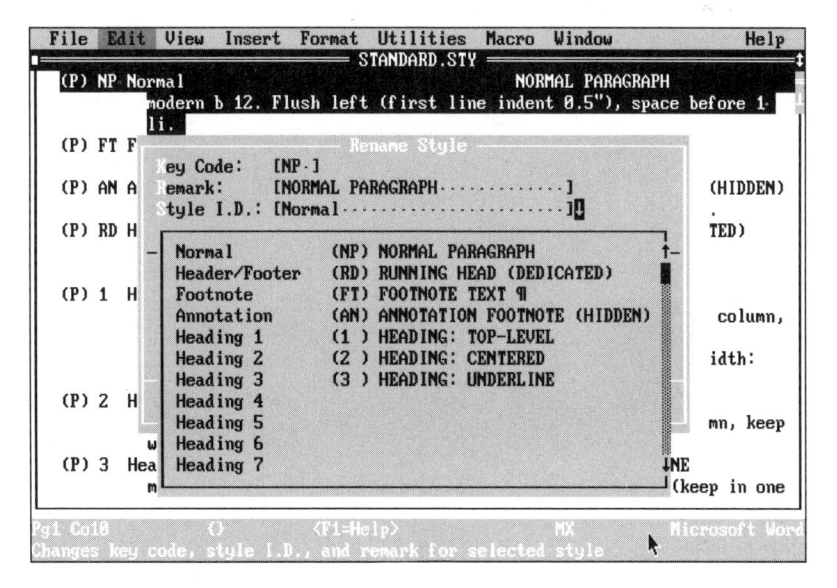

When you're editing a document and the style bar is turned on, the key codes of paragraph styles are displayed in it. Paragraph styles are used most often; hence they justify the broadest range of key codes. In addition, the codes of section styles are displayed to the left of section breaks.

You can use any letters or numbers for key codes, but the following choices make sense as a standard (and standards make sense as a hedge against confusion):

- ♦ A letter, followed by C, for character styles
- ♦ A letter, followed by S, for section styles
- ♦ Any other two letters, for paragraph styles

Try to make key codes suggestive of their uses: NP for "Normal Paragraph" and UC for "Underlined Character," for instance.

Modifying a Style's Formatting

You format or modify a style primarily though the use of the menu of commands that appears above the style sheet window. Working in the style sheet window:

1. Select the style (or styles) whose formatting you want to alter. When you select a style, both its name and formatting description are highlighted. An easy way to change the currently selected style is with the Up and Down direction keys. To extend the selection instead of moving it, press F8 first or hold down the Shift key.

2. Use the Format commands as if you were formatting text. In general, all the commands normally on the Format menu are available except for the last four. These four, Apply Style, Record Style, Define Style, and Attach Style Sheet, relate specifically to the use of style sheets from inside a document window and hence are not relevant or available when you are in a style sheet window. In addition, if a character style is all that is selected, only Format Character will be available (other choices will be grayed). If a section style is all that is selected, only the Format Margins, Format Section, and Format Header/Footer commands will be available.

3. When you are finished with your modifications, use the File Save command to save the amended style sheet. You can then close the window or press Ctrl+F6 to move to a different window.

NOTE: *It is also possible to edit the formatting of a style from within a document by highlighting text that is formatted appropriately and then using the Format Record Style command. Move to the Style I.D. drop-down list box, and press the Down direction key or Alt+Down direction key, to choose the I.D. of the formatting you want to modify. Press Enter when you have selected the appropriate style.*

Creating a Style Sheet

You've seen how to add a style to a style sheet by recording formatting; but what if you want to create a brand-new style, and an example of the desired formatting does not exist either in the current document or in another style sheet? The answer is to use the style sheet window's Insert New Style command.

The following example shows how to use the Insert New Style command to create a paragraph style that, when applied to a paragraph, turns that paragraph into a top-level heading. Such a style is particularly useful if you want to use Word's outlining feature.

Be sure you are in a style sheet window. Position the highlight on the style above the place you want the new style to be inserted. The choice of where to put a new style is entirely up to you. Word doesn't care where a style appears in a style sheet, but for ease of reference you will probably prefer to group similar styles together. If the style sheet window is blank, containing no existing styles, you don't have a choice as to where a style will be inserted—it will be inserted at the end mark.

CHAPTER TWENTY-FOUR: Style Sheets

When the highlight is in position, choose the Insert New Style command. Type a one-character or two-character code of your choice in the first field, which is labeled *Key Code.* In this case, type *H1* to assign the key code H1 to the style. Then

1. Press the Tab key to move to the Style Type drop-down list box, which has three choices: *Character*, *Paragraph*, and *Section*. You're creating a paragraph style, the default choice.

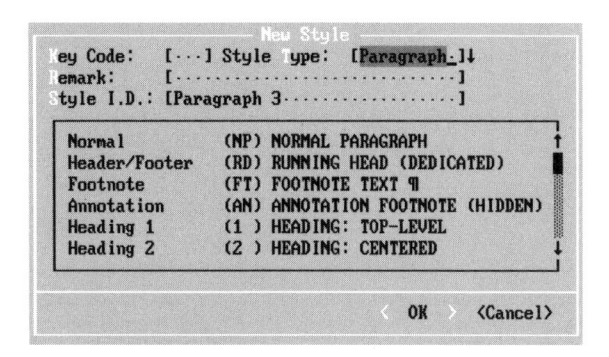

```
                      New Style
 ey Code:     [...] Style  ype: [Paragraph ]
 emark:       [................................]
 tyle I.D.: [Paragraph 3..................]

 Normal           (NP) NORMAL PARAGRAPH
 Header/Footer    (RD) RUNNING HEAD (DEDICATED)
 Footnote         (FT) FOOTNOTE TEXT ¶
 Annotation       (AN) ANNOTATION FOOTNOTE (HIDDEN)
 Heading 1        (1 ) HEADING: TOP-LEVEL
 Heading 2        (2 ) HEADING: CENTERED

                            <  OK  >   <Cancel>
```

2. Press the Tab key again, moving to the Remark field. Consider typing a remark in all capitals so that it will stand out among the other notations in the style sheet window.
3. Press the Tab key to move to the Style I.D. field. You can type in the I.D. of a style you want to define, provided the name you type is one of the 125 accepted by Word and is not already in use. If you prefer—and you probably will—you can press Tab one more time to move to the list box of both used and unused styles. You want to find an unused one so that you can use it. Used styles have parentheses after their I.D.s, and a key code might be enclosed in these parentheses. Unused styles do not have parentheses.
4. When you have highlighted the name of a style you want to create, press Enter. That's all it takes.

That leaves only the tasks of formatting the style as you want and saving the style sheet.

A Sample Style Sheet

A style sheet that has a single style can be very useful under the right circumstances. For example, it can redefine the margins of all documents that are formatted with it. A tiny style sheet has the advantage of not being very intimidating.

At the other end of the spectrum are full-featured style sheets containing dozens of styles. The advantage of a big style sheet, provided it is thoughtfully constructed, is that it provides a wide range of formatting options. The disadvantage is that a big collection of styles can be a bit overwhelming at first.

But if you agree with the theory that it is better to be a little overwhelmed at first but get the full benefit in the long run, you might want to take a look at the style sheet COR-SEM.STY in MasterWord. You can use this style sheet as it is or as the basis of a system of interchangeable style sheets.

CHAPTER TWENTY-FIVE

Merge

A few facts before we get on with the fun:

- Word's Merge feature allows you to create documents with contents that vary by recipient and circumstance. In other words, it lets you create individualized form letters.
- Merge has the ability to use *conditionals*. That is, it can decide on a copy-by-copy basis whether or not to include a particular message, word, or number in a document. Use conditionals thoughtfully, and you can produce a series of letters, each well tailored to its recipient.
- Merge can ask you for information until it knows enough to put a letter together and print it.
- Merge can print a finished letter for each person on your mailing list, or it can print letters for only recipients you specify. Merge can create your letters one by one, in succession, and print them as it goes, or it can create the letters and place them in a separate disk file for you to preview and edit before printing.

But let's not get bogged down in descriptions. The way to understand Merge is to see it in action.

THE SCENE

You are Sarah Torayo, a professional photographer living in Seattle, Washington. Your work frequently appears in *Photo Fiesta* magazine. Most weeks you receive several letters from people who want to purchase a color print of one photograph or another. You used to spend an afternoon each week typing replies and quoting prices. Soon you knew most paragraphs by heart.

Then you bought a computer and an elementary word processor, and your work was cut in half. You could use the same letter over and over in different forms by simply changing the name and address of the recipient and the title and purchase price of the photograph. When quoting a price of more than $150, you'd add a sentence offering a smaller, less expensive print. If the potential customer lived in Washington State, you'd include your phone number and a suggestion that he or she stop by your studio. If the person lived elsewhere, you'd include only a vague invitation. Often, but not always, you'd add a personal comment. So, even with a word processor, it was a fair amount of work.

Then you discovered Word and its Merge feature. Today, your correspondence takes a few minutes a week. You write a few letters while watching television. You do a few more during a brief break from writing a photography textbook.

Merge in Action

One day, you answer four letters while a friend watches.

Your first reply is to Thelma Matlow, who lives in San Francisco. To begin, you load an all-purpose reply letter called LETTER.DOC. Then you execute the File Print Merge command, and a moment later Word begins to request information, which you provide item by item by typing a response in the RESPONSE field and pressing Enter.

First Word presents you with a dialog box that asks you to *Enter today's date*. You type *August 27, 1991*.

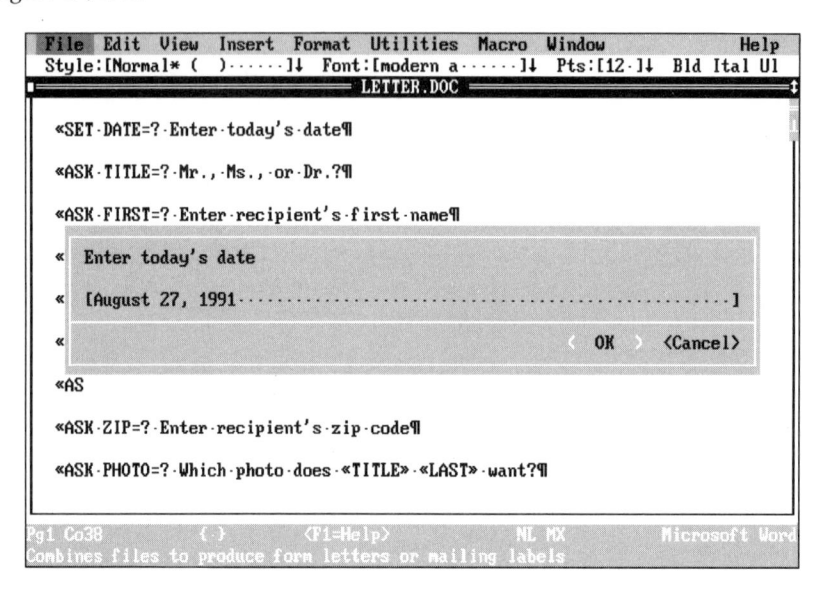

CHAPTER TWENTY-FIVE: Merge

Word moves to the next request:

```
Mr., Ms., or Dr.?
[............................................................]
                                              OK    <Cancel>
```

After you've typed *Ms.*, Word moves through a series of questions. Once the basics are taken care of, your friend sees Word personalize the questions it asks:

```
Which photo does Ms. Matlow want?
[_...........................................................]
                                              OK    <Cancel>
```

You respond

```
Which photo does Ms. Matlow want?
[Moonset......................................................]
                                              OK    <Cancel>
```

Word continues with the next request. You answer again

```
Enter price of "Moonset" (no $ please)
[250_.........................................................]
                                              OK    <Cancel>
```

and Word asks

```
Any personal message for Thelma Matlow?
[............................................................]
                                              OK    <Cancel>
```

You glance again at Ms. Matlow's stationery, with its handpainted picture of unicorns playing Frisbee. You type

```
Any personal message for Thelma Matlow?
[Your stationery was quite original!·······························]
                                          < OK >    <Cancel>
```

The message *Printing page 1* appears, your printer comes to life, and this is the letter it prints:

August 27, 1991

Mr Lonnie Blackmore
2523 N. Starr, No. 2
Tacoma, WA 98403

Dear Mr. Blackmore:

    I'm pleased you enjoyed my photograph "House of Cards" enough to want a copy. Unfortunately, my contract with <u>Photo Fiesta</u> doesn't permit me to sell my work in the 12 months after publication. I'd be happy to provide a copy in about a year. The price will be $220 for an unframed 11-by-14 color print from the original negative. An 8-by-10 would be somewhat less.

    Perhaps there is another photograph you'd like as well as "House of Cards." I can be reached at 555-8374.

    Thank you for your interest.

                                            Sincerely,

                                            Sarah Torayo

Observe that the recipient's full name, including courtesy title, is in the heading of the letter. Yet the salutation (*Dear Ms. Matlow*) omits the first name. That's possible because, when it was quizzing you, Word asked for the courtesy title, first name, and last name separately. The name and price of the photograph are included in the body of the letter. The price is more than $150, so, according to your usual practice, the letter mentions a smaller, less expensive print.

Because the recipient lives several hundred miles away, the second paragraph contains a polite, but vague, invitation to visit your studio. The concluding paragraph begins with your personal message. Now compare this letter with the following three.

The second letter

Your friend watches as you answer Word's inquiries about the next letter. He notices that the questions are the same as before, but Word doesn't request the date. "Does the computer remember the date from the first letter?" he asks. You simply grin and type, providing this information:

TITLE	Mr.
FIRST name	Lonnie
LAST name	Blackmore
STREET address	2523 N. Starr, No. 2
CITY	Tacoma
STATE	WA
ZIP code	98403
PHOTO name	House of Cards
PRICE in $	220

You don't want to include a personal message to Mr. Blackmore, so you press the Enter key when Word asks

```
Any personal message for Lonnie Blackmore?
[_................................................................]
                                              < OK  >   <Cancel>
```

Almost immediately, Word begins to print the second letter.

This letter begins like the letter to Ms. Matlow except for the name and address and the photo's name and price. But note that this correspondent is a resident of Washington State, so the second paragraph both encourages him to visit your studio and offers your telephone number. Word did this tailoring for you.

```
                                              August 27, 1991

   Ms. Thelma Matlow
   2111 Kirkham
   San Francisco, CA  94107

   Dear Ms. Matlow:

        I'm pleased you enjoyed my photograph "Moonset" enough
   to want a copy. Unfortunately, my contract with Photo Fiesta
   doesn't permit me to sell my work in the 12 months after
   publication. I'd be happy to provide a copy in about a year.
   The price will be $250 for an unframed 11-by-14 color print
   from the original negative. An 8-by-10 would be somewhat
   less.

        If this interests you please write again in several
   months. In the meantime, if you happen to be in the Seattle
   area, I'll gladly show you some of my other work.

        Your stationery was quite original! Thank you for your
   interest.

                                              Sincerely,


                                              Sarah Torayo
```

The third and fourth letters

The third letter is created like the preceding two. You provide this information:

TITLE	Mr.
FIRST name	Will
LAST name	Gyles
STREET address	Tamiami Trail South
CITY	Sarasota
STATE	FL
ZIP code	33581
PHOTO name	Sky Climber
PRICE in $	125
PERSONAL message	(None)

and Word prints the letter.

CHAPTER TWENTY-FIVE: Merge

```
                                                August 27, 1991

    Mr. Will Gyles
    Tamiami Trail South
    Sarasota, FL  33581

    Dear Mr. Gyles:

        I'm pleased you enjoyed my photograph "Sky Climber"
    enough to want a copy. Unfortunately, my contract with Photo
    Fiesta doesn't permit me to sell my work in the 12 months
    after publication. I'd be happy to provide a copy in about a
    year. The price will be $125 for an unframed 11-by-14 color
    print from the original negative.

        If this interests you please write again in several
    months. In the meantime, if you happen to be in the Seattle
    area, I'll gladly show you some of my other work.

        Thank you for your interest.

                                    Sincerely,

                                    Sarah Torayo
```

Mr. Gyles is a friend of your uncle's, so you've quoted less than your usual price for "Sky Climber." And because the photograph is less than $150, the sentence about smaller, less expensive color prints is not included. Mr. Gyles is from far-off Florida, so only the vague invitation to visit is included.

Your fourth and last letter is a response to Dr. Kris Terminus, who has written to request a copy of "Sky Climber" for his office waiting room. You enter the usual price for this photograph and add a personal comment:

TITLE	Dr.
FIRST name	Kris
LAST name	Terminus
STREET address	1070 S.E. Taylor
CITY	Port Orchard
STATE	WA
ZIP code	98366
PHOTO name	Sky Climber
PRICE in $	175
PERSONAL message	I think you're right. The photo would look good in a waiting room.

This letter is produced:

> August 27, 1991
>
> Dr. Kris Terminus
> 1070 S.E. Taylor
> Port Orchard, WA 98366
>
> Dear Dr. Terminus:
>
> I'm pleased you enjoyed my photograph "Sky Climber" enough to want a copy. Unfortunately, my contract with <u>Photo Fiesta</u> doesn't permit me to sell my work in the 12 months after publication. I'd be happy to provide a copy in about a year. The price will be $175 for an unframed 11-by-14 color print from the original negative. An 8-by-10 would be somewhat less.
>
> Perhaps there is another photograph you'd like as well as "Sky Climber." I can be reached at 555-8374.
>
> I think you're right. The photo would look good in a waiting room. Thank you for your interest.
>
> Sincerely,
>
> Sarah Torayo

Because "Sky Climber" is priced at more than $150, this letter mentions the availability of a smaller, less expensive copy. The letter also contains the invitation to Washington residents and the personal message.

When this letter is completed, you press the Esc key to cancel the File Print Merge command. You spent only a few minutes creating the four letters, and all you did was answer some questions. Your friend has watched in silence, but now he bursts forth: "How do you make Word do that?"

THE SECRET REVEALED

"Making Word do that" is a two-step process. First you create a main document, which includes instructions and conditionals that actually make your document a simple program. Then, to print letters, you use the File Print Merge command, which merges additional information into the main document, causing a printed (or *merged*) document.

CHAPTER TWENTY-FIVE: Merge

In this case, the main document LETTER.DOC looks like this on the screen:

```
«SET DATE=? Enter today's date¶ ─────────── 1
«ASK TITLE=? Mr., Ms., or Dr.?¶ ─────────── 2
«ASK FIRST=? Enter recipient's first name¶
«ASK LAST=? Enter recipient's last name¶
«ASK STREET=? Enter recipient's street address¶
«ASK CITY=? Enter recipient's city¶
«ASK STATE=? Enter recipient's two-letter state abbreviation¶
«ASK ZIP=? Enter recipient's zip code¶
«ASK PHOTO=? Which photo does «TITLE» «LAST» want?¶ ─── 3
«ASK PRICE=? Enter price of "«PHOTO»" (no $ please)¶ ─── 4
«ASK PERSONAL=? Any personal message for «FIRST» «LAST»?¶

¶
                        «DATE»¶ ─────────── 5

¶
¶
«TITLE» «FIRST» «LAST»¶ ─────────────────── 6
«STREET»¶ ──────────────────────────────── 7
«CITY», «STATE»  «ZIP»¶ ─────────────────── 8

Dear «TITLE» «LAST»:¶ ───────────────────── 9

     I'm pleased you enjoyed my photograph "«PHOTO»" enough ─── 10
to want a copy. Unfortunately, my contract with Photo Fiesta
doesn't permit me to sell my work in the 12 months after
publication. I'd be happy to provide a copy in about a year.
The price will be $«PRICE» for an unframed 11-by-14 color
print from the original negative.«IF PRICE>150» An 8-by-10 ─── 11
would be somewhat less.«ENDIF»¶

     «IF STATE="WA"»Perhaps there is another photograph ─── 12
you'd like as well as "«PHOTO»." I can be reached at 555-
8374.«ELSE»If this interests you please write again in
several months. In the meantime, if you happen to be in the
Seattle area, I'll gladly show you some of my other
work.«ENDIF»¶

     «IF PERSONAL»«PERSONAL» «ENDIF»Thank you for your ─── 13
interest.¶

                    Sincerely,¶

                    Sarah Torayo¶
```

NOTE: *The numbers down the right side of the preceding illustration are not part of the main document. They have been added in order to match each element of the on-screen display to its numbered description in the following section.*

Creating the Main Document

The first 11 paragraphs in LETTER.DOC are SET and ASK instructions that, when you execute the File Print Merge command, tell Word to request from you the information it needs in order to personalize the letter. In LETTER.DOC, as in all merge main documents, special markers known as chevrons are embedded in the document. To create these characters, you press the Control-[key combination for the left chevron («) and the Control-] key combination for the right chevron (»). You can use a paragraph mark (¶) instead of a right chevron, but you must always precede an instruction with the left chevron.

When you execute the File Print Merge command, Word carries out the instructions inside the chevrons as it encounters them in the document. Often an instruction tells Word to draw on a pool of information and use it in some way during printing. In our example, Word assembles the information individually for each letter when you answer its inquiries about such things as the name and address of the letter's recipient. But, as you'll see later, you can also give Word information in advance for a whole series of letters.

Let's go through LETTER.DOC a step at a time. The first four numbered explanations refer to the SET and ASK instructions at the beginning of the main document; references 5 through 13 are to parts of the letter that are printed.

SET and ASK instructions in LETTER.DOC

1. «*SET DATE=? Enter today's date*¶ The SET instruction lets you enter information that applies to a series of documents. In this case, the SET command instructs Word to ask you for text, and it instructs Word to assign the name DATE to the text. In Word's terminology, DATE becomes a *field name*.

    This instruction could also have been written as an ASK instruction («*ASK DATE=? Enter today's date*¶), but in that case, you would have to enter the date again and again, once for each letter you created. SET establishes a value that applies to *all* documents in a series, whereas ASK establishes a value for an individual document.

    Returning to the SET DATE instruction, notice that the phrase *Enter today's date* between the question mark and the right marker (in this case, the paragraph mark rather than the chevron) causes Word to display that message when it asks for the date. (Look at the first example in this chapter.) The instruction could be simplified to «*SET DATE=?*» or «*SET DATE=?*¶, which would cause Word to display the more generic message *Enter text for DATE*. (The reserved glossary name *dateprint* would be an even easier way to include the correct date. However, it would teach you nothing about File Print Merge.)

2. «*ASK TITLE=? Mr., Ms., or Dr.?*¶ The ASK instruction is identical to the SET command in all respects except that it causes Word to make the inquiry prior to each printing of a letter. In this case, it directs Word to ask you for the courtesy title to be used with the name of the recipient of the

particular letter. The optional message here is *Mr., Ms., or Dr.?*, but it could as easily be *Enter courtesy title* or any other appropriate reminder. Also, keep in mind that, when using File Print Merge to create an actual form letter, you aren't limited to the choices offered in the message. The message is a reminder to yourself, not a list of menu choices, so Word will accept *Professor* or *Lt.* as readily as it accepts *Mr., Ms.,* or *Dr.*

The ASK instructions requesting name, address, city, state, and zip code are identical in form to the ASK TITLE instruction. Again, any of these instructions can end in either a right chevron or a paragraph mark.

3. *«ASK PHOTO=? Which photo does «TITLE» «LAST» want?* ¶ The message of this ASK instruction differs from the preceding ones because it refers to information you supplied in response to earlier ASK instructions. When the message appears at the bottom of the screen, the entries «TITLE» and «LAST» are replaced by your earlier responses to the respective ASK instructions. Similarly, the message in the final ASK instruction (do you want a personal message in the letter?) uses the «FIRST» and «LAST» values established by earlier ASK instructions.

   When creating a main document of your own, be certain to establish values *before* trying to use them in messages. For example, if the ASK PHOTO instruction in this document preceded the ASK TITLE or ASK LAST instruction, Word would not know what information to use for «TITLE» and «LAST» in the ASK PHOTO message. Consequently, Word would beep and skip the ASK statement.

4. *«ASK PRICE=? Enter price of "«PHOTO»" (no $ please)* ¶ The message of this ASK instruction reminds you not to type a dollar sign as part of the price. The dollar sign already appears in the body of the document, so if you type it here, the price in your document will be preceded by two dollar signs, like this: *$$250*. Furthermore, a conditional instruction in LETTER.DOC asks Word to compare the value of «PRICE» with the number 150. If you type *$250* instead of *250* when you establish the value of «PRICE», Word becomes confused because you've given it more than simply a number.

Avoiding unwanted line spacing

Before we examine the printable part of LETTER.DOC, let's look again at its SET and ASK instructions. Each concludes with a paragraph mark (¶) rather than a right chevron (»). This maintains the proper vertical spacing of the document. If both the right chevron and the paragraph mark ended each instruction, the File Print Merge command would print each paragraph mark, placing extra blank lines in your document.

If you want to use right chevrons in SET and ASK instructions, employ one of two other ways to ensure that the instructions aren't treated as printable paragraphs. The first is to leave each instruction as a separate paragraph but use the Format Paragraph command to set the *line spacing, space before,* and *space after* fields to *0* for each. The second method is to run all the instructions into a single paragraph.

```
«SET·DATE=?·Enter·today's·date»«ASK·TITLE=?·Mr.,·Ms.,·or·
Dr.?»«ASK·FIRST=?·Enter·recipient's·first·name»«ASK·LAST=?·
Enter·recipient's·last·name«ASK·STREET=?·Enter·recipient's·
street·address»«ASK·CITY=?·Enter·recipient's·city»«ASK·
STATE=?·Enter·recipient's·two-letter·state·abbreviation»«ASK·
ZIP=?·Enter·recipient's·zip·code»«ASK·PHOTO=?·Which·photo·
does·«TITLE»·«LAST»·want?»«ASK·PRICE=?·Enter·price·of·
"«PHOTO»"·(no·$·please)»«ASK·PERSONAL=?·Any·personal·message·
for·«FIRST»·«LAST»?¶
```

The document proper

The remainder of LETTER.DOC is the part we normally think of as the letter. It's the part that is printed.

5. *«DATE»¶* Whatever you typed for DATE in the SET instruction will be printed at this location. Remember that DATE is a *field*. Word replaces any field with its current value when merge printing.

    In this case, both a right chevron and a paragraph mark are used. The right chevron signifies the end of the field, and the paragraph mark tells Word how to handle the line spacing of the preceding text.

6. *«TITLE» «FIRST» «LAST»¶* These fields follow the form of the preceding example. The spaces separating the fields provide spaces between the words when they are printed. You want *Ms. Thelma Matlow* not *Ms.ThelmaMatlow*.

7. *«STREET»¶* Although this is part of the address, it follows the form of «DATE».

8. *«CITY», «STATE» «ZIP»¶* Note the comma after the right chevron of CITY. Note also that there are two spaces before «ZIP» because two spaces generally separate a state name or abbreviation from a zip code.

9. *Dear «TITLE» «LAST»:¶* For the first time, we see text that will not change from letter to letter. *Dear* is a permanent part of the document, but the courtesy title and last name are variable.

10. *"«PHOTO»"* The field PHOTO will print as whatever value you gave in reply to the ASK instruction requesting the photograph name. The quotation marks are outside the chevrons because you want the name of the photograph to be enclosed in quotation marks: "Moonset." The item *$«PRICE»* represents a similar situation.

11. *«IF PRICE>150» An 8-by-10 would be somewhat less. «ENDIF»* This is your first encounter with a conditional statement. It causes everything between the «IF» and «ENDIF» statements to be printed *if* the condition expressed by the «IF» statement is true. In this case, if PRICE is greater than 150, Word prints *An 8-by-10 would be somewhat less*.

    The condition here is evaluated with the *operator* "greater than," expressed with this symbol: >. Word also accepts the operators "less than" (<); "equals" (=); "not equal to" (<>); "less than or equal to" (<=); and "greater than or equal to" (>=).

12. «*IF STATE="WA"*» *Perhaps...*«*ELSE*» *If this interests you...*«*ENDIF*» The «ELSE» statement extends the power of conditionals. If the condition expressed by the «IF» statement is true, then everything between the «IF» and «ELSE» statements is printed. If the condition isn't true, everything between the «ELSE» and «ENDIF» statements is printed instead.

    In the example, if *STATE* is "*WA*", Word includes the three sentences encouraging a visit and giving a telephone number. Otherwise, it includes the statement *If this interests you...other work.*

    The «IF» statement requires quotation marks around specific text to which a field is compared. That's why "*WA*" is in quotation marks. If the quotation marks are missing, Word assumes the text is supposed to be a number and gives an error message.

13. «*IF PERSONAL*»«*PERSONAL*»«*ENDIF*» This is a third variation of the conditional statement. When an «IF» statement contains a field name, such as «IF PERSONAL», Word interprets the statement as: "If a value has been assigned to the field, then this statement is true."

    In this case, Word looks to see whether you typed a personal message. If you did—even if all you typed was a blank space—Word considers the «IF PERSONAL» statement to be true. But if you pressed the Enter key without typing anything, Word considers the «IF PERSONAL» statement to be false.

    If the statement is true, Word prints everything between the «IF» and the «ENDIF» statements. In the preceding example, it prints your response to the ASK PERSONAL instruction plus the two blank spaces preceding «ENDIF». (The spaces separate the PERSONAL message from the final sentence.)

    If the «IF PERSONAL» statement is false, Word skips to whatever text follows «ENDIF».

    You could add an «ELSE» statement: *«IF PERSONAL» «PERSONAL» «ELSE» Thank you for your interest.«ENDIF»* In this case, the sentence *Thank you for your interest* would print only if you hadn't typed a personal message when Word asked for one in the preliminary instructions.

    You can type LETTER.DOC as a Word document and experiment with it if you want. When you understand it, you'll grasp all the essentials of constructing documents with conditionals. But Merge has other features and possibilities too.

MERGING DATA FROM A LIST

The good news: One of your photographs is so popular you're getting dozens of requests for it. The bad news: You have to answer the mail. Is there an even faster way than SET and ASK instructions to give Word the information it needs to create "personal" replies?

There is.

The Data Document

You can set up a separate *data document* containing the information to be merged into the main document. You don't need SET and ASK instructions at all with this method, although you can still use them to supplement information from a data document. This is how a data document would look for the four letters created earlier with SET and ASK statements:

```
TITLE,FIRST,LAST,STREET,CITY,STATE,ZIP,PHOTO,PRICE,PERSONAL¶

Ms.,Thelma,Matlow,2111 Kirkham,San
Francisco,CA,94107,Moonset,250,Your stationery was quite
original!¶

Mr.,Lonnie,Blackmore,"2523 N. Starr, No.
2",Tacoma,WA,98403,House of Cards,220,¶

Mr.,Will,Gyles,Tamiami Trial South,Sarasota,FL,33501,Sky
Climber,125,¶

Dr.,Kris,Terminus,1070 S.E. Taylor,Port Orchard,WA,98366,Sky
Climber,175,I think you are right. The photo would look good
in a waiting room.¶
```

We'll call this data document MAILLIST.DOC. (The spaces between the paragraphs in the example were created by paragraph formatting and exist only for ease of reading. They are not the result of extra paragraph marks between paragraphs.)

Each paragraph of a data document (except the first) is a *record*. There is one record for each merge document you want to print or might potentially want to print. For example, if you want to print 75 form letters, the data document would have 75 records—one for each merge document you want to produce. Each record contains all the data for one document.

Each record is composed of a series of fields. Each field represents a category of information. Instead of using an ASK statement to request a price, for example, one of the fields in each record can be dedicated to storing price information. In the sample data document MAILLIST.DOC, field entries are separated from each other by commas, but you can also separate field entries with semicolons or with tab characters. Tab characters have the virtue of laying out your data in neat columns. (If the decimal separator specified in the Decimal text box of the Utilities Customize dialog box is a comma, you must use either tab characters or semicolons to separate field entries.)

The first paragraph in the data document is a *header record*. It establishes an order for the fields of information; it is an order that every subsequent paragraph (record) must follow. In MAILLIST.DOC, the header record tells Word that the first field name in each record will be TITLE, the next field will be FIRST, the next field will be LAST, and so on, through PERSONAL. You can include up to 256 field names in a header record, provided that the same number of field records exists within each of the subsequent records. A field name can contain up to 64 characters, beginning with a letter and consisting of letters and numbers. No punctuation, other than the underscore character, is permitted.

If you have difficulties when attempting to print, double-check to be sure that the number and order of field entries in every record match the number and order of the fields in the header paragraph. If there is a field for which you have no entry, put in an extra comma, a tab character, or a semicolon to mark its place. You will notice that MAILLIST.DOC includes extra commas at the ends of the records for both Lonnie Blackmore and Will Gyles. Neither person is to receive a personal message, so for each the PERSONAL field is marked by a comma.

If you don't insert these field separators, you will have too few fields in the record and Word won't know which field is which. Merge is very powerful—and very unforgiving. You must get everything exactly right before it will work.

Notice, too, that the record for Lonnie Blackmore has the STREET field in quotation marks. That's because the content of the field includes a comma, and you must tell Word that this comma is part of the entry rather than a dividing point between fields. Quotation marks are needed around a field whenever it contains a comma, a tab character, a semicolon, or a quotation mark. To avoid possible oversights, you can routinely enclose all fields in quotation marks. It's a conservative, but safe, practice. (See the example of this in the "Database Programs" section at the end of this chapter.)

A simple database

One advantage to using tab characters rather than commas to mark the borders between fields in a data document is as follows: Tab characters organize the data so that you can view entries as a table—one in which all telephone numbers, for instance, are in the same column. This practice enables you to use Word's Column Selection mode (accessed with the Shift+Ctrl+F8 key combination) to rearrange or delete fields from all data records at one time. Ordering items in columns also allows you to use the Utilities Sort command to sort the order of the records. And, if you create a nonworking first field in which you simply number the records in a data document, such columns enable you to find the numbers of the records you need quickly—a great help if you use the File Print Merge command to create documents for some, but not all, of the records in your data document.

In a sense, setting up a data document with tab characters turns Word into a simple database program. For this to work, however, you must format all the paragraphs containing the records with the same tab stops. (A style sheet works well in this regard.) Make the distance between tab stops greater than the greatest number of characters in the respective fields. To do this, you might need to set the Format Margins command's Width field to a large value (22 inches is the largest possible) and scroll horizontally to see all your data. If 22 inches is not enough, try formatting the characters for a very small font size to get more on the line, and set the Line Breaks check box of the View Preferences command to Yes to show more on the screen.

If you're an old hand with database programs, the idea of a data document is familiar. If you're a newcomer to databases, you might be a little confused at first.

Even if you don't use tab characters to separate fields, it might help to think of a data document as a table of rows and columns. Each row is a record, a collection of related information. For instance, a data document for a form letter might have one row, or record, for each version of the letter that is to be printed. Each column in the table is devoted to a category of information. The first column, or field, might be reserved for first names, the second column for middle names, the third column for last names, the fourth for phone numbers, and so on.

Each field has a name, and the field name is placed at the top of the appropriate column in what is called the header record. For example, a simple data table might look like this:

	col. 1. (field)	col. 2 (field)	col. 3 (field)	col. 4 (field)
row 1 (header record)	FIRST	MID	LAST	PHONE
row 2 (record 1)	GERARD	T.	HANKS	555-5007
row 3 (record 2)	JODI	S.	GREAT	555-9999
row 4 (record 3)	GREG		SLINGSHOT	555-5555
row 5 (record 4)	JEFF	N.	TRISH	555-1982

Word will merge the data from this table, one record at a time, creating one printed document for each record (except the header record). Note that in row 4 (the third record) the second field is blank, perhaps because we don't know Mr. Slingshot's middle initial. It is important that this field have nothing in it so that the correct data appears in the correct place in the main document.

When you create a data table with Word, you don't use vertical lines to separate fields; you separate fields with commas or tab characters. And you don't use horizontal lines to separate records, you use paragraph marks. So, in Word, the data table used in the previous example would look like this:

```
FIRST,MID,LAST,PHONE¶
Gerard,T.,Hanks,555-5007¶
Jodi,S.,Great,555-9999¶
Greg,,Slingshot,555-5555¶
Jeff,N.,Trish,555-1982¶
```

Again, notice the third data record. The two consecutive commas indicate that the second field, MID, is blank.

The Main Document

Earlier in the chapter we analyzed a main document that obtained all the data it needed from SET and ASK statements. It contained text and field names and didn't rely on a data document. Most main documents do use a data document, however, and require a third kind of element—a data statement. The following are the three kinds of elements in a form letter or other main document.

CHAPTER TWENTY-FIVE: Merge

- An initial *data statement*, which tells Word the location and name of the corresponding data document. The data statement must be the first paragraph of the main document.
- *Text* that doesn't change from one printed document to the next.
- *Field names*, which are placeholders for the information from the data document.

When data from the data document is merged with the main document, the incoming information replaces the field names. The result is a complete, personalized form letter.

This is how the beginning of our main document looks when a data statement is added so that it can use the data document MAILLIST.DOC:

```
======================== LETTERS.DOC ========================
«DATA MAILLIST.DOC¶

«SET DATE=? Enter today's date¶

¶
                              «DATE»¶
```

The main document is largely identical to the earlier version, but the ASK instructions are gone and a DATA statement is at the beginning of the document. When you are using a data document, the DATA statement must be the first entry—not even a blank space or a blank line can precede it. If anything comes before it, you get an error message. The form of the DATA statement is

```
«DATA DATADOC.DOC»¶
```

where DATADOC.DOC represents the name of the data document. Omit the right chevron, leaving only the paragraph mark to end the statement, if you want the printer to omit the line spacing associated with the paragraph mark.

You can use a header paragraph as a document by itself if you find that's more convenient than having it at the top of the data document. The header paragraph could be a document called MAILHEAD.DOC, with this content:

```
TITLE,FIRST,LAST,STREET,CITY,STATE,ZIP,PHOTO,PRICE,PERSONAL¶
```

In this case, you would modify the DATA statement at the top of the main document to show the name of the header document, followed by the name of the data document:

```
«DATA MAILHEAD.DOC,MAILLIST.DOC»¶
```

You'll find this approach useful if you use the same main document with a string of data documents. Rather than place the header paragraph in each of the data documents, you put the header in a document of its own and refer to it in the DATA statement of the main document.

The instruction «SET DATE=? Enter today's date» was preserved in this version of the data document because it's convenient to type the date when executing the File Print Merge command. However, you could omit the instruction and type the date into the main document as regular text or, as mentioned earlier, you could use the *dateprint* entry from the glossary to insert the current date whenever the document is printed.

Regardless of which method you use to supply data for form letters—ASK and SET statements or a data document—the printed result is the same.

MERGE INSTRUCTIONS

You control Word's merge powers by incorporating any of seven instructions in a main document: DATA, SET, ASK, IF, SKIP, NEXT, and INCLUDE. Many of them will already be familiar to people who write Word macros. Like macro instructions, each merge instruction must be enclosed in chevrons (« and »). Here, for easy reference, is a brief rundown on each of the instructions.

DATA

The DATA instruction, which must be the first line in a main document, identifies the data document that contains the information to be merged. It can take any of several similar forms, including

«DATA datadoc.doc» The file *datadoc.doc* is the name of the data document, stored in the same directory as the main document.

«DATA c:\info\datadoc.doc» The file *datadoc.doc* is stored on the C drive in the *info* directory, which might or might not be the same directory that contains the main document.

«DATA datahead.doc,datadoc.doc» The file *datahead.doc* is a header document (containing only the header paragraph, which would otherwise be at the top of the main document), and *datadoc.doc* is the main document. Both are in the same directory as the main document, so no drive letter or subdirectory is listed before either name.

It is not necessary to include the .DOC extension, unless the file being referenced has a different extension.

SET

The SET instruction lets you give a variable a specific value, which Word uses throughout printing of a series of merged documents. The variable can have virtually any name, such as *x* or *amount* or *date*. The instruction can follow either of two forms:

CHAPTER TWENTY-FIVE: Merge

«*SET limit = 500*» The variable named *limit* has been set to 500. When you merge documents, references to «*limit*» in your main document will be treated as *500*.

«*SET limit = ?Please enter the credit limit now.*» When you choose the File Print Merge command, Word pauses the *first* time it encounters this instruction and asks you to type a value for the variable named *limit*. It prompts you with the message *Please enter the credit limit now*. If you type *750* and press Enter, Word will treat references to «*limit*» in your main document as *750*. The prompt *(message)* is optional.

ASK

The ASK instruction resembles the second form of the SET instruction: Word pauses while you type in a value for the variable specified in the ASK instruction. Unlike the SET instruction, however, ASK uses the value only for the current document; if you are printing 150 form letters, the ASK statement will ask you each time to establish a value for the variable. For example

«*ASK limit = ?Please enter the credit limit now.*» Word uses whatever you type only for the merged document about to be printed.

IF [...ELSE]...ENDIF

Like a macro IF instruction, a merge IF instruction tells Word to do something if a condition is true. Generally, a condition is an expression (a number or other constant or a variable), followed by an operator that makes a comparison, followed by another expression. For example, if the condition is «*IF limit < 500*», Word performs some particular action whenever *limit* is a number smaller than 500.

Comparison operators

These are the six *comparison operators* that can be used inside an IF statement:

Operator	Meaning
=	equal to
<	less than
<=	less than or equal to
<>	not equal to
>	greater than
>=	greater than or equal to

In addition, you can test whether any value exists for a variable. To use this technique, follow the word *IF* with the name of the variable you are testing; the condition «*IF limit*» would cause something to happen if (and only if) the variable *limit* had been assigned a value. (This is useful in a form letter in which some people have titles and others don't, because you can say in effect: "If the recipient has a title, print it.")

Math and logical operators

The math operators +, –, *, /, (, and) can be included in a condition. For example, the condition «*IF (limit*2) > amount*» tests whether the variable named *amount* was less than twice the variable named *limit*. You can read more about these operators later in the chapter.

Finally, a condition can be modified by or linked to another condition by one of three *logical operators*—AND, OR, or NOT. For example, an IF instruction might begin «*IF name = "Mark" OR name = "Sonya"*». The use of logical operators is described later in the chapter.

If true, then what?

When Word determines a condition to be true, it follows all directions between the «IF» and either the first «ELSE» or the first «ENDIF». Most often, this means printing text in a letter, as in: «*IF limit >400*»*Your credit is good here.*«*ENDIF*».

If the value of the variable named *limit* is greater than 400, Word prints the sentence *Your credit is good here*. Otherwise, Word ignores the sentence and doesn't print it.

An ELSE statement included in an IF instruction creates a branch from the main road that Word follows when executing the instruction. If the condition is true, Word follows the steps between the IF and the ELSE and ignores the steps between the ELSE and the ENDIF. On the other hand, if the condition is not true, Word follows only the steps between the ELSE and the ENDIF. In the following example, a modification of the previous example, if *limit* is not greater than 400, Word prints the sentence *We are reviewing your credit*: «*IF limit >400*»*Your credit is good here.*«*ELSE*»*We are reviewing your credit.*«*ENDIF*».

SKIP

The SKIP instruction tells Word not to print anything for the current record of the data document. Typically, SKIP is placed in an IF instruction so that under some conditions the record is skipped. For example, to print letters to women but not to men when the data document contains records for people of both genders, you might include an instruction such as this: «*IF sex = "M"*»«*SKIP*»«*ENDIF*».

NEXT

The NEXT instruction tells Word to continue working on the current merge document but to jump to the next record in the data document. This jump makes it quite different from the SKIP instruction, which tells Word to abandon work on the current merge document when it jumps to the next data document. For example, NEXT instructions let you print more than one mailing label on a single sheet of paper because a NEXT instruction says to Word: "Continue printing this sheet (or document), but move on to the next record to get more data." For an example of the NEXT instruction in use, see the tip titled "Mailing Labels" later in this chapter.

INCLUDE

The INCLUDE instruction tells Word to merge an entire document into the document you are printing with the File Print Merge Printer command. The two files are printed as one, although they aren't actually combined on disk. In the following example, the document to be included is called LEFTY.DOC: «INCLUDE lefty.doc».

TIPS ON USING MERGE

Some of the following tips will be more valuable than others, but as you become adept with Merge you'll probably find reason to use most of them at some time. These tips range from explanations of the lesser-known, simple merge instructions «SKIP», «NEXT», and «INCLUDE» to the use of the three logical operators AND, OR, and NOT to suggestions on how to maximize Word's performance. The chapter concludes with notes on using Merge with several popular database programs.

Merging to a Document File

Sometimes, particularly with a long or complex merge procedure, you might feel more comfortable reviewing—and perhaps editing—each document before sending it to the printer. To do so, choose the File Print Merge command (Alt+FM), and press the New Document command button. This brings to the screen the Print Merge To Document dialog box:

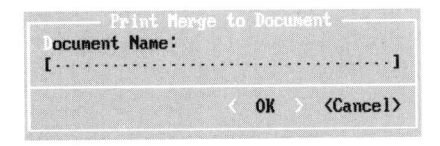

```
─── Print Merge to Document ───
 ocument Name:
[................................]

           < OK >   <Cancel>
```

In the dialog box's lone field, the Document Name text box, type the name of the document you want to create on disk. When you press Enter, Word will create the new document and insert into it the text of all the merged documents that otherwise would go to the printer. If the document name you specify is already used, Word asks if you want to overwrite the file. Choose Yes if you do.

For example, you might want to print to a new document when you debug a main document or data document that is not working properly. Rather than waiting for results to be printed on paper, simply print to a new document and then load the new document and review the results. You can use a generic name for the document, such as TEST.DOC, and close the window containing the document after each time you review it. In a matter of a few minutes, you might be able to experiment with several versions of your letter, eventually finding one that both works and suits your needs.

Merging documents to a separate file is something like putting them in a print queue, except that this "queue" is one you can look at and edit to ensure that each document will be printed exactly as you want it. You can, for example, check lines and pages to ensure that they break neatly on the printed output. If the document contains multiple columns or side-by-side paragraphs, you can use the View Layout command to preview their layout on the printed page. Or you can use the Print Preview feature to see running heads, absolutely positioned paragraphs, banner headlines, spreadsheets, and so on as they will be printed.

Optional Address Lines

Some of the people to whom you address letters have business titles; others don't. Some use a company name in their address; others do not. Some street addresses have one line; others have two. How can you vary the number of lines in an inside address without leaving unintentional blank lines?

One solution is to make the name and address a single field. The drawback is that if you do so, individual elements, such as first name and city, aren't available as discrete elements for other uses in the merge document.

A more elegant solution is to include conditional statements that allow additional lines only if they are needed. Study the following example. It handles everything by using IF statements and fields named BUSINESS TITLE, COMPANY, ADDR1, and ADDR2 in addition to the fields used in this chapter's photography example. (ADDR1 replaces the earlier example's STREET field.) When a particular letter is being merged and no value has been assigned to BUSINESS TITLE, COMPANY, or ADDR2, the line on which that element would appear is omitted:

```
«TITLE» «FIRST» «LAST»¶
«IF BUSINESS TITLE»«BUSINESS TITLE»¶
«ENDIF»«ADDR1»¶
«IF ADDR2»«ADDR2»¶
«ENDIF»«CITY» «STATE»   «ZIP»¶
```

You don't need to understand the example in order to use it as a model, but here's an explanation of why it works. Take the BUSINESS TITLE field as an example. If there is a business title, Word prints it, followed by a paragraph mark, as if the title had been typed there. But if, for a particular letter, no information has been provided for the BUSINESS TITLE field, everything up to the «ENDIF» on the next line is omitted—including the paragraph mark, which means the line doesn't print at all, not even as a blank line.

Mailing Labels

You can produce mailing labels relatively easily with Merge and a mailing list. You can choose from several approaches, depending on whether you're using single-column labels or multiple-column (often triple-column) labels.

Single-column labels

If you are using a dot-matrix printer, you might find pin-fed single-column labels to be most efficient. Use the Format Section command to set the top and bottom margins to 0 and the page length to 1 inch (or whatever the length of a single label happens to be). Then create a three-line, four-line, or five-line document containing the field

CHAPTER TWENTY-FIVE: Merge

names for the labels. Put the name of the mailing-list file in a data field at the beginning of the document, on the same line as the recipient's name field. The document might look like this:

```
«DATA MAILLIST.DOC»«TITLE» «FIRST» «LAST»¶
«STREET»¶
«CITY» «STATE»  «ZIP»¶
```

This example works well if every record in your data document uses only one line for «STREET» and if you don't need to include a «BUSINESS TITLE» or «COMPANY» field. However, if you need to print individual labels with different numbers of lines, refer to the previous section "Optional Address Lines."

When you choose the File Print Merge command, Word treats every label as a separate "page," albeit a small one.

Multiple-column labels

If the labels are multiple-column, set the Format Section command's Number field to the number of columns, and repeat the name and address fields (but not the DATA statement) an appropriate number of times. For example, if the blank labels come on sheets three across, your document looks like this:

```
«DATA MAILLIST.DOC»«TITLE» «FIRST» «LAST»¶
«STREET»¶
«CITY» «STATE»  «ZIP»¶
«NEXT»¶
«TITLE» «FIRST» «LAST»¶
«STREET»¶
«CITY» «STATE»  «ZIP»¶
«NEXT»¶
«TITLE» «FIRST» «LAST»¶
«STREET»¶
```

The «NEXT» statements after the first and second addresses tell Word to continue printing the same document (in this case, a three-column, 1-inch label) but to skip to the next record in the data document (mailing list). Without the «NEXT» statement, Word would not know what to print after the first of the three labels.

You might need to experiment somewhat with the right and left section margins until you get the placement you want. With labels that are several columns to a sheet, you might need to adjust the Space Between Columns field, as well, to ensure that the addresses are not printed too far to the left or right on the labels. When you've found the settings you want, save them on disk.

Skipping Records in a Data Document

Sometimes you might want to send a document to some but not all of the people on a mailing list. There are two ways you can go about choosing: You can do it yourself if some judgment is required, or you can have Word do it for you if you can give Word criteria and let it choose.

To continue this chapter's earlier example, suppose Sarah Torayo wants to send invitations to her best local customers, inviting them to an exhibition of her photographs. She could modify her mailing list, adding a field showing number of purchases or total dollar value of purchases and then create a main document that includes IF instructions that evaluate customers' purchases and their addresses, but the effort involved might be more work than it's worth. She might find it easier to print her mailing list, check off the names of the people she wants to invite, and tell Word to print invitations for them.

Even though you do not normally see any evidence of its bookkeeping ability in your data document on screen, Word can find a particular record by number in the document. If you tell it to merge record number 5, Word finds the fifth record in the data document, merges it with the main document, and prints the result (or sends it to a new document). Your means of specifying records is the Print Merge dialog box, which you encounter as soon as you choose the File Print Merge command.

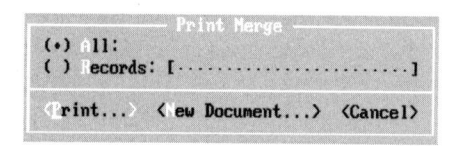

```
─────────── Print Merge ───────────
 (•) All:
 ( ) Records: [....................]
  <Print...>  <New Document...>  <Cancel>
```

If you choose the Records option button and fill in a record number or range of record numbers, Word will limit its merging accordingly. This would be Sarah Torayo's choice in issuing her invitations. After scanning her mailing list, she would use the Records text box to type in the numbers of the records corresponding to the names and addresses of people she wants to invite. Even if the record numbers were scattered throughout the mailing list, Sarah would have no problem; the field accepts up to 255 characters.

When you specify record numbers, separate individual numbers with commas and ranges of numbers with hyphens or colons; for example, *1,17,22* to specify the first, seventeenth, and twenty-second records, but *1-5,17-22* to specify the first through fifth and the seventeenth through twenty-second records.

Consider setting up a separate field for record numbers in your data document if you think you will be sorting your mailing list on a regular basis. If you make this field the first in each record, you should have little trouble finding the records you want on a printout of your data document (mailing list).

Sometimes you don't need to count. Sometimes Word can determine whether or not to merge a specific record. If the judgment required is simply a matter of comparing two items, you can use an IF instruction in your main document to tell Word what to do. If the condition is true, you can tell Word to skip the current record and use the next record in the data document.

Suppose, for example, you have a mailing list of clients. Some clients are mechanical engineers, others are electrical engineers, and still others are architects. You could set up your data document with a field, such as «PROFESSION», in which you identify your clients' specialties: EE for electrical engineers, ME for mechanical engineers, and AR for architects. Then, if you wanted to send a mailing to only one of these groups, you could include an IF instruction plus a SKIP instruction like this in your main document:

```
«IF PROFESSION<>"EE"»«SKIP»«ENDIF»¶
```

meaning "IF the entry in the field named *PROFESSION* is not *EE*, skip it and go to the next record."

Word evaluates a SKIP instruction no matter where it occurs in the main document. To ensure correct line spacing in the finished document, do not end a paragraph containing a SKIP instruction with both a right chevron and a paragraph mark. If you do, you'll find that Word adds the line spacing stipulated by the paragraph mark to every document that is printed.

Paths and Data Instructions

If a data document is on a different drive or in a different subdirectory, include the drive letter or pathname in the data instruction that begins the main document.

For instance

```
«DATA C:PHOTOS\MAILLIST.DOC»¶
```

Powerful and Easy: The «INCLUDE» Instruction

The «INCLUDE» instruction causes an entire document on disk to be inserted at the location of the statement. You can store often-used paragraphs as individual documents and insert them into any document with «INCLUDE». You can also combine «INCLUDE» instructions with «IF»...«ELSE»...«ENDIF» statements, causing passages to be printed only under certain conditions. You can even print the chapters of a book or report in proper order by creating a short document that is nothing more than a series of «INCLUDE» instructions and chapter titles:

```
«INCLUDE INTRO.DOC»¶
«INCLUDE CHAPTER1.DOC»¶
«INCLUDE CHAPTER2.DOC»¶
«INCLUDE CHAPTER3.DOC»¶
```

The File Print Merge command will cause the chapters to be printed in order, repaginating as it goes. Whether the numbering restarts with each chapter depends on the placement of section breaks and on how you set the Insert Page Number command's Start At text box.

Math Operators for Computation on the Fly

Word will compute the result of calculations involving field names and numbers, printing the result in a merge document. To accomplish this, you use math operators to act on numbers and/or field names. The entire expression must be inside chevrons in the main document.

The math operators are

Operator	Description
+	Add
−	Subtract
*	Multiply
/	Divide
%	Percentage

For example, a letter might include this sentence: "Your average daily balance of $«daily» is «daily/5» percent of our required minimum of $500." Or you could accomplish the same thing, using the percent sign, by including this sentence: "Your average daily balance of $«daily» is «daily/500%» percent of our required minimum of $500."

As noted earlier in the chapter, you can use mathematical operators inside a conditional instruction. This lets the content of your merged documents depend on the results of a calculation. For example, the previous example could be modified in this way to cause one of two sentences to be included, depending on the results of the calculation:

"Your average daily balance of $«daily» is «daily/500%» percent of our required minimum of $500. «IF daily/500%<100»Consequently, we need to review the situation. Could you please call for an appointment at your convenience? «ELSE» We appreciate your business and hope you will contact us if we can be of further service. «ENDIF»"

Logical Operators: AND, OR, and NOT

Three logical operators let you refine the Merge feature, working much as they do in macros. Essentially

- AND enables you to evaluate two conditions and perform an action (print a particular sentence, for example, or include a certain file) if both conditions are true (that is, if both match criteria you specify). In everyday life, this is equivalent to saying, "If tomorrow is sunny and warm, I will take a walk."

- OR enables you to evaluate two conditions and perform an action if *either* one *or* the other is true. To continue the example, this is like saying, "If tomorrow is sunny or warm, I will take a walk."

- NOT enables you to evaluate one or more conditions and perform an action if they are not true (do not match the criteria you specify). This lets you declare, "If tomorrow is sunny but not warm, I will take a walk."

There are many ways you can use AND, OR, and NOT in creating merge documents. A few examples should suffice to show you generally how they can be used. For further discussion of these logical operators, refer to Chapter 23.

Suppose you had the data document of mechanical engineers, electrical engineers, and architects mentioned previously. For the sake of simplicity, let's assume your data covers Washington, Oregon, and California and includes, in a field called MEMBER, a Y or an N indicating whether the person belongs to your chapter of a professional organization. Part of the data document (named LIST.DOC), including its header, might look like this:

```
LASTNAME,FIRSTNAME,PROFESSION,STREET,CITY,STATE,ZIP,MEMBER¶
Meyer,George,AR,12230 NE First,Kingsport,WA,90000,Y¶
Sanchez,Helen,EE,79 Second Street,Newtown,OR,90111,N¶
Waters,Bill,AR,9876 Third Place,Ventura Diego,CA,91000,N¶
Kimura,Tom,ME,3549 Fourth Avenue,Oldwest,OR,90111,Y¶
Smith,Martha,ME,183 Fifth Boulevard,Nez Perce,WA,90000,N¶
Thompson,David,EE,90123 Sixth Parway,Vista
Caliente,CA,91000,Y¶
```

Notice that each line except the last two is a separate paragraph, ending in a paragraph mark, and therefore is a separate record. The last two lines form a single record.

Suppose you want to send a letter to all members of your list, and in that letter you want to include a couple of paragraphs aimed specifically at mechanical engineers (ME) who live in Washington (WA). If the paragraphs to be included are in a file called NEWNEWS.DOC, place the following paragraph in the main document at the location where you want the paragraphs included.

```
«IF PROFESSION="ME" AND STATE="WA"»«INCLUDE NEWNEWS.DOC»«ENDIF»¶
```

Suppose now that you want the paragraphs in NEWNEWS.DOC to go out to all architects (AR), regardless of membership status, and to all engineers who are members of your organization. The beginning of the IF statement would become

```
«IF PROFESSION="AR" OR MEMBER="Y"»«INCLUDE NEWNEWS.DOC»«ENDIF»¶
```

Character Formatting

Text inserted from a data document or established with a SET or ASK statement has the same character formatting as the first character of the field name. If, using this chapter's earlier example, we always want the price of the photograph to be underlined, we would underline the first character of the field name «PRICE» in the document. You can format the characters of the whole field name if you prefer, but the only letter that matters is the first one.

Don't, however, confuse character formatting with uppercase and lowercase unless it is the uppercase created with the Format Character command's All Caps check box. Field names and merge instructions enclosed in left and right chevrons can be any combination of uppercase and lowercase. Uppercase has been used in this chapter only as a matter of convention.

Paragraph Marks and Formatting

If a paragraph mark that is enclosed in quotation marks in a data-document field is merged into a main document, the paragraph mark's formatting is too. This can be a rude surprise when you print. Possible solutions are

- Format your data document and main document identically.
- Use the same style sheet and styles for both the main document and the data document during the execution of the File Print Merge command. (You can use other style sheets if you want during the writing and editing of your main document and data document.)
- Avoid merging paragraph marks into your main document by deleting them from your data document when they are within fields (in other words, inside quotation marks). Place appropriately formatted paragraph marks in your main document instead.

Merging Quotation Marks

When you want to merge quotation marks from a data document into a document, double them: "He was ""honorably"" discharged." Whenever the quoted word or phrase is the first or last in a field, it must have a triple quotation mark: "The discharge was """honorable."""

Using Merge with Multiple Windows

Consider opening one window for your main document and another for your data document. This is useful when you're trying to find the causes of error messages or if you want to see the data while you write the main document.

You can also use two windows with the File Print Merge command to keep an often-used main document in a small window or in a window that is usually out of sight. You can work on other projects in other windows; whenever you want to print out a few form letters, use Ctrl+F6 or the Window menu to select the window containing the main document, and then execute the File Print Merge command. This works best if you use SET and ASK instructions exclusively rather than a data document. If you use a data document, revise either the «DATA» statement or the contents of the file before you use File Print Merge, or specify only selected records to merge. Otherwise, you'll create the same form letters over and over because the merging starts at the top of the data document each time you execute File Print Merge.

Unless you want to see it, the data document needn't be displayed on the screen at all. It does, of course, need to be on the disk.

Nesting Conditionals

Conditional statements can be nested inside each other. Imagine the variety you can give your documents by nesting one IF statement within another—and maybe even tossing in an «INCLUDE» statement or two.

Let's say you award bonus points to your customers and you want to write them letters listing the prizes for which they're already eligible. They get different prizes depending on whether they've accumulated 10 points, 25 points, 50 points, or 100 points. Assume the number of points is called «POINTS» in your main document, and the lists of prizes are kept on disk in separate documents called 10PTS.DOC, 25PTS.DOC, 50PTS.DOC, and 100PTS.DOC. This set of conditionals in the main document causes each letter to print with a list of prizes appropriate to the recipient:

```
«DATA POINTS»¶
«IF POINTS>99»«INCLUDE 100PTS.DOC»«ELSE»«IF
POINTS>49»«INCLUDE 50PTS.DOC»«ELSE»«IF POINTS>24»«INCLUDE
25PTS.DOC»«ELSE»«IF POINTS>9»«INCLUDE 10PTS.DOC»«ELSE»You
begin to qualify for prizes when you reach 10 points. So far
you have «POINTS» points.«ENDIF»«ENDIF»«ENDIF»«ENDIF»¶
```

It looks confusing, and it is. But it could save you a phenomenal amount of typing. The logic of it might be clearer to you in this form:

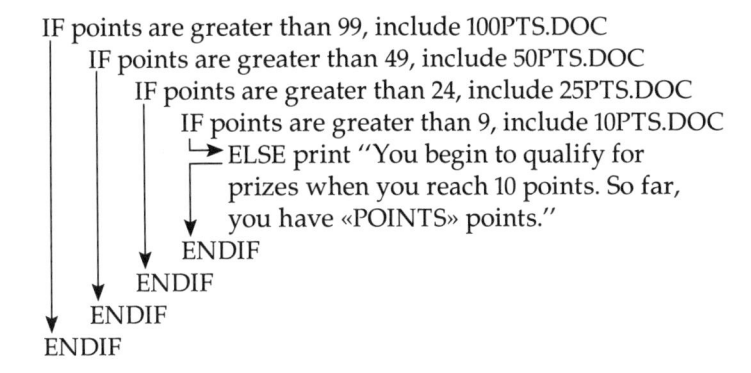

IF points are greater than 99, include 100PTS.DOC
    IF points are greater than 49, include 50PTS.DOC
        IF points are greater than 24, include 25PTS.DOC
            IF points are greater than 9, include 10PTS.DOC
                ELSE print "You begin to qualify for
                prizes when you reach 10 points. So far,
                you have «POINTS» points."
            ENDIF
        ENDIF
    ENDIF
ENDIF

If you want to derive the maximum power and flexibility from Merge, experiment with complex nested statements. You can make a letter take entirely different directions depending on the recipient's gender (indicated by courtesy title), place of residence, income, or other information found in a data document or supplied through SET and ASK instructions.

DATABASE PROGRAMS

Word's Merge facility can use mailing lists or other ASCII files from many database and filing programs. Most database programs have a command or utility for "exporting a delimited ASCII file," which is what Word needs.

The goal is to produce a series of records, separated by paragraph marks, in which all fields within a record are separated by commas. Database programs typically "export" data documents with quotation marks around the fields but with the commas outside the marks, like this:

```
"Ms.","Thelma","Matlow","2111 Kirkham","San
Francisco","CA","94107","Moonset","250","Your stationery was
quite original!"¶
"Mr.","Lonnie","Blackmore","2523 N. Starr, No.
2","Tacoma","WA","98403","House of Cards","220",¶
```

As you saw in the section "The Data Document," these quotation marks are correct—and are needed by Word whenever a data field contains a comma, tab character, or quotation mark.

Although merged printing is usually associated with form letters, you can use it as a powerful way to present information from a database program. Rather than printing out data records in raw form and then formatting them for a second printing, you can store the information in an ASCII file and use Merge to print it with Word's sophisticated formatting.

Following are tips on how to use five popular database and filing programs to create a data document for use with Merge. In each instance, the example assumes you want to create a mailing list limited to people who live in Washington State. In the examples, the mailing list is called MAILLIST.DOC and is generated from a database named ADDRESS.

R:BASE for DOS and R:BASE 5000

You can create a mailing list with R:BASE for DOS or R:BASE 5000. The steps are the same for either program. At the R prompt (R>), type *open address* to open the database (called *address* in our example). R:BASE responds: *Database exists*. This database will contain one or more tables, and you must choose one that you want to export to ASCII. (To see a list of tables, type *list tables* at the R prompt.) In our example, the table to be used is called *names*.

At the R prompt, type *output*, followed by the name of the mailing-list document you are creating. In our example, the name is MAILLIST.DOC. This command causes the output of R:BASE to be sent to the file named MAILLIST.DOC, not the screen. At the R prompt, type *unload data for names as ascii sorted by last name where state = WA*. At this point, your screen will look like this:

```
R>open address
  Database exists
R>output maillist.doc
R>unload data for names as ascii sorted by lastname where state = WA
```

When you press the Enter key, R:BASE will print a file named MAILLIST.DOC on the disk, which contains data from the records in the table called *names*. The only records included will be those in which the state is listed as WA. The data from the records will be alphabetized by last name.

Type *output screen* to cause the program to resume sending its output to the screen. Then quit R:BASE (type *exit* at the R prompt) and start Word.

When you load the document MAILLIST.DOC into Word, you might find spaces in places you don't want them if you're using R:BASE 5000 rather than R:BASE for DOS. The Replace command can remove unwanted spaces. First, use the Options command to make invisible characters visible on the screen. Then devise an appropriate version of the Replace command.

For instance, you might find that each record ends with two unwanted spaces, followed by the necessary paragraph mark, and then seven more unneeded spaces. To solve this problem, select the first character in the document and use Word's Edit Replace command. In the text field, press the Spacebar twice, type ^*p*, and then press the Spacebar seven more times. Press the Tab key to move to the With Text field, where you type ^*p*. Change the confirm field to No to save time, and press the Enter key.

> NOTE: *If you are using R:BASE for DOS, you can speed up this process and take advantage of the ease of utilizing menus by using the program's GATEWAY feature. At the DOS or R prompt, type* gateway, *type* 2, *type* 1, *and then answer the questions the programs asks.*

dBASE II, dBASE III, and dBASE IV

Creating a data document called MAILLIST.DOC that Word can use is easy with dBASE II, dBASE III, or dBASE IV. At the dot prompt, type

```
. use address
. copy to maillist.doc for state = "WA" delimited
. quit
```

To speed up the COPY TO command, you can use the appropriate INDEX file as part of the USE command. For example, in dBASE II, III, or III Plus: *USE ADDRESS INDEX STATE*.

If you want to limit MAILLIST.DOC to certain fields, specify them this way in the *copy to* line:

```
. copy to maillist.doc fields name,city,state,zip, for state = "WA" delimited
```

Paradox

Exporting an ASCII file with Paradox 2.0, 3.0, or 3.5 is a simple and fast task. If necessary, use the Query command to create an answer table that contains only the records you want—in the case of our example, records in which the state field is equal to WA. If you want the data document to contain only certain fields, use the F6 key to mark the ones you want before you create the answer table. Then, to actually create the ASCII file, press F10 to bring the main menu to the screen; press T for Tools; press E for ExportImport; press E for Export; press A for ASCII; and press D for Delimited. Paradox will ask for the name of the table you want to export. You can type the name of the table, or you can press the Enter key to choose from a list of available table names. After you press Enter, Paradox asks you which name you want to give the ASCII file you are about to create; type MAILLIST.DOC. Press Enter, and Paradox will create the ASCII file in a flash. Paradox is a Borland product.

Professional File

To create an ASCII delimited file with Professional File from Software Publishing Corp., start the program and press 6 to select and load the file Address. If necessary, press the Esc key several times to cause the main menu to appear. Type *463* to move rapidly through a series of choices. (The actual choices you make by typing *463* are *Copy, Export records,* and *Export to delimited ASCII.*) Professional File asks you to name the file from which you want to export (a source file); because this file name is already displayed, simply press Enter. Next the program presents you with three fields; press Tab twice to move to the third field, where you type the name for the ASCII file you want to create. If you want the document stored in a directory other than the one listed, press Ctrl+E to blank the field, type a new path, and then type the filename *MAILLIST.DOC*. If you want to use the proposed path (subdirectory), press the End key to move to the end of the field, and then type *MAILLIST.DOC*. Press Enter.

Professional File will display all the fields in Address. If you want to export the contents of all the fields, leave the spaces next to the fields blank. However, if you want to export only certain fields, number the desired files consecutively, beginning with 1. You can mark a total of 300 fields in this way. You can control the order in which the fields are listed in the records in this way too. If you list only certain fields and want to save the instructions for later use, press F2 and give the instructions a name; otherwise, press F10 to continue.

If you want to export only certain records from Address, use Professional File's Search instructions, as you would when searching for particular files to display on the screen. When you've tailored your request, press F10 to actually create the ASCII file.

PC-File version 5.0

ButtonWare's PC-File 5.0, like the earlier shareware programs PC-File+ and PC-File:dB, is simple to use but asks a lot of questions. You begin by loading Address and pressing F8 to reach the program's utilities. Then press E to choose Export, and specify a disk drive letter, path, and name for the ASCII file MAILLIST.DOC. (You don't need to include an extension on the file name you specify.) PC-File responds with a list of possible formats; from them, press M for "Mail-merge (comma delimited)".

PC-File asks if you want it to add an initial record to the ASCII file and place in that record the names of each field. This is an opportunity added to PC-File specifically for Word users, and you'll probably want to press Y for Yes *if* the field names in your main document match the names you use for fields in PC-File. The program asks if you want an extra comma added to the end of records that have blank last fields; you do not, so press Enter to accept the default answer of N for No. The next question is whether you want to "flip data"; this is a peculiarity of PC-File, but the default answer of Y won't hurt anything, so press Enter to accept it.

CHAPTER TWENTY-FIVE: Merge

PC-File asks you to press A if you want to export all fields or S if you want to export only selected fields. If you press S, a screen shows the names of all fields, and you can move the cursor next to any field that you want to include and press F10. When you've chosen all the fields you want, press F10 a second time.

Finally PC-File asks whether you want to export all records or only selected records. Press A for All or S for Selected. If you press S, you can make either a simple or a complex search for the desired records, as you do when looking up information with the program. After you make your choices and tell PC-File to proceed, it displays the first record and offers several choices. Pressing X causes PC-File to finish its work promptly.

CHAPTER TWENTY-SIX

Outlining

Some people draw up an itinerary before setting out on a journey. Others have only a vague idea of where they're heading. Either way, there's much to be said for having a map, both to trace where you've been and to see where you might be going.

Word's outlining feature provides ways to look at and think about what you write. Even before you start writing, you can outline major topics and subtopics, placing under each any notes, phrases, or bits of memorable prose that come to mind. As you write one section of the document, you can move instantly to any other section to check on organization or related topics. Partway through a document, you can review what you've already written and see it as concisely or in as much detail as you want. You can look ahead to ideas and passages that are only partly formed and judge where and how they fit into what you're fashioning. You can, in short, consult a map as you journey from the beginning of your document to its end.

"Outlining" is really a modest term to describe the organizational tools Word makes available. You can compose and print a formal outline, of course. Word will number the topics for you, if you want. But by itself, creating and printing an outline makes only small use of the feature. Outlining's special contribution is enabling you to see and edit, on an ongoing basis, an up-to-date model ("outline") of your document. You can collect ideas under headings and *collapse* the text so that only headings show. You can reorganize a document by moving headings from one place to another— Word moves the text that follows. And you can adjust not only the order of the headings and subheadings that remain but their relative importance, or *level*.

With a Word outline mapping your document, you don't need to scan through many screens to find an idea; instead, you find it summarized on a line in the outline model. You don't need to scroll through a long document to move a subsection; instead, you rearrange lines in the model, and the document reflects the changes automatically. Or you edit the document, and the outline updates itself. It is the unprecedented integration of document and outline that sets Word apart from most non-Microsoft outlining tools.

This integration of document and outline thus provides some practical opportunities that have little to do with outlines in any conventional sense. To be fanciful for a moment, consider the concept of *hyperspace,* an idea borrowed from science fiction. Because nothing can travel faster than light, the science-fiction writer faces a nasty problem. How can a spaceship leap to the center of the Milky Way, when it takes light 30,000 years to travel that far? The answer comes through an act of imagination.

The spaceship arrives almost instantly in the desired neighborhood by taking a shortcut through hyperspace, a place where normal rules don't apply.

You can use Word's *outline view* as a sort of hyperspace. Imagine that you've outlined a document. Now you're writing and want to jump to an idea many pages away. You press Shift+F2 to enter outline view, your entry into hyperspace. Then you press Shift+Alt+7 to collapse all regular text out of view, leaving only the headings and subheadings of your document. At a glance, you see the breadth of the document. The outline becomes a menu of places to which you can travel. You select a heading or subheading from a distant region and press Shift+F2 to return to normal *document view,* but at the selected destination. Many such uses for Word's outlining powers are possible. New ideas might suggest themselves to you.

If you've put off learning to use style sheets because you thought they'd be difficult or not worth the effort, you've lost your excuses. Outlining is more powerful, and in some respects easier, when you use a style sheet to format the appearance of documents.

Among the many styles possible in a style sheet are seven dedicated to various levels of headings. For each of these *Heading level* styles, you can design specific formatting. For example, you can decree that Level 1 headings are all in uppercase letters, boldfaced, underlined, and centered on the page and that Level 2 headings are all underlined and centered but neither uppercase nor bold. Level 3 headings might be flush left and underlined, and so forth.

With a style sheet in place, it doesn't matter whether you are working with a document or with its outline—you control headings in the same way. For example, you can turn a single-line paragraph into a Level 1 heading simply by selecting any character in the paragraph and pressing the style's key code. If the key code is H1, you could press Ctrl+YH1. Immediately the characters become boldfaced, underlined, and uppercase—or whatever you decided when you designed the style. Change your mind? Press the key code for a second-level heading, and the line becomes a Level 2 heading, formatted as you specified in the style sheet. When you're in outline view, headings are indented to reflect their relative levels. When you're in document view, the headings assume the layout dictated by the style sheet. Any time you change a heading's level in document view, the change is reflected in outline view, and vice versa. A lesson later in this chapter shows you step by step how to create and use a style sheet that you can put to work immediately.

Outlining is one of Word's strengths and one of its weaknesses. The strength is obvious from the foregoing discussion. The weakness becomes obvious as you wade into the next section of this chapter. The outlining feature employs a relatively large number of keys, many of which behave differently when used outside of outline view.

CHAPTER TWENTY-SIX: Outlining

Some keys change purpose again when you enter the outline-organize mode of outline view. Furthermore, unlike *Word for Windows* and *Word for the Macintosh*, there is not a good way to use outlining with a mouse—although there are some uses for the mouse, which are described later in the chapter. Still, even in its rudimentary forms, the outlining feature is wonderful for the opportunities it provides, and it deserves some patient attention. If you stick to basics and forget the rest, you can get a lot out of the outlining feature without extensive effort. I use outlining all the time, switching in or out of it perhaps as often as every five minutes, and can hardly imagine writing about certain topics without it.

THE BASICS

Early in Chapter 13 the differences between document view and outline view were described, and it was noted that once you are in outline view you can switch to a special outline organize mode. Briefly:

Document view is the standard mode in which you write, edit, and format a document.

Outline view is the mode in which you turn Word's attention to the outline of a document. You enter outline view by pressing Shift+F2 or by choosing Outline from the View menu. This is the mode you use when you want to look at and work on the structure of the document—its headings and the way they are organized. To return to document view, you press Shift+F2 again. Within outline view, you can work in

- *Outline edit* mode, in which you edit or add to the outline or edit any text that isn't collapsed out of view. Word puts you in this mode whenever you enter outline view, so in a sense you can think of it as "ordinary" outline view.
- *Outline organize* mode, in which you reorganize an outline—for example, move headings and text from one place in the outline to another. In outline organize mode, body text and subsidiary headings move when the headings they are under move. You enter outline organize mode from outline edit mode by pressing Shift+F5. To return to outline edit mode, press Shift+F5 again. To return from there to document view, press Shift+F2.

A few other terms are worth knowing in advance. These are *heading levels, body text, collapse,* and *expand.*

Heading levels are the elements of your outline. For example, the illustration below shows a few heading levels from the hands-on tutorial later in this chapter.

```
Part One: The Magic of Magic
    A Short History of Legerdemain and Illusion
    Magic by Any Other Name
```

In a standard outline, these heading levels might be assigned numbers and letters, like this:

```
I. Part One: The Magic of Magic
   A. A Short History of Legerdemain and Illusion
   B. Magic by Any Other Name
```

These heading levels are the elements of a document that you work with in either outline edit or outline organize mode. You create headings and assign them different levels of importance either in outline edit mode or with a style sheet.

Body text is the narrative portion of your document. In using the outlining feature, you can choose to display body text, or you can choose to "hide" it and view only the elements of your outline.

Collapsing and *expanding* are opposite actions you can perform to selectively display parts of your outline and body text. You can collapse all or part of an outline to display only certain heading levels, with or without the text that follows. Conversely, when you want to see collapsed portions of outline or body text, you can expand them back into view. Of course, returning to document view causes all text to come back into view.

Keystrokes

You use various keys and key combinations to work with an outline. The table on page 503 lists the keys and key combinations you use and the purposes they serve, with accompanying text explaining the functions in more detail.

Changing modes

The function keys F2 and F5 are used in conjunction with the Shift key to get you in and out of Word's outline modes. Holding down the Shift key and pressing F2 takes you out of normal document view and into outline view, a task you also can accomplish by executing the View Outline command (Alt+VO).

When you are in outline view, you can switch to the mode called *outline organize* by holding down the Shift key and pressing F5. Outline organize will be of increasing interest as you gain experience; but to keep things simple at first, stick as much as possible with *outline edit*, the mode you are in when you enter outline view.

Understanding one distinction between outline edit and outline organize is essential:

- In outline edit, you can type, select, and edit text within a single heading or paragraph. Although you can move from paragraph to paragraph, you cannot select or otherwise affect more than one paragraph at a time. In fact, you cannot delete a paragraph mark at all unless it is all the paragraph contains.
- In outline organize, on the other hand, you can select only whole paragraphs. Use outline organize to delete or move a paragraph or a group of paragraphs.

CHAPTER TWENTY-SIX: Outlining

To:	Press:
Move between document view and outline view	Shift+F2 or Alt+VO
Toggle between outline edit and outline organize	Shift+F5
Lower heading one level	Ctrl+0 (zero)
Raise heading one level	Ctrl+9
Add body text to outline	Ctrl+X; type text
Collapse subheadings and body text	Minus (on number pad) or Ctrl+8
Collapse body text below heading	Shift+Minus (on number pad) or Ctrl+Shift+8
Expand next heading level and body text	Plus (on number pad) or Ctrl+7
Expand body text below heading	Shift+Plus (on number pad)
Expand all headings to specified level	Alt+Shift; type desired heading level (use numbers on top of keyboard)
Expand all headings	Select entire outline (Shift+5); press * (on number pad)
Expand all body text	Select entire outline; press Shift+Plus (on number pad) or Shift+Ctrl+7

The possible ways to shift among the document view, outline edit, and outline organize modes are shown in this illustration:

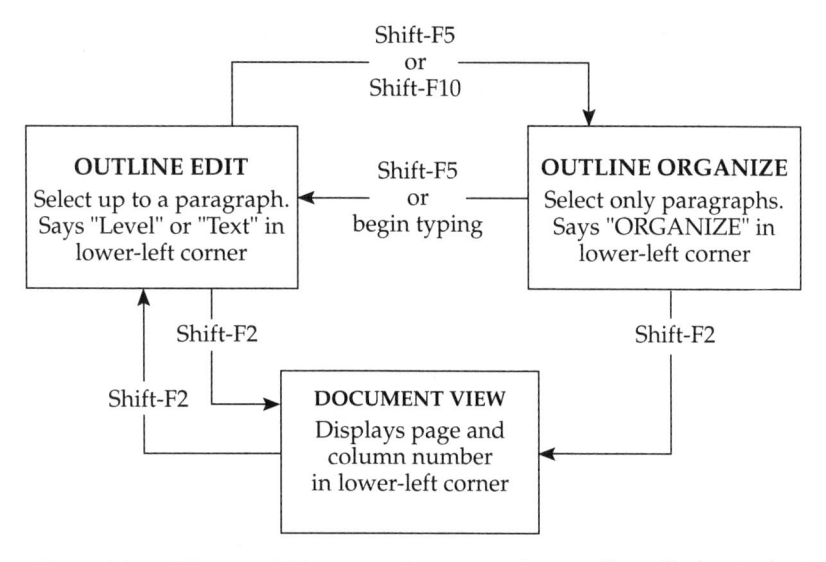

```
                         Shift-F5
                            or
                         Shift-F10
        ┌─────────────────────────────────────────┐
        │                                         ▼
┌──────────────────────┐              ┌──────────────────────┐
│    OUTLINE EDIT      │   Shift-F5   │  OUTLINE ORGANIZE    │
│ Select up to a       │      or      │ Select only paragraphs. │
│ paragraph.           │◄─begin typing│ Says "ORGANIZE" in   │
│ Says "Level" or      │              │ lower-left corner    │
│ "Text" in            │              │                      │
│ lower-left corner    │              │                      │
└──────────────────────┘              └──────────────────────┘
        │      ▲                              │
        │      │ Shift-F2              Shift-F2
        │      │                              │
Shift-F2│      │                              │
        ▼      │        ┌──────────────────┐  │
               └────────│  DOCUMENT VIEW   │◄─┘
                        │ Displays page and│
                        │  column number   │
                        │ in lower-left corner │
                        └──────────────────┘
```

Figure 26-1. Ways to shift among document view, outline edit (equivalent to outline view), and outline organize modes.

To get from document view to outline edit, press Shift+F2. To get from outline edit or outline organize back to document view, press Shift+F2. To get from outline edit to outline organize, press Shift+F5 or Shift+F10. (This latter key combination also selects the entire outline/document.) To get from outline organize to outline edit, press Shift+F5 or begin typing; when you type, Word knows you want to affect less than a whole paragraph, so it switches you to outline edit.

When you are in normal document view, the left side of the status bar displays a page and, if appropriate, a column number (a line number as well, if you've checked the Show Line Numbers check box of the View Preferences command). If the document has more than one section, you also see a section number such as *P7 S2*.

In outline edit, the status bar displays the word *Level* and a number that corresponds to the level of the heading currently highlighted in the main portion of the window. If a paragraph of body text is selected instead of a heading, the word *Text* is displayed.

In outline organize, the advanced mode, the status bar says *ORGANIZE*. It cannot show a level number because multiple paragraphs of different levels can be selected at the same time.

Promoting and demoting

Whether you create an outline in outline edit mode or create it with the help of a style sheet, Word uses indentations to visually distinguish one heading level from another. The first level of heading is flush left, and each successive heading level is indented four spaces to the right of the level above it. Thus, Level 1 headings have no left indentation, Level 2 headings have four spaces of indentation, Level 3 headings have an additional four spaces of indentation (eight altogether), and so forth.

An outline can have several levels of headings, and you might want to move ideas not only from one place to another but also from one heading level to another. Perhaps a topic you thought would make a chapter by itself seems less important now, so you incorporate it into another chapter and move it on the outline from Level 1 to Level 2.

In Word, this moving of headings from one level to another is a matter of *promoting* (raising to a higher level) and *demoting* (lowering to a lower level). To promote or demote a heading, you must first select part or all of it. If you are in outline organize mode, you can use the F8 key to select several headings and then promote or demote them all at once.

To promote a selected heading to a higher level, hold down the Ctrl key and type the number 9 (from the top line of the regular keyboard). To demote a selection, press Ctrl+0 (zero). At first glance, these keys might seem like peculiar choices for raising and lowering levels of an outline, but they are not. They were chosen because of the open and close parenthesis marks on the same keys. As you can see in the following figure, the (character on the 9 key "points" to the left—appropriate because Ctrl+9 moves an outline heading to the left (promotes it). Similarly, the) character on the 0 key "points" to the right—and that key demotes a heading.

Ctrl+9 promotes (raises) a heading, moving it to the left.

Ctrl+0 demotes (lowers) a heading, moving it to the right.

Figure 26-2. Promoting and demoting headings.

Key codes and styles If you have a style sheet that includes Paragraph Heading styles, you can use the key codes for these styles as a more powerful way to assign levels of headings in either an outline or a document.

For example, if you want to change a Level 1 heading to a Level 3 heading, press Ctrl+Y followed by the key code for the Level 3 style. This changes not only the heading level in the outline but also the style of the heading in the document. If the Level 1 style calls for a centered heading and the Level 3 style calls for a flush-left heading, changing a heading from Level 1 to Level 3 not only changes its relative importance in the outline, but it also causes the paragraph formats of the headings to change in the document.

This book assumes that if you are using a style sheet with Paragraph Heading styles, you will assign as a key code for each the letter H followed by the number that corresponds to the paragraph style variant, as shown here.

- Ctrl+Y followed by H1 for the Heading level 1 paragraph style
- Ctrl+Y followed by H2 for the Heading level 2 paragraph style
- Ctrl+Y followed by H3 for the Heading level 3 paragraph style
- Ctrl+Y followed by H4 for the Heading level 4 paragraph style
- Ctrl+Y followed by H5 for the Heading level 5 paragraph style
- Ctrl+Y followed by H6 for the Heading level 6 paragraph style
- Ctrl+Y followed by H7 for the Heading level 7 paragraph style

If you follow this convention, you concentrate control over heading levels in the number keys on the top line of your keyboard. Pressing Ctrl+YH1 through Ctrl+YH7 assigns the associated heading level style, and pressing Ctrl+9 or Ctrl+0 promotes or demotes headings regardless of whether there is a style sheet.

Even if you use styles (key codes Ctrl+YH1 through Ctrl+YH7) to assign levels of headings, you can still use the Ctrl+9/Ctrl+0 method. There are two circumstances in which you might want to do so:

- When you want to promote or demote a block of several headings and the headings are of different levels, Ctrl+9 will promote them all at once and Ctrl+0 will demote them all at once. Each heading will keep its place in the hierarchy, but the hierarchy will be promoted or demoted one level. If you select a Level 2, a Level 3, and a Level 4 heading together and promote them with Ctrl+9, they will become Level 1, Level 2, and Level 3 respectively. In contrast, if you select a group of headings and use a key code to apply a style, all the selected headings will assume the heading level controlled by the style.

- When you want help in keeping an outline correct in a formal sense, Ctrl+9 and Ctrl+0 help you. Technically, an outline or a document should never transit directly from a Level 1 heading to a Level 3 heading. With styles, you have the freedom to make a heading any level you want. You can follow a Level 1 heading with a Level 3, if that is your preference. But with the Ctrl+9/Ctrl+0 method, Word tries to protect you, and it won't let you promote or demote headings in such a way that levels are skipped. If you try, Word simply causes your computer to beep.

Promoting body text to headings and vice versa To promote body text to a heading, press Ctrl+9. This causes the selected body-text paragraph to assume the same level as whatever heading precedes it (is above it) in the document. From there, you can adjust the level with subsequent uses of Ctrl+9 and Ctrl+0. If you are using a style sheet, simply use the key code (Ctrl+YH1 through Ctrl+YH7) for the heading style you want.

To demote a heading to body text, use Ctrl+X if you are not using a style sheet or Ctrl+Y followed by the key code for a paragraph style if you are using a style sheet. In a style sheet that you'll create later, the key code for a normal paragraph is NP.

Expanding and collapsing

Much of the power of Word's outlining feature is the capability it gives you in outline edit and outline organize to collapse subheadings and text so that they disappear from the screen. With nonessential subheadings and text out of sight, you can examine the order and relationship of important headings to understand a document's underlying structure. If you need more detail on a point, you can get it by temporarily expanding a portion of the outline. When you reorganize elements in the outline, the document is reorganized accordingly.

After you create an outline, there isn't much point in using Word's outline feature unless you keep most body text collapsed. After all, with a lot of body text showing, the document isn't condensed, and you might as well be in regular document view.

If, on the other hand, you keep body text collapsed and most or all of the headings expanded (visible), the outline can be enormously useful, not only as a means of seeing the overall structure of a document but also as a means of jumping from place to place in it. So the first thing to learn is a reliable way to achieve this situation—all headings showing, no text showing.

This is easily accomplished: Simply hold down the Shift and Alt keys and press the 7 key on the main keyboard.

That might be all you need to know at first about expanding and collapsing outlines. Using this simple method,

- When you want to see the body text of the document, press Shift+F2 to enter document view.
- When you want to see the outline, press Shift+F2 to enter outline view, and then press Shift+Alt+7 if necessary.

CHAPTER TWENTY-SIX: Outlining

Every paragraph in any document is either expanded or collapsed. This isn't apparent in document view, where both kinds of paragraphs show on the screen and both kinds print. But in outline edit mode and outline organize mode, only expanded paragraphs appear, and the presence of collapsed paragraphs is indicated next to a visible heading by

- a *t* if the collapsed text is body text, or
- a *+* if it is a heading or a combination of heading and body text.

When you're in document view and you press the Enter key to create a new paragraph, the paragraph will be either expanded or collapsed, depending on what kind of paragraph the cursor was in when you pressed the Enter key. If the cursor (or the beginning of the selection) was in a collapsed paragraph, then any new paragraphs of body text you create will also be collapsed. They will remain collapsed until you expand them in outline view or unless they are or become formatted with heading styles. (Word expands any paragraph formatted with a heading style unless you have told Word not to display headings of the level of the style.)

On the other hand, if the cursor was in an expanded paragraph when you pressed the Enter key, any newly created paragraphs will also be expanded.

Again, none of this is apparent in document view. But when you switch to outline view, the collapsed paragraphs vanish, and the expanded paragraphs appear.

When subheadings or text are said to be *below* or *under* a heading or subheading, it means they are subsidiary—they are indented to the right of the heading or subheading, and they might or might not be collapsed from view. In other words, elements are below a heading if they come between that heading and another of the same level.

A heading that has subheadings collapsed below it is marked in the selection bar with a *+*. (The *+* also appears if there are both subheadings and body text collapsed below the heading.) A heading that has collapsed body text under it is marked in the selection bar with a *t*.

Selecting in outline organize Selecting characters when you are in outline edit is much like selecting characters in document view except that you cannot extend the selection to cover characters in more than one paragraph.

In outline organize, however, you can select whole paragraphs only. Consequently, several keys take on new meanings in outline organize:

- The Up and Down direction keys select headings at the same level as the heading currently selected; the Left and Right direction keys move up (Left key) or down (Right key) through headings regardless of level.
- The Home key moves you up in a document to the next higher level; the End key moves you to the last heading in the next lower level.
- The F8 key selects a highlighted heading and all its subheadings.

WARNING: *When you delete a heading in outline organize mode, you will also delete any subheadings or text collapsed beneath it.*

The Mouse

The mouse has limited uses in outlining. You can switch between document view and outline view by using the mouse to choose the View Outline command. If you're using a style sheet, you can promote or demote headings with the mouse by using it to choose the Format Style Sheet Attach command or the Style text box of the ribbon. If you're in outline organize mode, you can collapse a heading by pressing both mouse buttons or expand a heading by holding down the right mouse button.

But one of the most valuable aspects of using a mouse with outlines is the ability it gives you to select a place at which to begin working. There are instances in which you might have selected an entire outline by pressing Shift+F10. Afterward, the whole screen remains selected, and when you press a direction key, the document/outline scrolls to its beginning or end. Word loses track of the place that was selected before you pressed Shift+F10. With a mouse, however, you can point to the spot on the screen you want and click a mouse button to select it.

A PRACTICE SESSION

In the two lessons that follow, you'll create and experiment with an outline. Begin the first lesson with a blank document window. If NORMAL.STY or any other style sheet is attached to the document, use the Format Attach Style Sheet command, press Del to remove the style sheet's name, and press Enter. When Word asks *Do you want to convert style sheet's formatting to direct formatting?* choose No. Later we'll format the document with a style sheet, but for now you should experience Word's outlining feature without the benefit of a style sheet.

The subject of our outline will be the craft of the performing magician.

I: Fundamentals

From your blank screen, do the following:

Step 1. Enter outline view by holding down the Shift key and pressing the F2 key. The message *Level 1* will appear in the status bar. Press the Enter key a few times to create several blank paragraphs and to move the diamond-shaped endmark out of the way. Press the Up direction key to return to a line at or near the top of the screen, and on this line type *Part One: The Magic of Magic*.

CHAPTER TWENTY-SIX: Outlining

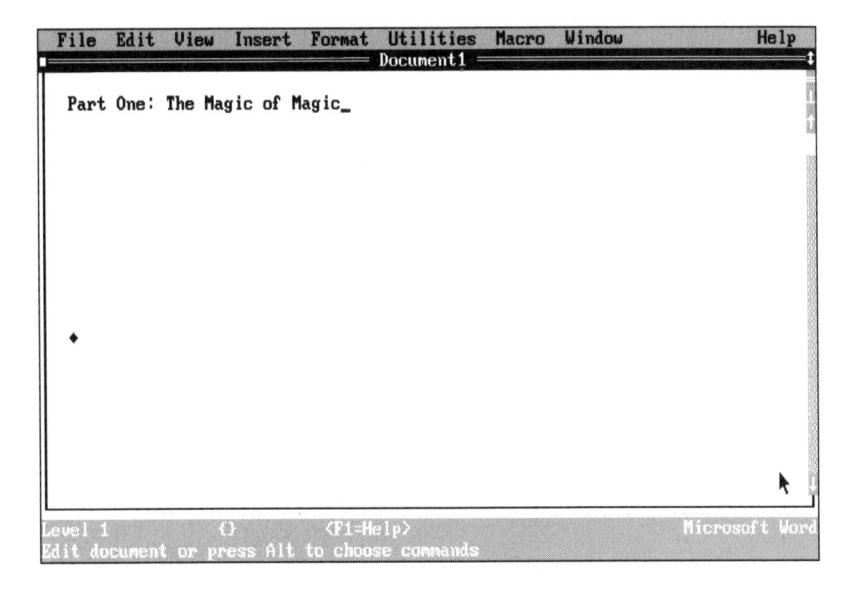

Step 2. At the end of the line, press the Enter key to end the paragraph and move to the next line. The status bar will still say *Level 1*. The cursor will be positioned directly under the first line.

Step 3. Hold down the Ctrl key and press the 0 key (on the top number row of the keyboard, not on the keypad). The selection moves four characters to the right, a demotion of one outline level. Consequently, the screen's lower-left corner displays the words *Level 2*. Type *A Short History of Legerdemain and Illusion*, and press the Enter key to move to a new line, which will be at the same level as the last line, Level 2.

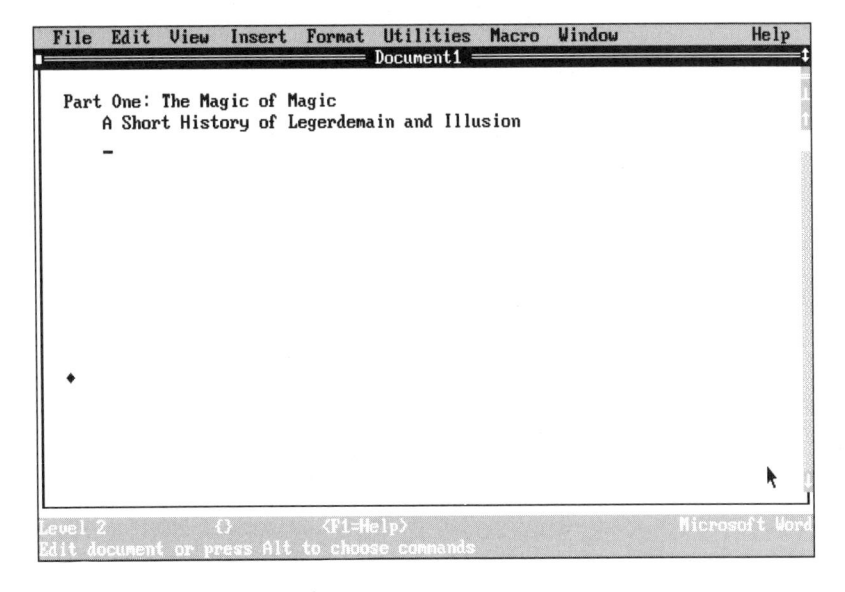

Step 4. Type *Magic by Any Other Name* and press Enter. So far you've typed the book's Part One name as a Level 1 heading and two chapter titles as Level 2 headings.

Step 5. Press Ctrl+0 to move to a third level. The screen's status bar now displays the words *Level 3.* Type *Illusionists.*

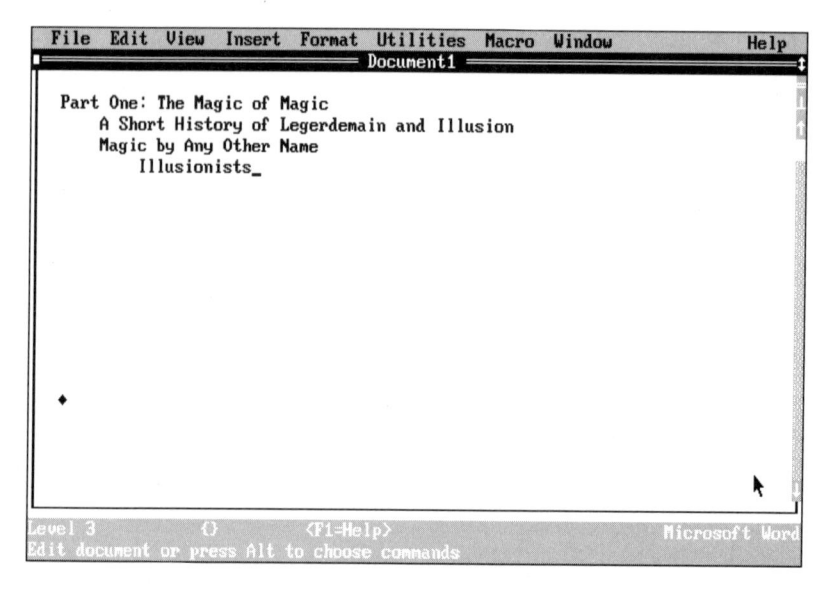

```
 File   Edit   View   Insert   Format   Utilities   Macro   Window              Help
                                    Document1
 Part One: The Magic of Magic
     A Short History of Legerdemain and Illusion
     Magic by Any Other Name
         Illusionists_




 ◆




Level 3              {}          <F1=Help>                          Microsoft Word
Edit document or press Alt to choose commands
```

Step 6. You can change a level of heading, even after the heading has been typed, with Ctrl+9 and Ctrl+0. Press Ctrl+9 twice to promote *Illusionists* up two levels. Now it is a Level 1 heading.

Step 7. You can change a heading into body text. Press Ctrl+X to turn the line that says *Illusionists* into body text. An uppercase *T* appears in the selection bar to the left of the line, and the lower-left corner of the screen says *Text,* as is shown in the illustration on page 511.

Step 8. You can change body text into a heading by pressing Ctrl+9. Body text turned into a heading always starts at the same heading level as the most recent previous heading. When the line is a heading, you can change its level by using Ctrl+9 or Ctrl+0.

Press Ctrl+9 to turn the *Illusionists* line into a heading. It becomes Level 2 because the heading above it is Level 2.

Step 9. Press Ctrl+0 to demote the line to Level 3. Pressing Ctrl+0 yet another time won't turn the paragraph into a Level 4 heading because it isn't correct for an outline to skip a level—in this case, a Level 2 heading can't be followed by a Level 4 heading.

Step 10. Press Enter and type *Manipulators.* Press Enter and type *Mind Readers.* These are both Level 3 headings. Press Enter again to move to a new line.

CHAPTER TWENTY-SIX: Outlining

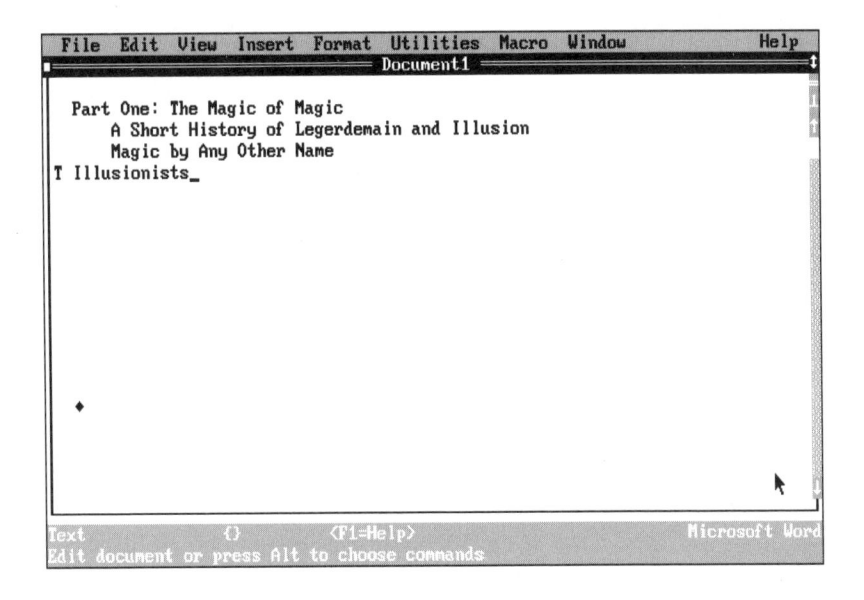

```
 File  Edit  View  Insert  Format  Utilities  Macro  Window              Help
═══════════════════════════════ Document1 ═══════════════════════════════
  Part One: The Magic of Magic
      A Short History of Legerdemain and Illusion
      Magic by Any Other Name
T Illusionists_
```

Step 11. Press Ctrl+0 to change the new line to Level 4. It is possible to move to Level 4 now because there is a Level 3 heading preceding it. Type *Mentalism* and press Enter. On the new line, type *Clairvoyance and telepathy*.

```
  Part One: The Magic of Magic
      A Short History of Legerdemain and Illusion
      Magic by Any Other Name
          Illusionists
          Manipulators
          Mind Readers
              Mentalism
              Clairvoyance and telepathy_
```

Step 12. You could go back and insert a new heading after the heading *Illusionists*. Press the Up direction key three times, and select the beginning of *Manipulators*. Type *Escape Artists*.

```
          Illusionists
          Escape ArtistsManipulators
          Mind Readers
```

Step 13. Press Enter, and Word inserts the new Level 3 heading.

Step 14. Move the selection back to the end of the Level 4 line *Clairvoyance and telepathy*, and press the Enter key. The new heading line thus formed will also be at Level 4.

Step 15. Press Ctrl+9 three times to change the line to Level 1. Type *Part Two: Old Standards*, and press Enter. Press Ctrl+0 to demote the new line one level, and type *Hat Tricks*. Continue typing, pressing Enter, and adjusting levels until you've filled your screen like this:

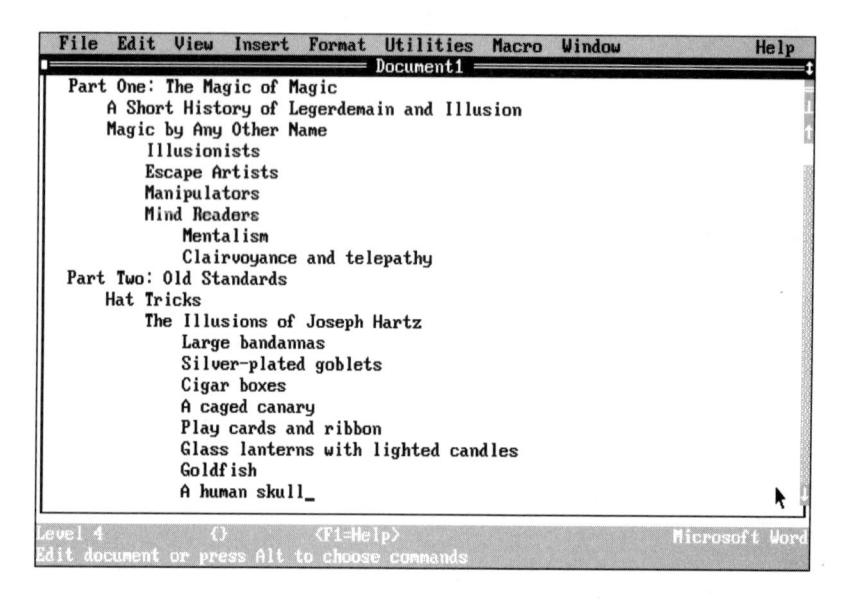

```
 File   Edit   View   Insert   Format   Utilities   Macro   Window              Help
                              Document1
 Part One: The Magic of Magic
     A Short History of Legerdemain and Illusion
     Magic by Any Other Name
         Illusionists
         Escape Artists
         Manipulators
         Mind Readers
             Mentalism
             Clairvoyance and telepathy
 Part Two: Old Standards
     Hat Tricks
         The Illusions of Joseph Hartz
             Large bandannas
             Silver-plated goblets
             Cigar boxes
             A caged canary
             Play cards and ribbon
             Glass lanterns with lighted candles
             Goldfish
             A human skull_

Level 4           {}         <F1=Help>                    Microsoft Word
Edit document or press Alt to choose commands
```

Step 16. You spot a typographical error. *Play cards and ribbon* should be *Playing cards and ribbon*. You can make editing changes in outline view the same way you make them in normal document view: Move the cursor up three lines, and add the needed *ing*.

Step 17. Use the File Save As command to save the document with the name *MAGIC1*.

So far you've used only outline view, which can be identified by the word *Level* or *Text* in the status bar. The other outline mode, outline organize, is more powerful. It is identified in the lower-left corner by the word *ORGANIZE*. Let's get a little taste of it.

Step 18. Move the cursor to the first character of the line *Goldfish*, and then switch to outline organize mode by holding down the Shift key and pressing F5. Word highlights the entire line because in outline organize the smallest unit that can be selected is a paragraph.

Step 19. Press F8 to turn on Extend Selection mode, and then press the Up direction key three times to extend the selection to include the two previous headings. Because you're in outline organize, whole headings are selected.

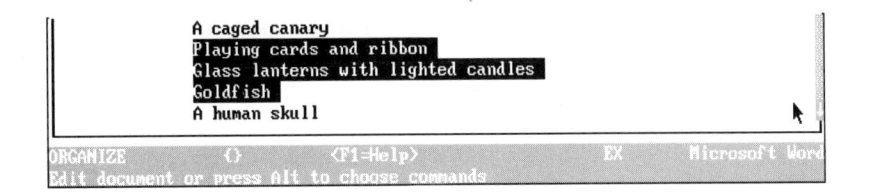

```
     A caged canary
     Playing cards and ribbon
     Glass lanterns with lighted candles
     Goldfish
     A human skull
ORGANIZE        {}        <F1=Help>              EX    Microsoft Word
Edit document or press Alt to choose commands
```

Step 20. Press Shift+F5 to return from outline organize to outline edit.

So far, you've done all your work in the outlining modes. It's time to see what it looks like in document view.

Step 21. Press Shift+F2 to switch to normal document view.

All the indentation disappears because you've been working in a document that has no paragraph formatting. The indentation was a characteristic of outline view.

```
Mentalism
Clairvoyance and telepathy
Part Two: Old Standards
Hat Tricks
The Illusions of Joseph Hartz
```

If your document doesn't look like the illustration above, it probably means there is a style sheet attached to it. Possibly it has the name NORMAL.GLY, which means you do not need to deliberately attach it to a document, and you might not know of its existence. If the style sheet attached to a document contains heading styles, they will govern the appearance of the headings you typed in the preceding steps—but the formatting will not be reflected on the screen until you leave outline view. As noted at the beginning of this section, you can detach any style sheet from your document by using the Format Style Sheet Attach command and pressing Del followed by Enter and then choosing No when Word asks you whether you want to convert the style sheet's formatting into direct formatting.

Step 22. Press Shift+F2 again to return to outline view, where the indentation shows. Press Shift+F2 once again, and you're back in document view.

You've had a taste of Word's outlining feature, but you haven't really used an outline for a specific purpose, nor have you seen the pleasing interaction of the outlining feature and a style sheet that contains heading styles.

II: With a Style Sheet

For this second tutorial, you will need a style sheet that contains heading level styles. If you have the COR-SEM style sheet or any of the other MasterWord style sheets, you're set. Otherwise, you can get by nicely for the purposes of this tutorial by creating the style sheet shown on page 514, which has only five styles. (These five styles are excerpted from COR-SEM.STY.)

If you need help creating this style sheet, refer to Chapter 24. In brief, you open a style-sheet window and use Insert New Style five times, once for each style. You then format each style as desired and save the resulting style sheet. You might call the style sheet HEADINGS, although you can use any name that suits you.

Before following the steps of this second tutorial, attach the style sheet to the document you created in the first tutorial. Do this by choosing the Format Attach Style Sheet command and typing (or choosing) the name of the style sheet that contains the heading styles.

```
(P) NP Normal                              NORMAL PARAGRAPH
       modern b 12. Flush left (first line indent 0.5"), space before 1
       li.
(P) H1 Heading 1                           HEADING: TOP-LEVEL
       modern b 12 Bold. Centered, space before 1 li (keep in one column,
       keep with following paragraph). Frame position: Inline,
       Horizontally centered in margins, 0.17" from text. Frame width:
       Single Column.
(P) H2 Heading 2                           HEADING: CENTERED
       modern b 12. Centered, space before 1 li (keep in one column, keep
       with following paragraph).
(P) H3 Heading 3                           HEADING: UNDERLINE
       modern b 12 Underlined. Flush left, space before 1 li (keep in one
       column, keep with following paragraph).
(P) H4 Heading 4                           HEADING: FLUSH LEFT
       modern b 12. Flush left, space before 1 li (keep in one column,
       keep with following paragraph).
```

If the style bar is not turned on, use View Preferences to turn it on. With the style bar turned on, MAGIC1 retains its familiar, indented form when viewed in outline view. However, now there are numbers in the style bar. Each number is the key code for the heading style that formats it. You'll also see that certain levels of heading have assumed character formatting. Level 1 headings are boldfaced, and Level 3 headings are underlined. This conforms to the formatting specified in the style sheet.

```
H1  Part One: The Magic of Magic
H2      A Short History of Legerdemain and Illusion
H2      Magic by Any Other Name
H3          Illusionists
H3          Escape Artists
```

Step 1. Just for fun and to see how powerfully styles can be used to assign and format heading levels, place the cursor in lines here and there in the outline, and apply different styles. For example, select the first line (Level 1), and use the key code H4 (press Ctrl+YH4). It becomes a Level 4 heading instantly, and its character formatting changes to conform to that specified in the style sheet. Select other lines and change their levels too by pressing Ctrl+Y followed by the key code. This is how your outline might look after changing levels.

```
H4              Part One: The Magic of Magic
H1  A Short History of Legerdemain and Illusion
H3          Magic by Any Other Name
H2      Illusionists
H1  Escape Artists
```

CHAPTER TWENTY-SIX: Outlining

Step 2. After you've finished experimenting with key codes and levels, return the headings to their original levels. Observe that the character formatting of heading styles is reflected when you're working in outline view, but the paragraph formatting is not. That's because a paragraph's indentation reflects its level in the hierarchy of outlines. It's time to look at the outline in document view.

Step 3. Press Shift+F2 or Alt+VO to switch to document view. The page number replaces the level number in the status bar, and the headings from the outline assume not only the character formatting but also the paragraph formatting specified for them in the style sheet.

Step 4. Position the cursor on the space (actually the paragraph mark) at the end of the Level 2 heading *A Short History of Legerdemain and Illusion.* Press Enter to create a new paragraph. This paragraph will be marked *H2* in the style bar, for "Level 2."

Step 5. Change the blank paragraph from Level 2 to standard by applying the style sheet's key code for a normal paragraph, NP. To do this, hold down the Ctrl key and press Y followed by *NP*. Now you can type normal paragraphs—and begin to fill in the outline and transform it into a document with body text.

Step 6. Type these paragraphs, pressing the Enter key at the end of each except the last one. Observe that the key code NP marks each as a normal paragraph. The style bar must be turned on in order for you to see key codes.

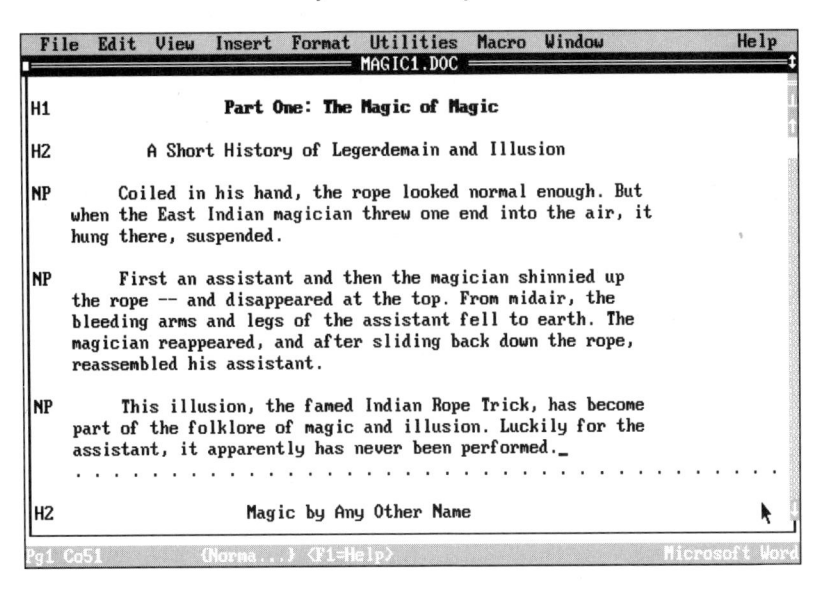

```
   File   Edit   View   Insert   Format   Utilities   Macro   Window          Help
================================= MAGIC1.DOC =================================
H1                        Part One: The Magic of Magic

H2              A Short History of Legerdemain and Illusion

NP         Coiled in his hand, the rope looked normal enough. But
     when the East Indian magician threw one end into the air, it
     hung there, suspended.

NP         First an assistant and then the magician shinnied up
     the rope -- and disappeared at the top. From midair, the
     bleeding arms and legs of the assistant fell to earth. The
     magician reappeared, and after sliding back down the rope,
     reassembled his assistant.

NP         This illusion, the famed Indian Rope Trick, has become
     part of the folklore of magic and illusion. Luckily for the
     assistant, it apparently has never been performed._
     . . . . . . . . . . . . . . . . . . . . . . . . . . . .

H2                       Magic by Any Other Name
Pg1 Co51          {Norma...} <F1=Help>                    Microsoft Word
```

Step 7. Press Shift+F2 to return to outline view. You'll see that the headings have resumed their outline-like indentations, but the body text retains its normal paragraph formatting. The paragraphs are expanded, but we want them collapsed.

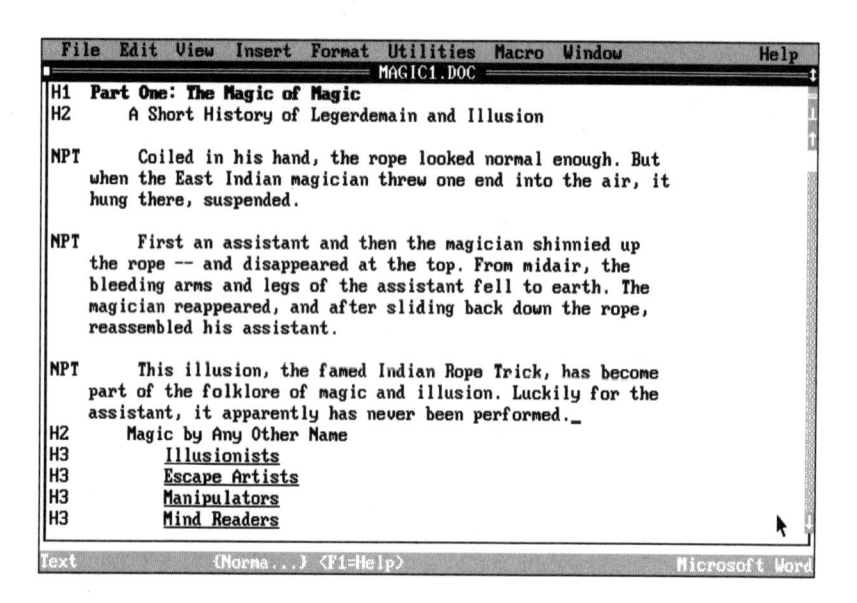

```
 File   Edit   View   Insert   Format   Utilities   Macro   Window              Help
===================================== MAGIC1.DOC =====================================
H1   Part One: The Magic of Magic
H2       A Short History of Legerdemain and Illusion

NPT      Coiled in his hand, the rope looked normal enough. But
         when the East Indian magician threw one end into the air, it
         hung there, suspended.

NPT      First an assistant and then the magician shinnied up
         the rope -- and disappeared at the top. From midair, the
         bleeding arms and legs of the assistant fell to earth. The
         magician reappeared, and after sliding back down the rope,
         reassembled his assistant.

NPT      This illusion, the famed Indian Rope Trick, has become
         part of the folklore of magic and illusion. Luckily for the
         assistant, it apparently has never been performed._
H2       Magic by Any Other Name
H3           Illusionists
H3           Escape Artists
H3           Manipulators
H3           Mind Readers
Text                   (Norma...) <F1=Help>                          Microsoft Word
```

Step 8. Position the cursor in any part of the heading above the body text, and press Shift+Ctrl+8 (8 on the top row of the normal keyboard) or Shift+minus (on the numeric keypad). The body text collapses from view, its presence indicated only by a lowercase *t* in the selection bar.

```
H1    Part One: The Magic of Magic
H2t       A Short History of Legerdemain and Illusion_
H2        Magic by Any Other Name
H3            Illusionists
```

Step 9. Toggle back to document view by pressing Shift+F2. You'll see that the text paragraphs that were collapsed in outline view are still apparent in document view. Position the cursor on the last space (the paragraph mark) of the last paragraph you typed, and press Enter. This creates a new normal paragraph, marked with the key code NP, below the paragraph that ends *never been performed*.

```
NP       This illusion, the famed Indian Rope Trick, has become
         part of the folklore of magic and illusion. Luckily for the
         assistant, it apparently has never been performed.

NP       _

H2                       Magic by Any Other Name
```

Step 10. Press Ctrl+YH4 to turn the paragraph into a Level 2 heading. Type *Harry Houdini*, and then press Enter to form a second Level 2 paragraph below the *Houdini* line. Apply the key code NP (Ctrl+YNP) to turn it into a normal paragraph, and then type the paragraph shown below.

```
NP      This illusion, the famed Indian Rope Trick, has become
        part of the folklore of magic and illusion. Luckily for the
        assistant, it apparently has never been performed.

H2                      Harry Houdini

NP      If the Indian Rope Trick is the most famous illusion,
        Harry Houdini is arguably the most famous magician. That his
        name brings to mind images of spectacular escapes under
        seemingly impossible conditions is testimony to his skill
        both as a performer and as a self-promoting publicist._

H2                  Magic by Any Other Name
```

Step 11. Return from document view to outline view by pressing Shift+F2. Press Ctrl+Home so that the Level 1 heading is selected. Press Ctrl+8 (on the top of the normal keyboard) or the minus key (on the keypad). This collapses all subheadings below it, so the next line appearing on the screen is the next Level 1 heading.

```
H1+  Part One: The Magic of Magic
H1   Part Two: Old Standards
H2      Hat Tricks
H3         The Illusion of Joseph Hartz
```

Step 12. Press Ctrl+7 or the plus key (on the keypad) to expand the next level, in this case Level 2. Observe that one of the Level 2 headings that appears has a + next to it, indicating there are more headings collapsed under it. You could expand these headings either by pressing the asterisk now or by moving the selection to the marked line and pressing Ctrl+7 or the plus key.

```
H1   Part One: The Magic of Magic
H2t     A Short History of Legerdemain and Illusion
H2t     Harry Houdini
H2+     Magic by Any Other Name
H1   Part Two: Old Standards
```

Let's say you want to delete the heading and paragraph on Harry Houdini that you just typed into the outline/document. You could select the *Harry Houdini* line and delete it while in outline edit, but that would delete only the heading and not the paragraph collapsed below it. To delete more than one paragraph at a time, you must switch to outline organize.

Step 13. Move to the *Harry Houdini* line. Press Shift+F5 to enter outline organize. The word *ORGANIZE* appears in the lower-left corner of the screen. Choose the Edit Cut command. The line is deleted, and, as you can see inside the scrap brackets at the bottom of the screen, so is the paragraph of body text that was collapsed under the *Houdini* line. The selection remains a full paragraph, the smallest it can be in outline organize.

```
H1   Part One: The Magic of Magic
H2t    A Short History of Legerdemain and Illusion
H2+    Magic by Any Other Name

ORGANIZE      {Har...9D}  <F1=Help>           MX         Microsoft Word
```

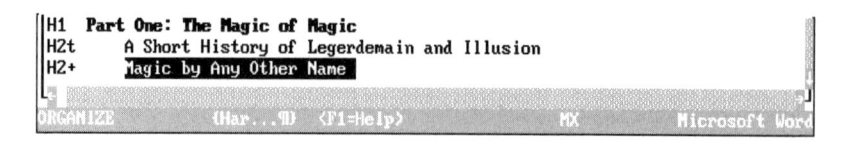

Step 14. To return to outline edit, press Shift+F5. To return to document view, press Shift+F2.

You've had a pretty fair taste of outlining, including some of the more demanding situations you can get into.

TIPS

A number of points might make outlining more useful.

- If you plan to collapse the first paragraphs from view, you must place a heading, at least temporarily, before the first body text in a document. After the heading is in place, you can collapse the text below out of view and then delete the heading. After the text is collapsed, it will stay that way.

- If you're using a style sheet and do not want to see the character formatting of headings while you are in an outline mode, you can remove the character formatting by temporarily breaking the link between the style sheet and the outline/document. Choose the Format Style Sheet Attach command, press Del, and then press Enter. Or attach a different style sheet, one that has no special character formatting associated with its heading level paragraph styles. When you switch back to document view, use Format Style Sheet Attach again to reattach the style sheet that contains the character formatting.

- Sometimes you might see a + in the selection bar, but pressing the plus key doesn't cause anything to happen. Pressing Shift+plus (on the keypad) might cause text to appear, but that doesn't explain why there was a + instead of a *t* in the selection bar. Likely as not, the heading has a lower-level heading collapsed below it (possibly one you added by key code while you were in document view). A way to get this to show is to select the heading that has the + in the selection bar and press the asterisk key on the numeric keypad. This will reveal all levels of collapsed headings. Then, if you want body text to appear, press Shift+F12 or Shift+plus.

- There is something to be said for making section marks first-level headings. This way, they will always appear when you're in outline view or outline edit, and you'll know when you are moving across a section boundary.

- When you are moving or copying text between windows, you might think your Ins (or Shift+Ins) key has stopped working, but it hasn't. If the original text is collapsed (but visible in a document window) and you insert it into an outline, it will seem not to be there. It will remain collapsed. You won't see the collapsed text you've inserted until you expand it or until you switch from outline view to document view. Then, if you've pressed Ins (or Shift+Ins) several times, you'll find several successive copies of what was in the scrap.

Certain tricks pertain specifically to document view:

- When you are in document view and want to delete a heading and all the text that follows it, a fast technique is to select the heading and press Shift+F2, Shift+F5, Shift Del, and then Shift+F2 to return to document view. The deleted material will be in the scrap and can be inserted elsewhere in the document.
- Assuming text is collapsed and you're in document view, you can move to the next heading by pressing Shift+F2 twice in a row. However, if a heading is selected when you use this technique, you will move to that heading.

NUMBERING AND SORTING

The Utilities Renumber and Utilities Sort commands give you the means to number and alphabetize elements in a document. The general use of these commands is covered in Chapter 16. But the rules change in some respects when you are in outline mode; the commands assume special characteristics and powers.

The Utilities Renumber Command

When you're in normal document view, the Utilities Renumber command will update or remove existing numbers and letters that start paragraphs, but it won't assign numbers to paragraphs on its own. Because Word can only guess which elements in a document you want numbered, it doesn't try. But in an outline, matters are considerably different. Word "knows" the conventional ways of numbering an outline, and it assumes you want every element numbered (or lettered). It will number from scratch if you want.

For example, if you execute the Utilities Renumber command while you are in outline edit, you'll normally get a numbering scheme such as this:

```
I. Part One: The Magic of Magic
    A. A Short History of Legerdemain and Illusion
    B. Magic by Any Other Name
        1. Illusionists
        2. Escape Artists
        3. Manipulators
        4. Mind Readers
            a) Mentalism
            b) Clairvoyance and telepathy
II. Part Two: Old Standards
    A. Hat Tricks
        1. The Illusions of Joseph Hartz
        2. The Secrets of Joseph Hartz
            a) Large bandannas
            b) Silver-plated goblets
            c) Cigar boxes
```

If you type *1.* at the beginning of the first line of an outline that has no numbers and then execute the Utilities Renumber command, you'll get a double-numeration (or "legal-style") scheme, often used in technical documents.

```
1. Part One: The Magic of Magic
    1.1 A Short History of Legerdemain and Illusion
    1.2 Magic by Any Other Name
        1.2.1 Illusionists
        1.2.2 Escape Artists
        1.2.3 Manipulators
        1.2.4 Mind Readers
            1.2.4.1 Mentalism
            1.2.4.2 Clairvoyance and telepathy
2. Part Two: Old Standards
    2.1 Hat Tricks
        2.1.1 The Illusions of Joseph Hartz
        2.1.2 The Secrets of Joseph Hartz
            2.1.2.1 Large bandannas
            2.1.2.2 Silver-plated goblets
            2.1.2.3 Cigar boxes
```

These two numbering systems are built into Word. If you have other preferences, Word will try to oblige. It will mimic a numbering system if you give it, at the beginning of the first instance of each outline level, an example of the kind of numbering (or lettering) you want for that level. For example, if you type *A.* at the beginning of the first Level 1 line in an outline and *i)* at the beginning of the first instance of a Level 2 line, Word will letter your first-level headings and give lowercase Roman numerals to your second-level headings. (If you try this, be certain to show Word what type of numbering/lettering you want for each level of heading your outline contains. If you do not, Word will resort to its built-in numbering for any levels you did not identify.)

Regardless of which numbering system you use, the numbers not only appear in outline view but become part of the document.

A useful facet of the Utilities Renumber command is that every group of subheadings is numbered separately. However, if you have a group of subheadings you want to number consecutively, you can do it if you're using a style sheet with heading level styles. For example, if you want to number all the Level 2 headings in a document consecutively, without regard for occasional Level 1 headings, temporarily apply a style for a lower level, such as Level 7 (Ctrl+YH7), to the Level 1 styles. This permits the Level 2 headings to be numbered consecutively.

If you do not want certain paragraphs numbered, precede them with a hyphen (-), an asterisk (*), or a square bullet (■). (For a bullet try either ASCII character 22 or ASCII character 254. Turn on Num Lock, hold down the Alt key, and type 22 on the numeric keypad. If that doesn't print, try Alt and 254.)

Finally, you can trick Word into assigning numbers to a list that's not meant to be an outline. Simply put the list in outline form temporarily: Type *1.* or *1)* at the beginning of the first line of the list; then enter outline organize (Shift+F2 followed by Shift+F5), select the elements in the list, make them Level 1 by pressing Ctrl+9 as many times as necessary, and then execute the Utilities Renumber command.

The Utilities Sort Command

Word's Utilities Sort command operates differently from document view when it alphabetizes or puts in numeric order elements in an outline.

The advantage of sorting in outline view is that you can keep groups of paragraphs together and sort the order of a document on a group-by-group basis. The position of a group of paragraphs in a document will be based on the alphabetic or numeric value of the beginning of the group's first paragraph. You do this by making the first paragraph of each group a Level 1 heading in the outline and by making other paragraphs lower levels that follow the Level 1 heading. Utilities Sort will put the Level 1 paragraphs in order, moving the associated lower levels with them.

CHAPTER TWENTY-SEVEN

Indexes

Indexing is no picnic, even with Word's sophisticated help. Human judgment is required to produce a high-caliber index. Index headings and subentries must be chosen with care.

Although Word can't help you decide the content of an index, it can increase your efficiency enormously. Word reduces the tedium of indexing by compiling, alphabetizing, and recording page numbers. It also simplifies or eliminates the chore of formatting an index to look the way you want it to.

There are three broad stages to indexing with Word.

The first stage is *coding,* in which you embed in the body of a document hidden instructions that indicate the words, phrases, or lines you want Word to compile into an index. This coding must be formatted as hidden text, so to see what you're doing, you'll probably want to select Hidden Text in the View Preferences dialog box.

The second stage is *compiling,* which Word does for you when you execute the Insert Index command. Word uses the hidden coding to pull together a compilation of content and page numbers, which it can then assemble into an index.

The optional third stage is *formatting,* in which you make the index look the way you want it to. As you might recall from the discussions of the Insert Index command in Chapter 14, Word can do substantial formatting when it compiles an index. It can even follow formatting instructions from a style sheet.

Page numbers aren't all Word can insert in an index. Word can also include table and figure numbers. You do this by incorporating cross-referencing markers (for example, figure numbers) when you code the entries for an index. When Word compiles the index, it adds correct page numbers or series numbers. (For more on cross-referencing, see Chapter 21.)

Step 1: Coding

The first stage in indexing with Word is identifying all of the places in the document at which you have words, phrases, or ideas you want referenced in the index. You need to mark each location with hidden coding, a task you can accomplish manually or with the assistance of a macro.

Coding follows a simple form: You begin each word or phrase to be indexed with *.i.* (or *.I.*), formatted as hidden text. You end the word or phrase with a semicolon (;), which presumably you'll also want to have hidden, although technically you don't need to. These two codes, *.i.* at the beginning and *;* at the end, identify the intervening text as an index entry.

```
This .i.sentence; has its second word marked for indexing.
```

Word does not care whether the text between *.i.* and *;* is formatted as visible or as hidden. You can place the hidden coding on either side of visible text that's already in your document, as in the preceding example, or you can make the entire instruction hidden. For instance, in the following sentence, the word *jetliners* has been marked as an entry for the index, even though the word isn't part of the visible text. (Note also that the visible text, *Boeing 757*, is marked as a separate index entry.)

```
The .i.jetliners;.i.Boeing 757; symbolizes humanity's quest for
```

In this example, the word *jetliners* was placed before the name *Boeing 757*. Placing hidden instructions immediately before the visible text to which they refer ensures that, after repagination, both will be on the same page.

Coding subentries

The simplest indexes have entries with only one level, the heading. More commonly, books and reports have two levels, headings and subentries.

Word handles multiple-level entries nicely. When coding an index subentry, you can designate a path of words or phrases leading from a heading to the relevant subentry. The method of marking, which is derived from conventional notation used by professional indexers, is to put a colon (:) between levels of a multiple-level entry instruction. For example, if page 35 of this book contained a discussion of horizontal scrolling with the mouse, you could add to the manuscript at that point a hidden instruction—*.i.Scrolling:horizontal:with mouse;*—and Word would later construct from it an index entry with three levels:

```
Scrolling
   horizontal
      with mouse                               35
```

In this example, the page number appears only after the bottom-level line. To instruct Word to place the page number on all three lines, you would code three successive index instructions, all of which could be run together like this:

```
.i.scrolling;.i.scrolling:horizontal;.i.scrolling:horizontal:with mouse;
```

Word allows up to five levels in an index, and at your request it will format up to four of these with a style sheet. Generally, people use two or three.

Even though you might not plan to use subentries in your index, it is sound practice during the initial coding to include at least one subentry following each main-level heading in an index instruction. You can always delete some of these subentries later if they prove unhelpful. But, as the authoritative *The Chicago Manual of Style* puts it: "It is important to have them on hand at later stages in making the index, because if you do not, you may end up with nothing but unmodified headings followed by long strings of page numbers. These make an index all but useless."

Referencing series items

You can include in an index any figures, tables, maps, and other such series items you've already coded with a sequence holder for automatic numbering at print time. (For details, see Chapter 21.) For example, suppose the third table in your document is a population table that is to be printed on page 30. The table lists census figures for the ten most densely populated cities in the United States.

To have Word number the table at print time, you type *table:* and press F3 to include a sequence holder like this in the caption:

```
Table (table:). The ten most densely populated cities.
```

The sequence holder (*table:*) tells Word to number the table when you print the document, so the printed caption will read *Table 3. The ten most densely populated cities.*

To further identify this table for cross-referencing purposes as the one listing city populations, you can highlight the table and its caption and give it a bookmark name of *census*. Within the document, you can now add cross-references, such as *See Table (table:census)* or *See page (page:census)*, and Word will print the references as *See Table 3* or *See page 30*.

When you code index entries, you can add a final instruction to the table:

```
Table (table:). The ten most densely populated cities..i.New
York:Population:Table (table:census);
```

Now, when Word compiles your index, it will paginate the document and include an index entry that looks like this:

```
New York
  Population
    Table (table:census)                    30
```

and is printed out like this:

```
        New York
          Population
            Table 3   30
```

Tips on coding

- Because semicolons (;) and colons (:) have special meanings when used as coding in index instructions, you must enclose in quotation marks any index instruction that uses these characters as punctuation. For example, the book title *Magic: Beyond the Illusion* would mislead Word if it were marked as an index entry. Word would assume *Magic* was supposed to be a main index heading and *Beyond the Illusion* a second-level index sub-entry. By placing the entire title (but not .i. or ;) inside quotation marks, you signal that the colon inside the quotation marks is to be treated as punctuation, not index coding. Format the quotation marks as hidden text.
- You can place *See* and *See also* cross-references in your document by placing a hidden colon immediately before the semicolon that ends the coded instruction. The colon suppresses the page number that Word would otherwise add when it compiled the index. For example, in the passage on the Boeing 757 you might insert .i.757. *See* Boeing 757:; formatted as hidden. Word would include 757.*See* Boeing 757 in the index, alphabetized under 757. No page number would follow it. (A *See* entry is used when the information can be found under a different heading: *Leona Helmsley.* See *Helmsley, Leona.* A *See also* entry is used to direct the reader to additional information. Generally, the words *See* and *See also* are italicized.)
- The .i. must be formatted as hidden text. Anything else, including the final semicolon, can be visible. But unless you want the semicolon to print, hide it.
- Instead of using a semicolon to end an index instruction, you can use a paragraph mark. This is a handy option if you're coding a document heading that ends in a paragraph mark anyway. (Technically, a section mark can end an index instruction too.)
- If your Word document has been typeset, you can still index it. Use the Format Margins command to enlarge the page size or to narrow the margins so that at least as many characters appear on a Word page as on

any typeset page. Scroll through the document and place new-page characters (Ctrl+Enter) at exactly the places where they occur in the typeset version. Repaginate your Word document, and its page numbering will match that of the typeset version. This permits you to code the document with confidence that the page references in the index will be accurate.

Faster coding

There are ways to speed up the coding of a document. One is to copy the hidden-text code *.i.* to the glossary, giving it a simple name such as *i*. To insert the code, you type *i* (or whatever glossary name) and press F3. Similarly, you can insert both *.i.* and a hidden-text heading jointly by making both parts one glossary entry. This is handy when a particular index heading is used repeatedly with different subentries. You include as a single glossary entry *.i.*, the heading, and the semicolon.

When used with the F3 key, the glossary doesn't work as well for inserting hidden semicolons at the ends of index entries because a glossary name, in order to work with the F3 key, must be typed after a blank space, or else the name must be more than one character long and be selected. However, you can insert a hidden semicolon from the glossary if you save it with a control code. For example, format and save a hidden semicolon with a control code such as Ctrl+YSE (for "semicolon"). At the end of an index entry press Ctrl+YSE, and the hidden semicolon will be inserted directly after the last character of the index entry. Alternatively, without using a glossary entry, you can type a hidden semicolon rapidly by pressing Ctrl+H followed by a semicolon. Then you can press Ctrl+Spacebar to turn off the hidden-text formatting, or you can leave the hidden-text formatting behind by moving away with a direction key or by clicking elsewhere with the mouse.

Edit Replace When a topic appears numerous times in a document, you can partly automate the coding of a key word or phrase that is repeated. You can replace every instance of *Boeing 757* with *.i.Boeing 757;* for example. Unfortunately, this technique won't insert formatting, so whatever text it inserts will be visible. You must manually select and hide every *.i.* and semicolon.

You can speed up this manual formatting by using a mouse, which gets you around the screen quickly, or by using Edit Search and the F4/Shift+F4 key combination.

Search and F4 Recall that F4 repeats the last editing act and Shift+F4 repeats the last execution of the Edit Search command. Use the Edit Search command to find and highlight the first instance of *.i.* Press Ctrl+H to format it as hidden text. Press Alt+F6 as many times as necessary to highlight the semicolon at the end of the word or phrase. In the case of *Boeing 757;* press Alt+F6 three times—once to highlight *Boeing*, once to highlight *757*, and once to highlight the semicolon. Press the F4 key to repeat the last editing act, which in this case turns the highlighted semicolon into hidden text. Press the Right direction key once to eliminate the highlight, and then press Shift+F4 to search for the next occurrence of *.i.*, and then press F4 to hide it (repeating the last editing act). Press Alt+F6 again, until the semicolon is highlighted, and then press F4, and so on. Don't worry that the blank space after the semicolon is highlighted when you press F4. Word won't hide the space, even though it's highlighted. However, when punctuation such as a period or comma follows the semicolon, use the Shift+Left direction key to ensure that only the semicolon, and not the period or comma, is highlighted. Then press F4.

Another variation: Replace *757* with *.i.Boeing 757;757* throughout a document, and then use Edit Search to find the first instance of *.i.Boeing 757;*. When it is highlighted, apply the hidden text format (Ctrl+H or Ctrl+AH). This will leave only the original word *757* as visible text. Press Shift+F4 to search for the next instance of *.i.Boeing 757;* and press F4 to apply the hidden format. This method reduces the amount of typing you have to do, and it causes all text references to either *Boeing 757* or *757* to be indexed as *Boeing 757*.

Macros If all of the foregoing sounds complicated…well, it is. But a macro can do much of the work of marking index entries. Simply highlight the word or phrase to be coded, and press the macro's control code. One such macro comes with Word. It has the control code Ctrl+VI, and comes in a glossary file called MACRO.GLY.

An alternative macro, with the control code Shift+Ctrl+IN, is included with MasterWord and is reproduced below. You can type this macro into a document, highlight it, and use the Macro Edit command to define it as a macro.

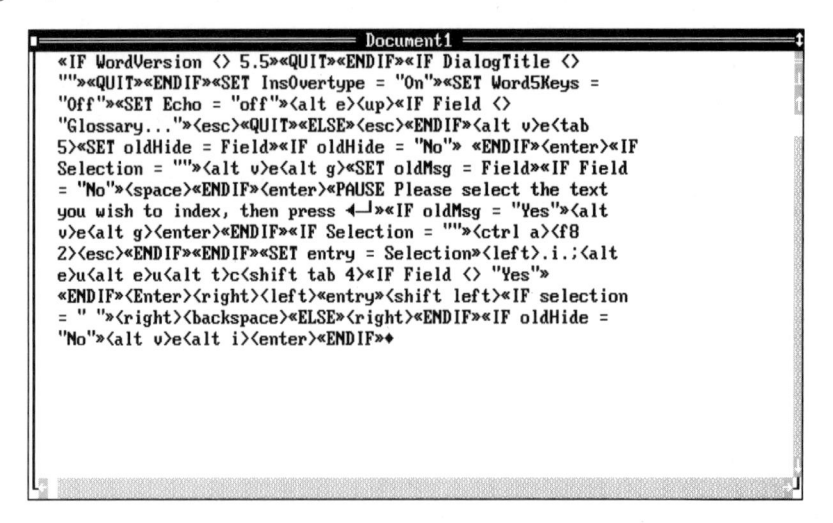

```
«IF WordVersion <> 5.5»«QUIT»«ENDIF»«IF DialogTitle <>
""»«QUIT»«ENDIF»«SET InsOvertype = "On"»«SET Word5Keys =
"Off"»«SET Echo = "off"»<alt e><up>«IF Field <>
"Glossary..."»<esc>«QUIT»«ELSE»<esc>«ENDIF»«alt v>e<tab
5>«SET oldHide = Field»«IF oldHide = "No"» «ENDIF»<enter>«IF
Selection = ""»<alt v>e<alt g>«SET oldMsg = Field»«IF Field
= "No"»<space>«ENDIF»<enter>«PAUSE Please select the text
you wish to index, then press ⏎»«IF oldMsg = "Yes"»<alt
v>e<alt g><enter>«ENDIF»«IF Selection = ""»<ctrl a><f8
2><esc>«ENDIF»«ENDIF»«SET entry = Selection»<left>.i.;<alt
e>u<alt e>u<alt t>c<shift tab 4>«IF Field <> "Yes"»
«ENDIF»<Enter><right><left>«entry»<shift left>«IF selection
= " "»<right><backspace>«ELSE»<right>«ENDIF»«IF oldHide =
"No"»<alt v>e<alt i><enter>«ENDIF»♦
```

This macro does basically the same things as the one that comes with Word, but it has a couple of advantages. First, it senses when the highlighted text you want to code ends with an unneeded trailing space. This means that you can highlight words and phrases by pressing F8 or Alt+F6 or by using the right mouse button, without concern as to whether you have selected unwanted space following the word. The other advantage of the Ctrl+IN macro is that it places a second copy of the index entry into your document in hidden-text form rather than simply putting hidden coding around your existing entry. This makes it easier to modify the entry if you want the wording in the index to differ somewhat from the wording in the body of your document.

Step 2: Compiling

By now, your work's almost done. Compiling the indexing instructions into an index is as easy as running the Insert Index command, which was described in Chapter 14. Turn off the Hidden Text field of the View Preferences command before executing the command so that page numbering won't be thrown off.

Long documents might take a while to index. Have patience. Word is doing a lot: reading the document for index entries, figuring out up to five levels of heading, alphabetizing the entries by level, adding appropriate page numbers, and formatting the results.

In addition to creating the index, the Insert Index command adds a couple of things to the document's content: some hidden markers and a section mark.

Hidden markers The first line of the compiled index will say *.Begin Index.*, and the final line will say *.End Index.*. Both lines are in hidden text. If you want to keep the existing version of the index and yet run the Insert Index command again to compile an updated version, delete the existing version's *.Begin Index.* line.

The section mark Word starts a new section at the end of the body of the document, before the index. The section mark appears on the screen as a series of colons stretching across the text window (::::::::::::). Word inserts this boundary between body text and index because it's trying to be helpful. It assumes you'll want to format the overall look of index pages differently from earlier pages. The section mark lets you format the regions on either side individually, using the Format commands or section styles from a style sheet. For each section, you can make different choices regarding the number of columns on a page, the format of page numbers, the width of page margins, and the content and format of headers and footers.

If the section mark Word inserts before an index confuses you, the following discussion might be useful. Otherwise, you might want to skip it.

The section formatting of text is stored in the section mark that comes *after* the text. When an index or other text isn't followed by a section mark, it is governed by the document's "standard" section format. This "standard" format is set by

- The Section Standard style, if you are using a style sheet that has this style defined.
- Or the built-in section format, if you are not using a style sheet or if you are using a style sheet that doesn't include a Section Standard style. (The built-in section format was introduced early in Chapter 3.)

If you change the section formatting of the index, Word will add a section mark after the index.

You might find after compiling an index that *two* section marks precede it. This means one was already at the end of the document when the Insert Index command added another. The second mark has no effect because there's no text between it and the mark above it. You can delete it.

Fixing up content

Few indexes of any substantial length are perfect at first. You'll have overlooked one thing or another. For example, you might find that you have coded *jetliner* on some pages and *jetliners* on others. These will be listed separately in the index, but you probably want to consolidate them with a single list of page numbers. You can either recode the document's index entries and execute the Insert Index command again, or you can fix up the index by editing it.

Alphabetization In some circumstances, you might second-guess the alphabetic order Word uses for main index headings. Dictionaries follow a system of alphabetization called *letter-by-letter,* in which every letter is taken into account regardless of spaces between words. *Halfback* comes before *half sister* because *b* comes before *s*.

The other major alphabetization system, called *word-by-word,* is used in telephone books. It follows the letter-by-letter scheme only until the end of the first word. *Half sister* comes before *halfback* because *half* comes before *halfback*. However, the letters of the second and subsequent words are taken into account when two or more headings begin with the same word or words. Hence, *half nelson* comes before *half sister* in both systems.

As a practical matter, there usually is little difference between indexes alphabetized according to the two systems. The following words were chosen to emphasize differences:

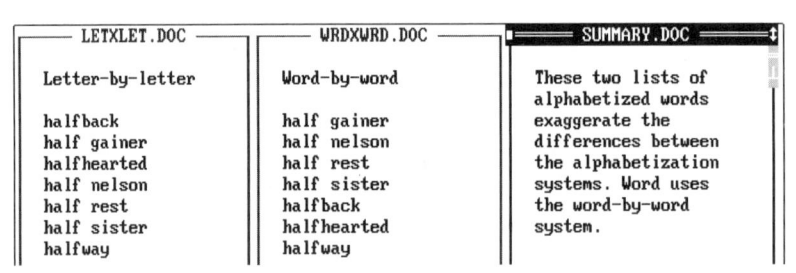

LETXLET.DOC	WRDXWRD.DOC	SUMMARY.DOC
Letter-by-letter	Word-by-word	These two lists of alphabetized words exaggerate the differences between the alphabetization systems. Word uses the word-by-word system.
halfback	half gainer	
half gainer	half nelson	
halfhearted	half rest	
half nelson	half sister	
half rest	halfback	
half sister	halfhearted	
halfway	halfway	

Word uses the word-by-word system, as do most microcomputer programs. If you prefer the letter-by-letter system, you can edit the order of the headings after you compile them in index form. Alternatively, you can omit the space between multiword headings when you code a document with index instructions. Omitting spaces forces a strict letter-by-letter sequence, but you must edit the compiled index to restore the spaces between words.

Subentries With subentries, a certain amount of editing is often appropriate. There can be outright mistakes. Your judgment about what is important might sharpen when

CHAPTER TWENTY-SEVEN: Indexes   531

you survey the results of your indexing. You might want to delete references that seem unimportant or to gather them together at the end of the entire entry under the sub-entry mentioned.

Page numbers Changes to page numbers may be appropriate too. If an entry lists pages 37, 38, and 39, and you know the numbers refer to a single extended discussion, you might edit the entry to read *37–39*.

Consider two versions of part of the same index:

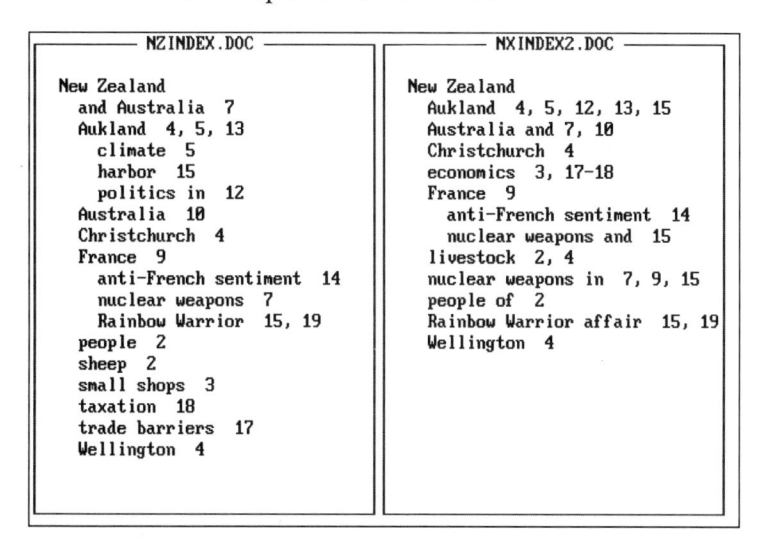

```
─────── NZINDEX.DOC ───────
New Zealand
   and Australia  7
   Aukland  4, 5, 13
      climate  5
      harbor  15
      politics in  12
   Australia  10
   Christchurch  4
   France  9
      anti-French sentiment  14
      nuclear weapons  7
      Rainbow Warrior  15, 19
   people  2
   sheep  2
   small shops  3
   taxation  18
   trade barriers  17
   Wellington  4
```

```
─────── NXINDEX2.DOC ───────
New Zealand
   Aukland  4, 5, 12, 13, 15
   Australia and  7, 10
   Christchurch  4
   economics  3, 17-18
   France  9
      anti-French sentiment  14
      nuclear weapons and  15
   livestock  2, 4
   nuclear weapons in  7, 9, 15
   people of  2
   Rainbow Warrior affair  15, 19
   Wellington  4
```

The left example shows an index entry for the heading *New Zealand* before editing. It is displayed in Word's normal format for indexes. It has 14 subentries, of which two, *Auckland* and *France,* have sub-subentries. The right example shows the same index entry after preliminary editing. The format hasn't changed, but the content has been consolidated.

Step 3: Formatting

By choosing the Insert Index command and making choices in its dialog box, you make basic decisions about how the index will look. The fields of the dialog box are described in Chapter 14.

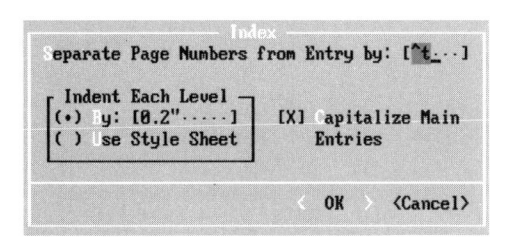

```
┌──────────────── Index ────────────────┐
│ Separate Page Numbers from Entry by: [^t...] │
│                                        │
│ ┌─ Indent Each Level ─┐                │
│ │ (•)  By: [0.2"....] │  [X] Capitalize Main │
│ │ ( )  Use Style Sheet│      Entries   │
│ └─────────────────────┘                │
│                                        │
│                      <  OK  >  <Cancel> │
└────────────────────────────────────────┘
```

If you don't change the default settings, Word inserts a right-aligned space between the end of each heading or subentry and the page number that follows; every heading (top-level entry) begins with a capital letter; and every sub-subentry is indented 0.2 inch relative to the higher-level entry above it.

You might not want these default settings. For instance, you might want Word to insert two spaces, or a comma and a space between each heading or subentry and its associated page numbers. To make either change, type two spaces, or a comma and a Spacebar space in the Separate Page Numbers From Entry By text box of the Insert Index command.

Indexing with a style sheet

When you use the Use Style Sheet option in the Insert Index dialog box, the program disregards the command's Indent Each Level By text box. Instead of directly formatting the paragraphs of the index, Word formats each paragraph indirectly by assigning it one of four styles and giving the styles sole control over the indentation and line spacing of the paragraphs.

- Each top-level index heading (including any heading with no subentries) is linked to the Index 1 paragraph style.
- Each subentry is linked to the Index 2 paragraph style.
- Each sub-subentry is linked to the Index 3 paragraph style.
- Each sub-sub-subentry is linked to the Index 4 paragraph style.

The four index styles are no different from other paragraph styles in the way you create or format them in the style sheet window. They are automatic styles, like Normal or Footnote, in that they are automatic to a particular purpose. If you choose the Use Style Sheet option button, Word applies these styles to your document's levels of index headings and subentries. It is as if you had selected each line of the index individually and applied styles with key codes. In this sense, they are similar to other automatic styles, such as the Paragraph Standard style, which Word applies to all paragraphs that are not deliberately formatted in some other way.

Here is a sample style sheet, which contains four Index-level paragraph styles as well as a Paragraph Standard style and a character style for hidden text. Note that the key codes for the four index styles are I1 through I4, the key code for standard paragraphs is NP, and the key code for hidden character is HC.

```
(P) NP Normal                               NORMAL PARAGRAPH
        modern a 12. Flush left (first line indent 0.5"), space before 1
        li.
(P) I1 Index 1                       INDEX LEVEL 1 (MAIN ENTRIES)
        modern a 12. Flush left, Left indent 0.6" (first line indent -
        0.6").
(P) I2 Index 2                                  INDEX LEVEL 2
        modern a 12. Flush left, Left indent 0.8" (first line indent -
        0.6").
(P) I3 Index 3                                  INDEX LEVEL 3
        modern a 12. Flush left, Left indent 1" (first line indent -0.6").
(P) I4 Index 4                                  INDEX LEVEL 4
        modern a 12. Flush left, Left indent 1" (first line indent -0.4").
```

If you use these sample index styles, your index will look the same initially as it would if you accepted the default settings in the dialog box of the Insert Index command. But by changing the formatting of the styles—either before or after an index is compiled—you can change the look of the index. For instance, you could change formatting of the Index 1 style (key code I1) so that main headings print in bold type and are preceded by half a line of blank space. You could change the Index 2 style so that subentries print with a deeper left indent and in italics. And so on. This is how the first two Index styles might appear after their formatting had been modified:

```
(P) I1 Index 1                              INDEX LEVEL 1 (MAIN ENTRIES)
    modern a 12 Bold. Flush left, Left indent 0.6" (first line indent
    -0.6"), space before 0.5 li.
(P) I2 Index 2                              INDEX LEVEL 2
    modern a 12 Italic. Flush left, Left indent 1.1" (first line
    indent -0.6").
```

Word will let you choose the Use Style Sheet option button even if the style sheet doesn't have the Index styles or if no style sheet is attached to the document. It will still "format" the index with the style names, but if no formatting instructions exist for the styles, the index paragraphs will not have proper indentation—at least, not at first. Later you can attach a style sheet or create the index styles after the index has been compiled. Word will know which style to apply to which index level.

NOTE: *If you ask Word to create a five-level index entry, it formats the lowest level with the paragraph style named Normal. Of course, you can select the fifth-level paragraphs and apply a different style to them manually.*

Indented or run-in format?

Indexes that have subentries fall into one of two typographic styles, *indented* or *run in*. In either case, all lines are set with a hanging indent, which means the first line is flush and the rest are indented. (This is also called *flush and hang,* and you obtain it in Word by giving a paragraph—or a style-sheet style—both a left indent and a negative first-line indent.)

An indented index indents subentries, uses a new line to start each, and can have sub-subentries. (And sub-sub-subentries, and so on.) Word compiles indexes in the indented style, the preferred method for complicated indexes.

More common is the run-in index. It uses a single paragraph for each index entry. All subentries are gathered together and tacked onto the end of the heading, following a colon. A semicolon follows the page numbers for each subentry. A run-in index typically uses less space than an indented one.

Here is the index entry you encountered earlier, shown on the left in its original indented style and on the right in run-in style. Note that in the run-in version, the double space following each subentry has been replaced with a comma and a space. This was accomplished by typing a comma and a space in the Separate Page Numbers From Entry By text box of the Insert Index command. Also note that in the run-in entry, the subentry *France* is repeated several times to accommodate the sub-subentries under it. This is awkward, but it makes three levels possible in a run-in index.

```
New Zealand                          New Zealand: Aukland, 4, 5, 12,
    Aukland  4, 5, 12, 13, 15           13, 15; Australia and, 7,
    Australia and  7, 10                10; Christchurch, 4; eco-
    Christchurch  4                     nomics, 3, 17-18; France, 9;
    economics  3, 17-18                 France, anti-French senti-
    France  9                           ment, 14; France, nuclear
        anti-French sentiment  14       weapons and, 15; livestock,
        nuclear weapons and  15         2, 4; nuclear weapons in, 7,
    livestock  2, 4                     9, 15; people of, 2; Rainbow
    nuclear weapons in  7, 9, 15        Warrior affair, 15, 19;
    people of  2                        Wellington, 4
    Rainbow Warrior affair  15, 19
    Wellington  4
```

To convert an indented index, as compiled by Word, into a run-in index, you must convert each entry individually. Follow these steps:

1. Be sure the indented index you are transforming has a comma and a single space before page numbers. You can assure yourself of this by typing a comma and a space in the Separate Page Numbers From Entry By text box of the Insert Index command's dialog box before using the command to compile the index.

2. Type a colon followed by a space (:) immediately after the last character on the heading line. In the example, you would type the colon and space after the *d* that ends *New Zealand*. If the heading is followed directly by page numbers, type the colon and space after the last page number.

3. Press the Right direction key to move the cursor to the last character in the heading line. This character is the paragraph mark, which might be invisible, depending on the setting of the View Preferences command. You can position the cursor on the paragraph mark even if it is invisible: Press the Right direction key until the cursor moves to the first character of the next line, and then press the Left direction key once to return to the paragraph mark.

4. Press Shift+Del to delete the paragraph mark and place it in the scrap. If you have turned off the Use INS for Overtype check box of the Utilities Customize command's dialog box, press Del instead of Shift+Del. Or if you're unsure of which method deletes the paragraph mark to the scrap, simply use the Edit Cut command (Alt+ET). Regardless of how you get the paragraph mark into the scrap, the heading becomes indented like the subentries below it and joins the next paragraph.

5. Move the cursor to the paragraph mark that ends the line of the last subentry. Again, you can use the technique described in Step 3 to find the paragraph mark even if it isn't visible on the screen.

6. Insert the paragraph mark from the scrap into the paragraph. Again, how this is accomplished depends on how you've set the Use INS for Overtype Key check box of the Utilities Customize command. If the box is checked, you press Shift+Ins. If the box is not checked, you press Ins.

Or you can use the Edit Paste command (Alt+EP). Regardless, the result is that the new paragraph mark's formatting governs the paragraph, so the last line of the entry moves left as it assumes the formatting that used to belong to the entry's first paragraph. Another result of inserting the paragraph mark from the scrap is that the former paragraph mark is moved to a line of its own. The cursor moves to the new line, too.

7. Press the Del key to get rid of the old paragraph mark, the one that has been moved to a line of its own.

8. Press the Left direction key once to move the blinking cursor to the apparent position of the paragraph mark you inserted from the scrap. It is only the "apparent" position, because (as Concept 3 in Chapter 2 described) the real location of the cursor is an "insertion point" to the immediate left of the blinking underline.

9. Press F8 to turn on Extend Selection mode, and press the Up direction key until the entire entry is highlighted. The paragraph mark itself will not be highlighted, because the selection begins at the insertion point to the left of the cursor. It doesn't matter whether *all* of the first line (the line that says *New Zealand*, in our example) is highlighted, but some of it must be.

10. Choose the Edit Replace command. In the Text to Search for field, type ^p (Shift+6 followed by *p*). This is the symbol for a paragraph mark. In the Replace with field, type a semicolon followed by a space (;). Turn Confirm Changes off, and press the Enter key to execute the command.

That does it. The entry will become a single run-in paragraph, governed by the formatting of the final paragraph mark—the paragraph mark that you moved down from the end of the first line.

NOTE: *The sample run-in paragraph has been narrowed by giving it a 2.8-inch right indent. To achieve narrow columns, you might want to print your index in multiple columns using the Format Section command. Also, the sample was hyphenated with the Utilities Hyphenate command.*

Multiple columns

If your index is part of a manuscript, you'll probably want a single wide column, possibly in the run-in style. But if you are publishing a finished product, you might want the index in two or three columns. To accomplish this, set the Number field of the Format Section command. Presumably, you'll want to be sure that the index is in a separate section (or has been copied to be a separate document altogether) before you switch to a multicolumn layout.

You can center the word *Index* at the top of a multiple-column page by using any one of three techniques:

♦ You can place a section mark below the word *Index* and use the Format Section command to set the Section Start field to *Continuous*. This lets you format the top of the page as a single column and the bottom as multiple column by using the Format Section command twice, once on each side of the section mark.

- Or you can highlight the paragraph containing the word *Index* and choose the Format Position command. Choose *Left* (*Centered*, if you prefer) relative to *Margin* as the horizontal position, *Inline* relative to *Margin* as the vertical position, and *Between Margins* as the paragraph width.
- Or you can center the word *Index* at the top of the multicolumn page by making it a deep header that is formatted (with the Format Header/Footer command) to print only on the first page of the section.

Any of these methods work—but, as with most aspects of indexing, that's exactly what they are...work.

CHAPTER TWENTY-EIGHT

Tables of Contents

When you choose the Insert Table of Contents command, Word compiles a table of contents or any other kind of table based on page numbers, such as a list of illustrations.

These tables can be simple or sophisticated. They can have a single level with a few entries or as many as four levels and dozens of entries. They can follow a straightforward built-in format, or they can be formatted elaborately, and quite automatically, with a style sheet. Leaf forward a few pages, and you'll see some samples.

Numerous similarities exist between creating a table of contents and creating an index. Both tasks involve three stages: coding the document with hidden instructions, compiling the instructions into a table or an index, and formatting the results for best appearance. It is assumed here that you've read about indexing in Chapter 27 and will refer back as necessary to Chapter 14, where specifics of the Insert Table of Contents command are discussed.

CODING

By the time you begin coding a document with hidden table-of-contents instructions, you've already done most of the real work. This is because the toughest part about making a good table of contents is organizing the document itself. If your report, book, or other document is well ordered and you understand the kind of table of contents that you want, the remaining steps are relatively simple.

A table of contents lets a reader find information quickly and see which subjects are covered and how they are organized. The comprehensiveness of a table of contents is governed partly by the author's preferences but largely by the type of document.

Although some books list only chapters and others (such as this one) list both parts and chapters, long reports, papers, and technical textbooks generally have tables of contents that include headings and even subheadings from within chapters. One caution: Don't get so carried away with subheadings and sub-subheadings that the reader finds it difficult to discern the overall organization of the book from looking at the table of contents.

Two rules are paramount. First, the wording of a title or heading in a table of contents must exactly match its wording in the document. If the chapter is titled "Space Travel and Human Destiny," you can't call it "Space Travel and Destiny" or "Human Destiny and Space Travel" in the table of contents. Word makes it easy to follow this rule because the table is compiled from the actual words in the document.

Second, be consistent. If you include a subheading from one chapter, you must include every subheading of identical level from every chapter.

Letting Word Do the Coding

You can totally eliminate the task of coding table-of-contents entries—*if* you've used Word's outlining feature to outline your document and *if* you're willing to have as table-of-contents entries the headings from your document. The Insert Table of Contents command lets you tell Word whether to generate a table of contents from an *outline* or from *codes*. If you have created an outline, as described in Chapter 26, creating a table of contents from it can be as simple as following these steps:

1. Saving the document (to make memory usage as efficient as possible).
2. Choosing the Insert Table of Contents command.
3. Pressing the letter O to choose Outline in the dialog box's Create Table of Contents From field.
4. Pressing Enter.

(For details on the fields of the Insert Table of Contents command, refer to Chapter 14.)

More quickly than you might imagine, a complete table of contents drawn from the outline levels in the document appears below a section mark at the end of the document.

The only additional work you need to do is format the elements of the table of contents as you want. And you can even eliminate this step if a style sheet is attached to the document and if it contains Table styles designed specifically for formatting the elements of a table of contents. (Such styles are illustrated later, in the section "Formatting the Table.") Choose the Use Style Sheet option button of the Insert Table of Contents command to tell Word you want the degree of indentation of the various levels of the table governed by the styles of your style sheet. Almost instantly, Word creates a table of contents formatted as you want it.

An impressive argument for using Word's outlining feature? Absolutely. But if you don't use outlining or, more important, if you want to compile additional tables—of charts, graphics, or figures, for example—you'll need to add hidden codes to your document.

Coding Manually

If you choose not to let Word use headings as table-of-contents entries, you're in for a little work. But at least the mechanics of coding a document are straightforward. You code a document for the Insert Table of Contents command in the same general way you code it for the Insert Index command, and you can automate the coding to a large extent by using Word's glossary feature or a macro. There are some important differences, however, between coding for an index and coding for a table of contents.

- Begin a table instruction with the hidden-character code .c. or .C. instead of .i., which is used for indexing.
- Actually, you can use almost any letter in a table instruction. The Insert Table of Contents command expects you to use the code .C. unless you tell it otherwise. However, you can employ .f. for figures, or you can use almost any other letter. (Avoid using D, G, L, and P because Word uses them for other features.) You can even use .i. if you want a table of your index entries. By coding different elements in a document with different letters, you can compile various tables with successive passes of the Insert Table of Contents command.
- Although a hidden semicolon will end a table instruction, it usually isn't necessary to include semicolons. Most table instructions apply to heading lines that end with a paragraph mark anyway. The semicolon isn't needed if the paragraph mark is there. Similarly, you can type all of the text of an index instruction in hidden characters—but as a practical matter you'll probably want to use the existing wording.
- If you generate a table from codes rather than from an outline, you can indicate that marked text is to be moved to a lower level in the table by placing hidden colons immediately after .c. (or whatever letter you use instead of c). That is, adding one colon after the code (.c.:) marks the passage for inclusion at the second level in a table. Adding two colons (.c.::) marks it for the third level, and adding three colons (.c.:::) marks it for the fourth. These colons generally don't have any text between them, unlike index instructions.
- You can type a hidden colon at the end of any instruction for which you do not want to have a page number printed. For example, in the table of contents for this book, the major sections do not have page numbers listed, although the individual chapters do. Here is a sample instruction that would mark a heading as a first-level table entry for which there is to be no page number printed.

```
.c."PART ONE: THE MAGIC OF MAGIC":
```

- When text contains a colon or semicolon, the text must be enclosed in quotation marks. (Observe in the preceding example that hidden quotation marks—indicated by the dotted underline—surround the text. This is because the text contains a colon.)
- When the text contains printable quotation marks, you must enclose them within a second set of hidden quotation marks. This means that if a passage contains both printable quotation marks and a colon, you must put one set of hidden quotation marks around the printable quotation marks and another set around the entire passage.

Coding with Macros

Just as a macro can speed up the coding of entries for an index, a macro can speed up the coding of table-of-contents entries. In fact, the two macros are almost the same; only the coding each inserts into your document changes.

The glossary file MACRO.GLY that comes with Word includes a macro called *toc_entry* that codes highlighted phrases or lines as table-of-contents entries. To use it, simply highlight the text you want to code and press Ctrl+V5. (Of course, in order to do this you first must load the MACRO.GLY file by using the Macro Edit command's Open Glossary or Merge command button.) Unfortunately, this macro doesn't recognize when you have highlighted text that ends in a paragraph mark, and in this instance it will insert a hidden semicolon at the beginning of the following line, which is annoying.

Reproduced below is a macro that improves considerably on the Ctrl+V5 macro that comes with Word. It has the control code Shift+Ctrl+TC (for "Table Compile" or "Table of Contents") and is easier to use. One advantage of this macro is that it recognizes when you have highlighted a passage that ends in a paragraph mark. In this instance, it does not insert a hidden semicolon at the end of the entry. This means you can designate that a paragraph be coded by pressing Alt+F10 to highlight the whole paragraph, and then pressing the control code—a fast procedure. Another advantage is that this macro inserts (in hidden text) a whole copy of the passage you have highlighted so that you can modify the wording of the table-of-contents entry without affecting the wording in the document. Finally, the Shift+Ctrl+TC macro lets you designate which heading level the table-of-contents entry will have; you type the number of the desired level when asked, and the macro inserts the appropriate hidden colons for you.

To use either the Ctrl+V5 or Shift+Ctrl+TC macro, highlight the phrase to be coded, and then type the control code. Basically, it's that simple.

Here is the text of the Shift+Ctrl+TC macro. It is excerpted from MasterWord, but you can make personal use of it if you type it in as shown here.

```
«IF WordVersion <> 5.5»«QUIT»«ENDIF»«SET InsOvertype =
"On"»«SET Word5Keys = "Off"»«IF DialogTitle <>
""»«QUIT»«ENDIF»«SET Echo = "Off"»<alt e><up>«IF Field <>
"Glossary...">«(esc)«QUIT»«ELSE»<esc>«ENDIF»«IF Selection =
""»«ASK temp =? Please select (highlight) the word or phrase
you want to code for a table of contents, then press
Shift+Ctrl+TC.»«QUIT»«ENDIF»<alt v>e<alt i>«SET hidSave =
Field»«IF Field = "No"»<space>«ENDIF»<enter>«ASK level =
?Which level? (Enter 1, 2, 3, or 4, or simply press Enter
for level 1)»«SET oldScrap = scrap»<alt e>t.c.:<shift left
4><alt t>c<alt h><alt h>«IF Field <>
"Yes"»<space>«ENDIF»<enter><right><left>«IF level =
"2"»:«ENDIF»«IF level = "3"»::«ENDIF»«IF level =
"4"»:::«ENDIF»<alt e>p<shift left>«IF selection = "^p"»<alt
e>t<right><alt e>p«ELSE»<right>«ENDIF»«SET Scrap =
oldScrap»«IF hidSave = "Yes"»<alt v>e<alt i><enter>«ENDIF»♦
```

COMPILING THE TABLE

After you've coded the document, compile the instructions into a table of contents with the Insert Table of Contents command. For details on the command and its fields, see Chapter 14. Be sure to turn off the Hidden Text check box of the File Print Options dialog box before executing the Insert Table of Contents command so that page numbering will be correct.

As it does with indexes, Word adds a section mark and hidden markers to the end of the document when it compiles a table. The comments in Chapter 27 on the section mark and the Insert Index command are equally relevant to the Insert Table of Contents command and should be noted. The first line of a compiled table is marked with a line that says *.Begin Table.*, and the final line says *.End Table.* Both lines are hidden.

To update a table, execute the Insert Table of Contents command again. Word will highlight the existing table and ask you *Do you want to replace the existing table? Choose YES to replace or NO to append the new table.* If you want to keep the present version of the table, press N before completing the command.

Multiple Tables

You can compile a second or subsequent table if the Insert Table of Contents command's Codes text box is set to a different letter for each table. This causes Word to bring together a different set of table instructions. For instance, you could compile separate tables for figures (*.f.*), maps (*.m.*), and charts. (For charts, you can use any letter, except *.c.* if you used that code for the table of contents. Also, it is best to avoid the letters D, G, I, L, and P because Word uses them for other features.)

When creating more than one table for a document, compile the table of contents last because you'll want it to include correct page numbers for the other tables.

Moving a Table

As you know, Word places a table in a new section it creates at the end of a document. You probably don't really want a table of contents at the end, but inserting new pages for a table near the beginning of a document would throw off all following page numbers, rendering the table obsolete from the moment it appeared.

The neatest way around this is to compile the table a first time, format it to proper length, and then move the whole thing, including the hidden *.Begin Table.* and *.End Table.* lines, to the position in the document where you want it to appear. If you want, set it off from surrounding pages either with a new-page break (which you create by pressing Ctrl+Enter) at top and bottom or, if you want to format its page layout specially, with section marks (which you create by pressing Alt+IB, choosing Section, and pressing Enter). Run the Insert Table of Contents command again, replacing the existing version. Word will insert the newly compiled table with correct page numbers in the document at the same location as the previous table rather than at the end of the document; it will not add a section mark at the end of the document.

Alternatively, you can keep the table at the end of the document or make it a separate document altogether for purposes of printing and then you can insert the table into the document's sequence of pages after printing. You can keep page numbers consecutive by adjusting fields of the Insert Page Numbers command or by manually inserting the correct number of blank pages at the proper place in the document. Simply force blanks with the page-break character.

FORMATTING THE TABLE

By filling in the dialog box of the Insert Table of Contents command, you make basic decisions about how the index will look. These fields are described in Chapter 14.

If you don't change the default settings in the dialog box, several things will happen: Word will look for table instructions coded with *.c.*; a single tab character (^t) will be inserted between the end of each heading or subheading and the page number that follows; every subheading will be indented 0.4 inch relative to the next higher-level heading above it; and styles from a style sheet will not be used to format the paragraphs of the table.

The printout on the following page shows how the beginning of a table of contents looks when it is printed with the default settings. (Page numbers for Parts One and Two were deleted manually.)

Not perfect? You can change the default settings of the Table of Contents dialog box and thereby the formatting of the paragraphs. For example, if you want to change the Separate By field, you can replace the default of a single tab character (^t) with a comma and some spaces or simply some spaces. Or, more powerfully, you can fill in the field with a space followed by two tab characters (^t^t). The strategy behind twin tab characters is discussed in the next chapter, but briefly, it lets you include leader

CHAPTER TWENTY-EIGHT: Tables of Contents

```
Part One: The Magic of Magic
     1. A Short History of Legerdemain and Illusion     2
     2. Magic by Any Other Name                         7
          Illusionists                                  7
          Escape Artists                                9
          Manipulators                                 11
          Mind Readers                                 13
               Mentalism                               13
               Clairvoyance and telepathy              14
Part Two: Old Standards
     3. Hat Tricks                                     17
          The Illusions of Joseph Hartz                18
          The Secrets of Joseph Hartz                  19
               Large bandannas                         19
               Silver-plated goblets                   20
               Cigar boxes                             20
               A caged canary                          21
               Playing cards and ribbon                21
               Glass lanterns with lighted candles     21
               Goldfish                                22
               A human skull                           22
          Howard Thurston's Inflated Balloons          23
     4. Cups and Balls                                 25
     5. String Tricks                                  29
```

characters that stop short of the page numbers to which they are leading. The following macro, excerpted from MasterWord, executes the Insert Table of Contents command and uses the two-tab-stop approach:

```
«IF WordVersion <> 5.5»«QUIT»«ENDIF»«IF DialogTitle <>
""»«QUIT»«ENDIF»«SET Echo = "Off"»«SET PromptMode =
"User"»<alt e><up>«IF Field <>
"Glossary..."»<esc>«QUIT»«ELSE»<esc>«ENDIF»«ASK temp =?
Press ⏎ to compile a table of contents from codes, H to
use outline headings, or Q to quit this macro.»«IF
MID(temp,1,1) = "q"»«QUIT»«ENDIF»<alt i>c«IF MID(temp,1,1) =
"h"»<alt o>«ELSE»<alt c>«ENDIF»<alt s>^^t^^t<alt u><enter>♦
```

You are free to make personal use of this macro.

Look what happens to the previous table of contents when you use the macro or do the same thing manually—put a space and two tab characters in the Separate By field and choose the Use Style Sheet option.

```
PART ONE: THE MAGIC OF MAGIC
    1. A Short History of Legerdemain and Illusion......  2
    2. Magic by Any Other Name........................  3
        Illusionists..................................  3
        Escape Artists................................  5
        Manipulators..................................  7
        Mind Readers..................................  9
            Mentalism.................................  9
            Clairvoyance and telepathy................ 10
PART TWO: OLD STANDARDS
    3. Hat Tricks..................................... 13
        The Illusions of Joseph Hartz................. 14
        The Secrets of Joseph Hartz................... 15
            Large bandannas........................... 15
            Silver-plated goblets..................... 16
            Cigar boxes............................... 16
            A caged canary............................ 17
            Playing cards and ribbon.................. 17
            Glass lanterns with lighted candles....... 17
            Goldfish.................................. 18
            A human skull............................. 18
            Howard Thurston's Inflated Balloons....... 19
    4. Cups and Balls................................. 21
    5. String Tricks.................................. 25
```

These are the styles from the style sheet that performed the formatting.

```
(P) T1 Table 1                          TABLE LEVEL 1
       modern a 12 Bold Underlined Uppercase. Centered, space before 3
       li, space after 1 li.
(P) T2 Table 2                          TABLE LEVEL 2
       modern a 12 Bold. Flush left, Left indent 0.2" (first line indent
       -0.2"), space before 1 li. Tabs at: 5.6" (left flush, leader
       dots), 6" (right flush).
(P) T3 Table 3                          TABLE LEVEL 3
       modern a 12. Flush left, Left indent 0.6" (first line indent -
       0.2"). Tabs at: 5.6" (left flush, leader dots), 6" (right flush).
(P) T4 Table 4                          TABLE LEVEL 4
       modern a 12 Italic. Flush left, Left indent 1" (first line indent
       -2"). Tabs at: 5.6" (left flush, leader dots), 6" (right flush).
```

CHAPTER TWENTY-EIGHT: Tables of Contents

Simply by changing the style sheet, you can make the same table look like this:

```
                    PART ONE: THE MAGIC OF MAGIC


  1. A Short History of Legerdemain and Illusion.........   2

  2. Magic by Any Other Name ............................   3
         Illusionists.....................................   3
         Escape Artists...................................   5
         Manipulators.....................................   7
         Mind Readers.....................................   9
              Mentalism...................................   9
              Clairvoyance and telepathy..................  10


                    PART TWO: OLD STANDARDS


  3. Hat Tricks..........................................  13
         The Illusions of Joseph Hartz....................  14
         The Secrets of Joseph Hartz......................  15
              Large bandannas.............................  15
              Silver-plated goblets.......................  16
              Cigar boxes.................................  16
              A caged canary..............................  17
              Playing cards and ribbon....................  17
              Glass lanterns with lighted candles.........  17
              Goldfish....................................  18
              A human skull...............................  18
         Howard Thurston's Inflated Balloons..............  19

  4. Cups and Balls .....................................  21

  5. String Tricks ......................................  25
```

These are the styles that created that look:

```
(P) T1 Table 1                         TABLE LEVEL 1
       Courier 12 Bold Underlined Uppercase. Centered, space before 3 li,
       space after 1 li.
(P) T2 Table 2                         TABLE LEVEL 2
       Courier 12 Bold. Flush left, Left indent 0.2" (first line indent -
       0.2"), space before 1 li. Tabs at: 5.6" (left flush, leader dots),
       6" (right flush).
(P) T3 Table 3                         TABLE LEVEL 3
       Courier 12. Flush left, Left indent 0.6" (first line indent -
       0.2"). Tabs at: 5.6" (left flush, leader dots), 6" (right flush).
(P) T4 Table 4                         TABLE LEVEL 4
       Courier 12 Italic. Flush left, Left indent 1" (first line indent -
       0.2"). Tabs at: 5.6" (left flush, leader dots), 6" (right flush).
```

By changing the style sheet yet again without changing the content of the document or index at all, you get this:

PART ONE: THE MAGIC OF MAGIC

1. A Short History of Legerdemain and Illusion 2

2. Magic by Any Other Name 3
    Illusionists 3
    Escape Artists 5
    Manipulators 7
    Mind Readers 9
        Mentalism 9
        Clairvoyance and telepathy 10

PART TWO: OLD STANDARDS

3. Hat Tricks 13
    The Illusions of Joseph Hartz 14
    The Secrets of Joseph Hartz 15
        Large bandannas 15
        Silver-plated goblets 16
        Cigar boxes 16
        A caged canary 17
        Playing cards and ribbon 17
        Glass lanterns with lighted candles 17
        Goldfish 18
        A human skull 18
    Howard Thurston's Inflated Balloons 19

4. Cups and Balls 21

5. String Tricks 25

These are the styles that did it (on a Hewlett-Packard LaserJet printer):

```
(P) T1 Table 1                         TABLE LEVEL 1
       HELV 14/12 Uppercase. Centered, space before 3 li, space after 1
       li.
(P) T2 Table 2                         TABLE LEVEL 2
       TMSRMN 10/12 Bold. Flush left, Left indent 0.2" (first line indent
       -0.2"), space before 1 li. Tabs at: 5.6" (left flush, leader
       dots), 6" (right flush).
(P) T3 Table 3                         TABLE LEVEL 3
       TMSRMN 10/12. Flush left, Left indent 0.6" (first line indent -
       0.2"). Tabs at: 5.6" (left flush, leader dots), 6" (right flush).
(P) T4 Table 4                         TABLE LEVEL 4
       TMSRMN 10/12 Italic. Flush left, Left indent 1" (first line indent
       -0.2"). Tabs at: 5.6" (left flush, leader dots), 6" (right flush).
```

For insight into style sheets, see Chapter 24. In addition, you might want to review the discussion of the relationship of style sheets and indexing in Chapter 27.

Adjusting Page Numbering

With all but informal documents, for purposes of formatting you'll probably want your table of contents to be a separate section or even a separate document. "Front matter" pages—those that contain such things as the table of contents, the introduction, and so on—generally are numbered with lowercase Roman numerals, which require separate section formatting from the rest of the document. A table of contents typically starts on page v or page vii.

If you're producing a manuscript, your table of contents should list all page numbers as *000*. Later, the publisher will insert the correct pages. There are several more-or-less automatic ways of getting your tables to list *000* for all page numbers.

One is to instruct Word, through the Format Section command, to start numbering your document at, say, *9500*. The Insert Table of Contents command will produce a table of contents with numbers that all begin with *95* and end with two additional digits. After the table has been compiled, select it and use the Edit Replace command to change *95??* to *000*. If the document that was indexed has more than 100 pages, also replace *96??* with *000*. If it has more than 200 pages, replace *97??* with *000*, and so forth. Before your document is printed, remember to change the page numbering back to something reasonable.

CHAPTER TWENTY-NINE

Columns, Tables, and Forms

At its simplest, creating and printing a document involves little more than starting Word, typing the text, and choosing the File Print command. But not all finished documents are streams of prose flowing from margin to margin, line after line down the printed page. In some documents, tables mingle with the text; in others, point-by-point comparisons benefit from side-by-side layout for visual impact; in other documents, page design, personal preference, or tradition call for a multiple-column presentation. And then there are forms, those things few of us like but all of us have to deal with.

Word offers a collection of tools that let you create effective multiple-column layouts, tables, and forms. To create a framework for understanding, let's begin by giving two distinct meanings to the word *column*. In tables and in forms, a column is usually a *column of information:*

MONTH	DAYS	HOLIDAYS
January	31	2
February	28	1
March	31	0
April	30	0
May	31	1
June	30	0
July	31	1
August	31	0
September	30	1
October	31	1
November	30	2
December	31	1

In multiple-column layouts, however, a column is a *column of type:*

```
Multiple-column        Normally one long      from the View menu,
layout is used in      column is shown on     you will see the
newspapers and         the screen but if      columns in their
newsletters.           Layout is chosen       correct positions.
```

Unless you use an appropriate style sheet, it is rare for a table, a set of side-by-side paragraphs, or a multicolumn layout to jump from your mind to your computer screen in full perfection. Most of the time, these types of layout require some tinkering before they are satisfactory. Success depends on your familiarity with, and ability to use, certain of Word's tools. These tools are as follows:

Tabs The basics of using tab characters and of applying tab formatting are explained in the discussion of the Format Tabs command in Chapter 15. That chapter also examines the distinction between format and content as it pertains to tabbing—a vital matter, because a tab *character* (created by pressing the Tab key) is part of a document's content, but a tab *stop* is part of a document's formatting.

Changing default tab widths When you have set no other tab stops in a paragraph, Word places evenly spaced default tab stops across the page. Normally, these stops occur every 0.5 inch, but you can change this default spacing with the *Default Tab* text box of the Utilities Customize command. Why might you want to change 0.5" to something else? Suppose you change the font size from 12 points (pica size) to 10 points (elite size). A setting of 0.5" provides five spaces of pica-size type (P10). To maintain default tab stops of 0.5 with the smaller elite-size type (P12), use a setting of 0.42". Then too, computer programmers often need tab stops eight characters apart so that lines in a program are indented for easier reading. A setting of 0.8" works.

Selecting one or more columns Word's Column Selection mode lets you select vertical, rather than horizontal, groups of characters—for example, columns of numbers in a table. You activate the Column Selection mode by holding down the Shift and Ctrl keys and pressing the F8 key. After you select a column of characters, you can delete them all at one time (an easy way to rearrange columns in a table), or you can add (or perform other simple math on) any numbers in the selection.

Multiple columns and side-by-side paragraphs You can format paragraphs for side-by-side or multiple-column printing with the Format Paragraph command, the Format Section command, or the Format Position command. These subjects are discussed in detail later in this chapter.

Using multiple windows Opening more than one window that looks at the same document can be useful when you're working on a table that is too large to see at one time on the screen. You can, for example, look at the table's headings in one window and the portion of the table that you are editing in another window. Similarly, you can split a single window to get two views of it.

CHAPTER TWENTY-NINE: Columns, Tables, and Forms   551

Style sheets and macros Both style sheets and macros can be of immense help in creating tables, multiple-column layouts, and forms. Use them to record the formatting, the setup operations, or both so that you don't need to reinvent the procedure each time you want to create a similar table. A complicated financial document, for example, might have different formatting requirements for each of many different lines. If you use a style sheet, the formatting instructions for various lines are conveniently stored as separate paragraph styles. If you use a macro, you can "play back" the steps in creating the document.

Data entry into forms Word lets you turn a document into a form (such as an order form) that you can fill in on the screen and print when it's complete. The key difference between a form and a conventional document is the presence of a » character, formatted as hidden text, at every location at which you might want to enter data. For example, if the form includes the word *Name* followed by a blank space, you could put a hidden » between the word and the space.

When filling in a form, you can jump from one » to another. To jump to the next marker, hold down Ctrl and press the > key; to jump to the previous marker, hold down Ctrl and press the < key.

Because it is in hidden text, the » does not normally print. You place the character in your document by holding down the Ctrl key and pressing the] (right bracket) key and then formatting it as hidden.

Hidden text Imagine you are designing a form for on-screen use and want to place a hidden-text » marker before a fill-in blank. You do one of two things:

- Move the cursor to the position at which you want the marker. Turn on hidden text by holding down the Ctrl key and pressing the H key. Type the marker character by holding down the Ctrl key and pressing the] key.
- Type the » marker by holding down the Ctrl key and pressing]. Then highlight the » and format it as hidden by holding down the Ctrl key and pressing the H key.

COLUMN MANIPULATION

Word lets you select columns of text or numbers—actually rectangles of any size— and move them, delete them, format them, or perform calculations on the numbers contained within them. This feature is called *column manipulation*, and a simple demonstration shows its usefulness.

We'll make a three-column table showing the daily and Sunday circulations of nine major U.S. newspapers. We'll use a style sheet, and it need have only one style, to which we've assigned the arbitrary key code NC:

```
(P) NC Paragraph 1                         NEWSPAPER CIRCULATION PAPER
        Courier 12. Flush left. Tabs at: 2.6" (left flush, leader dots),
        4.2" (right flush), 5.9" (right flush).
```

(It is not vital that you understand style sheets to learn how to manipulate columns. This style is reproduced for those trying to learn how to create styles for tables. Note that the style could have had the Format Paragraph command's Together check box checked, ensuring that any table formatted with it would never split across more than one page, provided the table was less than a page long.)

With the assistance of the style, let's type the following table:

```
   R[·······1·······2····.L···3·········4·R······5·······R6········7···
NC  Newspaper                         Daily          Sunday
NC
NC  Boston Globe..............        510,261        793,151
NC  Chicago Tribune...........        762,882      1,145,387
NC  Denver Post...............        244,953        356,986
NC  Honolulu Star-Bulletin....        113,608        200,462
NC  Los Angeles Times.........      1,057,536      1,321,244
NC  New York Times............        226,038      1,593,107
NC  S.F. Chronicle............        539,458        706,150
NC  Seattle Times.............        226,038        473,155
NC  Washington Post...........        768,288      1,042,821
```

If you're following along at your computer, using this as a tutorial, press the Tab key twice after the name of each newspaper—one tab for the leader character stop (at 2.6 inches) and one for the *Daily* column stop (at 4.2 inches). After typing the daily circulation figure, press the Tab key once and type the Sunday circulation figure. Press Enter at the end of each line.

To avoid having leader characters on the first line of the table (after the word *Newspaper*), press the Spacebar until the selection reaches the 2.6-inch mark on the ruler. (It will be marked by an *L*, showing a left-aligned tab stop.) These Spacebar spaces "use up" the space that otherwise would be filled with leader characters. (An alternative approach would be to create a second style in the style sheet, intended specifically for formatting the first line. This style would be identical to the other one except that it would not have the tab stop at 2.6 inches.)

With the table complete, we'll turn on the Tabs check box in the View Preferences dialog box so that tab characters show up on the screen (and leader characters disappear from view). You need to see the location of the tab characters when you execute the next steps. We'll also turn on the Paragraph Marks and Spaces check boxes.

Tab characters are displayed as small right arrows. Spacebar spaces are displayed as small dots, and you can see these dots between words and after the word *Newspaper* in the following example. (Recall that you typed Spacebar spaces after the word *Newspaper* to keep leader characters from appearing there.)

```
   R[·······1·······2····.L···3·········4·R······5·······R6········7···
NC  Newspaper················→        Daily→         Sunday¶
NC  ¶
NC  Boston·Globe→             →       510,261→       793,151¶
NC  Chicago·Tribune→          →       762,882→     1,145,387¶
NC  Denver·Post→              →       244,953→       356,986¶
NC  Honolulu·Star-Bulletin→   →       113,608→       200,462¶
NC  Los·Angeles·Times→        →     1,057,536→     1,321,244¶
NC  New·York·Times→           →       226,038→     1,593,107¶
NC  S.F.··Chronicle→          →       539,458→       706,150¶
NC  Seattle·Times→            →       226,038→       473,155¶
NC  Washington·Post→          →       768,288→     1,042,821¶
```

CHAPTER TWENTY-NINE: Columns, Tables, and Forms   553

Observe that the tab character immediately following the word *Daily*, on the top line, is selected. The cursor becomes a single-character selection whenever you first turn on column-selection mode. With column-selection mode on, the letters *CS* appear on the bottom line of the screen, and you are ready to make a rectangular selection. This is the situation displayed in the previous illustration. The single selected character, in this case the tab character, will be one corner of what you select.

Press the Down and Right direction keys (or move the mouse), extending the selection until it reaches the character just to the left of the last paragraph mark on the screen. As you can see below, we've selected a rectangle—a column of numbers and the tab characters (right arrows) that precede them:

```
   R[········1·········2·····L···3·········4·R······5·······R6·········7···
NC  Newspaper················→         Daily→         Sunday¶
NC  ¶
NC  Boston·Globe→            →         510,261→        793,151¶
NC  Chicago·Tribune→         →         762,882→      1,145,387¶
NC  Denver·Post→             →         244,953→        356,986¶
NC  Honolulu·Star-Bulletin→  →         113,608→        200,462¶
NC  Los·Angeles·Times→       →       1,057,536→      1,321,244¶
NC  New·York·Times→          →         226,038→      1,593,107¶
NC  S.F.·Chronicle→          →         539,458→        706,150¶
NC  Seattle·Times→           →         226,038→        473,155¶
NC  Washington·Post→         →         768,288→      1,042,821¶
```

As an aside, if you were to press the F2 key now, Word would add all the numbers that are selected and put the sum in the scrap. In this case, the sum would be 7,632,463, the combined Sunday circulations of the nine newspapers. You could insert the sum from the scrap anywhere into the document if you wanted.

But instead of adding the numbers in the selected column with the F2 key, let's delete the column entirely.

Use the Edit Cut command to delete the selected column, placing it in the scrap. Observe that the scrap contains a little box. This indicates the ends of lines, reminding you at a glance that the scrap contains a column selection.

```
Pg1 Co43              {→Su..1■}  (F1=Help)                      Microsoft Word
```

To insert the column from the scrap back into the document at a different location, use the Edit Paste command. Before doing so, we must move the cursor to the point where we want it to reappear. We do this by positioning the cursor in the document where we want the upper-left corner of the column to be positioned.

In this case, let's move to the tab character preceding the word *Daily*.

```
        R[········1·········2····.L·3··········4·R·······5········R6·········7···
     NC Newspaper················→             Daily¶
     NC ¶
     NC Boston·Globe→            →             510,261¶
     NC Chicago·Tribune→         →             762,882¶
     NC Denver·Post→             →             244,953¶
     NC Honolulu·Star-Bulletin→  →             113,608¶
     NC Los·Angeles·Times→       →           1,057,536¶
     NC New·York·Times→          →             226,038¶
     NC S.F.·Chronicle→          →             539,458¶
     NC Seattle·Times→           →             226,038¶
     NC Washington·Post→         →             768,288¶
```

The next step is to insert the column back into the document by using the Edit Paste command. When that is done, choose the View Preferences command, and restore the Tabs, Paragraph Marks, and Spaces check boxes to their original settings. The document will look much as it did when you started, except that the two columns of numbers have exchanged positions.

```
        R[··········1·········2·········3··········4·········5·········6·········7···
     NC Newspaper                         Sunday          Daily
     NC
     NC Boston Globe..............        793,151         510,261
     NC Chicago Tribune...........      1,145,387         762,882
     NC Denver Post...............        356,986         244,953
     NC Honolulu Star-Bulletin....        200,462         113,608
     NC Los Angeles Times.........      1,321,244       1,057,536
     NC New York Times............      1,593,107         226,038
     NC S.F. Chronicle............        706,150         539,458
     NC Seattle Times.............        473,155         226,038
     NC Washington Post...........      1,042,821         768,288
```

Some points to keep in mind about column manipulation:

- When moving a column, include a set of tab characters on one side or the other of the column of numbers (or text) you want. If you select and delete only the numbers, you'll leave behind an extra set of tab characters that will probably spoil the appearance of the document. Furthermore, if you leave the tab characters behind, you'll miss their effect when you insert the selection back into the document somewhere else.
- You can generate a column of tab characters by selecting the column in which you want the characters to appear (with Shift+Ctrl+F8) and pressing the Tab key. This technique is handy, particularly when you want to add a tab character to the end of each line of a table in preparation for moving the last column of the table to a new location.
- By selecting a column and using the Utilities Sort command, you can rearrange the order of the lines in a table.
- Column selection is impossible when Word is in outline view. This safety measure protects you from the havoc you could wreak on a document if, for example, it were in outline form with subheadings or text collapsed

from view and you deleted a column. You would mistakenly delete all kinds of things you couldn't even see, and you wouldn't discover the damage until you returned to document view.

♦ If all the lines in a column don't fit neatly into a rectangle, it probably means the tab stop is center aligned or decimal aligned. If all else fails, you can temporarily change the alignment of the tab stop by using the Format Tabs command or, if you are using a style sheet, by temporarily changing the tab formatting of the relevant style(s).

♦ Don't forget the Edit Undo command. If you insert the column into a place that isn't quite right, use the Undo command right away and try inserting the column at a different location.

SIDE-BY-SIDE PARAGRAPHS

One question posed by users of Word is "How do I get a page that has both single-column and double-column (or triple-column) text on it at the same time?"

Another question is "How can I juxtapose text so that related paragraphs appear next to each other instead of one after the other?"

Still another is "How can I have multiple-line side heads in the margins of my document?"

Word has always been able to print "snaking columns," in which a whole page or several pages are formatted to print in multiple columns, like a newspaper article. But this capability, which is controlled through Word's section formatting, wasn't designed to let you specify exactly which paragraphs should print adjacent to each other.

There are other ways to work with side-by-side text. When you turn on the Side by Side check box of the Format Paragraph command, you open the door to various possibilities. Additional options are opened by the Format Position command. These possibilities are touched on later in this chapter and are covered in considerable depth in the next chapter. For now, let's examine side-by-side paragraphs.

```
         From version 3.0            Beginning with version
      onward, a field in the      5.0, you have additional
      Format Paragraph command is options opened by the
      called side by side.        Format Position command.
```

In the Word 5.5 Document View, the above passage looks like this:

```
LS      From version 3.0
        onward, a field in the
        Format Paragraph command is
        called side by side.

RS                                              Beginning with version
                                                5.0, you have additional
                                                options opened by the
                                                Format Position command.
```

In this example of side-by-side paragraphs, the first paragraph (marked in the style bar with the key code *LS*) is indented from the right so that it prints on the left side of the page. The second paragraph (marked in the style bar with the key code *RS*) is indented from the left so that it prints on the right side of the page. The key codes indicate that the two paragraphs were formatted with styles from a style sheet. These are the two styles (LS and RS) plus one more (MI):

```
(P) LS Paragraph 46                     LEFT SIDE OF SIDE-BY-SIDE
        CourierLegal 12. Flush left (first line indent 0.5"), right indent
        3.3", space before 1 li. Place side by side.
(P) MI Paragraph 47                     LINE BETWEEN SIDE-BY-SIDE
        CourierLegal 12. Flush left, Left indent 2.8", right indent 2.8",
        space before 1 li. Place side by side. Vertical Bars at: 3".
(P) RS Paragraph 48                     RIGHT SIDE OF S-B-S
        CourierLegal 12. Flush left, Left indent 3.3" (first line indent
        0.5"), space before 1 li. Place side by side.
```

You might recognize these styles as being from COR-SEM, the sample style sheet presented at the end of Chapter 24. The MI style, not used in the sample, provides a vertical line between side-by-side paragraphs formatted with the LS and RS styles.

You could use the Format Paragraph command to format paragraphs for side-by-side printing, but using styles is easier by far. (See the following discussion.) With one style of your style sheet dedicated to each position on the page at which you want side-by-side paragraphs to appear, you format any paragraph for proper placement simply by selecting it and typing the corresponding key code. The style takes care of all details, including the appropriate indentations and the side-by-side feature.

Notice that the LS (left-side) paragraph style has a right-side indentation of 3.3 inches. This forces the paragraph to be printed only on the left, in a column width of 2.7 inches (6 inches minus the 3.3-inch right-side indent). Note also that the side-by-side feature is in effect, making any paragraph formatted with this style eligible to be printed beside another paragraph. (Activating the side-by-side feature is important, but it is easy to forget when you're not using a style sheet. Remember to specify it; otherwise, you might find perfectly formatted paragraphs being printed one below the other instead of next to one another as you expected.)

If you weren't using a style to format a left-side paragraph, you could obtain the same formatting by selecting a paragraph, choosing the Format Paragraph command, and filling in the fields of the command this way:

CHAPTER TWENTY-NINE: Columns, Tables, and Forms

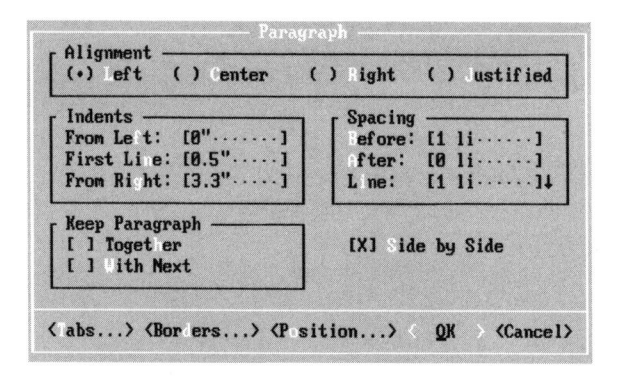

```
┌─────────────────────── Paragraph ───────────────────────┐
│ ┌─ Alignment ─────────────────────────────────────────┐ │
│ │ (•) Left    ( ) Center    ( ) Right    ( ) Justified│ │
│ └─────────────────────────────────────────────────────┘ │
│ ┌─ Indents ──────────────┐ ┌─ Spacing ──────────────┐  │
│ │ From Left:  [0"·····]  │ │ Before: [1 li·····]    │  │
│ │ First Line: [0.5"····] │ │ After:  [0 li·····]    │  │
│ │ From Right: [3.3"····] │ │ Line:   [1 li·····]↓   │  │
│ └────────────────────────┘ └────────────────────────┘  │
│ ┌─ Keep Paragraph ──────┐                              │
│ │ [ ] Together          │     [X] Side by Side         │
│ │ [ ] With Next         │                              │
│ └───────────────────────┘                              │
│  <Tabs...> <Borders...> <Position...>  OK   <Cancel>   │
└─────────────────────────────────────────────────────────┘
```

Notice that the RS (right-side) paragraph style has a left-side indentation of 3.3 inches, which forces the paragraph to be printed at a width of 2.7 inches on the right side of the page. It also has the side-by-side feature turned on. The formatting looks like this when expressed in the dialog box:

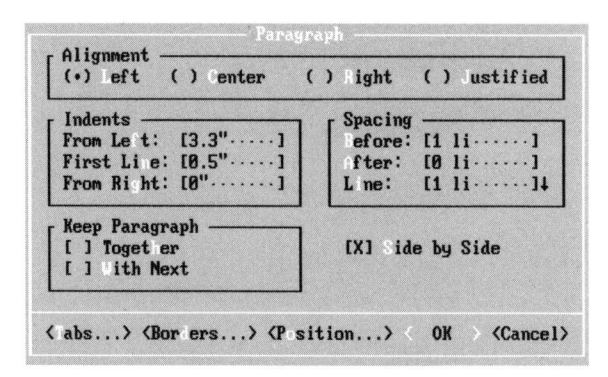

```
┌─────────────────────── Paragraph ───────────────────────┐
│ ┌─ Alignment ─────────────────────────────────────────┐ │
│ │ (•) Left    ( ) Center    ( ) Right    ( ) Justified│ │
│ └─────────────────────────────────────────────────────┘ │
│ ┌─ Indents ──────────────┐ ┌─ Spacing ──────────────┐  │
│ │ From Left:  [3.3"····] │ │ Before: [1 li·····]    │  │
│ │ First Line: [0.5"····] │ │ After:  [0 li·····]    │  │
│ │ From Right: [0"·····]  │ │ Line:   [1 li·····]↓   │  │
│ └────────────────────────┘ └────────────────────────┘  │
│ ┌─ Keep Paragraph ──────┐                              │
│ │ [ ] Together          │     [X] Side by Side         │
│ │ [ ] With Next         │                              │
│ └───────────────────────┘                              │
│  <Tabs...> <Borders...> <Position...>  OK   <Cancel>   │
└─────────────────────────────────────────────────────────┘
```

Although the example shows only two paragraphs side by side, Word can juxtapose any number of them, provided each has Side by Side set to Yes and is indented from the right and left margins in such a way that it doesn't occupy the same space as another paragraph.

As a practical matter, columns get pretty narrow when you place more than three side by side on a letter-size page. But five or even more columns are feasible when you choose a small enough type font, use wide paper, or use letter-size paper printed sideways (as is possible with the landscape mode of a laser printer or with a Postscript printer or an HP LaserJet III printer).

To increase the average number of characters that print on a line in a narrow column, you might want to use the Utilities Hyphenate command. Allowing words to break from one line to another at syllabic divisions often improves the appearance of short lines by filling them out more fully.

The Rules Word Follows

So far you've learned enough to use side-by-side paragraphs but perhaps not without occasional confusion. You can gain insight by understanding the rules Word follows when it prints paragraphs that are formatted to be side by side. When you grasp these rules, you can predict what Word will do. Understanding how Word "thinks" removes any mystery—and mystery, nice as it might be in other realms, is the enemy when it comes to word processing.

These are the rules Word follows:

1. When Word encounters the first paragraph marked for side-by-side printing, it considers it the beginning of a *cluster* of paragraphs that are to be printed in juxtaposition to each other.
2. Word examines the succeeding paragraphs, looking for the last one in the cluster. The cluster ends when

    —Word encounters the last paragraph marked to be printed side by side,
    or
    —It reaches a paragraph that has a left indent less than that of the side-by-side paragraph that came before it,
    or
    —It reaches the 31st successive paragraph marked to be printed side by side.

3. Word draws an imaginary line across the page at the location of the first line that is available for printing the beginning of the first paragraph of the cluster. This line is the *ceiling* for the cluster, and Word uses it as the vertical starting point for printing any side-by-side paragraphs that are formatted to appear to the right of the first paragraph in the cluster. (In Word 5.0 and 5.5, the ceiling is a blank line if the first paragraph of the cluster is formatted with a *space before* setting other than *0*. Earlier versions of Word used the first printed line of the first paragraph as the ceiling for the cluster.)
4. Word checks to see if the whole cluster will fit on the remainder of the page currently being printed. If not, Word begins a new page to start printing the cluster's paragraphs.
5. Word prints the first paragraph.
6. Word looks at the second paragraph. If the paragraph is indented so that it will fit to the right of the first paragraph, Word prints the paragraph there, pressed up against the ceiling. If the second paragraph won't fit to the right of the first paragraph (because it tries to occupy some of the same space as the first paragraph), Word prints it below the first paragraph.

CHAPTER TWENTY-NINE: Columns, Tables, and Forms   559

7. Word continues in this fashion. Each paragraph is given horizontal placement according to its indentation from the left and right page margins, and each is printed as high on the page (as close to the cluster's ceiling) as possible.
8. When it reaches the end of the cluster, Word resumes printing normal paragraphs or, if the next paragraph is marked to be printed side by side, Word starts a new cluster and begins the process over again.

NOTE: *If a cluster of paragraphs is too large to fit on a single page, Word isn't sure how you want the paragraphs aligned. So it gives up, essentially, and prints one column to a page. Take this as a signal to break the cluster into smaller pieces before printing it again.*

Now that you know the rules, let's consider some typical uses for side-by-side paragraphs and see a few ways to achieve the effects we want.

Tables and Scripts

Perhaps the most common use for side-by-side paragraphs is to create a table or script in which related paragraphs appear next to each other.

For instance, if you're a financial consultant, you might produce a newsletter that compares investment opportunities point by point in two or more columns. This is easy to do, either with the Format Position command or with side-by-side paragraph formatting (especially if you use a style sheet to handle paragraph indentation).

The paragraphs in a cluster will print next to each other, lined up against the ceiling. Each time Word encounters a paragraph formatted to have less left-side indentation than the preceding paragraph, it starts a new cluster. In this way, you control which paragraphs print in direct juxtaposition.

Imagine that you want to print three side-by-side paragraphs for each of four investment opportunities. This forms a grid of twelve paragraphs, three wide and four deep. You would mark each paragraph for side-by-side printing and use different indentations for the paragraphs in each column. The illustration on the following page shows the first two clusters (rows). The page margins are 6 inches apart, each of the three columns is 1.8 inches wide, and the columns are separated by a 0.3-inch gutter.

Word starts a new cluster for each row because the first paragraph of each row has a smaller left indent than the paragraph that preceded it. For example, Paragraph 4 has a left indent of 0 inches, and the paragraph preceding it, 3, has a left indent of 4.2 inches. (The possible exception is Paragraph 1, which might not have a smaller left indent than the paragraph before it. Presumably, the paragraph before it is not marked for side-by-side printing.)

You can also print two or more successive paragraphs in the same column by keeping indentations the same for each. In the illustration, for example, Paragraph 6 would have printed below Paragraph 5 if the indentations for the two had been the same. The same side-by-side techniques can be used to create those kinds of scripts, such as radio scripts, that require blocks of type to be beside each other.

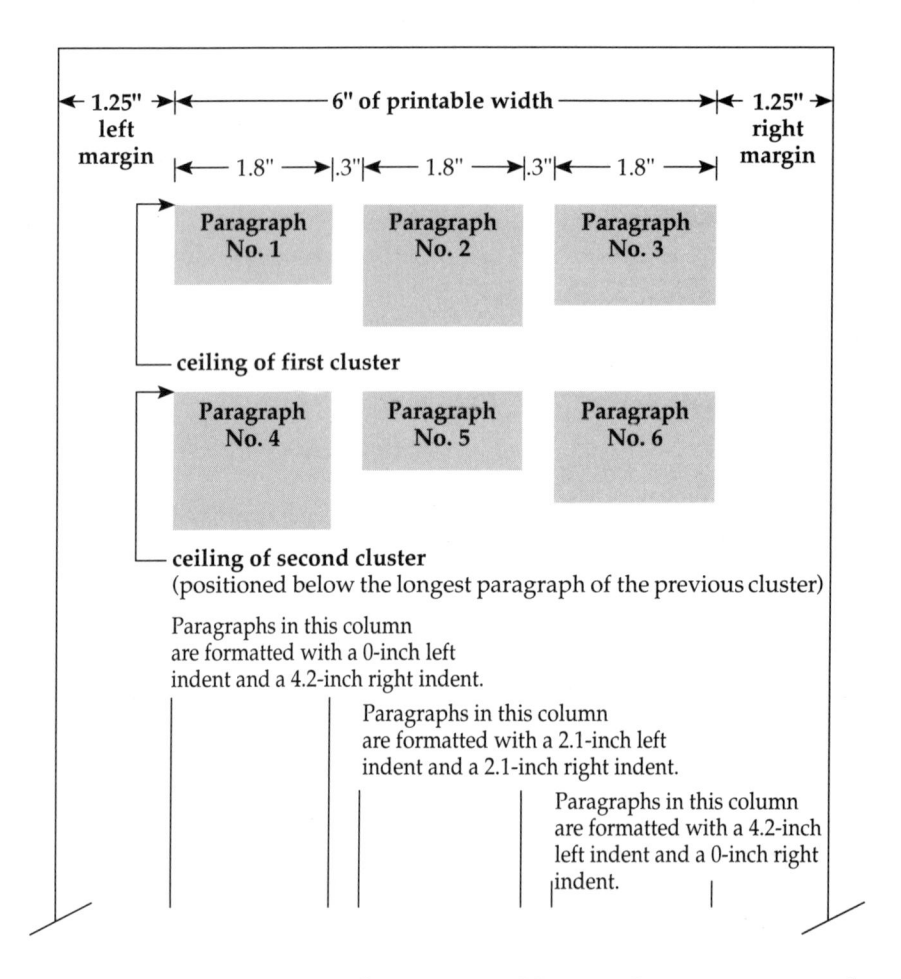

```
← 1.25" →|← ———— 6" of printable width ———— →|← 1.25" →
   left                                              right
  margin  |← — 1.8" —→|.3"|← — 1.8" —→|.3"|← — 1.8" —→|  margin

          ┌→┌─────────┐  ┌─────────┐  ┌─────────┐
            │Paragraph│  │Paragraph│  │Paragraph│
            │  No. 1  │  │  No. 2  │  │  No. 3  │
            └─────────┘  └─────────┘  └─────────┘
          └─ ceiling of first cluster

          ┌→┌─────────┐  ┌─────────┐  ┌─────────┐
            │Paragraph│  │Paragraph│  │Paragraph│
            │  No. 4  │  │  No. 5  │  │  No. 6  │
            └─────────┘  └─────────┘  └─────────┘
          └─ ceiling of second cluster
            (positioned below the longest paragraph of the previous cluster)

          Paragraphs in this column
          are formatted with a 0-inch left
          indent and a 4.2-inch right indent.

                        Paragraphs in this column
                        are formatted with a 2.1-inch left
                        indent and a 2.1-inch right indent.

                                      Paragraphs in this column
                                      are formatted with a 4.2-inch
                                      left indent and a 0-inch right
                                      indent.
```

This approach is one answer to the question: "How can I juxtapose text so that related paragraphs appear next to each other instead of one after the other?" Later in this chapter, we'll see how another technique—absolute positioning—could accomplish much the same result.

Side Heads

Word's capacity for side-by-side printing is distinguished by its flexibility. Not only can text print in any number of columns that fit, but individual columns can be of different widths. Among other things, this means that Word does well with side heads.

The example on the following page is composed of six paragraphs, all but one of which had Side by Side set to Yes. It was printed on the Hewlett-Packard LaserJet printer, using the Z font cartridge and the printer description file HPLASMS.PRD.

                                This side head   Side heads are effective in certain kinds of
                                is on the left   publications, including newsletters. The
                                                         Microsoft Word manual uses them extensively.

                                                         Word's ability to align paragraphs side by
                                                         side, even when the paragraphs are of different
                                                         widths, makes it easy to use side heads.

                    Side heads can appear on either side of a page.
                    Frequently, side heads are put on the left side   **This side head**
                    of even-numbered pages and on the right side of   **is on the right**
                    odd-numbered pages.

The section formatting was set so that the page had 6.5 inches of printable width. (To achieve this, the left and right margins were both set to 1 inch.)

The first paragraph in the document is the sentence *This side head is on the left*. The character formatting is HELV 14. The paragraph formatting has a 5.1-inch right indent, line spacing is set to *1.5*, and Spacing Before is *1*.

The second paragraph, which begins *Side heads are effective*, has a left indent of 1.8 inches to make room for the side head to the left of it. The Spacing Before text box of the Format Paragraph command's dialog box is set to *1* to more or less match the vertical spacing of the left-side paragraph.

The third paragraph (beginning *Word's ability*) is identical in format to the second one. This could be a standard paragraph format for text that is to appear to the right of a side head. This paragraph ends the first cluster because the next paragraph has a smaller left indent.

The fourth paragraph has no printable content. It is a paragraph mark placed in the document solely to create extra blank space between examples. Significantly, it is not formatted to print side by side.

The fifth paragraph begins *Side heads can appear* and starts the second cluster. It is placed in the document *before* the side head that prints to the right of it. When paragraphs are to be printed side by side, the one to the left must always come first in the document.

The paragraph is formatted with a right indent of 1.8 inches, to make room for the side head, and a Spacing Before setting of *1* line.

The sixth paragraph is the side head that says *This side head is on the right*. The character formatting is HELV 14. The paragraph formatting has a 5.1-inch left indent, line spacing is set to *1.5*, and the Spacing Before text box is set to *1*.

Multiple Columns

If you want to print a document with multiple columns, and you don't care which paragraphs are adjacent to each other, a simple solution might suffice. The Number text box of the Format Section command lets you specify any number of columns on a page: Simply type in the number, and Word does the rest.

All you need do is start a new section where the number of columns changes and set the Section Start field of this section to Continuous. Word then takes care not only of changing the number of columns but of balancing the columns above the change so that they are laid out attractively on the page.

In addition, you can force a column break wherever you want one by using the Insert Break command and specifying *Column*. Word displays the break as a dotted line the width of the column and treats it much as it does a page break.

Combining the Continuous setting of the Format Section command with manual section breaks, the View Layout command, and of course, the File Print Preview command gives you flexibility in designing and setting up multiple-column pages.

ABSOLUTE POSITIONING

In some situations, absolute positioning gives you superior control when juxtaposing paragraphs. In other situations, it is simply an alternative to side-by-side formatting. It is accomplished by using the Format Position command or by using a style that has been formatted with the Format Position command.

Suppose you have a set of three paragraphs, like the following, that you want to print side by side on a page otherwise devoted to a single, wide column of text:

```
Finally, respondees were asked their opinion about the
importance of maintaining a strong military presence in
troubled areas. The responses were:


In Favor:   39%        Opposed:   47%        Undecided:   14%

Reasons most           Reasons most          Reasons most
often given:           often given:          often given:
international          belief in self-       preference for
peacekeeping           determination for     deciding on a
responsibility         such areas and        case-by-case
and effective          possibility of        basis and not
deterrence             increased             enough available
measure                hostilities           information
```

CHAPTER TWENTY-NINE: Columns, Tables, and Forms

The Format Position command gives you an easy-to-use alternative to formatting these paragraphs as columns or with side-by-side paragraph formatting:

♦ Select the text at the left, beginning with *In favor* and ending with *measure*. Then use the Format Position command, as shown here, to define a "frame" for the text:

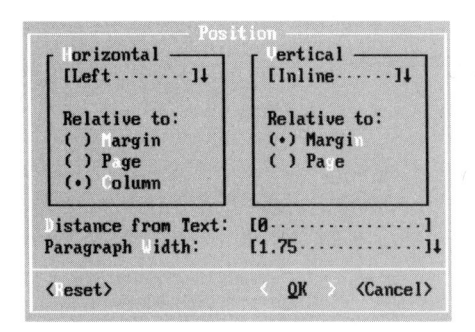

```
┌─────────────────── Position ───────────────────┐
│ ┌─ Horizontal ──────┐  ┌─ Vertical ──────┐    │
│ │ [Left········]↓   │  │ [Inline·····]↓  │    │
│ │                   │  │                 │    │
│ │ Relative to:      │  │ Relative to:    │    │
│ │ ( ) Margin        │  │ (•) Margin      │    │
│ │ ( ) Page          │  │ ( ) Page        │    │
│ │ (•) Column        │  │                 │    │
│ └───────────────────┘  └─────────────────┘    │
│                                                │
│ Distance from Text: [0················]        │
│ Paragraph Width:    [1.75············]↓        │
│                                                │
│ <Reset>             <  OK  >   <Cancel>        │
└────────────────────────────────────────────────┘
```

The horizontal position setting of Left relative to Margins ensures that Word will frame the text in an invisible "cage" at the left side of the page, relative to the left and right margins. The vertical position setting of Inline ensures that the text will be printed *in-line*—that is, where it occurs naturally in the flow of surrounding paragraphs. The paragraph frame width of 1.75 inches is the actual measurement that determines the width of the text on the printed page. By specifying such a frame width, you are telling Word the width of the frame in which it is to enclose the text. In practice, this is more or less equivalent to specifying left and right paragraph indents with the Format Paragraph command. The value 1.75 inches was chosen to allow three frames to fit comfortably between left and right page margins of 1.25 inches.

♦ Select the text beginning with *Opposed* and ending with *hostilities*. Use the Format Position command, and set the Horizontal option to Centered. Or use the same settings shown earlier.

♦ Select the text beginning with *Undecided* and ending with *information*. Again use the Format Position command, this time setting Horizontal to Right but otherwise using the same settings as before.

If you want to see the page before you print, use the File Print Preview command:

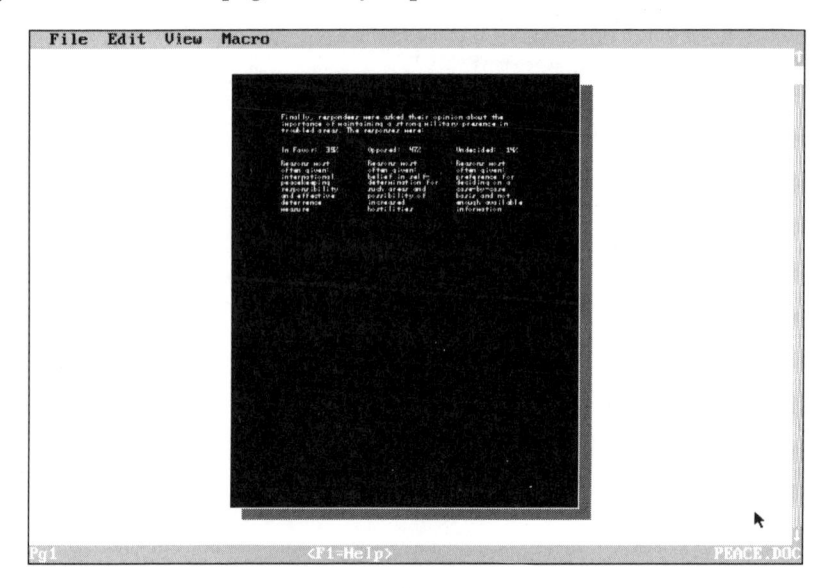

Now suppose you want these paragraphs to be positioned in a prominent spot—let's say at the top of the page, as follows:

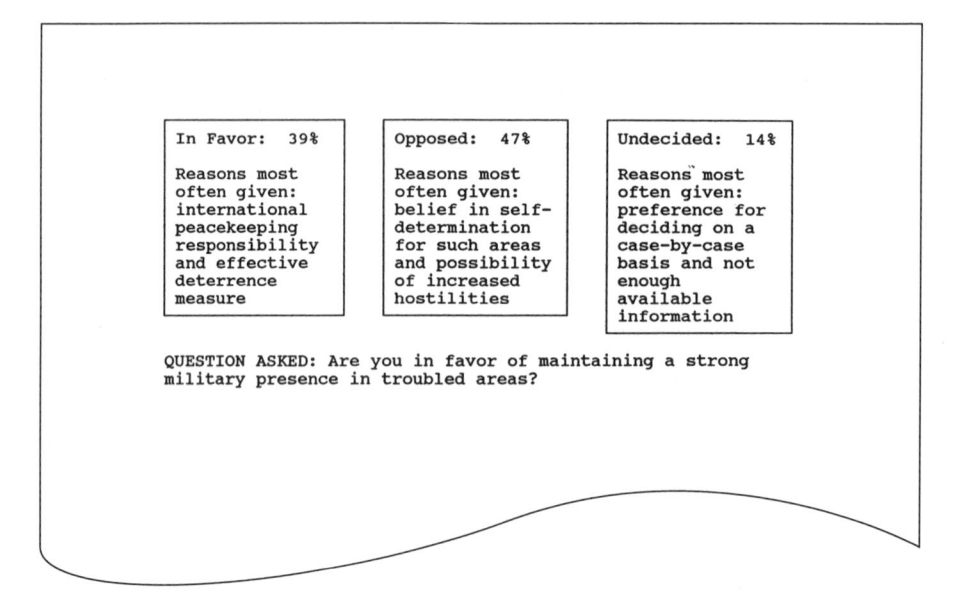

```
In Favor:   39%        Opposed:   47%         Undecided:   14%

Reasons most           Reasons most           Reasons most
often given:           often given:           often given:
international          belief in self-        preference for
peacekeeping           determination          deciding on a
responsibility         for such areas         case-by-case
and effective          and possibility        basis and not
deterrence             of increased           enough
measure                hostilities            available
                                              information
```

QUESTION ASKED: Are you in favor of maintaining a strong
military presence in troubled areas?

CHAPTER TWENTY-NINE: Columns, Tables, and Forms   565

If you check the Side by Side check box of the Format Paragraph command's dialog box, you can't assume that your juxtaposed paragraphs will appear at the top of a new page. Serendipity might make this happen if the preceding pages break just so. But that's an outside chance. Forcing a page break just before these paragraphs could also ensure that they appear at the top of a new page. But then the preceding page might well turn out to be too short. Again, the solution is the Format Position command. To create this look, the paragraphs have been given the same Format Position settings used earlier, with one change: Vertical has been set to Top rather than Inline. The change is dramatized by the boxes added with the Format Border command, but the only essential change has been the shift in vertical position from Inline to Top.

When you begin experimenting with the Format Position command and tables, you'll find it possible to lay out a table like this:

```
Item                List            Discount
                    Price           Price*
Chocolate
truffles            $1.20 ea.       $0.90 ea.
Peppermint
sticks              .30 ea          .15 ea.
Amaretto
fudge balls         .75 ea.         .50 ea.
------------
*Units of 100 or more.

As can be seen in the table of this page, the savings to all
customers purchasing Aunt Marie's candy in quantities of 100
or more units (pieces, pounds, and so on) are substantial.
At the same time, lower profits from such volume sales are
offset by the savings in production, packaging, and shipping
costs when compared with sales of the same items in smaller
quantities. Our overall profit margin is, in fact, slightly
higher for volume sales than for smaller sales, and so sales
representatives are urged to emphasize the availability of
discount prices to prospective customers.
```

which is positioned at the top of the page in a frame the width of a single column, or like the following printout, which is horizontally positioned at the right of the page and vertically positioned at the top of the page.

```
As can be seen in the table    Item            List       Discount
of this page, the savings to                   Price      Price*
all customers purchasing       ───────────────────────────────────
Aunt Marie's candy in quan-    Chocolate
tities of 100 or more units    truffles      $1.20 ea.   $0.90 ea.
(pieces, pounds, and so on)    Peppermint
are substantial. At the same   sticks          .30 ea      .15 ea.
time, lower profits from       Amaretto
such volume sales are offset   fudge balls    .75 ea.      .50 ea.
by the savings in produc-      ---------------
tion, packaging, and ship-     *Units of 100 or more.
ping costs when compared       ───────────────────────────────────
with sales of the same items in smaller quantities. Our
overall profit margin is, in fact, slightly higher for vol-
ume sales than for smaller sales, and so sales representa-
tives are urged to emphasize the availability of discount
prices to prospective customers.
```

Notice how the surrounding text flows around the invisible frame assigned to the table. (By the way, you can type this text either above or below the table, and Word will still position the table correctly.) As for the remainder of the formatting shown, the only real "trick" required was in the drawing of the horizontal lines. The top two lines were drawn by the Format Border command, but the bottom line was drawn by a right-aligned tab stop. An underline border could have been used for the bottom line as well but would have narrowed the spacing between the lines of text to the left and below the underline. Using a tab stop equalized the line spacing to produce the print-out shown here.

Tables and Scripts

You can use absolute positioning instead of side-by-side paragraphs to format the paragraphs illustrated on page 560. Use a frame width of 1.8 inches and left, centered, and right horizontal positioning as shown in the questionnaire example presented earlier. If you want the paragraphs at a particular location on the page, choose a vertical position of Top, Centered, or Bottom, or specify an exact vertical starting position, such as 2", from (relative to) the page margins or the page itself. If you want the paragraphs printed as they occur within surrounding paragraphs of narrative text, set the vertical position to Inline.

NOTE: *If you encounter problems with the spacing or indentation of narrative text following absolutely positioned paragraphs, one simple solution is to add an extra, blank paragraph above the first narrative paragraph. (Move the highlight to the first character of the narrative paragraph and press Enter.) Set the Spacing Before of the blank paragraph to 1, and the paragraphs should print as you want them to.*

Side Heads

Absolute positioning greatly eases the task of positioning side heads.

To create the same group of paragraphs used in the illustration on page 561, use these settings with the Format Position command:

The first paragraph (*This side head is on the left*) is HELV 14 and has line spacing of *1.5* and a Spacing Before setting of *1 li*. These choices are made with the Format Paragraph command. The position dictated by the Format Position command is Left horizontal placement relative to Column, Inline vertical placement relative to Margins, and a frame width setting of *1.4"*.

The second and third paragraphs (from *Side heads are* through *to use side heads*) have line spacing of *1* and a Spacing Before setting of *1 li*. The Horizontal setting is Right, the first relative to setting is Column, the Vertical setting is Inline, the second relative to field is set to Margins, and the width (paragraph width) is set to *4.7"*.

The fourth paragraph (*Side heads can appear*) is Courier 12 with line spacing of *1* and a Spacing Before setting of *2*. (Notice that this space before of two blank lines eliminates the need to add an extra, blank paragraph as in the side-by-side formatting.) The Horizontal setting is Left, the first Relative To field is set to Column, Vertical is set to Inline, the second Relative To setting is Margins, and frame width is *4.7"*.

The fifth paragraph (*This side head is on the right*) is, again, HELV 14 with line spacing of *1.5*. Like Paragraph 4, and for the same reason, it has a Spacing Before setting of *2* lines. The Horizontal setting is Right, the first Relative To setting is Column, Vertical is Inline, the second Relative To setting is Margins, and paragraph width is *1.4"*.

Keep in mind, too, that side heads positioned with Format Position can be printed in the margins of a document on the inside or the outside of the page. Choose the appropriate horizontal position for the side head (Left or Right, Inside or Outside), and make the position relative to Page, not to Margin or Column. Be sure that the margin (set with Format Margins) is wide enough to accommodate the side head, and you can produce a page like the one on the following page:

If font sizes differ between side heads and normal text, you might need to experiment with line spacing and extra space before the text to align the text as you want. Use File Print Preview frequently.

> **This side head is on the left**
>
> Side heads are effective in certain kinds of publications, including newsletters. The Microsoft Word manual uses them extensively.
>
> Word's ability to align paragraphs side by side, even when the paragraphs are of different widths, makes it easy to use side heads.
>
> Side heads can appear on either side of a page. Frequently, side heads are put on the left side of even-numbered pages and on the right side of odd-numbered pages. **This side head is on the right**

TABLES

Before looking in some detail at a couple of the features Word offers, let's consider some general strategies and ideas that can make tables easier to manage. The following are some tips on tables (and no jokes about waiters, please).

A Single Page

You will almost always want a table less than one page long to print on a single page rather than breaking across two pages.

The easiest and most effective way to guarantee that a short table does not break across two pages is by using the Format Position command. Provided that the table is less than a page long, Format Position places the table exactly where you want it on the page and ensures that surrounding text fills out the page by "flowing" around the position occupied by the table. Format Position is especially useful when, for visual appeal, you want to print a table at either the top or the bottom of a page, across the width of the page, or within a smaller block of space.

Another simple way to guarantee that a table will be printed on one page is to make the whole table one paragraph by inserting new-line characters (with the Shift+Enter key combination) rather than paragraph marks (with the Enter key) at the ends of lines. Then choose the Together check box of the Format Paragraph command's dialog box. This single-paragraph method works with all versions of Word, but it has one drawback: You must use the same tab stops throughout the table because you can change tab stops only from one paragraph to the next.

A superior alternative lets you keep a table composed of different paragraphs (with the potential for different tab stops) on the same page. For each paragraph in the table except the last paragraph, check the With Next check box in the Format Paragraph command's dialog box.

A third alternative is to use the Utilities Repaginate Now or File Print Preview command to preview page breaks. If a break occurs in the middle of a table, force a new page to begin immediately before the table by pressing Ctrl+Enter or by using the Insert Break command. The table will print on a single page (unless it's more than one page long).

A fourth alternative is to use the new-line character (created by pressing Shift+Enter) with the Format Border command to create the table as a single paragraph within a box border. Provided that the table is less than one page long, Word will print the entire table, box included, on the same page. Use the File Print Preview command before printing to see whether printing the table on a single page will cause Word to create an unduly short page preceding the table.

Revising Formatting

Because of Word's ability to treat format and content independently, you have some freedom to change the design of an existing table without affecting its content. If you're not using a style sheet, you can select the paragraph or paragraphs in question and change the locations of tab stops by using the Format Tabs command, the ruler at the top of the screen, or both. If you are using a style sheet, matters are simpler still. You can change the formatting of any style that controls part of your table.

Spaces versus Tabbing

Using Spacebar spaces to line up tabular material can cause problems when you use more than one font or font size or when you use a proportionally spaced font. See the Tip "Tabbing and Spacing in Tables" in Chapter 8.

Leaders

Here's a tip about Word's leader characters that will improve the look of nearly any table that uses leaders.

Recall from the discussion of the Format Tabs command that a leader is a series of dots (......), hyphens (----), or underline characters (___) that can be added to the formatting of a tab stop to "lead" the reader's eye across a table to corresponding information in other columns. If you choose a leader character, a leader of dots, hyphens, or underlines leads from left to right across to the tab stop. (Of course, this happens only at those tab stops you've actually used. You "use" a tab stop by pressing the Tab key to add a corresponding tab character to the content of the document.)

For example, the table on the next page uses leader dots to carry the eye across the page.

```
Table 1: New home sales.

                        Region 1        Region 2        Region 3
Under $75,000 .......... 12 ............... 9 ............ 22
$75,001-$100,000 ....... 17 ............... 12 ........... 13
$100,001-125,000 ....... 15 ............... 17 ........... 19
$125,001-150,000 ........ 9 ............... 7 ............ 10
$150,001-175,000 ........ 3 ............... 0 ............. 8
$175,001-200,000 ........ 0 ............... 1 ............. 4
Over $200,000 ........... 2 ............... 0 ............. 3
```

In the body of the table, right-aligned tab stops with leader dots are set at 2.6 inches, 4.1 inches, and 5.6 inches. You can lessen the crowding of such leader characters by assigning the leader character to a tab stop to the left of the tab stop you actually need. To create even more space, use alternating tab stops with and without leader characters. Here, for example, are the additional tab stops used:

Tab setting	Leader character
2.3 inches	Dots
2.7 inches	None
3.8 inches	Dots
4.2 inches	None
5.3 inches	Dots

To refine the earlier table:

```
Table 1: New home sales.

                     Region 1     Region 2     Region 3
Under $75,000 ....... 12        ......... 9    ......... 22
$75,001-$100,000 .... 17        ......... 12   ......... 13
$100,001-125,000 .... 15        ......... 17   ......... 19
$125,001-150,000 ..... 9        ......... 7    ......... 10
$150,001-175,000 ..... 3        ......... 0    ......... 8
$175,001-200,000 ..... 0        ......... 1    ......... 4
Over $200,000 ........ 2        ......... 0    ......... 3
```

CHAPTER TWENTY-NINE: Columns, Tables, and Forms

Another example of using leader characters is in a table of contents. Although you probably would not consider a table of contents to be a table at all, stretch your interpretation a bit and view a table of contents as a two-column table made up of chapter or section titles and their corresponding page numbers. Perhaps this table has no leader characters and has entries such as the following:

```
    L[········1·········2·········3·········4·········5········R·]·········7···
 TA  Chapter 5: Poodles and Rodents                              76_
```

Observe in the above illustration that the page number is lined up with a right-aligned tab stop. (You can tell it is a right-aligned tab stop because of the *R* in the ruler. The ruler shows the formatting of whatever paragraph is selected or contains the cursor.) In this example, the space between the end of the chapter title and the beginning of the page number was created by pressing the Tab key once to add one tab character to the document.

Notice what happens when a leader character, in this case the hyphen, is added to the tab stop.

```
   -R[········1·········2·········3·········4·········5·······-R·]·········7···
 TB  Chapter 5: Poodles and Rodents-----------------------------76_
```

The *R* in the ruler is now preceded by a hyphen (*-R*), indicating that the right-aligned tab stop has a hyphen leader character. The hyphens extend from the end of the chapter title to the beginning of the page number. Professionally designed tables generally cut off leaders at least a couple of characters short of the right-hand column. You can eliminate the extra hyphens by adding another tab stop, setting the leader character of this new tab stop to hyphens, eliminating the leader character in the formatting of the original tab stop, and pressing the Tab key an extra time between the chapter name and the page number when typing the document. Word places two tab characters between the end of the chapter title and the beginning of the page number. The first of these tab characters will match up with the first tab stop (the one that has the leader character), and the second tab character will match up with the second tab stop (the one at which page numbers are typed).

```
    R[········1·········2·········3·········4·········5···-R···R·]·········7···
 TC  Chapter 5: Poodles and Rodents------------------------  76_
```

An additional, optional refinement is to type a Spacebar space at the end of the chapter title so that the leader character starts one space to the right of the end of the title. This makes the line look like this:

```
    R[········1·········2·········3·········4·········5···-R···R·]·········7···
 TC  Chapter 5: Poodles and Rodents  ----------------------  76_
```

The preceding examples were created with a simple, temporary style sheet containing only three styles. Studying the style sheet and the examples might help you understand tables and style sheets and the relationship of the two. Observe that the key codes for the three styles (TA, TB, and TC) appear in the style bar on the far-left side of each example. (The style bar must be turned on by using the View Preferences command in order for you to see this on your computer screen.) This is the style sheet:

```
(P) TA Paragraph 1                              TABLE 1 -- DEMO STYLE
       Courier 12. Flush left. Tabs at: 5.8" (right flush).
(P) TB Paragraph 2                              TABLE 2 -- DEMO STYLE
       Courier 12. Flush left. Tabs at: 5.8" (right flush, leader
       hyphens).
(P) TC Paragraph 3                              TABLE 3 -- DEMO STYLE
       Courier 12. Flush left. Tabs at: 5.4" (right flush, leader
       hyphens), 5.8" (right flush).
```

Macros for Setting Tabs and Creating Tables

Word comes with four macros that help you set up tables. They are contained in the file MACRO.GLY on the Utilities disk, and they let you more easily set tab stops at the positions you specify. The macros are named *table*, *tabs*, *tabs2*, and *tabs3*. They can be useful, but bear in mind that you must still do the work of deciding where you want table columns to appear and what type of alignment they should have. Briefly, this is what the macros do:

- *table* sets as many tab stops as will fit on the printable line. When you press Ctrl+V4 to run the macro, it asks you for the position of the first tab stop in inches and then asks how far apart you want the tabs to be set. The macro sets left-aligned tab stops, beginning at the location you specified for the first and extending across the page to the right margin or to the right paragraph indent. Preexisting tab stops remain in effect.
- *tabs* gives you more flexibility than *table*. When you press Ctrl+V1 (the number one, not the letter L) to run the macro, it prompts for the position and alignment of a tab stop, *in characters*. The macro repeats this question, setting a tab stop for each set of answers you give, until you type *0* to end the macro. As with *table.mac*, the tab stops are added to any existing ones in the paragraph(s).
- *tabs2* is a hybrid between *table* and *tabs*. When you press Ctrl+V2 to run the macro, it first asks how many columns you want in your table. Next it asks where you want the first column to be positioned and then asks for the type of alignment you want. The macro sets the tabs accordingly. Like *table*, this macro spaces tabs equally across the printable page and lets you specify the type of alignment you want. It gives all tab stops the same type of alignment. (It doesn't mix left, right, and decimal, for example.)

- *tabs3* is the most impressive of the table macros that come with Word. When you press Ctrl+V3, the macro asks how many columns you want and whether you want to specify the widths for these columns by entering a number of inches or by typing your longest entries for each and letting Word compute widths. It asks you for information about each column in turn. The macro produces a boxed table, complete with vertical rules between columns.

These macros don't handle errors well, and with the exception of *tabs3*, they don't give you much flexibility. However, if used carefully they meet simple needs.

MasterWord contains two macros that make creating and modifying tables much easier. Unlike Microsoft's macros, which create tab stops, the MasterWord macros use side-by-side paragraphs. The advantage is that any cell in a table can have multiple lines of wrapping text. The two macros do this:

- *Create Table* creates a table with as many rows and columns as you specify. When you press Shift+Ctrl+CT, the macro poses a series of questions. How many rows and how many columns do you want? Do you want vertical lines, horizontal lines, or a box around the table? If so, how heavy should the lines be? Should the headings or the entire table be shaded? How should the table be aligned on the page? What is the desired width and alignment of each column? What is the text for each heading? And so forth. After posing the questions, the macro builds the table.
- *Adjust Table* lets you change the widths of columns within any table created with *Create Table*. When you press Shift+Ctrl+AT, the macro analyzes the existing table, presenting the width of each column and asking how you want to change it.

Tables can be challenging, but with good enough macros you will hardly notice.

CREATING A FORM

Although Word does not rank alongside database products that specialize in the creation of forms, you can use many of its features to create and fill in all manner of forms, including forms to be used with the print merge feature and those, such as medical-insurance forms, that have been preprinted with blanks. Whether you want to create a form to be filled in by others by hand or you want to complete a preprinted form on your computer, Word can help do the job.

Bear in mind, however, that Word does not have a "forms" feature as such. Rather, you employ combinations of other features to create and fill in forms. A form is simply a document with formatting that generally includes lines and blank areas in which you can add information later. Consequently, working with forms is a two-step process.

- Initially you create the basic document, the form. To a large extent, this means drawing lines and deciding where the blanks for new text will appear.
- Later you or someone else fills in the form.

This chapter is organized with the two-step nature of forms in mind. This section offers tips on designing common elements found in forms, whereas a later section suggests efficient ways to fill in forms.

Forms take on their distinctive appearances by combining text with lines and sometimes shaded regions. The lines can be underlines, vertical rules, or horizontal rules; or they can meet to create small or large boxes. Word offers you several approaches when it comes to creating these elements. You can place a line on the page by using underlining, tab stops formatted with leader characters, Word's line-drawing feature, or Word's paragraph-boxing feature.

Circumstances can dictate one approach or another. For example, if you plan to print your document using a fixed-pitch (typewriter-like) font such as Courier or Pica, Word's line-drawing and boxing features make a lot of sense because they yield fast results. But if you are using a proportional font, such as HELV or TMS RMN, with many printers you might be better off using tab stops to create lines. (Word's line-drawing characters are fixed-pitch fonts and therefore do a poor job of boxing paragraphs composed of proportional type. However, nothing says you can't use a line-drawing font for the lines and a proportional font for the text.)

Let's look at some of the elements you might want to include in a form.

Underlining

Underlines are simple to produce, although laying them out can become something of a challenge if you are designing a complex form. For an underline, you can use any of four features: underline characters created with the underline key or with character formatting, linedraw characters, tab stops with an underline leader character, or a paragraph formatted with a line border above or below.

Of these, underlining character by character is probably the least efficient because you must press either the underline key or the Spacebar repeatedly to create a long line. The line-drawing feature, which you turn on by running the Utilities Line Draw command (Alt+UL) and turn off by pressing the Esc key, gives you a choice of line types, including dots and circles and thick, thin, and shaded lines. It draws the line one character at a time, although it does so quickly and in whatever direction you indicate by pressing a direction key. There are good uses for the line-drawing feature, but drawing a simple underline is not necessarily one of them.

With the Tab key

Setting multiple tab stops, some with an underline leader character and some with a blank leader character, is a useful approach for underlining, especially when you want two or more separate underlines to be aligned across the page. For example,

CHAPTER TWENTY-NINE: Columns, Tables, and Forms   575

Such lines can be handy in a form, as follows:

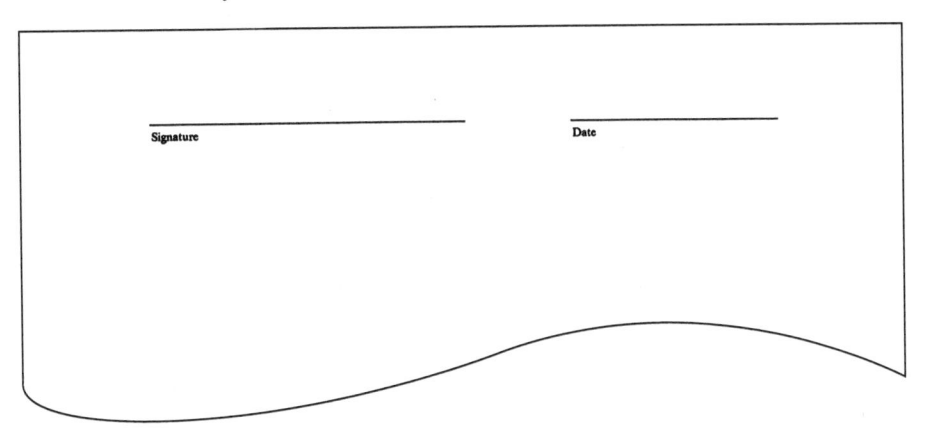

_____   _____
Signature   Date

Although it is likely you will choose different tab stops for your own forms, you can duplicate this example by formatting a paragraph with the following tab stops: 3 inches, left alignment, underline leader character; 4 inches, left alignment, blank leader character; 6 inches, left alignment, underline leader character. For the Signature/Date paragraph, format the paragraph for single (one-line) spacing with no blank lines above, and set a tab stop with blank leader at 4 inches. Format characters for whatever small, attractive typeface your printer can handle. (The previous example shows 8-point TMS RMN type on a LaserJet printer.) In your own forms, you will also want to preview page layout or use the Together and With Next fields of the Format Paragraph command to ensure that the underline prints on the same page as its related text.

A somewhat more obscure way to produce an underline with associated text is with the Format Border command:

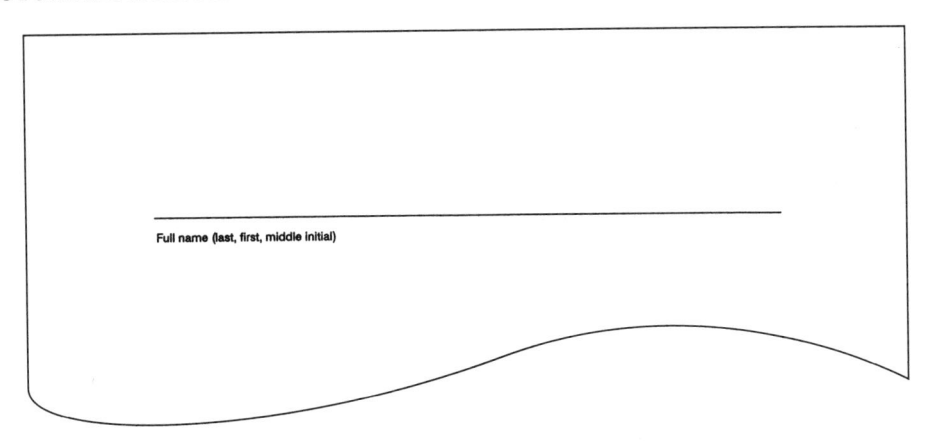

_____
Full name (last, first, middle initial)

Here, the paragraph has single spacing with a Spacing Before of 1 line. The underline is created with the Format Borders command with Border Type set to Lines, with the Top check box checked, and with Line Style set to Normal. For variety, the font and font size shown here are 8-point HELV. As for most other examples in this chapter, the printer is a Hewlett-Packard LaserJet with the Microsoft Z font cartridge.

If you enjoy using paragraph borders, here is another approach you can try:

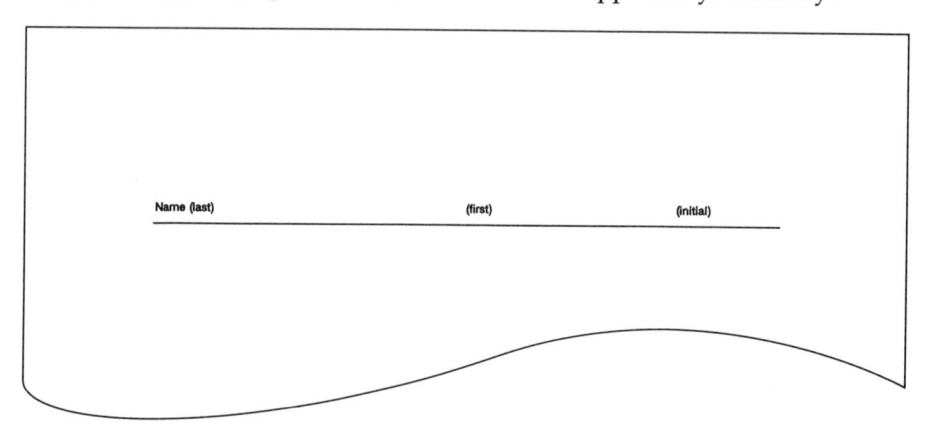

    Name (last)   (first)   (initial)

This paragraph, like the one in the preceding illustration, has single spacing with a blank line above. Here, however, the Format Borders command is set to draw the line below the text (Lines is set to Bottom), and left-aligned tab stops are set at 3 inches and 5 inches for the text. The characters are formatted in 8-point HELV.

NOTE: *Before you invest time and effort in creating a form that includes paragraph borders, try printing a box border as a test. Because different printers use different character sets, not all produce clean, continuous border lines; some, such as an Epson FX-85 running in Epson rather than IBM mode, will replace lines with bars and hyphens. You can test by printing a box to see what your printer will produce for horizontal and vertical border lines. If your printer does not produce lines, check the manual. You might, as with the Epson, be able to switch the printer over to an IBM-compatible mode that will handle the line drawing you want, although doing so might cause loss of some other printer feature, such as near-letter-quality printing. Alternatively, you might be able to format the space at which you will begin to draw lines, using a different font—a font that contains the linedraw characters in its character set. By far the easiest way to do this is with a style sheet that includes an appropriately formatted Line Draw character style.*

Dotted lines

If you prefer dotted lines to solid lines in your form, use the Utilities Customize command to set the linedraw character to a dot, or use a dot leader character for a tab stop. To place the dots close together on the line, specify a small font size and a proportional font such as TMS RMN or HELV. For example, the following illustration is created with the same tab stops as in the earlier Signature/Date example, but both the dotted-line paragraph and the text paragraph are formatted for 10-point TMS RMN:

....
Signature   Date

Grids

Sometimes a form contains intersecting lines that form a grid:

	In	Out	In	Out	In	Out	In	Out
Monday								
Tuesday								
Wednesday								
Thursday								
Friday								

Employee Name: Week of:

Overtime:

Date: From: To:

You could create such a form with Word's line-drawing feature most easily, but that works only with fixed-pitch (nonproportional) fonts. Instead, you might want to create this sample grid by using the Format Borders command and vertical tab stops. Specifically,

- ♦ The lines above and below the grid are regular text paragraphs formatted in 12-point TMS RMN type with left-aligned tab stops at 2 and 4 inches.
- ♦ The rows of the grid are boxed paragraphs, single-spaced, with a 0.2-inch right indent that makes the width of the last column equivalent to that of its companions. (The right indent varies for different printers. This example is for a LaserJet; if you have a different printer, you might need to experiment a bit to find the setting that's right for you.)
- ♦ The vertical bars are created with vertical tab stops 0.6 inch apart, at 1.0 inch, 1.6 inches, 2.2 inches, 2.8 inches, 3.4 inches, 4.0 inches, 4.6 inches, and 5.2 inches.
- ♦ The words *In* and *Out* in the top row are aligned with the following centered tab stops: 1.3 inches, 2.0 inches, 2.6 inches, 3.2 inches, 3.8 inches, 4.4 inches, 5.0 inches, and 5.6 inches.

Again, as with the linedraw characters, check to see whether your printer can produce lines and boxes as they appear on screen. If it cannot, vertical lines will be printed as vertical bars, and horizontal lines will be printed as rows of hyphens.

If you work on forms like these, a handy way to determine spacing is to work it out roughly in your head or on paper and then set the tabs directly on the ruler at the top of the document window so that you can see where each tab is being set.

Sometimes, especially in forms designed to gather information for data entry, you will see boxes like these, each of which is meant to hold a single character:

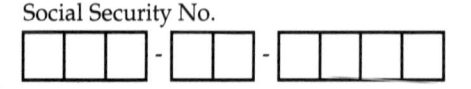

Social Security No.
☐☐☐-☐☐-☐☐☐☐

Here the line-drawing feature is the best approach. In this example, each of the squares is three characters across and three down. The hyphens between the sets of boxes were typed by turning off line drawing, typing the hyphen, and turning line drawing back on. This is what the boxes look like on screen, with paragraph marks displayed:

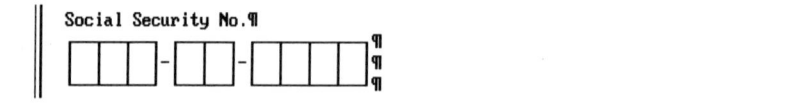

Social Security No.¶
☐☐☐-☐☐-☐☐☐☐¶

Boxes like these are also useful for questionnaires, especially if you create one set, positioned where you want it, copy it to the scrap or glossary, and then reproduce it down the page by inserting it over and over.

Organizational Charts and Illustrations

After you've tried your hand at drawing lines and creating boxes in forms, you'll find that the same skills let you make simple charts and illustrations. Here is an organizational chart created with the line-drawing feature:

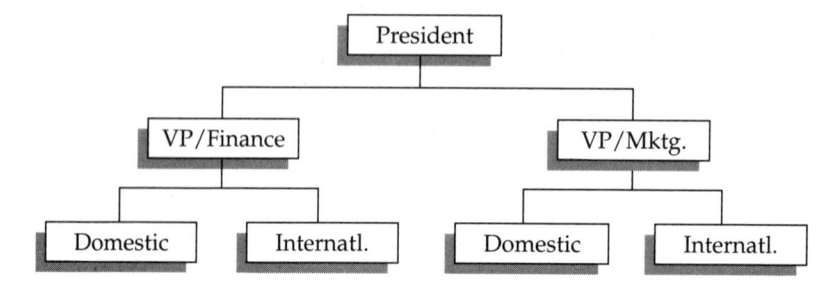

```
                    President
          ┌────────────┴────────────┐
      VP/Finance               VP/Mktg.
      ┌────┴────┐              ┌────┴────┐
   Domestic  Internatl.     Domestic  Internatl.
```

To create this type of form, you might find it helpful first to draw a rough sketch on paper—graph paper is best. That way, you can work out approximate locations and spacing for the boxes and lines of the chart, and you can make notes on measurements to use. (The heavy shadow effect was created by switching to a heavier linedraw character.)

Inserting Hidden Markers

The final step in creating a form is inserting a hidden marker at the beginning of each blank you want to have filled in when the form is used. This is an optional step because a form needn't have the markers, but it's worthwhile because the markers will give you a way to jump from blank to blank when you fill in the form.

The marker is a right chevron—the same » symbol you use in merge and macro instructions. To create this character, hold down the Ctrl key and press the right bracket key (]). Then press Shift+Left direction key once to select the marker, and press Ctrl+H to format it as hidden. (Alternatively, you can make the marker hidden in the first place by turning on hidden text before you type the character: Press Ctrl+H, type the marker, and press Ctrl+Spacebar to turn the hidden-text formatting off again.)

This is what a form looks like when markers have been added. Notice the dot(s) below each marker, indicating that each is formatted as hidden text:

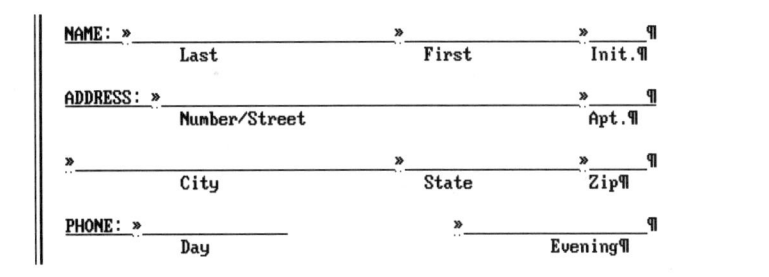

```
NAME: »_____  »_____  »_____¶
            Last                      First                  Init.¶
ADDRESS: »_____                          »_____¶
            Number/Street                                    Apt.¶
»_____   »_____  »_____¶
            City                      State                  Zip¶
PHONE: »_____  »_____¶
            Day                            Evening¶
```

NOTE: *Even though solid lines, as in this illustration, might be broken on screen by the dots indicating hidden text, don't be concerned. The lines will print perfectly on paper.*

If you have a large or complex form that requires many markers, consider typing a single marker and formatting it as hidden text. Save it in the glossary with a control code (such as Shift+Ctrl+MK) or a name (such as *mrk*) that's easy to type. You can then add appropriately formatted markers wherever necessary by positioning the highlight and inserting the glossary entry.

One word of caution is in order if you save the marker as a named glossary entry and insert it by pressing the F3 key. If your form contains field names followed by colons, leave a space between the colon and the name of the glossary entry—for example, *Name: mrk*, not *Name:mrk*. If there is no space between the colon and the glossary name, Word interprets the colon as part of a series name for numbering at print time and transforms the entire string of characters into a sequence holder like this instead of inserting a hidden marker for filling in forms.

FILLING IN A FORM

Whether a form is one you created with Word or a preprinted form you re-created for on-screen data entry, you can automate the process of filling in the blanks. If the form is to be filled in on screen, you can jump from one hidden marker to the next to fill in field after field. If the form is designed to gather information from a mailing list or another such data file, you don't need to fill it in at all. You can use the File Print Merge command instead.

Jumping to markers

To employ hidden markers that are present in a form, position the highlight at the beginning of the form and press Ctrl+> (greater-than sign). Word moves the highlight to the space immediately following the first marker on the form, so you can simply type whatever information belongs in that field. Press Ctrl+> again, and Word jumps to the next marker. Each time you press Ctrl+>, Word skips to the next marker, so you can move from field to field, filling out the form as you go and never worrying about needing to position the highlight on the screen. If you overshoot a marker, press Ctrl+< to jump back to the previous marker.

Ctrl+> and Ctrl+< work whether or not hidden text is displayed on screen, but you'll probably want to check the Hidden text check box of the View Preferences command to avoid confusion. When printing the completed form, be sure that the Hidden text check box of the File Print (Options) command is not checked to ensure that the markers are not printed.

Saving the form

After you have filled in all the fields of a form, you might want to save the form before or after printing it. Habit suggests that you simply use the File Save command, but that might be a mistake. You probably want to save the document with a new name, thereby making a new copy of it, so that the original form (not filled in) remains on disk with the original name, whereas the filled-in form is also saved on disk with a name of its own. This idea of giving a filled-in form a new name can be confusing; people sometimes assume they should use the File File Management (Rename) command. But you don't want to rename the existing form; rather, you want to save a new version of the form and give it its own name—something you accomplish with the File Save As command.

When you load a form for the purpose of filling in new copies, consider checking the Read Only check box of the File Open command. That way, it will be impossible for you to save the document without changing its name.

Macros

If you are comfortable with macros, you might want to consider writing one that automates filling in a form, especially if your form will be filled in by others who are not as familiar with Word as you are. Your macro might, for example, load the form as read-only, set Hidden text check boxes of the View Preferences and File Print (Options) commands, and later request a new name for the completed form.

Forms and the Merge feature

Often a form is used to organize quantities of information that already exist in a database such as a mailing list or an inventory. If you have such information on disk, either as a database file or as a Word data document, you can create a form and use the File Print Merge command to fill in the blanks for you. Any of the approaches already described for creating a form are acceptable for creating a Merge form. The only difference is that your merge form is a main document created and saved for the merge feature to use: It need not include hidden markers, but it must include field names describing the information in your data document.

To indicate where information is to be added to your form, you include the field names, enclosed in left and right chevrons, at appropriate places in the form. For example, here is the earlier name/address/phone form translated into a Merge document:

```
NAME:  «lastname»                    «firstname»        «init»_ ¶
              Last                       First           Init.¶

ADDRESS:  «address»                                      «apt»_ ¶
              Number/Street                              Apt.¶

«city»                              «state»              «zip»_ ¶
    City                              State              Zip¶

PHONE: «dayphone»                   «evephone»                  ¶
           Day                                          Evening¶
```

Note that field names in left and right chevrons take the place of markers in the previous example. However, the chevrons are not formatted to be hidden because a document containing them will be merged rather than printed.

Here is a sample record from the data document named FORMLIST.DOC:

```
lastname,firstname,init,address,apt,city,state,zip,dayphone,evephone¶
Jordan,Michelle,D,3372 Primrose St.,,Palmer Lake,CO,30372,555-6718,555-9845¶
```

And here is the completed form:

```
NAME: Jordan                    Michelle              D
        Last                     First              Init.

ADDRESS:    3372 Primrose St.
            Number/Street                            Apt.

Palmer Lake                      CO                   30372
        City                    State                 Zip

PHONE: 555-6718                  555-9845
        Day                                         Evening
```

Creating and using such a form is nothing more than creating and using a main document and a data document, as described in Chapter 25. Thus, you can use ASK and SET instructions or conditional statements if you want, and you can print your forms with the File Print Merge command.

If the idea of using Merge to fill in forms sounds complex, think for a moment about the definition of a form. At heart, a form is nothing more than a document that contains spaces waiting to be filled. A form letter is a form; you just might not think of it as one. A preprinted invitation to a birthday party is a form too. So is your tax return. Thus, if the information for filling in the form resides on disk as a data document, you can create the form itself as a main document and then use Merge to fill in the blanks.

CHAPTER THIRTY

Graphics, Layout, and Positioning

Style without substance is hollow, but substance without style can be pretty drab. So, in the end—after you've polished your prose, compiled your data, drawn your graphs, sketched your pictures, crunched your numbers—you put all your work together on the printed page. It's time to add some visual style, and Microsoft Word can help mightily by letting you print finished or semi-finished pages that have sophisticated layouts, including graphics images and a world of typographical fonts.

Some documents should look bland. Legal briefs, past-due notices, raw manuscripts, and cover letters can or sometimes should appear as if they came from a typewriter rather than a typesetting machine.

But what of reports, proposals, resumes, fliers, newsletters, directories, catalogs, and even books? Polished documents are becoming increasingly common as relatively inexpensive computer-based tools gain popularity. People are combining images and text on their desktop computers and printing them with laser printers or taking them on disk to service bureaus to have the finished pages produced on typesetting machines. Results are sometimes clumsy, but expectations are rising. Today you might startle people with great-looking business documents. Tomorrow you might startle people if your documents don't look great.

Word offers a broad array of choices for the appearance of documents. Word has always been a leader in supporting proportional fonts and laser printers. In fact, version 1.0 of Word supported desktop laser printers before any were on the market. Word 5.5 makes it easier than ever to include various typefaces. You can position and size graphics images and cause other text to flow naturally around these fixtures. You can position headlines or blocks of type on the page and have other type flow around them, with the number of columns changing as needed. You can draw lines and box text. You can even shade the boxes.

And you can refine your results rapidly, because Word lets you see on the screen how each page of your finished document will look—including headlines, scanned photographs, drawings, and charts.

Taking advantage of these "desktop publishing" possibilities of Word requires skills rather different from those used for writing. You might find yourself struggling now and then as you try to master graphics, layout, and fonts. But keep at it.

You might want to begin by reviewing Chapter 7, then turn again to this chapter.

YOUR PUBLISHING NEEDN'T BE "DESKTOP"

Microsoft Word is not a complete desktop publishing system, but it does most or all of what typical computer users expect of one. Users of true desktop publishing programs such as Aldus PageMaker and Ventura Publisher are sometimes startled at how much Word can accomplish.

Still, if your primary interest is document design and you have sophisticated desires and tastes, you're better off using Word only to create documents and using a desktop publishing program to format them. For example, PageMaker lets you see fonts on screen that match the shape and size of those that will print; "pick up" sections of type or graphics images and move them around with a mouse; create a document in layers so that you can overlay one element on another; and lay text closely around the edges of irregularly shaped graphics images. Word was not designed for these tasks.

However, most people simply don't need the services of a full desktop publishing package, and a lot of people won't begin to tap all of Word's capabilities. Simple, but interesting, documents can be among the most effective. Sometimes, when you want something a bit fancier but don't want to learn a lot of new skills that you won't use often, it is easier to employ Word as a sort of typesetting machine and then cut out the elements and paste them together as finished pages. On the other hand, the more of these mechanical tasks you let Word do, the less you have to worry about lines that aren't straight or columns of text that don't fit next to each other.

Even if your time is limited, consider paying a little attention to learning something about the art of layout. In aesthetic matters, taste often wins over technical expertise, although it is nice to have generous amounts of both.

A WHIRLWIND TOUR

It is hard to venture into the world of graphics without a sense of where you are heading. A whirlwind tour can whet your appetite and give you a sense of what to expect and what is available to explore.

The following tutorial guides you through several of Word's graphics-related commands and features, including the use of hidden text. This provides a glimpse of what is to come as you take control of Word's powers.

Step 1. You use the File New command to open a new document window that's blank, unless you already have a blank document window active on the screen.

CHAPTER THIRTY: Graphics, Layout, and Positioning

Step 2. If the style sheet NORMAL.STY is attached to the blank screen, detach it by choosing the Format Attach Style Sheet command (Alt+TA), pressing the Del key, and pressing the Enter key. Choose No if Word asks you: *Do you want to convert style sheet formatting to direct?*

This step breaks any possible link between the document you are going to create and the style sheet NORMAL.STY. You want to sever the link so that your document initially is governed by Word's default (built-in) formatting rather than by whatever formatting might be stored in a NORMAL.STY file.

Step 3. Check to be sure a printer file (.PRD file) is installed. Do this by choosing the File Printer Setup command (Alt+FR) and looking at the Printer File text box. The name there usually will bear some obvious relationship to your printer—for example, D630A.PRD is for the Diablo 630, and HPLASMS.PRD is for the HP LaserJet printer with a Microsoft font cartridge. Press Esc after verifying this.

If no printer is listed, press the Down direction key to choose one from the list of printer files that the SETUP program has placed in the Word program directory. If the printer file you need is not listed, quit Word and run the SETUP program again, specifying your printer when the program asks for it. (See Appendix A for information on the SETUP program.)

Step 4. Be sure you are in a graphics mode, preferably 25, 30, or 34 lines of 80 characters each. In a graphics mode, italics appear italic and the mouse pointer most likely appears as an arrow rather than as a bright or blinking box.

To be sure you are in a graphics mode, choose the View Preferences command and either press Alt+D or press the Tab key 15 times to move to the Display Mode drop-down list box. Once the list box is highlighted, press the Down and/or Up direction key to move through the available choices.

Preparations are out of the way. Now we'll do some fancy, but easy, document formatting. Because not everyone's printer can produce graphics, this tutorial uses a simple boxed paragraph as its "graphic." Some printers can shade a box to give it a little more weight, but whether you shade yours or not doesn't materially affect the tutorial.

If, as you follow the remaining steps, you find that your screen is somewhat different from the images in this book, you might want to use the File Printer Setup command to install the printer file HPLASMS.PRD (or HPLASMS2.PRD). This printer file is for HP LaserJet printers using the Microsoft Z font cartridge. You needn't actually have the printer and the Z cartridge in order to install the printer file, but you need to tell Word's SETUP program that you do in order for the printer file to be decompressed and placed in your Word program directory. If you install HPLASMS.PRD, the File Print Preview command will show what a document would look like if printed with the LaserJet and a Z cartridge. If you use a different printer file during this tutorial, what you see on the screen might differ from what you see in this book. If you use a printer file for a printer that is not capable of graphics (for example, a daisy-wheel printer) Word will not display the graphics, although it will leave room for them on the screen, and it will print them. Regardless of which printer file you use during the tutorial, if you change it now you should switch back to a printer file appropriate to your printer after completing the tutorial.

Step 5. Press the Enter key to create a fresh paragraph, and then press the Up direction key once. This pushes the end mark (the little diamond on the screen) away from where you are working.

Step 6. Hold down the Shift key, and press the Enter key three more times. Then release the Shift key. This creates a paragraph that is four lines long but has no printable content.

Step 7. Choose the Format Border command (Alt+TB). Press Alt+B to choose Box Each Paragraph and then Alt+P to move to the Percentage text box. Type *10* in the text box and press Enter.

This boxes the paragraph. Note that the box extends across the screen, even though the lines of text are as short as lines can be (so short, in fact, that they have no content). The box is wide because it surrounds the greatest line length that is *possible,* not the line length you are actually using.

Step 8. Choose the File Print Preview command. The image of the page appears. Note that the box extends across the printable region of the page, from margin to margin. If the printer file is HPLASMS.PRD or another one that allows shading, the box will be shaded (because of actions you took in step 7). This is what it looks like:

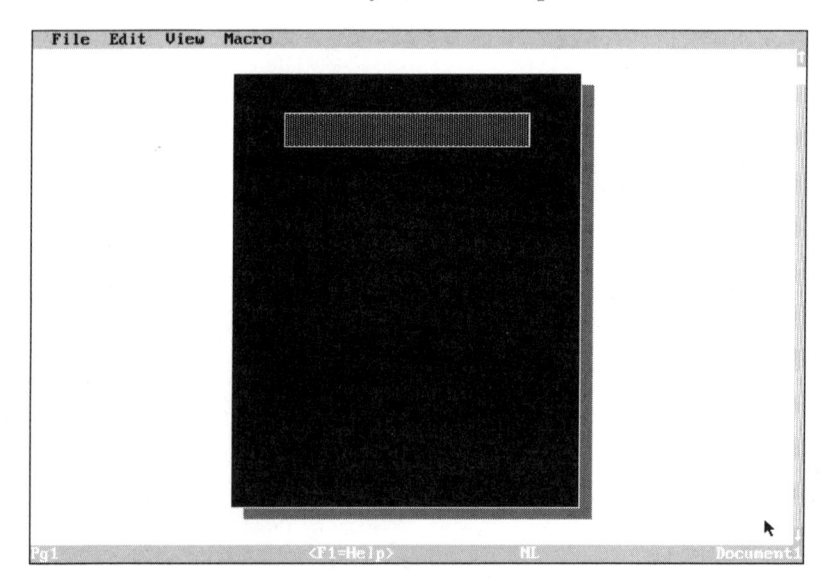

Step 9. Press the Esc key to leave preview mode.

Step 10. Be sure the cursor is inside the boxed paragraph, and then choose the Format Position command (Alt+TO). Do not press Enter yet.

CHAPTER THIRTY: Graphics, Layout, and Positioning

The Format Position command turns a normal paragraph into one that has a fixed position on a page. It also controls the width of a paragraph's invisible frame and the breadth of the space that will surround the four sides of the frame.

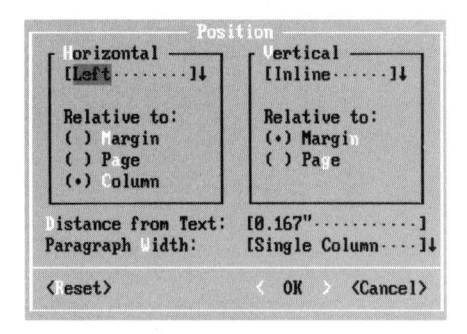

```
┌─────────────────── Position ───────────────────┐
│  ┌─ Horizontal ──────┐   ┌─ Vertical ──────┐   │
│  │ [Left········]↓   │   │ [Inline······]↓ │   │
│  │                   │   │                 │   │
│  │ Relative to:      │   │ Relative to:    │   │
│  │ ( ) Margin        │   │ (•) Margin      │   │
│  │ ( ) Page          │   │ ( ) Page        │   │
│  │ (•) Column        │   │                 │   │
│                                                │
│  Distance from Text:  [0.167"··········]       │
│  Paragraph Width:     [Single Column····]↓     │
│                                                │
│  <Reset>              <  OK  >   <Cancel>      │
└────────────────────────────────────────────────┘
```

Step 11. Press Alt+W to move to the Paragraph Width text box.

Word's proposed response is *Single Column*. Because the page layout has only the one column, this response would stretch the paragraph's frame the entire distance from the left to the right page margin. But we're going to narrow the paragraph's frame to only 3 inches.

Step 12. Type *3"* in the Paragraph Width text box, and press the Enter key to carry out the command.

In response, the paragraph is reduced in width to 3 inches.

Step 13. Choose the File Print Preview command. Note that the box has narrowed to cover a much smaller proportion of the width of the page. Press Esc to exit from the print preview mode.

Step 14. Press the Down direction key as many times as necessary to move the highlight below the boxed paragraph. (You might need to press it only once.)

Step 15. Type some text. It can be anything, even random characters. Your object is to create dummy text for formatting. Press the Enter key periodically to break the text into paragraphs. You can use the F4 key, which repeats your last editing act, to speed up your creation of text. Type enough characters so that the screen scrolls at least three or four times. At the conclusion, hold down the Ctrl key and press the Home key to move back to the top of the document.

Step 16. Choose the File Print Preview command. Observe that the boxed paragraph remains at the beginning of the "printed" document.

We say that this paragraph is "in line" because it will be printed on paper in the same position at which its content appears in the file—in this case, at the beginning.

Step 17. Press Esc to exit the print preview mode.

Now we're going to position the boxed paragraph somewhere other than in line. We're going to put it near the middle of the page, both horizontally and vertically.

Step 18. Choose the Format Position command again. The Horizontal text box is highlighted initially.

This field lets you choose either a specific or a relative horizontal location for the paragraph and its frame. To choose a specific horizontal location you would type a distance, such as *2.3"*, that positions the left edge of the paragraph that distance from the left side of the column, margin, or page. But here we want to specify a relative horizontal position.

Step 19. Press Alt+Down (or click on the down arrow with the mouse) to drop down a list of possible relative positions. The choices are Left, Centered, Right, Inside, and Outside. Highlight the word *Centered*. Do not press Enter yet.

Step 20. Press the Tab key to move to the next field, the Relative To option buttons (the drop-down list will close, leaving the word *Centered* showing in the text box of the drop-down list). Choose the Page option button to tell Word that you want the horizontal position measured relative to the page margins. In this case, you're saying you want the paragraph centered relative to the page. Do not press Enter yet.

Step 21. Press the Tab key to move to the Vertical drop-down list. The proposed response is Inline. We want to change that, so press Alt+Down to drop down a list of other relative positions. The choices are Inline, Top, Centered, and Bottom. You could type a specific number, but we want to center the paragraph vertically relative to the top and bottom margins of the page.

Step 22. Highlight the word *Centered*, and press the Enter key (or choose OK) to carry out the command. The paragraph doesn't appear to move, but it has been given a specific position that will be reflected when the page is printed or previewed.

Step 23. Choose the File Print Preview command. Observe that the paragraph is now centered vertically and horizontally on the page. Press the Esc key to exit the preview mode.

Step 24. Choose the Format Section command (Alt+TS). Type *2* in the Number text box to indicate you want a two-column layout, and press Enter to carry out the command.

Step 25. Choose File Print Preview one last time. You can see by the screen on the following page that the boxed paragraph remains in the center of the page, but now two columns of type flow around either side of it.

Step 26. Press Esc to exit the preview mode.

Now that you've seen some of the possibilities, you're ready to delve into the intricacies of Word's layout and graphics powers.

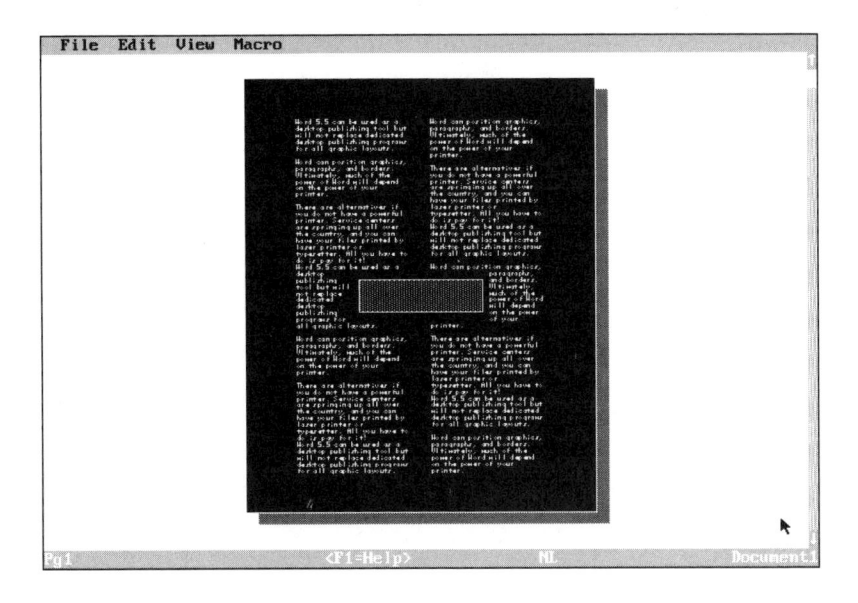

CREATING A LAYOUT

Laying out pages needn't be tricky, but it can be. The level of challenge depends on your demands. If you want conventional, single-column pages that look as if they might have been produced by a typewriter, Word's built-in section formatting lets you simply start the program, type, and print. You don't even need to think about page layout. If you want multiple columns, you can turn to the section-formatting technique described in Chapter 7 or the side-by-side-paragraphs technique described in Chapter 29. But if you want to get fancier, you turn to a collection of commands that often must be used in combinations.

As outlined in Chapter 7, these commands for sophisticated layout are

- ♦ Format Margins, which controls the size of the page and the size of its margins
- ♦ Format Section, which controls the number of columns
- ♦ Format Paragraph, which controls the left and right indents and the space before and space after paragraphs
- ♦ Insert Picture, which imports graphics created outside of Word and controls their size so that Word treats them as paragraphs
- ♦ Format Position, which fixes certain text or graphics paragraphs to particular places on the page and controls the width of the invisible frames that contain paragraphs

Full command of Word's layout powers requires that you learn how to use these commands together, not simply individually. A good place to begin is with an understanding of the concept of the paragraph frame.

Frames and Flowing Text

As you've already learned, every paragraph in a Word document has an invisible frame around it. It doesn't matter whether the paragraph contains text or whether it is a graphic imported from another program. Either way, the frame is a type of armor, a protective shield that stops other text from overlapping it. A frame carves out space in a document, reserving it for the paragraph. The actual content of the paragraph can be text, a graphic, or both, and it does not need to use all of the frame.

You can adjust a frame to fit snugly around the text or graphic it protects, or you can place adjustable buffers of blank space between the paragraph's content and its frame. These buffers at the top, bottom, left, and right are like the matting around a framed lithograph—they surround the artwork, but they are inside the frame. You can control the width of these inside buffers individually with the Format Paragraph command's Before, After, From Left, and From Right text boxes.

Although a frame is invisible, you can visualize a paragraph's text and its frame, as shown in Figure 30-1 on the following page.

In this example, the paragraph is formatted (with Format Paragraph) to have spacing Before of 1 line, spacing After of 0, an indent From Left of 0, and an indent From Right of 0. Consequently, the frame clings to the text, except for the area at the top, which is the one line of "before" space. The frame is wide enough to accommodate the maximum possible line length—in this case, 6 inches, the distance between the page margins. Observe that the first line of the paragraph is indented 0.5 inch, a bit of formatting accomplished by setting the Format Paragraph dialog box First Line text box to *0.5"*. The frame is unaffected by this or any indentation.

If we use Format Paragraph to set a left indent and a right indent of 1 inch each, the paragraph's text is indented at both left and right, as shown in Figure 30-2 on page 592, but the frame remains the same width. However, because the lines are shorter, more of them are necessary, and the bottom of the frame adjusts downward to accommodate the deeper paragraph.

Again, the frame is unaffected because indents control the space *between* the frame and the text. Changing an indent alters the length of the lines of text, not the location of the left or right side of the frame.

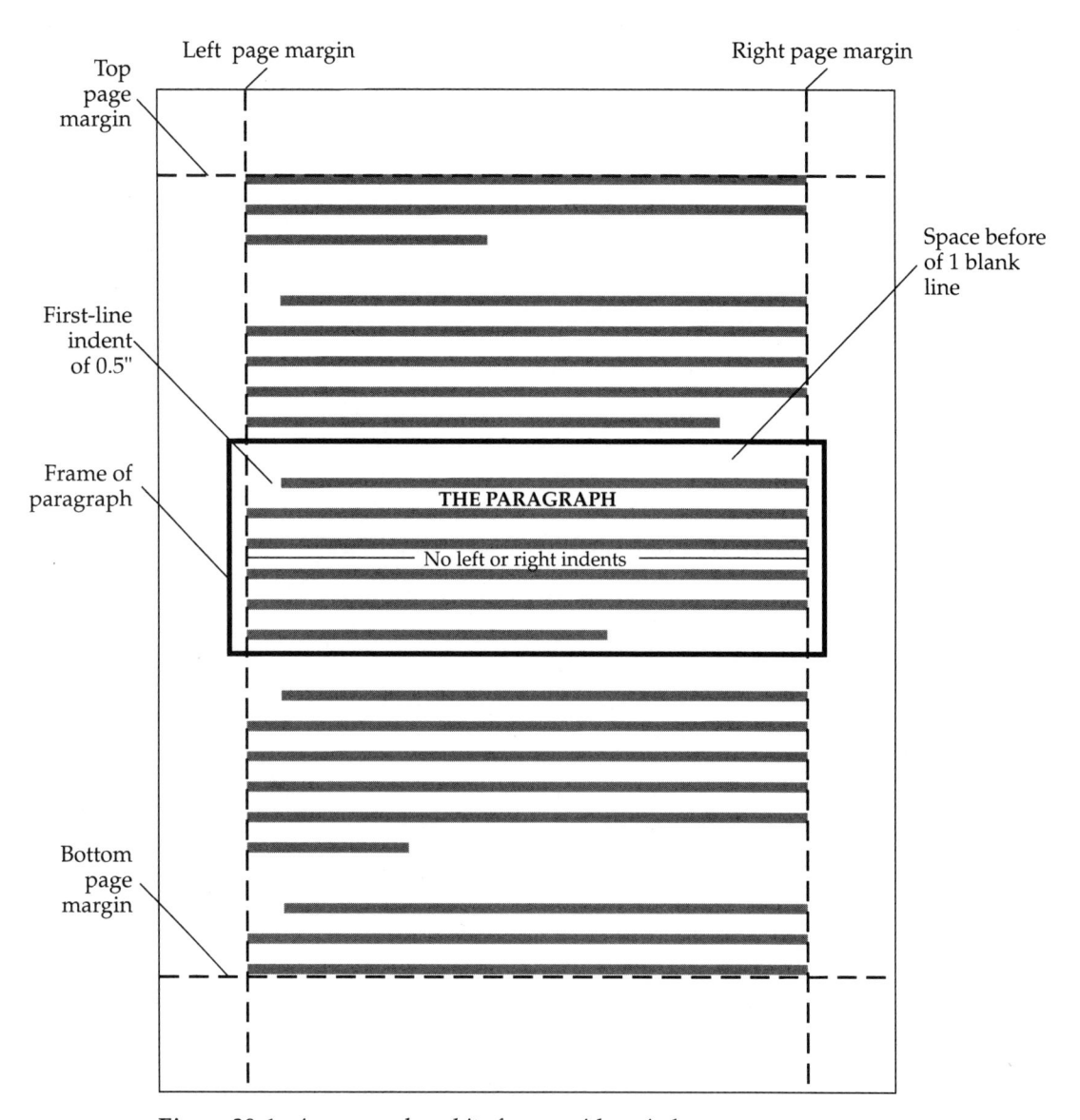

Figure 30-1. A paragraph and its frame, with no indents.

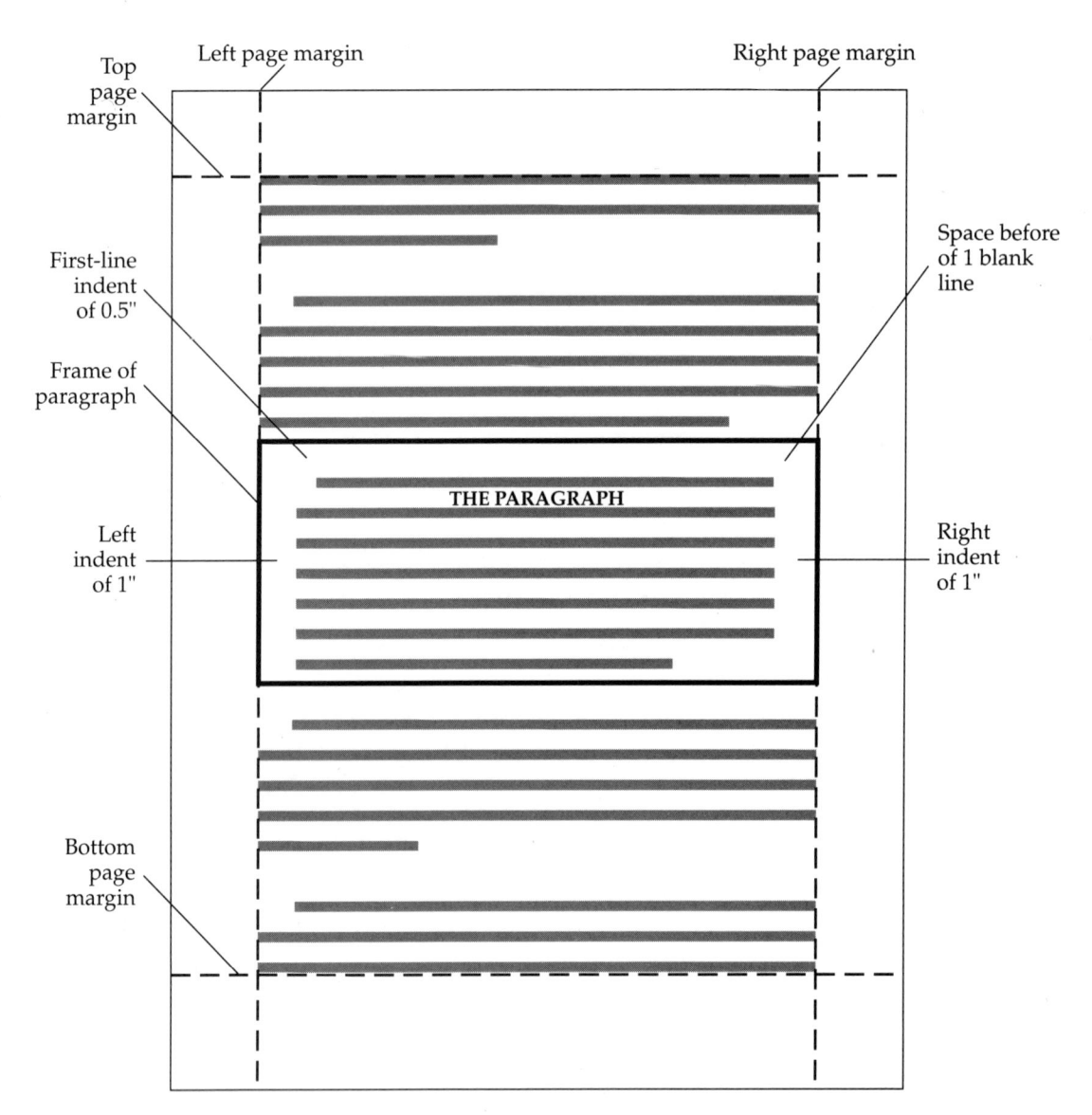

Figure 30-2. A paragraph and its frame, with left and right indents.

Positioning Elements

How can we narrow the frame itself? By using the Format Position command, which also lets us fix the paragraph to a specific location on the page. First let's select the paragraph (by placing the cursor somewhere within it) and use the Format Paragraph command to return our left and right indents to 0. This returns the text to its full width inside the frame. Now we'll use the Format Position command to narrow the frame.

When you choose Format Position, you see the Position dialog box:

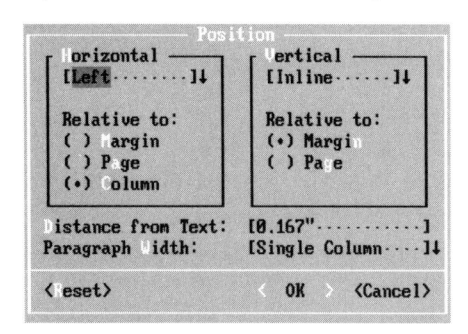

```
┌─────────────────── Position ───────────────────┐
│  ┌─ Horizontal ──────┐  ┌─ Vertical ──────┐   │
│  │ [Left········]↕   │  │ [Inline······]↕  │   │
│  │                   │  │                  │   │
│  │ Relative to:      │  │ Relative to:     │   │
│  │ ( ) Margin        │  │ (•) Margin       │   │
│  │ ( ) Page          │  │ ( ) Page         │   │
│  │ (•) Column        │  │                  │   │
│  └───────────────────┘  └──────────────────┘   │
│                                                │
│  Distance from Text: [0.167"··········]        │
│  Paragraph Width:    [Single Column····]↕      │
│                                                │
│  <Reset>           <  OK  >      <Cancel>      │
└────────────────────────────────────────────────┘
```

The Format Position command can alter a paragraph's nature in the following three important ways:

- It can fix the position of the paragraph on the printed page.
- It can narrow the paragraph's frame to less than the width of the text column if you want. A narrowed frame leaves room for text from other paragraphs to flow around the positioned paragraph.
- It can create an additional buffer on two or four sides of the *outside* of a paragraph's frame. This outside buffer holds the text of adjacent paragraphs at bay, providing a more generous margin around a paragraph that has been fixed to a certain position.

In other words, using the Format Position command causes a paragraph to take on a special status and special qualities. To learn how to harness this power, let's look at each field of the command.

Horizontal

The Horizontal drop-down list and its companion field, the Relative to option buttons, together let you tell Word to put a paragraph in the horizontal center of the page, in the center of a column, or so many inches from the left side of the column, the margins, or the page. If you type a specific number in the Horizontal field, Word will place that number of inches of space between the left edge of the frame and the left side of the column, margins, or page (which are the three option buttons of the Relative to field). This presumes that you have selected *In* (for "inches") in the Measure drop-down list of the Utilities Customize dialog box. You can use a unit of measure other than inches in the Horizontal field by typing it after the number: for example, *2.5 cm* or *16 pt*.

If you press Alt+Down or click with the mouse on the down arrow to the right of the Horizontal field, Word offers the choices *Left, Centered, Right, Inside,* and *Outside*. The first three choices are self-explanatory. *Inside* places the paragraph frame to the left on odd-numbered pages and to the right on even-numbered pages, and *Outside* has the opposite effect.

Vertical

The Vertical drop-down list and its companion field, the Relative To option buttons, let you tell Word to print the paragraph at the top, bottom, or vertical center of either the page or the region of the page that is inside the margins. Alternatively, the Vertical field lets you specify that the paragraph should appear "in line"—that is, printed immediately after the paragraph that precedes it on the screen and immediately before the paragraph that follows it on the screen.

If you type a specific number in the Vertical field, Word will place that number of inches of space between the top edge of the frame and the top side of the margins or page (depending on which of the two option buttons you select in the Relative To field). Again, this assumes you have selected In (for inches) in the Measure field of the Utilities Customize command. You can use a unit of measure other than inches by typing it after the number.

Instead of typing a number, you can press Alt+Down to drop down a list of choices: Inline, Top, Centered, and Bottom. Again, Inline means the paragraph is not to be positioned in any special place. The remaining three choices are formatted relative to either the page margins or the page edges, depending on which option button you choose in the Relative to field.

Frame width

Format Position lets you narrow the paragraph's frame to less than the width of the text column. A narrowed frame leaves room for text from other paragraphs to flow around it.

To leave room for other text to flow around the selected paragraph, specify a value in the Paragraph Width drop-down list of the command's dialog box. The proposed width is Single Column, but you can choose almost any width. You can even make a frame wider than the column, causing the text (or graphic) stored in the paragraph to extend into a page margin.

If you prefer, you can press Alt+Down to drop down a list of choices. In addition to Single Column, a choice that is always available is Width of Graphic. This choice lets you specify that the frame will hug the boundaries of a graphics image that you have incorporated into the document by using the Insert Picture command.

If your document is formatted to have more than one column, the list has two additional choices in the Paragraph Width field: Double Column, which causes the paragraph frame to span two columns, and Between Margins, which causes the paragraph's frame to stretch from the left margin of the page to the right margin without regard for individual columns. These are handy choices, for example, when you want to format a paragraph that contains a headline so that the paragraph spans either two columns or all the columns on the page.

CHAPTER THIRTY: Graphics, Layout, and Positioning 595

Of course, you don't need to use choices from Word's list. If you have a five-column layout and you want one paragraph's frame to span three of those columns, you can compute the correct value for the Paragraph Width field, or you can experiment until you get it right. (File Print Preview is a great help if you decide to experiment, because it gives quick feedback.)

Distance from Text

The additional buffer on two or four sides of the outside of a paragraph's frame holds the text of adjacent paragraphs at bay, providing a more generous margin around a paragraph that has been fixed to a certain position. Normally, the Format Position command proposes a buffer of 0.167 inches, which is about a ⅙ inch, equivalent to one standard line. You can change the width of the buffer by adjusting the command's Distance from Text field.

The Distance from Text field is a tad tricky, for several reasons.

First, you must keep in mind that the total amount of white space on any given side of a paragraph is the sum of two different buffers—the *outside buffer*, controlled by the Format Position command's Distance from Text field, plus the *inside buffer*, controlled by the relevant text box of the Format Paragraph command's dialog box: Before, After, From Left, or From Right, as shown in Figure 30-3 on the following page.

Second, it's impossible to adjust the widths of a paragraph's four outside buffers independently. The Distance from Text text box controls all directions at once. (But, as just noted, you can adjust the overall amount of buffer in any given direction by using fields of the Format Paragraph command.)

Third, regardless of the measurement in the Distance from Text text box, the outside buffer might or might not be in effect. Whether the buffer is active is dictated by the choices you make in other fields of the Format Position command's dialog box. To activate the top and bottom outside buffers, you must choose something other than Inline in the Vertical drop-down list. This makes sense because you probably don't want an extra border of white space above or below a paragraph's frame unless the paragraph is positioned in some special place. To activate the left and right outside buffers, you must specify a frame width that is narrower than the column width. This also makes sense, because if the frame is not narrower than the column there's no room for other text to flow around the paragraph, and hence no need for an extra buffer of white space on the left or right.

To continue with the example, if you select the sample paragraph and use the Format Position command to set Paragraph Width (which is the "frame width") to 3" and leave Distance from Text set to the proposed *0.167"* (which is one line), a printed copy will look somewhat as shown in Figure 30-4 on page 597.

The frame is drawn in for the sake of illustration, but in reality it is invisible. Observe that the text of the paragraph became narrower even though there is no left indent or right indent. This is because the frame is narrower—only 3 inches instead of 6. Observe also that there is an extra buffer to the right of the paragraph's frame.

This outside buffer was set with the Format Position command's Distance from Text field, which was activated in the horizontal orientation because the measurement in the Paragraph Width drop-down list box is narrower than a single column.

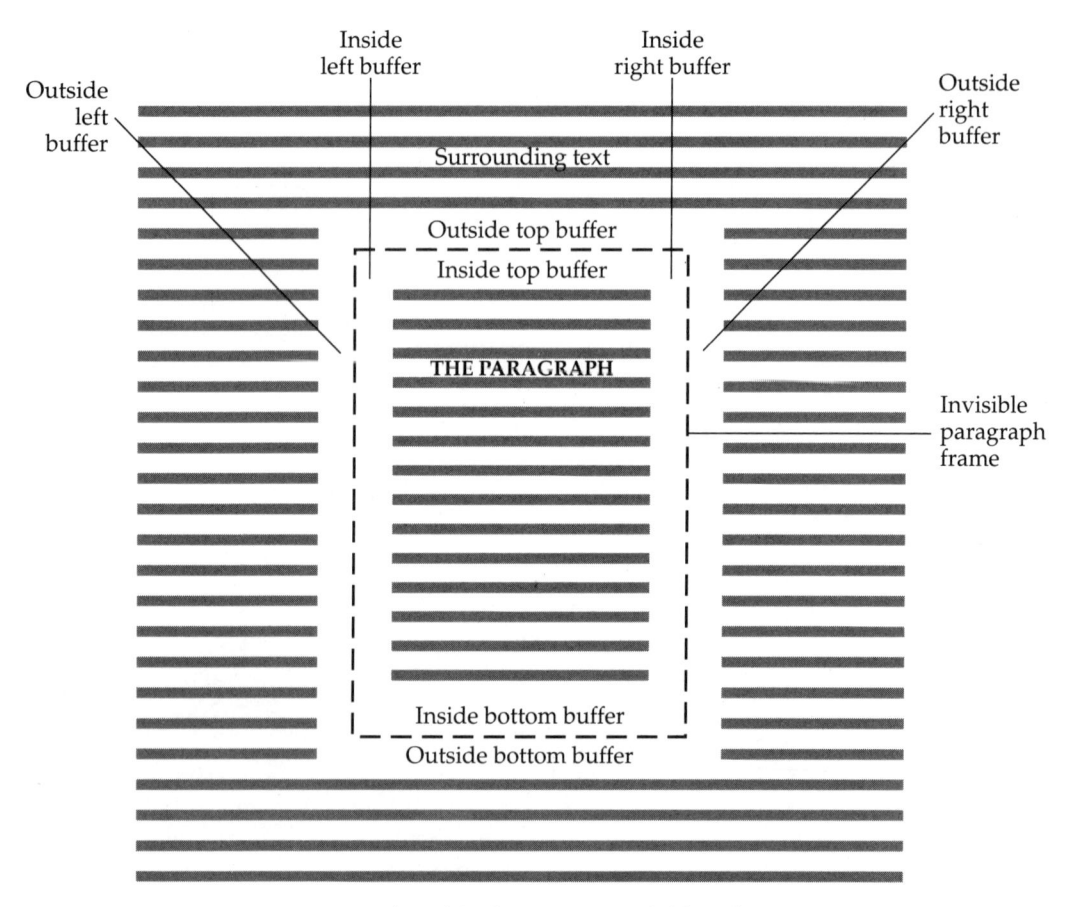

Figure 30-3. A paragraph and its frame, surrounded by other text.

If you want to create an outside buffer above and below the positioned paragraph, you must select something other than *Inline* in the Format Position command's Vertical drop-down list. If you select the paragraph again and choose the Format Position command one more time, you can type 3" in the Vertical drop-down list box. The result is shown in Figure 30-5 on page 598.

The paragraph is no longer "in line," meaning Word will not necessarily print it in the position shown on the editing screen. Instead, the paragraph is contained in a 3-inch frame that begins 3 inches from the top margin. It doesn't matter what else is on the page or whether anything else is on the page; the position of the paragraph on the printed page won't change. Observe that an outside buffer now exists above and below the frame of the paragraph, as well as to the right of it as before. This is because the paragraph is no longer "in line."

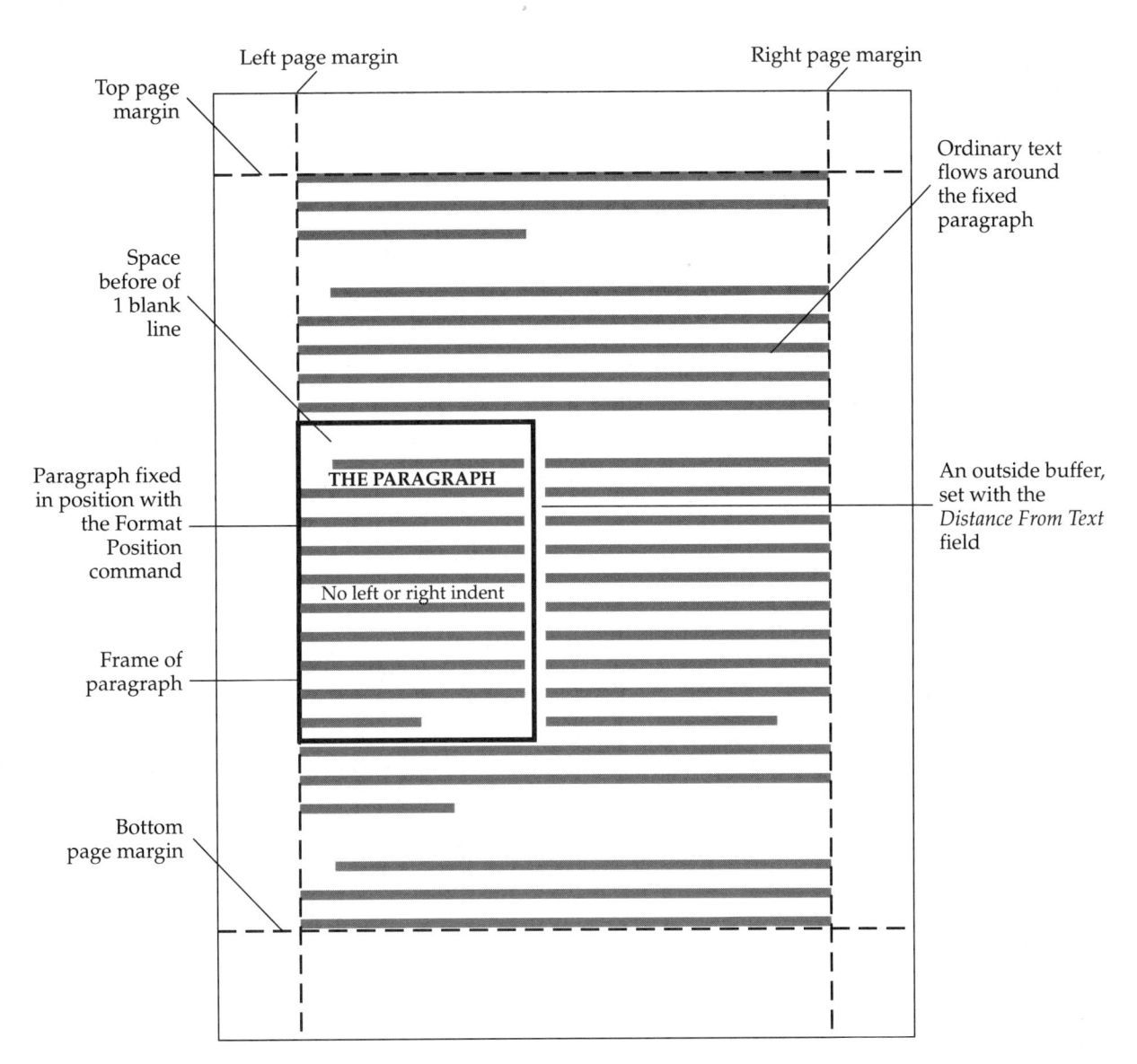

CHAPTER THIRTY: Graphics, Layout, and Positioning

Labels on figure:
- Top page margin
- Left page margin
- Right page margin
- Space before of 1 blank line
- Ordinary text flows around the fixed paragraph
- Paragraph fixed in position with the Format Position command
- THE PARAGRAPH
- No left or right indent
- An outside buffer, set with the *Distance From Text* field
- Frame of paragraph
- Bottom page margin

Figure 30-4. A paragraph and its frame, with a Paragraph Width of 3 inches and a Distance from Text of 0.167 inches.

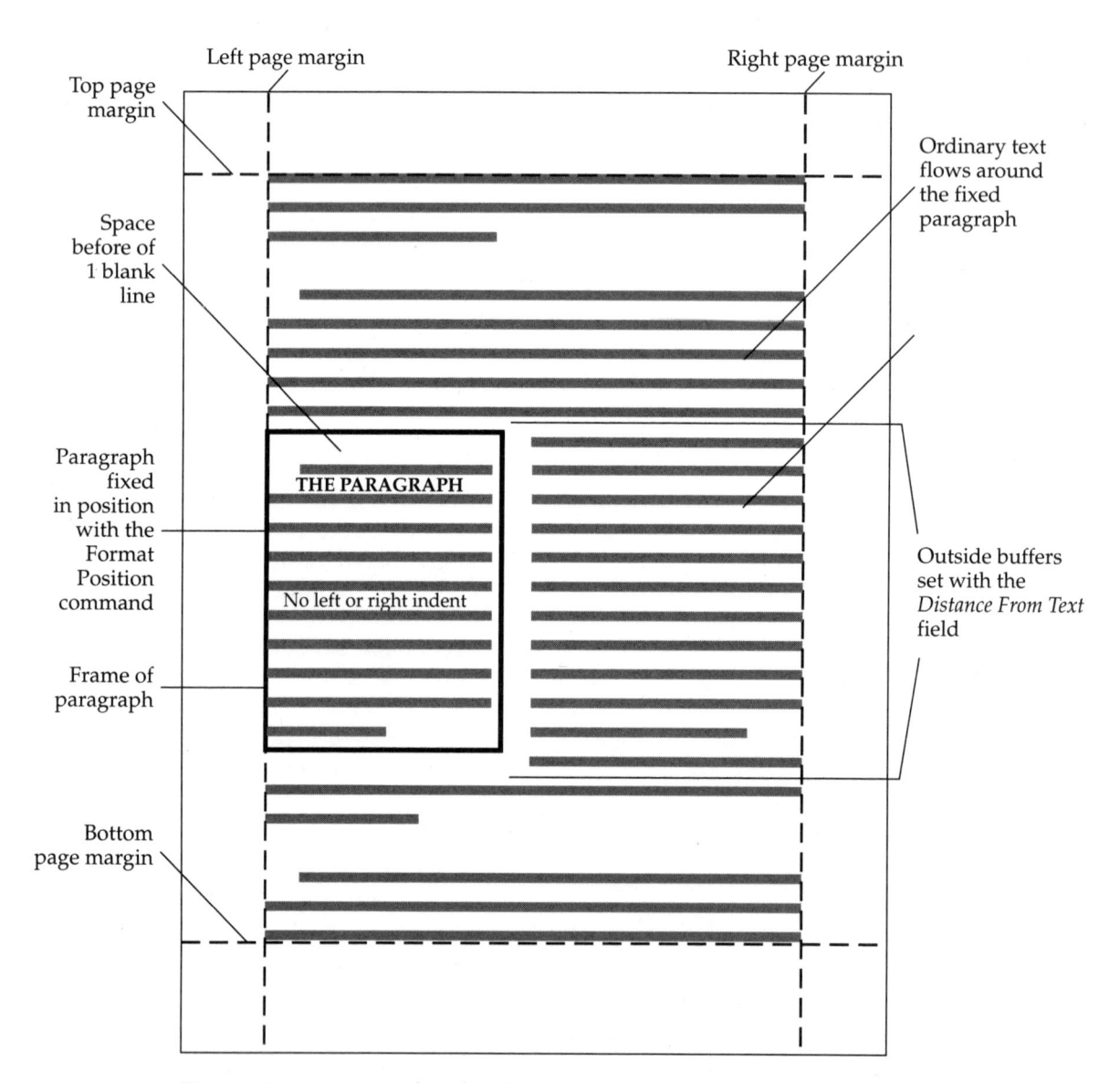

Figure 30-5. *A paragraph and its frame, with a Vertical position of 3 inches.*

CHAPTER THIRTY: Graphics, Layout, and Positioning   599

IMPORTING GRAPHICS

Word can incorporate graphics of various kinds into a document and print them. The graphics can come from a variety of sources, including output files from leading software packages that print graphics. For example, you can print graphs from Microsoft Excel or Lotus 1-2-3, charts from CHART-MASTER or Harvard Graphics, drawings or other images from Microsoft Windows applications, photographs or artwork digitized with a scanner, or images captured and cropped from your screen.

When creating a file containing a graphics image, crop the image so that it contains only the portion you want to appear in the Word document. Although Word can change the size of a graphics image and even let you stretch the image in one dimension and not another, it does not let you remove portions of the image that you do not want to print. However, almost all programs that create graphics images let you clip or crop them, so there is no difficulty.

Step 1: Creating an Image

The first step is to create a file on disk that contains the image you want to incorporate in your document. Almost any program that can print a graphics image, such as a chart, can be the source of a file that you can import into Word. Additionally, scanners that translate photographic or other hard-copy images into graphics files are becoming relatively affordable.

The particulars of using other programs to create graphics files are beyond the scope of this book, but as an example, suppose you want to copy a chart from the Microsoft Windows spreadsheet program, Microsoft Excel, to the Windows clipboard: While running Microsoft Excel, select the chart, choose the Copy Picture command from the Edit menu, and then hold down the Shift key while you choose OK.

Importing the image into Word depends on the version of Windows and the mode it is running in. If you are using Windows 3 in real or standard mode, you must convert the clipboard image into a graphics file and then import the file.

1. Start the Windows 3 accessory graphics program Paintbrush. (You might want to quit Excel first to save valuable memory.)
2. Paste the clipboard image onto the screen.
3. Save the image as a .PCX file. (Use the Options command button in the Save As dialog box.)
4. Crop the image if you want to import an image that is less than the full screen. Use the Pick tool to select the portion of the image to be imported and then use the Copy command to create a new .PCX file.

The file can then be imported using the Insert menu's Picture command.

If you are using Windows 2 or 2.1, Windows/286, Windows/386, or Windows 3 running in 386 enhanced mode, you can import the image directly.

If you quit Microsoft Excel and start Word (without quitting Windows), the image of the chart will be available to Word through the Insert Picture command (discussed a little later in this chapter) or through the reserved glossary name *clipboard*. (However, you can't import more than one color of a color image unless you use Windows/386 or Windows 3. In Windows/386, you can't import graphics from the clipboard if Word is in a VGA graphics mode (30, 34, or 60 lines on the screen).

In addition to creating graphics images with other programs, you can use the Capture program that comes with Word 5.5 to take a "snapshot" of whatever is on your computer screen, pretty much regardless of the program you're using. This snapshot can be of the full screen or, if you are running in a graphics mode, a cropped image of a desired portion of the screen. Capturing an image from the screen is one of the easiest ways to create a graphics file that you can incorporate into a Word document. A disadvantage, however, is that a screen image might not be of as high quality as an image deliberately exported from a graphics package. You should not use Capture if you are running Windows.

Capture is a terminate-and-stay-resident (TSR) program, which means it stays active in your computer's memory even when you run a different program. Capture takes up about 20 KB of RAM, which should present little problem for most users. In any case, you can remove Capture from memory at any time by typing *capture /e* at the DOS prompt. (You can run it only from DOS, not from OS/2.)

You load Capture into memory before starting Word or any other program from which you want to capture an image. To do this, type *Capture* at the DOS prompt. (You can place the instruction *Capture* in your AUTOEXEC.BAT file, if you like.) Then start your application program (such as Word or Lotus 1-2-3). That's all there is to it. Now, regardless of the program you are using, you can take a "snapshot" of some or all of your computer screen and later bring that image into a Word document.

Setting up Capture

Capturing an image is simple, involving little more than holding down the Shift key and pressing the PrtSc key, but setting up Capture for this task has a few wrinkles.

The first time you use Capture, or whenever you want to change its settings, you type */s* after the command name: *capture /s*. (If you want Capture to remember the settings in future editing sessions, switch to the directory containing CAPTURE.COM before typing *capture*. Typing *capture* takes you into a special setup mode, in which you can express various preferences by choosing topics from a menu.

Before you make these choices, it is important to know whether the application program from which you will capture an image runs in graphics or text mode. Some application programs, such as Word, can run in either text or graphics mode, computer hardware permitting. (To see or change the mode in which Word operates, choose the View Preferences command and look at the Display Mode drop-down list box.

You also need to know whether you want the images you will capture (and then import into Word) to be in text form (ASCII) or graphics form (bitmapped). Usually, you will want images to be bitmapped, which means that every little point of light or darkness on the screen will be recorded. When you capture a bitmapped image, you

CHAPTER THIRTY: Graphics, Layout, and Positioning

can crop it, and when Word imports such an image, it lets you control the image's vertical and horizontal dimensions. However, if the application from which you are capturing an image is running in text mode, you might prefer to capture the image as text; this causes it to be saved as an ASCII file, which can be treated like any other unformatted document. A text image cannot be cropped or sized, although after you import it into Word you can edit its content and change the size of the font in which it is displayed.

When you enter *capture /s*, this is the screen you see:

```
                          CAPTURE.COM
             Screen capture program version 1.0 for Microsoft Word
         (C) Copyright 1989 Jewell Technologies, Inc. - All rights reserved

    Use the menu below to select your display adapter and choose your options.
    When you press a letter for an option, a screen will appear to describe
    the option in more detail.

    ┌─────────────────────────────────────────────────────────────────────┐
    │ TO                                                           PRESS  │
    ├─────────────────────────────────────────────────────────────────────┤
    │ Select display adapter                                         D    │
    │ Enable/Disable text screens as pictures                        T    │
    │ Enable/Disable saving in reverse video                         V    │
    │ Enable/Disable clipping                                        P    │
    │ Enable/Disable 90 degree rotation                              R    │
    │ Enter number of text lines per screen                          N    │
    │ Quit and save settings                                         Q    │
    └─────────────────────────────────────────────────────────────────────┘
```

The most important choice on the Capture setup menu is the first one, *Select display adapter*. Press D to choose this item from the menu and to see another menu of choices. Each of these secondary choices represents a video mode in which Capture can operate. Most computer systems let you use choice 0 (zero), and you want to use 0 if at all possible because it provides the most flexibility. If you find later that this option doesn't work with your system, you can run Capture with the /s option again and make a different selection. After you've made a choice, press Enter to return to the main setup menu.

The second setup-menu choice, Enable/Disable text screens as pictures, is relevant only if the screen is running in text mode *and* you previously chose 0 for Select display adapter. In this situation, Capture normally will capture a screen image as text. If, instead, you want to capture the text image as a bitmapped file so that you can crop and size it, press T. The program then asks: *Do you want screens in text mode to be saved as pictures (Y/N)?* Press Y.

The next three choices, indicated by the letters V, P, and R, are relevant only if you are running in a graphics mode. Pressing V lets you control whether the captured image will be in reverse video (with light and dark areas reversed, as most in this book are). Pressing P lets you choose whether Capture lets you crop (select only a portion of) an image before you capture it. You'll probably want to leave this set to Y, for "Yes," unless you are going to capture a Windows screen. Pressing R lets you choose whether to rotate images 90 degrees clockwise. You'll probably want to leave this set to N, for "No."

The next menu choice, indicated by the letter N, is relevant only if you previously chose a number other than 0 for *Select display adapter*. It lets you tell Capture how many lines appear on the screen. The default is 25, so you probably don't need to change this setting in any case.

When Capture is set up as you want it, press Q to quit. Word will remember your settings until you start Capture with the /s option again.

As a shortcut that sidesteps the setup menu, you can avoid the /s option and instead type *capture* followed by:

Type *capture* and this:	To achieve this:
/d=nn	The *nn* is the display adapter number as it appears in the setup menu. (As noted earlier, you want to leave this set to *0* if at all possible.)
/t=y or /t=n	If you are set to display adapter 0, you can capture a text screen as a graphics screen with /t=y or as a text screen with /t=n.
/v=y or /v=n	In graphics mode, this option saves screens in reverse video (/v=y) or in normal video (/v=n).
/r=y or /r=n	In graphics mode, this option rotates screens 90 degrees clockwise (/r=y) or does not (/r=n).
/p=y or /p=n	In graphics mode, this option enables the cropping feature (/p=y) or turns cropping off (/p=n).

For example, if you type *capture /v=y /r=n*, the Capture program saves the image in reverse video (black as white and vice versa) and does not rotate the image 90 degrees.

Using Capture

To capture an image, hold down Shift and press the PrtSc key. The program responds by proposing a name for the file that will contain the image you are about to capture. This name appears at the top of the screen; it starts with *CAPT*, followed by a four-digit number, and ends in either *.SCR* (if the screen is in a graphics mode) or *.LST* (if the screen is in a text mode). The numbers in the proposed names increment, so if the last one used was CAPT0004.SCR, the next one proposed would be CAPT0005.SCR. You can accept a proposed name by pressing Enter, or you can type a more descriptive name and then press Enter. If you change your mind, press Esc to cancel the capture.

```
| File Name:  capt0001.scr                                              |
```

CHAPTER THIRTY: Graphics, Layout, and Positioning

Capture isn't very smart. Unless you set *Select display adapter* to 0, for example, it can't tell whether your screen is running in a graphics mode or a text mode. It handles this dilemma by assuming the screen is in a graphics mode and by capturing images in bitmapped form. If the screen is actually running in a text mode, a bitmapped capture results in garbage rather than an image of the screen being placed in the file on disk. There is a way around this. If you are using a display adapter setting other than 0 and are running in text mode, capture a screen by holding down Shift and pressing PrtSc and then *immediately* pressing the Esc key. A .LST (text) file will result.

If you are saving a screen image in text form, the image is captured as soon as you press Enter to accept the name. The resulting file is composed of ASCII characters only and can be incorporated into your document using the Insert File command. It is not a graphics file, so you cannot use the Insert Picture command.

On the other hand, if you are saving the screen in graphics mode and did not turn off Capture's cropping feature when making setup choices, you have an opportunity to crop the image before saving it on disk. To crop, you box the region of the screen you want captured. The boxing is achieved by pressing the direction keys to move four cropping lines—one for the top of the box, one for the bottom, and one for each of the remaining two sides.

Before you press any of the direction keys, the cropping lines are at the outer edges of the screen, indicating that the entire screen is to be saved. By pressing the Left and Right direction keys, you move the side lines left and right. By pressing the Up and Down direction keys, you move the top and bottom lines. If the direction keys move the left line and you want to move the right one instead (or vice versa), press the Tab key. Similarly, use the Tab key to switch between the top and bottom lines.

As you press the direction keys, the lines move in small increments. This gives you fine control. If you want to move the lines more quickly, press the plus key (+) on the numeric keypad. To have the crop lines move in smaller increments, press the minus key (–) on the keyboard.

To cause the top and bottom lines or the left and right lines to move simultaneously, press the Ins key. To unlink the movement of the two lines, press Del.

When you have moved the cropping lines so that the screen is cropped as desired, press Enter. There will be a delay, possibly a substantial one, while the bitmapped file is created on disk. When the file is complete, the program beeps. If you change your mind about capturing the screen, press Esc to cancel the capture.

NOTE: *Files created by Capture are in a proprietary variant of the PCX file format that only Word uses. This format is fine if you only want to import screen images into Word or if you never want to use a paint program to edit an image between the time you capture it and the time you import it into Word.*

Step 2: Incorporating the Image

The next step is to incorporate the image into your Word document. You accomplish this with the Insert Picture command, which places appropriate hidden text in the paragraph and formats it in certain ways. As noted in Chapter 7, the hidden text specifies the file on the disk that contains the graphic, the width and height of the graphic, and the graphics file format in which it is stored.

Specifying a file

When you choose the Insert Picture command, the fields of its dialog box prompt you for the information that Word will turn into the hidden-text instruction line:

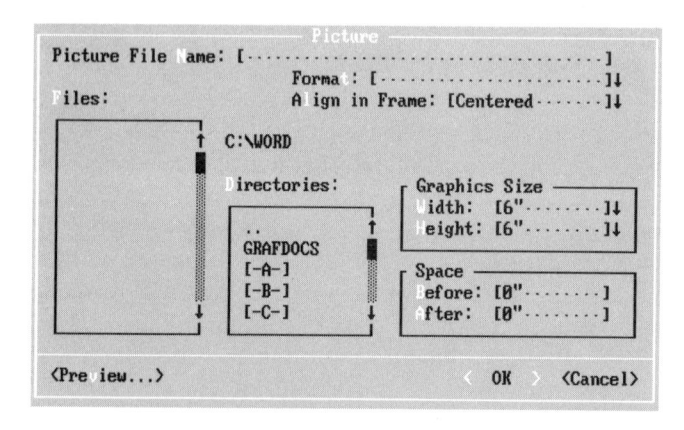

```
┌─────────────────────── Picture ───────────────────────┐
│ Picture File Name: [·······························]   │
│                Format: [···················]↕         │
│  Files:        Align in Frame: [Centered······]↕      │
│  ↑  C:\WORD                                           │
│  ▒                                                    │
│  ▒   Directories:    ┌─ Graphics Size ─────┐          │
│  ▒                   │ Width:  [6"········]↕│          │
│  ▒   ..              │ Height: [6"········]↕│          │
│  ▒   GRAFDOCS     ↑  └─────────────────────┘          │
│  ▒   [-A-]        ▒  ┌─ Space ─────────────┐          │
│  ▒   [-B-]        ▒  │ Before: [0"········]│          │
│  ↓   [-C-]        ↓  │ After:  [0"········]│          │
│                      └─────────────────────┘          │
│  <Preview...>                  < OK >  <Cancel>       │
└───────────────────────────────────────────────────────┘
```

In the Picture File Name text box, type the name of the file that contains the image you are importing. Include the filename extension, such as *.TIF*.

Instead of typing a name, you can press Alt+F to move to the Files list, which shows the names of all files in the picture directory. (Word remembers the drive and directory from which you last inserted a picture, even during a different session of Word, and proposes the same drive and directory as the location of your next insertion. If you have never inserted a picture in the past, Word shows the current directory in the Files list.) You can highlight the name of a desired graphics file from this list, or you can use the Directories list to change to a different drive and/or directory.

If you are running Word through Microsoft Windows (except Windows 3 in real and standard modes), the choice *Clipboard* will appear at the top of the Files list.

After choosing the name of the graphics file you want to insert into your document, look to the dialog box's Format drop-down list box. Word will fill in this field for you if it recognizes the format of the graphics file you named. However, there are three file formats that Word can use but does not recognize: HPGL, Postscript, and "print file." If the graphics file is in one of these formats, you must type its name or press Alt+Down to choose it from a list of the three formats.

File formats

A little background will help you understand the difference between types of file formats. The three basic categories of files are *bitmapped files,* *metafiles,* and *print files.* A

CHAPTER THIRTY: Graphics, Layout, and Positioning

bitmapped file contains information on every pixel in the image. A metafile contains instructions that let software draw the image; it is a formula, in other words. A print file is one that is ready to be output to a particular printer.

Word is great with bitmapped images; it handles some kinds of metafiles; and it can send any print file along to a printer, although the print file might contain instructions to the printer that cause difficulties.

The PIC format is a simple metafile format. Word handles it well. The HPGL format also is a metafile.

PostScript is a very complicated metafile format that Word treats more or less as a print file. Word sends the image to the printer but interprets enough of the metafile code in a PostScript file to ensure that the image will print.

In contrast, a print file image often won't print correctly. The file might contain, for instance, a form-feed character that causes the printer to spit out the image on a fresh sheet of paper. You can use Word to edit a print file and try to remove the offending characters that were put there by the software that created the file, but this method requires patience plus some knowledge of the control-code sequences used by the printer for which the file was created.

Although all PostScript images will print, only encapsulated PostScript images are displayed on the print preview screen. Normal PostScript images will not show up on the print preview screen because Word does not interpret a sufficient amount of PostScript to create the image. It lets the printer do that work.

File formats Word recognizes

Word recognizes the following specific formats and, when printing, can resize images stored in any of them to fit the dimensions you specify:

PCX Bitmapped picture files generated by PC Paintbrush (and certain other programs, including some screen-image-capture programs and the software that accompanies many scanners) use this format. PC Paintbrush also is marketed as Microsoft Paintbrush and often comes bundled with the Microsoft Mouse. Other programs that can generate PCX include Microsoft Windows 3 Paintbrush, Harvard Graphics, the HP Graphics Gallery, and the HP Scanning Gallery.

PCC Bitmapped picture files generated by PC Paintbrush (and Microsoft Paintbrush) use this format. This is a close variant of PCX and is used to store on disk a *cutout picture file*, which is a cropped portion of a Paintbrush picture.

PIC Graphics files generated by Lotus 1-2-3 use this format. Paradox produces graphics in this format, too.

TIFF Bitmapped graphics files produced by many scanners use this format. There are four kinds of TIFF files, and Word can read and manipulate three of them. *TIFF B Uncompressed* stores a black-and-white image, and *TIFF B Compressed* stores the same image but in a more compact form. Scanner software commonly can produce both of these formats, and Word can use either of them. *TIFF G Uncompressed* stores an image that has up to 256 shades of gray (a "gray scale"). In other words, any given pixel (dot in the image) can be in one of 256 shades, from white to black. Word can also use this format. Because these files can be long, there is a fourth format, called *TIFF G Compressed*, which contains all the gray-scale information but is more compact. Word cannot use *TIFF G Compressed* files, however. If you scan an image and save it in one of the TIFF formats Word does support, you will get better results if you avoid dithered images.

Clipboard This is the file format listed when the file has been imported into Word from the Microsoft Windows clipboard (but not the Presentation Manager clipboard). It is a bitmapped format, so graphics images stored on the clipboard as metafiles cannot be imported into Word. Some Windows applications let you use either a bitmapped format or a metafile format when storing a graphics image on the clipboard; other applications limit you to one or the other.

When using Windows 3, you must be running in 386 enhanced mode rather than real or standard mode in order to use the clipboard to transfer graphics to Word. If you have a computer that cannot run in 386 enhanced mode, you might be able to use your Windows application to save a graphic in a different file format, one that Word can handle. For example, you can use the Windows 3 Paintbrush program to save an image in PCX format.

Capture This is the name listed in the Format field when the image being imported by the Insert Picture command was created with Capture. It is similar to PCX but unfortunately is not interchangeable with PCX.

File formats Word uses but doesn't recognize

If the Format field remains blank after you've specified a file in the previous field, the file is not in one of the preceding formats. You can supply one of three additional formats that Word can use. If the image on disk is one of these formats, you can type the name in the Format field or press Alt+Down to choose the format from the list. The three formats are as follows:

HPGL Hewlett-Packard plotters use this metafile format. Any software program that can print to an HP plotter and a file can, in turn, create an HPGL file that Word can use. HPGL comes in several variants, however, for plotters of various degrees of sophistication. Word supports only the least-complex subset of the total range of HPGL instructions. This is the subset designed for the HP 7440 Plotter.

Programs that can produce HPGL suitable for Word's use include AutoCAD, CHART-MASTER, Energraphics, Graph-In-The-Box, Harvard Graphics, HP Graphics Gallery, Lotus Freelance Plus, Microsoft Chart, and Microsoft Excel.

PostScript PostScript files printed to disk use this metafile format. This is not encapsulated PostScript. Word is able to scale an image in this format (change its dimensions), but not much more.

Print file This is the format various programs use to print to a file instead of to a printer. Using this format is the method of last resort because, as mentioned earlier, there is a fair chance that the results will not be what you had hoped for. This format was included in Word 5.0 and 5.5 chiefly to retain backward compatibility with Word 4.0 so that people who have created documents in 4.0 can continue to use those documents.

Aligning the image

The Align in Frame drop-down list box lets you specify that the graphic either will be centered horizontally or will be pushed to the left or right inside the frame of the paragraph that contains the graphic.

Your choice in this field is meaningful only if the width of the graphics image is different from the paragraph frame—a decision you make by using the Width drop-down list box, which is described a little later in this chapter. If the image is exactly as wide as the frame, it fills the whole frame and alignment is irrelevant.

To a certain extent, the Insert Picture command's Align in Frame field plays the same role for graphics paragraphs that the Format Paragraph command's From Left and From Right fields play for text paragraphs. Either way, you are establishing the horizontal placement of the paragraph's content within the paragraph's frame.

To establish vertical placement within the paragraph's frame, use the Insert Picture command's Before and After fields. These perform precisely the same functions as the fields of the same names in the Format Paragraph command: They let you add blank space before or after a paragraph's content (but inside the paragraph's frame).

Sizing the image

The Insert Picture command's Width field lets you specify how wide the graphic will be. Word initially proposes a width that is identical to the width of the frame that contains the graphic. You can change this by typing a different width (in inches, for instance).

If you press Alt+Down instead of typing a distance, you will see a list of one or more possible widths. These widths might be expressed with quite a bit of precision, such as *7.678" (natural size)*—a choice that says "Include this graphic in the document at its natural size, which is 7.678 inches wide." Another choice might be *6" (same as frame width)*—a choice that says "Include this graphic in the document, but change its width to match that of the paragraph frame." Word might list other choices but not explain them. For example, if the image's natural size were 7.678 inches, Word might list the choice *3.839"* because it is half the image's natural size.

Use the Height field to control the height of the graphic. Word initially proposes a height that would keep the aspect ratio of the image true to its original shape. For example, if the original graphic is twice as high as it is wide and in the Width field you told Word to print the graphic 3 inches wide, Word would propose that the printed graphic be 6 inches high.

By typing a new number, you can change the height to whatever you like; this offers you a way to, among other things, distort the image.

Instead of typing a number, you can press Alt+Down to look at a list of possibilities. For example, Word always offers you the opportunity to print the graphic exactly as tall as it is wide—regardless of whether the original graphic was square or not. This is the Same As Width choice. Another option is to make the graphic its natural size.

Remember, though, that making the graphic its natural height won't make it look natural unless its width is also natural or nearly natural. In general, to avoid distortion and make the image look natural, you want to choose Preserve Aspect Ratio.

Hidden coding

When you use Insert Picture to tell Word to incorporate a graphics image into the printed version of a document, Word places a special instruction line in the document instead of putting the actual graphic there. The instruction line starts with a code formatted as hidden text so that it normally does not print. The instruction line follows this form:

1. The characters .G., indicating that this is a graphics instruction. These characters, are formatted as hidden.
2. The drive, pathname, and filename (including filename extension) of the graphics file, followed by a semicolon. For example, if the graphics file had the name PROGRESS.PCX and were stored in the ART directory of the C drive, the characters would be *C:\ART\PROGRESS.PCX*—formatted, again, as hidden text. However, if the graphics file is in the same directory as the document, Word will insert only the name of the file, not its path.
3. The width of the graphic, followed by a semicolon.
4. The height of the graphic, followed by a semicolon.
5. The name of the file format in which the graphic is stored, such as PCX or TIF.

For example, if the graphics file *PROGRESS.PCX* were 4.2 inches wide and 2.75 inches tall, the hidden-text instruction line would be:

```
.G.C:\ART\PROGRESS.PCX;4.2";2.75";PCX
```

Step 3: Positioning the Image

The third step in importing a graphic and positioning the image on the page takes us back to the use of the Format Position command. Although there are differences, you position a paragraph that contains a graphic much as you position a paragraph that contains text. (Remember, a paragraph doesn't really *contain* a graphic; it contains a hidden-text instruction that causes a graphic to print. But, practically speaking, we say that such a paragraph contains a graphic.)

You position and size the frame of a graphics paragraph by filling in the dialog box of the Format Position command, exactly as you would if you were positioning a text paragraph. Similarly, you control the width of the frame's outside buffers exactly as you would for a text paragraph, by adjusting the dialog box's Distance from Text field. And you adjust the top and bottom inside buffers by typing a value in the Before and After fields of the Insert Picture command (or the Format Paragraph command).

But when it comes to creating left and right buffers inside the frame, you cannot use the From Left and From Right fields of the Format Paragraph command, as you would for a text paragraph.

Instead, if you want the graphic to be less than the full width of the frame, you specify the desired width in the Width field of the Insert Picture command. A graphic actually can be wider than its frame, but more often you'll want the graphic to be the same size as the frame or narrower. If you made it narrower by setting the Width field to a smaller number than that to which the Paragraph Width field of the Format Position command is set, you would have blank space on either side or both sides of the graphic. To split the blank space evenly between the two sides, set the Insert Picture command's Align in Frame field to Centered. If you want all the blank space to be to the right, set the field to Left. If you want all the space to be to the left, set the Align in Frame field to Right.

This technique provides slightly less control over the horizontal placement of graphics within a paragraph's frame than you get with text. But most of the time, like most of Word's other pseudo–desktop publishing facilities, it will do nicely.

CHAPTER THIRTY-ONE

Printing and Fonts

If you've turned to this chapter first, it might have been in frustration. Getting printers to work properly can be aggravating because of the complex interactions of computer hardware, computer software, printer hardware, and—when you're using downloadable fonts—printer software. On the other hand, a printer that is working properly is a joy that is soon taken for granted.

This chapter begins with the basics of printing but rapidly broadens into a survey of the issues involved in printing, with an emphasis on laser printers and fonts. Whole books could be written (and have been) on the subject, but the following review might at least help you down the road toward successful laser printing.

PRINTER BASICS

Printers fall into four main categories:

- *Dot matrix*—a fast printer that doesn't equal other types in print quality but can look surprisingly good when it is a 24-pin model operated in a slow (near-letter-quality) mode.
- *Laser*—a fast, flexible type of printer that emulates a typesetting machine or a typewriter with equal ease and produces originals that look like good photocopies (which, in a sense, they are). Most laser printers are Hewlett-Packard LaserJets or competitors that are compatible with LaserJets. Increasing in popularity, and with good reason, are PostScript-based laser printers.

- *Ink-jet*—a printer that shares some of the advantages of a laser printer, at lower cost. However, as laser printers descend into the range of a few hundred dollars, you should think about buying a laser printer instead of an ink-jet printer, particularly because an ink jet costs more to operate.
- *Daisy wheel*—an all-but-forgotten technology, in which a mechanical ball or wheel strikes a ribbon and impresses a letter or other character on the page. Although slow and loud, this printer creates output that is indistinguishable from typewritten, making it ideally suited for high-end correspondence applications, in which a typewritten look is preferred.

Printers are classified as *parallel* or *serial,* depending on how computers communicate with them. A parallel printer must be connected to a *parallel port,* located on the back or side of the computer; a serial printer must be connected to a *serial port* (also called an *asynchronous communications adapter*). All else being equal, you might consider using a parallel printer before a serial one. Most computers have only two serial ports, and you might need them for hooking up modems, serial versions of the mouse, and another printer manufactured in a serial version only.

If you choose a serial printer, your computer and your printer must be matched to each other. This matching (configuring) takes many factors into account, among them the specification of certain settings such as transmission rate, that are handled by means of the DOS Mode command. Typically, the Mode command is placed in your AUTOEXEC.BAT file so that it executes automatically whenever you start or reboot your computer. For a LaserJet printer, the relevant line often is *mode com1:96,n,8,1,p,* indicating that communication between printer and computer will be on serial port 1, at a speed of 9600 baud, with no parity checking, and with 8 data bits and 1 stop bit.

WHAT IS A FONT?

If you're confused about exactly what constitutes a font, perhaps it is because the computer industry is somewhat confused itself.

Terms such as *font* and *typeface* are thrown about rather imprecisely—with Word being one of the offenders because what Word considers a font is, in fact, a typeface.

We'll define the term *font* and explain why what Word calls a font really isn't a font at all, and then we'll go right on calling it a font because that's what Word calls it.

A true font (as opposed to what Word considers a font) is a cohesive collection of characters that assigns one distinct appearance to each character or symbol. In a given font, the uppercase A can appear only one way although it might increase or decrease in size or be underlined. It cannot be italicized or boldfaced or condensed, because these variations each constitute a new font.

A typeface is a family of fonts, related by appearance and name. A typeface has an overall design, leaving a stylistic impression. When we boldface or italicize a font, we are actually using a different font of the same typeface.

For instance, each of these examples relies on a different font of the Helvetica typeface:

24-pt. Helvetica

24-pt. Helvetica

24-pt. Helvetica

WHEN A FONT IS NOT AVAILABLE

Sometimes a printer is asked to print a font that is not available. In such a case, the printer attempts to choose a similar font, which is why you might find that your printed documents don't always match the character formatting you have specified.

For example, when you request a font that the Hewlett-Packard LaserJet doesn't have, it compares all the fonts it does have against the following criteria:

- **Orientation**—The LaserJet printer first eliminates any of its fonts that fail to match the orientation of the desired font. For example, if the requested font is in *portrait* orientation, the printer eliminates those fonts that are in *landscape* orientation. In portrait orientation, the page is taller than it is wide; in landscape orientation, the opposite is true.

- **Character set**—The printer next eliminates fonts that have a different character set (also called *symbol set*) than the requested font. A character set describes which characters can be produced with the font. Of more than 1000 characters and symbols typically available in a font, only 256 distinct characters can be included in a character set. The font's character set defines which characters shall be included and which excluded, and it associates each of the included characters with one of 256 numbers. For example, the number 206 is associated with a graphics character of two vertical lines intersecting with two horizontal lines (╬) in the character set used on your computer screen, but it produces a close-quotation mark character (") when printed on a PostScript printer.

- **Spacing**—If the requested font is *proportionally spaced*, the printer disregards fonts that are monospaced. Similarly, if the requested font is *monospaced*, the printer disregards proportionally spaced fonts. A proportional font is one in which characters assume different widths, depending on their proportions. These provide a typeset look. Monospaced fonts, most notably Courier, cause every character to use the same amount of space, whether the character is a period (.) or a capital W. This results in a typewritten look.

- **Pitch**—If the font is monospaced and measured by the number of characters per inch (the *pitch*), Word eliminates other fonts that are dissimilar in pitch. Pitch is a term from the typewriter world: a Pica typewriter, producing 10 characters per inch, is *10-pitch;* an Elite typewriter, producing 12 characters per inch, is *12-pitch*. See the boxed discussion of points versus pitch.

- **Height**—Next the printer removes from consideration those fonts that do not match the height of the desired font. *Font height* is measured in points (pts). There are 72 points to the inch; Word deems one standard line as 12 points, or ⅙ inch. Somewhat confusingly, a 10-point monospaced font is 12-pitch, whereas a 12-point monospaced font is 10-pitch. See the boxed discussion of points versus pitch.
- **Shear**—*Shear* refers to whether or not a font is italic. Of the remaining pool of available fonts, the printer eliminates those whose shear does not match that of the requested font.

DISTINGUISH BETWEEN POINTS AND PITCH

Learn to distinguish between the two type-size measurements—points and pitch—Word uses. Both measurements are related to inches, but they have different meanings:

- Typographically, a *point* is approximately 1/72 inch. The higher the point number, the taller the characters.
- *Pitch* is a unit of width, as in *10-pitch* or *12-pitch*. The number tells how many monospaced (nonproportional, or typewriter-like) characters will fit side by side in an inch of space. The higher the pitch number, the more characters to the inch and, generally, the narrower the width of each character.

If you are used to thinking in terms of typewriters, you might know that "normal" 10-pitch type is called Pica and "normal" 12-pitch type is called Elite. Pica type is taller and wider than Elite. Keep this in mind, and remember that for most printers Word assumes that

- Pica is 12-point but 10-pitch.
- Elite is 10-point but 12-pitch.

When you are formatting documents, you choose type size by specifying a point size in the Point Size drop-down list box of the Format Character command's dialog box. Daisy-wheel and many dot-matrix printers tend to measure character size in pitch (also known as *characters per inch*, or *cpi*).

- **Weight**—*Weight* reflects the relative boldness of a font. The LaserJet next casts aside those choices that don't match the weight of the requested font.
- **Typeface**—If multiple fonts meet the preceding criteria, the printer attempts to give you the typeface you requested—Bookman instead of Times Roman, for example.

Let's use this list to predict what a LaserJet will do when it does not have a requested font. Imagine that a document's formatting calls for 12-point Courier italic, but the printer does not have this font available. It does, however, have 12-point Courier (nonitalic), 12-point Courier bold, 10-point Prestige Elite italic, and 12-point Times Roman italic. When the request for 12-point Courier italic reaches the LaserJet, it works its way though the list of criteria, eliminating fonts until only one remains.

To convert pitch to points, divide 120 by the pitch. To convert points to pitch, divide 120 by the points. For example, if you know that a font is 8-point and you want to know its pitch, divide 120 by 8. You'll find that the font is a 15-pitch font.

Here are some common conversions:

Points	Pitch (characters per inch)
6	20
7.5	16
8	15
8.5	14
9	13
10	12
11	10.9
12	10
13	9.2
14.5	8.3
15	8
16	7.5
18	6.7
20	6
24	5
30	4

For the sake of our example, we'll assume that the orientation and character set of all the fonts are identical and match those of the requested font. This means that the first two criteria do not reduce the number of fonts competing to stand in for 12-point Courier italic.

The third criterion, spacing, causes 12-point Times Roman italic to be cast aside. Although it is 12-point and italic, this font is proportional whereas the Courier italic is monospaced (nonproportional).

The fourth criterion, pitch, eliminates 10-point Prestige Elite italic. It is a monospaced italic font, but it is 12-pitch whereas the desired font is 10-pitch.

The fifth criterion, height, has no bearing because the height of both remaining fonts is 12 points.

The sixth criterion is shear. The desired font is 12-point Courier italic, which means that any nonitalic font remaining should be rejected. However, neither of the remaining fonts is italic, so shear is ignored as a factor.

The seventh criterion is weight, and here there is a difference. The desired font is not bold, but one of the two remaining candidates is bold. So 12-point Courier bold is eliminated, leaving 12-point Courier as the sole remaining candidate. It is this font that is printed as a substitute for the unavailable 12-point Courier italic.

CHARACTER SETS

A font isn't the finest unit of differentiation between characters, however. That honor lies with the character set. As already noted, a character set maps numbers to specific characters in a given font.

A character is represented inside a personal computer by a number from 0 through 255. Several of these numbers are reserved for special purposes and hence have no printable representation (and are thus referred to as *nonprinting characters*). Some of these numbers represent different characters in different situations.

A character set associates each character number with a symbol in a given font. The ASCII standard symbol set, used in PCs and Macintoshes, reserves the first 128 characters (0 through 127). For example, ASCII character 97 is the lowercase *a*. The remaining 128 characters, in the range 128 through 255, represent different characters depending on the character set in use. Often you can choose from among several symbol sets for a single font. Bitstream's downloadable fonts, for example, can be installed with your choice of character sets. You might choose a character set that has graphical symbols so that lines appearing on your screen print identically; or you might choose a character set with mathematical symbols or one optimized for writing in French.

Most fonts adhere to the ASCII standard for the first 128 characters, but some do not. For example, a math font might assign mathematical symbols in lieu of letters of the alphabet, and the PostScript Dingbats font uses a character set that replaces all normal letters of the alphabet with check boxes, copyright symbols, and various other ornaments useful for commercial publications. The LaserJet's legal character set substitutes a few of the 128 characters to meet the needs of legal documents. For instance, number 94 is a caret (^) in the normal ASCII character set but a copyright symbol (©)

CHAPTER THIRTY-ONE: Printing and Fonts   617

in the legal character set. Word lets you mix and match fonts on a single line. The character set of your screen does not change when you change the character set used by the printer. For example, one of the Dingbat characters is a check mark, which is character 052 formatted with the Dingbat font. On your screen, character 052 is the numeral 4. If you type a 4 and leave it formatted in Courier or Helvetica or any other conventional face with a conventional character set, it will print as a 4. But if you format the character with the Dingbat font, it will print as a check mark because the font uses a different character set.

Character sets diverge most dramatically in the characters they assign to ASCII numbers above 127. IBM chose a set particularly heavy in graphics characters for use on computer screens, and most other computers use the same set for their screens. Hewlett-Packard calls this the PC-8 set, and it is available from several sources, including the LaserJet Y font cartridge. In other words, anything on the screen will print the same way when the Y cartridge is installed in a LaserJet printer. Advertisements for dot-matrix printers often refer to this character set as the *IBM character set*.

When the character set used by your printer differs from the character set used by your screen, the characters printed can differ markedly from the characters that appear on the screen. Generally you can remedy this by printing with a different character set (which might mean a different font) or by using (or constructing) a different printer file, one that calls into play the character set you want.

TECHNICALLY, WHAT IS A FONT?

So far we've talked about a font from the perspective of you, the user. Now let's consider it from the standpoint of the computer.

Fonts rely on different technologies. The most common kind of font, though this is changing, is a *bitmap*. This kind of font maps a number from 0 through 255 to a *bitmap*, a sequence of 1's and 0's that indicates which dots to paint black and which dots to leave white. When you print an ASCII 97 (the character *a*), the printer looks up in the current font the bitmap associated with ASCII 97 and displays a replica of the 1's in the bitmap. The printer is not acting intelligently; it is simply using a stencil to knock out a character of given size and appearance. When you use a font product that must individually download each size to the printer, you are using a bitmap font. Bitmap fonts are simple, inflexible, and extremely demanding of hard-disk space. However, they print quickly because they are straightforward; after all, the printer is merely using a stencil.

A more sophisticated kind of font defines a character as a sequence of lines and curves rather than as a finite number of bits in an array. Thus, when a printer is asked to print the letter *a*, it looks up entry 97, extracts a formula that creates the needed sequence of lines and curves, and draws each in turn. The resulting composite picture is the requested character. Because the printer has access to the internal form of a character, it often can apply stylistic variations, such as italicizing or scaling, by modifying the lines and curves. Fonts that behave in this manner are called *outline fonts* because the sequence of lines and curves can be thought of as describing the outline of the character, or *scalable fonts* because a single formula can be scaled up or down to define a character of any size (typically, from 3-point to 120-point or more).

Taken to an extreme, an outline font can be a collection of programs that each renders a single character. Thus, when a printer wants to print the character *a*, it simply runs the *a* program. Of course, the result will only look like an *a* if the program happens to actually draw an *a*; this is the case most of the time, but it does not have to be. A single font can be scaled, outlined, filled, italicized, shadowed, rotated, or contorted because it is based on a formula, and the formula can be manipulated.

As might be expected, this increased complexity and sophistication comes with a cost: speed. Because a program might have to do a lot of computation, it can take a long time to draw using an outline font or one of these *program* fonts. Because of this, most printers that use outline fonts use a memory cache that stores a bitmapped image of each character after it has been created by a program and formula. In this way, the computation required to generate any character needs to be done only once per document.

Traditionally, LaserJet printers have relied on bitmaps, whereas PostScript printers have been the most prominent examples of printers that work with formula-based, scalable fonts.

With the advent of the LaserJet III, however, scalable fonts are becoming more common, and PostScript is losing a little bit of its grip on the market for scalable fonts. It would seem that bitmapped fonts are, in the long run, more or less doomed.

THE PRINTER FILE

You choose fonts with the ribbon or Format Character, but how does Word know which choices are available? It consults the Word printer file.

Word can use any of a large number of printers with differing capabilities and requirements. Initially, you tell Word which printer make and model you have when you run its SETUP program. If you have more than one printer, you tell Word about each one. Word then copies the printer files (.PRD files) that it needs in order to work with the printer (or printers) you have named.

After you use SETUP to tell Word about each of your printers, you can link Word to a specific printer file by using the File Printer Setup command. Word displays the name of the printer file to use. You can choose among any printer files that were decompressed and made available by the SETUP program. (In the event that you need a printer file that you didn't instruct SETUP to decompress, you can run SETUP again. Details are in Appendix A.)

By loading a printer file, you give Word the specific information that enables it to work with your printer—information such as the fonts and type sizes it can use and how to communicate accurate font data to the printer. Such information, stored in the printer file, lets Word present a list of available fonts and sizes in the fields of the Character dialog box or the fields of the ribbon.

But printing matters aren't always straightforward. For one thing, the font capabilities of laser printers and certain other printers can change, depending on how

CHAPTER THIRTY-ONE: Printing and Fonts

you've set up the printer and your computer and on what options you are using. In such cases, it might take more than a single printer file to describe the fonts that are available on a printer. The classic case involves Hewlett-Packard LaserJet printers and printers that emulate LaserJets. The font capabilities of the LaserJet vary, depending on which fonts are available. All LaserJets have Courier in the 12-point size, and you can load additional fonts by using cartridges that plug into the printer. Furthermore, all but the original LaserJet let you download fonts. When you download a font, your computer stores the information needed for the printer to create a particular font and supplies this information as needed. Because a large number of downloadable fonts are available and because printers such as the LaserJet II allow two font cartridges, as well as downloadable fonts, to be used simultaneously, a whole array of printer files is needed to reflect the possibilities. Broadening the choices even more is the advent of the LaserJet III, which provides scalable fonts. The upshot is that you might need to switch among various printer files, depending on what you want to format and print.

Word works with any printer that works with your computer, but it makes the best use of printers that have printer files written specifically for them. If you're thinking of buying a printer, there's some logic in choosing one for which a Word printer file exists—although nearly all popular printers now have printer files, and for those that don't, generic "standard" .PRD files (TTY.PRD, TTYBS.PRD, TTYFF.PRD, and TTYWHEEL.PRD) allow the basic features of any printer to be used with Word. Each autumn, *PC Magazine* does an impressive roundup of printers. (One such issue was published November 13, 1990.)

Some printer manufacturers supply printer files for Word, but you'll find several hundred of them on the printer disks and supplementary disks for Word 5.5.

Word 5.5 can use printer files created for Word 5.0, but Word 5.0 cannot use printer files created for Word 5.5. That's because additional features are built into the Word 5.5 printer drivers, and Word 5.0 is not equipped to interpret the information. In general, if you are using Word 5.5 you are better off with printer drivers created specifically for it.

In addition, Word comes with two printer-file management programs, one of which is easy to use, the other more difficult. The first one is MergePRD, which lets you assemble custom printer files based on existing printer files. It also lets you make small modifications to a printer file, such as changing the line-drawing character set (useful if you are unable to get your printer to produce the lines that show on the screen).

The more challenging program is MakePRD, which converts a printer file into a readable form so that you can modify it in sophisticated ways, thereby better tailoring the operation of your printer to your needs.

For information on the use of both of these programs, as well as for specific information on how to download fonts, see the separate "Printer Information for Microsoft Word" manual that comes with Word 5.5.

GENERIC FONTS

Word thinks of fonts in generic terms, such as modern a, modern b, decor e, and roman i. In all, Word can accommodate 64 fonts at a time. Here is a list of the 64 generic font names and the literal font names that Microsoft suggests be associated with each.

Font number	Generic font name	Reserved for
0	Modern a	Pica/Courier/Titan
1	Modern b	Courier/Pica-D
2	Modern c	Elite
3	Modern d	Prestige/Elite-D
4	Modern e	Lettergothic/Gothic/NLQ
5	Modern f	Gothic-PS/NLQ-D
6	Modern g	Cubic-PS
7	Modern h	Lineprinter
8	Modern i	Helvetica
9	Modern j	Avant Garde
10	Modern k	Spartan
11	Modern l	Metro
12	Modern m	Presentation
13	Modern n	APL
14	Modern o	OCR-A
15	Modern p	OCR-B
16	Roman a	Printer's Standard Roman
17	Roman b	Emperor-PS/Trend-PS/Modern-PS
18	Roman c	Madeleine/Karena
19	Roman d	Zapf Humanist
20	Roman e	Classic
21	Roman f	Optional, serif font
22	Roman g	Optional, serif font
23	Roman h	Optional, serif font
24	Roman i	Times Roman
25	Roman j	Century
26	Roman k	Palatino
27	Roman l	Souvenir
28	Roman m	Garamond

CHAPTER THIRTY-ONE: Printing and Fonts

Font number	Generic font name	Reserved for
29	Roman n	Caledonia
30	Roman o	Bodoni
31	Roman p	University
32	Script a	Script
33	Script b	Script-PS
34	Script c	Optional, serif cursive font
35	Script d	Optional, serif cursive font
36	Script e	Commercial Script
37	Script f	Park Avenue
38	Script g	Coronet
39	Script h	Optional, serif cursive font
40	Foreign a	Greek
41	Foreign b	Kana
42	Foreign c	Hebrew
43	Foreign d	Optional
44	Foreign e	Russian
45	Foreign f	Optional
46	Foreign g	Optional
47	Foreign h	Optional
48	Decor a	Narrator/Orator
49	Decor b	Emphasis
50	Decor c	Zapf Chancery
51	Decor d	Optional decorative font
52	Decor e	Old English/Old World
53	Decor f	Optional decorative font
54	Decor g	Optional decorative font
55	Decor h	Cooper Black
56	Symbol a	Symbol/Pi
57	Symbol b	Linedraw/Forms
58	Symbol c	Math 7
59	Symbol d	Math 8
60	Symbol e	Bar 3 of 9
61	Symbol f	EAN/UPC
62	Symbol g	PCLine
63	Symbol h	Optional symbol font

The generic name modern a is Pica on a Diablo 630 but Courier on a LaserJet. If you format characters to be Pica when the Diablo printer file is installed, Word considers the characters to be modern a. It shows them as Pica for your convenience as long as it thinks you'll be printing the document on a Diablo printer. But when you install an appropriate LaserJet printer file, Word starts calling the modern a characters Courier.

The virtue of this system is that you can format a document with one printer in mind and then switch to a different printer with at least some confidence in the printed page that will result.

SOURCES OF FONTS

Two general sources of fonts are available for laser printers, aside from those that are built in: cartridge fonts and downloadable fonts. In either case, the fonts provided can be bitmaps of formulas (scalable fonts).

Cartridge Fonts

Cartridge fonts plug into a slot in the printer and, when they provide bitmaps, offer a few different faces. This is a relatively expensive way to acquire fonts, but it has the distinct advantage of making the fonts available to the printer on an instant's notice. A cartridge might cost $250 and contain only a few fonts, although some companies now are providing large numbers of fonts—sometimes dozens—in cartridges costing only a few hundred dollars.

Downloadable Fonts

A more flexible (and sometimes more economical) source is downloadable fonts. These fonts are stored on your computer's disk and are sent to the printer as needed. It takes time for this information to be passed, but downloadable fonts provide the flexibility of myriad sizes and variations. And by having a large number of fonts available on your disk, you have a whole library of typefaces available for your documents. Downloadable fonts range widely in price, and virtually all of them work with Word.

Generally, before you can use a downloadable font, you must process it with a font manager that puts it in an appropriate form for Word. (Be sure that the manager is appropriate for your specific version of Word.) Font managers generally create matching printer files too. In addition, Word must have access to a .DAT file that matches any printer file you will be using with the downloadable fonts.

SAMPLE FONTS

To get you thinking about fonts, here are the fonts typically supplied in a PostScript printer. Keep in mind that while these fonts are printed here in a single size, each one can be scaled to more than 100 different sizes.

CHAPTER THIRTY-ONE: Printing and Fonts

Times
Times Bold
Times Italic
Times Bold Italic

Courier
Courier Bold
Courier Oblique
Courier Bold Oblique

Helvetica
Helvetica Bold
Helvetica Oblique
Helvetica Bold Oblique

Helvetica Narrow
Helvetica Narrow Bold
Helvetica Narrow Oblique
Helvetica Narrow Bold Oblique

ITC Avant Garde Book
ITC Avant Garde Demi
ITC Avant Garde Book Oblique
ITC Avant Garde Demi Oblique

New Century Schoolbook Roman
New Century Schoolbook Bold
New Century Schoolbook Italic
New Century Schoolbook Bold Italic

Palatino Roman
Palatino Bold
Palatino Italic
Palatino Bold Italic

(continued)

continued

ITC Bookman Light
ITC Bookman Demi
ITC Bookman Light Italic
ITC Bookman Demi Italic

Zapf Chancery Medium Italic

Symbol— αβχδεφγηιφκλμνοπθρστυϖωξψζ
ΑΒΧΔΕΦΓΗΙϑΚΛΜΝΟΠΘΡΣΤΥς
ΩΞΨΖ0123456789−=∴;∍,./ ♣ ♦ ♥ ♠
(!≅#∃%⊥&*)_+|{ }[]: ∀ <>?~•÷≠

Zapf Dingbats—✡✜✢✣✤✥✦✧★☆✩✪✫✬✭✮✯✰
✱✲✳✴✵✶✷✸✹✺✻✼✽✾✿❀❁❂●○■□❏❐▲▼◆❖
❘❙❚❛❜✓✔✗✘✙✚✛✜✝✞✟✠✡✢✣❞❡
❩❪❨❫❬❭❮❯❰❱❲❳❴❵❛❜❝❞

PART IV
Appendixes

APPENDIX A

Setting Up and Setting Options

Setting up Word gets easier all the time because Microsoft's setup procedures keep improving. This appendix tells you what equipment you need to run Word, explains how to run it on a network or from floppy disks, briefly describes how to install Word, lists the choices you have when you start Word, summarizes how you set options to tailor Word to your preferences, and offers tips on how to run Word through Microsoft Windows or with OS/2 rather than DOS.

EQUIPMENT YOU NEED

You need a computer with at least two floppy-disk drives or, preferably, one floppy-disk and one hard-disk drive. Word takes advantage of the capabilities of relatively powerful computers, such as IBM ATs, IBM PS/2s, or 386/486 machines. But Word works satisfactorily even on original PCs with only floppy-disk drives. Because it runs on such a wide range of hardware, Word is an ideal choice for offices or for people who have more than one computer.

You can use Word and Word for Windows side by side. For instance, you might use Word for Windows on your 386-based or 486-based computer and use Word on your laptop or home computer. Or an office might be set up with the majority of the people using Word but a few people (such as page designers) using Word for Windows to refine and print the critical work of others. Word for Windows can read and write Word files.

In addition to a computer, you need either MS-DOS version 2.0 (or later) or OS/2. For Word 5.5, a computer with a hard disk needs a minimum of 384 KB of free memory under DOS 3.3. As a practical matter, you should have at least 512 KB of memory (preferably more) available before you start Word. To check whether you do, use the DOS

CHKDSK command at the DOS prompt before you start Word. This command reports the status of your hard disk, reports on the amount of conventional memory that DOS recognizes in your system, and then reports how much is available.

More is better, but just adding memory to your computer might not be enough. Beyond 640 KB, the memory must be configured as expanded memory. Whether or not you must configure it deliberately depends on your hardware, your version of DOS, whether you are running Windows, and other factors beyond the scope of this appendix.

Display and Adapter

The information Word employed to work with the various combinations of adapters and displays used to be built into earlier versions of the program. But the number of possibilities has grown so great that Word now uses separate *drivers* for each kind of display adapter. Word's SETUP program creates and installs the appropriate driver and gives it the name SCREEN.VID. Without SCREEN.VID, Word runs only in character (text, or nongraphics) mode.

The following chart lists the video modes supported by .VID files that ship with Word. Microsoft might release other .VID files, or other manufacturers might choose to release .VID files that support Word. In the chart, the letters (A through DD) are arbitrary and have meaning only in the context of this discussion.

(A)	Text mode, 25 lines × 80 characters, 2 colors	(M)	640 × 480 res, 30 lines × 80 characters, 2 colors
(B)	Text mode, 25 lines × 80 characters, 16 colors	(N)	640 × 480 res, 60 lines × 80 characters, 2 colors
(C)	640 × 200 res, 25 lines × 80 characters, 2 colors	(O)	Text mode, 50 lines × 80 characters, 2 colors
(D)	640 × 200 res, 25 lines × 80 characters, 16 colors	(P)	640 × 480 res, 30 lines × 80 characters, 16 colors
(E)	Text mode, 25 lines × 80 characters, 16 colors	(Q)	Text mode, 25 lines × 80 characters, 16 colors
(F)	640 × 350 res, 25 lines × 80 characters, 2 colors	(R)	640 × 480 res, 60 lines × 80 characters, 16 colors
(G)	Text mode, 43 lines × 80 characters, 16 colors	(S)	Text mode, 50 lines × 80 characters, 16 colors
(H)	640 × 350 res, 43 lines × 80 characters, 2 colors	(T)	1024 × 768 res, 38 lines × 102 characters, 16 colors
(I)	640 × 350 res, 25 lines × 80 characters, 16 colors	(U)	1024 × 768 res, 48 lines × 128 characters, 16 colors
(J)	Text mode, 25 lines × 80 characters, 16 colors	(V)	720 × 348 res, 25 lines × 80 characters, 2 colors
(K)	640 × 350 res, 43 lines × 80 characters, 16 colors	(W)	720 × 348 res, 43 lines × 90 characters, 2 colors
(L)	Text mode, 43 lines × 80 characters, 16 colors	(X)	Ramfont mode, 25 lines × 80 characters, 2 colors

APPENDIX A: Setting Up and Setting Options

(Y)	Ramfont mode, 35 lines × 90 characters, 2 colors	(BB)	Text mode, 66 lines × 80 characters, 2 colors
(Z)	Ramfont mode (no mouse), 25 lines × 80 characters, 16 colors	(CC)	1008 × 728 res, 66 lines × 80 characters, 2 colors
(AA)	Ramfont mode (no mouse), 35 lines × 90 characters, 16 colors	(DD)	640 × 400 res, 25 lines × 80 characters, 2 colors

Various display adapters are listed below, along with the video modes from the above list that they support.

Monochrome Display Adapter (MDA)—Mode A. This adapter is inexpensive, relatively high in resolution, and scrolls and updates the screen quickly; however, it allows no color or graphics. Italicized text, for example, appears underlined. The adapter has a parallel printer port, which is handy.

Color Graphics Adapter (CGA)—Modes B and C. This adapter was once a standard for IBM PCs, but now newer adapters and displays provide far better resolution. Definitely not recommended.

Enhanced Graphics Adapter (EGA) with 64 KB of video memory—Modes A through H. The resolution (640 by 350 pixels) is slightly lower than for either the monochrome or the Hercules card, but the resolution difference seems negligible. The EGA card permits using Word with a condensed 43-line by 80-character screen display.

Enhanced Graphics Adapter (EGA) with 128 KB or 256 KB of video memory—Modes A through L. The resolution of this adapter is acceptable for word processing, but it's not as good as that of a monochrome system.

Multicolor Graphics Array (MCGA) (IBM Personal System/2 Model 25 or 30)—Modes A, M, N, and O. This is a junior version of the VGA and lacks some of its modes.

Video Graphics Array (VGA) (IBM Personal System/2 Model 50, 60, or 80)—Modes A through S. This adapter has emerged as the new standard in video adapters. It has improved resolution (640 by 480 pixels) compared with the EGA, which makes it possible to see as many as 60 lines of text displayed on the screen.

IBM 8514/A—Modes A through U. If this adapter is running under OS/2 rather than under DOS, the B, S, T, and U modes are not available. This is a superset of the VGA.

Hercules GB101, GB102—Modes A, V, and W. This adapter, not available under OS/2, has the virtues of the monochrome card, but with graphics. Graphics mode is not as fast as text mode, however, and shows 90 characters per line instead of 80. Most of the inexpensive monochrome graphics adapters are clones of Hercules adapters.

Hercules Plus GB112—Modes V, W, X, and Y. This adapter is not available under OS/2. If you run Word on a system with both a Hercules Ramfont GB112 and a Hercules Color adapter GB200, the GB112 must be set to Full using the utility provided with the adapter by Hercules.

Hercules GB222 (Ramfonts or Color Support)—Modes V, X, Y, Z, and AA. This adapter, not available under OS/2, does what the Hercules Plus Card GB112 does, and it also lets you display color in graphics mode if you have an EGA-compatible color display monitor.

Genius—Modes BB and CC. This adapter, not available under OS/2, lets you preview complete 8.5-inch by 11-inch pages before printing, because the monitor has a vertical rather than a horizontal orientation.

AT&T 6300—Modes B and DD. This adapter supports a 640-pixel by 400-pixel monochrome mode in addition to the normal text mode.

COMPAQ Portable III or Portable 386—Modes B and DD. This adapter supports a 640-pixel by 400-pixel monochrome mode in addition to the normal text mode.

Ericsson—Modes B and DD. This adapter supports a 640-pixel by 400-pixel monochrome mode in addition to the normal text mode.

Hewlett-Packard Vectra—Modes B and DD. This adapter supports a 640-pixel by 400-pixel monochrome mode in addition to the normal text mode.

Toshiba T3100 Personal Computers—Modes B and DD. This adapter supports a 640-pixel by 400-pixel monochrome mode in addition to the normal text mode.

The Microsoft Mouse

The mouse is handy, but both its hardware and software must be installed before you can use it. Your mouse manual covers the installation of the hardware, and the SETUP program installs the basic mouse software.

You should install the mouse driver supplied with Word 5.5 on your system, even if you have already installed a mouse driver. The new mouse driver will work with existing software, including Windows 3.0. If you use a mouse that isn't compatible with the Microsoft Mouse, contact the manufacturer for the latest mouse driver.

Printers and Other Peripherals

Most people use a printer, and by the time you buy this book you might already have one. For a basic discussion of printers and how they are used with Word, see the beginning of Chapter 31.

A variety of other peripherals might be useful:

A *modem* for telecommunications makes better sense each year, as the price goes down and as the number of people and services relying on electronic transmissions goes up. Purchase as fast a modem as you can afford because the costs of long-distance telephone calls and connect charges to services such as CompuServe soon eat up any savings you achieve through purchasing a slow modem. Today, anything slower than 2400 baud is a slow modem.

Scanners are becoming popular, although they remain expensive. A scanner converts a printed image into electronic form in one of two ways.

- In the first, the printed page or portion of a printed page is treated as a graphics image. Such an image can be imported into Word and printed as a picture by using the Insert Picture command. Text captured as a graphics image is only a picture to Word—you cannot edit it as text. Graphics images consume vast amounts of disk space, although various compression schemes can cut file size quite substantially.
- In the second type of conversion, text is "recognized" by software and converted into a document file that can be edited in Word. For example, the software package Wordscan Plus, by Calera, can read a great number of typefaces, differentiate between normal text and boldface or italic text, check words against a spell checker dictionary, and save the resulting document in Word 5.5 format (which is the same as Word 5 format). Character-recognition software packages, such as Wordscan Plus, are not perfect, but they are acceptable.

NETWORKS AND ENVIRONMENT VARIABLES

If you are setting Word up on a network or on a floppy-disk system, you might want to read this section to better understand the role of environment variables.

You can communicate your desires to Word through its menus, with the function keys, or with a mouse. Another way to pass important information to Word is through *environment variables*, a method often overlooked because you use it before you even start Word.

DOS reserves a region of memory, called the *environment,* so that symbolic names and values can be associated with each other. Programs such as Word (and DOS itself) can read information from the environment that often tells the program how to behave. For example, your AUTOEXEC.BAT file should contain a Path statement that defines for the computer a list of directories in which to look when you type a command name. This list is stored in the environment.

To use environment variables to tailor Word's performance, you enter them with the DOS Set command, either by typing them at the DOS prompt or by placing them in the AUTOEXEC.BAT file. The Set command defines an environment variable name and its value. However, you should set environment variables before you load any terminate-and-stay-resident programs, such as SideKick or Capture, the screen-image-capture program that comes with Word. If you try to set an environment variable after running a TSR, you might receive the following message: *Out of environment space.*

Word 5.5 monitors two environment variables, *TMP* and *MSWNET55.* (If you also have an old version of Word 5.0 loaded, your computer will monitor *MSWNET* too. The version of Word 5.0 shipped with Word 5.5 pays attention to *MSWNET55* rather than *MSWNET.*)

You can use the DOS statement *SET TMP = C:\temp* to write temporary files created by Word to the *\temp* directory of the C drive. If you use only floppy disks, you can use the statement *SET TMP = B:* to write the files to the B drive because the Word Program disk in the A drive might not have much room in temporary files. Similarly, you can specify that temporary files be written to some other directory of some other drive or to a *RAM disk*. (A RAM disk isn't really a disk at all but an area of random-access memory.)

You can use the DOS statement *SET MSWNET55 = drive\directory* in the AUTOEXEC.BAT file of a workstation that is connected to a network to do three things. First this statement notifies Word to run in network mode. Second it tells Word upon startup to check the specified drive and directory (called the *local Word directory*) for *configuration files*—files that instruct Word exactly how to set itself up. MW.INI and SCREEN.VID are examples of such files. Similarly, this statement tells Word at the end of the Word session to write the MW.INI file to the local Word directory. The third result of creating an MSWNET55 environment variable is more subtle. It tells Word to set the Default Path text box of the File Open (Options) command to the MSWNET55 directory when you choose File Open (Options) and then press Del to remove the existing directory name from the field. This works only if the corresponding Always Use as Default check box is not checked. If the environment variable is not set, this procedure causes the start-up directory to be listed in the Default Path text box. (The start-up directory is the directory that was active when you typed *word* to start the program.)

Each workstation can have its own *MSWNET55* environment variable; hence, Word can practically treat each workstation as a separate computer rather than as a station on a network. This lets the user of one workstation run a color monitor and keep menus displayed on the screen at all times while the user of another workstation runs a monochrome monitor and keeps menus turned off.

For example, if the environment variable on your workstation were set up as *SET MSWNET55 = C:\word*, Word would run in network mode and would expect to find individual configuration files, such as MW.INI, stored on the Word directory of the C drive. (For information on the MW.INI file, see the discussion titled "What Word Remembers" in Chapter 8.)

USING SETUP

Word's SETUP program prepares Word for your computer, display, printer, and mouse (if you have one). SETUP is simple to run and steps you through the installation procedure by asking for information, such as the directory in which you want to install the Word program files, or by requesting you to tell it about your computer system by choosing from lists it displays. Along the way, SETUP prompts you to insert the disks it needs, and it tells you what is happening each time your disk drives start up. There's no need to hurry because SETUP waits patiently for you to continue. And if, at any time, you become confused or make a mistake, SETUP allows you to quit and start over.

Word can run under either MS-DOS or OS/2, and either on a stand-alone computer or on a network. It's clever enough to look around, find out where and on what type of machine it's running, and act accordingly. The only real differences in the way you install Word depend on two factors.

APPENDIX A: Setting Up and Setting Options   633

- Whether you install on floppy disks or on a hard disk.
- Whether you install on an independent (stand-alone) computer or on a network workstation.

And neither of these differences is at all problematic.

For example, if you have a floppy-disk system with 360-KB drives, SETUP will place Word 5.5 on three disks for you: one that you use to start the program, another that stays in place during most of the time you use Word, and one that you slip into the disk drive, at Word's request, when you want to do such specialized things as check spellings, find a synonym, or ask for online help. For example, if you ask for help Word will in turn ask you to insert a disk containing the file MW.HLP. You then insert your help disk (whether it is Microsoft's original help or MasterWord Help) in a disk drive, removing the document disk if necessary. When you are through reading the help, you return to working on your document, replacing the help disk with the document disk.

On the other hand, if you have a hard disk, the SETUP program combines several smaller files into one large one on your disk so that Word operates as fast as possible.

Before you run the SETUP program, you need the following information:

- The type of computer you have. If it is an IBM-compatible computer, you should know the IBM model to which it corresponds (PC, XT, AT, or PS/2). If your computer is 386-based or 486-based, it is considered part of the AT family.
- The type of display adapter and/or monitor you have. (SETUP checks your video card and tells you what it thinks it has found, asking you to confirm that it is correct.)
- The make and model of printer you will be using and the port to which it is connected (usually LPT1: for a parallel printer; COM1: for a serial printer).
- If you will be using a mouse, whether it is of the bus or serial variety. A bus mouse plugs into a circuit board specifically designed to host the mouse and possibly other peripherals, whereas a serial mouse plugs into a serial port.

After you are armed with information about your hardware, your next step depends on whether you are installing Word on floppy disks or on a hard disk. If you are installing on floppy disks, set aside a generous supply of blank formatted disks. If you are installing on a hard disk, choose a directory to hold Word. You can install a Word update in the directory currently occupied by an earlier version; SETUP will take care of replacing old program files with new ones. If you choose a nonexistent directory, the SETUP program will create it for you.

Now you're ready. Turn on or restart your computer, set the active (current) drive to A, and insert the SETUP disk in drive A.

If you are installing Word on a single-user system, type

setup

Press the Enter key, and follow the instructions that appear on your screen.

If you are installing Word on a network workstation (not the main network server), change to the server directory in which the Word program has previously been installed, and type

setup user

Press Enter, and follow the on-screen instructions.

SETUP first asks what sort of a setup you want. Use the direction keys to highlight one of the following options, and then press Enter to proceed.

- **Set up hard disk**—Choose this option to set up Word on your hard disk; you will be asked to specify a directory to which SETUP can copy the Word program files.
- **Set up floppy disk**—Choose this option to set up Word on a series of floppy disks.
- **Set up network**—Choose this option to set up Word to run from a network server.
- **View the README file**—README is a file that contains new information about the Word program—information not contained in the printed documentation. The README file also corrects known errors in the documentation.
- **Exit Setup**—Choose this option to cancel the setup operation. To cancel SETUP at another point in the program, press Ctrl+X.

After you choose what type of SETUP you want to run, Word prompts you for information about the configuration of your computer system—for example, what type of computer you have and what printer(s) you use. This tells SETUP what files Word needs in order to work properly with your hardware. You will also be asked whether you want to install Word's spell checker, thesaurus, and Learning Word files. Learning Word is a collection of interactive tutorials.

After SETUP knows what files to install, it asks whether you want to customize Word's settings. If you so choose, you can take this opportunity to set such options as the default page size and decide whether to start Word in text or graphics mode. If you choose not to customize the settings, Word will start with Microsoft's default settings. In either case, you can change any setting later, either from within Word or, if you have MasterWord, with the WordSet utility.

SETUP then prompts you to insert particular disks. Files from these disks are decompressed and copied to your Word program directory (if you are installing on a hard disk) or on floppy disks.

Finally, when Word is installed and customized, SETUP ends the installation by asking you to confirm changes it will make to AUTOEXEC.BAT and CONFIG.SYS, two files that affect your whole computer system. AUTOEXEC.BAT contains start-up instructions that are carried out each time you start or restart your computer. Among other things, AUTOEXEC.BAT on a hard-disk system can include a Path command that tells the operating system where to look for program files, such as Word. CONFIG.SYS is similar to AUTOEXEC.BAT in that your operating system carries out its commands each time you start or restart your computer. The difference between the two files is that CONFIG.SYS contains commands that describe your computer hardware. Among the commands that can be included in CONFIG.SYS are *DEVICE=* commands that tell the system about devices, such as a mouse, that you've attached to the computer.

When SETUP asks you to confirm its proposed changes to the AUTOEXEC.BAT and CONFIG.SYS files, tell it to go ahead. It will then modify the Path command in AUTOEXEC.BAT to include the Word program directory. If a Path command does not exist, SETUP will create one for you.

If you are working on a network workstation, SETUP also adds to your AUTOEXEC.BAT file the command *SET MSWNET55=<directory>*, where *<directory>* is the name of the Word directory you use on your computer. (The role of *MSWNET55* was discussed earlier in this appendix, in the section on environment variables.)

For your CONFIG.SYS file, SETUP will add or modify a line to read *FILES=20*, meaning that the system can maintain 20 open files and, if you have a mouse, will add or change a line to read *DEVICE=MOUSE.SYS*, identifying your mouse and the program that controls it.

When all of this is complete (it doesn't take long), SETUP runs through a few closing screens and ends the installation procedure. Word is now ready to go to work.

DECOMPRESSING A FILE

Most files on the Word disks are compressed to save disk space. Such files have an extension ending in a dollar sign ($). When you set up Word, those files the program believes you will need are decompressed and placed on your hard disk (or on your working floppy disks). In the event you want other files from the disks, such as a new printer file, you can run SETUP in a mode that decompresses a single file.

The syntax for decompressing a single file is

setup /d *filename$ filename*

The decompression switch is /d. The name of the compressed file is *filename$* (with the dollar sign). The name you give the decompressed file is *filename* (without the dollar sign). For example, to decompress the HPLASMS.PRD and store it in the WORD directory of the C drive, type

setup /d hplasms.prd$ c:\word\hplasms.prd

NOTE: *Word's executable (.EXE) files are read-only. Before you can delete an executable file, you must turn off its read-only attribute. Many utility programs can do this, as can the DOS (or OS/2) ATTRIB command.*

STARTUP CHOICES

After typing *word*, you have the option of typing a space and the name of a document you want Word to load. You can also type a forward slash (/) and a letter, called a *switch*, that starts Word in a particular way. A space before the slash is optional.

/l When you type *word/l*, Word starts up and also loads the last document you were working on. It even scrolls the document to the last place you were working and selects the same character(s) that were highlighted when you quit Word.

/i If you find a blinking cursor distracting or annoying, type *word/i* to turn off the blink. This will work only when you are running in a graphics mode.

/m macroname To have Word run a macro when it starts, type *word/m* followed by a space and then the name of the desired macro. If you want to run a particular macro each time you start Word, place it in your NORMAL.GLY file with the name AUTOEXEC.

/k If you have an enhanced keyboard (12 function keys) and an IBM-compatible computer that isn't fully compatible, your keyboard might not work properly. This can also occur when certain RAM-resident software is in memory while you use Word. Starting Word with the /k switch causes the computer to treat the keyboard as if it were not an enhanced model. This means you lose the use of the F11 and F12 keys, but you lose your problems too.

/bnnnn The /b switch influences how much conventional and expanded memory Word sets aside for disk buffering. The memory is measured in 512-byte units; you can type any number up to 1500 after the *b*. For example, typing *word/b300* would tell Word to set aside 150 KB of memory for disk buffering; typing *word/b1500* would tell Word to set aside the maximum amount of memory (750 KB, assuming you have that much memory available). If you don't use the /b switch, Word allocates 25 percent of free memory (both conventional and expanded) for buffers that can hold document information from disk. If you use the switch to increase the number of disk buffers, Word might perform document-intensive operations, such as scrolling and replacing, more quickly. However, increasing the number of buffers can slow certain other Word operations because less unreserved memory will be available.

/t If you are used to the way Word 5.0 uses function keys and the Insert and Delete keys and want to use them the same way in Word 5.5, start Word by typing *word/t*.

/p To return the function keys and the Insert and Delete keys to their default Word 5.5 functions, start Word by typing *word/p*.

/n On a Novell network, type *word/n* the first time you start Word. After you have used the /n switch, there's no easy way to change back; Word will remember the setting from one editing session to another. MasterWord's WordSet utility lets you turn the /n switch on and off, or you can delete the MW.INI file, thereby clearing Word's memory of all of its settings.

APPENDIX A: Setting Up and Setting Options

/w Ignores line spacing at the top of a page so that the first line printed on a page can print as high as the margins allow. If you are using Word 4.0 files formatted with small fonts or double line spacing, start Word with *word/w* to avoid excess line spacing at the tops of pages.

/x If you have expanded memory but do not want Word to use it, type *word/x* to start Word without it.

/y Type *word/y* to control how far Word scrolls up when you are typing and you reach the end of the last line of the screen. Prior to version 5.0, Word would scroll up one-half screen so that subsequent text you typed would appear beginning in the middle of the screen. In Word 5.0 and 5.5, however, the screen scrolls only a line at a time so that all your typing appears on the bottom line. If you prefer to have Word scroll one-half screen, as it did prior to Word 5.0, use the /y switch. You need to do this only once because Word remembers your preference indefinitely.

/z Starting Word by typing *word/z* reverses the effects of the other switches, returning them to the Word 5.5 defaults. For example, if you have used the /y switch previously to change the way Word scrolls up when your typing reaches the end of the screen, the /z switch returns the scrolling to its original behavior. The only exception is the /n switch, which cannot easily be returned to the Word 5.5 default.

SETTING OPTIONS

Word will tailor itself to your needs, preferences, and equipment (your printer, for example). Word remembers your chosen options even when the computer is turned off, so you needn't set most options more than once for any particular computer setup. Word remembers the settings by storing them on the Program disk or on the hard disk in the file called MW.INI. When you quit Word (by using File Exit Word), Word updates the MW.INI file. Whenever you start Word, it reads MW.INI, so it knows how to set the options.

Some of this tailoring is done when the SETUP program offers you choices for customizing Word. Additional choices can be made with internal Word commands.

View Preferences command Use this command to establish a customized look for your Word screen by choosing a display mode, by setting colors, and by turning the scroll bars, window borders, and other screen elements on or off.

Utilities Customize command Do you want Word to paginate as you type? How wide do you want a default tab stop to be? Do you want to type measurements in centimeters or in inches? These and other technical specifications are set in the dialog box of this command.

File Printer Setup command or File Print (Options) command Use these two commands to choose a .PRD file, set graphics resolution, and otherwise instruct Word on how to print documents.

You can also establish any of these settings with MasterWord's WordSet utility.

USING WORD THROUGH WINDOWS

The distinction between running Word *for* Windows and running Word *through* Windows can be confusing.

Word *for* Windows is a separate word processor that runs only in the Windows graphics environment. It offers a greater range of features than Word 5.5 and gives a true "What you see is what you get" screen display. It is not as fast as Word 5.5, however, and it seems that for every person who prefers to read the on-screen text of the Word for Windows screen, someone prefers the on-screen text of Word 5.5.

Running Word *through* Windows refers to starting Windows 3 or 3.1 and then running Word 5.5. Viewed in this way, Windows in effect becomes an extension of DOS. Provided you have a computer with some muscle—preferably a 386-based or 486-based machine with 2 MB or more of memory—running Word through Windows is advantageous. It guarantees access to expanded memory, and it lets you switch rapidly from one program to another by pressing Ctrl+Esc. (If you are running Word on a Hercules display adapter and are in a graphics mode, you cannot press Ctrl+Esc to switch to a different program. Instead, you must quit Word to return to Windows.)

After you have set up Word, you can install the program in Windows 3 by following these steps:

1. Start Windows, and open its Program Manager window if it is not open already.
2. Use the Program Manager's File New command, choose the Program Group option button, and then choose OK (Enter). (If you already have a program group into which you want to install Word 5.5, skip both this step and the next one.)
3. When the Program Group Properties dialog box appears, type *Microsoft Word 5.5* (or some title you prefer) in the Description text box. Choose OK (Enter). You've now defined a program group for Word 5.5.
4. Choose File New again, this time selecting the Program Item option button. Choose OK (Enter).
5. In the Command Line text box, type *c:\word\word.pif*, where *c:\word* is the name of your Word program directory. Choose OK (Enter).

This completes the installation under Windows 3. If you want to be able to run Word's tutorials through Windows, repeat the procedure for Learn (using *learn.pif* in place of *word.pif*).

You can also have Windows set up multiple applications at one time by using the Windows Setup program (in the Main program group) and choosing the Set Up Applications command from the Options menu. Windows will search your hard disk and list all your applications. Choose the applications you want to add, and Windows will do the rest, placing all the Word-related applications in the Non-Windows Applications program group.

If you run Word under Windows 2.1, delete *word.pif* from your Word directory, and copy the file *word.pi2* from the Word Program disk 1 to your Word directory.

Rename this file *word.pif*, and use it to start Word under Windows 2.1. (If you want to run Learn Word under Windows 2.1, follow the same procedures, with *learn.pif* instead of *word.pif*.)

Windows 3 can be run in any of three modes: standard, real, or 386 enhanced (protect). Which mode you use depends on your hardware and on what switches you use when starting Windows. If you type only *win* to start Windows, the program will start in the most capable mode that it can. In other words, it will start in enhanced mode if possible, standard mode failing that, or real mode as a last resort. One advantage of real mode is that applications created for Windows 2.1 run without difficulty in Windows 3 real mode.

Real mode is used on 8086-based or 8088-based computers that have at least 640 KB of memory and on 286-based computers that have less than 1 MB of memory (640 KB conventional memory plus any extended memory).

Standard mode is used on 286-based computers that have 1 MB or more of memory and on 386-based computers with 1 to 2 MB of memory (conventional plus extended memory). In standard mode, Windows does not use expanded memory, so you can devote this memory to Word.

Enhanced mode is used with 386-based and 486-based machines that have at least 2 MB of memory (conventional plus extended memory). You can use the Windows Clipboard with Word only if you are running in 386 enhanced mode. In this mode, you can determine how much expanded memory is available to Word by using the .PIF editor (a Windows accessory) to modify the settings of *word.pif*.

In general, configuring Word to use expanded memory is an excellent idea. Certain operations benefit greatly from the presence of ample expanded memory.

USING WORD UNDER OS/2

The men and women who wrote Microsoft Word 5.5 use OS/2 rather than DOS as their operating system. Some might have a DOS machine running somewhere in their office, but OS/2 is their operating system of choice. Of course, they have powerful PCs (486-based, as a rule) and plenty of memory—factors that make a major difference.

The advantages of OS/2 include superior management of memory. Under DOS people sometimes bump against practical limits on such things as the number of index entries that Word can handle. These limitations are much higher under OS/2 because so much more memory is available to Word.

OS/2 has some drawbacks. Some of Word's utility programs cannot be run under OS/2 and instead must be run in DOS compatibility mode. Also, Word cannot use a mouse when in a graphics mode and running under OS/2 version 1.0, 1.1, or 1.21 in protect mode. The mouse lessons of Learning Word are not available, either. However, in the DOS compatibility box the mouse and all lessons of Learning Word are available, provided you are running in a CGA or an EGA mode.

If you run Word through the OS/2 Presentation Manager, be sure that the Menus check box of the View Preferences command is checked.

APPENDIX B

Keyboard

You realize extra efficiency in your writing, editing, and formatting by mastering the many possibilities of the Word keyboard.

Actions possible with the keyboard fall into several categories: entering and editing both printable characters and spacing characters such as paragraph marks; using commands (both general procedures and specific techniques); moving in a document and selecting text; formatting; and operating in special modes such as outline view.

The following pages list the keyboard possibilities for Word 5.5. Earlier versions of Word, including 5.0, use key combinations that are sometimes quite different.

The organization of this appendix roughly matches that of Chapter 5, which is devoted to the use of the mouse and the keyboard. As in that chapter, this appendix has considerable overlap because certain keys and key combinations fall into more than one category. For example, F8, the Extend Selection key, is listed under Function Keys, Turning Modes On and Off, and Selecting.

A Strategy for Avoiding Keystroke Conflicts

In Word 5.5, the Ctrl key is used for many different functions, including applying built-in formats, using the ribbon, applying styles, and running macros. To help keep all these straight, be systematic about using the Ctrl key. To avoid potential conflicts, use the following key combinations:

- Ctrl+Y to apply styles.
- Ctrl+S to use the Styles field of the Ribbon.
- Ctrl+F to use the Font field of the Ribbon.
- Ctrl+P to use the Pts field of the Ribbon.
- Ctrl+E, V, or W as potential hot keys for resident programs (TSRs).

- Ctrl+Esc to reach the task list of Microsoft Windows (if you are running under Windows 3). This lets you move to other running applications whether or not they are in visible windows.
- Shift+Ctrl to run macros.

KEYS AND COMBINATIONS

We begin with a listing of basic keys and key combinations. In this section, you are told "Press this to do that." Later sections of the appendix are organized by tasks rather than keys; you are told "To do this, press that."

Keys That Shift Other Keys

Some keys don't do anything directly but rather change the functions of other keys or the way in which Word operates.

Press:	To cause Word to:
Shift	Change the case (capitalization) of newly typed letters, or
	Select text with the direction keys rather than by moving the cursor
Ctrl	Interpret a letter as a speed-formatting key, or
	Go to the Style, Font, or Pt box of the ribbon (when followed by S, F, or P, respectively), or
	Interpret letters as a macro key code
Ctrl+Y	Interpret the succeeding letters as a style key code
Alt	Interpret letters as accelerator keys (menu and dialog box shortcuts)
Alt (with NumLock on)	Interpret keypad numbers as ASCII character codes
Shift+Ctrl	Interpret letters as macro control codes, or
	Interpret letters as style key codes

Function Keys

Press:	To:
F1	Request on-screen help
Alt+F1 (or F11)	Move cursor to next field (the first character after the next right chevron: »)
Alt+Shift+F1 (or Shift+F11)	Move cursor to previous field (the first character after the previous right chevron: »)
F2	Calculate highlighted expression
Shift+F2	Turn outline mode on or off (View Outline)
Ctrl+F2 (or Ctrl+Shift+F2)	Choose formatting for characters (Format Character)
Alt+F2	Name and save current file (File Save As)
Alt+Ctrl+F2	Open existing file (File Open)
Alt+Shift+F2	Save active file (File Save)
Alt+Ctrl+Shift+F2	Print active file (File Print)
F3	Expand previous or selected glossary term
Shift+F3	Toggle case of selected text
Ctrl+F3	Record macro (Macro Record)
Alt+F3	Copy selected text to scrap
F4	Repeat last edit or macro (Edit Repeat)
Shift+F4	Repeat last search
Ctrl+F4	Close active window (Window Close)
Alt+F4	Exit Word and return to DOS or OS/2 (File Exit Word)
F5	Jump to specified location (Edit Go To)
Shift+F5	Toggle between edit and organize modes (in outline view)
Ctrl+F5	Restore document window to an unmaximized state (Window Restore)
Alt+F5	Toggle overtype mode
Shift+Ctrl+F5	Insert bookmark (Insert Bookmark)
F6	Move to next pane in active window
Shift+F6	Move to previous pane in active window
Ctrl+F6	Move to next window
Alt+F6	Select word in which cursor appears or, if that word is already selected, select next word
Shift+Ctrl+F6	Move to previous window

(continued)

continued

Press:	To:
F7	Use the spell checker (Utilities Spelling)
Shift+F7	Use the thesaurus (Utilities Thesaurus)
Ctrl+F7	Move active window (Window Move)
Alt+F7	Toggle Show Line Breaks (View Preferences)
F8	Turn on extend-selection mode, and select a character, word, sentence, paragraph, or entire document (depending on how many times you press it)
Shift+F8	Shrink selection (if F8 key has been pressed more than once)
Ctrl+F8	Adjust size of active window (Window Size; press Enter when done)
Alt+F8	Select sentence in which cursor appears or, if that sentence is already selected, select next sentence
Shift+Ctrl+F8	Turn column-selection mode on or off
F9	Update links to other files (established with Insert File)
Shift+F9	Print active document (File Print)
Ctrl+F9	Preview how document will look when printed (File Print Preview)
Alt+F9	Toggle between last two display modes
F10	Activate menu bar
Shift+F10	Select entire document
Ctrl+F10	Maximize (zoom) all windows (Window Maximize)
Alt+F10	Select paragraph in which cursor appears or, if that paragraph is already selected, select next paragraph
Shift+Ctrl+F10	Move cursor to ruler
F11 (or Alt+F1)	Move cursor to next field (first character after next right chevron: »)
Shift+F11 (or Alt+Shift+F1)	Move cursor to previous field (first character after previous right chevron: »)
F12 (or Alt+F2)	Name and save active file (File Save As)
Shift+F12 (or Alt+Shift+F2)	Save active file (File Save)
Ctrl+F12 (or Alt+Ctrl+F2)	Open existing file (File Open)
Shift+Ctrl+F12 (or Alt+Shift+Ctrl+F2)	Print active file (File Print)

APPENDIX B: Keyboard

Function Keys for Word 5.0 Emulation

When the Use 5.0 Function Keys field of Utilities Customize has been checked, the function keys perform more or less like Word 5.0 function keys. The main exception is the F1 key: F1 is permanently assigned to Help in Word 5.5, so you must use the Alt+Shift+F1 key combination rather than F1 to move to the next window.

Press:	Word 5.0 emulation:
F1	Request on-screen help
Shift+F1	Undo last editing act
Ctrl+F1	Toggle between Maximize and Restore (zooming)
Alt+F1	Move to ruler to set tab stops
Alt+Shift+F1	Move to next window
F2	Calculate highlighted expression
Shift+F2	Turn outline mode on or off
Ctrl+F2	Format current paragraph as a header or footer (in a dialog box)
Alt+F2	Format current paragraph as header or footer (in a dialog box)
Alt+Ctrl+F2	Open existing file
Alt+Shift+Ctrl+F2	Print active file
F3	Expand previous or selected glossary term
Shift+F3	Record macro
Ctrl+F3	Toggle macro step mode
Alt+F3	Copy selected text to scrap
F4	Repeat last editing action
Shift+F4	Repeat last search
Ctrl+F4	Toggle case of selected text
Alt+F4	Toggle layout view
F5	Toggle overtype mode
Shift+F5	Toggle between its edit and organize modes (in outline view)
Ctrl+F5	Toggle line draw mode
Alt+F5	Go to specified location (Edit Go To)
Shift+Ctrl+F5	Insert bookmark
F6	Turn on extend selection mode
Shift+F6	Toggle column selection
Ctrl+F6	Use thesaurus
Alt+F6	Check spelling
Shift+Ctrl+F6	Move to previous window

(continued)

continued

Press:	Word 5.0 emulation:
F7	Select previous word
Shift+F7	Select previous sentence
Ctrl+F7	Open existing file
Alt+F7	Toggle the Show Line Breaks option
F8	Select next word
Shift+F8	Select next sentence
Ctrl+F8	Print active file
Alt+F8	Choose character formatting (in dialog box)
Shift+Ctrl+F8	Turn column-selection mode on or off
F9	Select previous paragraph
Shift+F9	Select line that contains the cursor
Ctrl+F9	Preview how document will look when printed
Alt+F9	Toggle between last two display modes
F10	Select next paragraph
Shift+F10	Select entire document
Ctrl+F10	Save current file
Alt+F10	Record formatting as style
Shift+Ctrl+F10	Move cursor to ruler
F11	Collapse current heading (in outline view)
Shift+F11	Collapse body text (in outline view)
F12	Expand current heading (in outline view)
Shift+F12	Expand body text (in outline view)
Ctrl+F12	Expand all text and headings (in outline view)
Shift+Ctrl+F12	Print current document

ENTERING AND EDITING TEXT
Copying, Deleting, and Inserting Text

To:	Press:
Insert (paste) text stored in glossary	F3
Copy selected text to scrap	Ctrl+Ins (or Alt+F3)
Delete character to left of cursor	Backspace
Delete word to left of cursor	Ctrl+Backspace

The functions of the Insert and Delete keys in Word 5.5 change depending upon the status of the Use INS for Overtype Key field in the Utilities Customize dialog box. If the field is checked (turned on), follow the instructions in the second column of the table. If it is not checked (turned off), follow the instructions in the third column.

To:	Effect with INS for Overtype on:	Effect with INS for Overtype off:
Permanently delete (kill) selected text	Del	Shift+Del
Delete (cut) selected text to scrap	Shift+Del	Del
Insert (paste) text from scrap	Shift+Ins	Ins

Spacing Characters

To insert:	Press:
Normal space	Spacebar
Nonbreaking space (keeps both words on same line)	Shift+Ctrl+Spacebar
Tab character	Tab
Paragraph mark	Enter
New-line character (forces new line, same paragraph)	Shift+Enter
New-column character (forces new column)	Shift+Ctrl+Enter
New-page character (forces new page)	Ctrl+Enter
New-section character (forces new section)	Alt+IB; choose Section; press Enter
Optional hyphen (appears only when a word breaks at end of a line)	Ctrl+Hyphen (on top row of keyboard)
Nonbreaking hyphen (keeps both words on same line)	Shift+Ctrl+Hyphen (on top row of keyboard)

Printable Characters

To type:	Press:
Number	Numbers on top row or, if Num Lock key is on, the keypad
Symbol such as $, %, or @	Shift and simultaneously press key showing the symbol (Caps Lock key won't work)
Nonbreaking hyphen (keeps both words on same line)	Shift+Ctrl+Hyphen (on top row of keyboard)
Optional hyphen (appears only when word breaks at end of a line)	Ctrl+Hyphen (on top row of keyboard)
Dash	Alt+Ctrl+Hyphen (on top row of keyboard) twice in a row
Foreign, mathematic, or graphics character	Turn on Num Lock, and then hold down the Alt key and type the character's number code on the keypad. (Examples are given at the end of Chapter 20.)

APPENDIX B: Keyboard

SCROLLING, MOVING, AND SELECTING

You *scroll* when the text displayed on the screen moves but the cursor remains stationary. You *move* when the cursor changes position on the screen. You *select* when the cursor becomes an extendable "selection" that highlights text.

Scrolling

To scroll:	Press:
Up one window	PgUp
Down one window	PgDn
Up one line	(Scroll Lock on) Up direction key
Down one line	(Scroll Lock on) Down direction key
To beginning of document	Ctrl+Home
To end of document	Ctrl+End
Left (one-third of window)	(Scroll Lock on) Left direction key
Right (one-third of window)	(Scroll Lock on) Right direction key

Cursor Movement

To move cursor to:	Press:
Beginning of next word	Ctrl+Right direction key
Beginning of previous word	Ctrl+Left direction key
Beginning of line	Home
End of line	End
Beginning of next paragraph	Ctrl+Down direction key
Beginning of previous paragraph	Ctrl+Up direction key
Beginning of first line in window	Ctrl+PgUp
Beginning of last line in window	Ctrl+PgDn
Beginning of document	Ctrl+Home
End of document	Ctrl+End

The cursor can also be moved one character at a time using the direction keys.

Selecting (Highlighting)

Extend Selection Mode

F8 turns on Extend Selection Mode. Pressing F8 a second time selects the word in which the cursor appears; pressing it repeatedly extends the selection to the sentence, the paragraph, and the entire document. Shift+F8 reverses the process. You can also use the direction keys to select text in Extend Selection Mode. To select forward from the cursor, sentence by sentence, press the period (.) key. Press Esc to turn off Extend Selection Mode.

Other ways to select text

To select:	Press:
The word containing the cursor	Alt+F6
The sentence containing the cursor	Alt+F8
The paragraph containing the cursor	Alt+F10
A column or rectangular block	Shift+Ctrl+F8; and then use direction keys to adjust highlight
An entire document	Ctrl+5 (keypad) or Shift+F10
Forward, character by character	Shift+Right direction key
Backward, character by character	Shift+Left direction key
Forward, word by word	Shift+Ctrl+Right direction key
Backward, word by word	Shift+Ctrl+Left direction key
Downward, paragraph by paragraph	Shift+Ctrl+Down direction key
Upward, paragraph by paragraph	Shift+Ctrl+Up direction key
Downward, screen by screen	Shift+PgDn
Upward, screen by screen	Shift+PgUp
Forward to end of line in which cursor appears	Shift+End
Backward to start of line in which cursor appears	Shift+Home
Everything from cursor to end of document	Shift+Ctrl+End
Everything from cursor back to beginning of document	Shift+Ctrl+Home

APPENDIX B: Keyboard

USING COMMANDS

Instructions for using Word commands fall into two categories: general techniques and rules that apply to many commands, such as details of filling in a dialog box; and keystrokes relevant only to a specific command.

General Techniques for Using Commands

The following is a brief review of the general rules for using commands, recapping information presented in Chapter 4.

Using the menu bar

Press Alt or F10 to activate the menu bar. Press the emphasized character (accelerator key) of the command family you want. Then press the emphasized character of the command in the drop-down menu. You can also use the direction keys to move around in the menu bar. Press Esc to cancel the menu bar.

To undo a command, press Alt+Backspace or choose Edit Undo (Alt+EU).

Using keys in dialog boxes

To:	Press:
Move to next option	Tab
Move to previous option	Shift+Tab
Move to specific option	Alt+emphasized letter of the option
View options on drop-down list (in fields with down arrows after them)	F4 or Alt+Down direction key
Select item in list box	Direction keys
Toggle check boxes on and off	Spacebar (or Alt+emphasized letter of the field)
Select options in option box	Direction keys
Execute command, when all options are set	Enter
Cancel dialog box and lose any option changes made	Esc

Shortcuts for Specific Commands

For the most part, these shortcuts don't work if you have turned on the Use Word 5.0 Function Keys check box of the Utilities Customize command.

To choose this command:	Press:
File Open	Alt+Ctrl+F2 (or Ctrl+F12)
File Save	Alt+Shift+F2 (or Shift+F12)
File Save As	Alt+F2 (or F12)
File Print	Alt+Shift+Ctrl+F2 (or Shift+F9 or Shift+Ctrl+F12)
File Print Preview	Ctrl+F9
File Exit Word	Alt+F4
Edit Undo	Alt+BackSpace
Edit Repeat	F4
Edit Cut	Shift+Del (Del if Use INS for Overtype Key is on)
Edit Copy	Ctrl+Ins
Edit Paste	Shift+Ins (Ins if Use INS for Overtype Key is on)
Edit Go To	F5
View Outline	Shift+F2
Insert Bookmark	Shift+Ctrl+F5
Format Character	Ctrl+F2 (or Shift+Ctrl+F2)
Utilities Spelling	F7
Utilities Thesaurus	Shift+F7
Utilities Calculate	F2
Macro Record	Ctrl+F3
Window Maximize	Ctrl+F10
Window Restore	Ctrl+F5
Window Move	Ctrl+F7
Window Size	Ctrl+F8
Window Close	Ctrl+F4
Help Index	F1

APPENDIX B: Keyboard

Help commands

Except for when you have requested help while inside a dialog box, Word's help system permits you to jump from topic to related topic by highlighting terms that appear in <brackets> and pressing Enter or by clicking on those terms with a mouse.

Help from within a dialog box is limited to a single set of help windows from which you cannot jump to other topics (unless you are using MasterWord Help).

To:	Press:
Get context-sensitive help (help with command, dialog box, or message displayed on the screen)	F1 (or click with mouse on the <F1=Help> button on bottom of screen)
Go to the help index so that you can choose a help topic (doesn't work when a dialog box or message is displayed)	Alt+HI; F1; or click with mouse on <F1=Help> button
Return (backtrack) to previous Help topic, when help window is active	Backspace (or click with mouse on Back button)
Return (backtrack) to previous Help topic, when help window is not active	F1 followed by Backspace (or click with mouse on Back button)
Exit Help (close help window)	Esc (or click with mouse on window-close icon or Exit button)

If you use MasterWord Help, the expanded help system that replaces Word's original online help, you have additional opportunities, some of which are listed here.

To:	Press:
Get extra help, when a dialog box (or help with a dialog box) is displayed	Shift+F1
Reach tree of topics	F1+Enter if you are not in the help window, or click the <2=Tree> button if you are in the help window.
Reach index of topics	F1 and then first letter of topic
Exit Help (move the help window to background but not close it)	Click the <5=Exit> button

Print commands

To:	Press:
Print current file	Shift+F9 or Alt+FP (File Print command)
Stop printing	Esc
Print in the background so that you can continue editing	Select File Printer Setup (Alt+FR), and turn on Use Print Queue in the dialog box
Preview how the current document will look when printed	Ctrl+F9 or Alt+FV (File Print Preview command)
To scroll in print preview	PgUp; PgDn; Ctrl+End to go to end of document; Ctrl+Home to go to beginning of document
To exit print preview	Esc or Alt+FX (File Exit Preview command)

Spelling commands

To check the spelling of an entire document, do not select any text. To check the spelling of a specific word or section of text, select the desired text.

To:	Do this:
Check a spelling	Press F7, or choose Utilities Spelling
Correct a spelling	Choose Change or Remember Correction
Ignore an unknown word	Choose Ignore
Add a word to the dictionary	Choose Add
Undo your decision regarding the previous unknown word	Choose Undo
Change how the spell checker works	Choose Options
Exit spell checker	Choose Close, or press Esc

Thesaurus commands

After selecting the word for which you want a synonym, you can do any of the following.

To:	Do this:
Activate thesaurus	Press Shift+F7, or choose Utilities Thesaurus.
See synonyms for a synonym	Highlight the synonym in the list box, and then choose Synonyms.
Replace term with a synonym	Highlight the synonym; choose Replace.
Cancel thesaurus without replacing selected term	Choose Cancel, or press Esc.

APPENDIX B: Keyboard

Macro commands

To:	Press:
Record keystrokes as a macro	Ctrl+F3
Interrupt running macro	Esc
Repeat macro	F4
Turn Step Mode on or off	Esc, Alt+S (in dialog box), Enter

Window commands

To:	Press:
Open blank window	Alt+FN, Enter.
Move to next window	Ctrl+F6.
Move to previous window	Ctrl+Shift+F6.
Close current window	Ctrl+F4 or Alt+WC or Alt+FC. (With a mouse, click the window close icon, the small square in the upper-left corner of the window.)
Adjust size of the current window	Ctrl+F8 or Alt+WS; use direction keys to size window; press Enter.
Move current window	Ctrl+F7 or Alt+WM; use direction keys to move window; press Enter.
Maximize all windows	Ctrl+F10 or Alt+WX. (With the mouse, click the maximize icon in upper-right corner of window.)
Restore maximized windows to their previous size	Ctrl+F5 or Alt+WR. (With the mouse, click the maximize icon in upper-right corner of window.)
To split window into panes	Alt+WT; use direction keys to position the split line; press Enter.
To remove a window split	Alt+WS; press Up direction key until split is at top of window; press Enter.
To open or close a footnote pane	Alt+VF (View Footnotes/Annotations command).
To move between panes	To move to the next pane, press F6. With a mouse, click anywhere on the desired pane.
To open a new window containing the same document	Alt+WN (Window New command).
To arrange windows so that none overlap	Alt+WA (Window Arrange All command).

FORMATTING

Using the Ribbon

To:	Do this:
Turn the ribbon on and off	Press Alt+VB (View Ribbon command).
Move the cursor to the Style field	Press Ctrl+S (Ctrl + AS if necessary).
Move the cursor to the Font field	Press Ctrl+F (Ctrl + AF if necessary).
Move to the Pts field	Press Ctrl+P (Ctrl + AP if necessary).
Apply a style, font, or point size listed on the ribbon	With text selected, use direction keys to scroll to the desired option in a list box; press Enter.
Leave the ribbon without making changes	Esc.

Using the ribbon with a mouse

To:	Do this:
Turn ribbon on and off	Point to the ruler icon (⊥), and click the right mouse button.
See a list box of style, font, or points options	Click on the arrow (↓) following the field.
Apply a style, font, or point option	Click on the option in a list box.
Make characters bold, italic, and/or underlined	With text selected or cursor positioned to begin typing, click on Bld, Ital, and/or Ul.
Make text plain, when Bld, Ital, or Ul is highlighted	With text selected, click on highlighted option(s).
Leave the ribbon without making changes	Click on the document window.

APPENDIX B: Keyboard 657

Using the Ruler

To:	Press:
Turn the ruler on and off	Alt+VR (View Ruler command)
Move cursor to the ruler (and turn it on if it is not on already)	Shift+Ctrl+F10
Return cursor to document and save changes made in the ruler	Enter
Return cursor to document without making changes with the ruler	Esc

Adjusting custom tab stops with the ruler

Each of the five types of tab stops is shown on the ruler by a different character: L for left alignment, R for right alignment, C for center alignment, | for vertical alignment, or D for decimal alignment.

To:	Do this:
Insert custom tab stop	Use direction keys to position cursor; press first letter of tab type (L, C, R, D, or V).
Move custom tab stop	With cursor on tab stop, hold down Ctrl and use the Left and Right direction keys to reposition tab.

Three types of leader characters can be used with a tab stop: - - - (hyphens), ... (periods), or _____ (underscore).

To:	Do this:
Add leader characters to tab stops	With cursor on the tab stop, press period (.), hyphen (-), or underscore (_).
To delete custom tab stops	Move cursor to tab stop with direction keys; press Del.

Adjusting indents with the ruler

Three paragraph indents are shown on the ruler: ¦ for first-line indent, [for left indent, or] for right indent.

The location of these can be changed with the mouse. Position the mouse cursor on the indent character, press the right mouse button, reposition the character, and release the button.

Speed Formatting with Built-In Formats

Character formats

If you have macro codes that begin with Ctrl rather than Shift+Ctrl, you might need to press Ctrl+A before you can use a built-in character format. For example, press Ctrl+AB rather than Ctrl+B to make characters bold.

If a style sheet is attached, Ctrl+Spacebar gives the selected characters whatever formatting is specified in the character portion of the governing paragraph style.

To make characters:	Press:
Bold	Ctrl+B (Ctrl+AB if there is a macro conflict)
Italic	Ctrl+I (Ctrl+AI)
Small caps	Ctrl+K (Ctrl+AK)
Underlined	Ctrl+U (Ctrl+AU)
Double underlined	Ctrl+D (Ctrl+AD)
Superscripted	Ctrl+Plus (Ctrl+A+Plus)
Subscripted	Ctrl+= (Ctrl+A=)
Hidden	Ctrl+H (Ctrl+AH)
Standard (remove all character formats)	Ctrl+Spacebar (Ctrl+A+Spacebar)
Standard (remove character formats except font and size)	Ctrl+Z (Ctrl+AZ)

APPENDIX B: Keyboard

Paragraph formats

If you have macro codes that begin with Ctrl rather than Shift+Ctrl, you might need to press Ctrl+A before you can use a built-in paragraph format. For example, press Ctrl+AC rather than Ctrl+C to center paragraphs.

Format:	Press:
Centered	Ctrl+C (Ctrl+AC if there is a macro conflict)
Left alignment	Ctrl+L (Ctrl+AL)
Right alignment	Ctrl+R (Ctrl+AR)
Justified	Ctrl+J (Ctrl+AJ)
Increase left indent	Ctrl+N (Ctrl+AN)
Decrease left indent	Ctrl+M (Ctrl+AM)
Hanging indent (indent all lines but the first)	Ctrl+T (Ctrl+AT)
Indent from both left and right (for block quotations and so on)	Ctrl+Q (Ctrl+AQ)
Single line spacing	Ctrl+1 (Ctrl+A1)
Double line spacing	Ctrl+2 (Ctrl+A2)
Open paragraph spacing (blank line before paragraph)	Ctrl+O (Ctrl+AO)
Normal paragraph	Ctrl+X (Ctrl+AX)

TURNING MODES ON AND OFF

Word operates in a variety of *modes*. Although only certain of these are called modes by Microsoft, all of the following key combinations cause Word to shift its method of operation in a significant way.

To turn this mode on or off:	Press:
Extend Selection (on/off)	F8/Esc
Column Selection	Ctrl+Shift+F8
Numeric Lock	Num Lock
Scroll Lock	Scroll Lock
Uppercase letters	Caps Lock
Overtype	Alt+F5 (or Ins if the Utilities Customize command's Use INS for Overtype key check box is checked)
Macro Record	Ctrl+F3
Step Macro	Alt+MR and then Alt+S (in dialog box) and then Enter
Line Draw (on/off)	Alt+UL/Esc
Show Line breaks	Alt+F7
Previous video mode	Alt+F9
Print Preview (on/off)	Ctrl+F9/Esc
Outline View	Shift+F2

Layout View

To enter Layout View, choose View Layout (Alt+VL). The characters *LY* will appear on the status line.

To move to:	Press:
Beginning of previous paragraph	Ctrl+Up direction key
Next column or element (to the right)	Alt+5(keypad)+Right direction key
Previous column or element (to the left)	Alt+5(keypad)+Left direction key

OPERATING IN SPECIAL MODES

Outline View

The purposes of several keys change when you move from normal document view to outline view. Outline view has two modes: outline edit and outline organize.

To:	Press:
Move between document view and outline view	Shift+F2 or Alt+VO
Toggle between outline edit and outline organize	Shift+F5
Lower a heading one level	Ctrl+0 (zero)
Raise a heading one level	Ctrl+9
Add body text to the outline	Ctrl+X; type text
Collapse subheadings and body text	Minus sign (keypad) or Ctrl+8
Collapse body text below a heading	Shift+minus sign (keypad) or Ctrl+Shift+8
Expand next heading level and body text	Plus sign (keypad) or Ctrl+7
Expand body text below a heading	Shift+Plus sign (keypad)
Expand all headings to a specified level	Alt+Shift; type desired heading level (use numbers on top of keyboard)
Expand all headings	Select entire outline (Shift+5); press * (keypad)
Expand all body text	Select entire outline; press Shift+plus sign (keypad) or Shift+Ctrl+7

Outline organize mode only

When you are in organize mode, the word ORGANIZE will appear on the status line.

To:	Press:
Select previous heading of the same level as current heading	Up direction key
Select next heading of the same level as current heading	Down direction key
Select previous heading of any level	Left direction key
Select next heading of any level	Right direction key
Select nearest heading at the next highest level	Home
Select last subheading at next lower level	End
Extend selection to subsequent headings of same level	F8+Down direction key

KEYS FOR MICROSOFT WINDOWS

If you run Microsoft Word as a non-Windows application under Microsoft Windows 3.0, certain key combinations let you move between Word and the Windows environment.

To:	Press:
Switch to next application (program) or minimized icon	Alt+Esc
Switch to next application, restoring applications that are running as icons	Alt+Tab
Switch to the Windows Task List to choose among all programs currently running	Ctrl+Esc
Copy screen to Windows clipboard	Print Screen
Switch Word to windowed application (386 Enhanced mode only)	Alt+Enter

WHEN WORKING WITH A FORM

To move to:	Press:
Next field (indicated by »)	Alt+F1 (or F11)
Previous field (indicated by »)	Alt+Shift+F1 (or Shift +F11)

APPENDIX C

Mouse

Unlike earlier versions of Word, in which the mouse pointer assumed various distinctive shapes, the mouse pointer for Word 5.5 is always an up arrow. It tilts slightly to the left (↖) unless it is in the vertical selection bar, which runs alongside the left edge of a window. In the selection bar, the arrow tilts slightly to the right (↗), which indicates that if you click the left mouse button once you will select a line, if you click it twice you will select a paragraph, and if you click both buttons at one time you will select the entire document.

If you are running in a text mode rather than in a graphics mode, the mouse pointer will appear as a solid rectangle. If you have a color monitor and run Word in a text mode, the pointer will change to a different color when it is in the selection bar.

The selection bar is an unusual feature of the Word screen because its presence is revealed solely by the changed appearance of the mouse pointer. Other features of the screen that are sensitive to the mouse or that can be manipulated by the mouse have distinctive appearances. Figure C-1 on the following page shows the Word screen with several of these icons and other mouse-sensitive elements identified.

In this appendix, as in the rest of the book, *click left* means "press and release the left mouse button," *click right* means "press and release the right mouse button," *double click* means "press and release the left mouse button twice in rapid succession," and *drag* means "hold down the left mouse button while you move the mouse pointer across the screen."

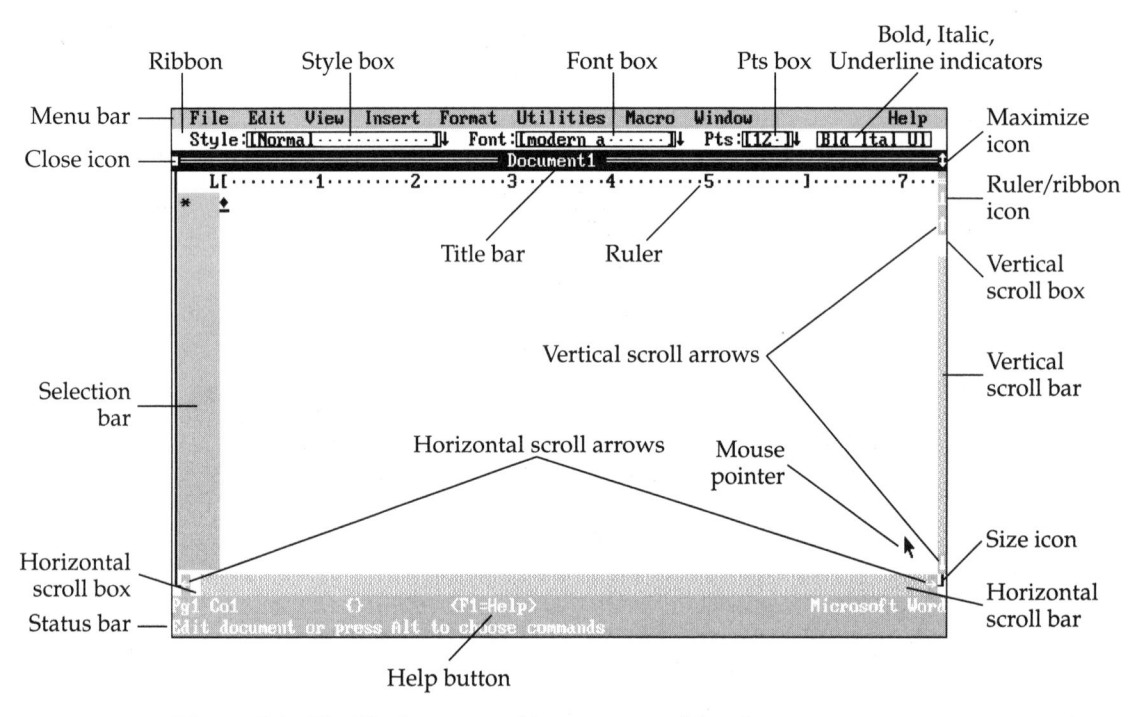

Figure C-1. The Word screen and its mouse-sensitive elements.

Editing

To:	Point to:	And do this:
Move selected text	Its destination	Ctrl+click right
Copy selected text	Its destination	Shift+Ctrl+click right
Copy character format	Character with desired format	Shift+Ctrl+click left
Copy paragraph format	Paragraph with desired format	Shift+Ctrl+click left

APPENDIX C: Mouse

Scrolling

To scroll:	Point to:	And do this:
Continuously	Scroll arrows or scroll bar	Hold down left mouse button
Up or down by line	Up or down scroll arrow	Click left
Left or right by character	Left or right scroll arrow	Click left
Up or down by screen	Vertical scroll bar, above or below its scroll box	Click left
Up or down by multiple screens	Vertical scroll box	Drag up or down a proportionate distance
To start of document	Vertical scroll box	Drag to top of vertical scroll bar
To end of document	Vertical scroll box	Drag to bottom of vertical scroll bar
To a relative horizontal position	Horizontal scroll box	Drag left or right a proportionate distance
Left or right by one-third of window's width	Horizontal scroll bar, left or right of the scroll box	Click left

Selecting

To select:	Point to:	And do this:
Word	Word	Double-click left or click right
Sentence	Sentence	Ctrl+click left
Line	Selection bar beside line	Click left
Paragraph	Selection bar beside paragraph	Double-click left or click right
Document	Selection bar	Click both

Using Menus

To:	Point to:	And do this:
Browse menus and commands	Menu bar	Hold down left
Drop down a menu	Name on menu bar	Click left
Choose a command	Name in drop-down menu	Click left

Using Dialog Boxes

To:	Point to:	And do this:
Select option or button	Option or button	Click left
Select item from list	Item	Click left
Select item from list and execute command	Item	Double-click left
Drop down a list	Drop-down arrow	Click left
Carry out a command	OK button	Click left
Cancel a command	Cancel button	Click left

Shortcuts for Specific Commands

To choose this command:	Point to:	And do this:
Edit Go To	Status bar	Double-click left
Format Section	Section mark	Double-click left or click right
Help Index	<F1=Help> button	Click left
Format Character	Font box or Pts box in ribbon	Double-click left
Format Apply Style	Style box in ribbon	Double-click left

APPENDIX C: Mouse

Using Windows and Panes

To:	Point to:	And do this:
Split window into two panes	Window split icon	Drag icon down window border
Open footnote/annotation pane	Window split icon	Shift+drag icon down window border
Size pane	Window split icon	Drag icon in window border
Close pane	Window split icon	Double-click or drag to top or bottom of window
Close window	Window close icon	Click left
Maximize/restore window	Maximize icon	Click left
Size window	Size icon	Drag
Move window	Window title bar or left border	Drag
Activate visible window	Window	Click

Using the Ribbon and Ruler

To:	Point to:	And do this:
Turn ruler on/off	Ruler/ribbon icon	Click left
Turn ribbon on/off	Ruler/ribbon icon	Click right
Adjust font	Font box in ribbon	Click left
Adjust font size	Pts box in ribbon	Click left
Choose Format Character	Font box or Pts box in ribbon	Double-click left
Choose paragraph style	Style box in ribbon	Click left
Choose Format Apply Style	Style box in ribbon	Double-click left
Move paragraph indents	Indent marks	Click right and drag
Set tab stops	Ruler positions	Click left
Change alignment of tab stops	Alignment character at left of ruler	Click until choice appears
Change leader character	Space to left of ruler	Click until choice appears
Clear tab stops	Tab stops in ruler	Drag off ruler
Move tab stops	Tab stops in ruler	Drag to new position

Index

Note: Italicized page numbers refer to illustrations and figures.

Special Characters

" (quotation marks) 180–81, 426
$ (dollar sign) in filename extension 635
% (percent sign) 434, 490
& (logical AND operator) 179, 180
( ) (parentheses) 181, 434, 484
∗ (multiplication operator) 342, 484, 490
∗ (wildcard character) 165, 180
+ (addition operator) 342, 434, 484, 490
, (field separator) 479
, (logical OR operator) 179, 180
- (logical NOT operator) 179, 180
– (subtraction operator) 342, 434, 484, 490
… (ellipsis) 157, 159
/ (division operator) 342, 434, 484, 490
: (colon) 524, 539
:: (double colon) 399–400
; (semicolon) 524
< (less-than operator) 179, 181, 434, 483
<= (less-than-or-equal-to operator) 434, 483
<> (not-equal-to operator) 419, 434, 483
= (equal-to operator) 434, 483
> (greater-than operator) 179, 181, 434, 483
>= (greater-than-or-equal-to operator) 434, 483
? (wildcard character) 165, 180, 212
^ (caret) 180, 212, 312, 426
{} (scrap brackets) 74, 209
~ (tilde) 180

A

absolute positioning 305–6, 562–66
   of side-by-side paragraphs 566–67
   of side heads 567–68
accelerator keys 61–62, 100, 156–57
active window 58, 85
addition operator (+) 342, 434, 484, 490
alarm, muting 352
all caps 279
alphabetizing in indexes 530
Alt key 642
ampersand (&) 179, 180
anchors, bookmark 256
AND logical operator 179, 180, 435, 484, 490
Annotation dialog box 259–61
Annotation paragraph style 109
annotations 259–61
   jumping to 219, 221
   viewing 236
Apply Style dialog box 72–73, 112–13, 313–14, 458
array variables 427–28
ASCII characters 98, 384–85, 446, 616–17
ASCII files 170–72
ASK instruction
   macro 419, 421, 438
   merge 474–75, 483
asterisk (∗)
   as multiplication operator 342, 484, 490
   as wildcard 165, 180
Attach Style Sheet dialog box 106–7, 317
AUTOEXEC.BAT file 384, 631, 634–35
AUTOEXEC macro 129, 447
automatic styles 128, 452–53
autosave feature 149, 347–48

B

background screen color 243
backup (.BAK) files 168
.BAK filename extension 168
bitmapped graphics 604–5
body text, outline 502
   expanding/collapsing 506–7
   promoting/demoting 506
boldface characters 278
bookmarks 255–56, 394–96
   anchors for 256
   creating 255–56
   cross-referencing documents using 400–403

bookmarks *(continued)*
  importing document sections using 256
  jumping to 219, 220–21
  as place markers 395
  reorganizing documents with 395–96
Boolean variables 432–33
borders
  formatting 302–5
  using to underline 576
  window, displaying 77, 240
bottom margin 295
boxes 577–78
braces () 74, 209
Break dialog box 246–48
breaks, inserting 246–48
built-in formats 34
  for characters 26, 38–39, 658
  keyboard shortcuts for *36, 38,* 658–59
  for paragraphs 26, 35–37, 659
  for sections 34–35
  vs. formatting applied with styles 458–59

C

calculations 342–45
capital letters, small 279
Caps Lock (CL) mode 75
Capture file format 606
Capture program 600–603
caret (^) 180, 212, 312, 426
case
  changing 279, 382–83
  and macros 422–23
  replacing 382–83
  and sorts 341
centering paragraphs 283
Character dialog box 68–69, 276–80
character formatting 26, 275–80
  boldface 278
  built-in formats 38–39, 658
  case 279
  displaying attributes in ribbon 66
  eliminating direct 460
  as glossary entries 409
  hidden 279, 280–81
  italics 278
  keyboard commands for *38,* 658
  in merged documents 491–92
  overriding 452
  search and replace 214, 217, 393–94

character formatting *(continued)*
  small capitals 279
  strikethrough 279
  with styles 452
  subscripts/superscripts 250, 280
  underlining 278
characters
  adding to formatted character string 383
  ASCII (*see* ASCII characters)
  case (*see* case)
  color 278
  extended character set 98
  hidden (*see* hidden text)
  leader (*see* leader characters)
  new-page vs. page-break 346
  selecting 22
  spaces as 24–25
  special 98, 648
character sets 613, 616–17
checked reserved variable 432–33
CL (Caps Lock) mode 75
Clipboard file format 606
coding indexes 263–64, 523, 524–29
colon (:) 399–400, 524, 539
colors
  characters 278
  on-screen 242–44
Colors dialog box 242–44
column breaks 247, 562
columns, multiple 550, 562. *See also* tables
  columns of information vs. columns of type 549–50
  formatting 138–41, 291, 562–67
  formatting indexes as 535–36
  number of and space between 291
Column Select (CS) mode 75, 98, 445–46, 550
comma (,) 179, 180, 479
command-key shortcuts 62, 100, 652–55
command menus 155–56
commands 60–65, 99–100
  backing out of, before executing 64
  choosing from menus 61–62, 100, 156–57
  executing 64
  help for a specific 370
  toggle 62–63
  using 155–59, 651–55, 666
comments in macros 417–18
comparison operators 434
concatenation 437

conditional statements
    in macros 419, 439, 441, 442
        merging documents using 476–77, 483–84, 493
CONFIG.SYS file 254, 634–35
content vs. format 25–26, 297–98
control codes 118, 119–20, 354, 357
Copy command 211
copying
    files 185–86
    formatting 383–84
    to glossary 211
    with mouse 382
    to scrap 209–11
    styles 209
    text 211
COUNTRY command 254
cross-references
    document 396, 400–403
    index 526
CS (Column Select) mode 75, 98, 445–46, 550
Ctrl (Control) key 91–92, 642
    avoiding keystroke conflicts 641–42
    speed formatting with 34
<ctrl esc> macro key 426
curly braces ({}) 74, 209
current directory 188–89
    changing 189–90
CurrentDir reserved variable 188, 431
cursor
    extending, to select material 22–24
    inserting text with 20–22
    moving 99, 380, 649
    selecting text with 22–24, 99, 650
    speed options 240
Customize dialog box 347–52
cut-and-paste technique 209–11
Cut command 98, 209–10

D

daisy-wheel printers 612
database programs 493–97
data documents 200–201, 478–80
DATA merge instruction 482
date and time formatting 351
date glossary name 225–26
dateprint glossary name 225–26
dBASE 495

debugging macros 444–45
decompressing files 635
Del (Delete) key 93, 98, 210, 350
desktop publishing 131, 137, 584
dialog boxes 63–65, 157–59
    exiting 64
    fields in 63–64, 157–59
    navigating 64–65, 100, 651, 666
DialogTitle reserved variable 431
dictionaries, spelling
    adding words to 322
    naming 350–51
    standard 321–22
    user-created 322–23
direction keys
    avoid using in dialog boxes 159
    selecting with 22
    vs. Spacebar 24, 25
directories 188–92
    changing 189–90
    current 188–89
    default 166–67
    program 188–89
    specifying files in 164–67, 190–92
    start-up 188–89, 431–32
Directories list box 190–92
direct text, printing 194, 197–98
direct vs. indirect formatting 28–30, 107, 274, 458–59
display and adapter setup 628–30
display mode 241–42
division formatting. *See* section formatting
division operator (/) 342, 434, 484, 490
.DOC filename extension 117, 165
document markers. *See* bookmarks; page breaks; paragraph marks; section marks
document-retrieval feature. *See* File File Management command
documents
    checking spelling in 320–26
    content vs. format 25–26, 297–98
    copying 185–86
    creating 19–20
    cross-referencing 400–403
    deleting 184
    displaying (*see* graphics, layouts using)
    .DOC extension 117, 165
    formatting (*see* formatting)

documents *(continued)*
  indexing of 523–36
  inserting 251–54
  layout *(see* layout)
  linking 253–54
  listing 182–83
  navigating in 98–99, 649–50
  new 129
  numbering items in 396–400
  organizing with glossary 405–9
  previewing 136–37, 198–200
  printing *(see* printing)
  renaming 184–85
  reorganizing with bookmarks 395–96
  repaginating 345–47
  returning to 380
  saving 168–74
    autosave 149, 347–48
    file formats for 170–72
  search and replace in 215–17, 388–93
  sections of 26, 138–40
  styles *(see* styles; style sheets)
  summary sheet *(see* summary sheets)
  vs. windows 30–31
document view 230, 501, 507
document windows 76–87
DOS, running from Word 186–87
DOS Commands command 186–87
dot-matrix printers 486–87, 609
dotted lines 576–77
double-clicking mouse buttons 94–96, 663
draft mode 136, 196
drop-down menus 61, 156–57

E

echo reserved variable 418, 420, 428
Edit commands 7–8, 207–8
  for style sheets 227–28
Edit Copy command 211
Edit Cut command 209–10
Edit Glossary command 221–27, 406
Edit Go to command 218–21
editing command shortcuts 647, 665
Edit Macro dialog box 356–59, 422
Edit menu 207
Edit Paste command 211
Edit Rename Style command 114, 227–28, 460–61

Edit Repeat command 209
Edit Replace command 215–18, 389, 390–93
Edit Search command 212–15, 388–90
Edit Undo command 208–9, 380
ellipsis (…) 157, 159
endmark 43, 76
EndMark reserved variable 433
Enhanced Graphics Adapter (EGA) 241, 629
environment variables 631–32
equal-to operator (=) 434, 483
Esc (Escape) key 64, 187
EX (Extend Selection) mode 22–23, 75, 98, 650
Exit Word command 187
extended characters 98

F

<F1=Help> 74
Field reserved variable 431
fields 474, 476, 478–80
File Close All command 168
File Close command 167–68
File commands 6–7, 161–62, 193
File Directories list box 190–92
File DOS Commands command 186–87
File Exit Word command 186–87
File File Management command 174–86
file formats 170–72
File New command 162–63
File Open command 85, 164–67
File Print command 193–98
File Printer Setup command 204–6, 637
File Print Merge command 200–201, 474
File Print Preview command 136, 198–200
File Print Queue command 202–4
files
  ASCII 170–72
  copying 185–86
  decompressing 635
  deleting 184
  formats for saving 170–72
  inserting 251–54
  listing 182–83
  loading 164–67
  marking 177
  naming 169
  printing to disk 195
  read-only 165, 168
  renaming 184–85

INDEX 673

files *(continued)*
   Rich Text Format (RTF) 172
   saving 168–74
   saving all 174
   viewing 183
File Save All command 174
File Save As command 169–74
File Save command 168
flush-right alignment 283
fonts 277, 612–16
   bitmapped 617–18
   cartridge 622
   character set 613–14
   displaying in ribbon 66
   downloadable 622
   generic 620–22
   orientation 613
   outline 617–18
   pitch 613–14
   point size of 68, 69, 614–15
   and printer file 66–68
   sample 622–24
   scalable 618
   selecting by name 67–68
   skipping downloading of 205–6
   sources of 622
   spacing 613
footers 309–12
Footnote dialog box 248–50
footnote glossary name 225, 226
Footnote paragraph style 109
footnotes 248
   deleting 249
   jumping to 221
   limitations 250–51
   numbering 248
   reference marks for 248–50
   and section formatting 251, 291
   superscripts 250, 280
   using window panes with 250
   viewing 236
Format Apply Style command 112, 313–14, 458
Format Attach Style Sheet command 106, 117, 316–17, 459
Format Borders command 302–5
Format Character command 26, 275–81
Format commands 11–13, 274–75
Format Define Styles command 113–14, 316

Format Header/Footer command 290, 309–12
Format Margins command 26, 138, 290, 294–96
Format menu 274
Format Paragraph command 26, 138, 281–88
Format Position command 138, 142, 305–8, 562–63, 565, 567, 568, 593
Format Record Style command 110, 314–16, 383–84
Format Section command 26, 140–41, 288–93, 562
Format Tabs command 296–302
formatting 26–28
   "at any time" concept 27
   built-in formats for 34–39, 658–59
   characters (*see* character formatting)
   columns 138–41, 291, 562–67
   commands for 656–59
   content vs. format 25–26, 297–98
   copying with keyboard 383–84
   direct vs. indirect 8–30, 107, 274, 458–59
   indexes 523, 531–36
   paragraphs (*see* paragraph formatting)
   recording in style sheets 316, 454
   replacing 217–18, 393–94
   sections (*see* section formatting)
   and Select-Do concept 20
   of styles 115–16, 462
   with styles 457–59
   tables of contents 268–69, 542–47
   using glossary entries 409–12
form letters 465–72
forms 573–79
   boxes on 577–78
   dotted lines in 576–77
   filling in 580–82
      and merge feature 581–82
   grids on 577–78
   hidden markers in 551, 579
   key commands for 662
   organization charts and illustrations 578–79
   saving 580
   underlining in 574–77
Found reserved variable 432
frames, paragraph 138, 282, 305–8, 587–96
   distance from text 308, 595–98
   flowing text in 590–92
   horizontal position of 306–7, 593–94

frames, paragraph *(continued)*
   relative to other page elements 307, 308
   vertical position of 307–8
   width of 308, 594–95
function keys 92
   list of 643–44
   remapping for macros 443
   Word 5.0 emulation 92–94, 645–46

G

glossaries 221–22, 405–9
   copying to 211
   creating entries 406–7
   deleting entries 224
   formatting with entries 409–12
   inserting entries into documents 407
   loading files 224–25
   merging entries 225, 359
   NORMAL.GLY file 125, 129
   organizing with 405–9
   outlining with glossary names 407–8
   preparing entries for 406–7
   printing 194
   saving entries to 225
   saving macros to 124–25, 358
   tutorial on 410–12
   vs. scrap 211
Glossary dialog box 224–25
glossary names 223, 406–7
   numbers as 408
   permanent 225–26
   using as outline 407–8
Go to dialog box 219–21
graphics 132
   bitmapped 604–5
   file formats 261, 604–5
   importing 141–42, 261–63, 599–609
   layouts using *(see* layout*)*
   on-screen 133–37
   printing 143
   resolution of 197
   tutorial on 584–89
graphics mode vs. text mode 133–34, 241–42, 275
greater-than operator (>) 179, 181, 434, 483
greater-than-or-equal-to operator (>=) 434, 483
grids 577–78

H

hardware requirements 627–31
Header/Footer dialog box 309–11
Header/Footer paragraph style 109
header records 478
headers 309–12
heading levels, outline 501–2
Heading paragraph style 109
Help About Help command 369
Help commands 16–17, 369–70, 653. *See also* MasterWord
help feature
   dialog box help 371–72
   help windows 371, 380
   message help 372–73
Help Index command 369, 370–71
Help Keyboard command 369
Help Learning Word command 369
Help menu 369
Help reserved variable 433
Help Using Help command 369
Help Word 5.0 to 5.5 command 369
hidden text 246, 279, 280–81
   displaying 238, 280
   formatting text as 279
   in forms 551, 579
   in indexing 263, 264, 524, 529
   printing 197
   in tables of contents 266, 267–68, 539–40
highlighting. *See* selecting
HPGL file format 261, 605, 606
HYPH.DAT file 329, 332
Hyphenate dialog box 330–32
hyphenation 328–30
   nonbreaking hyphens 329
   normal hyphens 328
   optional hyphens 237, 329, 330
hyphenation point 331, 332

I

IBM PC keyboards 90–91
IF...ELSE...ENDIF statement
   macro 419, 439
   merge 476–77, 483–84
images. *See* graphics
importing graphics 141–42, 261–63, 599–609
INCLUDE merge instruction 484, 489

indentation
  in macros 419, 445–46
  numbering in outlines 504
  paragraph 284–85
  removing with Edit Replace command 391
  in table of contents 268–69
  vs. margins 146, 294
Index dialog box 264–66
indexes 523
  alphabetizing 530
  coding 263–64, 523, 524–29
    automating with search and replace 527–28
    macros for 528–29
    series items 525–26
    subentries 524
  compiling 264, 523, 529–31
    editing 530–31
    hidden markers 529
    page-number spans 531
    and section markers 529
    subentries 530–31
  cross-references in 526
  formatting 523, 531–36
    indented vs. run-in 533–36
    multiple columns 535–36
    with style sheet 265, 532–33
  hidden text in 263–64, 524
  indentation in 265–66, 533
  using macros to create 528–29
Index paragraph style 109
indirect vs. direct formatting 28–30, 107, 274, 458–59
Insert Annotation command 259–61
Insert Bookmark command 10, 245, 255–56, 389, 394–96, 401
Insert Break command 138, 246–48
Insert commands 10–11, 245–46
  for style sheets 270–71
Insert File command 251–54
Insert Footnote command 248–51
Insert Index command 263–66, 529, 531, 532
insertion point 20. *See also* cursor
Insert menu 245
Insert New Style command 270, 462–63
Insert Page Numbers command 256–59, 290
Insert Picture command 138, 141, 261–63
Insert Style Sheet command 271
Insert Table of Contents command 266–69, 538, 541, 542

Ins (Insert) key 93–94, 98, 210, 350
InsOverType reserved variable 430
INT (integer) function 436
italics 278

J

justified paragraph alignment 284

K

keyboard 90–94
  applying built-in formats with 658–59
  avoiding keystroke conflicts 641–42
  keys for copying of formatting 383–84
  keys for cursor movement 99, 649
  keys for executing commands 651–55
  keys for outline view 502–4, 661
  keys for scrolling 649
  keys for selecting text 99
  keys for setting tab stops 300–301
  keys for spacing of characters 647
  keys for text editing 647–48
  manipulating windows with 84–87
  navigating dialog boxes with 159, 651
  shortcuts 61–62, 100
    accelerator keys 61–62, 100, 156–57
    command-key 62, 100, 652–55
    speed-formatting keys 34–39, 65, 100
  vs. mouse 95

L

laser printers 611, 612, 613, 615–19
layout. *See also* graphics
  creating 587–96
  frames for 590–92
  positioning elements 593–98
  viewing 231–33
Layout View (LY) mode 75, 136, 231–33, 660
LD (Line Draw) mode 75, 98, 388–89
leader characters 299, 569–72
left-aligned paragraphs 283
left margin 295
LEN function 420, 436
length2 reserved variable 418
length reserved variable 418, 420
less-than operator (<) 179, 181, 434, 483
less-than-or-equal-to operator (<=) 434, 483

letters, form 465–72
line breaks, displaying 238–39
linedraw characters 338, 350
line drawing 338–39
   grids created with 577–78
   organizational charts created with 578–79
Line Draw (LD) mode 75, 98, 338–39
line numbers 241, 292
line spacing 276–77, 285
live ruler 234
logical operators 178–81, 435, 484, 490–91
LY (Layout View) mode 75, 136, 231–33, 660

M

Macro commands 15, 353, 655
Macro Edit command 125, 356–59, 414–15
MACRO.GLY file 118, 540, 572
macro-instruction language for scripting
   ASK instruction 419, 421, 438
   COMMENT...ENDCOMMENT
      instruction 417–18, 438–39
   IF...ELSE...ENDIF instruction 419, 439
   ignored characters 417
   MESSAGE instruction 439–40
   PAUSE instruction 440
   QUIT instruction 441
   REPEAT...ENDREPEAT instruction 419, 421, 441
   SET instruction 419–20, 441–42
   WHILE...ENDWHILE instruction 419, 442
Macro menu 353
Macro Record command 119, 354
Macro Record (MR) mode 75, 98, 121
macro rules
   array variables 427–28
   constants 426
   functions 420, 435–37
   instructions 419–20, 437–43
   names of keys 417, 420–21, 424–26
   operators 419–20, 433–35
   reserved variables 428–33
   variables 418–19, 427
Macro Run command 123, 354–56
macros 104, 117–19, 413–14
   AUTOEXEC 129, 447
   capitalization in 422–23
   chevrons in 418, 426, 445, 448
   comments in 417–18
   conditionals in 419, 439, 441, 442
   control codes for 118, 119–20, 354, 357
   debugging 444–45
   deleting 357
   DOS commands in 447
   editing 356–59, 414–15
   ignored elements in 417–18
   indentation in 419, 445–46
   index coding with 528–29
   naming 119, 354, 422
   playing back 122–24, 354–56
      in step mode 124, 355–56
     recording 119–22, 446
      in Record mode 354
     vs. writing 118
   reducing paragraph marks in 447
   rules governing (*see* macro rules)
   running 122–24, 354–56
      in step mode 124, 355–56
   saving 124–25
   setting tabs with 572–73
   for single-page printing 126–28, 448–50
   special characters in 446–47
   start-up 447
   step mode 124, 355–56, 444
   tables created with 572–73
   tables of contents coding with 540–41, 543
   vs. styles 104–5
   for word counting 415–17
   writing vs. recording 118
mailing labels 486–87
MakePRD program 617
manuscript-revision feature 335–38
margins 294–96
   default 147
   gutter 295
   left/right 295–96
   mirror 296
   top/bottom 295
   vs. indents 146, 296
Margins dialog box 294–96
marks. *See* bookmarks; page breaks; paragraph marks; section marks
MasterWord 374–75, 572–73, 421, 458, 653
mathematical calculations 342–45
mathematical operators 434, 490
Maximized reserved variable 433
Maximize (MX) mode 75
maximizing windows 86, 363–64

INDEX

measurement, units of 135, 276–77, 351
memory 147–48, 627–28
menu bar 60, 651
<menu> macro key 425
menus 60–65, 156–57
   displaying 239
   drop-down 61, 156–57
   using commands in 155–59, 651–55
   using mouse for 666
merge feature 200–201, 465
   and character formatting 491–92
   chevrons in 474
   comparison operators in 483
   conditional statements in 465, 476–77, 483–84, 493
   and database programs 493–97
   data document 200–201, 478–80
   delimiters 479, 493–94
   field separators 479
   fields in 474, 476, 478–80
   header records in 478–79
   logical operators 484, 490–91
   mailing labels 486–87
   master (main) document 200–201, 480–82
      body text 481
      creating 474–77
      data statements 480, 481
      field names 474, 481
   mathematical operators in 484, 490
   merged printing 200–201
   merge instructions 482–85
      ASK instruction 474–75, 483
      DATA instruction 482
      IF...ELSE...ENDIF instruction 476–77, 483–84
      INCLUDE instruction 484, 489
      NEXT instruction 484, 487
      SET instruction 474, 482–83
      SKIP instruction 484, 489
   merging data from a list 477–82
   merging to a document file 201, 485–86
   merging with INCLUDE instruction 485, 489
   multiple windows used with 492
   optional address lines 486
   quotation marks in 492
   records in 478–80
   skipping records 484, 487–89
MergePRD program 617

merging style sheets 271
message bar 76, 240
MESSAGE macro instruction 439–40
metafiles 604–5
"mickeys" 97
Microsoft Windows 2.1 638–39
Microsoft Windows 3.0 101, 638–39, 662
Microsoft Word 5.5
   hardware requirements 627–31
   installing 632–34
   memory use 147–48, 627–28
   on networks 130, 149, 167, 226–27, 432, 631–32
   and OS/2 639
   quitting 187
   setup 632–34
   startup options 636–37
   tutorial for 39–55
   vs. version 5.0 4–5, 30–31, 349
   and Windows 2.1 638–39
   and Windows 3.0 101, 622, 638–39
   and Word for Windows 627
MID function 436–37
minus sign (–) 342, 434, 484, 490
modems 630
mouse 94–97, 630
   controlling mouse pointer 94, 663
   copying text with 382
   double-clicking buttons 94–96
   installing 630
   list of uses 96
   manipulating windows with 84
   "mickey" units 97
   navigating dialog boxes with 100, 159, 165, 666
   scrolling with 79–80, 665
   selecting with 95–96, 665
   setting tab stops with 301–2
   shortcuts *664–67*
   vs. keyboard 95
mouse pointer 94, 663
MR (Macro Record) mode 75, 98, 121
MSWNET55 environment variable 167, 432, 631–32
multiplication operator (∗) 342, 484, 490
MW.HLP file 373
MW.INI file 149–50, 236–37, 432, 637
MX (Maximize) mode 75

N

networks
  environment variables for 167, 432, 631–32
  NORMAL files on 226–27
  setup on 631–32
  storing MW.INI files on 149
New (File) dialog box 163
new-page character 247, 346
NEXT merge instruction 484, 487
nextpage glossary name 225
NL (Num Lock) mode 75
nonprinting characters, displaying 237
NORMAL.GLY file 125, 129
Normal paragraph style 108, 109
NORMAL.STY file 106, 117, 128–29
not-equal-to operator (<>) 419, 434, 483
NotFound reserved variable 632
NOT logical operator 179, 180, 435, 484, 491
numbering/renumbering items 332–35
  in documents 333–34, 396–400
  in multipart documents 398–99
  in outlines 334, 519–20
  removing numbers 335
  using numbered passages as glossary names 408
numeric keypad 98
Num Lock (NL) mode 75

O

online help 369–73
Open dialog box 157–58, 164–65
Open Glossary dialog box 357–59
operators
  comparison 434
  logical 178–81, 435, 484, 490–91
  in macro instructions 433–35
  mathematical 434, 490
  in merge instructions 483–84, 490–91
Options dialog box 166–67
organizational charts, creating 578–79
OR logical operator 179, 180, 435, 484, 490
orphans 349
OS/2 operating system 186, 639
OT (Overtype) mode 75
outline edit mode 501, 502–3, 504
outline organize mode 501, 502, 504, 661
outline view 81–82, 231, 232, 500, 501, 661

outlining feature 499–508
  body text 502, 506–7
  changing modes 502–4
  expanding and collapsing body text 506–7
  generating tables of contents from 267
  heading levels 501–2
  headings 504–6
  key combinations in 502–4, 661
  mouse in 501, 508
  numbering 519–20
  promoting/demoting body text 506
  sorting 521
  status bar in 82, 504
  style sheet for 500, 505–6, 513–14
  tutorial on 508–18
  using glossary names as outlines 407–8
Overtype (OT) mode 75
overtyping 210, 211, 350

P

page breaks 247
  confirming 345–47
  new-page characters vs. page-break markers 247, 346
page formatting. *See* section formatting
page glossary name 225
page numbers 256–59
  aligning 258–59
  background pagination 345, 346, 348–49
  formatting 258
  in headers 312
  index spans 531
  printing 256–57
  repagination 345–47
  in tables of contents 268, 547
Page reserved variable 431
pages
  default page size 289
  jumping to 219–20
  layout (*see* layout)
  margins (*see* margins)
  new-page character 247, 346
  printing 125–28, 195–96
  sizes of 289, 294–95
panes 83
paper feed 195
paper size 289, 294–95
Paradox database 495–96

INDEX

paragraph formatting 26, 281–88
   alignment 283–85
   borders 302–5
   breaking paragraphs across pages 285–86
   built-in formats 35–37, 659
   frames for 138, 282, 305–8, 587–96
   as glossary entries 409
   headers/footers 309–10
   indentation 284–85
   line spacing 285
   markers (*see* paragraph marks)
   "normal" 35
   search and replace 215, 218, 393–94
   side-by-side paragraphs 286–87, 555–62
   spacing between paragraphs 285
   styles for 108–9, 452
paragraph marks 145, 282–83
   deleting 145
   displaying 237
   as glossary entries 409
   reducing number of, in macros 447
   removing with Edit Replace command 391
Paragraph paragraph style 109
paragraphs
   absolute positioning 305–6, 562–67
   breaking across pages 285–86
   side-by-side 286–87, 555–62
   spacing of 285
parallel ports 610
parentheses ( ) 181, 434, 484
Paste command 98, 211
pathnames 164–65, 166, 189
paths 188–89
PAUSE macro instruction 440
PCC file format 605
PC-File database 496–97
PCX file format 261, 599, 605
percent sign (%) 434, 490
picas 277
PIC file format 261, 605
Picture dialog box 141–42, 262–63
piece table 147
pitch 611–12
   vs. points 614–15
place markers 389, 395
plus sign (+) 342, 434, 484, 490
point size
   vs. pitch 68, 69, 614–15
ports 610
Position dialog box 306–8, 593–96

PostScript file format 605, 606
PRD files 194, 202, 619, 637
Preferences dialog box 236–42
printable characters 648
Print dialog box 158, 194–98
Print Direct Text dialog box 197–98
printer drivers. *See* printer files
printer files 202–3, 618–19
   font description in 66–67
   setup 204, 618
printers 611–12
   paper feed 195
   recording in MW.INI file 205
   sending keystrokes directly to 194, 197–98
   setup 204–6
   types of 611–12
Printer Setup dialog box 204–6
print files 604, 605, 606–7
printing
   direct text 194, 197–98
   documents 184, 194
   in draft mode 136, 196
   to file 195
   glossaries 194
   graphics 143, 197
   hidden text 197
   keyboard shortcuts for 654
   merged documents 200–201
   number of copies 194–95
   page numbers 256–59
   previewing 136–37, 198–200
   queued 202–4, 205
   range of pages 195–96
   single page
      with macro 126–28, 448–50
      without macro 125–26
   style sheets 194
   summary sheets 184, 194, 196
   two-sided 196
   widow/orphan control in 349
Print Merge dialog box 200–201
Print Options dialog box 196–97
Print Page macro 126–28, 448–50
print preview mode 136–37, 198–200
Print Queue dialog box 203–4
Professional File database 496
program directory 188–89
ProgramDir reserved variable 188, 431
PromptMode reserved variable 428–29

Q

question mark (?) 165, 180, 212
queued printing 202–4, 205
QUIT macro instruction 441
quitting Word 5.5 187
quotation marks (") 180–81, 426

R

R:BASE 494–95
read-only files 165, 168, 177, 187
Record Macro dialog box 119–21, 354
records in merge data documents 478–80
Record Style dialog box 110–11, 315–16
redlining 335–38
REMEM-XX.COR file 325
Rename (File) dialog box 184–85
Rename Style dialog box 114–15, 227–28
Renumber dialog box 334–35
renumbering 332–35, 519–20
Repaginate Now dialog box 345–47
REPEAT...ENDREPEAT macro instruction 419, 421, 441
Replace dialog box 216–18
reserved macro variables 428–33
result reserved variable 418
revision marks. *See* redlining
Revision Marks (RM) mode 75, 336
ribbon 65–73
   accessing fonts in 66–69
   character attributes in 66
   displaying 66, 233
   keyboard commands for 656
   mouse commands for 667
   recording styles via 108–11, 458
Rich Text format (RTF) file format 172
right margin 296
RM (Revision Marks) mode 75, 336
ruler 78
   commands for 657, 667
   live 234
   scalable 234–35
   sliding 135, 235
   and tab stops 300–302
   using mouse with 301–2
Run Macro dialog box 123–24, 355–56
running heads. *See* headers

S

Save As dialog box 169–70
SAVE indicator 74
save reserved variable 433
saving
   autosave feature 149
   documents 168–74
   file formats for 170–72
   forms 580
   glossary entries 225
   macros 124–25
   style sheets 116–17
scalable ruler 234–35
scanners 630–31
scrap 74, 209–11
   copying to 211
   cutting text to 98, 209–10
   vs. glossary 211
scrap reserved variable 418, 430
screen 58–76
   colors 242–44
   splitting 83–84, 366
   text mode vs. graphics mode 133–34
   in View Layout (LY) mode 135–36
SCREEN.VID file 432, 628
scroll bars 78–80
   displaying 240
   in Styles list box 71
   using mouse in 79–80
scrolling 25, 98
   with keyboard 649
   with mouse 79–80, 665
Scroll Lock (SL) mode 75
scrp reserved variable 418–19, 420, 421
search and replace 388–93
   coding indexes by 527–28
   replacing formatting using 217–18, 393–94
Search dialog box (Edit menu) 63–65, 212–14
Search dialog box (File File Management command) 178–82
section breaks 247–48, 293
section formatting 26, 288–89
   built-in formats 34–35
   creating multiple-column documents with 138–41, 291
   default 288–89, 296
   and footnotes 251, 291
   as glossary entries 410
   and headers/footers 310–11

section formatting *(continued)*
    and line numbers 292
    and margins 294–96
section marks 138–39, 146, 247, 288, 293, 529
sections 138–40
Select-Do concept 20
selecting
    with cursor 22–24
    keys for 99, 650
    with mouse 95–96, 665
    single characters 22
    single-sentence paragraphs 381
selection bar 80, 663
Selection reserved variable 418, 420, 431
semicolon (;) 524
serial ports 610
SET command (DOS) 631, 632
SET instruction
    macro 419–20, 441–42
    merge 474, 482–83
SETUP program 632–34
<shift ctrl esc> macro key 426
Shift key 91, 642
shortcut keys
    accelerator keys 61–62, 100, 156–57
    command-key 62, 100, 652–55
    speed-formatting keys 34–39, 65, 100
side-by-side paragraphs 286–87, 555–62
    rules for 558–59
    side heads created with 560–61
    styles 556–57
    tables and scripts created with 559–60
side heads
    placed with absolute positioning 567–68
    for side-by-side paragraphs 560–61
SKIP merge instruction 484, 489
slash (/) 342, 434, 484, 490
sliding ruler 135, 235
SL (Scroll Lock) mode 75
small capital letters 279
sofar reserved variable 418, 420
Sort dialog box 339–41
sorting 339–40
    alphanumeric vs. numeric 340, 341
    ascending/descending 340
    and case 341
    outlines 521
    primary 340–41
    secondary 340–41

Spacebar
    creating spacing characters with 24–25, 146, 237
    vs. direction keys 24, 25
    vs. Tab key 146
spacing characters
    changing with Edit Replace command 391–92
    keys for 647
special characters 98
SPECIALS.CMP file 323
speed-formatting keys 34–39, 65, 100
    vs. styles 458–59
spell checker 320–26
    dictionaries
        adding words to 322
        naming 350–51
        standard 321–22
        user-created 322–23
    keyboard shortcuts for 654
Spelling dialog box 323–26
SPELL-XX.LEX file 321–22
start-up directory 188–89
StartupDir reserved variable 188, 431
status bar 73–76, 97–98, 236
step macro mode 124, 355–56, 444
strikethrough text 279
ST (Step Macro) mode 75, 444
.STY filename extension 117, 165, 460
style bar 80–81, 111
    displaying 239
styles 70–73, 104, 452
    adding to style sheets 454, 462
    applying 111–13, 313–14, 457–59
    automatic 128, 452–53
    character formatting 452
    copying 209
    creating with Insert New Style command 270, 462–63
    formatting with 111–13, 313–14, 457–59
    I.D. for 111
    key codes for 81, 110, 113, 452
    names of 108–9, 128, 455–56
    Normal 71, 128, 455
    for outlines 500, 505–6, 513–14
    paragraph formatting 452
    recording 106–11, 314–16
    renaming 227–28, 460–61
    scrolling through 71

styles *(continued)*
  searching for and replacing 215, 218, 393–94
  section formatting 289, 452
  for side-by-side paragraphs 556–57
  tutorial on 106–17
  types of 110–11
  viewing 80–81
  vs. built-in formats 458–59
  vs. macros 104–5
style sheets 70–71, 451, 459–60
  attaching 117, 316–17, 459
  creating 462–63
  detaching 106–7, 317
  Edit commands for 227–28
  for indexing 265
  Insert menu commands for 270–71
  merging 271
  modifying formatting in 115–16, 462
  modifying style names 114–15
  NORMAL.STY file 106, 117, 128–29
  printing 194
  renaming 114–15
  saving 116–17
  tables of contents 268–69, 544–47
  viewing 113–14, 453–54
subscripts 280
subtraction operator (–) 342, 434, 484, 490
summary sheets 175, 182, 349
  creating 172–74
  printing 184, 194, 196
  searching 178–82
superscripts 250, 280
synonyms. *See* thesaurus

T

Tab key
  creating spaces with 25, 146
  navigating dialog boxes with 159
  underlining with 574–77
Table of Contents dialog box 267–69
Table paragraph style 109
tables 568–73
  column manipulation 551–55
  leader characters in 569–72
  macros for 572–73
  single-page 568–69
  tabs and spacing in 146
tables of contents 537
  coding 266–67, 537–41

tables of contents *(continued)*
  compiling 266–69, 541–42
  formatting 268–69, 542–47
  hidden text in 266, 267–68, 539–40
  indentation in 268–69
  leader characters in 571–72
  moving 542
  multiple 541
  style sheet for 268–69, 544–47
  using outlines to create 267
tabs 296–97
  alignment 298
  default width 350, 550
  displaying 237
  and Format Tabs command 298–300
  formatting 298–300
  keyboard and mouse shortcuts 651
  leader characters 299
  macros used to set 572–73
  and ruler 300–302
  setting with mouse 301–2
  tab characters vs. tab stops 297, 550
  in tables 569–73
  vs. Spacebar spaces 146
Tagged Image File Format (TIFF) 261, 605–6
text
  applying a style to 111–13, 313–14, 457–59
  bookmarking (*see* bookmarks)
  centering 283
  copying 211
  copying with mouse 382
  cutting 98, 209–10
  deleting 98
  direct printing 194, 197–98
  formatting (*see* character formatting; formatting)
  hidden (*see* hidden text)
  inserting 98
  keys for entering and editing 647
  moving to/from scrap 98
  moving unconnected passages 381–82
  pasting 98, 211
  place markers in 389
  replacing 215–18
  search and replace 212–18, 388–93
  storing (*see* glossaries; saving)
  strikethrough 279
text files 170–72
text mode vs. graphics mode 133–34, 241–42, 275
Text Only file formats 170–72

thesaurus 326–28, 654
Thesaurus dialog box 326–28
TIFF file format 261, 605–6
tilde (~) 180
time glossary name 225–26
timeprint glossary name 225–26
title bar 77
TMP environment variable 631–32
toggling 62–63, 157
top margin 295
total reserved variable 418
tutorials
   glossary 410–12
   graphics and layout 584–89
   Microsoft Word 39–55
   outlining 508–18
   styles 106–17
typefaces 610–11. *See also* fonts

U

underlining 278
   double 278
   in forms 574–77
Undo command 208–9, 380
units of measure 135, 276–77, 351–52
UPDAT-XX.CMP file 322
Utilities Calculate command 342–45
Utilities commands 13–14, 329–20
Utilities Customize command 347–52, 637
Utilities Hyphenate command 328–32
Utilities Line Draw command 338–39
Utilities menu 319
Utilities Renumber command 332–35, 519–20
Utilities Repaginate Now command 345–47
Utilities Revision Marks command 335–38
Utilities Sort command 339–41, 521
Utilities Spelling command 320–26
Utilities Thesaurus command 326–28
Utilities Word Count command 338, 420, 421

V

variables
   environment 631–32
   macro 418–19, 427–33
Video Graphics Array (VGA) 241, 629
.VID files 628–29

View commands 9–10, 229–30
View Footnotes/Annotations command 236
View Layout command 135–36, 232–33
View Layout (LY) mode 75, 136, 231–33, 660
View menu 229
View Outline command 82, 229–32, 502
View Preferences command 236–44, 637
View Ribbon command 66, 233
View Ruler command 78, 233–35
views
   document 230, 501, 507
   layout 231–33
   outline 81–82, 231, 232, 501
View Status Bar command 9, 230, 236
virus detection 149

W

WHILE conditional statement in macros 419, 442
widow/orphan control 349
wildcards 165, 180, 212
Window Arrange All command 86, 362–63
Window Close command 86, 167, 366–67
Window commands 15–16, 361–62
Window [Document Name] command 367
Window Maximize command 86, 367
Window Move command 365
Window New Window command 362
Window reserved variable 428, 430
Window Restore command 364
windows 58–60, 83–37
   closing 366–67
   controlling with keyboard 655
   controlling with mouse 77, 84, 667
   displaying borders 77, 240
   listing 367
   maximizing 86, 363–64
   maximum number 362–63
   moving 365
   opening new 362
   panes in 83
   resizing 363–64, 365–66
   splitting 83–84, 366
      vs. multiple 84–87
   vs. documents 30–31
   zooming (*see* windows, maximizing)
Windows 3.0. *See* Microsoft Windows 3.0
Window Size command 365–66

Window Split command 83–84, 366
Word. *See* Microsoft Word 5.5
Word5Keys reserved variable 429–30
word count 338, 415–17
wordversion reserved variable 418, 431

Z

zooming windows. *See* maximizing windows

Other Titles From Microsoft Press

MICROSOFT® WORD 5.5:
Microsoft® Quick Reference

Peter Rinearson

Now you can have instant answers to your Word 5.5 questions! This compact, action-oriented quick reference lets you use the features of Word 5.5 as you need them—you needn't know specific menu commands. Simply look up a task. Entries are arranged alphabetically, and you'll find clear, direct information on all the basics plus instructions on creating multiple columns, using macros, merging files, setting up style sheets, and performing dozens of other tasks. This book is a great source of quick refreshers and instant answers to your Word 5.5 questions, plus a great complement to *Running Microsoft Word 5.5*.

208 pages, softcover   4 $3/4$ x 8   **$7.95**   Order Code QRWO5

RUNNING MS-DOS® 5th ed.

Van Wolverton

"This book is simply the definitive handbook of PC-DOS and MS-DOS...written for both novices and experienced users."   **BYTE magazine**

Now updated to include DOS 5, RUNNING MS-DOS, 5th ed., is the ideal book for all levels—from novices to advanced DOS users. For novices, this is a solid introduction to basic DOS concepts and applications. For seasoned users this book provides all you need to achieve DOS mastery—precise, real-world examples, thoughtful discussions, and understandable descriptions. Throughout, the author addresses the exciting improvements in DOS 5 while providing in-depth coverage of every major version of DOS. You'll discover how to control your entire computer system—manage a hard disk, use the built-in text editor, increase your productivity with batch files, and even tailor the system to your needs and preferences. The example-rich command reference—completely revised and updated—is a valuable resource for every DOS user.

608 pages, softcover   7 $3/8$ x 9 $1/4$ **$24.95**   Order Code RUMS5

DESKTOP PUBLISHING BY DESIGN
Blueprints for Page Layout Using Aldus® PageMaker® on IBM® and Apple® Macintosh® Computers

Ronnie Shushan and Don Wright

DESKTOP PUBLISHING BY DESIGN is filled with how-to information, layout ideas, and inspiration for anyone new to design, publishing, or computers. The authors offer a primer on the use of basic design elements—typeface, page layout, and graphics. And they provide a wide-ranging and imaginative portfolio of promotional flyers and brochures, newsletters and magazines, catalogs, data sheets, and forms that highlight good design and constitute a sourcebook of inventive ideas. DESKTOP PUBLISHING BY DESIGN is a fact-filled, design-oriented resource you'll turn to again and again.

408 pages, softcover   8 $1/2$ x 11   **$24.95**   Order Code DEPUDP

Updated edition available June

*Microsoft Press books are available wherever quality computer books are sold.
Or call* **1-800-MSPRESS** *for ordering information or placing credit card orders.*[*]
Please refer to **BBK** *when placing your order.*

[*] In Canada, contact Macmillan of Canada, Attn: Microsoft Press Dept., 164 Commander Blvd., Agincourt, Ontario, Canada M1S 3C7. In the U.K., contact Microsoft Press, 27 Wrights Lane, London W8 5TZ.

Peter Rinearson

Journalist Peter Rinearson has been using word processors since 1976. He has received several national writing awards, including a Pulitzer Prize for an account of the creation of the Boeing 757 jetliner, published in *The Seattle Times*. He is the creator of the MasterWord™ companion software for Microsoft® Word version 5.5 and has written another book for Microsoft Press, *Quick Reference Guide to Microsoft® Word for the IBM® PC*.

The manuscript for this book was prepared and submitted to Microsoft Press in electronic form. Text files were processed and formatted using Microsoft Word.

   Principal word processors: Debbie Ken and Judith Bloch
   Principal proofreaders: Cynthia Riskin and Deborah Long
   Principal typographer: Carolyn Magruder
   Interior text designer: Darcie Furlan
   Principal illustrators: Kim Eggleston and Connie Little
   Cover designer: Tom Draper
   Cover color separator: Color Services, Precision Photo

   Text composition by Microsoft Press in Palatino and Helvetica, with display type in Palatino Bold, using the Magna composition system and the Linotronic 300 laser imagesetter.

Printed on recycled paper stock.

If you like this book, you'll love MasterWord

Peter Rinearson's MasterWord places readable information about every nuance of Microsoft Word 5.5 at your fingertips. It even performs hundreds of useful tasks for you. Plus you get macros, style sheets, utilities, and a desktop reference.

If you've given up on the help screens that come with software, MasterWord will change your mind—and the way you use Microsoft Word.

MasterWord begins with more than 2,000 screens of on-line help, written by Peter Rinearson, the author of this book. In fact, MasterWord's help works hand in hand with *Running Word 5.5*.

The help screens, which are indexed in a variety of easy-to-use ways, provide insightful summaries of each Word command, feature, dialog box, and message, backed up with as much or little detail as you like. Special topics make it easier to learn Word 5.5 if you already know WordStar, WordPerfect, or an earlier version of Word. And MasterWord's help is *active*—it performs tasks for you.

See page xv, and the other side of this card, for details about MasterWord.

Get three free gifts and a guarantee!

MasterWord is unconditionally guaranteed for 30 days. Return it, and keep these as gifts:

1. WordSet is a control panel that gives great control over screen colors and Word settings.

2. Intro is a demonstration of useful features.

3. Touch Me Not is a screen saver.

Fold here, fill in order form below, and mail postage-free. Tape the sides if enclosing a check (no staples).

We pay for air shipping, and ship quickly.

To order, call 800-669-WORD or 206-286-2600. Or, complete the order form and mail to:
Alki Software Corporation, 219 First Ave. N., Suite 410, Seattle, WA 98109.
FAX orders to 206-286-2785. Shipped by 2-day air to the United States, or air mail to Canada and abroad. Thirty-day money-back guarantee.

NAME _____
COMPANY _____
STREET _____
CITY _____ STATE _____ ZIP _____
PHONE (___) _____ NATION _____

	Quantity		Total
MasterWord Indicate size of disks: ☐ 5.25-inch ☐ 3.5-inch	_____	$ 99.95	$ _____
Microsoft Dictionaries Circle your choice(s): Legal, Medical, British, Dutch, French, German, Italian, Spanish, Swedish	_____	$ 69.95 ea.	$ _____
	Foreign orders, add $15 Canada, AK, HI add $5.00		$ _____
	WA residents add 8.2% tax		$ _____
	Order Total		$ _____

☐ Visa ☐ MasterCard ☐ American Express ☐ Check or money order (in U.S. funds, payable to Alki)

Card # ☐☐☐☐ ☐☐☐☐ ☐☐☐☐ ☐☐☐☐
Signature _____ Exp. Date _____

Call today toll-free **1-800-669-WORD**

MasterWord features include:

- **MasterWord Help** — Extensive details on Word; easy to use.

- **Macros** — More than 100, each a new "command" or function.

- **Style Sheets** — A comprehensive set, with sample documents.

- **MasterWord Calc** — Offers all of the financial and math functions of Microsoft Excel 2.2.

- **MasterWord Seek** — Search your hard disk for files by name or content; view what you find.

- **Desktop Easy Reference** — A keyboard template and reference card containing vital information about Word and MasterWord.

Microsoft Word is multilingual

Microsoft Word is the top-selling word processor outside the United States, with versions sold in many languages. Now you can use your English version of Word to check spellings and hyphenate in other languages, with Microsoft's own dictionaries.

Spanish. French. German. Italian. Swedish. Dutch. And even British English. Now you can spell-check and automatically hyphenate documents written in any of these languages with the American English version of Word 5.0 or Word 5.5. If you purchase the French Dictionary, for example, you get the same Microsoft spell-checking and hyphenation files you would get if you purchased a French version of Word in Paris.

Medical and Legal Dictionaries help professionals. Replace your American English spell-checking dictionary with an expanded version that includes all of the original words plus either 20,000 legal terms or 24,000 medical terms. More than 150,000 words in all. Invaluable in professional offices.

These dictionaries are produced under license from Microsoft.

Fold here, fill in order form on other side, and mail postage-free. Tape the sides if enclosing a check (no staples).

BUSINESS REPLY MAIL
FIRST CLASS MAIL   PERMIT NO. 75428   SEATTLE, WA

POSTAGE WILL BE PAID BY ADDRESSEE

Aiki Software Corporation
219 First Ave N Suite 410
Seattle WA 98109-9803

NO POSTAGE NECESSARY IF MAILED IN THE UNITED STATES